CHAPLIN

His Life and Art

CHAPLIN

His Life and Art

David Robinson

COLLINS
8 Grafton Street, London W1
1985

William Collins Sons and Co. Ltd
London · Glasgow · Sydney · Auckland
Toronto · Johannesburg

British Library Cataloguing in Publication Data

Robinson, David, 1930–
Chaplin: his life and art.
1. Chaplin, Charles, 1889–1977
2. Moving picture actors and actresses –
United States – Biography
I. Title
791.43′028′0924   PN2287.C5

ISBN 0-00-216387-X

First published 1985
Text copyright © David Robinson 1985
All material quoted from the Chaplin archives
is copyright © Roy Export Company Establishment.

Photoset in Linotron Sabon by
Rowland Phototypesetting Ltd
Bury St Edmunds, Suffolk

Made and Printed in Great Britain by
William Collins Sons & Co. Ltd, Glasgow

CONTENTS

Preface
Acknowledgements

1	A London boyhood	1
2	The young professional	43
3	With the Guv'nor	71
4	In Pictures	101
5	Essanay	134
6	Mutual	156
7	Penalties and rewards of independence	221
8	Escape	273
9	A WOMAN OF PARIS	302
10	THE GOLD RUSH	334
11	THE CIRCUS	363
12	CITY LIGHTS	387
13	Away from it all	420
14	MODERN TIMES	446
15	THE GREAT DICTATOR	484
16	MONSIEUR VERDOUX	509
17	LIMELIGHT	544
18	Exile	573
19	A COUNTESS FROM HONG KONG; and the final years	608

Notes 633

Appendices

I	Chaplin Chronology	643
II	Tours of 'The Eight Lancashire Lads', 1898–1900	678
III	Tours of 'Sherlock Holmes', 1903–6	682
IV	Tours of 'Casey's Court Circus', 1906–7	686

V	Three Keystone scenarios	689
VI	Filmography	699
VII	Shooting schedules and ratios	746
VIII	Chaplin, Epstein and the Circle Theatre	747
IX	The FBI v. Chaplin	750
X	A Chaplin Who's Who	757
	Bibliography	778
	Index	783

ILLUSTRATIONS

All photographs unless otherwise specifically acknowledged are the copyright of the Roy Export Company Establishment.

Section 1, between pages 72 and 73

Page 1
Photograph, c. 1870, believed to be Spencer Chaplin.
Charles Chaplin Senior aged 20.

Page 2
Hannah Chaplin.
Charles Chaplin Senior aged 30. (Author's collection)

Page 3
Music hall bill, 1898, featuring Charles Chaplin Senior. (Author's collection)
Leo Dryden's 'card'. (Author's collection)

Page 4
The Hanwell Schools. (Inman Hunter Collection)
Charles Chaplin at Hanwell Schools, 1897. (National Film Archive/GLC Archive)

Page 5
Chaplin as one of the Eight Lancashire Lads. (National Film Archive)
Chaplin as Sammy the Newsboy, 1903. (Author's collection)

Pages 6 and 7
Chaplin as Billy the Page in *Sherlock Holmes*, 1903. (Author's collection)
Chaplin's two Sherlock Holmes: William Gillette (Roy Waters Collection) *and* H. A. Saintsbury. (Author's collection)

Pages 8 and 9
Sydney, aged 18.
Chaplin in *Repairs*, 1906.
Casey's Court Circus, 1906. (Author's collection)

Page 10
The real Dr Walford Bodie. (Garrick Club)
Chaplin's impersonation of Dr Walford Bodie, 1906.

Page 11
Fred Karno. (Author's collection)
Workers leaving the Karno Fun Factory. (Author's collection)

Page 12
Chaplin c.1909
Chaplin as Archibald in *Skating*.
Sydney as Archibald in *Skating* with his wife, Minnie

Page 13
Chaplin as The Inebriate, c.1910

Pages 14 and 15
The Karno troupe en route for America, 1910.
On tour in USA.
On tour with the Karno troupe. At Solano, Philadelphia. (Ted and Betty Tetrick)

Page 16
Chaplin with Karno poster, Spokane.
With an Indian pedlar.
With posters at Exeter, California.

Section 2, between pages 232 and 233

Page 1
The Keystone Studios. (Bison Archives: Marc Wanamaker Collection)
Mack Sennett. (Bison Archives: Marc Wanamaker Collection)

Page 2
The Essanay Studio. (Bison Archives: Marc Wanamaker Collection)
The Majestic Studio. (Bison Archives: Marc Wanamaker Collection)

Page 3
Mabel Normand. (Author's collection)
Making a Living. (Bison Archives: Marc Wanamaker Collection)

Page 4
Essanay publicity, 1915. (Bison Archives: Marc Wanamaker Collection)

Page 5
Essanay picture postcards, 1915. (Author's collection)

Pages 6 and 7
The cast and crew of *The Bank*, 1915. (Author's collection)

Page 8
Chaplin's first day at the Lone Star Studios. (Bison Archives: Marc Wanamaker Collection)
Filming *The Vagabond*, 1916.

Page 9
Edna Purviance. (Author's collection)
Edna's star hat, *The Count*.

Page 10
The old mansion in the grounds of the Chaplin Studio.
Chaplin and Sydney visit the site of the projected studio.

Page 11
Building the studio, 1918.
Chaplin on the studio site.

Pages 12 and 13
Cartoon by Cami, 1917.
Anticipation of *Shoulder Arms*, 1918.
Aerial views of Chaplin Studio.

Page 14
A Dog's Life, 1918.

Page 15
A Dog's Life: Chaplin with Mut.
A rehearsal at the studio, posed for *How to Make Movies*, 1918.

Page 16
Visitors to the studio: Helen Keller with Annie Sullivan (*above*); Douglas Fairbanks and Harry Lauder (*below*).

Section 3, between pages 328 and 329

Page 1
Chaplin addressing a Bond rally in Wall Street, 1918.
Chaplin at a Bond rally in Washington, 1918.

Page 2
Shoulder Arms: sets for the abandoned prologue and epilogue.
Shoulder Arms: Chaplin getting into his tree costume.

Page 3
Chaplin with Dorothy Rosher during the making of *The Bond*.
The Bond: Chaplin and Edna.
A break during filming of *The Bond*.

Page 4 and 5
Douglas Fairbanks vaults the gate of the Chaplin Studio.
Tea break during shooting of *Sunnyside*.
Mildred Harris Chaplin. (Author's collection)

Page 6
A Days Pleasure: between shots.
(Author's collection: Jack Wilson
Archive)
The Kid: Chaplin practises flying.
The Freak. (Jean-Baptiste Thierrée)

Page 7
The Professor. (Both author's
collection: Jack Wilson Archive)

Pages 8 and 9
The Kid: Chaplin with Jackie Coogan,
Edith Wilson and her baby.
(Author's collection: Jack Wilson
Archive)
Handing over the negative of *The Kid*.

Pages 10 and 11
Aboard the *Olympic*, 1921. (National
Film Archive)
Chaplin leaving the *Olympic* at
Southampton. (National Film
Archive)

Page 12
Portrait of Max Linder.
Chaplin directs Lord Moutbatten in
Nice and Friendly.

Page 13
Chaplin in his cutting room, *c.*1920.
Lady Mountbatten in *Nice and
Friendly*.

Pages 14 and 15
Pola Negri. (Author's collection)
A Woman of Paris, 1923.
A Woman of Paris: Lydia Knott, Carl
Miller, Edna Purviance. (Inman
Hunter Collection)

Page 16
The United Artists. (Author's
collection: Jack Wilson Archive)
Jack Wilson photographs the four
United Artists. (Author's collection:
Jack Wilson Archive)
Chaplin rehearsing with Abe Lyman's
orchestra, 1925.

Section 4, between pages 424 and 425

Page 1
The Gold Rush: Lita Grey with
Chaplin at the signing of her
contract.
Chaplin on set.

Pages 2 and 3
The Gold Rush: on location at
Truckee.
Chaplin performs the Dance of the
Rolls out of costume.
Preparing to film a travelling shot
between takes on location.

Pages 4 and 5
The Gold Rush: Lita Grey as leading
lady.
Georgia Hale as leading lady.

Page 6
Chaplin's first Hollywood home.
(Author's collection)
His house on Summit Drive. (Author's
collection)

Page 7
The Circus: Merna Kennedy.
Chaplin succumbs to exhaustion.
(Author's collection: Jack Wilson
Archive).

Page 8
The Lita Grey divorce: Lita takes the
oath. (Author's collection)

Page 9
After the studio fire.

Page 10
Sea Gulls (A Woman of the Sea): the
cast and crew on location. (Inman
Hunter Collection)
Edna Purviance. (Inman Hunter
Collection)

Page 11
Sea Gulls: Edna Purviance and Gayne
Whitman. (Inman Hunter
Collection)

Pages 12 and 13
City Lights: Chaplin at the camera.
The studio back lot during the shooting
of *City Lights*.
Chaplin with Ralph Barton on the set.
Chaplin in the costume of the Duke.
Al Jolson visits Chaplin on the set.

Pages 14 and 15
Hannah Chaplin in 1921. (Pauline
Mason)
Hannah Chaplin in Hollywood.

Hannah Chaplin's grave in the
Hollywood Cemetry. (Author's
collection)
Chaplin's sons, Sydney (*left*) and
Charles Jr.
Chaplin at home, 1930.

Page 16
Chaplin with Mr and Mrs Albert
Einstein at the première of *City Lights*.
The première of *City Lights* at the Los
Angeles Theatre, 30 January 1931.

Section 5, between pages 552 and 553

Page 1
The 1931 world tour. Chaplin at the
Majestic Hotel, Nice.
Sydney with May Reeves at St Moritz.

Page 2
Paulette Goddard.
Chaplin with Paulette Goddard at the
première of *Modern Times*.

Page 3
Paulette Goddard, photographed by
Hurrell.

Page 4
Modern Times: principal members of
the Chaplin unit at this period.
Set design for the department store
skating sequence.

Page 5
Chaplin as Napoleon, 1925. (Bison
Archives: Marc Wanamaker
Collection)
Chaplin as Napoleon, mid 1930s.

Page 6
The Great Dictator.
Chaplin and Roland Totheroh.
The last meeting with Douglas
Fairbanks, on the set of *The Great
Dictator*.

Page 7
The Great Dictator: Chaplin at a music
recording session.
Chaplin at the New York press
conference for *The Great Dictator*.

Pages 8 and 9
Chaplin with Oona in Hollywood,
1944.
Monsieur Verdoux: Chaplin and
Martha Raye.
Chaplin and Margaret Hoffmann.

Page 10
Chaplin directing at the Circle Theatre,
Hollywood. (Jerry Epstein)
Limelight: Chaplin with Wheeler
Dryden and Claire Bloom.

Page 11
Limelight: the screen debuts of
Geraldine, Josephine and Michael
Chaplin.
The flea circus routine.

Page 12
Chaplin in conversation with Oona,
1965.

Page 13
A Countess from Hong Kong: the first
script session.

Pages 14 and 15
Oona Chaplin.
Family group on the set of *A Countess
from Hong Kong*.
Manoir de Ban, Corsier-sur-Vevey,
Switzerland.

Page 16
The Chaplin Studio, 1983. (Author's
collection)
The last official portrait, 1977.

PREFACE

The world is not composed of heroes and villains,
but of men and women with all the passions that God
has given them.

The ignorant condemn, but the wise pity.

CHARLES CHAPLIN, prefatory title to
A Woman of Paris, 1923.

Those big shoes are buttoned with 50,000,000 eyes.

GENE MORGAN, Chicago newsman, 1915.

Charles Chaplin's autobiography appeared in 1964. He was then
seventy-five years old. The book ran to more than five hundred pages
and represented a prodigious feat of memory, for it was in large part
done without reference to documentation. At the time, indeed, the feat
seemed too prodigious to some reviewers, who were incredulous that
anyone could remember in such detail events that had taken place a
long lifetime before.

Since Chaplin's death, I have had the privilege of examining the
great mass of his working papers – some of them unseen for more than
half a century. In the public archives of London and in old theatrical
records I have been able to uncover many long-forgotten traces of the
young Chaplin and his family. In addition, a number of people in
England and America have generously shared their memories and
papers.

Sifting this mass of documentation has only served to heighten
regard for the powers of Chaplin's memory and the honesty of his
record. An instance of the kind of detail which is constantly corroborated by the archives is the recollection, from his thirteenth year, that

when his brother first went to sea he sent home thirty-five shillings from his pay packet: Sydney Chaplin's seaman's papers – which were not available to Chaplin when he wrote – exactly confirm the sum. Even small inaccuracies attest to rather than discredit his memory. He remembers a childhood ogre, one of his schoolmasters, as 'Captain Hindrum', an old vaudeville friend of his mother's as 'Dashing Eva Lestocq' and the friendly stage manager at the Duke of York's Theatre as 'Mr Postant'. In fact their names turn out to have been Hindom, Dashing Eva Lester and William Postance. Chaplin probably never saw any of the names written down, and no doubt he recalled them simply as he heard them as a child. In themselves the slips clearly show that Chaplin's record is the result of a phenomenal memory rather than the product of *post facto* research and reconstruction. So regularly is his memory vindicated by other evidence that where there are discrepancies without proof one way or the other, the benefit of the doubt seems best given to Chaplin.

The present volume, written twenty years after Chaplin's own account of his life, serves in part to complement *My Autobiography*. Subsequent research makes it possible to add further documentation and detail to the subject's sometimes random recollections. In their study *Chaplin: Genesis of a Clown*, Raoul Sobel and David Francis complained of the lack of hard facts and dates in the early chapters of *My Autobiography*. 'To try to keep a running time scale while reading *My Autobiography* is rather like having to navigate by the stars on an overcast night. By the time one reaches the next break in the clouds, the boat may be miles off course.' This is true, perhaps: the special charm of those first chapters of *My Autobiography* is the free range of memory, unrestrained by the cold collaboration of any ghostly researcher. It is hardly to be wondered at if, at six or seven years old, the infant Chaplin was a trifle confused about the order of the workhouses and charity schools into which he was thrust. The importance of the autobiography is that it recorded his feelings in the face of these misadventures. The present volume can, at risk of pedantry, tidy up the facts and chronology.

While *My Autobiography* is a strikingly truthful record of things witnessed, Chaplin might sometimes have been misled in the case of things reported to him. Like any mother, Mrs Chaplin must have tried to shield her children from unpleasant facts when she was able to do so. Some critics of the autobiography doubted whether Chaplin's childhood could really have been as awful as he described. New discoveries suggest that Mrs Chaplin kept the worst from her children. The Chaplin boys seem never to have known, for example, of the sad fate of his maternal grandmother as she declined into alcoholism and vagrancy. Charles always believed that this grandmother was a gypsy, whereas the gypsy blood came with his *paternal* grandmother. Again it was a natural misunderstanding for a child. Grandma Chaplin died years before his birth. Told that his grandmother was a gypsy, he could only assume it to mean the grandmother he had known.

Chaplin was an accurate and truthful chronicler of what he had seen. He was not always a comprehensive one. There are large and deliberate areas of omission from the autobiography. His description of friends, acquaintances and affairs was selective. Some relationships are described in the autobiography with great frankness and humour, while other people who at one time or another were very close to him are not even mentioned. To an extent, gallantry may have played a part in the selection. Most of the people left out were still living: Chaplin may have felt that they would have been too easily hurt or offended. As it happened, a lot were offended by being left out.

His reticence about his own work was more disappointing. He discussed very few of his films, and then had little to say about the way he made them. Later in his career, visitors were discouraged on his sets, and he would explain his reluctance to let people into his working secrets by saying, "If people know how it's done, all the magic goes." This, though, was probably only a small factor in Chaplin's secretiveness. It may be that he came to feel more and more that he was unable to unveil the mysteries, simply because the essential part of the mysteries remained veiled for him, too. How could he ever explain, to himself or to anyone else, how it was that he was able, one afternoon in 1914, to walk into the Keystone wardrobe hut, pick out a costume, and on the spot create a character which was so soon to become the most universally recognized representation of a human being in the history of mankind? In later years, Chaplin and his apologists would rationalize the appeal of the Tramp; but no one could ever figure why it was he, and that moment, that were chosen for the mystical birth of Charlie.

There were more practical reasons for leaving his work out of the autobiography. Chaplin wrote the book in the spirit of the entertainer that, his whole life, he was. Like most people, he saw no particular glamour in his job: he once told someone that his working life was no more exciting than that of a bank clerk. He probably felt that it would simply be boring to tell people how his films were made. If genius is computed at 10 per cent inspiration and 90 per cent perspiration, that 90 per cent should be reckoned much higher in Chaplin's case. No one was ever more dogged in the pursuit of the best of which he was capable.

Ironically, considering his legendary secrecy during his lifetime, Chaplin has left a more comprehensive record of the processes of his creativity than any other film maker of his generation (or generations, for Chaplin's whole working life spanned eight decades). For this reason alone, it has seemed important to explore these at length in this book. The reader must judge if Chaplin was justified in his fears that the daily work even of a comic genius was too humdrum to be interesting.

The worknotes, the studio records and the out-takes and rushes that have survived tell us what Chaplin was reluctant to tell about his methods and his indefatigable application to the quest for perfection. Part of this book is devoted to reconstructing the way that Chaplin created his comic visions – the long and painful processes of refining and polishing plots and gags; the mechanical problems involving resources, studios, apparatus, sets; the choice of collaborators and working relations with them; the endless repetitions, trials, rehearsals, shooting, reshooting, rejection, revision; and finally the months of editing until the finished product should betray nothing of the labour, but seem as simple and natural (in the phrase of Alistair Cooke) 'as water running over stones'.

When I began this book, I intended to deal only with Chaplin's work. The private biography seemed to have been recorded more than enough times, and at first sight the two elements of his life appeared clearly distinguishable. Chaplin himself described the way he divided his life: when he was at work on a film, his creative concentration left him no time for other pursuits. It quickly appeared, however, that Chaplin's life was not in fact so easily divisible. His mind, said one collaborator, was like an attic, in which everything that might one day come in handy was stored away for future use. He may have forgotten about his private life when he was at work; but he never forgot work at the other times. Again and again we can recognize the people and incidents and feelings of his personal life transposed into incidents in the films.

Readers who like biographers to supply post-Freudian interpretations for every action and incident may be frustrated. I have no personal liking for that genre of biography; I do not feel qualified for psychoanalysis; and finally I think that Chaplin's singular life story would defy the process. The childhood, for a start, made up of experiences that few people can even comprehend, let alone share, and felt through a sensibility that was already out of the ordinary, had to leave its impression upon his attitudes to people, work, money, wives, families, politics, himself. Then he was an actor, with the actor's ability to stay ahead, to adapt his personality to suit the occasion and the company. His protean quality was often puzzling. People who knew him well enough to record their impressions have described him as modest, vain, prodigal, mean, generous, shy, show-off, ruthless, timid, kind, patient, impatient . . . Most likely he was all these things, since he was human. Perhaps the most remarkable achievement of his life, in fact, was to stay fallibly, recognizably human, despite the adulation amounting to apotheosis at the peak of his fame; despite experiencing public revilement as passionate as the affection he had known; despite having lived the most dramatic of all the rags to riches stories ever told. There is no wonder if he was a complex creature. For all we can learn about Chaplin's life and thought, it will still not be easy to explain him. But we can try to understand.

ACKNOWLEDGEMENTS

My principal thanks are of course to Lady Chaplin, who gave me full access to Sir Charles's working papers, without seeking to impose the restraints implied in an "authorized" biography, which this assuredly is not. I am also grateful to her children for their kindness and patience. It was in large part due to the urging of Victoria Chaplin, her husband Jean-Baptiste Thierrée and their friend David Gothard that I first undertook the book. Nor could it have been possible without the wholehearted cooperation of Miss Rachel Ford, who has been responsible for ordering and maintaining the Chaplin archives, and her assistant in Paris, Madame Pam Paumier. I have been very conscious of the courtesies and warmth of the household staff at Vevey – Renato, Gino, Mirella, Fernanda and "Kay-Kay" McKenzie—during my stays there.

Perhaps the most important personal link with Chaplin has been Jerry Epstein. He was Chaplin's producer and assistant, and has become my agent. More important is his great gift of friendship, which, like Chaplin himself, I have been privileged to share. He encouraged me to embark upon this book for several years before I was finally persuaded to put pen to paper.

In sharing the mass of material they assembled during the years of research for their incomparable film series *Unknown Chaplin*, Kevin Brownlow and David Gill have far exceeded any ordinary calls of friendship or scholarship. Not a week has gone by without an envelope in the post addressed in Brownlow's meticulous hand, containing some new discovery turned up in his monumental files. My friends Al and Candy Reuter have shown equal generosity in finding for me rare stills and posters not represented in the Chaplin collection. Inman Hunter has freely made available the treasures of his own collection, including the papers of Edna Purviance, which are now in his safe-keeping.

I am particularly indebted to the pioneer researches of Harold Manning and David Clegg, who have spent years combing public archives and the volumes of *The Era* in the Birmingham Public Library. Mr Manning is the most vital nonagenarian of my acquaintance, with a store of vivid theatrical memories that go back to his first Christmas pantomime in 1899. He is, in addition, a scrupulous and indefatigable scholar, whose advice has been invaluable. David Clegg's own listings have made a major contribution to the record of Chaplin's theatrical appearances in the appendices.

Research in the archives of the Greater London Record Office has produced much new evidence of Chaplin's childhood years; and here I owe a particular debt to Mr Alan Neate, the Record Keeper for the Director-General, who has over the years carefully noted every Chaplin reference. Mr Neate also drew my attention to the discovery by Mrs Weston of the record of Hannah Chaplin's and her father's adult baptisms.

Others in this country to whom I am especially grateful are Roy Waters, who has helped me with research on *Sherlock Holmes* and has lent or given me rare photographs from his collection; Peter Cotes, whose *The Little Fellow*, written with the late Thelma Niklaus, remains one of the best appreciations; Colin Sorenson of the Museum of London who has passed on a note of any Chapliniana that has come under his eye; Tony Barker, for music hall references; John Whitehorn of Francis, Day and Hunter for dating the songs of Charles Chaplin Senior; Bill Douglas and Peter Jewell for advice and pictures; Ken Wlaschin, whose eagle eye has often spotted a reference, a postcard or a music sheet; Miss Kathleen Saintsbury for memories of her father; Mrs Fred Karno Junior for her recollections of the Karno troupes; I am also grateful to the Garrick Club and its librarian Dr Geoffrey Ashton for access to their files of *The Era*; and especially Pauline Mason (*née* Chaplin) for her family recollections.

In the United States my first debt is to Mark Stock, the most dedicated Chaplinian of my acquaintance, who gave me every possible help in Hollywood. Marc Wanamaker was also of inestimable assistance in driving me around the wildernesses of California, giving helpful leads and supplying photographs. Paul and Betty Tetrick were

Acknowledgements

generous hosts and wonderful informants about life at the Chaplin Studio; they also loaned me rare and precious photographs. Moreover they introduced me to Wyn Ray Evans, with her precise and fascinating reminiscences of her parents' days with Karno and her own meetings with Hannah Chaplin.

Of those who worked with Chaplin, I enjoyed long conversations with Hans Koenekamp, who photographed the first film in which Chaplin appeared in the famous costume; with Georgia Hale, the exquisite leading lady of *The Gold Rush*; with Eugene Lourié, the great designer who was art director on *Limelight*. I spent a memorable day with Dan James at his cliff-edge eyrie at Carmel. Anthony Coogan talked to me of his father, and Steve Totheroh of his grandfather. I was also able to speak to Virginia Cherrill Martini, Chaplin's leading lady in *City Lights*; to Lita Grey Chaplin; to David Raksin; to Tim Durant; to Dean Riesner (once the Horrid Child in *The Pilgrim*) and to the nonagenarian Nellie Bly Baker, Chaplin's first studio secretary.

A special debt of gratitude is due to Charles Mandelstam in New York, for obtaining the FBI files on Chaplin in time to make use of them in this book. I would also like to record with particular appreciation the support I have received, in friendship, interest and encouragement, from Alexander Walker; from Mo and Lynn Rothman; from Peter Rose and Albert Gallichan; and from my endlessly patient friends Roger Few and Harry Ogle who gave invaluable help in laborious proofreeding. Finally, at Collins I must thank Christopher MacLehose and Roger Schlesinger who nursed the book along, Ronald Clark and Marian Morris who designed it, and my editor, Ariane Goodman.

Embleton, Northumberland
June 1984.

The Chaplin Family

Table 1

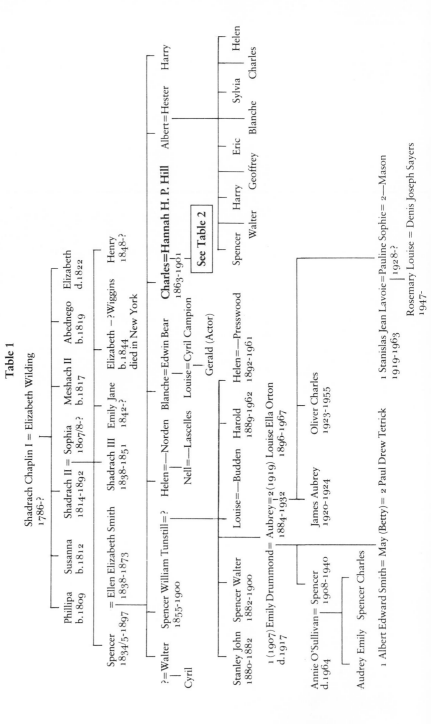

Shadrach Chaplin I = Elizabeth Wilding
1786-?

Phillipa b.1809 — Susanna b.1812 — Shadrach II 1814-1892 = Sophia 1807/8-? — Meshach II b.1817 — Abednego b.1819 — Elizabeth d.1822

Spencer 1834/5-1897 = Ellen Elizabeth Smith 1838-1873

Shadrach III 1838-1851 — Emily Jane 1842-?

Elizabeth b.1844 died in New York = ?Wiggins — Henry 1848-?

Spencer William Tunstill = ? 1855-1900

Helen = —Norden — Blanche = Edwin Bear — Louise = Cyril Campion

Nell = —Lascelles

Gerald (Actor)

Charles = Hannah H. P. Hill 1863-1901

See Table 2

Albert = Hester — Harry

Spencer — Harry — Eric — Sylvia — Helen
Walter — Geoffrey — Blanche — Charles

?= Walter

Cyril

Louise = —Budden — Harold 1889-1962 — Helen = —Presswood 1892-1961

Stanley John 1880-1882 — Spencer Walter 1882-1900

Aubrey = 2 (1919) Louise Ella Orton
1884-1932   1896-1967

1 (1907) Emily Drummond =
d.1917

James Aubrey 1920-1924 — Oliver Charles 1923-1955

Annie O'Sullivan = Spencer
d.1964   1908-1940

Audrey Emily   Spencer Charles

1 Albert Edward Smith = May (Betty) = 2 Paul Drew Tetrick

1 Stanislas Jean Lavoie = Pauline Sophie = 2 —Mason
1919-1963   1928-?

Rosemary Louise = Denis Joseph Sayers
1947-

Table 2

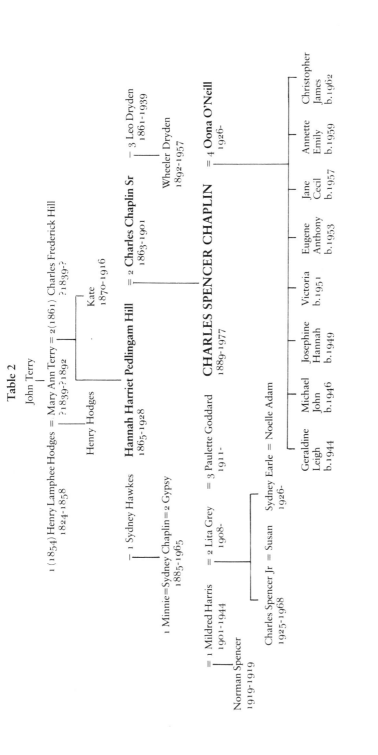

John Terry

1 (1854) Henry Lamphee Hodges = Mary Ann Terry = 2 (1861) Charles Frederick Hill
1824-1858   ?1839-?1892   ?1839-?

Henry Hodges

Kate
1870-1916

Hannah Harriet Pedlingam Hill
1865-1928

= 2 Charles Chaplin Sr
1863-1901

— 3 Leo Dryden
1861-1939

Wheeler Dryden
1892-1957

— 1 Sydney Hawkes

1 Minnie=Sydney Chaplin=2 Gypsy
1885-1965

CHARLES SPENCER CHAPLIN
1889-1977

= 4 Oona O'Neill
1926-

= 3 Paulette Goddard
1911-

= 2 Lita Grey
1908-

Sydney Earle = Noelle Adam
1926-

= 1 Mildred Harris
1901-1944

Norman Spencer
1919-1919

Charles Spencer Jr = Susan
1925-1968

Geraldine Leigh b.1944

Michael John b.1946

Josephine Hannah b.1949

Victoria b.1951

Eugene Anthony b.1953

Jane Cecil b.1957

Annette Emily b.1959

Christopher James b.1962

The London of Chaplin's Youth

1 *York Road*
CC lived at number 164 with Hodges family, 1895.

2 *14 Lambeth Square*
CC's mother lived here, May 1890.

3 *Canterbury Music Hall,*
Westminster Bridge Road.
CC recalled seeing father perform here.

4 *Christchurch,*
Westminster Bridge Road.
CC's mother and paternal grandfather baptized here as adults, 10 January 1898.

5 *South London Palace,*
92 London Road, Lambeth.
Hannah appeared in a benefit performance here on 27 May 1886, and Charles Chaplin Senior frequently performed. Chaplin also remembered that this was where he first saw a Karno company, about 1903.

6 *West Square*
CC's parents lived together here, c.1890.

7 *Broad Street,*
(now Black Prince Road)
Spencer Chaplin, CC's uncle, landlord of Queen's Head, c.1890-1900.

8 *3 Pownall Terrace*
CC lived here with mother, early 1903.

9 *Kennington Road*
CC lived with Mr and Mrs Alfred Jackson at 5 Kennington Mansions, April 23 - May 3, 1900.

10 *Renfrew Road*
Lambeth Workhouse.

11 *Chester Street*
CC lived here with mother, and worked in barber's shop, c.1901.

12 *289 Kennington Road*
CC and Sydney stayed here with father and 'Louise', September-November(?) 1898.

13 *39 Methley Street.*
CC's mother lived here, November 1898 - August 1899 and subsequently.

14 *Kennington Park*
Mrs Chaplin and her sons spent the day of their 'escape' from the Lambeth Workhouse here, in August 1898.

15 *10 Farmer's Road*
(now Kennington Park Gardens)
CC's mother lodging here, July 1898.

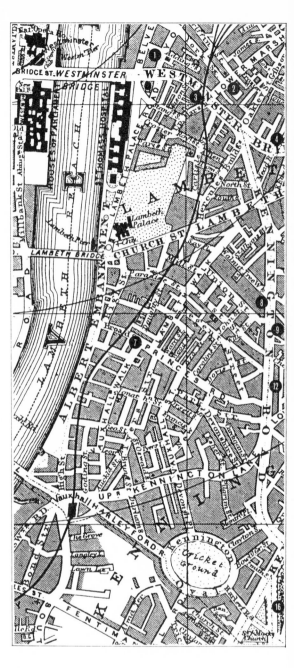

16 *Brixton Road*
CC and Sydney rented a flat here, in Glenshaw Mansions, 1906 - 1912.

17 *57 Brandon Street*
CC's parents living here at time of Sydney Chaplin's birth (16 March 1885) and their marriage (22 June 1885).

18 *St John's Church, Larcom Street*
CC's parents married here 22 June 1885;
Sydney baptized here.
19 *11 Camden Street*
(now Morecambe Street)
CC's maternal grandparents living here
at time of Hannah Chaplin's birth, 1865.

19 *68 Camden Street*
CC's parents living here, March 1890.
20 *East Street*
CC believed he was born here
16 April 1889.

The Cradle.

On the 15th ultimo, the wife of Mr Charles Chaplin (*nee* Miss Lily Harley), of a beautiful boy. Mother and son both doing well. Papers please copy.

Chaplin's first press notice -
The Magnet, 11 May 1889. Contrary
to this announcement, Chaplin always
celebrated his birthday on 16 April.

I

A London boyhood

The Chaplin family lived for generations in Suffolk. The name suggests that they were descended from Huguenots, who had settled in great numbers in East Anglia. Chaplin's great-great-grandfather, Shadrach Chaplin, was born in 1786 and became the village boot-maker in Great Finborough, Suffolk. Shadrach inherited the taste for Old Testament names, so that the Chaplin family descent has the appearance of a biblical genealogy. Shadrach, as well as three daughters, begat Shadrach II (1814), Meshach (1817) and Abednego (1819). Shadrach II married a woman named Sophia, seven years older than himself, who came from Tunstall, Staffordshire: it became a Chaplin family tradition to give children the middle name 'Tunstall', though, depending on · the parish clerk, it sometimes became 'Tunstill'.[1]

In 1851 Shadrach II was described as a 'master brewer'. He lived in Carr Street, Ipswich,[2] where he established an inn and eating house and conducted a pork butchery. Perhaps these enterprises did not prosper, however, for in the early 1870s he had given up the catering business altogether and taken up his father's trade of boot and shoe maker. He seems still to have been in this business at the time of his death in 1892, when he bequeathed his stock-in-trade, his shoemaker's tools and his estate of £144 to his widow.[3] Poor Sophia had very temporary benefit from her bequest, since she died the day after her husband.

Shadrach II inevitably begat Shadrach III, but his eldest son – the great Charles Chaplin's grandfather, who was born in 1834 or 1835 – had been named, for a change, Spencer. Spencer was trained to the trade of butcher. It is with Spencer that the first touch of poetry enters the Chaplin history, for on 30 October 1854, still a minor, he married a seventeen-year-old gypsy girl called Ellen Elizabeth Smith, in the parish church of St Margaret, Ipswich.[4] The witnesses to the marriage included the girl's father, who was illiterate, but no Chaplin, so perhaps the family were not happy with the match. Ellen Elizabeth died in 1873, at thirty-five,[5] and no photograph of her survives, so we can only speculate that it might have been she who originated the striking looks, jet hair and fine eyes that became the Chaplin heritage.

The marriage may have been precipitated, for only eight months later, in June 1855, the couple's first child, Spencer William Tunstill (*sic*), was born in Ipswich.[6] Shortly after this event the young Chaplins moved to London. Spencer continued to work as a journeyman butcher, though he was later, in the 1890s, to become a publican and the landlord of the Davenport Arms, Radnor Place, Paddington. On 18 March 1863 a second son, Charles, was born at 22 Orcus Street, Marylebone.[7] This Charles was the future father of the more famous Charles Chaplin.

Towards the end of Sir Charles Chaplin's life, an admirer sent him an old poetry book she had found which bore a school prize label. It had been awarded at St Mark's Schools, Notting Hill in 1874 to Charles Chaplin in Standard 4.[8] The registers of the school no longer exist, so we can discover no more details about this Charles Chaplin to confirm that he was, indeed, Chaplin's father. However the St Mark's Schools in Lancaster Road were only a mile or so from the only addresses we know for Grandfather Spencer Chaplin. In 1874 Charles Chaplin Senior would have been ten or eleven, the appropriate age for Standard 4. Moreover, the registrations of births in the years 1862–1864 indicate no likely contender of that name for the prize in the London area. The balance of evidence seems to confirm Charles Chaplin as the diligent scholar thus rewarded.

Apart from this brief tantalizing glimpse, the elder Charles's early life is shrouded in obscurity until the age of twenty-two, when he met and married Chaplin's mother, Hannah Hill.[9] The Hills appear to have been if anything more humble people than the Chaplins. Hannah's father, Charles Frederick Hill, the son of a bricklayer, was born on 16 April 1839 – fifty years to the day before his famous grandson. There was a family tradition that he had come from Ireland, though in this respect it may be remarked that he seems to have been and remained a Protestant. His whole working life was spent as a journeyman shoemaker: considering that Charlie Chaplin would come to be symbolized by a pair of disintegrating boots, it is curious that the making and mending of footwear should appear so often as an occupation of his ancestors.

With the Hills the Chaplin story moves to South London. On 16 August 1861 Charles Hill, then living in Lambeth Walk, married Mary Ann Hodges.[10] Both had been married before. There is no record of Charles Hill's first wife; but Mary Ann's previous marriage was to have some relevance to the early years of the younger Charles Chaplin. Socially, Mary Ann seems to have been a cut above her second husband. Her father was John Terry, a mercantile clerk. On 15 May 1854 she had married Henry Lamphee Hodges, a sign-writer and grainer.[11] After four and a half years of marriage however, poor young Hodges fell off an omnibus and suffered a fatal concussion.[12]

When she married Charles Hill, Mary Ann brought with her a five-year-old son by Hodges, also called Henry. Four years later a daughter was born at 11 Camden Street and christened Hannah Harriet Pedlingham Hill.[13] A second daughter, Chaplin's Aunt Kate, followed on 18 January 1870.[14]

Charles Hill's boot-making appears not to have given the family much stability, and they moved from lodging to lodging – always in Lambeth or Southwark – with bewildering frequency. The census of 1871 records them at 77 Beckway Street, Walworth. They are described as Charles Hill, boot riveter, aged thirty-two; his wife, Mary Ann Hill, boot binder, aged thirty-two; their son Henry, boot-maker, aged fifteen; and their daughters Harriet (Hannah), aged five, and Kate, aged one.[15]

While their step-brother, known as young Harry, stuck to the boot business, Hannah and Kate grew up into strikingly attractive women. As the music hall songs of the time delighted to relate, the streets of London were full of perils for young girls. Hannah became pregnant. In later years she told her sons that she had run off to South Africa with a rich bookmaker called Hawkes, but it is now impossible to verify either the trip or Mr Hawkes. All that is certain is that on 16 March 1885 Hannah gave birth to a boy, who was named Sidney John. When the birth was registered and again when he was baptized at St John's Church, Larcom Street, the father's name was not entered.

3

Sidney John was not to remain fatherless for long.*

The accouchement took place at 57 Brandon Street,[16] the premises of Joseph Hodges, trading as a general dealer and most likely the brother of the unfortunate Hodges who fell off the omnibus.[17] It seems probable that Hannah had left the paternal home and taken refuge with her mother's former brother-in-law. At some point Charles Chaplin Senior took up residence in Joseph Hodges' house, and less than fourteen weeks after Sydney's birth Charles Chaplin and Hannah Hill were married. Both gave their address as 57 Brandon Street. One of the two witnesses at the ceremony at St John's Church, Larcom Street, Walworth, was Mary Ann Hill, the mother of the bride.[18]

Charles Chaplin described himself on the registration of the marriage as 'professional singer'. In fact, however, there is no evidence that either Charles or Hannah had begun a career as professional entertainer until after their marriage. Certainly *The Era*, the weekly

1885 - Marriage certificate of
Charles Chaplin Senior and
Hannah Harriett Hill.

* The correct spelling of the name of the elder Chaplin brother can not be resolved. He was baptized 'Sidney', but the records of the local authorities and institutions generally spell the name as 'Sydney'. During his days with Karno the forms Sidney, Sydney, Sid and Syd all occur. As an adult Sydney-Sidney himself used the 'y' form, but Charles consistently used the 'i' in writing his brother's name. (It was said that Chaplin and his then wife Lita Grey disagreed over the spelling of the name of their son, Sydney Earle Chaplin, because Chaplin thought the 'y' was pretentious. The present Chaplin family consider that uncle and nephew are differentiated as, respectively, 'Sidney' and 'Sydney'.) The solution adopted for this book is to adopt the 'y' form in the main text, but to retain whatever form is adopted by the writers in quoted texts.

journal of the British theatrical profession, which provided exhaustive records of theatrical presentations, lists no appearances by either of them before 1886 (Hannah) and 1887 (Charles). There is no record or family tradition to suggest what lured these two young people, with no previous connexion with show business, into the theatre.

Still, it was not surprising that the music halls should beckon young people with looks and even a small talent. This was the start of the great era of the British music hall. In London, the London Pavilion had just been handsomely reconstructed, the Alhambra had recently established itself as a variety house, and the Empire, Leicester Square was to be opened in 1887. In all, London boasted thirty-six music halls of varying class in 1886, while throughout the rest of the country, from Aberdeen to Plymouth, there were no less than 234 halls with weekly bills to fill. Dublin alone had nine music halls, Liverpool eight and Birmingham six. The opportunities were immense, and perhaps more apparent in Lambeth than in any other quarter of London. The first music hall agent, Ambrose Maynard, had set up his offices in Waterloo Road in 1858, and shortly afterwards moved to York Road, where he was soon followed by rival firms. York Road ran into Westminster Bridge Road, where the Canterbury and Gatti's Music Halls stood. Proceeding further south from Westminster Bridge Road was Kennington Road, with a parade of public houses – The Three Stags, The White Horse, The Tankard and above all The Horns – which were favourite resorts of the music hall professionals. Large numbers of performers lived in Kennington, though the more successful preferred the somewhat smarter Brixton, immediately to the south. No doubt Charles and Hannah Chaplin were as dazzled by the glamour of the élite of the music halls, at their Sunday morning get-togethers in the Kennington pubs, as their son was to be fifteen years later.

Both Hannah and Charles were evidently talented. Chaplin's descriptions of his mother's gifts for observation and mimicry are certainly not inspired by sentiment alone; and he was a shrewd judge of talent. Hannah may simply have been unlucky: perhaps her particular talent was out of tune with the time. Her career was brief and not triumphant. Her recorded performances were all in small provincial music halls, and at the bottom of the bill – 'among the wines and spirits' as they said in a day when music halls were still often also drinking places, and the artists' names were followed on the printed programme by the tariff of refreshments. Still, Hannah's brief time as a music hall artist was sufficient to supply glamorous memories with which to stir the imagination of her worshipping young sons in later years.

Debutants like Hannah and Charles would in those days have gained their experience of entertaining audiences with one-night engagements in the 'free-and-easies' and public houses which provided nightly entertainment for their guests. Hannah's first advertised professional engagements were at the end of 1885, when she appeared at The Star, Dublin. By this time she had acquired an agent, Frank Albert, and by the start of the new year was sufficiently encouraged to place her 'professional card' in *The Era*. These 'cards' have been an almost unchanging feature of British theatrical journals for well over a century: they serve to announce a performer's success, his availability, even his mere existence.

When Hannah placed her first card, to appear on 2 January 1886, there was still apparently some doubt as to the spelling of her professional name. The announcement read:

> That Charming little Chanter.
> L I L L I E   H A R L E Y,
> just finished a most successful Engagement Star,
> Dublin. Now appearing with great success in BELFAST.
> Agent, Frank Albert.

The following week's card read:

> New Song, "He might have sent on the gloves," J. Bowess.
> L I L L I E   H A R L E Y,
> just finished, grand success Nightly, Star, Dublin, and
> Buffalo, Belfast. SCOTIA, GLASGOW, Monday next.
> Booking dates fast. Sole Agent, Frank Albert.

Next week Hannah's stage name appeared in its definitive form:

The Refined and Talented Artist
LILY HARLEY
complimented by Proprietors, the Public and Press
Heaps of notices in different papers every week
Pleasing success SCOTIA GLASGOW
A few good songs required. Agent, F. Albert

Perhaps something more than a few good songs was required, for after this Lily Harley's card vanished for periods of several weeks, and her engagements seem to have been sporadic. On 27 May 1886 she appeared (as 'Miss Lilly Harley') in London at a benefit concert for William Bishop at the South London Palace. On this occasion she figured rather low on a bill whose stars were Vesta Tilley, The Great Vance and Chirgwin. Below her, however, at the very bottom of the bill, was the sixteen-year-old Marie Lloyd, soon destined to become the greatest star of British music hall. In the autumn there was a run of bookings ('Lily Harley – The Essence of Refinement') at M'Farland's Music Hall, Aberdeen, M'Farland's, Dundee and The Folly, Glasgow. After this, both 'cards' and bookings cease altogether.

The disappointments of Hannah's own career must have been aggravated by watching the success of a friend, 'Dashing Eva Lester', with whom for a while she shared the same agent. Billed as 'The California Queen and England's Queen of Song', Eva had a brashness which Hannah lacked. *The Era* wrote of her performance at the Metropolitan in September 1886: 'Miss Eva Lester, one of the prettiest and most fascinating serio-comic songstresses we have. In a delineation of a romp, Miss Lester, by her piquancy, won much applause . . .' In his autobiography Chaplin recalls how a dozen or so years later, when they were themselves upon hard times, they found poor Eva in the street, a sick, dirty, shaven-headed derelict. The boy Charlie was horrified and ashamed to be seen with her but kindly Hannah took her in for the night and cleaned her up.

Charles's career had a slower start than Hannah's but a more promising progression. His first recorded professional engagement was in the week of Queen Victoria's Golden Jubilee, 20 June 1887, at the Poly Variety Theatre.[19]

At first he worked as a mimic, but soon developed into what was called a 'dramatic and descriptive singer' with a strong attraction for his audiences. He was a pleasant-looking man, with no very evident facial similarity to his son. Chaplin described him as a quiet, brooding man with dark eyes, and said that Hannah thought he looked like Napoleon. The portraits that appear on the sheet music of his song successes show him with dark eyes that seem somewhat melancholy despite the broad prop grin.

Charles sang songs in the character of a masher, a man about town, or an ordinary husband and father, bedevilled by problems all too familiar to his audiences such as mothers-in-law, landladies who

1886 - Handbill for benefit concert
at the South London Palace,
including Hannah Chaplin
(as Miss Lilly Harley).

wanted to be paid, nagging wives and crying babies. The clearest sign of his success is that between 1890 and 1896 the music publishers Francis, Day and Hunter issued several of his song successes, with

1893 – Illustrated cover of song sung
by Charles Chaplin Sr.

his portrait prominent on the cover. This honour was accorded only to artists whose reputation the publishers were certain would sell copies. These years were the peak of Chaplin's career. Without ever achieving the rank of contemporaries like Herbert Campbell, Dan Leno, Arthur Roberts, Charles Coborn or Charles Godfrey (to whom he was considered to have a striking physical resemblance), he was a star: as late in his career as 1898 he could share (with the 'Beograph' moving pictures) top billing at the New Empire Palace Theatre of Varieties, Leicester:

**VERY IMPORTANT AND WELCOME RETURN OF
ONE OF LEICESTER'S GREATEST FAVOURITES, MR
CHARLES CHAPLIN
STAR DESCRIPTIVE VOCALIST AND CHORUS COMEDIAN
IN HIS LATEST SUCCESSES AND OLD FAVOURITES
"DEAR OLD PALS"**

All this, however, and much unhappiness besides, was before him on Tuesday 16 April 1889, when his first son, Charles Spencer Chaplin was born. At that moment he was playing a week's engagement at 'Professor' Leotard Bosco's Empire Palace of Varieties, Hull.[20] Perhaps in later years the elder Chaplin told his son stories of the colourful Professor Bosco, because Chaplin was twice to use the name for characters in his films. The expectant Hannah had, presumably, stayed at home in London to await her baby.

Charles and Hannah were not so meticulous in registering Charles's birth as Sydney's; and it has tormented historians and biographers for decades that there is no official record of the birth of London's most famous son. The fact is not especially remarkable. It was easy enough, particularly for music hall artists, constantly moving (if they were lucky) from one town to another, to put off and eventually to forget this kind of formality; at that time the penalties were not strict or efficiently enforced. In the early days of his cinema fame, Chaplin said that he was born at Fontainebleau, in France. This may have been one of the colourful stories with which Hannah seems to have endeavoured to brighten her sons' lives. Later Chaplin was certain that he was born in East Lane, Walworth, just round the corner from Sydney's birthplace in Brandon Street.

It is a certain mark of a Walworth native that Chaplin refers to the street as 'East Lane'. On the map it has never appeared otherwise than as 'East Street', but the locals, like Chaplin, have never known it as other than 'East Lane'. For Londoners a street with a market is characteristically described as a 'Lane' (as with Petticoat Lane, the other side of the river). East Lane market is still as flourishing now as when Chaplin was a child. For some reason the East Lane traders seem to have a greater bent for drama, and the food that is cooked there has more variety and pungency than in any other London market. Practically nothing survives from the time of Chaplin's child-hood, apart from one or two ruinous shops at the west end and The Mason's Arms, a building whose theatrical flamboyance must have been thrilling to a small boy. Even so, the colour and vitality, the tumult of fruit and fish and pop music and old clothes still evoke an atmosphere as close, perhaps, as we may come to Chaplin's London.

Chaplin recalled that soon after his birth, the family moved to much smarter lodgings in West Square. West Square has somehow survived the destruction of the little streets and community life of the area by insensitive urban development. In 1890, as today, it must have been a strange oasis in a perennially depressed region: an elegant Georgian square of tall brick houses, with gardens in the centre. The move was made possible by Charles Chaplin's growing success. In the months after his son's birth, he was getting regular engagements, and in the year 1890–1 the music publishers Francis, Day and Hunter regarded him as such a 'comer' that they published no less than three of his song successes – 'As the Church Bells Chime', 'Everyday Life' and 'Eh, Boys?', which was written by John P. Harrington and George Le Brunn, 'the Gilbert and Sullivan of the halls' who wrote most of Marie Lloyd's greatest successes, including 'Oh Mr Porter'.

The portrait that appears on the cover of 'Eh, Boys?', with the singer in silk hat, frock coat and floppy orange bow tie, shows some resemblance between the elder and the younger Charles Chaplin. One of the verses – illustrated by a comic vignette on the cover – ominously touches upon one of the real-life domestic troubles of the Chaplin family:

> When you're wed, and come home 'late-ish'
>   Rather *too* late – boozy, too,
> Wifey dear says, 'Oh, you *have* come!'
>   And then turns her back on you;
> Only gives you 'noes' and 'yesses',
>   Until, with a sudden bound,
> She quite fiercely pokes the fire up,
>   And then spanks the kids all round.
>
>   CHORUS
> We all of us know what *that* means – Eh, boys? Eh, boys?
> We all of us know what that means, – Eh, boys? Eh?
>   When first she starts to drat you,
>   And then throws something at you,
> We all of us know what that means – it's her playful little way.

Drink was the endemic disease of the music halls. The halls had evolved from drinking establishments and the sale of liquor still made up an important part of the managers' incomes. When they were not on stage the artists were expected to mingle with the audiences in the bars, to encourage conviviality and consumption – which inevitably was best achieved by example. Poor Chaplin was only one of many who succumbed to alcoholism as an occupational hazard.

In 1890, however, he was still leaping from success to success. In the summer he was invited to sign for an American tour, and in August and September was appearing in New York at the Union Square Theatre.[21] The stay appears to have been pleasant and sociable. Charles's aunt Elizabeth had married a Mr Wiggins and now lived in New York. Through her he met and made friends with Dr Charles Horatio Shepherd, who had a dentist's practice, and Mrs Shepherd. 'We had some delightful hours together,' recalled Dr Shepherd, a quarter of a century later.[22]

J. P. Harrington, the song-writer, recalled an incident that occurred just before Chaplin's departure for America:

> One of our first clients was Charlie Chaplin, father of the famous film 'star'. Chaplin was a good, sound performer of the Charles Godfrey type, although he, of course, lacked the latter's wonderful talent and versatility. We wrote the majority of Charlie's songs for some considerable time: in fact at one period, all three of the songs he was nightly singing were from our pens.
>
> In this connexion, an incident which strikes me as far more amusing now than when it happened, occurs to me. We had made an appointment with Mr David Day, head of Francis, Day and Hunters, the music publishers, to hear the three songs played over and sung in his office, with a view to their publication. In due course, Chaplin, Le Brunn and I arrived: the songs were played over by George and were sung by Charlie, and David was delighted with all three.
>
> The cheque book appeared on the scene. 'Terms? The usual, I suppose?'
>
> Trio of course, in delightful unanimity: 'Certainly, Mr Day.'
>
> The cheque book is opened – the pen is raised – then, George Le Brunn, anxious to paint the lily and gild refined gold, says: 'You know, he'll sing all these songs in America as well, Mr Day.'
>
> Pen suspended in mid-air.
>
> 'Ah, yes?' murmurs Mr Day, softly. 'And when do you go to America, Mr Chaplin?'
>
> 'Week after next,' says Charlie.

'How long for?'

'Four months.'

'Snap!' Cheque book returned to its little nest in the desk-drawer; pen carefully laid aside.

'Come and see me again, when you come back from America. It won't be any use publishing the songs while you're singing them on the other side of the Atlantic!'

'The things Charlie Chaplin and deponent said to George Le Brunn when we got outside that office would not look well if set down in this veracious narrative.'[23]

The American trip, however, seemed to mark the final break-up of the Chaplins' marriage. No doubt Hannah had been making new friends in Charles's absence. Certainly she had a new friend by the autumn of 1891, another music hall singer who over the years frequently appeared on the same bill as Charles Chaplin. He was Leo Dryden.

Dryden's real name was George Dryden Wheeler, and he was born in Limehouse, London, on 6 June 1861. He had first gone on the halls in 1881 but had little success for several years until one of the great stars of Victorian variety, Jenny Hill, noticed him and introduced him to her own agent, Hugh Didcott. From then onwards his career prospered. His greatest hit came early in 1891 when he presented his sentimental ballad 'The Miner's Dream of Home', depicting the nostalgia of an emigrant in the Australian gold fields. From this time on, Dryden, with his square-jawed, handsome face, was established as the minstrel of England, Empire and patriotism. His later songs included 'The Miner's Return', 'India's Reply', 'Bravo, Dublin Fusiliers', 'Freedom and Japan', 'The Great White Mother', 'The Only Way' and 'Love and Duty'. Unfortunately the stoic nobility of the characters he presented on stage does not seem to have distinguished his private life. He was from all accounts erratic and given to violence. He is said to have given each of his three wives a rough time. In 1919, irked at finding his star fading, he sought publicity by singing his songs in the streets.

In October 1891 he was engaged at the Cambridge, a large music hall in Shoreditch. The popularity of 'The Miner's Dream of Home' obliged the management to extend his engagement week by week until Christmas. During these twelve weeks in London Dryden brought his affair with Hannah Chaplin to fruition. We have comic evidence of his courtship. As he became more successful, Dryden took to inserting flamboyant advertising in the professional papers. A typical example reads:

OCTOBER 31. 1891

> MR. LEO DRYDEN,
> "Love and Duty," Published by Maynard.
> "Struck 'ile." "Struck 'ile." "Struck 'ile" again.
> "Love and Duty," the Premier Descriptive Song, but
> I have "Struck 'ile" with a Song that will be the Song,
> a Song that will be Sung in every home,
> where the "Mother Tongue" is spoken.
> On Tuesday, Oct. 20th, I produced at the Cambridge
> "The Miner's Dream,"
> Written and Composed by Will Godwin and L. D.
> I was to have finished on the following Saturday, but directly
> Mr E. Page the Manager, saw and heard
> "The Miner's Dream,"
> he immediately rescinded the Notice, and made arrangements
> for me to stay on, and took me from 8 10 Turn and put me
> "Star Turn." 10 20. Such facts speak volumes
> On Monday next I produce "The Miner's Dream" at the
> Foresters', with Special Scenery and Effects.
> Managers are cordially invited to see and hear
> "The Miner's Dream."
> ALHAMBRA (Second Week) 8 20
> FORESTERS' (Second Week).... 9 20
> CAMBRIDGE (Fifth Week).. ... 10 20
> Messrs Francis, Day, and Hunter have Paid the Highest
> Price they have ever paid for any Song for
> "The Miner's Dream of Home."
> Owing to certain unprincipled Artistes (?) taking mean
> advantage of my knowledge of the Law of Copyright, the Song
> I Reconstructed and made so Popular in Birmingham, Liverpool, Birkenhead, Newcastle, and Sunderland, I have entirely
> discarded
> Remember, It was the Singer, not the Song.
> "The Miner's Dream"
> is both Singer and Song, and will eclipse all previous productions. I shall shortly produce a Descriptive Monologue,
> in Three Scenes, entitled "Hard Times,"
> in which I shall introduce the success of successes,
> "The Miner's Dream,"
> which will ensure the success of the Monologue.
> Representatives, Messrs Healy and Cooke.

It was a feature of these advertisements that Dryden aggressively asserted his rights in his songs, offering licences for performances outside London, and threatening legal proceedings against anyone who infringed his rights. One exceptional announcement in November 1891, however, introduced, for those who could recognize it, a romantic touch:

> In answer to many letters received, I beg to inform those ladies who have written that I intend to retain the London Right for myself. Re "Opportunity," Artistes wishing to secure the Pantomime Rights (£1 1s.) may apply to me for same.
> Middlesbrough Right Secured by Miss Kittie Fairdale.
> No other Artiste has my permission to Sing the above but Miss Kittie Fairdale and Miss Lillie Harley.
> Proprietors and Managers kindly note.

Miss Kittie Fairdale had, of course, paid her guinea. Miss Lillie Harley – Hannah Chaplin – had presumably not; nor was she very likely to take advantage of her rights, since she had no apparent engagements at which she could sing 'Opportunity'. Still, the announcement must have found her vulnerable indeed. This was the first time for more than five years that her name had appeared in the professional press, and now it was linked with the star of the day. Dryden was thirty and handsome, and the flattery of his announcement must have been irresistible. The advertisement appeared on Friday 28 November. Nine months and three days later, on 31 August 1892, Hannah gave birth to Leo Dryden's son, also George Dryden Wheeler.

Thus the young Charles Chaplin found himself fatherless, but with another half-brother. He was three and a half; Sydney was four years older. In his autobiography he recalls that at this time the children and their mother were still living in some affluence. He attributed the cause to his mother's work on the stage, and recalled that she would tuck the two boys in bed and leave them in the care of a house-maid while she went to the theatre. Since there is no record of Hannah working at this period, and since Charles's payments for the support of his sons seem to have stopped quite early, it can only be supposed that Leo Dryden was providing this temporary prosperity. What were the domestic arrangements of Leo and Hannah is not clear. Years later their son – he had adopted the professional name of Wheeler Dryden – said that according to information he had received from his father, they lived 'for a year or two as man and wife',[24] but neither Charles nor Sydney recorded any recollection of Leo Dryden.

The comfort which sheltered Chaplin's first three or four years was soon to end. Hannah's liaison with Leo did not long survive the birth of their child. Hannah seems to have been a devoted, affectionate and protective mother, and to have loved the new baby as fiercely as she did her older sons. It is then easy to appreciate the shock that she must have suffered in the spring of 1893 when the appalling Dryden entered her lodgings and snatched away their six-month-old son. The baby was to vanish from the lives of the Chaplins for almost thirty years.

Poor Hannah had only wanted to be Lily Harley and to dream of the glamour of the stage. Now her life became a nightmare. Other troubles came on her at exactly the moment that her baby was stolen from her. Her mother, Chaplin's Grandma Hill, had apparently left

15

Grandfather Hill: family tradition said that her husband had caught her in a compromising situation with another man. Since the separation, Grandma Hill had gone from bad to worse. She had taken to drinking heavily, and supported herself by hawking old clothes. She became more and more eccentric and, in the village-like community of Lambeth and Southwark, must have been a grave embarrassment to her family. Eventually, in February 1893, she was taken off the streets into the Newington Workhouse, and from there transferred to the Infirmary.

The doctors recorded: 'She is incoherent. She says that she sees beetles, rats, mice and other things about the place. She thinks that the doctors at the Infy. tried to poison her. She makes a lot of rambling statements and frequently contradicts herself.'[25] After some days she was 'much more noisy and troublesome', and on 23 February she was certified insane and committed to the London County Asylum at Banstead.[26] Dr Williams, who signed the certificate, found her still imagining rats and mice, and beetles in her bed. He noted that her condition had been deteriorating for several months, and attributed her madness to drink and worry. Cheap gin was a perilous liquor. Mary Ann was now fifty-four years old. Her husband was ordered to pay four shillings a week towards her support.

The collapse of her mother must have been appalling for Hannah, even if she had no foreboding of her own eventual fate. Yet she appears to have kept the catastrophe from her boys – hard as that must have been in the gossipy intimacy of the Lambeth streets. Chaplin only remembered his grandmother as 'a bright little old lady who always greeted me effusively with baby talk'. Mary Ann survived in Banstead Asylum for two more years.

Hannah now found herself without any means of livelihood. Leo had gone out of her life and Charles appears to have contributed little or nothing to the support of his sons. Chaplin remembered that she earned a little money by nursing and by dressmaking for other members of the congregation of Christchurch, Westminster Bridge Road: she had turned to religion in search of some kind of spiritual comfort. She seems also to have tried to take up her stage career again. As autobiographer, Chaplin generally proves phenomenally accurate in reporting those events in which he was personally involved, so there is no reason to question his version of his own first appearance on the stage, which he described more than once. It appears to have been in about 1894. Hannah had succeeded in getting an engagement at the Canteen, Aldershot. Her health had already begun to deteriorate, and during the performance her voice failed her. The Aldershot audience – mostly soldiers – was notoriously rough, and became vocally hostile. When Hannah left the stage, the manager, who had seen little Charlie do turns to amuse Hannah's friends backstage, led him on as an *extempore* replacement. Unabashed, the child obliged with a song which the coster comedian Gus Elen had made a hit in 1893, ''E Dunno Where 'E Are', and which described the dismay of his former pals at the airs put on by a coster who had come into an inheritance:

> Since Jack Jones come into a little bit of splosh,
> Why 'E dunno where 'E are!

The performance was a great success and to Charlie's delight the audience threw money on to the stage. His business sense was born that night: he announced that he would resume the performance when he had retrieved the coins. This produced still greater appreciation and more money; and Chaplin continued to sing, dance and do impersonations until his mother carried him off into the wings. He noted that this night marked his first appearance on the stage and his mother's last, but this is not quite accurate (unless he much misjudged his own age at the time) since in his later book *My Life in Pictures* he illustrates a handbill advertising a one-night appearance of 'Miss Lily Chaplin, Serio and Dancer' at the Hatcham Liberal Club on 8 February 1896.

Hannah's financial situation must have been desperate, but her sons were to remember more vividly than the privations her efforts to bring gaiety and small pleasures into their lives: the weekly comic, bloater breakfasts and an unforgettable day at Southend after Sydney had providentially found a purse containing seven guineas but no means of identifying its owner. She was, when well, a constantly amusing companion. She would sing and dance her old music hall numbers and act out plays to them. In his old age Chaplin still recalled the emotion aroused in him by her account of the Crucifixion and of Christ as the fount of love, pity and humanity.

The music halls may not have appreciated her gifts, but she had the greatest of audiences in her young sons. She undoubtedly had a talent, and – consciously or not – she applied herself to cultivating the innate gifts of observation that both children seemed to share. Chaplin recalled in 1918:

If it had not been for my mother I doubt if I could have made a success of pantomime. She was one of the greatest pantomime artists I have ever seen. She would sit for hours at a window, looking down at the people on the street and illustrating with her hands, eyes and facial expression just what was going on below. All the time, she would deliver a running fire of comment. And it was through watching and listening to her that I learned not only how to express my emotions with my hands and face, but also how to observe and study people.

She was almost uncanny in her observations. For instance, she would see Bill Smith coming down the street in the morning, and I would hear her say: 'There comes Bill Smith. He's dragging his feet and his shoes are polished. He looks mad, and I'll wager he's had a fight with his wife, and come off without his breakfast. Sure enough! There he goes into the bake shop for a bun and coffee!'

And inevitably during the day, I would hear that Bill Smith had had a fight with his wife.[27]

He had paid touching tribute to his mother in an earlier press statement, an 'autobiography' published by *Photoplay* in 1915:

It seems to me that my mother was the most splendid woman I ever knew ... I have met a lot of people knocking around the world since, but I have never met a more thoroughly refined woman than my mother. If I have amounted to anything, it will be due to her.

Soon after Charlie's sixth birthday, the family's situation reached a new crisis. Hannah became ill – it is not certain with what, but Chaplin recalls that she suffered from acute headaches. On 29 June she was admitted to the Lambeth Infirmary, where she stayed until the end of July. On 1 July Sydney was taken into Lambeth Workhouse,[28] and four days later placed in the West Norwood Schools, which accommodated the infant poor of Lambeth. As Poor Law institutions went, Norwood was pleasant enough. It stood on the slope of a hill facing green fields, on the boundary of Croydon and Streatham, which were then still quite rural. The building, in which Sydney shared a dormitory with thirty-five other boys between nine and sixteen, had been erected only ten years before. There was a steam-heated swimming bath, and the children were not uniformed. Under each bed was a wicker basket for the children to store their clothes at night. Each child had his own towel, brush and comb, but at an inspection a year or two after Sydney's stay there, it was noted that 'only a few of them are provided with tooth-brushes'. Sydney remained at Norwood until 17 September: he was lucky not to stay longer than the autumn, for the inspectors were gravely concerned about the inadequate heating arrangements in the Schools. Strangely, when Sydney was discharged, he was given into the care of his step-father, so perhaps Hannah was still not well enough to care for the boys.[28]

In Charlie's case, the Hodges – Grandma Hill's relations by her first marriage – came to the rescue: and Charlie was lodged, at 164 York Road, with John George Hodges, son of the Joseph Hodges from whose house Charles and Hannah had married, and nephew of the unfortunate Henry Lamphee Hodges who fell from the omnibus. He had, as it happened, taken up the same profession as his deceased uncle, and was a master sign-writer. John George entered Charlie into Addington Road Schools, along with his own son, who was a year or so younger. Charlie appears to have stayed in the school only a week or two: he was never to undergo any prolonged period of day-school attendance.[29]

Only eight months after Sydney's discharge from Norwood Schools, both Chaplin boys were to experience in earnest life in charity institutions. Hannah was again taken into the Infirmary, and Sydney and Charlie, now eleven and seven, were admitted to the workhouse, 'owing to the absence of their father and the destitution and illness of their mother'.[30] Charles Chaplin Senior was traced and reluctantly appeared before the District Relief Committee. Somewhat heartlessly, he told them that while he was willing to take Charlie, he would not accept responsibility for Sydney, who was born illegitimate. The Committee retorted that since Chaplin had married the boy's mother, he was now legally liable for Sydney's maintenance. At this stage, however, Hannah intervened to reject the idea of the boys living with their father as wholly repugnant, since he was living with another woman. Charles was not slow to point out her own adultery. No doubt somewhat bewildered by the family bickering, the Relief Committee decided that it was desirable to keep the boys together and that the best solution would be to place them in the Central London District Poor Law School at Hanwell. It was ruled that Chaplin should pay the sum of fifteen shillings a week towards the cost of keeping them: 'The man is a Music Hall singer, ablebodied and is in a position to earn sufficient to maintain his children.' On 1 July, a fortnight after the boys had been transferred to Hanwell, the Board of Guardians reported to the Local Government Board that Chaplin had consented to this arrangement.

It was one thing to get Chaplin to consent; quite another to get

6 Chaplin

3. Your Committee recommend that the collector be instructed to collect the sum of 15/ per week from Charles Chaplin of 15 Hunters Grove, Fulham, in respect of the maintenance of his two children, Sydney aged 12 and Charles aged 7 about to be sent to Hanwell School

Dated this 9th day of June, 1896

C G Hamel

On behalf of the Committee

17th June   6

My Lords & Gentlemen,

In accordance with article 10 of the Outdoor Relief Regulation Order, December 15th, I beg to report what appears to be a departure from the regulations therein contained.

Two children, Sydney Chaplin, 10, and Charles Chaplin, 7, were admitted to the Workhouse owing to the absence of their father and to the destitution and illness of their mother who was residing with them at this Union.

Enquiries were made for the father and eventually he appeared before the Outdoor Relief Committee. On that occasion he stated he was willing to take the younger boy but wished the Guardians to keep the elder, who was born illegitimate. As however Chaplin married the boy's mother he is legally liable for the boy's maintenance.

Subsequently to the admission of the boys to the Workhouse the mother became chargeable on the Guardians' Infirmary. The idea of the boys being given up to her husband was not pleasant to her as I was obliged he was now living with another woman and this she was able not deny. It was also stated that the mother herself had committed adultery in the absence of her husband

1896 – Extracts from minutes of
Southwark Board of Guardians.

him to pay. Throughout the following year the Board of Guardians was receiving regular reports of Chaplin's non-payment.

The boys, however, knew nothing of this. On 18 June 1896 they were driven the twelve miles to Hanwell in a horse-drawn bakery van, and Chaplin always recalled with a pleasant nostalgia the adventurous drive through the then beautiful countryside on the way. He thought Hanwell less sombre than Norwood, though it was not so up-to-date. Part of the buildings had been adapted from a much older institution; others were one-storeyed corrugated iron structures; but it had a swimming pool and large play areas, and the heating arrangements were at least efficient. In one respect Sydney and Charles were fortunate. Only six or seven years earlier massive reform and reorganization had taken pace at Hanwell. Before that it had long been notorious as a forcing ground for the contagion of ophthalmia: many children who had entered the school healthy left it either wholly or partially blind from the disease.

By 1896 modern treatments and the isolation of sick children had checked the spread of the most infectious diseases. It was harder to control vermin, and Charlie had the misfortune to be one of the thirty-five children who picked up ringworm in the course of the year. He retained bitter memories of having his head shaved, iodined and wrapped in a bandana. Remembering the contempt of the other boys for the ringworm sufferers, he carefully avoided being seen by them looking out of the window of the first-floor ward where those so afflicted were confined.

Life at the school was healthy, with games and exercises, country walks and emphasis on hygiene. The administration was by and large humane and the food sufficient. (Charlie recalled that Sydney worked in the kitchen and was able to smuggle out rolls and butter, but that for all his pleasure in the thrill of stolen fruits he had no actual need for extra nutrition.) The boys remembered with a thrill of horror the weekly punishments by cane or birch administered to infant malefactors by 'Captain' Hindom, the school drill master.[31] Once Charlie found himself, quite unjustly, included in the punishment list: he had been innocently using the lavatory at the moment it was discovered some boys had set fire to some paper there, and received three strokes of the cane from Hindom as presumptive arsonist.

The worst part of institutional life was separation from Sydney. The adversities of their childhood had created an unusually close bond of understanding between them, which was to survive throughout their lives. Writing not long before her death in 1916, their Aunt Kate Mowbray wrote: 'It seems strange to me that anyone can write about Charlie Chaplin without mentioning his brother Sydney. They have been inseparable all their lives, except when fate intervened at intervals. Syd, of quiet manner, clever brain and steady nerve, has been father and mother to Charlie. Charlie always looked up to Syd, and Sydney would suffer anything to spare Charlie.'[32] For his own part, Sydney wrote to his brother, almost forty years after their Hanwell days, 'It has always been my unfortunate predicament or should I say fortunate predicament? to concern myself with your protection. This is the result of my fraternal or rather paternal instinct. . .'[33]

Charlie was very soon to be deprived, at least temporarily, of this protection. In November 1896 Sydney was transferred to the Training Ship *Exmouth*, moored at Grays, in Essex. The *Exmouth* was an old wooden-walled, line-of-battle ship which had seen service at Balaclava, and since 1876 had been used by the Metropolitan Asylums Board 'for training for sea-service poor boys chargeable to metropolitan parishes and unions'.[34] The children came from all parts of London and the Board were selective about entrants. There was, indeed, some difficulty in maintaining the full complement of six hundred boys since there was 'not unnaturally, a disinclination on the part of the various school authorities to part with *all* their finest "show" boys'.[35] Boys became eligible at the age of twelve, and Sydney's selection was a tribute to his physique, intelligence and athletic prowess. Life on the *Exmouth* was tough but varied. The boys' first task 'is to learn how to mend and patch their clothes, and thus acquire the deftness of using their fingers, which every real sailor displays. They also learn to wash their own clothes and to keep their lockers (one of which is set apart for each lad) and their contents in good order and condition. Each boy has his own hammock, which is neatly stowed away during the day, leaving the decks free from all encumbrance, in the shape of bedding.'[36] The general schooling was good, and the boys learned seamanship, gunnery and first aid. Sydney was to turn to his subsequent advantage the emphasis in the *Exmouth*'s curriculum upon gymnastics and band training. He learned to be a bugler. Sydney left the *Exmouth* with generous enough memories of the ship and its veteran captain-superintendent, Staff-Commander W. S. Bourchier. Years afterwards, he took the trouble to arrange and finance special treats and entertainments for later generations of youthful crewmen.

The two boys stayed in their respective institutions throughout 1897. There is little trace of how or where Hannah lived during this period, though at one point she was resident at 133 Stockwell Park Road. Meanwhile the Southwark Board of Guardians wrestled with the problem of extracting from Charles Chaplin Senior the weekly contribution of fifteen shillings he had agreed to pay towards the maintenance of his sons. The first problem was to find him, though had the guardians been more assiduous readers of the music hall professional press they would have been aware that he was still in good work around the provinces and occasionally in London.[37]

Early in 1897 Dr Shepherd, the New York dentist with whom Charles had become friendly on his 1890 American tour, visited London and recalled that he was given 'a very, very Royal time' during his three months' stay, not only by Charles but also by Charles's brother Spencer and their father, also Spencer. When Dr Shepherd left London, they presented him with several pieces of Doulton ware, which was produced locally, and for those days was comparatively costly. Charles was clearly not in want of money at this period.[38]

Very soon after Dr Shepherd's visit Charles's father died. He drew up a will one week before his death on 29 May 1897. It contained a curious provision, requiring 'that my son, Charles Chaplin, doth carry on the business of The Davenport Arms, Radnor Place, Paddington for a period of 12 months, during which time he is to find a home for Mrs Machell. At the expiration of 12 months, the business is to be sold and the proceeds equally divided amongst my children unless an amicable arrangement can be made amongst themselves.'[39] Grandfather Chaplin's intention may have been to try to introduce some stability into the life of his undeniably feckless son. If that was the intention, however, it was frustrated, for Charles managed, through some technical flaw in the will, to evade responsibility for the paternal pub and the mysterious Mrs Machell.

The Southwark Board of Guardians, however, was not to permit him so easily to shuffle off his family responsibilities. After more than a year during which he had not paid one penny of the agreed contribution,[40] the Guardians applied for a warrant for Chaplin, for neglecting to maintain his children, and offered a reward of one pound for information leading to his arrest. Happily there seemed to

be the same kind of fraternal bond between Charles Chaplin Senior
and his brother Spencer, eight years his senior, as there was between
his two sons. Spencer stepped in with the back payments – amounting
to the then very considerable sum of £44 8s – and averted Charles's
arrest. The Guardians had clearly had enough of Chaplin, and at
their meeting on 11 November 1897, it was moved that the two boys
should be returned to their father within fourteen days. Again the
problem was to find him. On 16 November the Clerk to the Guardians
wrote to the long-suffering Spencer:

> Dear Sir,
>   I shall esteem it a favour if you will kindly inform your brother Charles
> Chaplin that the Guardians desire him to relieve them of the future
> maintenance of his two children Sydney and Charles within 14 days from
> this date: – I am compelled to write to you not knowing his address.[41]

Evidently Spencer was unable or unwilling on this occasion to help,
and again, two days before Christmas, the Guardians applied for a
warrant for Charles's arrest. A helpful citizen named Charles Creasy
supplemented his Christmas budget by informing on poor Charles,
and claiming the one pound reward. This time Charles paid up
£5. 6s. 3d, but passed on future responsibility to Hannah, by requesting that the boys should be discharged to the care of his wife.
So on 18 January 1898 Charlie came home again. He had been an
inmate of Hanwell Schools for exactly eighteen months. Sydney's
return from the *Exmouth* two days later completed the family
reunion.

Charlie later remembered that they moved from one back room to
another: 'It was like a game of draughts: the last move was back to
the workhouse.' In the early summer they were living in a room at
10 Farmers Road, a little row of cottages directly behind Kennington
Park. It was from here that on 22 July 1898 the three of them trundled
three quarters of a mile up Kennington Park Road, to the Lambeth
Workhouse in Renfrew Road, to throw themselves once more on the
mercy of the parish authorities. They stayed ten days in the workhouse, then Sydney and Charles – now thirteen and nine – were sent
off to Norwood Schools. This time however they stayed only a
fortnight, for Hannah announced her intention of taking herself and
the boys away from the workhouse. Sydney and Charles were duly
brought back from Norwood and on Friday 12 August the three of
them were discharged.[42] It was only a ruse of Hannah's to see her

sons again. Charles vividly remembered that day, and the joy of meeting his mother at the workhouse gates in the early morning. Their own clothes had been returned to them, rumpled and unpressed after obligatory steam-disinfection by the workhouse authorities. With nowhere else to go they spent the day in Kennington Park – a rather cheerless patch of green, though it had recently been glorified with a fountain by Doultons' popular sculptor-ceramist George Tinworth.

The resourceful Sydney had saved ninepence, which they spent on half a pound of black cherries to eat in the park, and a lunch of two halfpenny cups of tea, a teacake and a bloater which they shared between them. They played catch with a ball which Sydney improvised out of newspaper and string, and after lunch Hannah sat crocheting in the sun while her children played. Finally she announced that they would be just in time for tea in the workhouse, and they set off again up Kennington Park Road. The workhouse authorities, Charles recalled, were very indignant when Hannah demanded their re-admission, since it involved not only paperwork but also a fresh disinfection of their clothes. An added bonus of the day out was that Sydney and Charles had to remain in the workhouse during the weekend, and so spend more time with their mother. On Monday they were sent back to the Norwood Schools.

This adventure which Hannah had devised for them remained a joyous memory for her sons to the end of their lives.* Ironically, the courage to carry it out was probably a sign of her growing mental instability. On 6 September – just three weeks after the outing to Kennington Park – she was taken from the workhouse to the infirmary. The intervening period in the workhouse had left her in poor physical condition. She had dermatitis, and her body was covered in bruises. No one troubled or dared to inquire into the cause of her injuries; they were most likely explained by violent encounters with

* This account is based on Chaplin's version of the event. Sydney's recollection of it, related to an interviewer in the 1920s, did not materially differ, although he suggests that the idea had originated with the boys rather than with Hannah:

> Finally we hit upon a plan. I had made ninepence doing odd jobs and had carefully hoarded it.
>   I got word to our mother and we all checked out of the institution. They gave us back our clothes all wrinkled up from having been packed away. Hand in hand, we went out. I spent the ninepence for some cakes and cherries and we sat all day together in the park. When night came, we all went back to the workhouse and went thru all the formalities of entering again – greatly to the disgust of the officials.[43]

other patients as a result of her mental condition. She was committed to Cane Hill Asylum, the doctors reporting:

> Has been very strange in manner – at one time abusive & noisy, at another using endearing terms. Has been confined in P[added] R[oom] repeatedly on a/c of sudden violence – threw a mug at another patient. Shouting, singing and talking incoherently. Complains of her head and depressed and crying this morning – dazed and unable to give any reliable information. Asks if she is dying. States she belongs to Christ Church (Congregation) which is Ch. of E. She was sent here on a mission here by the Lord. Says she wants to get out of the world.[44]

When she was admitted to the hospital she had given her occupation as 'machinist' – so she was still apparently supporting the family by sewing whilst in Farmers Road – and gave her first name as 'Lily'. The workhouse authorities corrected it to Hannah Harriet. As a true theatrical, she had had the presence of mind to tell them that she was twenty-eight: her real age at that time was just over thirty-three.

When Hannah and her children re-entered the workhouse in July, the Board of Guardians had resumed their pursuit of Charles Chaplin Senior. He was now living at 289 Kennington Road*, a few minutes away from Spencer's pub, The Queen's Head, on the corner of Broad Street and Vauxhall Walk. A fortnight after Hannah was committed to the asylum, Sydney and Charles were discharged from Norwood Schools to the care of their father.

When they were delivered – again in a bakery van – to the house, Charles remembered seeing his father only twice before. Once, he said, was on stage at the Canterbury Music Hall in Westminster Bridge Road; another time Charles had actually addressed him when they had met outside the house in Kennington Road. On that occasion Charles Chaplin Senior was accompanied by the woman with whom he was still living, and who is only identified in Chaplin's autobiography as 'Louise'. 289 Kennington Road was (and remains) a large, handsome late Georgian terraced house, set back behind a small front garden. Charles Senior occupied the two first-floor rooms with Louise and their four-year-old son (another half-brother for Charlie). The arrival of the two boys cannot have been convenient. In fact Sydney and Charles lived with their father for no more than two months,

---

* This is the address in the records of the Board of Guardians. Chaplin, whose memory was generally reliable, thought it was 287, not 289, and a commemorative plaque placed there in 1980 marks No. 287.

but it clearly seemed like years to them. Louise was surly and resentful and took particular dislike to Sydney (who on one occasion took his revenge by threatening her with a sharpened button-hook). When she drank she only became more morose. Yet in retrospect Chaplin felt a kind of sympathy for her. She had the remains of beauty, and sad, doe-like eyes; Chaplin sensed that she and his father were genuinely in love. Life with the elder Chaplin could not have been easy. He was drinking heavily by this time, and rarely came home sober. There were moments when he was attentive and charming and full of amusing stories about the music halls, but more often Charlie remembered the fights between Charles and Louise, and the occasions when he himself was locked out of the house. One of these occasions led to a visit by the Society for the Prevention of Cruelty to Children.

At this period Hannah's illness was subject to periods of remission. On 12 November 1898 she was discharged from Cane Hill Asylum,[45] and soon afterwards gathered up her sons from 289 Kennington Road. The three of them moved into a room at 39 Methley Street, behind Haywards' pickle factory which exuded a pungent atmosphere throughout the neighbourhood. Their home was next to a slaughterhouse; and Chaplin remembered the horror with which he realized that a merry slapstick chase after a runaway sheep was destined to end in tragedy and the slaughter of the entertaining animal.

Apart from this, life in Methley Street appears not to have been too uncomfortable. Charles Chaplin Senior was making occasional contributions to his sons' support, presumably to ensure that they did not return to disrupt the dubious harmony of Kennington Road. Hannah had returned to church and sewing, putting together blouses that were already cut out for a sweat shop which paid her a penny-halfpenny apiece. (In early versions of Chaplin's script for *Limelight* he describes Terry's mother as a worn but still beautiful woman, bent over a sewing machine in their attic room.) About this time Sydney took a job as a telegraph boy at the Strand Post Office. Louise, at the insistence of the Board of Guardians, had sent Charlie back to the Kennington Road Schools. He did not enjoy it very much, and to the end of his life complained of the failure of so many teachers to stir the imagination and curiosity of their pupils.

He spent his last day at Kennington Road Schools on Friday 25 November 1898.[46] Charlie Chaplin was now to become a professional entertainer. In early interviews he occasionally gave rather romantic accounts of his discovery by William Jackson, the founder of the Eight Lancashire Lads:

> One day I was giving an exhibition of the ordinary street Arab's contortions, the kind so common in the London streets, when I saw a man watching me intently. 'That boy is a born actor!' I heard him say, and then to me, 'Would you like to be an actor?' I scarcely knew what an actor was in those days, though my mother and father had both been connected with the music hall stage for years, but anything that promised work and the rewards of work as a means of getting out of the dull rut in which I found myself was welcome, and I listened to the tempter with the result that a few days later I was making my appearances in London suburban music halls with the variety artists known as the Eight Lancashire Lads.[47]

This was the kind of story newspaper reporters and readers loved in the 1920s. In his autobiography Chaplin explained, more mundanely but more credibly, that his father knew Mr Jackson and persuaded him to take on his son. Hannah was convinced: the arrangement was that Charlie would get board and lodging on tour, and Hannah would receive half a crown a week. William Jackson and his wife were evidently reliable people to whom to entrust her son. They were devout Catholics; they allowed their own children to perform in the troupe; and they proved conscientious about enrolling the Lads in schools in the towns where they appeared – though Charlie was only too well aware that these weekly attendances did not greatly benefit his education. Mr Jackson's least appealing habit was to pinch the boys' cheeks if they looked pale before they went on: he liked to boast that they did not need make-up since they had naturally rosy cheeks. A writer in a music hall paper, *The Magnet*,[48] described the act at the time that Charlie was a part of it:

> A bright and breezy turn, with a dash of true 'salt' in it, is contributed to the Variety stage by that excellent troupe, the Eight Lancashire Lads, whose speciality act we cannot speak too highly of. Mr William Jackson presents to the public eight perfectly drilled lads, who treat the audience to some of the finest clog dancing it is possible to imagine. The turn is a good one, because it gets away from the usual, and plunges boldly into the sea of novelty. The Lancashire Lads are fine specimens of boys and most picturesque do they look in their charming continental costumes: indeed, they are useful as well as ornamental, and treat us to a most enjoyable ten minutes' entertainment. The head of the troupe is William Jackson, and with this gentleman I had an interview recently. Mr Jackson

some years ago commenced his career in Liverpol where he acquired a thorough knowledge of dancing. I was advised, he said to me, to go in for it professionally, so I gave up my work as a sculptor, and devoted myself to the stage. [Chaplin understood that Jackson had originally been a school teacher.]

Mr Jackson told the interviewer that the Lads

made their first appearance at Blackpool, achieving a big success there, and afterwards going to the chief halls in the provinces. You see, the turn was quite new and caught on at once . . . and we are always endeavouring to improve the show. After this we were engaged for pantomime at the Newcastle Grand, and scored again in a most satisfactory way . . . After the run of this engagement I brought the lads to London, and they made their appearance at Gatti's [Westminster Bridge Road]; this being followed by other halls and also the Moss and Thornton tour.

Asked if any of his own sons appeared in the act he replied, 'Yes, two of them are included in it; and the other six are pupils. They have all been trained under my personal supervision, and in this direction my wife gives me much assistance.' Again Chaplin's recollection was slightly different: he believed that four of the Lads were Jackson offspring, though one of these was a girl with her hair cut like a boy's. In any event, the *Magnet* correspondent concluded: 'Jackson's Eight Lancashire Lads are all charming little fellows, well cared for, and an inspection of them was sufficient to satisfy me that they are all endowed with that which is most delightful to youth – good health and spirits. They take as much interest in their work as does [*sic*] Mr and Mrs Jackson themselves; and the public need never fear of having their interests neglected by the eight boys from Lancashire.'

Charlie remembered that he had to rehearse his clog dancing for six weeks before he was allowed to appear – almost paralysed with stage fright. His debut may then have been at the Theatre Royal, Manchester, where the troupe appeared in the Christmas pantomime *Babes in the Wood* which opened on Christmas Eve. If so, Charles Chaplin Senior would have been on hand to watch his son's first steps: he opened on Boxing Day at the Manchester Tivoli. Certainly Charlie was working with the troupe by 9 January 1899, when he was enrolled by Mrs Jackson at the Armitage Street School, Ardwick, Manchester.[49]

William Jackson's youngest son, Alfred, a year older than Charlie, remembered the new boy, not quite ten, being taken on.

He was living with an aunt and his brother Sydney above a barber's shop [now a draper's] in Chester Street, off the Kennington-road. He was a very quiet boy at first, and, considering that he didn't come from Lancashire, he wasn't a bad dancer. My first job was to take him to have his hair, which was hanging in matted curls about his shoulders, cut to a reasonable length.

He came to stay with us at 267 Kennington-road, and slept with me in the attic under the tiles. While we were in London we all went to the Sancroft-street Schools [opposite Kennington Cross], and he began to brighten up as he got to know us better. He was a great mimic, but his heart was set on tragedy. For weeks he would imitate Bransby Williams in 'The Old Curiosity Shop' wearing an old grey wig and tottering with a stick, until we others were sick of him.[50]

Charlie himself had vivid memories of his Bransby Williams impersonation. Mr Jackson had seen him entertaining the other boys with imitations of Williams in his 'Death of Little Nell, from *The Old Curiosity Shop*', and had decided it should go into the act, but it was disastrous. Charlie wore his regular Lancashire Lads costume of blouse, knickerbockers, lace collar and red dancing shoes, with an ill-fitting old man's wig, and his inaudible stage whisper irritated the audience into stamping and cat-calls. The solo experiment was not repeated.

Charlie had, in fact, a number of opportunities to study Bransby Williams. The Eight Lancashire Lads got engagements at the major London and provincial halls and shared the bill with Williams and other top artists of the time. Chaplin clearly remembered seeing Marie Lloyd and remarking how seriously she approached her work, though he felt he had not seen Dan Leno, who was on the same bill at the Tivoli in April 1900, in his prime.

Chaplin, however, made the acquaintance of the English music halls at their zenith. In the years since his father's debut, new civic organization and safety regulations had closed many of the innumerable tiny fleapit theatres, and in every urban centre opulent new Empires and Palaces had sprung up. These grander theatres and a conscious move towards respectability by the highly organized new managements, had begun to attract a more discerning middle class audience. The huge salaries that star artists could earn attracted a lot of talented people from the legitimate theatre, Bransby Williams and Albert Chevalier among them. In 1897 Charles Douglas Stuart and A. J. Park, the first historians of the music halls, could write:

The position occupied by the variety stage today is as conspicuous everywhere as it is unique. Neither drama nor opera has had erected to its service more numerous or more palatial temples, and neither branches of art can count so many professors and supporters as those devoted to the cause of this peculiar and popular form of entertainment. But if the music hall has a glowing and interesting past, it has a still more golden and attractive future.

Keeping, as before, in close and sympathetic touch with the great beating heart of the people and enlisting in its service, as its sphere of usefulness extends and broadens, the active and artistic co-operation of the best authors, the best artistes and the keenest intelligence of its day, it will necessarily yield still better and brighter results, and the cultured audience of the twentieth century – when, melancholy prospect! the present writers have been gathered to their fathers – may sit through a programme in which Shakespeare and the Henry Irvings of the future may collaborate to glorify and adorn.[51]

Even to a ten-year-old in a troupe of clog dancers, the music halls of those times must have provided an incomparable schooling in method, technique and discipline. A music hall act had to seize and hold its audience and to make its mark within a very limited time – between six and sixteen minutes. The audience was not indulgent, and the competition was relentless. The performer on the music hall could not rely on a sympathetic context or build-up: Sarah Bernhardt might find herself following Lockhart's Elephants on the bill. So every performer had to learn the secrets of attack and structure, the need to give the act a crescendo – a beginning, a middle and a smashing exit – to grab the applause. He had to learn to command every sort of audience, from a lethargic Monday first-house to the Saturday rowdies.

The best of music hall was invariably rooted in character. There were the eccentrics, such as Nellie Wallace or W. C. Fields (who as a tramp juggler was as popular on both sides of the Atlantic) who always presented the same well-loved character; or there were the singers like Marie Lloyd, Albert Chevalier, George Robey or Charles Chaplin Senior himself, who would create an entire and individual character within each song. Hetty King, who was beginning her career at this time, was to bill her act as 'Song Characters True to Life'. The 'true to life' was important. The audience was keenly alive to falsehood, and comedy had to observe its own laws of dramatic and psychological activity.

Charlie seems to have toured with the Eight Lancashire Lads

throughout 1899 and 1900. The registers of St Mary the Less School, Lambeth, reveal that Mrs Jackson enrolled him there during the Lads' engagement at the Tivoli. He was evidently still with them at the end of the year, when the pantomime season came round. Alfred Jackson remembered, 'Charlie accompanied us on tour and played in the first Cinderella pantomime at the Hippodrome as one of the cats. Finally, he left the Lancashire Lads for the "legitimate".'[52] This confirms Chaplin's own very circumstantial memories of *Cinderella*, although William Jackson's boys do not appear on the programme. Such a popular act might be expected to receive advertisement, but it is not entirely surprising that it did not on this occasion. The cast of a spectacular pantomime presentation at this time could be huge, with scores of extras and speciality acts. Mr Jackson too may have felt that work as pantomime animals, though profitable, was slightly demeaning. The cast list ends: 'Members of the Prince's Hunting Party, Guests at the Bar, Foreign Ambassadors and their Retinues, etc. etc.' Charlie and the Lads may have been the etceteras.

Opened in January 1900, the Hippodrome was London's latest theatrical marvel. The impresario Sir Edward Moss had set out to give Londoners 'a circus show second to none in the world, combined with elaborate stage spectacles impossible in any other theatre'. The building was the masterpiece of a genius of theatrical architecture, Frank Matcham. The centrepiece of this palace of marble, mosaic, gilt and terracotta was the great arena, which could be flooded with 100,000 gallons of water, or converted within sixty seconds to a dry performing space by raising up platforms which lay at the bottom of the artificial lake. For animal acts, shimmering grilles could be automatically raised in moments around the whole area. In its first years the Hippodrome presented a unique combination of variety, circus and aquatic spectacle. As time went on seats were built over the arena, and a more conventional style of variety took over.

There is a persistent but unlikely legend that Charlie was an extra in the first production at the Hippodrome, *Giddy Ostend*, which opened on 15 January 1900. At that time the Eight Lancashire Lads were playing in *Sinbad the Sailor* at the Alexandra, Stoke Newington. The Hippodrome *Cinderella* which was produced by Frank Parker and ran from Christmas Eve 1900 until 13 April 1901, was more like one of the spectacular ballet spectacles that made up the second half of the programmes at the Alhambra and the Empire Music Halls. The first half of the programme was made up of eleven variety acts including Captain Woodward's Seals and Sea Lions, Lockhart's Elephants, Leon Morris's Educated and Comedy Ponies, the Aquamarinoff troupe of Russian Dancers, equestrian acts, trapeze artists, Captain Kettle and Stepsons (comical acrobats), and Gobert, Belling and Filpe, 'The Famous Continental Grotesques'. The ninth act on the bill was Gibbons' 'Phono-Bio-Tableaux', an early attempt to combine sound with moving pictures.

Cinderella was perhaps more a fairy play than a conventional pantomime. It was written by W. H. Risque, with music by George Jacobi, formerly the Alhambra's Director of Music, and dances arranged by Will Bishop. It was in five scenes and an aquatic display; and the setting for the ball was so elaborate that even with the Hippodrome's stage machinery it required a pause of several minutes. The cats and dogs provided by the Lancashire Lads presumably figured in the scene 'The Baron's Kitchen'.

Buttons was played by the French clown Marceline, who was to remain a favourite on Hippodrome bills for some four years, billed as 'Continental Auguste' or simply 'The Droll'. Chaplin never forgot the impression made on him by this young clown, and the description in his autobiography is one of the rare accounts we have of Marceline, who subsequently faded into obscurity and committed suicide in 1927, when he was fifty-four. Chaplin recalled how Marceline would perch on a camp stool beside the flooded arena, and fish with a rod for the chorus girls who had disappeared under the waves – anticipating Busby musicals of later years. For bait he used diamond necklaces and bracelets. There is something perfectly Chaplinesque about the impertinence of angling in the Hippodrome's grand arena, as there seems also to have been in the little poodle who shadowed Marceline's every movement.

Chaplin also recalled from *Cinderella* his own first comic improvisations. He played a cat (which had the privilege of tipping up Marceline in the kitchen scene) and at one of the children's matinées introduced some very unfeline comic business, sniffing at a dog and raising its leg against the proscenium. According to Chaplin's own account the laughs were gratifying but repetitions were strictly forbidden. The Lord Chamberlain in those days was very watchful for any impropriety in music hall performances.

Chaplin's explanation of his departure from the Eight Lancashire Lads was that William Jackson became tired of Hannah behaving like a stage mother, and constantly complaining that her son looked peaky. If this were so, it would most likely have happened during the troupe's prolonged London season at the Hippodrome. Perhaps there was some justice in Hannah's fears. In 1912 Chaplin, then starring with the Karno troupe, told a Winnipeg reporter:[53]

> Those were tough days sure enough. Sometimes we would almost fall asleep on the stage, but, casting a glance at Jackson in the wings, we would see him making extraordinary grimaces, showing his teeth, pointing to his face and making other contortions, indicating that he wanted us to brace up and smile. We would promptly respond, but the smile would slowly fade away again until we got another glance at Jackson. We were only kids and had not learned the art of forcing energy into listless nerves.
>
> But it was good training, fitting us for the harder work that comes before the goddess of success began to throw her favors around.

Despite Jackson's grimaces and his way of massaging roses into small boys' cheeks, Chaplin retained a feeling of wry gratitude towards him. In 1931 when he was in Paris Chaplin met the Jacksons – William and his son Alfred – again. The old man was then over eighty, but in very good form. Chaplin was touched when he told him, 'You know, Charlie, the outstanding memory I have of you as a little boy was your gentleness.'

Hannah's life as usual had not been easy during her son's frequent absences from London. Her father, Grandfather Hill, was now sixty and had not been doing well since Grandma Hill had left him to go to the dogs. Gout and rheumatism had made it hard to work at his cobbling, and for some years he had been moving from lodging to lodging almost as frequently as his daughter. In July 1899 he was homeless, and moved into Hannah's little room in Methley Street. After five days he was admitted to Lambeth Infirmary, and after that spent a month or so in the workhouse.[54] The return of Grandfather Hill into their lives could have its compensations. Charlie remembered that during one of his infirmary periods, Grandfather worked in the kitchen and was able to smuggle bags of stolen eggs to his nervous grandson when he came to visit him.

While Charlie was appearing in *Cinderella* Sydney decided to go to sea, taking advantage of the qualifications he had acquired aboard the *Exmouth*. He was still only sixteen, and seems to have added three years to his age, to improve his prospects: throughout his seagoing career, his personal documents invariably gave his date of birth as 1882, instead of the correct 1885. On 6 April 1901 he joined the Union Castle Mail Steamship Company Line's SS *Norman*, embarking on the Cape Mail run. He was engaged as an assistant steward and bandsman, on the strength of his aptitude with the bugle. Sydney was to make seven voyages in all, and from each his work and conduct were recorded on his Continuous Certificate of Discharge as 'Very Good'.[55] Throughout his life Sydney seems to have undertaken everything he did with the same conscientious zeal. More than thirty years after his first voyage, he recalled:

> When I first went away to sea as a steward and was seventeen years old, they put me to scrub a stairway that led down to the hold of the ship, and was used merely for the purpose of carrying down empty bottles and all waste matter used on the ship. These stairs were filthily black and with the aid of silver sand and holystone, I succeeded in getting these stairs so white that you could eat your meals off them. It was noticed by the captain, who sent for me, and told me that he had been captain for nineteen years and had never seen those stairs look so clean. He congratulated me, and told me that if I was always as conscientious in all my work, that I was bound to make a success in life and I have never forgotten that lesson, and the captain's praise.

Evidently such industry also brought more immediate rewards. When the Master of the *Norman* transferred to the *Kinfairns Castle*, Sydney was engaged for four successive voyages on that ship.

Before sailing, Sydney sent £1. 15s. out of his first pay instalment to his mother.[56] The officer making out the Seaman's Allotment Note entered her name as 'Annie' – a misinterpretation no doubt resulting from the weak aspirates of London speech.*

It was apparently on the strength of this very small fortune that Hannah and Charlie improved their conditions and moved into two rooms over a barber's shop in Chester Street.** This must have been at Number 24, where Frederick Clarke had the only hairdressing business in the street. Chester Street (now Chester Way) is a turning off Kennington Road, very close to the house where the boys had

---

* On more than one occasion Hannah's name appeared thus as 'Anna' or 'Annie' in official documents, presumably because of weak Hs. In the London *Star* of 3 September 1921, a childhood acquaintance of Charlie's recalled: 'Charlie's mother always struck me as being very refined, quiet and sad. He always said her name was Lily, so I don't know how 'Annie' got in the school register.' (A school register which the newspaper had traced but which has since disappeared.)

** Presumably the rooms previously rented by Aunt Kate *c.f.* p. 30.

lived with Charles and Louise. Chaplin's memories of Chester Street were still apparently vivid in 1943, when he made a transatlantic broadcast to Lambeth, and could still remember the names of the shops: Edward Ash the grocer at Number 18; Francis William Healey, the greengrocer, on the other side of Clarke's barber's shop, at Number 27; and round the corner, at 225 Kennington Road, Jethro Waghorn, who had only recently taken over the butcher's shop.

Charles Chaplin Senior was dying. He was only thirty-seven, but his constitution had been undermined by his drinking. He was suffering from cirrhosis of the liver and dropsy.* When, ultimately and inevitably, he succumbed, *The Era* wrote that its readers 'will hear with regret but without surprise of the death of poor Charles Chaplin, the well-known mimic and music-hall comedian ... Of late years poor Chaplin was not fortunate, and good engagements, we are afraid, did not often come his way ...' His last recorded engagement was the week of September 1900, at the Granville Theatre of Varieties, Walham Green.** Charlie remembered seeing him a few weeks before his death in The Three Stags, a public house at the northern end of Kennington Road, and being shocked at his changed appearance. On that occasion, he remembered, his father was very pleased to see him, and for the first time in his life took him in his arms and kissed him.

Perhaps at the end of Charles's life he and Hannah may have drawn close again. When he was taken to St Thomas's Hospital on 29 April, it was from 16 Golden's Place, a lane of mean houses just off Chester Street; and when Hannah gave her own address, as informant on her husband's death certificate, that, too, was 16 Golden's Place. Charles died on 9 May 1901.

Hannah, of course, had no money for a funeral, and the Lambeth parish authorities, perhaps at the instigation of the hospital, granted a pauper's grave in the cemetery at Tooting. Hannah proposed to go to the Variety Artists' Benevolent Fund to ask for the other costs of the funeral: no doubt she employed the Chester Street undertaker, Albert Mummery, who shared his premises at Number 34 with his relation Thomas Alfred Mummery, a maker of wine casks. The

---

* The cause of death is given on the death certificate as 'cirrhosis of the liver', but both Chaplin and *The Era* speak only of dropsy. At this time the cause of 'hob-nail liver' was too familiar, and perhaps cirrhosis was not considered a polite disease to acknowledge.

** Built by Frank Matcham in 1898 as a 'try-out' theatre for the great comedians Dan Leno and Herbert Campbell.

Chaplin family, however, were opposed to a charity funeral. Fortunately Charles's younger brother Albert, who had done well for himself in South Africa, was visiting London at the time. *The Era* reported: 'Poor Charles Chaplin was buried at Tooting on Monday [13 May 1901] at 12.30. The chief mourners were the widow and only child [*sic*], his brother and sister and sister-in-law. Mr and Mrs Harry Clarke also followed. At the graveside were Mr R. Voss, the song-writer, and Mr Fredericks of De Voy, Hurst and Fredericks. The coffin was of polished oak. The expense of the funeral was borne by Mr Albert Chaplin, from South Africa, the brother of the deceased comedian.' Afterwards, Charlie remembered, the Chaplins stopped off for lunch at one of the public houses they owned, after dropping off Hannah and himself to go home to an empty larder and no immediate prospects of filling it. Fortunately on 31 May Sydney docked at Southampton; his pay and more than three pounds he had earned in tips ensured the three Chaplins a comparatively luxurious summer, with bloaters, crumpets, cake and ice-cream, that Charlie was never to forget.

On 1 September Sydney returned to sea. This time he was a fully-fledged steward on the *Haverford*, and signed on for the voyage to New York and back. Much to the alarm of his mother and brother, this voyage lasted much longer than the anticipated three weeks. Sydney appears to have been put ashore in New York on account of sickness; and had to wait until 5 October before he could get another boat for his return. He signed on as steward on the *St Louis* out of New York on a North Atlantic voyage, and arrived back in England on 23 October.[57]

The chronology of the next year and a half of Charles Chaplin's life is somewhat unclear: even he admitted that 'my memory of this period goes in and out of focus'. During much of the time Hannah, with Charlie and sometimes Sydney, was living at 3, Pownall Terrace, though there were interludes during which they stayed with one of Hannah's fellow church members, a devout lady called Mrs Taylor, and with a less austere friend who was being kept in style in Stockwell by an old military gentleman, though she still kept up her younger gentleman caller.

For some reason Chaplin always had more vivid memories of the garret in Pownall Terrace than of any other of the many houses of his childhood. Perhaps it was simply that he spent longer there than anywhere else. When he made his triumphal return to Britain in 1921, he made a sentimental visit to the place one night. It was then occupied by a war widow called Mrs Reynolds, who told the newspaper reporters,

> He said, 'Many's the time I've banged my head on that sloping ceiling, and got thrashed for making so much noise.'
>
> He asked me where I did my cooking, and I showed him my old fireplace, and said if it wasn't so late I'd show him the loft. Charlie said, 'I know it. I've often hidden in there. I'd like to spend just one night here.' I said he could spend two if he liked, and I'd go somewhere else.
>
> One of the gentlemen said, 'It's not like your hotel, Charlie,' and he said, 'Never mind my hotel. This is my old room, where I used to sleep twelve years ago [*sic*].' And they went on laughing and talking and smoking cigarettes. He asked me what I paid for rent, and I said five shillings a week, though eight years ago, when I took it, it was only half a crown. He said when he was living here he paid 3s. 6d.[58]

More than twenty years later, in his 1943 transatlantic broadcast to Lambeth, Chaplin said:

> Although I left Lambeth thirty-five years ago, I shall always remember the top room at 3, Pownall Terrace, where I lived as a boy; I shall always remember climbing up and down those three flights of narrow stairs to empty those troublesome slops. Yes, and Healey's the greengrocer's in Chester Street, where one could purchase fourteen pounds of coal and a pennorth of pot herbs and a pound of tuppeny pieces at Waghorn's the butcher's; and Ash's the grocer's where one bought a pennyworth of mixed stale cake, with all its pleasant and dubious surprises.
>
> Yes, I went back and visited that little top room in Pownall Terrace, where I had to lug the slops and fourteen pounds of coal. It was all there, the same Lambeth I had left, the same squalor and poverty. Now they tell me that Pownall Terrace is in ruins, blasted out of existence by the German blitz.
>
> I remember the Lambeth streets, the New Cut and the Lambeth Walk, Vauxhall Road. They were hard streets, and one couldn't say they were paved with gold; nevertheless the people who lived there are made of pretty good metal.

In one respect Chaplin was misinformed. It was not the Germans who destroyed Pownall Terrace, but the urban developers, and not until 1966. In 1984 the site still remained empty and unused.

After the ill-fated New York voyage, Sydney appears to have remained in London for more than ten months, during which his savings must have dwindled away. On 6 September 1902 he embarked

on the first of four Cape Mail voyages on the SS *Kinfairns Castle*.
Each trip lasted seven weeks, with a fortnight's shore leave between.
Charlie, having clearly by this time given up all thought of school,
turned his mind to ways of earning a little money. While he still had
a mourning band on his arm following the death of his father, he
tried selling flowers round the Kennington pubs, successfully but
briefly since Hannah did not approve. He worked as a barber's boy
(presumably for Mr Clarke in Chester Street) and a chandler's boy.
He worked as a doctor's boy for a partnership called Hool and
Kinsey-Taylor at 10, Throgmorton Avenue. This must have been
quite early in 1901, since the doctors moved from that address during
the course of the year.[59] He lost the job because he was too small to
cope with cleaning the windows, but the Kinsey-Taylors took him on
as a page boy in their house in Lancaster Gate. As he reflects, he
might eventually have achieved a long career as a butler, if Mrs
Kinsey-Taylor had not sacked him for fooling around, improvising
an alpenhorn from a length of drain pipe. He lost a job with W. H.
Smith when they discovered he was under age, and lasted only one
day in a glass factory. A period with Strakers the stationers, feeding
an enormous Wharfedale printing press, seems to have been an augury
of his battles with machinery in *Modern Times*. Two odd jobs from
this period seem particularly to have caught his imagination. He first
described his efforts as a hawker of old clothes, in 1916:

> I conceived the idea of wanting to earn money to support the members
> of the family. I had observed the street merchants in Petticoat Lane*
> raking in the shekels, so I ransacked the house for all the discarded
> garments I could find and hurried to the famous street and, mounting on
> a box, began in a thin, boyish voice to auction off my wares.
> The pedestrians stopped in amazement and watched me for a short
> time and then out of kindness purchased my meagre stock. I returned
> home that night with a shilling and sixpence for the afternoon's work;
> but small as the sum was, it helped out.[60]

Fifty years later, his version of the experience had not changed
greatly, except that he remembered the takings as only sixpence, the
price of a pair of gaiters which Hannah declared should have realized
more.

He was always fascinated by his memory of the two Scots who

---

* Petticoat Lane sounded better for the press. In *My Autobiography* Chaplin
says it was Newington Butts.

made penny toys out of old shoe-boxes, grape cork, tinsel and scrap wood. Charlie helped them in the mews behind Kennington Road where they worked, and afterwards set up in business making toy boats on his own account. The experiment did not last long: Hannah found the odour and hazards of the glue too great when she was working at sewing her blouses. He told May Reeves, in 1931: 'If I were to lose everything one day and not be able to work any more, I would make toys . . . When I was a child I made little boats out of newspaper and sold them on the streets so as not to die of hunger.' 'How often,' Miss Reeves added, 'he repeated, during our friendship, "If I were one day to lose all my money . . ."'[61]

Ill fortune had not done buffeting the Chaplins. On 24 March 1903 Sydney embarked on what was to be the last of his voyages on the *Kinfairns Castle*. By the beginning of May Charles was aware that his mother was sick again. She had grown listless, seemed unconcerned when the sweat shop for whom she sewed stopped giving her work and took back the sewing machine, and neglected the little room. On Tuesday 5 May Charlie arrived home to be told by other children around the door that his mother had gone insane. He had the job of leading her to the Infirmary in Renfrew Road, and then, as her nearest known relative, reporting the case to the authorities. He had just turned fourteen. The medical certificate records: 'Charles Chaplin, son, 3 Pownall Terrace, Kennington Road, states she keeps on mentioning a lot of people who are dead and fancies she can see them looking out of the window and talking to imaginary people – going into strangers' rooms etc.' Hannah's delightful window entertainments had moved into the region of madness.[62]

Charlie remembered being dealt with by a kindly young doctor at the Infirmary. This was probably Dr M. H. Quarry, who examined Hannah: 'She is very noisy and incoherent, praying and swearing by turns – crying & shouting – She says the floor is the river Jordan and she cannot cross it. At times violent and destructive.' The relieving officer stated that she was dangerous to others, since she was inclined to strike people. After interviewing Charlie, he recorded on Hannah's documents that it was not known whether any near relative had been afflicted with insanity, which seems to confirm that Hannah had successfully concealed the matter of Grandma Hill's certification from her sons. Again Hannah's occupation appears on her documents as 'machinist'; and again, even in these straits, she had the presence of mind to subtract five years from her age. She is recorded as being thirty-three years old; she was in fact nearing thirty-eight.

1903 – Part of the 'Order for the
Reception of a Pauper Lunatic'
relating to Hannah Chaplin, 9 May 1903,
including the evidence given to Dr Quarry
by the fourteen-year-old Charles Chaplin.

Dr Quarry asked Charlie what he would do now; and terrified of being sent back to Norwood he quickly replied that he would be living with his aunt. In fact there is some evidence that he did at some periods stay with Aunt Kate; but on this occasion he went back to 3, Pownall Terrace to wait for Sydney's return. The autobiography eloquently describes the misery and anguish of these days, how he cried in the solitude of the wretched and now lonely little room, and the kindness of the landlady who allowed him to stay on and gave him food when he was not too proud or shy to take it. Six days after he had taken her to the Infirmary, Hannah was sent back to Cane Hill Asylum. This time she was to stay for almost eight months.

Sydney was due back in England on 9 May but his return to

London seems to have been delayed. (Chaplin believed that this was the voyage during which Sydney was kept abroad by his illness, but this is not corroborated by Sydney's personal documents.) While waiting for Sydney's return, Charlie remembered making friends with some wood-choppers – also working in a mews behind Kennington Road – and that one of them treated him to a gallery seat at the South London Music Hall in London Road, Lambeth. The star act was Fred Karno's *Early Birds*. This was his first encounter with the company in which he was first to achieve fame.

Sydney finally arrived home, and Charlie at last could share his troubles. They went to Cane Hill to visit Hannah and were shocked at how ill she looked. Charlie was long and deeply troubled by her reproach, 'If only you had given me a cup of tea that afternoon I would have been all right.'

Sydney announced that he had come home for good. He had saved enough to live on for the next few months, and had determined to go on the stage. It was an ambition which his younger brother shared. Many years later he was to tell his son (a third Charles Chaplin): 'Even when I was in the orphanage, when I was roaming the streets trying to find enough to eat to keep alive, even then I thought of myself as the greatest actor in the world. I had to feel that exuberance that comes from utter confidence in yourself. Without that you go down to defeat.'[63]

2

The young professional

Even at eleven or twelve, touring with William Jackson's Lancashire Lads, Chaplin's ambition to be a star was formed. 'I would have liked to be a boy comedian – but that would have taken nerve, to stand on the stage alone.'[1] With another of the Lancashire Lads, Tommy Bristol, he planned a double act, which they would call 'Bristol and Chaplin, the Millionaire Tramps'. The idea never came to anything, but more than a decade later Chaplin was impressed to meet Tommy Bristol in New York, where he and a partner were earning $300 a week as comedians.[2]

Bert Herbert, a minor English variety comedian, remembered another project from this period, and there is enough circumstantial detail in his account to give it credibility:

> After Charlie had left the Lancashire Lads my uncle brought him to our house (Thrush Street, Walworth), and asked my parents if they would agree to my brother and I joining another boy to tour as a dancing trio.
>
> My people agreed, and Charlie took over his duties straight away. Charlie was an excellent dancer and teacher, but I am afraid we did more larking about than dancing – we were between ten and fourteen years.
>
> Eventually we mastered six steps (the old six Lancashire steps) and got a trial show at the Montpelier, in Walworth, at that time, I believe a Mr Ben Weston was the proprietor.
>
> I remember that we had no stage dresses, and went on in our street clothes. Charlie and my brother wore knickerbockers, and as I had long trousers I had to tie them up underneath at the knee to make them look like knickers.
>
> How Charlie laughed when I went wrong, because one leg of my trousers started to come down as soon as I commenced to dance.

My uncle then went to America, and as we had no money to carry on, we had to let the Trio fall through. It was to have been called 'Ted Prince's Nippers'.

I lost sight of Charlie for some time, but I met him again when he was with Mr Murray in 'Casey Court' [*sic*] (a troupe of lads).

At the time I am speaking of Charlie lived in the buildings in Munton-road, off New Kent-road, and I rather fancy he went to Rodney-road school.

He certainly was not a 'gutter snipe'. My mother used to admonish my brother and I with the remark, 'Why aren't you good like little Charlie? See how clean he keeps himself and how well behaved he is.'

Of course, I could have told her that he was as bad as us when she was out of the way, but then, as now, he could pull the innocent face at a moment's notice.

I have heard it said that Charlie was always funny as a boy but, on the contrary, I found him just the reverse. I think he himself would bear out my statement.

His one ambition was to be a villain in drama. We often used to set a drama in the kitchen, and Charlie always wanted to be a villain. He certainly did not have awkward feet, as some people have suggested.

He was an ingenious kid. I remember often going to his house in Munton-road and playing with a farthing-in-the-slot machine, which he had made. It was an exact miniature model of the 'penny-in-the-slot' machines seen at fairs, etc., and worked admirably.[3]

Munton Road is not recorded anywhere else as an address for the Chaplins, but it is well within that small area of Lambeth and Southwark where all Chaplin's childhood was spent. If Bert Herbert's recollection about 'a Mr Ben Weston' is accurate, it would place these incidents somewhere around Chaplin's fourteenth birthday, in the early part of 1903, when Benjamin Dent Weston took over management of the Montpelier Palace in Montpelier Street, Newington, from Francis Albert Pinn.[4]

Quite suddenly young Charlie Chaplin's luck changed. In fact initiative and determination must have had as much to do with it as luck. It must have required some nerve for the shy and shabby fourteen-year-old to register with one of the better-known theatrical agencies, H. Blackmore's in Bedford Street, Strand. He clearly already had the looks, vivacity and charm of later years, and made an impression: within a short time of his registering, the Blackmore agency sent a postcard asking him to come in about a job. He was seen by Mr Blackmore himself, and sent off to the offices of Charles Frohman, whose wide-ranging interests as an impresario included management of the Duke of York's Theatre in London; later Frohman was also to lease the Aldwych and the Globe and at one time had five London theatres under his control. He was to die in the sinking of the *Lusitania* in 1915. Frohman's manager, C. E. Hamilton, engaged Chaplin on the spot to play Billy the pageboy in a tour of William C. Gillette's *Sherlock Holmes* due to start in October. His salary would be £2. 10s. a week.

Meanwhile, Mr Hamilton advised him, there was a likely part for him in a new play, *Jim, A Romance of Cockayne*, written by H. A. Saintsbury, who was to play Holmes in the forthcoming tour. Hamilton gave the boy a note to take to Saintsbury at the Green Room Club. To present himself in those august premises must have tested the boy's courage.

Saintsbury was a dedicated professional of the old Victorian repertory school. Born in Chelsea on 18 December 1869 he came from a good middle-class background and was educated at St John's College, Hurstpierpoint. He started his working life as a clerk in the Bank of England, but he was irretrievably stage-struck. At eighteen he was in Kate Vaughan's revival of *Masks and Faces*, and soon afterwards became a professional. He toured in the standard repertory of Victorian melodrama – *The Silver King, The Harbour Lights, The Lights o' London*, and *Under the Red Robe*, and a repertoire of classic parts. His great role, however, was Sherlock Holmes. Chaplin thought he looked just like the *Strand Magazine* illustrations of the great detective. Saintsbury was to play Holmes for almost thirty years, and for some 1400 performances. His own plays and adaptations reveal his romantic streak: as well as *Jim*, they included *The Eleventh Hour, Romance* (after Dumas), *The Four Just Men, Anna of the Plains, King of the Huguenots* and *The Cardinal's Collation*.

Saintsbury clearly took to Charlie on sight, and handed him the part there and then. The boy was much relieved that he was not asked to read on the spot, because he still found it very difficult to make out words on the page. Sydney read the part for him, however, and in three days he was word-perfect. The brothers were amazed and moved at their good fortune. Sydney said that it was the turning point of their lives – and promptly went off to Frohman's office in an unsuccessful attempt to up Charlie's salary.

Chaplin admired Saintsbury, and learned much about stagecraft working in his companies. Saintsbury, for his part, encouraged the boy. No doubt thanks to Saintsbury's interest, Master Chaplin was generally mentioned in the press copy which the company sent each week to *The Era*. Unfortunately *Jim, A Romance of Cockayne* was not a success. Its author described it as 'an original modern play', but it was very like Jones and Hermans' old warhorse, *The Silver King*, written twenty years before. Mr Saintsbury himself played Royden Carstairs, a young man of aristocratic lineage, inconveniently given to going off into cataleptic fits, who is down on his luck and sharing a garret with Sammy, a newsboy – Chaplin's part – and Jim, a flower girl who sleeps, for decorum's sake, in a cupboard. The play is packed with dramatic incident, improbable coincidences, a stolen sweetheart, a long-lost child, a murder, false accusations, and a lot of self-sacrifice.

As Sammy, Chaplin had a meaty supporting comedy role. His best scene is where he returns to the garret to find a detective searching the cupboard which is Jim's quarters:

SAMMY: Oi, you. Don't you know that's a lady's bedroom?

DETECTIVE: What! That cupboard? Come here!

SAMMY: The cool cheek of him!

DETECTIVE: Stow that. Come in and shut the door.

SAMMY: Polite, ain't you, inviting blokes to walk into their own drawing rooms?

DETECTIVE: I'm a detective.

SAMMY: What – a cop? I'm off.

DETECTIVE: I'm not going to hurt you. All I want is a little information that will help to do someone a good turn.

SAMMY: A good turn indeed! If a bit of luck comes to anyone here, it won't be through the cops!

DETECTIVE: Don't be a fool. Would I have started by telling you I was in the force?

SAMMY: Thanks for nothing. I can see your boots.

The critic of *The Era* praised the play ('The dialogue is polished and epigrammatic, and the story of remarkable interest.') but neither his fellow critics nor the audience shared his enthusiasm. *Jim* opened at the Royal County Theatre, Kingston-upon-Thames on 6 July 1903, moved to the Grand Theatre, Fulham for the following week, and closed finally on 18 July.

Chaplin, however, had earned his first press notices. Reviewing the first week, the *Era* critic wrote: '. . . mention should be made of . . . Master Charles Chaplin, who, as a newsboy known as Sam, showed promise.' Reviewing the Fulham performance, the critic praised him again: 'Master Charles Chaplin is a broth of a boy as Sam the newspaper boy, giving a most realistic picture of the cheeky, honest, loyal, self-reliant, philosophical street Arab who haunts the regions of Cockayne.'

His best notice though was in *The Topical Times* which ended its slaughter of poor Saintsbury's play with:

> But there is one redeeming feature, the part of Sammy, a newspaper boy, a smart London street Arab, much responsible for the comic part. Although hackneyed and old-fashioned, Sammy was made vastly amusing by Master Charles Chaplin, a bright and vigorous child actor. I have never heard of the boy before, but I hope to hear great things of him in the near future.

The premature demise of *Jim* seems to have hastened *Sherlock Holmes* into rehearsal, and provided for one or two extra dates prior to commencing the main tour. Chaplin played Billy for the first time on Monday 27 July 1903 at the Pavilion Theatre, Whitechapel Road. Seating an audience of 2650, it was an awe-inspiring place for a small, fourteen-year-old actor. The first provincial engagement was in Newcastle on 10 August 1903.

The management and Mr Saintsbury were concerned about the well-being of the youngest member of the company, and decided that Mr and Mrs Tom Green, the stage carpenter and wardrobe mistress, should be his guardians whilst on tour. In his autobiography Chaplin said that by mutual agreement they abandoned this arrangement after three weeks: it was not, he said, 'very glamorous', the Greens sometimes drank, and it was tiresome to eat what and when they ate. He felt it was probably more irksome to them than it was to him. In fact the shyness which was to remain characteristic may have led him to underestimate Mrs Green's concern for him. Almost thirty years later she recorded her recollections of the period, and though she was a year out on her dating, in all other respects, where her anecdotes can be checked against verifiable facts, she proves a remarkably accurate witness. At the time she was interviewed, in 1931, she was living in Scarborough as Miss Edith Scales. Mrs Tom Green, she said, was her 'stage name', so the liaison with Tom the carpenter may have been just temporary and informal.

> We opened our tour at the Pavilion Theatre, Mile End Road in July 1904 [*sic*]. I became his guardian a week later when we went to Newcastle to play at the Theatre Royal.* Charlie was all right when we were in London because he was at home, but when we started touring he had no one to look after him. There was a matinée on the Saturday, but Charlie, who had failed to leave his address, knew nothing about this matinée, and when he did not turn up for the opening, we had to get his understudy into his clothes. The show had started when up came Charlie proudly carrying under his arm a five-shilling camera he had just bought. Poor boy, he started to cry when he heard he was late for the matinée, but I told him to dry his eyes and rushed off to get the understudy out of his clothes again. Charlie was not due on until the second act, and so I rushed him off into the ladies' dressing room and we got him ready in time.[5]

The five-shilling camera which Chaplin had bought with his first week's wages from *Sherlock Holmes* remained an interest of his for some time. He had retained the mercantile spirit of the hard times of his first search for work in London, and set up as a part-time street photographer – it was a common itinerant trade at that time – taking portraits for threepence and sixpence a time. The sixpenny ones were framed: he had found a shop where he could buy cardboard frames for a penny. Miss Scales said that he generally sought out the working class streets for his trade.

Miss Scales remembered that Charlie did his own processing and printing:

> Whenever we went to new rooms, Charlie would ask the landlady, 'Have you got a dark room, ma?' One landlady asked Miss Scales to fetch Charlie for his dinner, but she could not find him anywhere in their rooms upstairs, so she called out. There was a knocking from inside the wardrobe, and Charlie's voice: 'Don't open the door! You'll spoil my plates if you do.'
>
> I was very much annoyed, then he came out and I discovered he had burnt the bottom of the landlady's wardrobe with his candle.
>
> 'It will be jolly fine if she charges you for the damage before we go,' I told him. 'Don't worry, she won't notice it,' said Charlie. 'I'll put a piece

---

* A Newcastle magazine, *Northern Gossip*, noted: 'Other characters are in very capable hands, but a special word of praise is due to Master C. Chaplin, for his wonderfully clever acting as Billy.' (15 August 1903)

of clean paper in the bottom and cover it over.' He did, and we heard no more about it.[6]

The Frohman tour proper began on 26 October 1903 at the Theatre Royal, Bolton. In the third week of the tour Miss Scales and Charlie found themselves in the magistrates' court and the local papers, as witness of a fracas that sounds like a try-out for *Dough and Dynamite*.

They were playing at the Theatre Royal, Ashton-under-Lyne, and lodging with Mrs Emma Greenwood in Cavendish Street. On Tuesday 10 November Mrs Greenwood was baking in the kitchen. Charlie was hovering: 'Charlie was an expert at getting round landladies,' Miss Scales remembered. 'When it was baking day, they could never resist his appeals for hot cakes.' Suddenly there was a loud knocking on the front door: it was a drunken chimney sweep called Robert Birkett who was notorious in the district for his violence and foul language. When Mrs Greenwood opened the door, he began to swear at her, told her her chimney was on fire, and insisted upon seeing it for himself.

> Complainant said he came into the house and when he saw the fire he said, 'Give me a lading can full of water.' She said she had not a can, and gave him a jugfull. He threw the water on the fire to put it out. He said, 'Give me another,' and she did, which he also threw on the fire. He then said, 'I will make you pay for this.' She told him if she had to pay she would do so. He then said, 'I want one shilling,' and came out with bad langauge. She opened the door and told him he had to go out, as she would give him no shilling. The defendant then caught hold of her and pulled her into the backyard where he thrashed her shamefully. He got hold of her arms in front and kicked her legs. – Defendant: I never lifted my foot up. – The Clerk: How was he for drink? – Complainant: He was not sober and was not drunk. – Defendant: Didn't you hit me with the poker? – Complainant: No. – Charles Chapman [*sic*], a boy, said he saw it all, and the complainant's evidence was quite true.[7]

As Miss Scales recalled the incident, she had been resting in her room when Charlie rushed in, woke her, told her a man was attacking him, and rushed out again. 'Of course, thinking a lot about the boy, I was off like a shot.' She arrived in time to see Mrs Greenwood putting Bob Birkett out, ably asisted by Charlie who was threatening him with a poker.

> We were at Stockport the following Monday when they sent for us to appear in court, and we had to return to give evidence. Charlie first went into the witness box, but no one could understand his cockney accent.

The sergeant kept touching him on the shoulder and saying, 'Will you speak a little more clearly please.' But Charlie was very excited and indignant about the man kicking the landlady. After a lot of fun he got his story out, however, and the man was sent to prison, I believe for about three months.

Then Charlie asked the sergeant, what about our expenses? The sergeant replied, there's no fine and so there's no pay. Charlie was very vexed, but despite his indignation at such treatment, the court allowed us no expenses. Charlie chattered and grumbled all the way to the station about this, and it took him a long time to forget it. 'To think we have had to come all this way and pay our own fares,' he complained.[8]

The week before this excitement in Ashton-under-Lyne, when the *Sherlock Holmes* company was playing in Wigan, Charlie had bought two tame rabbits, and Miss Scales' Tom – 'a very kind-hearted man' – had made him a box covered over with canvas to keep them in.

Charlie had a great affection for his two pets, and kept them for several months. When one got worried, he vowed vengeance and searched all over for the cat or dog that had done it, walking through all the streets in the district, but of course he did not find it. He took the rabbits wherever we went, and when we were travelling he used to put them on the luggage rack and take the cover off the box to give them plenty of air. Once he let his rabbits run away in the landlady's sitting room and of course they made a mess and annoyed the landlady. That was the only time I really had to chastise him. He could make those pets do all sorts of tricks.[9]

This story of the rabbits corroborates Chaplin's own autobiographical recollections, though he records only one of them, presumably the survivor of the worrying, which ultimately met its own fate at the hands of a landlady with a cryptic smile. He remembered that this was in Tonypandy, which the *Holmes* tour did not hit until 3– 8 April 1905, so the rabbit had retained his affection for seventeen months. The following week they played at Ebbw Vale, where the landlady's son was a pathetic, legless human frog. Charlie concealed his revulsion and bravely shook the poor thing's hand when he left the house.

Miss Scales was constantly impressed by young Charlie's financial acumen. On a later tour, in August 1905, she remembered:

One day, while we were at the Market Hotel, Blackburn, he went into the sitting room and delighted all the farmers by singing to them. It was market day and the place was full. He finished up by showing them the clog dance, and he could do that dance too. But the farmers had to pay for the entertainment. Yes, Charlie went round with the hat when he had finished. I got hauled over the coals for allowing him to do that, but I wasn't there to stop him. But everyone liked Charlie. He was a wonderfully clever boy and had wonderfully perfect teeth and hair. We had Robert Forsyth playing as Professor Moriarty in the company. He was a great friend of Charlie's. Another friend of Charlie's was H. A. Saintsbury . . .[10]

When the time came to settle with the landlady, Charlie would carefully inspect the bill and knock out any item he had not had. 'He allowed no overcharging. If he had been out to tea, for instance, he would deduct the amount chargeable for one tea from the bill.'[11]

This kind of touring must have been an extraordinary schooling in life for a bright boy to whom Hannah Chaplin had passed on her gift of observation. They toured all over Britain, from London to Dundee, from Wales to East Anglia. Mostly, though, they travelled through the sooty industrial towns of the Midlands and North – Sheffield, Blackburn, Huddersfield, Manchester, Bolton, Stockport, Rochdale, Jarrow, Middlesbrough, Sunderland, Leeds. At the time, even the smallest town had its theatre: if you included the Co-op halls and corn exchanges, there were well over five hundred active professional theatres in the British Isles.

Despite Mr and Mrs Green, Chaplin remembered that he became melancholy and solitary, and began to neglect his personal appearance. Meanwhile Sydney, whose theatrical aspirations had long predated his brother's but who had not yet succeeded in finding stage work, had taken a job as bar tender at the Coal Hole in the Strand (one of London's first song-and-supper rooms, it had by this time long since reverted to the role of an ordinary pub). In December 1903, however, Charlie persuaded the *Sherlock Holmes* management to give his brother a part as Count Von Stalberg; and for the remainder of the 1903–4 tour, which closed on 11 June at the Royal West London Theatre in Church Street, Edgware Road, the brothers were together.

The casting of Sydney in an aristocratic – albeit foreign – role raises the question of the Chaplin brothers' diction at this time. We have seen that Charlie's cockney accent was so pronounced that he was hardly comprehensible in Ashton-under-Lyme (before the days of radio, people were generally less accustomed to regional accents different from their own). Even after his arrival in Hollywood, interviewers occasionally referred in passing to his 'cockney' accent. Later, as we know from the talking films, there was no trace of such an accent.* Sydney's speech, however, retained evidence of his London origins to the end of his life. It might be supposed that an accent would be a handicap in a theatre committed to 'correct' English diction. Both in the music hall and the legitimate theatre, however, there was a formal 'Thespian' style of speech, which the ordinarily accomplished performer could adopt as readily as he put on make-up. A good example of stage accents was Gus Elen, whose song "'E Dunno Where 'E Are' is supposed to have been Chaplin's debut performance. Born in London, Elen retained a South London accent to the end of his life. He performed his coster songs with quite different diction, which still kept the Dickensian cockney's interchange of 'W' and 'V'. A gramophone record made at the time of a come-back in 1930, however, includes a speech of thanks to his public declaimed in full 'Thespian formal'. No doubt the Chaplin boys would have been thus equipped to rise to any role on the stage. The music hall style of 'Thespian formal' is admirably demonstrated in Chaplin's flea circus number in *Limelight*. The diction of the song that he sings as the circus proprietor is remarkably like that of the famous music hall star George Bastow, performing 'Captain Gingah' or 'Beauty of the Guards'.

For part of the tour the whole Chaplin family was reunited. Hannah had had one of the periodic remissions characteristic of her illness, and on 2 January 1904 was discharged from Cane Hill. For a week or two she joined her sons on tour. Charlie was touched and saddened. Their relationship had changed. Her sons had ceased to be children, and she in her way had become a child. On the tour she did the shopping and cooking, and bought flowers for their rooms: Chaplin remembered that even at their poorest she would manage to save a penny for a bunch of wallflowers. But, he said, 'She acted more like a guest than our mother.' After a month, Hannah decided she should go back to London, and rented the apartment over the hairdresser's in Chester Street again. The boys helped her furnish it, and sent her twenty-five shillings out of their weekly earnings.

Some time before Hannah's discharge from Cane Hill, the brothers had moved their London base from Pownall Terrace to smarter rooms

---

* Georgia Hale recalls that Chaplin was upset when Ivor Montagu referred to his 'cockney' accent around 1929.

in Kennington Road. Now that Hannah had a home again, they seem
to have given up the new rooms. Chaplin confessed with slight shame
and regret that when they stayed with her in Chester Street in the
summer of 1904, after the close of the *Sherlock Holmes* tour, he
secretly looked forward to the extra comforts they were able to
provide themselves with in theatrical lodgings.

On 20 August 1904, just over two months after the end of the
Holmes tour, the following advertisement appeared in *The Era*:

MR ERNEST STERN presents
" FROM   RAGS   TO   RICHES.'
" FROM RAGS TO RICHES."
" FROM RAGS TO RICHES."
Now running with enormous success in America.
Specially Selected Cast, including
Master CHARLIE CHAPLIN,
as NED NIMBLE, the Newsboy.
Everything carried.
Magnificent Plant of Printing
by the Best American and English Firms.
New York Times says :—Most exciting melodrama seen
locally for a long time. Interest never flags.
Cleveland Daily World says :—Last night's audience
went into paroxysms of delight at the heroic work of
Ned Nimble, the gutter boy, who works his way from
gutter to palace.
Vacant Dec. 26 and onwards, with exceptions.
Also First-class Suburban Theatre for Production.
Apply, JOHN A. ATKIN,
Bramoote Lodge, Sunbury-on-Thames.

The critical quotes refer somewhat misleadingly to the play's original
American presentation. This British production, promising young
Charles his first starring role, was apparently still only in the planning.
The advertisement continued to appear through the rest of August
and September and during the first two weeks of October, but there
was no announcement of any engagements, so perhaps the production
never progressed beyond rehearsals – for which, in 1904, the artists
would almost certainly have been unpaid. In his later days, however,
Chaplin spoke with some pleasure of the role.

He was next offered his old role as Billy in a new tour of *Sherlock
Holmes*, starting on 31 October 1904. Sydney's role was filled, so he
went back to sea, as assistant steward and bugler on the *Dover Castle*
to Natal. He sailed from Southampton on 10 November, and did not
return until 19 January 1905.[12] It was on this voyage that he discovered his gifts as a solo comedian. On 2 December he wrote home:

Union Castle Line
SS 'Dover Castle'
2nd Dec 04

Dear Mama,

I hope you received my last letter from Las Palmas. I have had a most enjoyable trip up till now. The weather has been splendid, not too hot, but just like an English summer. I am afraid I shall not make the money on these boats like I did on the Mail boats. I have done all right up till now. I had three passengers to Las Palmas. They gave me half sovereign between them, & when they had gone ashore, I had four more passengers

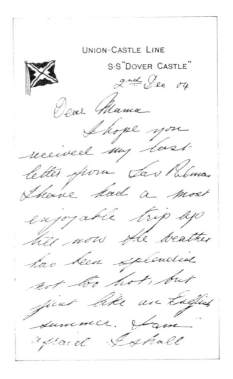

1904 - Letter from Sydney Chaplin
to his mother, written while at sea
on the Cape mail run.

3 to Cape Town & one to Natal. I think they will all give me half sovereign each. I had to march in front of the Fancy dress ball procession with the Bugle & play a march, & then a couple of days after the Scotchmen all dressed in kilts & I had to blow them round the deck, so

the sports committee have just called me into the smoking room & gave me 10/– not so bad is it? I have also made half a crown on the afternoon tea table, so altogether I can consider I have made £3 - 2 - 6. I have still got coast passengers to come yet besides my passengers home again so I may clear over £5. Thank God my health has been splendid & I do so hope your leg is better. Whatever you do take great care of yourself. I suppose the weather is getting very cold in London. I hope you will enjoy your Xmas. Try and get invited out somewhere. You don't want to be too much alone. How is little Charlie getting on? I hope he is in the best of health and taking great care of himself. Give him my love tell him so. I hope he will have an enjoyable Xmas & send him heaps of Kisses for me and heaps for yourself. You will be pleased to hear that I made a terrific success at the concert on board. I gave an impersonation of George Mozart* as the 'Dentist'. They simply roard and would not let me off the platform until I had sung them 'Two Eyes of Blue'. There is another concert on tonight and why [while] I am writing this they have sent down three people to ask me to oblige. They tell me the audience are shouting for the Bugler and the boy who has just got up to recite 'The Boy stood on the Burning Deck' has been hissed off. Fancy the quiet old Syd becoming a comedian. I have told them to tell the chairman I don't feel up to it tonight. The fact is I have undressed. I am lying on my bunk in my pyjamas. It is best to leave them wanting. My histrionic [word illegible] have become the talk of the boat the last two days. Give my love to Grandfather. I shall go & see him when I come home. Remember me to Miss Turnbull give her my Xmas Greetings. Best Love and Kisses to your own dear little self,

From your loving son,
Sydney

Charlie's new tour of *Sherlock Holmes* began at the end of October. At this time Frohman had three *Holmes* companies on the road, designated as 'Northern', 'Midland' and 'Southern'. Charlie was with the Midland Company, with Kenneth Rivington in the role of Holmes.

Chaplin was appearing in Hyde during the week of 6 March 1905 when news came of Hannah's relapse. Neighbours had taken her to Lambeth Infirmary on 6 March. Three days later Dr Marcus Quarry examined her and concluded that she was 'a Lunatic and a proper person to be taken charge of and detained under care and treatment . . . She is very strange in manner and quite incoherent. She dances

---

* George Mozart (1864–1947) was a popular English character comedian.

sings and cries by turns. She is indecent in conduct & conversation at times and again at times praying and saying she has been born again.'[13]

One week later a Justice of the Peace, Charles William Andrews, signed the necessary Lunatic Reception Order, and two days after

1904 – Letter from the great pioneer
music hall manager Charles Morton
in reply to Sydney's application
for an audition for Charles.

that Hannah was returned to Cane Hill. She was never to recover. On the statement of her particulars she was described as a widow and a stage artist (the boys' success must have revived the old dreams) and her age was given as thirty-five – she was of course forty. Sydney must have been away from home, as the only name of a relative entered on the forms was that of her sister, Kate Hill, then living at

27 Montague Place, Russell Square. Charlie was unable to visit Hannah until the tour ended on 22 April.[14] The homecoming must have been bleak.

In Hannah's lucid moments she would write to her children, and it is not hard to imagine the pain that her pathetic pleas must have

1905 – Letter from Hannah Chaplin to her sons written from the Cane Hill Lunatic Asylum. Instead of an address she writes, 'Best known to you'.

given them. In one letter, she could not even bring herself to write the name of the asylum.

This was evidently written soon after her arrival in Cane Hill. A few weeks later she seems more resigned, even jocular: the uncharacteristic mis-spelling of the address may itself be an Old Testament joke:

Cain Hill Asylum
Purley
Surrey.
3/7/05

My Dear Boys,

— for I presume you are both together by this time, altho Charlie has not written. Never mind, I expect you are both very busy, so I must forgive you. Oh, I do wish you had gone and seen about my ('Ta – yeithe') I mention this word as [illegible] know what I mean. *Do* see what you can do about *them*, as I am most uncomfortable without them, & if W.G.* should pay me a visit on this coming Monday, I am afraid he will not renew his offer of a few years back & I shall be 'on the shelf' for the rest of my life, now don't smile.

But joking apart you might have attended to small matter like that whilst you were in Town. Now I must draw to a close as it is Bedtime & broad daylight. Guess how I feel? Anyhow, good wishes & God Bless & prosper you both is always the Prayer of

your Loving Mother,
H. H. P. Chaplin.

Send me a few stamps and if possible *The Era*. Do not forget this, there's a dear.

Mum

Tons of Love & Kisses, for you both.

Hannah's request for *The Era* shows that she still liked to read about her old music hall acquaintances.

Charlie was out of work for fifteen weeks, but no doubt he had saved enough on his tours to support himself until August, when he was on the road again. The new tour was a distinct come-down. The touring rights of *Sherlock Holmes* had been taken over by Harry Yorke, lessee of the Theatre Royal, Blackburn, who had got together a pick-up company with one H. Lawrence Layton in the title role. Charlie was obliged to accept a reduced salary of thirty-five shillings a week, but had the consolation of being the seasoned pro of the troupe, laying down the law about the way things were done in the Frohman Company. He was aware that this precocity did not endear him to the rest of the cast.

---

* The significance of this reference is lost.

58

The tour opened in Blackburn at Mr Yorke's own theatre, then went on to Hull, Dewsbury, Huddersfield, Queen's at Manchester and the Rotunda at Liverpool. In the seventh week, when they were playing at the Court Theatre, Warrington, there came a miraculous reprieve in the form of a telegram from William Postance, stage manager to the celebrated American actor-manager William Gillette (1855–1937). Gillette was not only co-author, with Arthur Conan Doyle, of the dramatic version of *Sherlock Holmes*, but was also the greatest interpreter of the role. He had first played Holmes in New York at the Garrick Theatre on 6 November 1899, and scored a tremendous success with the play in London at Irving's Lyceum, in September 1901.

Gillette had just returned to London with a new comedy, *Clarice*, in which his leading lady was the exquisite Marie Doro, who had played opposite him in New York the year before in *The Admirable Crichton* and had made her mark in January 1905 with her London debut in *Friquet*. *Clarice* opened in London at the Duke of York's Theatre on 13 September 1905. It was not a success. The London critics not only disliked the play but they disapproved of Gillette's American accent. Gillette decided to reply with a joke, a little after-piece to be called *The Painful Predicament of Sherlock Holmes*, 'a fantasy in about one-tenth of an act', in which he would appear, but not speak. The playlet had only three characters: Holmes, his page Billy and a mad woman. The idea was that despite the efforts of Billy to keep her away from Holmes, the mad lady bursts into his room and talks incessantly and incoherently for twenty minutes, defeating all his efforts to get a word in. Holmes, however, manages to ring the bell and slip a note to Billy. Shortly afterwards two attendants come in and carry the lady off, leaving the last line to Billy: 'You were right, sir – it was the right asylum.' The unfortunate mad lady, Gwendolen Cobb, was to be played by one of the most gifted young actresses on the London stage, Irene Vanbrugh, wife of Dion Boucicault. Gillette required a Billy, and the Frohman office, who ran the Duke of York's and were managing Gillette, had the very boy. Hence the telegram from Mr Postance.

After his last Saturday performance in Lancashire, Charlie hurried to London, and after a couple of days of rehearsals was a West End actor. *The Painful Predicament of Sherlock Holmes* went onto the programme on 3 October. Unfortunately Gillette's good-humoured little joke still failed to save the day, and the doube bill ended its short run on 14 October, to be replaced after three days by a revival of the infallible *Sherlock Holmes*. Charlie, who had clearly made the same hit with Gillette as with everyone else with whom he worked, was kept on as Billy. Another veteran of the Frohman tours, Kenneth Rivington, who had played Watson to Saintsbury's Holmes and taken over the title role for the 1904–5 tour, was cast as Gillette's Watson. Marie Doro played Alice Faulkner for the first time; and the sixteen-year-old Chaplin fell desperately and agonizingly in love with this radiant young woman, seven years older than himself. The play repeated its original success: on 20 November there was a Royal Gala performance in honour of the King of Greece, who attended the show with Queen Alexandra, Prince Nicholas and Princess Victoria. Chaplin remembered that in a tense moment in the third act, when he and Gillette were alone on stage, the Prince was evidently explaining the plot to the King whose strongly accented voice boomed out in agitation, 'Don't tell me! Don't tell me!'

Saintsbury had taught the young Chaplin something of his stage-craft (one of his lessons, Chaplin recalled, was not to 'mug'* or move his head too much when he talked). Working with Gillette provided other valuable lessons. Gillette was highly intelligent and very successful. His father was a senator and he was himself educated at Harvard, the University of Boston and the Massachusetts Institute of Technology. Though his whole background was intellectual, he brought an aggressively populist approach to the theatre, both as actor and playwright. The dramatist, he said, should not study dramaturgy, but the public. He held that the drama should be derived from observation of life and not from concerns about correctness of grammar, diction and aesthetics. He reacted against current melodramatic, declamatory conventions of acting, adopting a casual, down-played style which suited light comedy rather better than love scenes. His guiding principle was that the actor must always strive to convince the audience that what he is doing he is doing for the first time. He set out this principle in an essay published in 1915, 'Illusion of First Time Acting'.

Someone in the company or the Frohman office at this time very clearly had Chaplin's interests at heart: it may have been Gillette himself, or Mr Hamilton or even William Postance, whom Chaplin remembered long afterwards with affection. (He was to call the kindly

---

* 'Mug. *v. slang . . . threat.* To "make a face"; to grimace' – Oxford English Dictionary.

impresario played by Nigel Bruce in *Limelight* Mr Postant: this seems to be intended as a tribute to Mr Postance, whose name is similarly misremembered as 'Postant' in the autobiography.) Two privileges which Chaplin enjoyed during the Duke of York's run of *Sherlock Holmes* were certainly exceptional for a small-part child actor in the West End. He was procured a seat at the funeral of Henry Irving, which took place two days after *Sherlock Holmes* opened.

GAUTIER'S
FAMOUS
COGNAC.

Supplied to the principal London Theatres

The Popular American Whisky
HUNTER
BALTIMORE
RYE.
Sold at the Bars of this Theatre.

H. L. SAVORY & Co.,
47, PICCADILLY, W.
Cigarette Manufacturers
By Special Appointment to
His Majesty King Edward VII.
Exclusively supply this Theatre.

TOM SMITH'S CRACKERS.

Fuller's
209, REGENT ST., W.
AMERICAN CONFECTIONERY.
Table d'Hote Luncheons.
Afternoon Teas.
Sole Purveyors to this Theatre.

Duke of York's Theatre
ST MARTIN'S LANE W C
Proprietors ... ... Mr & Mrs Frank Wyatt
Sole Lessee and Manager ... ... CHARLES FROHMAN

CHARLES FROHMAN PRESENTS
A DRAMA IN FOUR ACTS
BY A. CONAN DOYLE
AND WILLIAM GILLETTE
ENTITLED

SHERLOCK HOLMES

BEING A HITHERTO UNPUBLISHED EPISODE
IN THE CAREER OF THE GREAT DETECTIVE
AND SHOWING HIS CONNECTION WITH THE

STRANGE CASE OF MISS FAULKNER

CHARACTERS IN THE PLAY					COMPANY APPEARING IN THE CAST
SHERLOCK HOLMES	...	...	...	...	WILLIAM GILLETTE
DOCTOR WATSON	...	...	...	...	KENNETH RIVINGTON
JOHN FORMAN	...	...	...	...	EUGENE MAYEUR
SIR EDWARD LEIGHTON	...	...	...	REGINALD DANCE
COUNT VON STAHLBURG	...	...	...	FREDERICK MORRIS
PROFESSOR MORIARTY	...	...	...	GEORGE SUMNER
JAMES LARRABEE	...	...	...	FRANCIS CARLYLE
SIDNEY PRINCE	...	...	...	...	QUINTON McPHERSON
ALFRED BASSICK	...	...	...	WILLIAM H. DAY
JIM CRAIGIN	...	...	...	...	CHRIS WALKER
THOMAS LEARY	...	...	...	HENRY WALTERS
"LIGHTFOOT" McTAGUE	...	...	...	WALTER DISON
JOHN	...	...	...	...	THOMAS QUINTON
PARSONS	...	...	...	...	G. MERTON
BILLY	...	...	...	...	CHARLES CHAPLIN
ALICE FAULKNER	...	...	...	MARIE DORO
MRS. FAULKNER	...	...	...	DE OLGA WEBSTER
MADGE LARRABEE	...	...	...	ADELAIDE PRINCE
THERESE	...	...	...	...	SYBIL CAMPBELL
MRS. SMEEDLEY	...	...	...	ETHEL LORRIMORE

THE PLACE IS LONDON
THE TIME TEN YEARS AGO

FIRST ACT—DRAWING ROOM AT THE LARRABEES—EVENING

SECOND ACT—SCENE I—PROFESSOR MORIARTY'S UNDERGROUND OFFICE—MORNING
SCENE II—SHERLOCK HOLMES' APARTMENTS IN BAKER STREET—EVENING

THIRD ACT—THE STEPNEY GAS CHAMBER—MIDNIGHT

FOURTH ACT—DOCTOR WATSON'S CONSULTING ROOM KENSINGTON—THE FOLLOWING EVENING

SCENERY BY ERNEST GROS   INCIDENTAL MUSIC BY WILLIAM FURST

INTERMISSIONS
Between the 1st and 2nd Acts 4 minutes
Between the 2nd and 3rd Acts 2 minutes
Between the 3rd and 4th Acts 6 minutes

MATINEE every Saturday at 2.15 o'clock

BUSINESS MANAGER—JAMES W MATHEWS   ACTING MANAGER—ROBERT M EBERLE
STAGE MANAGER—WILLIAM POSTANCE   MUSICAL DIRECTOR—JOHN CROOK

Hooper, Struve & Co's
Royal German Spa
Table Waters.
LONDON & BRIGHTON

MACKIE'S
WHITE HORSE
SCOTCH WHISKY
• 10 YEARS OLD •
Obtainable at all the bars of this Theatre. Estd 1742.

MACMINN'S
"CLUBLAND"
Highland Liqueur Whisky
Sole Proprietors
MACMINN RICHARDSON & Co.
This Celebrated Whisky is on Sale at all the Bars of this Theatre.

The Cream of Cocoas.
EPPS'S
COCOA
of the Choicest Nibs.
Contains all the nutriment

SUPPORT HOME INDUSTRIES.
BRYANT & MAY'S MATCHES.
Are used in the Bars of this Theatre.

1905 - Programme for *Sherlock Holmes* at the Duke of York's Theatre.

The funeral took place on October 19th, and a vast concourse assembled outside Westminster Abbey from an early hour, the signs of public mourning being as general as they were sincere and deep-seated. The Abbey itself was filled with a great and distinguished assemblage, including representatives of the King and Queen, eminent statesmen, and men and women renowned in art, literature and science, as well as in the profession of which Sir Henry Irving had long been the acknowledged head. The ceremony itself, with all the aids of a superb musical service,was profoundly impressive, and was conducted by the Dean and Canon

Duckworth. The pall-bearers, who were assembled with the chief mourners round the coffin, included Sir Squire Bancroft, Lord Aberdeen, Sir A. C. Mackenzie, Sir George Alexander, Mr Beerbohm Tree, Sir L. Alma-Tadema, Professor Sir James Dewar, Mr J. Forbes-Robertson, Mr A. W. Pinero and Mr Burdett-Coutts, MP.[15]

And so among the great and distinguished sat sixteen-year-old Charles Chaplin, who within a decade would have won far greater fame even than the departed actor-knight. He was seated, he recalled, between another celebrated actor-manager, Lewis Waller, and 'Dr' Walford Bodie, the current sensation of the music halls as hypnotist, healer and miracle worker. Chaplin was shocked by Dr Bodie's unseemly behaviour, 'stepping on the chest of a supine duke' to get a better view as the ashes were lowered into the crypt.

A more remarkable achievement was that Chaplin managed to secure an entry in the first edition of *The Green Room Book, or Who's Who on the Stage*. This was the forerunner of *Who's Who in the Theatre*, but contained many fewer entries and so was more selective and prestigious. Hence it is remarkable to find listed among the aristocracy of the Edwardian stage:

> CHAPLIN, Charles, impersonator, mimic and sand dancer; b. London, April 16th 1889; *s.* of Charles Chaplin; brother of Sidney Chaplin; cradled in the profession, made first appearance at the Oxford as a speciality turn, when ten years of age; has fulfilled engagements with several of Charles Frohman's companies (playing Billy in 'Sherlock Holmes', &c.), and at many of the leading variety theatres in London and provinces; won 20-miles walking championship (and £25 cash prize) at Nottingham. *Address:* c/o Ballard Macdonald, 1, Clifford's Inn, E.C.

There are other mysteries about this brief biography, apart fom how Chaplin managed to make his way into *The Green Room Book* at all. The 'impersonator, mimic and sand dancer' presumably refers to talents acquired with the Eight Lancashire Lads; but does his 'first appearance' really mean his 'first London appearance', since he seems to have been with the lads for at least three months before their seven-week season at the Oxford in April–May 1899 when Chaplin did, indeed, pass his tenth birthday. This, too, is the only known reference to the very substantial prize allegedly won in Nottingham, where Chaplin's sole recorded appearance was in the week of 17 July 1899, again with the Lancashire Lads.

Sherlock Holmes might have settled in for a long run at the Duke of York's, but that the theatre was booked for the first revival of Sir James Barrie's *Peter Pan*, with Cissie Loftus this year in the leading role. In the 1950s Chaplin finally squashed the long-standing legend that he played a wolf in this second production of the popular Christmas entertainment after *Sherlock Holmes* closed on 2 December. Instead, on 1 January he was on the road again with Harry Yorke's touring *Holmes* company.

This was to be Chaplin's farewell to the play after more than two and a half years. The tour opened at the Grand Theatre, Doncaster, then played Cambridge and four weeks around London – at the Pavilion, East, where Chaplin had played Billy for the first time, the Dalston Theatre, the Carlton, Greenwich and the Crown, Peckham. After a further week at Crewe and a week at Rochdale, the tour ended. Chaplin placed a 'card' in *The Stage*:

Master Charles Chaplin
SHERLOCK HOLMES CO.
Disengaged March 5th

Coms. 9 Tavistock Place, Tele., 2 187 Hop.

Chaplin might have continued in the legitimate theatre but for a display of pride in the foyer of the St James's Theatre, just before the end of the London run of *Sherlock Holmes*. Irene Vanbrugh's husband Dion Boucicault gave him a letter of introduction to Mr and Mrs Kendal, who needed a boy actor for their 1906 tour of *A Tight Corner*. Madge Kendal swept in imperious and late, and asked him to come back the next day at the same time, whereupon young Chaplin coolly retorted that he could not accept anything out of town and swept out, dignified but unemployed.

Fortunately Sydney was able to find him a job. Intoxicated by his success at ships' smoking concerts, Sydney had decided that his future lay in the music halls, and joined the Charles Manon sketch company as a comedian. In March 1906 he joined a new company set up under the management of one Fred Regina to tour a sketch, *Repairs*, written by the popular author and playwright, Wal Pink. It was advertised as 'A New Departure – A Novel Item. WAL PINK'S WORKMEN IN *REPAIRS*. A brilliant example of "How NOT to do it".' The setting represented 'The interior of Muddleton Villa, in the hands of those eminent house decorators, Messrs Spoiler and Messit.' The idea of a gang of inefficient painters, paperhangers and plumbers was to be affectionately recalled in the slapstick paperhanger sketch in *A King in New York*. The plot, with Sydney as a heavily moustachioed and beery agitator endeavouring to get the slow-witted workmen to strike, looked forward to several two-reeler plots including *Dough and Dynamite* and *Behind the Screen*.

Sydney secured the part of plumber's mate for his brother. He wore a green tam o'shanter which was an object of unreasonable irritation to the plumber. When instructed by the latter to hang it up, Charlie would knock a nail into a water pipe and soak himself. In exasperation, the plumber would seize the offending headgear, throw it to the ground and trample it in fury. Sydney told the journalist R. J. Minney that the sketch went well until they reached Ireland, where there was fury at the trampling of a green tam o'shanter. For subsequent performances a hat of different hue was substituted. A rare photograph of the sketch exists, which seems to show the plumber in the act of seizing a hat from Charlie. The seventeen-year-old Charlie himself stands with a red nose, clown-like make-up, short trousers, a hammer in his hand and a look of blank idiocy on his face.

Repairs opened at the Hippodrome, Southampton, on 19 March. It was extravagantly advertised with a full column in *The Era*, predicting a brilliant future for the act with a tour that would continue at The Duchess, Balham, the Zoo Hippodrome, Glasgow, and subsequently Boscombe, Belfast, Manchester, Wolverhampton, Liverpool, Portsmouth etc. In fact the show seems not to have lived up to expectations. Not all of these engagements can be traced and the advertisement was never repeated. After the week of 7 May, when *Repairs* was playing at the Grand Palace, Clapham, Chaplin left the troupe and his act was taken over by another youth, Horace Kenney (1890–1955), who was subsequently to become a music hall star in his own right.

Chaplin had answered an advertisement in *The Era* announcing that boy comedians were required for *Casey's Court Circus, or the Caseydrome* which was shortly to be produced. It was a follow-up to a show, *Casey's Court*, that had already proved successful. The setting for this was an alley, and the central figure, around whom a dozen or so juvenile comedians clowned, was 'Mrs Casey' – played in pantomime style by the comedian Will Murray (1877–1955), who continued to tour with the act until he was well into his seventies. Harry Cadle, the creator and impresario of the troupe, encouraged by the success of the original turn, had now decided to establish and tour a second company with Will Murray again as leading artist and general director. *Casey's Court Circus* was described as 'a street urchin's idea of producing circus'.

c1906 - Page from Sydney's directory
of good cheap theatrical lodgings.
The invaluable information was
shared by both brothers.

Chaplin appeared with *Casey's Court Circus* in its opening week at the Olympia Theatre, Liverpool, from 21 to 26 May 1906. There is a story, without documentary corroboration, that he did a tryout with the original *Casey's Court* at the Bradford Empire the previous week. There is, too, some uncertainty about the terms of his contract. In October 1927 the magazine *Picturegoer* claimed,

There is an interesting document still in existence dated May 26th 1906 which is the first legal document Charlie ever had. It is signed by his brother Sydney, as his guardian. In it he agrees to accept 45/= per week and his travelling expenses for his assistance in 'anything connected with the performance of "Casey's Court" that may be a reasonable request'.

A recent Chaplin biographer (Denis Gifford: *Chaplin*) quotes another circumstantial version of this alleged contract, without providing a source:

> I, the guardian of Charles Chaplin, agree for him to appear in *Casey's Court* wherever it may be booked in the British Isles only, the agreement to commence May 14th, 1906, at a salary weekly of £2. 5. 0. (two pounds five shillings) increasing to £2. 10. 0. the week commencing July 1906.

Will Murray, for his part, reminisced fifteen years later:

> I first met Charlie when I was running the sketch 'Casey's Court (Circus)'. These sketches, which were pure burlesque, met with a great measure of success throughout the country,
> To carry out a second edition of the sketch, I found it necessary to advertise for a number of boys between fourteen and nineteen years of age.
> Amongst the applicants was one little lad who took my fancy at once. I asked him his name and what theatrical experience he had had.
> 'Charlie Chaplin, sir,' was the reply. 'I've been one of the Eight Lancashire Lads, and just now [*sic*] I've got a part in the sketch [*sic*] 'Sherlock Holmes'.
> I put him through his paces. He sang, danced, and did a little of practically everything in the entertaining line. He had the makings of a 'star' in him, and I promptly took him on salary, 30s per week.[16]

Chaplin, whose memory for sums of money seemed infallible, remembered his salary as £3 a week. He also remembered that he was the star of the show and though the individual boys' names were not billed, this seems to be confirmed by his placing, seated beside Mr Murray, in a group photograph of the troupe in 1906. Certainly he was given the two plum turns in the Circus. The act included a number of burlesques of current music hall favourites. 'I particularly wanted a good thing made of Dr Bodie,' remembered Murray. 'Chaplin seemed the likeliest of the lot for the part and he got it.'

'Dr' Walford Bodie, whose indecorous curiosity had shocked Chaplin at the funeral of Sir Henry Irving, was at the peak of his celebrity. He was born plain Sam Brodie in Aberdeen in 1870, was apprenticed as an electrician with the National Telephone Company, but soon took to the variety stage as a conjuror and ventriloquist. By the time of his London debut, in 1903, at the Britannia, Hoxton, he had developed a new and original act, billed as 'The most remarkable man on Earth, the great healer, the modern miracle worker, demonstrating nightly "Hypnotism, Bodie force and the wonders of blood-less surgery".' He claimed among other benefits to mankind to have cured nine hundred cases of paralysis judged incurable by the medical profession. Those who revered him as a miracle man and those who regarded him as a fake, alike acknowledged he was a great showman. He was a handsome man with a fine head of hair, an upswung waxed moustache and penetrating eyes. He appeared in a frock coat of exquisite cut and a gleaming silk hat. Chaplin studied his make-up from the photograph in Bodie's advertisement in *The Era*, and had a studio portrait taken of himself adopting the identical pose. 'Re-hearsals were numerous,' remembered Will Murray,

> and Charlie always showed a keen desire to learn. He had never seen Bodie's turn, but I endeavoured to give him an idea of the Doctor's little mannerisms.
> For hours he would practise these in front of a mirror. He would walk for long spells backwards and forwards cultivating the Bodie manner.
> Then he would ring the changes with a characteristic twist to the Bodie moustache, the long flowing adornment which the 'Electric Spark' affected, not the now world-famous tooth-brush variety . . .[17]

Dan Lipton, a writer of comic songs who befriended the young Chaplin confirmed that Chaplin had never seen Bodie in performance: 'The way that boy burlesqued Dr Bodie was wonderful. I tell you he had never *seen* the man. He just put on an old dress suit and bowler hat, and as he marched onto the stage he swelled with pride.'[18]

When the act came south to the Richmond Theatre, *The Era* commented that 'the fun reaches its height when a burlesque imitation of "lightning cures on a poor working man" is given'. Six weeks later, when the *Casey's Court Circus* company played at the Stratford Empire, *The Era* noted that 'an extravagant skit on Dick Turpin's ride to York concludes the turn'. Chaplin was the star of this number also. Will Murray recalled:

> . . . he 'got' the audience right away with 'Dr Bodie'.
> Then came 'Dick Turpin', that old invincible evergreen standby of the circus. It all went well, but the climax was the flight after the death of 'Bonnie Black Bess'.
> You can imagine the position of poor Mr Turpin. He had to run, hide, do anything to get out of the way of the runners, and yet he had nowhere to go except round the circus track.
> Nevertheless, Charlie started to run – and run – and run. He had to turn innumerable corners, and as he raised one foot and hopped along a

little way on the other in getting round a nasty 'bend' the audience simply howled.

I think I can justly say that I am the man who taught Charlie to turn corners. Yes, that peculiar run, and still more weird one-leg turnings of corners, which seems so simple when you see it carried out in the pictures, is the very same manoeuvre that I taught Chaplin to go through in the burlesque of Dick Turpin. It took many, many weary hours of monotonous rehearsals, but I am sure Charlie Chaplin, in looking back over those hours of rehearsals, will thank me for being so persistent in my instructions as to how I wanted the thing done.[19]

The *Casey's Court Circus* tour ended on 20 July 1907, and Chaplin left the company. Young though he looked, he was probably considered already too old for a further season with a juvenile troupe. He was to remain three months without a job. Sydney however was now in regular work. After leaving *Repairs* he had signed a contract with Fred Karno's Silent Comedians. In July 1906, by this time a major Karno star, he signed a new contract for a second year at £4 per week. No doubt, as he had done before, he helped his younger brother over a lean period.

In this period between jobs, Charles lodged with a family in Kennington Road, and on his own admission lived a solitary, harum-scarum, boyishly dissolute life. He decided to work up a solo act as a Jewish comedian. Towards the end of the *Casey's Court Circus* tour, in June 1907, he had played the Foresters' Music Hall in Cambridge Road (formerly Dog Row), Bethnal Green. The management remembered his success as Dr Bodie and Dick Turpin, and agreed to let him do a week's unpaid try-out. His material – he later realized that it was not only poor but anti-Semitic – make-up and accent were not well calculated for the predominantly Jewish audience of the neighbourhood. The first – and only – night was a disaster, and Charles fled from the theatre and the catcalls and pelted orange peel. This nightmare experience undoubtedly helped to instill in him an eventual dislike of working before a live audience. He was to have triumphant successes with the Karno Company, but it was evidently a tremendous relief when he was finally able to abandon the live theatre. Nothing would ever again persuade him to perform in front of an audience. In 1915 he told the actor Fred Goodwins, who was then working with him at the Essanay Studios: 'Back to the stage! I'll never go back to the stage again as long as I live. No. Unless my money leaves me, not ten thousand dollars would tempt me back behind the footlights again.'[20] Very soon he was to be offered much larger sums than $10,000 but his decision was still unshakeable. More than fifty years later he told Richard Meryman: 'On the stage I was a very good comedian in a way. In shows and things like that. [But] I hadn't got that come-hither business that a comedian should have. Talk to an audience – I could never do that. I was too much of an artist for that. My artistry is a bit austere – it is austere.'[21]

Many great artists whose work depended upon the precision of a highly polished technique shared this mistrust of the unpredictable element offered by the audience. In the 1950s the great music hall artist Hetty King, after almost sixty years' stage experience, disliked following the still rumbustious Ida Barr in the veterans' programme in which they were appearing: 'I hate to follow that old woman. She gets the audience so unruly. I'm always terrified they will shout to me, talk to me. It throws me.' Max Miller, too, could be thrown off balance when audience reaction was not entirely predictable. It is possible that Chaplin had also inherited anxieties about audience reaction from his mother; fear of the public is a possible explanation of the lack of success of her career, despite her evident talents.

Not entirely daunted by the Foresters' fiasco, however, he wrote a comedy sketch *The Twelve Just Men*, the title probably suggested by his friend Mr Saintsbury's adaptation of *The Four Just Men*. The twelve men of Chaplin's plot, however, were the jury deliberating a breach of promise case. Their discussions were complicated by the presence in their number of a deaf-mute, a drunk, and other unlikely personages. Chaplin sold the sketch for £3 and was hired to direct it, but the backer pulled out after two or three days. Sydney had to break the bad news to the cast for him; in later years, when he was in command of his own studios, Chaplin could never bring himself to deliver bad tidings, like sackings and reprimands, in person, but always did it through intermediaries.

The Twelve Just Men was to come back and haunt him a quarter of a century later. Either Chaplin or his backer, a stage hypnotist called Charcoate, had subsequently managed to sell the sketch to the comedian Ernie Lotinga (one of the Six Brothers Luck and the first husband of Hetty King) for £5. Lotinga forgot about it until he came upon the manuscript again in 1932, and announced that he would produce this sketch written by Charlie Chaplin. Chaplin was distressed at the prospect and offered to buy back the rights for $5000. Lotinga, reckoning he was on to a good thing, refused, whereupon the offer was raised to $7500. Lotinga still refused but proposed that he and Chaplin should go into partnership in the production, and that Chaplin should play the drunk. When this proposal aroused no enthusiasm, Lotinga announced that he would produce the sketch in the form of a musical revue and play the leading role himself. No more was heard of it.

3

With the Guv'nor

The comedy sketch was a staple of the music halls in the early years of the century. Harry Tate's *Motoring, Golfing, Flying, Billiards* and *Fishing*; Will Evans' *Building a Chicken House, Harnessing a Horse, Papering the Parlour*; Joe Boganny's *Lunatic Bakers*, Charlie Baldwin's Bank Clerks, the Six Brothers Luck, the Boisset and Manon troupes were only the more celebrated acts of the kind. Fred Karno's Speechless Comedians, though, were supreme of their kind. They were the conjuncture and end of several traditions of English pantomime. There was, first, the clowning of the pantomime proper, that singular British theatrical institution. Chaplin recalled in 1917:

> Christmas in London in the old days, when it was hard scratching for me to get sixpence so that I might see the Christmas pantomime spectacle at Drury Lane, *Jack and the Beanstalk, Puss in Boots* or *Cinderella*. I used to watch the clowns in the pantomimes breathlessly. They were clever fellows. There were Montgomery, Laffin, Feefe, Brough, Cameron – all high-class performers. Every move they made registered on my young brain like a photograph. I used to try it all over when I got home. But what I think of now is the rapt attention with which six or seven thousand boys and girls would watch the clowns work.* It was slapstick stuff. Everybody used to say that sort of thing would be dead in another ten years. What has happened is that pantomime, through motion picture developments, has taken the lead in the world's entertainment. My early

* Chaplin may not have been accurately reported. Drury Lane in the years when he could have known it had a capacity of three thousand: even for the famous children's matinées, twice that number could hardly have been squeezed in. The names he quotes, also, are not familiar from Drury Lane programmes of the period.

study of the clowns in the London pantomimes has been of tremendous value to me. What I learned from them has been supplemented by original research.[1]

Pantomime, in the more general sense, was stimulated by the licensing laws of the eighteenth century which forbade dialogue except on the stages of the two Theatres Royal. Hence the unlicensed theatres developed styles of wordless spectacle, with music and mime to explain the plot. These entertainments became so popular at Sadler's Wells and the Royal Circus, that the Theatres Royal in Covent Garden and Drury Lane were obliged to adopt the genre themselves for afterpieces. In the music halls, the prohibition of dialogue lingered much longer, and so in consequence did the mime sketches. Perhaps the finest pantomimist of the later nineteenth century was Paul Martinetti (1851–1924), born to French parents in the United States. Making his first appearance on the British music hall stage in the late 1870s, he formed a pantomime troupe with his brother Alfred, performing highly melodramatic sketches like *Robert Macaire, A Duel in the Snow, After the Ball, A Terrible Night, Remorse* and *The Village Schoolmaster* right up to the time of the First World War.

The circus also made its contribution with a genre of spectacles which combined acrobatics, scenic effects, narrative and comedy. Out of this tradition developed troupes like the Ravels and the Hanlon-Lees. The Hanlon-Lees, who toured in Britain, France and the United States from the 1860s to the 1880s, consisted of the six Hanlon Brothers and a celebrated acrobat, 'Professor' John Lees. The description of their entertainment *Voyage en Suisse* at the Gaiety Theatre, London, in March 1880 sounds like the prototype for Karno or Keystone chaos: 'It included a bus smash, a chaotic scene on board a ship in a storm, an exploding Pullman car, a banquet transformed into a wholesale juggling party after one of the Hanlons had crashed through the ceiling on to the table, and one of the cleverest drunk scenes ever presented on the stage.'[2]

Fred Karno was heir to all these traditions; in turn he contributed his own gifts for organization, for invention, for spotting and training talent, for *mise-en-scène* and direction. Like most of the great figures of the English music hall, his origins were humble. He was born in Exeter on 26 March 1866. His father was a cabinet maker called Westcott, who moved around the country a good deal during the boyhood of Frederick, his eldest son. Eventually the family settled in

Photograph, c.1870, believed to be
Spencer Chaplin, grandfather of
Charles and Sydney Chaplin.

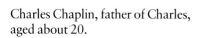

Charles Chaplin, father of Charles,
aged about 20.

Hannah Chaplin, mother of
Charles and Sydney, c.1885.

Charles Chaplin, father of
Charles, aged 30.

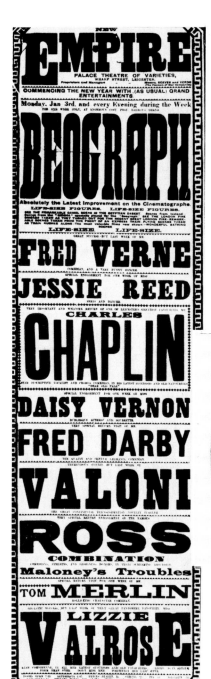

Bill for New Empire Palace Theatre
of Varieties, Leicester, featuring
Charles Chaplin Senior, 1898.

Leo Dryden's 'card' in *The Era*, 1902.

MR.

LEO DRYDEN,

Vocal Character Actor.

"LOVE AND DUTY."
"MINER'S DREAM OF HOME."
"THE MINER'S RETURN."
"SKIPPER'S DAUGHTER."
"INDIA'S REPLY."
"THE GREAT WHITE MOTHER."
"JOSEPHINE."
"MERCIA."
"BRAVO! DUBLIN FUSILIERS."
"THE ONLY WAY."
"MICE AND MEN."
"FREEDOM AND JAPAN."
"AN ACTOR AND A MAN."
"BACHELOR BOYS, FAREWELL."
"THE PRODIGAL SON."

All communications, c/o " The Era."

Cuckoo Schools, Hanwell.

Charles Chaplin at the time he was
touring with the Eight Lancashire Lads.

Left: Charles Chaplin at the
Hanwell Schools, 1897.

Right: Chaplin as Sammy the Newsboy
in *Jim, A Romance of Cockayne*, 1903.

Chaplin as Billy the Page
in *Sherlock Holmes*, 1903.

William Gillette

Chaplin's two Sherlock Holmes –
William Gillette (left) and
H.A.Saintsbury (below).

Sydney, aged 18, c.1903.

Below left: Chaplin in *Repairs*, 1906, with hammer and offensive tam-o'-shanter.

Casey's Court Circus, 1906. Chaplin (in bowler)
at Will Murray's left. Others in the group are
Hal Jones (back row, third from left),
George Doonan (back row, extreme right),
Tom Brown (? left of centre row), Eddie Emerson
(next to Murray), Herbert Kirk (next to Chaplin),
Fred Hawes, Hal Cheryl and Billy Leonard.

The real Dr Walford Bodie, from an advertisement in *The Era*.

Chaplin's impersonation of Dr Walford Bodie, 1906, clearly based on the *Era* advertisement.

Fred Karno in his office.

Workers leaving the Karno
Fun Factory, 1905.

Chaplin, c.1909.

Sydney as Archibald in *Skating*
with his wife, Minnie.

Chaplin as Archibald in *Skating*.

Chaplin as The Inebriate, c.1910.

Left: The Karno troupe en route for America, 1910, photographed aboard the *SS Cairnrona* by Alf Reeves. Chaplin is framed in life belt; the others in the group are, back row, left to right, Albert Austin, Bert Williams, Fred Palmer, unknown, Frank Melrose; front row, left to right, Stan Laurel, Fred Karno Jr, Mickey Palmer, (Chaplin), Arthur Dando (behind), Mike Asher, Amy Reeves

Below left: On tour in USA Chaplin is at right at left of right-hand train window. A note on the back says 'Charlie at $75 a week.'

Below: On tour with the Karno troupe. About to leave Solano railway depot, Philadelphia.

Chaplin in front of Karno
poster, Spokane.

On tour with the Karno troupe:
with an Indian pedlar.

Chaplin with posters at Exeter
(California) railway depot.

Nottingham where Fred started work when he was about fourteen in a lace factory, attending school in the afternoons. He moved on to work as a barber's boy, a costermonger, a bricklayer and a chemist's shop boy. Eventually he was apprenticed to a plumber. When this work took him to a gymnasium he was intrigued by the place, enrolled, and was soon a good enough gymnast to make his stage debut in an amateur competition at the Alhambra Theatre, Nottingham. Very soon he was partnering a professional gymnast, as the second half of Olvene and Leonardo. After a spell as a solo gymnast in north-country fairground shows, he toured for a year with Harry Manley's Circus. As luck would have it, Manley's was one of the last circuses still presenting pantomime sketches. Its repertory included *Dick Turpin, Mazeppa, The Bear and Sentinel, Love in a Tub, The Statue Blanche, Gregory's Blunder, The Prince and the Tinker, Black and White, or Tea for Two, The Wig Makers, Swiss Lovers, Where's Your Ticket?* and *The Copper Ballet.* Karno seems to have played in a good many of these.

Karno had varied fortunes in fairgrounds and music halls with different partners, and was obliged for a while to abandon show business and earn his living as a glazier (he claimed to have employed a boy to go ahead breaking windows – an idea which would reappear in Chaplin's film *The Kid*). In 1888 he put together an impromptu act with two other acrobats, Bob Sewell and Ted Tysall, to substitute for an act that had failed to turn up for their booking at the Metropolitan, Edgware Road. Shamelessly, they adopted the name of the absent act, The Three Carnos, but soon afterward adopted the spelling Karno, as more stylish (in 1914 Karno changed his name officially, by deed poll). The Karnos were a modest success, and Karno augmented his earnings with a solo act in which he demonstrated the Edison phonograph – still a comparative novelty – which he impertinently renamed the Karnophone. Always brash and energetic, he earned money by busking in the streets in the weeks when the act had no booking.

The Three Karnos presented their first sketch about 1894. Again it was an impromptu, to fill in for the pugilist Jem Mace in Portsmouth. The sketch was one of the old Manley's Circus standbys, *Love in a Tub*, but it was successful enough to give Karno the idea of creating original sketches and a company to play them. In 1895 he presented *Hilarity* at the Gaiety, Birmingham. It was to tour continuously for five years and to provide the prototype for the long succession of Karno pantomime comedies. In 1901 he presented *Jail Birds* at the Paragon, Mile End Road, and pulled off the first of the extravagant publicity stunts for which he was to become famous by carrying the company around in a Black Maria, which he even took to the Derby. *Early Birds* was a 'tale of slumland', in which Karno himself played a glazier. In *The New Woman's Club* which satirized the early feminist movement, he played a lady cyclist: it was his last stage appearance. His early productions were generally launched at the Paragon, Mile End Road. Subsequently the sketches were premièred as annual Christmas attractions at the Palace, Manchester, among them *His Majesty's Guests, Saturday to Monday, The Football Match* and *Skating*. A contemporary advertisement for *The Football Match* announces:

Grand Christmas Production

Of FRED KARNO'S latest Burlesque

"THE FOOTBALL MATCH."

Over 100 Auxiliaries.   **Catchy Music.**

Clever Comedians.   **Wonderful Scenery.**

Realistic Football Match—in the rain—with real Football Champions contesting, and the usual High-class Variety Entertainment.

Special Matinees Xmas Week—See future announcements.

TWICE NIGHTLY.

The *Pantomime Annual* described it as 'an entertainment that shall be unique in the history of amusements', vividly depicting 'the desperate struggle for supremacy between the Middleton Pie-Cans and the Midnight Wanderers'. *The Football Match* was characteristic of the elaborate scenic effects in which Karno specialized. The settings included a huge panoramic cloth with a great crowd of people painted on it. The painted figures had loose arms and hats which were activated be electric fans hidden behind a raked ground row. In front of these were supers, with very small people arranged behind larger ones, to produce an effect of perspective. In *The Wontdetainia*, presented at the Paragon, Mile End Road on 11 April 1910, and satirizing public enthusiasm for the great new luxury liners like the recently launched Lusitania and Mauretania, the effects were even more elaborate, with a practicable liner so huge that when it was made to move across the stage it was built up section by section in the wings. For *Mumming Birds*, which was to be closely linked to the fate and future of Charles Chaplin, a stage was built within the theatre stage, complete with boxes, proscenium and tabs. *Mumming Birds* grew out of a quickly concocted entertainment devised for a charity performance called *Entertaining the Shah* at the London Pavilion in 1904. It was extended and developed, and presented at the Star, Bermondsey, as *Twice Nightly, or a Stage upon a Stage*. In its second week at the Canterbury, it was finally renamed *Mumming Birds*.

Karno's publicity methods were as colourful, unconventional and ambitious as his sketches. He had his companies travel about in a bizarre collection of vehicles boldly painted with the words 'Karno's Speechless Comedians'. His own car was similarly inscribed in large letters and odious hues – to the grave embarrassment of his young son on parents' days at his smart boarding school. On the death of the Duke of Cambridge, Karno bought his state coaches; and there was some official embarrassment when the Karno comics galloped around London in them with the royal arms blazoned. Other Karno publicity methods included bands, balloons, advertising leaflets bearing testimonials wrung from audiences, and stunts like fake police chases through the towns in which the companies appeared.

Among Karno's first stars were Fred Kitchen, who had played Harlequin in the Drury Lane pantomime of 1896, *Aladdin*, which starred Dan Leno and Herbert Campbell. He was famous for his catch-line from Karno's *The Bailiffs*: 'Meredith – we're in!' Billie Reeves, who created the role of the drunk in *Mumming Birds* which Chaplin was later to take over and make famous, was the brother of Alfred Reeves, who managed Karno companies for many years before becoming general manager of the Chaplin film studios. Reeves had joined Karno in 1900, and since 1905 had spent a large part of his time in the United States. At the time that Sydney Chaplin joined him, in 1906, Karno had as many as ten companies regularly on tour. They were managed and serviced from Karno's 'Fun Factory', established in three houses at 26, 28a and 28 Vaughan Road, Coldharbour Lane, Camberwell. In 1906 Karno advertised a

> Magnificent NEW WING just added to the above, comprising a Paint Room, Rehearsal Room and Storage Dock . . . The new Paint Room is furnished with Two Frames capable of carrying any Cloths. The new Rehearsal Room, splendidly lighted, ventilated, and heated, is 72 feet long, 21 feet wide, and owing to the exceptional height (28 feet 6 inches) can be used as a Practice Room for any Gymnastic or Aerial Acts. The huge Storage Dock, thoroughly ventilated and dry, covers an area of 316 square yards, and has a cubic space of 32,648 feet.

Sydney's first contract with Karno was dated 9 July 1906. He was engaged as a 'pantomimist' at £3 a week, with a provision that he should be paid £6 a week if called upon to tour in the United States. He clearly made a rapid impression, because less than three months later he was selected for one of the two companies sent to America for Karno's second season there. Sydney played the drunk in *Mumming Birds* in a company managed by Arthur Forest; Billie Reeves was the star of the other company, playing *Early Birds*, under the management of Alf Reeves. Sydney was back in time for Christmas, to play in *The Football Match* in Manchester. The star role of Stiffy the Goalkeeper was played by Harry Weldon, a slow-talking Lancashire comedian. On 17 July 1907, when Charlie's tour with *Casey's Court Circus* was coming to an end, Sydney appeared in a brand new sketch, *London Suburbia*, at the Canterbury.

Sydney tried hard to persuade Karno to give Charlie, now unemployed, a job; but Karno showed no interest. In February 1908 he relented so far as to give Charlie a two-week trial with the chance of a contract if he proved satisfactory. He thought him, however, 'a pale, puny, sullen-looking youngster. I must say that when I first saw him, I thought he looked much too shy to do any good in the theatre, particularly in the knockabout comedies that were my speciality.' The try-out was in the vast London Coliseum, which had reopened a few weeks before. Charlie was to play the role of the comic villain who attempts to bribe Stiffy to throw the game. Ordinarily the character's appearance served only to prepare an entrance for Harry Weldon as Stiffy; but Chaplin, schooled in *Casey's Court Circus*, had worked out some laughs. He entered with his back to the audience, wearing a silk hat and opera cloak, and elegantly handling a cane.

The first laugh came when he rounded suddenly on the audience, and the svelte figure turned out to have a shocking crimson nose. He did a funny trip, got entangled with his cane and collided with a punching ball (the scene represented the team's training quarters). Weldon was surprised and disconcerted, particularly when Chaplin topped the laughs the star earned for improvised lines with his own quick ripostes. Chaplin had quite clearly earned his contract: it was signed on 21 February 1908, eighteen days after his first appearance with Karno. The agreement provided for one year at a weekly salary of £3 10s, a second year at £4 and a third year's option. For the first time in their lives the Chaplin brothers had security, and £7 10s a week between them since Sydney's salary had risen to £4. When Sydney returned to London from a provincial tour, they rented a flat in Brixton Road, at 15 Glenshaw Mansions, and furnished it from a second hand store, comfortably and with a touch of florid luxury provided by a Moorish screen and coloured lamps.

Chaplin felt that Weldon, eight years older than himself, was jealous of his success with the audience and his favour with Karno; this seems to be confirmed by the distinctly ungenerous tone of an article Weldon contributed some years later to *Pearson's Weekly*, a magazine run by Frank Harris:

> Charlie had undoubtedly a flair for pantomime, but in a speaking part he was rather out of it. Fred Karno, who always had an eye to new talent, was exceedingly impressed by him, and I know that Fred used to tell all the managers what a great find he had got.
>
> I know on one occasion when we were playing at the Olympic, Liverpool, I did Stiffy at the first house, and Chaplin, on the instructions of Karno, took on the part in the second house.
>
> I had the unique experience of sitting in a box and seeing my understudy perform. I cannot say that either the audience or myself were very impressed with the show that Charlie made. He did his best, but his slight physique prevented him from looking the part, and the audience were so cold to his Stiffy that he never appeared in goal – at least while I was in the company.
>
> Although Karno had such a high opinion of Chaplin, no one else in the company paid him much attention, but regarded him as one of the boys.

Other colleagues recorded impressions of the nineteen-year-old Chaplin. Karno himself said, 'He wasn't very likeable. I've known him go whole weeks without saying a word to anyone in the company.

Occasionally he would be quite chatty, but on the whole he was dour and unsociable. He lived like a monk, had a horror of drink, and put most of his salary in the bank as soon as he got it.' A young Karno-ite from Lancashire, called Stanley Jefferson, who was eventually to change his name to Stan Laurel, remembered on the other hand:

> To some of the company I know he appeared stand-offish and superior. He wasn't, he wasn't at all. And this is something a lot of people through the years don't know or refuse to believe about Charlie: he is a very, very shy man. You could even say he is a desperately shy man. He was never able to mix easily unless people came to him and volunteered friendship or unless he was among people who didn't know him. Then he wasn't so shy.[3]

Fred Goodwins, who knew him in the vaudeville days and worked with him in a few films in 1915, said that Chaplin always struck him as a dreamer

> – a builder of castles in the air – and I used to watch him interestedly and note the way he acted in the varying conditions into which his life brought him. He was ambitious, I think, in his own peculiar way. He has told me since how he used to wonder what it was like to be at the top of things and how he scoffed at himself for ever supposing that fame and fortune would come his way.
> He seemed to have some realization that a big bank balance was an invaluable aid in the battle of life and so he lived steadily and saved a goodly percentage of his salary. He was never mean or close – just thrifty. Neither was he ever an habitual drinker; in fact nothing but cheap scandal has ever held him otherwise than as the most abstemious of men. In all my experience of him I don't think I have found him addicted to a vice of any kind. He seldom smokes or drinks and, strangely enough, he has not even the vice of vainglory. True, he loves his success, and fights hard to retain and hold it, but only because he feels it is his due. He hates ostentation, and does not want to be lionised for the mere sake of it.
> Yet Charles is one of the lightest-hearted men I have ever known.
> He is very highly strung and given to extravagant expressions of delight when things go aright with him and his work; yet a little incident, the merest mishap to a fellow-actor, for example, will crumple him up completely and render further work impossible for the rest of the day. Sympathy, light-heartedness and his amazing common sense are perhaps his strongest characteristics . . .
> There is nothing stand-offish about Charlie; his preoccupied state of mind and his peculiar way of looking vaguely at his interlocutors, as he

does oftentimes, have misled many casual acquaintances into thinking his success has given him a 'swollen head'.

There never was a greater mistake in this world. Charlie is essentially 'one of the boys', a democrat, a staunch believer in the spirit of born camaraderie and fraternity.[4]

In his own account of himself at this time in *My Autobiography*, Chaplin gives the impression of a solitary, reclusive youth, but from the testimony of former Karno colleagues, it cannot have been always so. 'I have often thought,' Bert Weston (by this time a single act, 'The Mat Man'), wrote to him in 1918, 'of the time when you first came with the football match at Newcastle-on-Tyne, and we all travelled down to Blackburn together, and young Will Poluski had his 21st birthday, and we had the party.' Clifford Walton, then an officer in the Royal Air Force, just awaiting demobilization, wrote to him in March 1919:

It must be at least eight [years] since I left you outside your flat after coming back with you from the Holborn Empire. I remember my friend was very inebriated and insisted on reminding us every few minutes that he was very worried. Anyhow, the poor fellow has since died, after a short and very merry life. Well, old boy, I must first of all congratulate you upon your enormous success . . . You always did amuse me especially in the various digs we shared. I often go over those days in my mind again; after all we did not have such a bad time. Do you remember the week in Belfast and the little girl you were so keen on, also the incident with reference to Will Poluski and your box camera . . . My ideas of life have quite changed since those days although I still possess that roving spirit. Do you play poker nowadays? We used to have some very good games on Sundays, but usually rather disastrous to my financial resources, do you remember? I believe Harry Weldon was usually the lucky one. Am now going to turn into my campbed, so Cheerio Charlie. Hope to run across you somewhere again one day – Best of luck.

Your old pal
Clifford Walton.[5]

These memories give the impression of a young man who was not by any means unsociable, even though

People who were with Chaplin in the old Karno days tell all sorts of stories of his self-absorption in those times. On long train journeys when the other boys in the company were playing ha'penny nap, or reading the Sunday papers, or discussing football, or racing, or the girls, Charlie

would sit in a corner by himself, gazing, not at the scenery, but into space
. . . They thought he was moonstruck.[6]

Then, in the late summer of 1908, Chaplin fell in love. For anyone
else it would have been an adolescent infatuation, a temporary
heartbreak forgotten in a week. But Chaplin was not like anyone
else, and something in his sensibilities or rooted in the deprivations
of his childhood caused this encounter to leave a deep and ineradicable
impression upon him. The object of his feeling was a girl called
Henrietta Florence Kelly. She was born in Bristol, where her father
was an upholsterer, in October 1893.[7] It is not known what became
of her father, William Henry Kelly, but her mother Eliza Kelly had
arrived in London with her son and three beautiful daughters, for
whom she planned stage careers. Hetty was a dancer with Bert Coutts'
Yankee Doodle Girls when Chaplin met her. The act was on the bill
with the Karno troupe at the Streatham Empire. He saw her when
he was standing in the wings – 'a slim gazelle, with a shapely oval
face, a bewitching full mouth, and beautiful teeth'. When she came
off the stage she asked him to hold a mirror for her. The following
night, Wednesday, he asked her if she would meet him on Sunday
afternoon. He took her to the Trocadero (he had drawn £3 from his
bank), but the evening was a mild fiasco since Hetty had eaten
and Charlie had no appetite. Walking her home to Camberwell he
experienced a new sense of joy – 'I was walking in Paradise with
inner blissful excitement.'

On Monday morning he was up in time to call for her at seven
and walk her up Camberwell Road and Walworth Road to the
underground: she was rehearsing that week in Shaftesbury Avenue.
He collected and escorted her again on Tuesday and Wednesday, but
on Thursday when he met her, Hetty was cool and nervous and
would not hold his hand. She told him that she was too young, and
that he was asking too much of her. He was nineteen, she was fifteen.
Talk of love puzzled and alarmed her.

Chaplin could not resist walking to Camberwell Road the next
morning, but instead of Hetty he met her mother, who said that Hetty
had come home crying. He asked to see her, but Eliza Kelly at first
refused to let him. When she relented, and he went with her to the
house, he found Hetty cold and unfriendly. He remembered, more
than sixty years later, that she had just washed her face with Sunlight
soap, and the fresh smell of it.

Chaplin did not understand what had happened, and we can never know. The answer may be that Eliza Kelly did not intend her beautiful daughter to be wasted on a little vaudeville comedian with no prospects. Certainly she was, within a very few years, to see her three daughters married to husbands with money and position. From first sight to farewell, the affair had lasted eleven days, and apart from the Sunday meeting, they had never been together for more than twenty minutes. Chaplin never forgot; and both in his life and art he seemed for many years to be trying to recapture the ecstasy he had felt in the company of Hetty Kelly. Thirteen years afterwards, in 1921, he wrote:

> Kennington Gate. That has its memories. Sad, sweet, rapidly recurring memories.
>
> 'Twas here, my first appointment with Hetty (Sonny's sister). How I was dolled up in my little tight-fitting frock coat, hat, and cane! I was quite the dude as I watched every street car until four o'clock waiting for Hetty to step off, smiling as she saw me waiting.
>
> I get out and stand there for a few moments on Kennington Gate. My taxi driver thinks I am mad. But I am forgetting taxi drivers. I am remembering a lad of nineteen, dressed to the pink, with fluttering heart, waiting, waiting for the moment of the day when he and happiness walked along the road. The road is so alluring now. It beckons for another walk, and as I hear a street car approaching I turn eagerly, for the moment almost expecting to see the same trim Hetty step off, smiling.
>
> The car stops. A couple of men get off. An old woman. Some children. But no Hetty.
>
> Hetty is gone. So is the lad with the frock coat and cane.[8]

He was to describe the encounter again, in more detail, ten years later, adding, 'What happened was the inevitable. After all, the episode was but a childish infatuation to her, but to me it was the beginning of a spiritual development, a reaching out for beauty.'[9]

The life of a touring vaudevillian left little time for repining. In the autumn of 1909 he was sent with a Karno company to Paris, where they played at the Folies Bergères. Karno's pantomime sketches were eminently exportable, since they presented no language problems. Off stage the performers did experience some difficulties of communication, but Chaplin was not perturbed by them and was impressed and excited by all he saw in Paris. By his own account he toyed in a boyish way with the traditional carnal pleasures of the city. In the theatre he seems to have been performing the role which was to establish his fame in America, the Inebriate Swell in *Mumming Birds*, which had previously been played by Billy Ritchie, Billie Reeves and Sydney Chaplin.

The setting for *Mumming Birds* represents the stage of a small music hall, with two boxes at either side. The sketch opens with *fortissimo* music as a girl shows an elderly gentlemen and his nephew – an objectionable boy, armed with peashooter, tin trumpet and picnic hamper – into the lower O.P. box. The Inebriated Swell is settled into the prompt side box, and instantly embarks upon some business of a very Chaplinesque character. He peels the glove from his right hand, tips the waiting attendant, and then, forgetting that he has already removed his glove, absently attempts to peel it off again. He tries to light his cigar from the electric light beside the box. The boy holds out a match for him, and in gracefully inclining to reach it, the Swell falls out of the box.

The show within the show consisted of a series of abysmal acts. (Chaplin told a reporter that in some more benighted towns they visited – he instanced Lincoln – the public believed the acts were offered seriously, and received them with critical disapproval rather than laughter.) The acts changed over the years, but some remained invariable: ballad singer, a male voice quartet, and the Saucy Soubrette, delighting the Swell with her rendering of 'You Naughty, Naughty Man!' The finale was always 'Marconi Ali, the Terrible Turk – the Greatest Wrestler Ever to Appear Before the British Public'. The Terrible Turk was a poor, puny little man weighed down by an enormous moustache, who would leap so voraciously upon a bun thrown to him by the Boy that the Stage Manager had to cry out, 'Back, Ali! Back!' The Turk's offer to fight any challenger for a purse of £100 provided the excuse for a general scrimmage to climax the act.

There were clearly elements in the business and character which Chaplin was later to use in films; descriptions of his glare of mute distaste and the dismissive wave of the hand to indicate boredom anticipate the screen character. Chaplin played other leading roles in the Karno companies. Despite Weldon's contempt, he eventually took on the part of Stiffy with success, even though he had another unlucky experience with it. He was excited when Karno announced that he was to do the role at the Oxford, a major London music hall – perhaps too excited, because as the night approached he lost his voice. Since *The Football Match* was one of the dialogue sketches which now increasingly figured alongside the mimed pieces in the Karno repertory, Chaplin, to his bitter disappointment, was replaced by an understudy. By the spring of 1909, however, he was playing Stiffy in the provinces, and on the last day of the year he was finally billed in the role at the Oxford.

Sydney was now originating material for Karno, as well as starring in leading roles in the sketches. He was co-writer with Karno and a well-known pantomime author, J. Hickory Wood,* of *Skating*, which was presented in 1909 as 'A New and Original Pantomimical Absurdity on the Latest Craze'. Sydney created the role of Archibald Binks. A representative dialogue exchange between Archibald and his friend Bertie at the Olympia Rink runs:

'There we stood with our retreat cut off.'

'Our what cut off?'

'Our retreat cut off.'

'Oh stop it.'

'There we stayed for three days without food or water, think of it, not even a drop of water. What did we do?'

'We drank it neat . . .'

'How are your brothers getting along?'

'Do you remember my brothers?'

'I should say so. Two of 'em are bandy and the other knock-kneed.'

'Do you remember when they used to go out? The two bandy ones would walk on the outside and the knock-kneed one in the centre.'

'Yes, and when they walked down the street they spelt Oxo.'

'How's the world been treating you?'

'Oh, up and down.'

'Are you working?'

'Now and then.'

'Where are you working?'

'Oh, here and there.'

'Do you like it?'

'Well, yes and no.'

'What do you work at?'

'Oh, this and that.'

'You're always in work I suppose?'

'Well, in and out.'

---

* In 1905 Wood had written the biography of the great music hall and pantomime comedian Dan Leno.

'Do you work hard?'

'On and off.'

'How much do you earn?'

'That and half as much again.'

'Who do you work for?'

'Mr So-and-So.'

'Well – are you looking for work?'

'I'm afraid to, in case I find it.'[10]

Years later Chaplin was to commemorate this style of nonsense in the cross-talk scene in *Limelight*. While Sydney toured with the No. 1 *Skating* company, with Jimmy Russell in the part of 'Zena Flapper', a roller-skating flirt, Charlie toured with a second company performing the same sketch, with Johnny Doyle as the lady.

In April 1910 Karno offered Chaplin the leading role in a brand new act, *Jimmy the Fearless, or The Boy 'Ero*. It was planned in four scenes, with spectacular transformations. The sketch opens in a working-class parlour where mother and father are waiting up for Jimmy who arrives home late, brazenly explaining that he has been out 'with a bit o' skirt'. Mother dresses him down and leaves him to eat his supper by the light of the candle. As he eats he takes a penny dreadful out of his pocket and reads it avidly. After supper he draws his chair up to the fire and continues to read until he nods off to sleep.

In his dreams he wanders in the Rocky Mountains, encounters desperadoes in Dead Man's Gulch but overcomes them after a ferocious hand-to-hand struggle, and rescues the heroine. He is next seen with heroine and new-found riches in a palatial home, is about to save his poor old parents from eviction when . . . he awakens in the kitchen, with Father about to lay about him with his belt. 'It probably owes its inspiration,' guessed one reviewer, 'to Dickens. In *A Christmas Carol*, a superabundance of liquor produced the horrible nightmare which made of Scrooge a teetotaller [*sic*] but Jimmy's undoing was a too substantial supper allied to an orgy of "penny dreadfuls".'[11]

Chaplin for some reason turned the part down, and Karno gave it instead to a new boy, Stanley Jefferson:

I thought it was a wonderful sketch, so I jumped at the chance to play Jimmy . . . Charlie was out front the opening night, and right after the show he told Karno he had made a mistake. He wanted to play Jimmy.

And he did. No, I didn't feel bitter about it. For me, Charlie was, is, and will be always the greatest comedian in the world. I thought he should have played it to begin with. But after that I used to kid him – always very proudly – that for once in my life Charlie Chaplin was my replacement. Charlie loved to play Jimmy, and the memory of that role and of that production stayed with him all his life, I think. You can see *Jimmy the Fearless* all over some of his pictures – dream sequences, for instance. He was fond of them, especially in his early pictures. And when it comes down to it, I've always thought that poor, brave, dreamy Jimmy one day grew up to be Charlie the Tramp.[12]

Jimmy the Fearless, or The Boy 'Ero was an immediate success for Karno ('another winner – in which line of business he is as successful as Frohman') and for Chaplin. At the start of the tour he was not billed by name, but the critics noticed him: 'A word is due to the very capable comedian who played the dreamer, but whose modesty keeps his name off the programme'; 'The piece is capitally played by a strong company, including a comedian of original method in the role of the "'Ero".' By the time they reached Swansea his photograph was published in the local papers, with a brief biography:

Charles Chaplin, who plays the title role in *Jimmy the Fearless* at Swansea Empire this week, is only 21 years of age, and comes of an old stage stock, his father having been the late Charles Chaplin, a well-known comedian a few years back, and he started his own career when only nine years of age with the Eight Lancashire Lads. He is the youngest principal comedian in the Karno Companies, and has played 'Perkins' in *The G.P.O.* and *The Bailiffs*; 'Stiffy' in *The Football Match*; 'Archibald' in *Skating*; and the Inebriated Swell in *Mumming Birds*.[13]

The *Yorkshire Evening Post of* 23 July 1910 devoted a whole paragraph to him:

A RISING ACTOR

To assume the roles made famous by Fred Kitchen is no small task for a stripling of twenty-one, yet Mr Chas. Chaplin, who has caused so much laughter at the Leeds Empire this week as Jimmy the Fearless in Fred Karno's latest sketch, has done so with vast credit to himself. Mr Chaplin has only been three years with Mr Karno, yet he has played all the principal parts, and he fully realises the responsibility of following so consummate an artist as Fred Kitchen. He is ambitious and painstaking, and is bound to get on . . . Young as he is he has done some good work on the stage, and his entrance alone in *Jimmy the Fearless* sets the house in a roar and stamps him as a born comedian.

It was a sure sign of Chaplin's versatility and standing that he could take over the role of the bumbling and middle-aged Perkins in *The G.P.O.* and *The Bailiffs* which had been created by Karno's hitherto unrivalled star Fred Kitchen. Chaplin had clearly developed his gifts in his three years with Karno. A crude, ignorant and sadistic man, Karno had a touch of genius in the creation of comedy and comedians. He had an unerring instinct for what was funny. He understood the value of tempo and rhythm (his sketches always had special musical accompaniments). He strove for finesse and for faultless ensemble work. Until a company had been playing together for half a year he reckoned them unskilled, 'a scratch company'. Each player had to be perfect in his part, or rather in several parts, for it was necessary to be able to replace individual members of a cast like the parts of a precision machine.

Karno knew how to get the best out of his artists even if his methods of doing it sometimes lacked charm: a below-standard performance would be criticized with humiliating insults or simply a loud 'rasp-berry' blown from the wings. His treatment even of his stars could be brutish. Chaplin recalled that when he went to negotiate a new contract, Karno had arranged a plant at the other end of the telephone to pose as the manager of a theatre and confirm his view that Chaplin had no appeal and so was not worth any more money.

Another feature of the Karno style was to remain dominant in Chaplin's work. 'I do not remember if he was the one who originated the idea of putting a bit of sentiment right in the middle of a funny music hall turn,' Stan Laurel told John McCabe,

> but I know he did it all the time. I recall one or two instances of that. I forget the Karno sketch, but there was one in which a chap got all beat up – deservedly. He was the villain, a terrible person, and the audience was happy to see him get his [just deserts]. Then Karno added this little bit after the man was knocked down. He had the hero – who, mind you, had *rightfully* beaten up this bad man – walk over to the villain and make him feel easier. Put a pig's bladder under his head or what the hell have you. It got a laugh, and at the same time it was a bit touching. Karno encouraged that sort of thing. 'Wistful' for him I think meant putting in that serious touch once in a while. Another thing I seem to recall: you would have to look sorry, really sorry, for a few seconds after hitting someone on the head. Karno would say, 'Wistful, please, wistful.' It was only a bit of a look, but somehow it made the whole thing funnier. The audience didn't expect that serious look. Karno really knew how to sharpen comedy in that way.[14]

Karno taught his comedians other principles of comedy: that a slow delivery can often be more effective than hectic speed, but that in any event pace must be varied to avoid monotony; that humour lies in the unexpected, so it is funnier if the man is not expecting the pie that hits him in the face. The serious absurdity and the bizarre comic transpositions of the Karno sketches must often have resembled Chaplin gags. In one of them a man picks up a passing dog to wipe his hat. (Dogs figured in Karno sketches as they did in Chaplin films. Sydney's scenario for *Flats* contains the direction, 'This row outside wants to be a succession of shrieks, yells and noise. A dog can be obtained for the purpose or even two. It only requires their master to set them off in the first place and the shouts of the people will keep the dogs going.')

For the sixth successive year, Karno was to send a company on an American tour, with Alf Reeves as manager. 'The adroitness with which he has met the altered conditions of business,' noted *Variety*, 'so different from the methods obtaining in England, has won him the respect and friendship of the managers.' In the winter of 1910 he returned to London, and set about organizing a company for the next American season. Amy Minister, a charming soubrette in one of the Karno companies* told him, 'Al, there's a clever boy in the Karno troupe at the Holloway Empire. His name's Charlie Chaplin. He's a wonderful kid and a marvellous actor.' Reeves remembered in later years that on a foggy night he took a bus to Holloway, where Chaplin was playing *Jimmy the Fearless*.

> Just as I popped in he was putting great dramatic fire into the good old speech, 'Another shot rang out, and another redskin bit the dust!' . . .
>
> He looked the typical London street urchin, who knows every inch of the town as he darts through hurrying throngs and dodges in and out of rushing traffic, managing by some miracle to escape with his life. He had a cap on the back of his head and wore a shabby old suit, short in the sleeves and frayed at the cuffs – a suit he had long since outgrown.
>
> But it was not until he did something strikingly characteristic that I realised he was a real find. His father in the skit was ordering him to drop his novel and eat his supper. 'Get on with it now, m'lad,' and jabbing a loaf of bread at him. Charlie, I noticed, cut the bread without once taking his eyes off his book. But what particularly attracted my attention was

---

* In January 1911, during the Karno company's American tour, Reeves and Amy slipped off to the Cupid Bureau of New York City Hall to marry. Amy was at the time playing the Saucy Soubrette in *Mumming Birds*.

that while he absentmindedly kept cutting the bread, he held the knife in his left hand. Charlie's left-handed, but I didn't know it then. The next thing I knew, he had carved that loaf into the shape of a concertina.[15]

A few years later, Chaplin would use the same gag in his film *A Jitney Elopement*. Reeves went round to the dressing room after the act and asked Chaplin if he would like to go to America. 'Only too gladly, if you'll take me on,' he replied.

> I told him I'd have a talk with Karno. At hearing this he wiped the smudge of make-up off his face to give his smile full play, and I saw he was a very good-looking boy. I had made up my mind about him before leaving his dressing room.
> 'Well,' considered Karno, 'you can have him for the American company if you think he's old enough for the parts.' We were then giving *A Night in an English Music Hall*, *A Night in a London Club* and *A Night in a London Secret Society*.
> 'He's old enough,' I told Karno, 'and big enough and clever enough for anything.'[16]

Karno appears to have been happy to send Charlie in preference to Sydney because previous tours had resulted in a number of defections to the American vaudeville stage, and Sydney was too valuable to risk losing. Before he left, Chaplin solemnly assured the Guv'nor that there was no fear of his not returning. His contract was not due for renewal until March 1911, but a new one was drawn up and signed on 19 September 1910, just before the company set sail on the SS *Cairnrona*. The new agreement was to take effect from 6 March 1911, and provided for three years' engagement at £6 a week in the first year, £8 in the second and £10 in the third. After that there would be an option for a further three years.

The American company that year also included Stan Jefferson, Fred and Muriel Palmer, George Seaman, who doubled as stage carpenter, and his wife Emily, Albert Austin, who in later years worked in many Chaplin films, Fred Westcott, Karno's nineteen-year-old-son, and Mike Asher, who played the awful boy in *Mumming Birds*.

The *Cairnrona* docked at Quebec, and the troupe travelled by train via Toronto to New York, where they were to open on 3 October at the Colonial Theatre. Karno had insisted that they present a new sketch, *The Wow-Wows, or A Night in a London Secret Society*. The first scene was set in a summer camp, where the campers resolve to get even with the tight-wadded Archie by creating a phoney secret society. The second scene satirized the absurd initiation ceremonies of such arcane organizations. The cast were dismayed to open with a piece which they all regarded as silly and ineffective. As we can judge from the notices, only Chaplin's performance saved it from total disaster. *Variety* prophetically wrote that 'Chaplin will do all right for America, but it is too bad that he didn't first appear in New York with something with more in it than this piece.' Another reviewer wrote:

Now Charles Chaplin is so arriving a comedian that Mr Karno will be forgiven for whatever else the act may lack. The most enthusiastic Karno-ite will surely admit, too, the act lacks a great deal that might help to make it vastly more entertaining. Still, Mr Chaplin heads the cast, so the people laughed and were content.

He plays Archibald, a chappie with one end of his moustache turned up and the other turned down, a chappie with spots on his face betokening many a bad night, a chappie who declared himself in on everything though never paying his or any share.

His first appearance is made from a tent, one of several occupied by a camping party. He looks more than seedy, despite his dress being immaculate.

'How are you, Archie?' inquires a woman visitor, decidedly attractive, and of whom Archie appeared to be enamoured.

'Not well,' he responds. 'I just had a terrible dream.'

'Very terrible?' she asks solicitously.

'Oh, frightful!' says Archie. 'I dreamed I was being chased by a caterpillar.'

Archie makes such remarks as this in an exceedingly droll, ludicrous fashion. Outside Archie the company is composed of the most remarkable collection of blithering, blathering Englishmen New York has seen in many a day.[17]

After a month or two on tour, Chaplin and the company evidently built the business up until the sketch was tolerable. A rather later review noted that 'Nothing funnier has been seen in some time than the scene when Charles Chaplin, the fancy "souse", is initiated into the mysteries of the Wow-Wows. Chaplin is a real comedian. He is actually funny and *The Wow-Wows* might have been made to order for him.'[18]

During their three months around the New York circuit, the company dutifully played *The Wow-Wows*, but despite the improvement they wrought in it they were eager to be rid of it. At the

American Music Hall, Chicago, in the week of 30 January 1911 they offered a seventeen-minute sketch, in a single set, entitled *A Night in a London Club*. Some mystery surrounds this presentation, since it

1910 - Karno advertisement.

was apparently not repeated, and only briefly figured in Karno publicity. The most likely explanation was that, with the resourcefulness in which Karno players were trained, they had simply improvised a completely new act, using the club set from *The Wow-Wows*. It was related to an old Karno sketch, *The Smoking Concert*, but with elements taken from *Mumming Birds* and *The Wow-Wows*:

> The offering somehow suggests Dickens. Seeing it one is reminded of the gatherings of the Pickwick club. The caricatures of the individual members of the club are with a graveness which makes the comedy stand out. The comedy is rough but the characters are well drawn. Various members of the club are called upon to entertain. There is a woman singer who gets her key repeatedly but cannot strike it when she begins to sing, a precious daughter of one of them, who offers a childish selection to the plaudits of admiring friends and among others an ambitious tragedian who, after reminding the master of ceremonies several times, is at length permitted

to start a scene of a play, only to be interrupted by the 'drunk' (played by Charles Chaplin) which has come to be recognized as the leading comedy character of the Karno offerings. As seen Monday afternoon the only shortcoming of the farce was the lack of a big laugh at the finish.[19]

1911 - Cartoon of Chaplin in *A Night in a London Club*, in USA.

It is not too imaginative to suppose that, as the leading comedian, Chaplin would have played a major role in devising a new act of this sort, as he must also have done in an intriguing entertainment which the company put on as an extra turn at the American Music Hall in New York for their six-week Christmas season. It was billed as *A Harlequinade in Black and White: An Old Style Christmas Pantomime*. It was entirely played as a shadow show, behind a large white screen.

It brought forth our old friends, the Clown, Pantaloon, Harlequin and Columbine. The pantomime was much more interesting than one would imagine it to be by merely hearing about it, for the pantomimists were funny in their extravagant make-up and actions. There was plenty of action to it, a diversity of ideas shown, and much pleasure derived by the audience, judging by the way they received it.

First the characters indulged in a little general knockabout fooling, then they had fun with a stolen bottle, after which the policeman was relieved of his clothes, and another 'cop' was knocked out and laid upon a table to be dissected, his internal organs being brought forth one by one. The baby was stolen from the carriage of the nurse-maid, and all the characters had a 'rough house' experience while seeking lodgings. A droll duel brought forth two characters who grew and diminished in size rapidly as they fought, the phantom army appeared and paraded, and all the characters leaped 'up to the moon', the silhouettes showing them apparently jumping away up into the air and out of sight. They all jumped back again, and the act closed. It was quite a happy little idea for the holiday season, occupying about eleven minutes.[20]

Years later Chaplin was to use the same shadow technique for a wonderful scene which he in the end discarded from *Shoulder Arms*. In this case an antiquated form of entertainment was given such vitality that 'in a programme that embraces the best of every branch of vaudeville an astonishing hit was made by an act that may set the managers constantly striving . . .'[21] Within a few weeks the idea was borrowed by Gus Hill's *Vanity Fair*, for a number with shadow show-girls wearing strip tights and nighties.*

During the months in New York Chaplin lived in a brownstone house off 43rd Street, over a dry cleaner's. At first he found the city unfriendly and intimidating; in time he was stimulated by the energy of American life and the apparent classlessness of the country. After New York came a twenty-week tour, doing three shows a day on the Sullivan and Considine circuit. It provided a thrilling revelation of the country, from East to West – Chicago, St Louis, Minneapolis, St Paul, Kansas City, Denver, Butte, Billings, Tacoma, Seattle, Portland, San Francisco and Los Angeles, which Chaplin did not like. In Canada they played in Winnipeg and Vancouver, where they felt they were back among English audiences.

Stan Laurel told John McCabe:

> We were thrilled at the excitement of New York, but seeing the whole country, mile and mile, was really the way to see America. I was Charlie's roommate on that tour and he was fascinating to watch. People through the years have talked about how eccentric he became. He was a very eccentric person *then*. He was very moody and often very shabby in

---

* Among the few dozen press cuttings which Chaplin kept from this tour, several deal with this Christmas shadow show. His particular interest in it can reasonably be taken to indicate at the least a significant creative contribution to the turn.

appearance. Then suddenly he would astonish us all by getting dressed to kill. It seemed that every once in a while he would get an urge to look very smart. At these times he would wear a derby hat (an expensive one), gloves, smart suit, fancy vest, two-tone side button shoes, and carry a cane. I have a lot of quick little memories of him like that. For instance, I remember that he drank only once in a while, and then it was always port.

He read books incessantly. One time he was trying to study Greek, but he gave it up after a few days and started to study yoga. A part of this yoga business was what was called the 'water cure' – so for a few days after that he ate nothing, just drank water for his meals. He carried his violin wherever he could. Had the strings reversed so he could play left-handed, and he would practice for hours. He bought a cello once and used to carry it around with him. At these times he would always dress like a musician, a long fawn-coloured overcoat with green velvet cuffs and collar and a slouch hat. And he'd let his hair grow long at the back. We never knew what he was going to do next. He was unpredictable.[22]

Other members of the Karno companies confirmed Laurel's account of Chaplin's sartorial unpredictability. An anonymous columnist noted too that 'the world's greatest impersonator of inebriates and the biggest laughmaker on the vaudeville stage' (a striking encomium in 1911)

is one of the quietest and most non-committal of men – except just before, during and just after each performance. On these thrice-daily occasions he seems to enter heart and soul into the spirit of the impersonation and he's the most genial fellow one could meet. Then he lapses into a reserved state of mind during which he either sits quite still and thinks – thinks – thinks, or delves into the pages of the heaviest kind of literature he can find – philosophy preferred. It is said of him that, when in a small town where he could not secure a book to his liking, he purchased a Latin grammar and satisfied his peculiar mood for a time by devouring the dry contents as though it was a modern novel.[23]

Still, he was not unsociable. A gymnastic act called Lohse and Sterling was on the tour with them, and Chaplin struck up a warm friendship with Ralph Lohse, a big, handsome young Texan with ambitions to become a prize-fighter. They used to spar together, and became enthusiastic about a plan to quit show business and raise hogs in a big way. Chaplin lost his enthusiasm after reading up on techniques of castrating hogs, but Ralph Lohse was more dogged, and four years later wrote to Chaplin that though he was still in vaudeville – now with his wife in the act – he had a flourishing farm in Arkansas:

> I sold my first one and bought a second one and I have it running in great shape. I have in the neighbourhood of 600 hogs on it now and if conditions get better this fall I am going to put home-sugar-cured hams and bacon on the market, also pure pork farm sausage in little pound cartons. There is a great demand for such goods. My grandfather was considered one of the best sausage makers in the country and I know his process. And you was the durn fool that put all these notions in my head.
>
> Charlie I am glad to see you doing so well in pictures. We never go to a picture show unless you are in them and we manage to see nearly all of the pictures you are in. You will remember that all those Englishmen used to say that you would never amount to much if you ever lost out with Karno. Losing Karno was the best thing you ever done.[24]

1910 - Cartoon of Chaplin as the Inebriate in *A Night in an English Music Hall*, in USA.

94

Charlie had not lost all his chances of raising hogs, and making sausages: Ralph said that if ever he wanted 'to go in at round about $1800, let me know . . .'

Once out on the tour, the company thankfully revived the old faithful *Mumming Birds*, retitled for America *A Night in an English Music Hall*. Audiences had seen it before but welcomed it back joyously. Chaplin won his usual praise at every theatre. In Butte, Montana, he was said to prove himself 'one of the best pantomime artists ever seen here'. 'Charles Chaplin as the inebriated swell is a revelation and is given a big hand many times during the act.' 'Charles Chaplin, as the polite drunk, is an artist and even though doing the broadest burlesque, never gets out of the part for an instant. His falls in and out of the boxes are wonderful, and were he not a skilled acrobat, he would break his neck.'[25]

After the Sullivan and Considine tour, the company was booked for another six-week New York season by the William Morris Agency; then sent out for a further twenty-week Sullivan and Considine tour, which finally ended in May 1912 in Salt Lake City.

When the company arrived back in England in June 1912, they had been away for twenty-one months. For Charlie the homecoming was not particularly happy. He was met at the station by Sydney who

1910 - *A Night in an English Music Hall*: The Inebriate meets the Terrible Turk.

95

told him that he had married Minnie Constance, a Karno actress, and had given up the flat in Glenshaw Mansions. To be suddenly deprived like this of the first place he had recognized as his own home was a sharp blow to Charlie; for the first time in their lives there was a distance between the brothers. Hannah was still in Cane Hill, and not in any way improved. Now that they could afford it, Sydney and Charlie arranged for her to be moved to a private nursing home, Peckham House, Peckham Road. It was the place where Dan Leno had been cared for after his mental collapse.

Karno put the American company on the road, in suburban halls. Their year and a half together had polished them and sharpened their comedy, and they were very successful with the English audiences, but England seemed flat after the excitements of America, and Chaplin was glad to leave again for a new American tour. The company sailed from Southampton on 2 October 1912 on the SS *Oceanic*. (In his autobiography Chaplin refers to the ship as the *Olympic*, but the *Olympic* was laid up at this time, undergoing modifications following the sinking of the *Titanic*.) The only members of the last American company to remain with him were Alf and Amy Reeves, Stan Jefferson and Edgar and Ethel Hurley. One new member of the troupe was 'Whimsical Walker', the famous Drury Lane clown, who at this time was sixty-one years old. According to Walker he was engaged the night before sailing to fill a vacancy in the company, having met Alf Reeves and some members of the company by accident in a bar. He complained that he had not worked for such a low salary for years, but he was out of work and glad to take it.

They were again stuck with *The Wow-Wows* for much of the tour, which was not in any way a lucky one. Poor Walker's diction proved to be very bad. When they reached Butte, Montana, they found that the theatre had burnt down since their last visit and they had to play in a public hall. A number of the cast fell ill, and poor old Walker developed erysipelas and had to be hospitalized in Seattle. He did not rejoin the company.[26]

The third time round the Sullivan and Considine circuit, the sight-seeing had lost its novelty. Chaplin was growing tired of audiences which could be remarkably unsophisticated in the American sticks, as he discovered:

> ... we had been heavily billed as vaudeville, because vaudeville was a new thing there at the time. That fact was evident the first night, for the

people did not seem to understand that our work was merely burlesque. This was plainly brought home to us after the show. We were playing *A Night in an English Music Hall* during which a quartette renders a song in the most awful manner possible – the worse it is sung, the greater the fun produced.

Well, we had returned to the hotel and were compelled to listen to many uncomplimentary remarks. 'What do you think of the big act?' one Pennsylvania man asked another Pennsylvania man. 'Which big act?' was the reply. 'The Karno act,' responded the first speaker. 'Absolutely rotten,' snapped the other. 'Why,' he added, 'that quartette couldn't sing for sour apples. In fact, our local quartette could beat them in seven different ways!'[27]

Still, success brought economic consolations. On 8 October 1913 Chaplin was able to acquire $200 worth of shares in the Vancouver Island Oil Company: he was always preparing for a rainy day. It was time to be moving on, too. The week of 4 August, when the Karno company were playing in Winnipeg, Chaplin wrote one of his infrequent letters to his brother, from the La Claire Hotel:

My Dear Sid,

I hope you received my letter all right. I know there wasn't much news in it – 'they say no news is good news' but not in this case. I have quite a lot of good news to tell you this time. Did I tell you I met Sonny Kelly in New York? Yes, I met him and had a grand time – he took me all over the place. He has a lovely apartment on Madison Avenue which you know is the swell part of New York. Hetty was away at the time – so I never saw her but still I am keeping correspondence with Sonny and he tells me I am always welcome to his place when in New York. I do nothing else but meet people and old friends – right here in Winnipeg I met one of the old boys who use to be in the Eight Lancashire Lads. I dont know wether you would know him or not – Tommy Bristol – he use to be my bigest pal – now he's working the Orpheum turns with a partner getting about 300 dollars per – I tell you they are all doing well, even me. I have just to sign a contract for *150 Dollars a week*. 'Now comes the glad news.' Oh' Sid I can see you!! beaming now as you read this, those sparkling eyes of yours scanning this scrible and wondering what coming next. I'll tell you how the land lyes. I have had an offer from a moving picture company for quite a long time but I did not want to tell you untill the whole thing was confirmed and it practically is settled now – all I have to do is to mail them my address and they will forward contract. It is for the New York Motion Picture Co., a most reliable firm in the States – they have about four companies, the 'Kay Bee' and

'Broncho' [and] 'Keystone' which I am to joyne, the Keystone is the Comedy Co. I am to take Fred Mace place. He is a big man in the movies. So you bet they think a lot of me – it appears they saw me in *Los Angeles, Cal.* playing the Wow-Wows then they wrote to me in Philadelphia which was a long time after. I could have told you before but I wanted the thing settled. We had a week's lay-of in Phili so I went over to New York and saw them personaly. I had no idea they would pay any money but a pal of mine told me that Fred Mace was getting four hundred a week well I ask them for two hundred. They said they would have to put it before the board of Directors ('dam this pen!') Well we hagled for quite a long time and then I had to do all my business by writing them and you bet I put a good business letter together with the help of the dictionary. Finaly we came to this arrangement i.e. A year's contract. Salary for the first three months 150 per week and if I make good after three months 175 per week with no expences at all and in Los Angeles the whole time. I don't know whether you have seen any Keystone pictures but they are very funny, they also have some nice girls ect. Well that's the whole strength, so now you know. Of course I told them I would not leave this company until we finished the S.C.* circuit, so I will join them by about the beginning of Dec that will be about the time we get through. I have told Alf and of course he doesn't want me to leave but he says I am certainly bettering myself and he can't say otherwise. Mr Kessel tells me there is no end of advancement for me if I make good. Just think Sid £35 per week is not to be laugh at and I only want to work about five years at that and then we are independent for life. I shall save like a son of a gun. Well I am getting tired now so will draw to a close. Don't tell anybody about what Alf said because it may get to the Guvnor's ears and he will think Alf had been advising me. And if you know of any little Ideas in the way of synaros ect. don't forget to let me have them. Hoping you are in good health and Mother improving also I would love her and you to be over hear. Well we may some day when I get in right.

Love to Minnie
and yourself
Your loving Brother,
Charlie.

Chaplin left the Karno company in Kansas City on 28 November 1913. 'I missed him, I must say,' Stan Laurel told John McCabe.

Arthur Dandoe, a chap in the Karno company with whom I teamed one time in a vaudeville act, didn't like Charlie. Arthur didn't like him because he considered him haughty and cold. So in Kansas City on our last night

---

* Sullivan and Considine.

with Charlie, Arthur announced to everybody that he was going to present a special goodbye present. He told me what it was – about five pieces of old brown Leichner grease paint, looking just like turds, all wrapped up in a very fancy box. 'Some shit for a shit,' is the way Arthur put it. This was Arthur's idea of a joke.

1913 - Charles Chaplin's letter to
Sydney announcing he is going
into films.

I tried to argue him out of it but all Arthur said was, 'It'll serve the superior bastard right.'

The so-called presentation never took place however and later Arthur told me why. First of all, Charlie stood the entire company drinks after the show. That fazed Arthur a bit but the thing that really shamed him into not going through with the so-called gag was this:

just after his final curtain with us, Charlie hurried off to a deserted spot backstage. Curious, Arthur followed, and he saw haughty, cold, unsentimental Charlie crying.[29]

This story has a sad footnote. When Chaplin made his triumphal return to his native city in 1921, Arthur Dandoe, down on his luck, was working as a pavement artist in Trafalgar Square.[30]

Alf Reeves saw Charlie off at the Kansas City railroad depôt. As he stepped into the train he handed Alf a small package and said, 'Merry Christmas, Alf.' When the train had carried Charlie off, Alf opened the package and found a handsome pocket book, and inside it a $100 bill, with a note: 'A little tribute to our friendship. To Alf, from Charlie.' Not wanting to waste good money on something he might not like, Charlie wanted Alf to choose something for himself; but Alf kept the pocket book with the note intact for many years.

4

In Pictures

Accounts of how Chaplin came to be discovered by the Keystone Film Company vary. Mack Sennett, who ran Keystone for Adam Kessel and Charles Bauman, owners of the parent company, New York Motion Pictures, claimed that he had spotted Chaplin while spending a week in New York with his leading lady and girlfriend, Mabel Normand, 'late in 1912'. Chaplin was playing *A Night in an English Music Hall* at the American Theatre on 42nd Street and 8th Avenue.

> 'Feller's pretty funny,' Mabel said.
> 'Think he'd be good enough for pictures?' I said.
> 'He might be,' Mabel said . . .
> 'I don't know,' I said to Mabel. 'He has all the tricks and routines and he can take a fall, and probably do a 108, but that limey make-up and costume – I don't know.'[1]

By the time he came to write his autobiography, Chaplin was himself satisfied that Sennett's version was true, though his letter of 1913 to Sydney indicates that any of the motion picture people might have seen him with the Karno company at the Empress Theatre, Los Angeles. Other accounts allege that it was Adam Kessel or his brother Charles who had seen Chaplin in New York, at Hammerstein's Theatre. A more recent, and persuasive, version of events appears in a letter from T. K. (Kim) Peters to Kevin Brownlow. Peters had been interested in films since 1899 when he had shot some moving pictures in Paris; in 1913 he was in Hollywood. His letter, written in 1973, suggest it was another N.Y.M.P. executive who discovered Chaplin:

Harry Aitken . . . gave Charlie Chaplin his first job in movies . . . I had been moonlighting by painting some murals for the Pantage Theatre. In one of the murals I painted a beautiful semi-nude woman, after the fashion of Mucha . . . The manager of Pantage called me up shortly after they opened and asked me to come down as he had had several criticisms on the lady, as her breasts were bare. I went down and painted a veil over her breasts, and had stepped out into the lobby to go home when a well-dressed man who was looking at the billing photos . . . asked me if I was connected with the show . . . He said that he had heard that the show was interesting . . . The show was Karno's *Night in an English Music Hall* . . . He said that he was going to attend the matinée . . . He told me he was just in from New York . . .

I did not give it much thought, but he was Harry Aitken, owner of the major stock in the Keystone Comedies, and the actor was Charlie Chaplin. Harry hired Chaplin away from Karno . . . and it was my first meeting with Harry, which ripened into a life-long friendship.[2]

In any event, in the spring of 1913 Kessel and Bauman sent Alf Reeves a telegram which allegedly read (accounts of it vary in textual detail:

MAY 12 1913

ALF REEVES MANAGER
KARNO LONDON COMEDIANS
NIXON THEATRE, PHILADELPHIA

IS THERE A MAN NAMED CHAFFIN IN YOUR COMPANY OR SOMETHING LIKE THAT IF SO WILL HE COMMUNICATE WITH KESSEL AND BAUMAN 24 LONGACRE BUILDING BROADWAY NEW YORK.[3]

It was in response to this that Chaplin returned to New York for a day. He supposed that Kessel and Bauman must be lawyers, like most of the tenants of Longacre Building, and he speculated that perhaps his great-aunt, Mrs Wiggins, had died in New York and left him a fortune. Instead he was asked if he would consider signing up with the Keystone Company. From his letter to Sydney it is clear that Chaplin was told that he was to replace Fred Mace, the heavyweight star of the earliest Keystone comedies. In his autobiography, however, Mack Sennett says that his reason for asking Chaplin to join his company was the ever-growing demands of Keystone's other male star, Ford Sterling, and his fears that Sterling might at any time give in his notice. Sennett's version has been generally accepted by subsequent historians, but Chaplin's original understanding of the circumstances seems more likely. Tact, on the part of Kessel and Bauman, of course, would have made it more likely for Chaplin to be told that he was to replace a departing star than that he was required to stand by in case of the defection of a current leading player. But the date of the telegram is significant: Mace left Keystone at the end of April 1913: it would seem most likely that the company would be urgently seeking a successor a couple of weeks later. Moreover, Ford Sterling was only just coming into his own as the company's leading star with the removal of Mace's competition; and he was in fact to remain at Keystone for a further nine months, until February 1914.

Chaplin, tired of touring, was ready for a change. By July a contract was drawn up to engage Charles Chaplin of the City, County and State of New York 'as a moving picture actor to enact roles in the moving picture productions of the party of the first part in its companies, and such other companies as the party of the first part may hereafter form, for a period of one year commencing November 1st 1913 (unless sooner terminated by either party as hereinafter provided), for a salary of One Hundred and Fifty Dollars weekly.'

A remarkably uncomplicated, two-page document, the contract was signed in New York by Adam and Charles Kessel, as President and Secretary respectively of the Keystone Film Company, witnessed by a notary public and despatched to Chaplin on tour. Chaplin, however, evidently refused to sign: and a new version was drawn up, omitting the parenthetical phrase '(unless sooner terminated by either party as hereinafter provided)' and the associated provision that the contract was terminable by two weeks' written notice by either party. Chaplin at this stage of his career was not prepared to throw up security with Karno to run the risk of unforeseen unemployment within the year. The commencing date of the contract was changed to 16 December 1913.[4]

The signatures of Kessel and Bauman were witnessed on 15 September 1913, and the revised contract was sent to Chaplin, who signed it in Portland, Oregon, on 25 September. Curiously the contract makes no mention of the arrangement to raise Chaplin's weekly salary by $25 at the end of three months. Since Chaplin was equally certain in 1913 and in 1964 that these were the terms (and his memory was almost faultless in matters of business) this must have been the subject of a separate verbal agreement.

The origins and history of the Keystone Film Company have been fogged by the chronic mythomania of its presiding genius, the Canadian-Irish Mack Sennett, whose highly-coloured recollections were published long after the events they related. Among the few certain facts are that Sennett was born Michael Sinnott, to Irish parents, in Richmond, Quebec on 17 January 1880. While working

in writing, scenarios or in any other manner engage or assist others in any branch of the moving picture business, and that he will not, during the term of his employment hereunder, or at any time thereafter, enact for any others than the party of the first part, any of the roles to which he may have been assigned by the party of the first part during his employment, and that he will not, at any time during the continuance of his employment hereunder, appear in any public or private performance as an actor, lecturer, or entertainer, except with the written consent of the party of the first part.

This contract may be terminated by either par, upon two (2) weeks written notice to the other party hereto.

IN WITNESS WHEREOF, the party of the first part has caused these presents to be signed by its President and Secretary, and its corporate seal to be hereunto affixed, and the party of the second part has hereunto set his hand and seal, the day and year first above written.

THE KEYSTONE FILM CO.

By _____
President

_____
Secretary

_____ (L.S.)

1913 - Chaplin's first film contract: the first draft (above) which he did not sign, and the second (right) with his signature.

in an iron foundry in Northampton, Connecticut, he obtained from the local attorney – Calvin Coolidge – an introduction to the famous comedienne, Marie Dressler, who was appearing in town. Miss Dressler, in turn, sent him to David Belasco, the most prominent actor-manager of the day, who counselled burlesque as the proper *métier* for the raw-boned youth. Sennett, however, did not at once

in writing, scenarios or in any other manner engage or assist others in any branch of the moving picture business, and that he will not, during the term of his employment hereunder, or at any time thereafter, enact for any others than the party of the first part, any of the roles to which he may have been assigned by the party of the first part during his employment, and that he will not, at any time during the continuance of his employment hereunder, appear in any public or private performance as an actor, lecturer, or entertainer, except with the written consent of the party of the first part.

IN WITNESS WHEREOF, the party of the first part has caused these presents to be signed by its President and Secretary, and its corporate seal to be hereunto affixed, and the party of the second part has hereunto set his hand and seal, the day and year first above written.

THE KEYSTONE FILM CO.

By

A Kessel Jr
President

Chas Kessel
Secretary

Charles Chaplin (L.S.)

abandon ambitions to exploit his powerful baritone voice, and divided his time between touring burlesque and the chorus of musical comedy.

In 1908, like many another disappointed actor, Sennett was reduced to seeking work in 'the galloping tintypes', as movies were disparagingly styled. He claimed that it was on his twenty-eighth birthday, in January 1908, that he joined the Biograph Company at 11 East 14th Street, New York. With Irish luck, Sennett had chanced upon a time and place that were to prove historic. David Wark Griffith had arrived at Biograph a few months before, and was already embarked upon the period of prodigal creation which, in barely five years, was to explore and reveal the whole expressive possibilities of motion pictures, and to turn them into an art.

Sennett was inquisitive, ambitious, imitative, ingenious. He studied Griffith's work and determined to be a director himself. Soon he began to augment his income by writing scenarios. He recognized his natural bent for comedy, and he took note of the success of the anarchic, knockabout comedy films imported from France, where they were produced by the Pathé and Gaumont companies. In 1909 he played the leading role in a comedy directed by Griffith, *The Curtain Pole*. Humour was not Griffith's strong point, yet here too he applied his innate gift for discovering first principles. The farce was slight: Sennett played a tipsy Frenchman whose efforts to carry home a curtain pole wreak havoc in the streets of an unoffending township. Griffith however brought to the service of comedy all his discoveries of editing, suspense and timing.

In 1910 Sennett was appointed Biograph's principal director of comic productions, and between March 1911 and July 1912 directed upwards of eighty one-reel comedies. When Kessel and Bauman were looking for a man to run their new comedy studio, Sennett was the ideal candidate.* Keystone was established in the summer of 1912, and by early September Sennett had moved into the former Bison

---

* Sennett's characteristically highly-coloured version of events is that he conned Kessel and Bauman, 'two bookmakers', into going into partnership with him as a means of settling a $100 gambling debt. In fact Kessel and Bauman had given up bookmaking some four years earlier, and by this time were major film producers. Their prospering New York Motion Picture Company was the parent company for 101 Bison Films, producing Thomas Ince's western and historical spectacles, and for Reliance, specializing in dramas. Kessel and Bauman naturally now wanted to establish a comedy arm.

Studio at 1712 Allessandro Street, Edendale, California (the Edendale Studios). He brought with him Fred Balshofer as manager; Mabel Normand, Fred Mace and Ford Sterling as his stars; and Henry Lehrman who was to direct Keystone's second unit while Sennett directed the first. All had worked together at Biograph. The first Keystone releases were announced for 23 September 1912 and by February 1913 the studio was maintaining a steady production of eight reels a month.

As producer and director, Sennett shared many of Fred Karno's characteristics. He was a rough, tough, intelligent, uneducated man. He had an instinctive feeling for physical comedy. Because he was easily bored himself, he could tell what would keep the audience's attention happily engaged, and what would not. He could maintain discipline in his troupe of high-spirited and unruly clowns. At Biograph he had mastered film craft, and he passed on his lessons. The Keystone cameramen were dexterous in following the free flight of the clowns, and the dynamism of 'Keystone editing', adapted from Griffith's innovatory montage methods, soon became a byword.

Keystone films derived from vaudeville, circus, comic strips, and at the same time from the realities of early twentieth-century America. It was a world of wide, dusty streets with one-storey clapboard houses, grocery and hardware stores, dentists' surgeries and saloon bars; kitchens and parlours; the lobbies of cheap hotels; bedrooms with iron beds and rickety washstands; railroad tracks and angular automobiles that were just overtaking the horse and buggy; men in bowler hats and heavy whiskers; ladies in feathered hats and harem skirts; spoiled children and stray dogs. The stuff of comedy was wild caricature of the ordinary joys and terrors of daily life. At all events, the guiding principle at Keystone was to keep things moving, to leave no pause for breath or critical reflection. No excess of make-up or mugging was too great. In time the original group of comedians who had come west with Sennett was augmented by the recruitment of Roscoe 'Fatty' Arbuckle, cross-eyed Ben Turpin, gangling Charley Chase, the walrus-whiskered Chester Conklin and Billy Bevan, giant Mack Swain, Tom and Edgar Kennedy, Slim Summerville, Louise Fazenda, Polly Moran, Alice Davenport and others who could contribute acrobatic skill or outrageous characterization to the troupe. These were Chaplin's future colleagues.

He reached Los Angeles in early December 1913 and took a modest room at the Great Northern Hotel on Bunker Hill, close to the

Empress Theatre, where he had played. His first meeting with his new boss was accidental. On his first night in Los Angeles, very lonely, he went to the Empress. There he ran into Sennett, with Mabel Normand. Chaplin sensed Sennett's misgivings on seeing how young he appeared without stage make-up. Karno had had the same reaction, and received the same reassuring reply: 'I can make up as old as you like.'

The following day (according to his own recollections) Chaplin set out for the studio. Edendale was a district of shanty buildings and lumber yards and the studio itself was a strange-looking place. An area 150 feet square was surrounded by a green board fence. At the centre stood the stage, overhung with white linen to diffuse the sunlight. An old bungalow housed the offices and the women's dressing rooms; some converted agricultural buildings served as dressing rooms for the men. Chaplin arrived at lunchtime, was intimidated by the sight of the high-spirited actors surging out of the bungalow in quest of food, and fled back to his hotel. The same thing happened the next day; and only an anxious telephone call from Sennett got him beyond the gates on the third.

Sennett explained to Chaplin the Keystone method. There was no scenario; 'we get an idea, then follow the natural sequence of events until it leads up to a chase which is the essence of our comedy.' This did not entirely reassure Chaplin, accustomed to the months of polishing that perfected the team work of a Karno sketch. His first weeks at Keystone were far from happy: sometimes he began to think that he had made a mistake, and he was certain that Sennett felt the same. He came to films a complete novice, and had to master the basic notions: cutting; the shooting of scenes in discontinuity; the actor's problem of staying within the camera's range; the importance of sight lines, so that the direction of the actor's gaze in one shot will convincingly link with the object of that gaze in another shot. He felt that his own subtle and carefully paced comedy was going to be lost here, since the tempo of all the films seemed to be matched to the leaping and mugging of Ford Sterling's comedy. He was irked by enforced idleness: Sennett – perhaps intending him to watch and learn the techniques of film making – did not use him in a film until the end of January.

By this time, however, Chaplin already knew enough to doubt the competence of the director assigned to his first film. Henry Lehrman was born in Vienna in 1886 and had emigrated to the United States at the age of nineteen. He was working as a tram conductor when he first presented himself to D. W. Griffith at the Biograph Studios, claiming to have been a director with the Pathé Company in France. Griffith, no doubt seeing through the fraud, nicknamed him Pathé and passed him on to Sennett. Sennett, as we have seen, thought well enough of him to make him his second unit director when he opened his own studios. 'Pathé' Lehrman was to continue directing films until the mid-1930s, but he remained a mediocre man-of-all-work. History remembers him only as Chaplin's first director, and as the chief prosecution witness in the trial that ruined Roscoe Arbuckle seven years later.

Chaplin's first film, *Making a Living*, was one of Keystone's more elaborate productions. It had a comparatively well-developed story line, and was shot partly on the stage, partly in the gardens of a nearby house, and partly in the street, on Glendale Avenue. Chaplin's costume, make-up and character resembled Archibald Binks in *The Wow-Wows* and *A Night in a London Club*, with nothing as yet of the Charlie figure to come. He wore a grey top hat, check waistcoat, stiff collar, spotted cravat and monocle. Most surprising was the long, drooping moustache of a rather dejected stage villain. At the start of the film he established the fraudulence of his elegant pretensions by touching a passing friend (played by Lehrman) for a loan. The first characteristically Chaplin gag is where he disdainfully rejects the proffered coin as too mean, but then hastily grabs it before the friend can change his mind. In return for this favour, the Dude decides to steal his benefactor's girl, and sets to flirting with both the girl (Virginia Kirtley) and her mother (Alice Davenport) in the garden.

Lehrman plays a reporter, and most of the action is concerned with the Dude's attempts to muscle in on the job and scoop him. It all ends with a chase, a contretemps in a lady's bedroom (an almost indispensable incidental to Keystone films) and a grand finale on the cow-catcher of a moving train. The American critic Walter Kerr has pointed out that one small but striking gag established a permanent and productive pattern of Chaplin's screen personality, of 'adjusting the rest of the universe to his merely reflexive needs'.[5] The Dude is explaining his own merits to the newspaper editor, emphasizing his argument by banging him on the knee. When the editor withdraws his knee, the Dude pulls it back again so that he can continue his pummelling.

Chaplin hated the film. He was outraged when he saw the finished thing and discovered that in the cutting Lehrman had excised or mangled good gags which he had introduced. He was certain that Lehrman had deliberately tried to destoy his work, out of pique because Chaplin had been too free with suggestions for comic business during the shooting. In fact there was nothing to be ashamed of for a first film. It is a rough little effort, but so were most of the Keystone products. True, we can see in it very little of the Karno comedian of whom three years before one critic had written: 'Chaplin has been described, by some critics, as a genius. To say the least he carries the hallmarks of genius . . .' Nor was there as yet much, except these one or two little gags, to hint at the character he would ultimately create. But he emerges as a defined and dominant figure, already with a more consistent character, in his bland and airy malefactions, than was common in Keystone films. The trade press picked him out at once: 'The clever player who takes the part of a sharper . . . is a comedian of the first water.' If there is any truth in the legends passed on for seventy years that Sennett and his Keystone colleagues were convinced that the film and the new comedian were destined to flop, it can only be assumed either that they were startlingly unperceptive, or had pitched their expectations on some miracle.

Despite the appearance of chaos at the Keystone Studios, the films were made to a production-line formula. There were four main kinds of production. The simplest and probably the cheapest were the 'park' films, always shot in Westlake Park, and using park benches, promenades, a refreshment stand and (for the inevitable aquatic finale) Echo Lake as the setting for improvised mix-ups between courting couples. Another variety of production also used locations: Sennett would take advantage of some public occasion – a military parade, speedway event or horse-race meeting – and send a unit to film the comedians fooling and playing out some impromptu farce, with the crowd and the spectacle of the event as free background. More formal films were shot in sets which seem to have stood more or less permanently on the stage. The quintessential Keystone set, which Chaplin himself was to use and elaborate during the next few years, consisted of a hallway with a room on either side. This arrangement would variously represent a domestic setting, with parlour (always to the left) and kitchen (to the right); a hotel, with rooms facing each other across the corridor, ideally placed for nocturnal mix-ups; neighbouring offices; or perhaps a doctor's or dentist's surgery and waiting room, with the indispensable hall in between. Special settings might represent a restaurant, bar, hotel lobby, cinema or boxing booth; or the studio buildings might provide off-the-cuff sets. The fourth category of film, like *Making a Living*, combined location and studio sets.

Whatever the plan of the film, the director would restrict himself to no more than ten camera set-ups – a moving camera was practically unknown at Keystone. So far as possible all the material required in each set-up was filmed together: the ingenuity of a Keystone film lay in making, with as little waste as possible, a collection of shots which would join neatly together in the cutting room to make a coherent narrative. The usual number of shots for a one-reel film was between fifty and sixty. (Sennett did not recognize the principle of retakes – material once shot had to be used.)

It is too simple to dismiss these Sennett farces, machine-made at the rate of two a week, as crude and primitive, appealing to a naïve audience to whom all novelty was wonder. Walter Kerr, bringing to them the cultivated perceptions of seventy years later (perhaps too cultivated and too far removed in time) speculated:

> Perhaps we might have laughed too in 1914. At least we would have felt excitement.
>
> I say 'perhaps' we might have laughed, because I'm not entirely sure – though I'm certain we'd have felt the excitement. There is very little in the Sennett films, for all their breakneck pace and bizarre manhandling of the universe, that one would care to call humour under analytic examination. Normally it is possible to understand a joke that has faded, to recapture the principle that once provoked laughter while being unable to capture the laughter itself . . . Not so with Sennett for the most part. The jokes, as jokes, are rarely there . . . and all the activity is so headlong that there is scarcely time to pause for the 'constructed' quality of a jest . . . The films are successful agitations, successful explorations of elaborate visual possibilities; if laughter once accompanied them, it has to have been the laughter of breathlessness.[6]

It is true that to our unaccustomed vision, a Keystone comedy at first presents only a blurred impression of breakneck speed, running, jumping and wild gesticulation. If we take the trouble to view these films patiently, more times than once, and try to adjust to their pace, much more emerges. First the apparently senseless gesturing resolves itself into a quite deliberate and precise system of mime, not unlike that of classical ballet, and at certain moments as formal. One of the most striking instances appears in *Mabel's Married Life*, when Mabel Normand with a shrug of her shoulders, a gesture of pointing with her right index finger to the ring on her left hand, a quick and brilliant impersonation of the Chaplin waddle and an appeal to the camera with her big expressive eyes asks us, 'Why ever did I marry that man?'

A notable demonstration of this all but lost language is the fourth film which Chaplin made at Keystone, *Between Showers*. Henry Lehrman directed, and by this time Chaplin had adopted his definitive costume and was on the way to perfecting a screen character. At first sight it is one of the fastest, wildest, and most inexplicable Keystones. If we make the effort to penetrate its language, however, it presents quite a different appearance: a little story like the anecdote of a comic strip, yet even more (and the comparison is inevitable, not pretentious) like the scenario of the *commedia dell'arte*.

There are five main characters: Charlie and Ford Sterling, rival mashers; a pretty but faithless girl (Emma Clifton); a policeman (Chester Conklin) and the policeman's lady friend (Sadie Lampe). While the policeman is making love to his lady friend, Ford 'borrows' her umbrella, since it is raining and his own is broken. After the shower is over, he hands the umbrella to Emma for safe-keeping, while he goes to find a plank of wood to help her cross a large puddle. By the time he has returned, Emma has already found a new suitor to help her across the puddle, and now refuses to hand back the umbrella. Charlie arrives on the scene and defends Emma from Ford's wrath. Emma flounces off, leaving Charlie in firm possession of the umbrella. Ford goes off in search of assistance, and returns with a policeman. Unfortunately the policeman turns out to be Chester, who recognizes the stolen umbrella. Too late Ford attempts to disown the umbrella. Chester hauls Ford off to jail, leaving a happy Charlie to cock a snook after both of them.

It is a neatly-turned little anecdote, but it only emerges after two or three viewings and careful study of the mime. We have no means of knowing whether the audience of the day, by familiarity and enthusiasm, had developed more acute perceptions of the form than we are able to apply. Were they able to see, instantly and at first viewing, beyond the initial impression of aimless running, jumping, assault and mugging? Was this why they found the Keystone pictures funnier than Walter Kerr could do half a century later, and followed them with such enthusiasm?

The enigma ceases to be relevant with the arrival of Chaplin. In a film like *Between Showers* Chaplin still conforms more or less to the Keystone style, though already there are irrepressible touches of a different kind of character comedy, like his child-like pride in the eventual possession of the disputed umbrella. The traditional historical view of Chaplin's innovations at Keystone is that, despite the doubt and resistance of Sennett and the Keystone comedians, he succeeded in slowing down the helter-skelter pace, and introduced new subtlety to the gag comedy. This is true so far as it goes, but the difference lay deeper. Keystone comedy was created from without; anecdote and situations were *explained* in pantomime and gesture. Chaplin's comedy was created from within. What the audience saw in him was the expression of thoughts and feelings, and the comedy lay in the relation of those thoughts and feelings to the things that happened around him. The crucial point of Chaplin's comedy was not the comic occurrence itself, but Charlie's relationship and attitude to it. In the Keystone style, it was enough to bump into a tree to be funny. When Chaplin bumped into a tree, however, it was not the collision that was funny, but the fact that he raised his hat to the tree in a reflex gesture of apology. The essential difference between the Keystone style and Chaplin's comedy is that one depends on *exposition*, the other on *expression*. While the expository style may depend upon such codes as the Keystone mime, the expressive style is instantly and universally understood; that was the essential factor in Chaplin's almost instant and world-wide fame.

In his second film, Chaplin created the costume and make-up which were to become universally recognized. For many years it has been accepted that that second film, and the first appearance of Chaplin's tramp character, was *Kid Auto Races at Venice, California*. It now seems much more likely that the film was *Mabel's Strange Predicament*. In order of release, *Kid Auto Races* was certainly the first of the two. It was issued on 7 February 1914. *Mabel's Strange Predicament* came out two days later. Yet Chaplin clearly remembered that it was in *Mabel's Strange Predicament* that he first wore the costume, and his memory on such details rarely failed him. Hans Koenekamp, who was cameraman on *Mabel's Strange Predicament*, also remembers this as being the first appearance of the costume. The answer most likely is that *Mabel's Strange Predicament* was *shot* first. *Kid Auto Races* was one of Sennett's location films, said to have been filmed in forty-five minutes during a soap-box car rally, and consisting of no more than twenty shots. It could have been shot, cut, printed and slipped into the release schedule while the more elaborate film, *Mabel's Strange Predicament*, was being assembled.

The tramp costume, which was to be little modified in its twenty-two-year career, was apparently created almost spontaneously, without premeditation. The legend is that it was concocted one rainy afternoon in the communal male dressing room at Keystone, where Chaplin borrowed Fatty Arbuckle's voluminous trousers, tiny Charles Avery's jacket, Ford Sterling's size fourteen shoes which he was obliged to wear on the wrong feet to keep them from falling off, a too-small derby belonging to Arbuckle's father-in-law, and a moustache intended for Mack Swain's use, which he trimmed to toothbrush size. This neat and colourful version of the genesis of the tramp seems to have originated in the Keystone Studio, and was certainly never endorsed by Chaplin. In his autobiography he states that he decided on the style of the costume 'on the way to the wardrobe'. His idea was to create an ensemble of contrasts – tiny hat and huge shoes, baggy pants and pinched jacket.

It is easy enough to find precedents for the costume in the English music halls. Grotesquely ill-fitting clothes, tiny hats, distasteful moustaches and wigger-wagger canes were the necessary impedimenta of the comedian. Some of Dan Leno's stage costumes hint at Chaplin's; and Chaplin's old Karno colleague, Fred Kitchen, used to complain gently that it was he who had first originated the costume and the splay-footed walk. Elements of the character had been predicted in Chaplin's own stage career. His make-up in the single surviving photograph of Wal Pink's sketch *Repairs* somewhat resembles that of Charlie; and there is said to have been much of the costume in his get-up as a rag-and-bone man in Karno's *London Suburbia*.

Whatever its origins, the costume and make-up created that day in early February 1914 were inspired. Chaplin recalled how the costume induced the character, so that 'by the time I walked on to the stage he was fully born'.[7] We know from the films that this was not strictly true; the character was to take a year or more to evolve its full dimensions and even then – which was its particular strength – it would evolve during the whole of the rest of his career. It is a fair guess that the symbolic interpretations that Chaplin and his publicity staff gave to the individual elements of the Tramp's ensemble were the fruits of the hindsight of later years. From the first, though, certain traits were obvious: the derby, the cane, the bow-tie and close-trimmed moustache indicated brave but ineffectual pretensions to the dignity of the *petit bourgeoisie*.

The characteristic motions of the character had other origins. In 1916 Chaplin told an interviewer from *McClure's* magazine that he had based his characteristic shuffling walk on that of an old man called 'Rummy' Binks, who used to hold the horses for coachmen outside Uncle Spencer Chaplin's pub, The Queen's Head, at the corner of Broad Street and Vauxhall Walk.

> There was a cab stand near by and an old character they called 'Rummy' Binks was one of the landmarks. He had a bulbous nose, a crippled, rheumatic body, a swollen and distorted pair of feet, and the most extraordinary trousers I ever saw. He must have got them from a giant, and he was a little man.
>
> When I saw Rummy shuffle his way across the pavement to hold a cabman's horse for a penny tip, I was fascinated. The walk was so funny to me that I imitated it. When I showed my mother how Rummy walked, she begged me to stop because it was cruel to imitate a misfortune like that. But she pleaded while she had her apron stuffed into her mouth. Then she went into the pantry and giggled for ten minutes.
>
> Day after day I cultivated that walk. It became an obsession. Whenever I pulled it, I was sure of a laugh. Now, no matter what else I may do that is amusing, I can never get away from the walk.

We have already seen that Will Murray took credit for Chaplin's distinctive technique of rounding corners pivoting on one leg, with the other leg stuck out horizontally and revolving into the new direction of the run. According to Murray it had been developed for the grand chase in *Dick Turpin*. Billy Danvers, a fellow member of the Karno company, however, recalled that this mode of turning was in fairly general use in the company as an effective and laughable means of coping with the limited run permitted by small out-of-town stages.

Sennett took a hand in the direction of *Mabel's Strange Predicament*, no doubt because it starred his girlfriend, Mabel Normand. Mabel was born Mabel Ethelreid Normand in Providence, Rhode Island, the youngest of the three surviving children of Claude G. Normand, a Frenchman who played the piano in pit orchestras in small theatres, and his Irish-Catholic wife Mary Drury. Accounts of her birth date vary, but her family state that she was born on 9 November 1892. Her family, according to Sennett, 'was temperamental, improvident, and often in transit'. He also recalled that though she had had little formal education, Mabel was a great reader and had acquired a particular aptitude for geography. She was also an athlete, a fine swimmer and had been taught by her father to play the piano.

In her early teens she took a job in the pattern-making department of the Butterick Company in Manhattan, but was soon finding regular work as a model for illustrators. Among the popular magazine artists of the time for whom she is said to have sat were Carl F. Kleinschmidt, Henry Hutt, Penthlyn Stanlaws, Charles Dana Gibson and James Montgomery Flagg. In 1910 another model, Alice Joyce, encouraged her to try her luck in the movies, and Mabel began to get small roles in Vitagraph pictures. Soon afterwards she was recruited by Biograph where she met the aspiring young director Mack Sennett. When Sennett opened up the Keystone Studios he naturally chose her as his star.

Mabel was petite, beautiful, infectiously vivacious and exquisitely funny. Like Chaplin she was one of the rare artists who could establish a direct rapport between screen and spectator: more than half a century after her death her screen presence retains its immediacy and vivacity. After Chaplin achieved fame, she became known as 'the female Chaplin', which is an underestimation of the individuality of her own comedy. Certainly in this year at Keystone Mabel was to provide Chaplin with a very worthy foil and partner. Although after difficult beginnings they were to become good friends, the partnership was confined to work. Mabel had exceptional charms, but at this time in her life they were exclusively reserved for Mack Sennett.

In 1984 there still survived a witness of Chaplin's first scene in his tramp costume and character – perhaps, indeed, the most significant witness, since he was the cameraman who actually filmed it. Hans Koenekamp had arrived at Keystone in 1913 and stayed until 1918 or 1919; he retained the happiest memories of his days at the studio. He remembered Sennett as 'the mastermind' and Mabel as 'the nicest person I ever met. She was great.' He also recalled how the units would load all their equipment onto public streetcars to go on location in Westlake Park or elsewhere. 'Finally we got transportation of our own.' Half a dozen cameramen worked between as many units, turning out as many as three films a week. 'Sometimes we'd go out into a park and shoot and by the end of the day we came back, we had the film.' Working like this, it was often difficult to remember what films a cameraman had worked on and with whom. Even so, though he had forgotten the title, Hans Koenekamp very clearly remembered the film: 'Can't think of the title. Tried to remember it. I can still see the scene he's in though. It was a hotel lobby, and he acted like a half drunk with that cockiness with his foot and the hat and the cane. I shot him.'[8]

Before shooting the scene Hans Koenekamp had watched Chaplin come on the set:

> I can still see the little shack where he came out the dressing room. He'd come out and he'd kind of rehearse *himself* – that walk, the cane, the hat and things like that, you know.
>
> I can still see him when he came onto the set. He was supposed to be half drunk or something like that. He came into the lobby and tried to make eyes at women, and women ignored him and all that kind of stuff . . . I can remember that. Never forget that. So I really photographed the first scene he played in . . .
>
> Did it look funny there and then? Yes, it did. Well it was, because it was *fresh* . . . And his movements too. Wiggle the mouth and that moustache would kinda work. And the cane flapping around, swinging on his arm . . . and going around on one leg like he was skating.[9]

Mabel's Strange Predicament revolved around a standard Keystone theme – bedroom mix-ups in a small hotel. Sennett introduced Chaplin in a sequence in the hotel lobby. He enters, mildly inebriated, becomes entangled with the leash of Mabel's dog, takes some falls with a cuspidor, and evinces a flirtatious interest in every passing female. The humour lies in the air of precarious dignity with which he carries off both his tipsiness and the evident imposture of his presence in the hotel, down-at-heel as he is. Chaplin recalled with satisfaction how the rest of the Keystone players and technicians gathered round to watch rehearsals for the scene, and reassured him with their laughter. In subsequent sequences Charlie encounters Mabel, who has locked herself out of her room, wearing only her nightgown, and gives lecherous chase through the hotel corridors. When, ultimately and inevitably, there is a confrontation between Mabel, her admirer, the gentleman under whose bed Mabel has somehow found herself and the man's jealous wife, the bemused Charlie gets in the way of most of the blows. With this film, Chaplin won his first major point at Keystone. Sennett was so impressed with Chaplin's business in the lobby scene, and the favourable reactions of the bystanders, that he over-rode Lehrman's objections and let it run on for the full minute of the take, without the usual busy Keystone-after-Griffith intercutting.

Mabel's Strange Predicament was one of the company's more elaborate productions. *Kid Auto Races at Venice, California* was the most elementary type of impromptu shot in the course of a public event. The Kid Auto Races were held on a specially made track at the seaside resort of Venice. The competitors were boys in soap-box cars, which were laboriously pushed by the drivers and their team up a steep ramp erected at the beginning of the course. The run down this incline provided the momentum for the race. The film which Henry Lehrman shot against the background of the race and the crowds had only one joke: Lehrman is a film director; Chaplin is a nuisance who wants to get in the picture and constantly spoils the cameraman's shots. Chaplin later said that it was his idea, and had been suggested by an incident he had witnessed when he was touring with the Karno Company in Jersey. During the filming of the carnival procession there a fussy local official kept pushing himself into the picture.

Bits of business are already recognizable. Twirling his cane, he knocks off his own hat or injures his ankle. He pertly tips his hat to an official he has annoyed. The principal quality of the character Chaplin creates here is infantilism. He is a mischievous child, grimacing at a car that almost runs him down and sticking out his tongue at Lehrman. There is a long shot of him running, leaping and skipping down the track in crazed abandon. The final shot of the film is a huge close-up of a frightful grimace. Yet, as Walter Kerr wrote with admirable perception,

> He is elbowing his way into immortality, both as a 'character' in the film and as a professional comedian to be remembered. And he is doing it by calling attention to the camera as camera.
>
> He would do this throughout his career, using the instrument as a means of establishing a direct and openly acknowledged relationship between himself and his audience. In fact he is, with this film, establishing himself as *one among the audience*, one among those who are astonished by this new mechanical marvel, one among those who would like to be photographed by it, and — he would make the most of the implication later — one among those who are invariably chased away. He looked at the camera and went through it, joining the rest of us. The seeds of his subsequent hold upon the public, the mysterious and almost inexplicable bond between the performer and everyman, were there.[10]

The skirmishes of the film director and the persistent camera hog were a comic echo of the behind-the-screen relationship of Lehrman and Chaplin. After one more film, *Between Showers*, Sennett recognized that the partnership was unprofitable and assigned Chaplin to another director, George Nichols, a veteran from the pioneering days, now approaching sixty. Chaplin seems to have got on no better with him: he repulsed all the comedian's suggestions for business with the cry 'No time, no time!' and complained to Sennett when Chaplin talked back. Sennett responded by more closely supervising the films himself. *A Film Johnnie* was an elementary affair, shot around the studio and, like Chaplin's later films *The Masquerader*, *His New Job* and *Behind the Screen*, giving us evocative glimpses of life in the early American studios. Charlie goes to the cinema and falls for the star of the film. He therefore pursues her to the Keystone Studios, where he causes havoc among the productions. Fire breaks out and he is squirted by the fire brigade. In a crazy, funny little gag, he twists his ears and thereby gives the fireman a retaliatory squirt.

In *His Favorite Pastime* Chaplin plays the drunk again. He gets into a fight in a bar, follows a pretty young woman home, pays court to her coloured maid and ends up in a fracas with a jealous husband. Chaplin was able to introduce some virtuoso gags – the first of many *contretemps* with a swing door; and a memorable feat in which he somersaults from a balcony to land in sitting position on a sofa, his cigar still lit. The film had a special significance in Chaplin's personal life at the time. The girl is eighteen-year-old Peggy Pearce, Chaplin's first recorded Hollywood love. Peggy was an impregnably virtuous girl and lived with her parents. Chaplin felt that he was not yet ready to contemplate marriage and the affair was not of long duration. There is a touching, tangible memento of it, though: more than sixty years later Mrs Walter Matthau found in a Hollywood antique shop a plated cup won by Chaplin and Peggy in a dance contest.

Cruel, Cruel Love gave Chaplin the opportunity for parody melodrama: as a spurned aristocratic suitor he swallows a glass of water under the impression that it is poison and in his supposed death throes has hallucinations of hell. *The Star Boarder*, the most charming of this group of films supervised by Sennett, was partly shot in gardens and orchards, and has the verve and simplicity of a comic strip. Charlie is the pet of the landlady (Minta Durfee), carrying on a flirtation under the nose of her husband (Edgar Kennedy) who has his own extra-marital interests. All this is enthusiastically recorded by their mischievous son who possesses – just like the boy Chaplin in his *Sherlock Holmes* days – a box camera.

These four films occupied Chaplin throughout March and the beginning of April. During the same period Sennett took his male stars – Chaplin, Arbuckle, Sterling and Conklin – to a dance hall, where they improvised a knockabout film, *Tango Tangles*, on the theme of the rivalry of the first three over the hat-check girl (Minta Durfee). Except for Conklin, who put on Keystone Kop uniform, they are in their natty everyday clothes and without make-up. Sterling is the band leader, Arbuckle one of his musicians, and the handsome Chaplin a tipsy and smooth-shaven lounge lizard. The real patrons look on with unfeigned amusement and, to set the scene, the film opens with real demonstration dancers. Chaplin does an eccentric tango and in the fight scenes, menacingly twitching his protruded bottom, he looks forward to the pugilistic efforts of *The Knockout*, *The Champion* and *City Lights*.

Recognizing that Chaplin was getting on no better with Nichols than with Lehrman, and seeing that Chaplin and Mabel had struck up an amiable relationship, Sennett now made the mistake of assigning Mabel to direct the next film in which she and Chaplin were to co-star, *Mabel at the Wheel*. Chaplin from the start was not happy about taking direction from a girl several years younger than himself and with none of his stage experience. The happy working relationship evaporated rapidly as Mabel swept aside Chaplin's suggestions just as Lehrman and Nichols had done.

During the previous few months Pearl White had established herself as the heroine of dramatic adventure films, and the week before *Mabel at the Wheel* was begun had appeared on American screens in the first episode of the most famous of all serial thrillers, *The Perils of Pauline*. *Mabel at the Wheel* was a take-off of the Pearl White style, with Mabel as a race-track driver's girlfriend who takes over her boyfriend's car and wins the race when he is kidnapped by the villain. The villain, uncharacteristically, is Chaplin, dressed in a grey frock coat and silk hat, and with tufts of whisker on his chin in the style of Ford Sterling. He also has a magnificent new prop in the shape of a motor-cycle; in the first scene of the film he uses it to compete with Harry McCoy, as the racing driver, for Mabel's affection. Mabel unfortunately falls off the pillion into a puddle and there is a fine comic moment when Charlie feels behind him and finds her gone.

When Mabel, affronted by the incident with the puddle, abandons Charlie for Harry, Charlie and a couple of shady confederates kidnap

Harry and lock him in a hut. They then attempt to sabotage Mabel who has taken the car out herself. In one scene Charlie and his friends throw water on the track in front of Mabel's car. The trouble between them came to a head when they were shooting this scene. Chaplin suggested a bit of business to liven it up: he would step on the hose, peer into it to see why it had stopped, and then release his foot and soak himself. Perhaps Mabel was aware that this was, in historic fact, the oldest joke in the cinema: it was used by the Lumière Brothers (who had got it from a comic strip) in *L'Arroseur Arrosé*, for their first film programme in 1896. Mabel brushed the suggestion aside, Chaplin refused to work and sat down on the roadside. Mabel, the pet of the studio, was bewildered and the men in the crew were ready to beat up Charlie for upsetting her. Chaplin had himself grown attached to Mabel but, as he recalled in a significant phrase, '*this was my work*'. Nothing in his life was ever to take prior place to that.

They packed up for the day (it was already after five) and returned to the studio. Sennett, acutely sensitive to any hurt to Mabel (his turbulent and frustrated love affair with her was to survive her death, to his own) was furious. It was assumed on both sides that Chaplin's days at Keystone were finished, contract or no contract. Chaplin was therefore surprised the following day to find both Sennett and Mabel conciliatory: later he discovered that Sennett had had orders from the east for more Chaplin films, since sales of the first were already booming. Chaplin agreed to finish *Mabel at the Wheel* with Sennett's supervision, and took the opportunity to announce to Sennett that he was now ready and anxious to direct his own pictures. According to Chaplin Sennett was dubious, but accepted Chaplin's guarantee of $1500 – the money he had saved since his arrival in California – in case the film proved unshowable.

There is some doubt which film should be regarded as Chaplin's directorial debut. In his 1964 autobiography Chaplin said that it was *Caught in the Rain*. On 9 August 1914, however, he sent Sydney a list of the films in which he had appeared during his seven months at Keystone. On it he very deliberately marked as 'My Own' six films which he had already directed; these, in order of release, are *Twenty Minutes of Love* (released 20 April), *Caught in the Rain* (4 May), *Mabel's Married Life* (20 June), *Laughing Gas* (9 July), *The Property Man* (1 August) and *The Face on the Bar Room Floor* (released 10 August – the day after he sent the list to Sydney).

From this time to the end of his year at Keystone, Chaplin directed all the films in which he appeared except the feature *Tillie's Punctured Romance*, directed by Mack Sennett. It is notable that Chaplin does not include in the list of his own films three which existing filmographies record as collaborations with Mabel Normand: *Caught in a Cabaret* (27 April), *Her Friend the Bandit* (4 June), (Chaplin does not list this film at all and no existing copy is known) and *Mabel's Busy Day* (13 June). On the other hand he *does* include the fourth of these alleged collaborations, *Mabel's Married Life*.

1914 - Chaplin's first filmography,
written by himself, August 1914.

Chaplin might understandably have forgotten fifty years later that he directed *Twenty Minutes of Love,* or have simply written it off as apprentice practice, since it is the first and one of the slightest of the 'park' films. Nevertheless there are developing traits of the later Charlie character. There is a sweetness about his mischief and flirtations, and a touch of the romantic.

There was no danger of Chaplin's having to pay up the guarantee against the failure of *Caught in the Rain*. It proved one of the best and most successful Keystones up to that time. The film shows all the care of an apprentice's demonstration piece. Chaplin had made good use of his months at Keystone. In particular he had studied the work of the cutting room, and the jigsaw method of film construction that Sennett had inherited from Griffith. In addition, of course, he brought from Karno a highly developed skill in stagecraft. Already in his first film the *mise-en-scène* of each shot excels, or at least equals, the best work of the Keystone directors. This first effort shows him particularly conscious of the shot-by-shot method of narrative and assembly. The one reel contains far more shots than the average Keystone production, and though Chaplin would never again revert to this Griffith style of rapid montage, the logic and fluidity of the narrative are admirable.

The anecdote is absurd, but the telling is exemplary, and this remains one of the most accomplished films of Chaplin's year at Keystone. The film has clarity, verve, a musical or balletic rhythm in the rapid cutting; it is still entertaining and amusing after seventy years. He follows the ground rules of the studio, but he already has a special mastery of telling a story in images. Titles are used only for extra laughs, and as the action speeds up they are dispensed with altogether. As his own director, he is able to place and pace his gags as he wants and to introduce virtuoso comedy turns. He had chosen excellent supporting comedians in Mack Swain, who after this first partnership was to remain for more than a decade a favourite foil, and Alice Davenport.

Chaplin's next release, *A Busy Day*, has long been assumed to have been directed by him though he did not include it in the list of his films which he sent to Sydney in August 1914. Since it had been made only three months before, he clearly did not rate it very highly. Certainly it is one of Sennett's throwaways – it is only half a reel in length – but it is a curiosity for all that. It is one of the films in which Sennett has taken advantage of a local event – in this case a military parade – to provide a spectacular background, and the comic action takes place around a bandstand and grandstand.

Chaplin, for the first of three times in his film career, is dressed as a woman. In *The Masquerader* and *A Woman* the plots would call for him to disguise himself as a seductive and fashionable lady. Here he goes through the whole film as an angry little working-class termagant – almost a pantomime dame as she lays about her with her brolly, blows her nose very rudely on her skirt, and gives a preparatory hitch of her clothing and a wild leap in the air before setting off in pursuit of some victim. She and her husband Mack are spectators at the parade. Mack wanders off in the train of a prettier woman. The wife gives chase, on the way battling with several policemen, and getting in the way of a film cameraman, much as Charlie did in *Kid Auto Races*. Afer a lot of skirmishes and rough-houses, Mack very sensibly shoves the creature into the harbour, where she sinks in a flurry of bubbles. Apart from Chaplin's unwonted disguise, the film is curious for its technique. Whether Chaplin himself directed it or not, it has all the look of a study exercise in shot relations. Again and again the same effect of someone being thrown out of one shot and landing in another shot is repeated, for example:

8   Director throws wife off screen left.

9   Rear of bandstand. Wife is thrown into screen from right, and knocks over a policeman. The policeman throws her back off screen right.

10   As 8. Wife is thrown in from screen left. She picks herself up and starts to pose in front of movie camera. The director again throws her off screen left.

11   Rear of bandstand. Wife is thrown in, screen right, and lands on bandstand.

Fifty years later he regarded it as a serious shortcoming in old George Nichols that the only movie trick he knew was this one of throwing people out of one shot and into another. Still, for a comedy director, shot relationship was a useful lesson to learn.

In *The Knockout*, directed by Charles Avery, Chaplin played a two-minute supporting role as referee to a boxing bout between Roscoe Arbuckle and Edgar Kennedy. It is a lively little performance that anticipates *The Champion* and *City Lights*. Chaplin's refereeing is balletic, and introduces gags of a sophistication alien to the rest of the film. Worse hit than the pugilists, he lies down and drags himself around the ring by the ropes; then counts the loser out from a sitting position.

Chaplin's name was by this time already a sufficient draw for Keystone to advertise *The Knockout* as a Chaplin film. It is no longer clear whether he was deliberately added to the cast for his box-office value, or whether it was just part of the Keystone method of using any available talent at any time. More than fifty years later Chaplin told an interviewer that he had actually played bit roles as a Kop in Keystone films, though so far none of these appearances has been identified.

If we accept Chaplin's identification of his films in the letter to Sydney, we can discount *Mabel's Busy Day*, a rough and rowdy little piece, matching material shot at a race track with studio shots, which has generally been credited as a collaboration between Chaplin and Mabel. The film provides evidence of the growth of Chaplin's popularity. In *Kid Auto Races* the ordinary public at the sporting event show little interest in the proceedings of the film unit. In *Mabel's Busy Day* the crowds in the background are huge, and roped off from the performers. Clearly with Chaplin on hand the Sennett unit did not need to borrow the audience assembled for the sports event. Chaplin's very presence attracted all the audience they needed to provide a spectacular background.

In the succeeding six months Chaplin directed sixteen films, four of them two-reelers, running for half an hour. They are uneven; some are throwaways, some are sketches of ideas he will later elaborate and refine; but the speed with which he masters his craft is astounding.

Mabel's Married Life is as expert as *Caught in the Rain*, but with less tension in the cutting and more leisure for gags and character touches. Partly filmed in a park and partly on sets, the plot is concerned with the irritation inflicted by Mack, a hefty Don Juan, who taunts Charlie and pursues Charlie's wife Mabel. Mabel buys a punch-dummy to get Charlie into condition. Returning home drunk, Charlie takes it for his rival and fights it. The film contains much character comedy: Charlie's look of ineffable disapproval rudely cut short when the spring doors of the saloon knock him down; the *connaissance* with which he sizes up Mack's ample bottom before belabouring it with boot and cane; his panic when faced with an unexplained odour.

His next three films harked back in different ways to vaudeville. Dentists were a rich source for music hall jokes, and *Laughing Gas* explores the comic possibilities when the dentist's assistant substitutes for him. In *The Property Man* he is property man in a vaudeville theatre peopled by grotesque and unreasonably temperamental artists. Contemporary critics were shocked by the cruelty of the prop man's treatment of his aged and decrepit assistant; and shocked by the nursery rudeness of a scene in which, having concealed a glass of beer down the front of his trousers, he inadvisedly bends over. With a quick appeal of his eyes for the audience's understanding, he gingerly shakes the water down his leg. *The Face on the Bar Room Floor* is a parody in the *Casey's Court Circus* vein, and technically the least interesting of Chaplin's films – for the most part simply alternating lengthy titles with tableaux in comic illustration of Hugh Antoine d'Arcy's pathetic and then popular ballad of love betrayed. This and the two films that followed look like marking time: *Recreation* is a fast-improvised 'park' film. *The Masquerader* is simple knockabout set in a film studio, mainly notable for its behind-the-screen glimpses of the Keystone lot and for Chaplin's second female impersonation.

In his last three months at Keystone, Chaplin directed ten films which alternated improvisations like these (*His New Profession, Those Love Pangs, Gentlemen of Nerve. Getting Acquainted*) with more elaborately staged films which look like sketches for films to come. *The Rounders*, in which he was teamed with Roscoe Arbuckle, looks back over Chaplin's whole gallery of inebriates from Karno to Keystone, and forward to *A Night Out* and ultimately to the Tramp's nights on the town with the millionaire in *City Lights*. *The New Janitor* is the prototype for *The Bank*. Only seventeen days separated the releases of *The Rounders* and *The New Janitor*, yet in that short space of time, Chaplin's art seemed to take a massive leap forward both in approach to film narrative and in appreciation of the character that was developing within the tramp make-up and costume. The film conforms to the basic Keystone rules, using only eight static camera set-ups, yet out of his material Chaplin fashions a brilliant little narrative, clear, precise, with drama, suspense and an element of sentiment that goes deeper than the flirtations of Westlake Park. The animated strip cartoon of *Caught in the Rain* has developed into comic drama. The editing creates a real dynamic in the Griffith manner rather than simply providing a step-by-step progression of narrative incidents. Gags and character touches are developed without the Keystone rush and integrated into the story. Chaplin reveals his gift for observing behaviour: the secretary's brief, loving look at the manager's straw boater hanging in the hall intimates a whole past relationship. (See Appendix 5)

Chaplin's ambition led him to overspend his $1000 budget for

Dough and Dynamite. A worried Sennett withheld the $25 due to Chaplin as his director's fee, and decided that the only way to retrieve the loss was to release the film as a two-reeler. His anxiety was unfounded: it proved one of the most profitable of all Keystone pictures. The story is simple: Charlie and Chester are waiters in a teashop who take over the bakery when the bakers go on strike. The dastardly strikers secrete dynamite in a loaf before it goes into the oven, thus blowing the place up. The story is mostly an excuse for variations on the fun to be had from sticky dough and clouds of flour, but the film shows Chaplin developing new sophistication in his deployment of studio sets and restricted camera set-ups.

Chaplin at this time had not committed himself to a fixed method of film making. His technique in *His Musical Career*, an attractive film which provided the model for Laurel and Hardy's *The Music Box*, sixteen years later, is in marked stylistic contrast to *Dough and Dynamite*. The single reel consists of a mere twenty-seven shots: usually Chaplin and the other Keystone directors used up to ninety shots in a film of the same length. Here, as Buster Keaton was later to do, he bypassed the current fashion in editing, recognizing that each shot needed to be a stage for his own extended comedy routines. He declared this early that cutting was not an obligation but a convenience.

The last film which Chaplin directed and played in at Keystone was *His Prehistoric Past*, released on 7 December 1914. The discovery of the so-called Piltdown Man in 1912 and of some Neanderthal bits and pieces around the same time had aroused intense popular interest in man's ancient ancestors, and the subject was taken up by every popular cartoonist and not a few film comedians. Chaplin's film, recalling *Jimmy the Fearless*, was cast in the form of a dream. Charlie falls asleep on a park bench and dreams that he is Weakchin, a cave man. Weakchin runs into trouble when he starts up a flirtation with the favourite of the harem of King Lowbrow (Mack Swain). When the king finally catches up with him, he is forcibly struck on the head with a large rock – and wakes up again on the park bench where a policeman is roughly shaking him.

Tillie's Punctured Romance, which was released three weeks previously, was the last film in which Chaplin would appear under the direction of anyone else (if we exclude two or three brief guest appearances in the 1920s). It was also the first and only time in his film career that he played a supporting role to another star. Perhaps these factors explain his laconic dismissal of the film in his autobiography, even though it was his first feature picture, and a landmark in establishing him with the public. 'It was pleasant working with Marie [Dressler] but I do not think the picture had much merit. I was more than happy to get back to directing myself.'

The film was the first feature-length comedy. Before it no comic film made anywhere in the world had exceeded one third of its length of six reels (ninety minutes' running time). Sennett may have been stirred to this ambitious venture by a spirit of rivalry: his partner in Triangle Film Corporation, D. W. Griffith, was at the time embarking on *The Birth of a Nation*. The project was also undertaken under the influence of the current 'famous players in famous plays' policy of bringing stars and properties from the New York stage. It was natural enough that in looking for a theatrical success to film, Sennett should turn to *Tillie's Nightmare*. Written in 1910, the comedy had had a long and triumphant run on Broadway and its star, Marie Dressler, was America's greatest comic personality in the days before the First World War. Moreover Sennett may have felt a personal attachment to Dressler, remembering her counsel, discouraging though it may have been, in his own early days.

Sennett may, in fact, originally have intended to devise a new vehicle to star Miss Dressler. His unreliable memoirs mention that his writers spent some weeks struggling with a scenario, with Marie on the payroll at $2500 a week, before they decided to go ahead and film *Tillie's Nightmare* with a new title. After this, he recalled, the work went swiftly, though the fourteen-week production period was unprecedented at the studio.

It was natural enough, as box-office insurance, to use the two top stars of the studio, Chaplin and Mabel, to support Marie Dressler. Already there was a vast, international audience quite unfamiliar with even the greatest luminaries of Broadway. Marie, in her own memoirs offered a rather different (and patently mistaken) view of things: 'I went up on the lot and looked around until I found Charlie Chaplin who was then unknown. I picked him out and also Mabel Normand ... I think the public will agree that I am a good picker for it was the first real chance Charlie Chaplin ever had.' Marie was clearly not a picturegoer. Even so the enormous success of the film did make it a landmark in Chaplin's career. It was released on 14 November 1914 to a favourable press and ecstatic public acclaim, and it was constantly revived and still turns up fom time to time in cinemas in truncated, doctored and sound-synchronized versions.

Parts of the film betray its stage origin – the characters mouth conversations and soliloquies – but when the story gets under way and particularly in the final chase Sennett's direction exploits the vulgar, earthy knockabout with assurance. From the stage text, too, the film acquires some narrative and character strength: behind the slapstick and extravagant farce, there is a realistic and quite affecting theme of a stupid, good-natured country girl duped by a ne'er-do-well sharper. Dressler's warm personality wins through even though Chaplin and Normand's screen experience gives them an undoubted advantage. At moments Chaplin's characterization of the deft, funny, heartless adventurer anticipates Verdoux – even though Verdoux could never insult the footmen and an effeminate guest at a party as Chaplin does.

From the time he began to direct until his departure from Keystone, there is practically no record of Chaplin's private life. The reason is because he had virtually no life outside his work. He was fascinated by the new medium and absorbed in the task of mastering it. 'This was my work,' indeed. Throughout his career the pattern was to be repeated: committed to a job of work, a film, the private Charlie all but disappeared.

A modest private life was not entirely strange in Hollywood at that time. Publicists were already helping to promote, for the delight of avid fans, stories of the gaiety and high living of the movie world, but life in Hollywood must, a lot of the time, have been more sedate than the legend. At Keystone, as at every other successful studio, the film people worked long hours and six days a week: time for play was limited. We know of Chaplin's Sunday calls on Peggy Pearce. Once, he remembered, when they were on their way to a charity appearance, he kissed Mabel Normand but nothing came of it: Mabel told him they were not each other's type. In any case both had their loyalties to Sennett. Chaplin and Sennett undoubtedly grew fond of each other. Chaplin recalled that Sennett practically adopted him and that they ate together every night.

Certainly during his first months at Keystone he grew gregarious enough to surprise himself. It would indeed have been hard to resist the evident high spirits and good nature of the Keystone people. Hans Koenekamp remembers 'A whole bunch of 'em, actors as well, would pitch in if they had to build the set or something.' Chaplin shared the general habit of dropping into the Alexandria Bar on the way back to his hotel. In his early Hollywood days, too, he enjoyed going with the rest to see fights.

Later in the year, though, concentration on the work must have taken over. As in the Karno Company, some of his colleagues saw his abstractedness as a sign that he was unsociable and stand-offish. Even Hans Koenekamp felt that towards the end of his Keystone time 'he got to be a big shot. And he was a bit off-colour in politics.' Suspicion of Chaplin's libertarian instincts began this early, it seems.

Chaplin continued to live in a hotel and his thrift was marked. His only notable expenditure was when he signed an agreement on 10 February with the English Motor Car Company for the hire, for five months, of a 1912 Kissell Kar Roadster. This cost him $300 down and $100 per month.

Neither Sennett, nor the Keystone executives, nor Chaplin himself can have anticipated the effect of the first releases upon the public. We can only look back at the first few Keystone films and see a crude, unfinished form, and the earliest tentative search for a screen character. To the audiences of the time they arrived like rockets. Chaplin, from the very start, had created a new relationship with the audience, a new response that no one before in films or in any other medium had elicited.

In Britain the first Chaplin films were released in June 1914. Having already observed the phenomenon in America, the Keystone Company advertised:

ARE YOU PREPARED FOR THE CHAPLIN BOOM?

**There has never been so instantaneous a hit as that of
Chas Chaplin, the famous Karno comedian in Keystone Comedies.
Most first-rank exhibitors have booked every film in which he
appears, and after the first releases there is certain to be a
big rush for copies.**

The first seven films were shown to the trade press, and on 25 June, Keystone were able proudly to reprint their reviews. *Kine Weekly* reported:

> We have seen seven Chaplin releases, and every one has been a triumph for the one-time hero of 'Mumming Birds' who has leapt into the front rank of film comedians at a bound.

The Cinema's opinion was as favourable:

Kid Auto Races struck us as about the funniest film we have seen. When we subsequently saw Chaplin in more ambitious subjects our opinion that the Keystone Company has made the capture of their career was strengthened. Chaplin is a born screen comedian; he does things we have never seen done on the screen before.

Both Sennett and Chaplin were aware of Chaplin's fast growing value. Chaplin recalled that it was around the time of the outbreak of war in Europe that he and Sennett discussed the renewal of their contract. Chaplin announced that he would require $1000 a week for a further year, at which Sennett protested that that was more than he earned himself. Chaplin reminded him that it was not for Sennett's name that the public lined up outside cinemas, but for his. Sennett countered by pointing out that Ford Sterling was already regretting his decision to leave Keystone, to which Chaplin in turn replied that all *he* needed to make a comedy was a park, a policeman and a pretty girl.

Sennett apparently sought the advice of Kessel and Bauman, and came back with a counter-offer to Chaplin's demand for $1000 a week. He offered a three-year contract, at $500 a week for the first year, $750 for the second and $1500 for the third, the contract to become operative immediately. Chaplin said that he would agree if the terms were reversed – $1500 for the first year, $750 for the second and $500 for the third. Evidently baffled by Chaplin's economics, Sennett let the matter drop.

It was clear to Chaplin that the time had come to move on; and on Sunday 9 August – five days after the outbreak of the European War and presumably immediately after his conversation with Sennett – he sat down to write one of his very rare letters, to Sydney, in London:

Los Angeles Athletic Club,
Los Angeles, Calif.
Sunday Aug 9th

My Dear Sid,

You are doubtless realising who is addressing you. Yes. It really is your brother Chas. after all these years, but you must forgive me. The whole of my time is taken up with the movies. I write, direct, and play in them and believe me it keeps you busy. Well, Sid, I have made good. All the theatres feature my name in big letters i.e. 'Chas Chaplin hear today'. I tell you in this country I am a big box office attraction. All the managers tell me that I have 50 letters a week from men and women from all parts of the world. It is wonderfull how popular I am in such a short time and next year I hope to make a bunch of dough. I have had all kinds of offers at 500 a week with 40% stock which would mean a salary of or about 1000 a week. Mr Marcus Lowe [sic]*, the big theatre man over hear, has made me a proposition which is a certainty and wants me to form a comedy company and give me either a salary per week or 50% stock. This is a sure thing, any way, the whole matter is in the hands of my Lawyers, of course I shall finish out my contract with the Keyst. people, and if they come through with something better I shall stay where I am. This Marcus Lowe business is a sure I have a guarantee sale at all his theaters and then sell to the outside people. Anyway, I will let you know all about it in my next letter. He will finance the whole thing if it comes through it means thoullions to us. Mr Sennett is in New York. He said he would write to you and make you an offer. I told him you would do great for pictures of course he has not seen you and he is only going by what I say. He said he would give you 150 to start with. I told him you are getting that now and would not think of coming over hear for that amount. If you do consider it, don't sign for any length of time, because I will want you with me when I start. I could get you 250 as easy as anything but of course you would have to sign a contract. It will be nice for you to come over for three months with the Keystone and then start for ourselves. You will hear from Sennet [sic] but don't come for *less than 175 understand?* You will like it out hear it is a beautiful country and the fresh air is doing me the world of good. I have made a heap of good friends hear and go to all the partys ect. I stay at the best Club in the city where all the millionairs belong in fact I have a good sane, wholsome time. I am living well. I have my own valet, some class to me eh what? I am still saving my money and since I have been hear I have 4000 dollars in one bank, 1200 in another, 1500 in London not so bad for 25 and still going strong thank God. Sid, we will be millionaires before long. My health is better than it ever was and I am getting fatter. Well you must tell me how Mother is and don't forget to write me before you sign any contract because there is another firm who will pay you 250. They wanted me and I told them about you, as I could not break my contract of course. Mr Sennett is a lovely man and we are great pals but business is business. Of course he does not know I am leaving or that I have had these offeres, so don't say anything in case it gets back hear, you never know. I would not like to heart Sennet feelings he thinks the world of me. Now about that money for mother do you think it is safe for me to send you it while the war is on, or do you think it better for

---

* Marcus Loew, (1870–1927). American exhibition magnate and co-founder of Metro Goldwyn Mayer, which was long controlled by Loews Inc.

you to pay my share and then we will arrainge things later on. So long as I know the money will get there I will send it. Anyway tell me in your next letter what to do. I hope they don't make you fight over there. This war is terrible. Well that about all the important news. I have just finished a six real picture with Marie Dressler the American star and myself. It cost 50,000 to put [?] and I have hog the whole picture. It is the best thing I ever did. I must draw to a close now as I am getting hungry. Just this second my valet tells me I have friends to take me out Automobiling so am going to the beach to dine. Good night Sid, Love to Minnie

Your loving brother
Charlie

5

Essanay

Sydney arrived to start work at Keystone early in November 1914. He invented for himself a character called 'Gussle'; padded out to a grotesque pear shape, he wore a curious little boat-shaped hat and a moustache, tight jacket and cane which seemed like homage to his younger brother. His first film, to be released in December, was *Gussle the Golfer*. As for Charlie, the Loew proposal which he had outlined in his letter to Sydney had eventually come to nothing. By the time of Sydney's arrival in California he had still no firm offer from any other studio, and he was nervous. The apparent lack of interest may in fact confirm the oft-repeated stories that Sennett made strenuous efforts to prevent representatives of other film companies from reaching Chaplin, hoping that he would eventually come, by attrition, to accept Keystone's offer of $400 a week. Chaplin considered setting up his own production unit, but Sydney – to whom the film business as well as his own $200 salary was a startling novelty – opposed the idea.

Eventually, however, Chaplin received an emissary from the Essanay Film Manufacturing Company of Chicago, in the person of Jesse Robbins, a producer and director with the firm. The name 'Essanay' was made up from the initial letters of the names of the founders, George K. Spoor and G. M. Anderson. Spoor had started in the film business as an exhibitor and renter in Chicago; Anderson (1882–1971), born Max Aronson, made his acting debut in *The Great Train Robbery* (1903) and later, as Broncho Billy, became the cinema's first cowboy star. Spoor and Anderson went into partnership in Essanay in February 1907, taking as their trade-mark an Indian

134

head, borrowed from the copper one-cent piece. Anderson established a little studio at Niles, near San Francisco, in 1908, where he set an unbeatable record by producing and starring in a series of *Broncho Billy* films, turned out at the rate of one each week.

Anderson and Robbins had been greatly impressed by rumours that Chaplin was demanding $1250 per week and a bonus on signing of $10,000. Though the idea of the bonus was quite novel to him when Robbins mentioned it, Chaplin thought it best not to turn it down. Anderson agreed to the arrangement without consulting Spoor, who was greatly alarmed to learn that they would be paying about fifteen times the going rate for Essanay-featured players to a comedian he personally had never heard of. Chaplin signed, but became more and more suspicious when the $10,000 bonus failed to materialize, and it was poor Anderson who was left to placate him since Spoor, who was supposed to hand the money over, had tactically disappeared from the Chicago studios.

Fortunately Chaplin liked Anderson, an amiable if taciturn westerner. With him he visited Essanay's little glasshouse studio at Niles, and decided he did not care for it. In the last days of December 1914 therefore Anderson accompanied him by train to Chicago, Essanay's eastern headquarters, where the company had a studio at 1333 Argyle Street. Anderson returned to California on New Year's Day, 1915, leaving Chaplin to discover, with no small dismay, the chilliness of a Chicago January and the indifferent amenities of the studio. It still belonged to the era of 'film factories': after the creative chaos of Keystone, Chaplin found the cold, production-line style of the Chicago studio inimical. The worst affront was when he was told to collect his script from the scenario department, whose chief at that time was the future queen of Hearst columnists, Louella Parsons.

Other irritations were in store. Neither Spoor, bonus nor salary turned up. He found that the Essanay staff had little or no concern for the quality of their product, while with the absurd, penny-pinching, pound-foolish bookkeeper mentality of the place, they recklessly screened and edited the negatives rather than pay the few dollars needed for proper positive rushes and working material. Some compensation was provided by the acting talent on hand in Chicago. Ben Turpin, a wizened little man rather like a prematurely hatched bird, with permanently crossed eyes and a prominent adam's-apple dancing up and down his scrawny neck, was one of the best comedy partners Chaplin ever found. Leo White was a lean, fierce, volatile little man who originally came from Manchester but had worked in operetta and specialized in characterizing comic Frenchmen in goatees and silk hats. Bud Jamison – a former vaudeville performer, baby-faced, six feet tall and weighing nineteen stone – provided the same grotesque physical contrast to Chaplin that Mack Swain had done at Keystone. Two pretty extras in Chaplin's first Essanay film, Gloria Swanson and Agnes Ayres, were to become major Hollywood stars. Swanson plays a stenographer: Chaplin was disappointed when he gave her a tryout for a more ambitious role, only to find her wooden and unresponsive. Years later Swanson told him she had been deliberately unco-operative as she wanted to be a dramatic actress, not a comedienne.

We have a rare glimpse of Chaplin on the eve of starting work in Chicago. He was interviewed by Gene Morgan, a local reporter who was uncommonly perceptive and accurate in detail. One of his more striking revelations is that the legendary costume was at this period bought off the peg. Chaplin told him he had been shopping on State Street for a fresh costume and had had difficulty in getting boots large enough. He had also bought trousers. He told Morgan that he often followed people for miles to study character: 'Fortunately my types are all small men. I would hate to be found following a big man and imitating him behind his back.'

Morgan's summing up of the Chaplin personality deserves to be remembered if only for the haunting final phrase:

> You know him as a human gatling gun of laughs. He makes you chortle once every second. He has lots of flying black hair, and, do you know, it sort of grows on you. He wears an eloquent little moustache, which bounces on top of the funniest smile put on celluloid. He sports an unsteady derby hat, which he never fails to tip after kicking friends in the face. And he twirls a cane as if it were a blackthorn, Sousa's baton, a carpet beater and a lightning rod, all in one.
> And his feet –
> You can't keep your eyes off his feet.
> Those big shoes are buttoned with 50,000,000 eyes.

Chaplin's first film at Essanay was appropriately titled *His New Job*. As he had done in *A Film Johnnie*, he chose to set the action in a film studio. If nothing else this had the advantage that sets and props were ready to hand: at least he could limit his dependence on the Essanay scenic staff.

Chaplin is still the incorrigible Keystone Charlie, cheerfully causing chaos by his insouciant incompetence, tittering gleefully behind his hand at the spectacle of the destruction he has provoked, ever ready to apply a boot to the behind or a hammer to the head of anyone who presumes to protest. Chaplin clearly never worked out a scenario for the film. He adopts comedy props as they come to hand – cigarettes, matches, a pipe, a soda syphon, a saw and mallet, a swing door, a recalcitrant scenic pillar, an officer's uniform many sizes too large and with accompanying shako and exceedingly bendy sword. He goes though favourite routines with his cane (especially handy for hooking Ben Turpin's feet from under him) and hat. He was several times later to repeat and elaborate the business of being reprimanded for failing to remove his hat, which he here introduces. With child-like insolence he makes to replace the hat on his head and then at the last moment causes it to spring up into the air. He conscientiously searches the fur of the shako for fleas; and sizes up a piece of nude statuary with the affectation of disinterested connoisseurship he would later bring to the contemplation of the nude in the art shop window in *City Lights*.

After two weeks' work, *His New Job* was ready for release on 1 February. By this time Spoor was back in Chicago, now happily reconciled to the idea of his new star. To his surprise, business colleagues had rushed to congratulate him on his good fortune; and now *His New Job* chalked up more advance sales than any previous Essanay picture. Chaplin finally received his bonus, but neither that nor Spoor's strenuous efforts to make up for his previous offhandedness endeared him to his star. Unhappy with conditions in the Chicago factory, Chaplin announced that after all he would prefer to work in the company's Californian studio. Niles was the lesser of two evils.

Since the historian Theodore Huff compiled the first Chaplin filmography in the late 1940s, Chaplin chroniclers have trustingly followed his assertion that the Essanay films were photographed by Roland Totheroh. In fact Totheroh was not to become Chaplin's cameraman until 1916: his most regular cameraman at Essanay was Harry Ensign. Totheroh himself was wholly occupied on Broncho films. He nevertheless remembered his first meeting with Chaplin at Niles: 'We thought he was a little Frenchman.'[1] Broncho Billy Anderson suggested that Chaplin might like to live in one of the studio bungalows as he did. Chaplin was appalled however by the mean and squalid style in which the millionaire star lived, and soon moved to the Stoll Hotel nearby. Totheroh's description of his arrival affords a vivid picture of the informal and rural character of film studios of the period, as well as the austerity of Chaplin's own style of living in 1915:

> We had a bungalow in the studio. I had a corner one, and later on Ben Turpin had the next one . . . And Anderson had one about a block down the road further, his own bungalow, you know. It was anything but a palace, he had an old wood stove in the kitchen and everything. So Charlie had one handbag with him – just a little old one of those canvas-like handbags, you know. Jim said, Charlie's room will be this one here, and of course my room's in front, whatever it was. And they were saying, 'We've got the old wood stove going in the kitchen, and we heated up some tea or something. We had Joe heat up some tea, you know. Charlie was an Englishman . . . So we opened his bag to put the things out. All he had in it was a pair of socks with the heels worn out and an old couple of dirty undershirts, and an old mess shirt and an old worn out toothbrush. He had hardly nothing in that thing. So we didn't say anything. Joe said, Jeez, he hasn't got much in this thing, has he? . . . I'll never forget down there, nothing, he said, no bed and all this and that, and I felt like saying, yeah, and what the hell did you have? Jesus. Nothing in his handbag or anything.[2]

Years later visitors to the Chaplin studio would be no less surprised by the austerity of the star's quarters.

Chaplin began to build up his own little stock company. From Chicago he brought Ben Turpin, Leo White and Bud Jamison. He also recruited a former Karno comedian, Billy Armstrong, and another English artist, Fred Goodwins, who had been on the legitimate stage after an early career as a newspaperman. Paddy McGuire came from New Orleans via burlesque and musical comedy but typed well as an Irish bucolic. The essential task however, was to find a leading lady. One of Broncho Billy Anderson's cowboys, either Carl Strauss or Fritz Wintermeyer, recommended a girl who frequented Tate's Café on Hill Street, San Francisco. The girl was traced and proved to be called Edna Purviance. Born in Lovelock, Nevada, she had trained as a secretary but (at least according to later publicity biographies) had done some amateur stage work. She was blonde, beautiful, serious and Chaplin was instantly captivated by her. Only after he had engaged her did he have some qualms as to whether or not she had any gift for comedy. Edna convinced him of her sense of humour at a party the night before she started work, when she bet him $10 that he could not hypnotize her, and then played along with the gag, pretending to fall under his spell. She was to appear with him in thirty-five films during the next eight years and to prove his most enchanting leading lady, with a charm exceeding even that of Mabel Normand. For some time their association, both professional and private, was to be the happiest of Chaplin's youth.

Chaplin's first film at Niles was *A Night Out*. If stuck for an idea, he could always rely upon a restaurant for inspiration: he ordered the construction crew to build a large café set, complete with a fountain in the foyer as an extra source of havoc. In this film Chaplin and Ben Turpin form a beautiful double act, sharing a solemn, unselfconscious, childlike air of mischief. It is an interesting variation on the partnership of Chaplin and Arbuckle in *The Rounders*. Charlie and Ben are a couple of drunks, absorbed in the tricky business of staying upright to the exclusion of all other proprieties. They are aggressive, whether loyally defending each other against interfering policemen, waiters and other hostile strangers, or fighting between themselves, with fists and bricks.

Unlike *His New Job*, this comic pantomime depends upon comedy situations rather than comic incidents and props. It is so close to the Karno style that it is easy to imagine how it would have appeared on a theatre programme:

> Prologue: Outside the Bar-Room
> Scene 1: The Restaurant
> Scene 2: The Hotel
> Scene 3: The Other Hotel

In the prologue Charlie and Ben have an altercation with Leo White, as a Frenchified man-about-town. In Scene 1, much the worse for drink, they meet Leo again in a restaurant and proceed to harass him and his lady friend until they are thrown out by a gigantic waiter (Bud Jamison). In Scene 2, Charlie flirts with a pretty girl in the room across the hall, until he discovers that her husband is the same hostile waiter. He decides to move to another hotel, but the couple have the same idea; and Scene 3 is the kind of hotel room mix-up (very piquant for 1915) that did service in *Mabel's Strange Predicament* and *Caught in the Rain*.

Chaplin and Essanay still did not fully understand each other. Having completed shooting, Chaplin announced that he was going to San Francisco for the weekend. In his absence, Anderson, worried that they were behind schedule, asked Totheroh to help him edit

Chaplin's picture. According to Totheroh, Anderson's notion of editing his own pictures was to take a close-up of himself rolling his eyes around, and 'use it in any place. He just measured it at the tip of his nose to the length of his arm, and then he'd tear it off, and that was his close-up. He'd shove it in.'[3] Anderson and Totheroh had just started on the film when Chaplin, having changed his mind about the weekend, walked into the cutting room, and told them, very forthrightly, to take their hands off his picture.

He took this opportunity to tell them also that in future he would not conform to the studio practice of cutting the negative, but would insist on proper positive rushes. This required sending to Chicago for a new printer to be installed in the studio's laboratory. When the new machine arrived and was installed, it proved to be missing a vital part, so this in turn had to be sent for. Anderson fretted at the delay in starting the third Chaplin film, but the director-star was adamant. Evidently the cutting-room incident did not permanently injure relations with Totheroh; a year later, when Chaplin took charge of his own studios, he invited him to join his staff.

Chaplin next set to work on *The Champion*. The studio lot served admirably as the setting for a boxing training establishment. Much of the action takes place in front of the board fence surrounding the studio, and we also glimpse Essanay's glass-house stage, the bungalows and the dusty, open countryside. As interiors, Chaplin needed only rough, hut-like rooms for the gymnasium. Like other Essanay films, this seems a deliberate effort to retrieve opportunities lost at Keystone. Chaplin at this time loved boxing – going to prize-fights with members of his staff was his favourite leisure occupation – and he evidently found much satisfaction in developing the business of *The Knockout*.

Charlie is here quite firmly established as a vagrant: in the opening scene we see him on a doorstep, sharing his hot dog with his bulldog, a choosy pooch, who won't touch the sausage until it has been properly seasoned. He decides to try his luck as a sparring partner, and to enhance his chances slips a horse-shoe in his glove. The characters include a silk-hatted and moustachioed villain, straight from Karno's *The Football Match*, who tries to bribe him; and the *pièce de résistance* is the championship bout that ends the film. Running for six minutes, it is balletic in composition, with Charlie devising a series of exquisite choreographic variations. At one moment the opponents fall into each other's arms in a fox trot.

The delay in getting the new printing apparatus prolonged the production of *The Champion* to three weeks. To make up, Chaplin dashed off *In the Park* within a week. Having found a park at Niles that looked very like Westlake, he reverted to the reliable old Keystone formula, with Charlie intervening in the affairs of two distinctly star-crossed lovers. The Tramp is here at his least ingratiating. He is not only a pickpocket, but a cad as well. Having immobilized big Bud Jamison with a brick, he uses his victim's open mouth as an ashtray. He even makes awful grimaces behind Edna's back. Only one moment looks forward to the gallant Charlie of mature years. When Edna kisses him, he cavorts madly off under the trees in a satyr dance that anticipates *Sunnyside* and *Modern Times*.

Though Chaplin was never happy in the glass-covered studio at Niles, the open country around provided admirable locations for his next two films, *A Jitney Elopement* and *The Tramp*. The first was a conventional situation comedy with Charlie and Leo White competing for Edna's hand. (Leo purports to be a French count and Charlie masquerades in the same role.) The film ends with a spectacular and imaginative car chase: at one point the cars, shown in extreme long shot, waltz with one another. Chaplin also recorded for posterity the ingenious gag which Alf Reeves had admired when he saw him on stage as *Jimmy the Fearless*, and decided to recruit him for America. Attempting to take a slice from a French roll, Charlie continues in a spiral cut which turns the roll, in one of his most witty comic transpositions, into a concertina.

With this film, genuine romance begins to emerge in the love scenes. At our first sight of Charlie he is caressing a flower, as tenderly as the romantic vagabond of *City Lights*. Perhaps this new romantic element owed much to Chaplin's growing relationship with Edna. A charming note has survived, dated 1 March 1915, when they were at work on *The Champion*. Chaplin addresses his leading lady as 'My Own Darling Edna' and tells her that she is 'the cause of my being the happiest person in the world'. He was replying to a note which she had written to him: 'My heart throbbed this morning when I received your sweet letter. It could be nobody else in the world that could have given me so much joy. Your language, your sweet thoughts and the style of your love note only tends to make me crazy over you. I can picture your darling self sitting down and looking up wondering what to say, that little pert mouth and those bewitching eyes so thoughtful. If I only had the power to express my sentiments I would be afraid you'd get vain . . .'

The romantic element is still more pronounced in *The Tramp*. Made in only ten days, this remarkable film shows a staggering leap forward in its sense of structure, narrative skill, use of location, and

1915 - Two picture postcards:
'Charlie Chaplin in the Post Office'.

emotional range. Charlie is now clearly defined as a tramp. He saves a farmer's daughter from some ruffians, and subsequently foils the ruffians' plot to rob the farm. The pet of the place, he falls in love with Edna, but his happiness is crushed by the appearance of her handsome young fiancé. Charlie is disconsolate: his back alone expresses utter dejection. He departs from the farm, leaving a note:

> I thort your kindness was love but it aint cause
> I seen him good bye
>
> x x

For the first time, he makes his classic exit: he waddles sadly away from the camera up a country road, his shoulders drooped, the picture of defeat. Suddenly he shakes himself, and perks into a jaunty step as the screen irises in upon him.

Chaplin was anxious to get back to Los Angeles, and Anderson was hardly less anxious for his departure, since the Niles studio was proving too small to accommodate the productions of both of them. The move caused a break in the flow of production, and the next film, *By the Sea*, has all the appearance of having been shot in a day – on the breezy sea-front around Crystal Pier – to catch up on the schedule while the new studio was being made ready. It is the kind of scenario which would equally have served the *commedia dell'arte* or Keystone – a series of slapstick and situation variations skilfully managed within the restrictions of only nine camera set-ups.

Until this time Chaplin had respected the production-line methods of the time and maintained a steady rate of output. Now he declared his independence by taking much longer over his films. Twenty-seven days had elapsed between the release of *A Night Out* and *The Champion*; Essanay had to be content to wait still longer for subsequent releases. *By the Sea* was issued on 29 April 1915; *Work* did not appear until 21 June. The delay may in part be attributable to moving studios. For *Work* Chaplin temporarily took over the converted Bradbury Mansion at 147 North Hill Street, whose imposing approach serves for the exterior of the house seen in the film.

Some aspects of *Work* place it among the most remarkable comedies made up to that time. It apeared four months after D. W. Griffith's revolutionary *Birth of a Nation*, and within its circumscribed form and ambitions is as original. Painters, plumbers and paperhangers had been the stuff of slapstick on the music halls for years –

> When Father papered the parlour,
>   You couldn't see him for paste.
> Dabbing it here,
> Dabbing it there –
> Paste and paper everywhere.
> Mother was stuck to the ceiling,
> Kids were stuck to the floor.
> You never saw a blooming fam'ly
> So stuck up before.

Sydney and Charlie had appeared in Wal Pink's *Repairs*, and Karno toured a sketch called *Spring Cleaning*. Chaplin would later introduce paperhanging sketches into *The Circus* and *A King in New York*.

The basic notion of *Work* is that Charlie and his boss (Charles Insley) are decorators come to do over a middle class home. This gives rich scope for all the traditional business with planks, ladders, paste and paint. Charlie wrestles with sticky and disintegrating wallpaper and transforms a peaceful parlour into a quagmired battlefield. The situation is the richer since the household consists of a tetchy little husband (Billy Armstrong), angrily protesting because his breakfast is late, a flamboyant wife (Marta Golden), *en déshabillé* and rocketing around the house giving artistic instruction to the glazed-eyed workman, a pretty but inactive maid (Edna) and a gas stove given to periodic explosions. The mistress has also a secret lover (Leo White in French count style) who comes calling with flowers at the most awkward moment and has to be passed off, improbably, as one of the workmen. No opportunity for insult or assault with all the tools of the decorator's trade is allowed to pass. The grand finale is a massive explosion which leaves the heads of the ménage showing out of the rubble, Charlie's boss submerged in the bath, and Charlie himself feebly emerging from the guilty oven.

It is the introduction to this delirium of destruction that makes the film most memorable. Our first sight of Charlie is as he advances towards the camera down a busy city street, harnessed to a cart piled high with ladders, boards and buckets. The boss sits on the driver's seat, flicking at him with a whip. The cart gets stuck on the tramlines: Charlie drags it clear in the nick of time. He attempts a hill, but the cart again slides back into the path of an oncoming tram. In silhouette we see Charlie hauling the cart up the side of a 45-degree incline. The weight of the cart raises the shafts in front, with poor Charlie dangling helplessly in the air. The boss thoughtfully offers a heavyweight friend a lift, and Charlie must now drag the two of them. He disappears down an open manhole, but is hauled back, hanging on to the shafts and counterweighted by the cart.

It is a series of haunting, grotesque, horror-comedy images of slavery, with a degree of audacity and invention in the visualization that was hardly to be challenged until the Soviet avant-garde (idolaters of Chaplin) a decade later. The closest approximation to these first scenes of *Work* is to be found in Alexander Medvedkin's 1934 production, *Happiness*. Chaplin's aims in inventing the sequence were no doubt uncomplicated enough: it is funny; and it prepares the audience to accept as his proper deserts the ill-treatment that the boss will later receive at Charlie's hands. Yet, almost incidentally to his purposes, he has created a masterly and unforgettable image of the exploitation and humiliation of labour, the reverse of the Victorian ideal of the salutary virtues of work.

It was such aspects of Chaplin's vision that found the hearts of the great mass audience of the early twentieth century. There is another memorable moment of comic irony in a gag that sums up the ineradicable mistrust between middle and working classes. The lady of the house, having left the workmen alone in her dining room, suddenly remembers 'My silver!'. She rushes back and fixes them beadily with her eyes as she hastily gathers up her treasures and packs them into the safe. They watch her in cool amazement. Then, without a word, they carefully remove their watches and money from their pockets. These valuables are carefully placed in Charlie's right-hand trouser pocket. With his gaze mistrustfully fixed all the time on the woman, Charlie takes a safety pin and firmly secures the pocket.

Chaplin now moved into the old Majestic Studio on Fairview Avenue. Here he performed his third, last and best female impersonation in *A Woman*. It was a tempting exercise: female attire suited him disturbingly well; the role gave scope for a whole new range of character mime; and moreover Julian Eltinge's sophisticated female impersonations had brought the genre into vogue and respectability.

The female impersonation is remarkable: it was no small tribute that the film was banned in Scandinavia until the 1930s. Perhaps the most memorable image of the film however, is Charlie without moustache, hat or trousers suddenly transformed by the 'woman's' fox fur (= a ruffle), long pants (= tights) and striped underclothing (= knickerbockers) into a traditional clown figure – a guise in which he was to appear briefly again, many years later, in *Limelight*. Critics of the time were distracted from the charm and unforeseen poetry of the image by their disapproval of the film's improprieties. The pincushion bosom and the defrocking stirred a good deal of prudish protest, as did a throwaway scene in *Work* where Charlie puritanically covers the nakedness of a statuette with a lampshade, but then wiggles the lampshade to turn the figurine into a hula dancer. Chaplin was stung by charges of 'vulgarity'. Fred Goodwins wrote at the time:

His fame was at its zenith here in America when suddenly the critics made a dead set at him . . . They roasted his work wholesale; called it crude, ungentlemanly and risqué, even indecent . . . the poor little fellow was knocked flat. But he rose from his gloomy depths one day, and came out of his dressing room rubbing his hands. 'Well boys,' he said, with his funny little twinkly smile, 'let's give them something to talk about, shall we? Something that has no loopholes in it!' Thus began the new era in Chaplin comedies – clean, clever, dramatic stories with a big laugh at the finish.[4]

The Bank was not only a response to adverse criticism, however. Chaplin had been greatly struck by the praise he had received for *The Tramp* with its strong injection of sentiment and the ambivalence of the fade-out. Now he set out to emphasize the sentimental element still further. Working with Edna required no pretending in the love story. Again *The Bank* gave him an opportunity to rework an idea only partially realized in the hurly-burly of Keystone. The essential story of *The Bank* is the same as *The New Janitor*. Chaplin once more introduced the dream device from *Jimmy the Fearless*. Charlie's dreams of adventure and romantic success must remain merely dreams; the reality of the Little Fellow allows of no such escape from poverty.

The film opens with a surprise twist: Charlie enters the great city bank, descends to the vaults, makes great play with the combinations of a giant safe which he opens to produce – a pail, a mop and a janitor's uniform. Charlie the janitor is hopelessly in love with the pretty secretary, Edna, but her heart is set on another Charlie, the suave cashier. The janitor falls asleep and dreams that he rescues the fair Edna from a gang of bank robbers: he presses her to his side and caresses her hair, but wakes to find it is the mop he has in his arms. The reawakened Charlie, spurned, wanders back into his vaults, past Edna and her cashier, who are oblivious to his presence. He still holds in his hand the rejected bouquet he brought her: he tosses it down, gives it a kick, shrugs his shoulders and quickens his funny walk as he leaves us and the camera irises in.

A comedy with a sad end was something new. The scenes in which Charlie, with tragedy in his wide eyes, watches Edna contemptuously throw aside his declaration of love touched depths of pathos quite unfamiliar in film comedy. It was from this time that serious critics and audiences began to discover what the common public had long ago recognized, that Chaplin was not like anyone else before him.

Fred Goodwins recorded a rare, brief impression of Chaplin at work with his actors on *The Bank*:

> We had a scene in the vault – a burglary, with a creeping, noiseless entrance. All the time Chaplin sat beside the cameraman, whispering, almost inaudibly, 'Hush. Gently boys: they'll hear us upstairs!' It is infectious, it gets into the actors' systems and so 'gets over' on the screen.[5]

It was far from easy to discover new ideas for films, but Chaplin knew that a good setting or prop would at once set his imagination working. For *Shanghaied* he rented a boat, the *Vaquero*, which suggested a neat plot and a lot of funny business. Charlie is hired to shanghai a crew, but finds himself shanghaied as well. Moreover his loved one, Edna has stowed away, and the owner, Edna's father, has plotted to sink the ship for the sake of the insurance.

The ship proved a marvellous prop. To simulate its rocking motion, the cameraman, Harry Ensign, developed a pivot on which the camera could swing, controlled by a heavy counterweight. Chaplin also had a cabin built on rockers so that he could realistically recreate the hazards of a storm-tossed ship. *Mal de mer* was to remain a favourite joke: it figured in Chaplin's very last appearance on the screen, more than half a century later. The shipboard gags were also to provide prototypes for the first half of *The Immigrant*.

A good idea, he decided, will never wear out, so next he adapted his old Karno success *Mumming Birds* to the screen, as *A Night in the Show*. There is no evidence of any formal arrangement with Karno over the copyright, which is surprising since Karno was notoriously jealous of his properties. The *Mumming Birds* scenario is followed closely, with Chaplin in his old role of the drunk, here called Mr Pest.

Chaplin added new material, set in the foyer and auditorium of the theatre, to the original Karno scenario: a flirtation with Edna, altercations with the orchestra, much changing of seats, and the precipitation of a fat lady into the foyer fountain. Chaplin moreover plays a second role, Mr Rowdy, an outrageous tipsy working man in the gallery. This new character is forever needing to be rescued by his neighbours from tumbling into the pit below, and enthusiastically pelts the performers with rotten tomatoes. Finally, anticipating King Shahdov in *A King in New York*, he turns the fire hose on the fire-eater.

In his last days at Essanay Chaplin was reported to be working on a feature film called *Life* which was apparently to mark a new stage of realism in his comedy. The project was abandoned, but the time Chaplin spent on it may explain the long delays between the release of *The Bank* and *Shanghaied* (fifty-six days) and between *Shanghaied* and *A Night in the Show* (forty-seven days). Some ideas and material from *Life*, notably a fragmentary sequence in a dosshouse, were incorporated into *Police*.

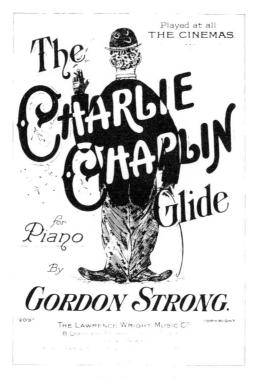

1915 - Chaplin music sheet:
The Charlie Chaplin Glide.

Chaplin's critics had confirmed his own growing recognition that the Charlie character acquired definition and dimension from the reality of his situations and milieu. Charlie belongs to the dirt roads and mean urban streets, and the solitude of vagrancy. The dosshouse scene is a tantalizing glimpse of what Chaplin may have intended in *Life*. There is a Cruickshankian touch of the macabre about the place. A remarkable troupe of derelicts includes a befogged old drunk, an unshaven heavyweight whose first menacing appearance is belied by a display of mincing effeminacy, a broken-down actor and a lean consumptive whose sunken cheeks and hacking cough Charlie callously impersonates when he perceives that such suffering is good for a free bed.

There is also a new irony. *Police* opens with Charlie coming out of prison: the title 'Once again into the cruel, cruel world' looks forward to *Modern Times* and Charlie's efforts in that film to get back to the security and protection of gaol. There is a foretaste too of later scepticism in the face of formal religion and its bigotries. Outside the prison gates Charlie meets a clergyman who begs him to 'go straight'. Within moments the man of the cloth has not only filched Charlie's last cent, but also pocketed the watch of a drunk which Charlie had passed up – easy pickings as it was – on account of his newfound, if temporary, Christian morality. The next cleric who offers help in going straight is swiftly seen off for his pains.

Chaplin's last film for Essanay was his sole essay in a style of parody then current. It was eventually released as *Charlie Chaplin's Burlesque on Carmen*. *Carmen* was the current rage of Hollywood. Sam Goldwyn (then still Sam Goldfish) and his brother-in-law Jesse Lasky had lured the beautiful, 33-year-old star of the Metropolitan Opera, Geraldine Farrar, to Hollywood with a salary of $20,000 for eight weeks, plus motor car, house, servants and groceries. Her extravagantly publicized first film was *Carmen*, directed by Cecil B. De Mille and adapted from Merimée and Bizet by De Mille's brother William.

De Mille's film was ready in October 1915, and was swiftly followed by a rival version directed by Raoul Walsh for William Fox, and starring the sultry Theda Bara. In the Essanay version, Don José, as played by Chaplin, became Darn Hosiery, with Edna as Carmen, sent by the smuggler chief, Lilias Pasta (Jack Henderson), to seduce this strutting Captain of the Guard. The film was due for release in December 1915, but after Chaplin's departure the company decided it would be more profitable as a feature than as a two-reeler. Leo White was called in to direct some completely new scenes with a new character, Don Remendado, played by Ben Turpin; Chaplin's scenes were extended by salvaging his out-takes, and by the time of its release on 22 April 1916 the film had grown to four reels. The horror of it sent Chaplin to bed for two days. The rambling, shambling knockabout of the film shows, by contrast, how taut and well-edited

Chaplin's own films had become. Some good things of Chaplin remain: the duel between Darn Hosiery and his rival of the Civil Guard (Leo White), though clearly longer and untidier than Chaplin intended it, contains some wonderful balletic passages. Audiences and serious critics were equally startled by the death scene, in which the hero stabs Carmen and then kills himself, and which was a good deal more realistically and movingly played than most genuine tragic death scenes of the period. Having shocked and silenced his audience with this scene, Chaplin then revealed how they had been fooled. His bottom suddenly twitches back to life, and he and Edna get up, laughing, to demonstrate the collapsing prop dagger with which the deed had been done.

These odd moments did not vindicate the film, and Chaplin looked for a remedy in the courts. In May 1916 Chaplin, through his lawyer Nathan Burkan, appealed for an injunction to prevent Essanay from distributing *Charlie Chaplin's Burlesque on Carmen*, claiming that he had not approved of the play; that his author's rights had been infringed; that it was a fraud upon the public; that his own role in the film had been garbled and distorted; and that he would be damaged by the production. The plea was heard on Monday 22 May before Justice Hotchkiss of the Supreme Court, State of New York. Chaplin's application for an injunction was dismissed; Justice Hotchkiss said:

> Whether plaintiff will suffer any damage from the production is problematical, while an injunction is certain to work loss for defendants.

While Nathan Burkan threatened that Chaplin would appeal to the Supreme Court and ask for a further $100,000 in damages, Essanay claimed for the recovery of half a million dollars' damages against Chaplin. The grounds of this counter-suit were that in July 1915 Chaplin agreed to 'aid in the production of' ten two-reel comedies before 1 January 1916. For each of them he was to receive a bonus of $10,000 over and above his salary of $1250 a week. One of the number was already completed: the company nevertheless retrospectively gave Chaplin his $10,000 bonus. (This must refer to *Work*.) Chaplin himself had decided that these comedies could be produced at the rate of one every three weeks. However he completed only five two-reel pictures before leaving the company, receiving the $10,000 bonus on each. 'The remaining four Chaplin failed to appear in, although the Essanay Company was prepared and still is ready to proceed with the making of these pictures. Under this arrangement the *Burlesque on Carmen* was produced and paid for.' The company's claim of $500,000 dollars was based on the estimated lost profit of $125,000 on each of the four films not made.

Justice Hotchkiss's ruling was encouraging enough for Essanay to prepare a further 'new' Chaplin comedy, three years after he had left the company. Two sections from the unfinished *Life* were retrieved. In one Edna is a down-trodden house maid, desperately scrubbing floors, while Charlie is the kitchen boy. The second is evidently a continuation of the dosshouse scene in *Police*: the old drunk has now become vocal and requires to be sedated with a bottle expertly applied to his cranium; a mad, vampiric sneak-thief filches from the other inmates. The scene has a wonderfully sinister quality, but it counts for little in the hotchpotch which Essanay concocted and called (for no good reason) *Triple Trouble*. Leo White was again engaged to direct additional scenes: a framing story about German spies, led by White himself, endeavouring to steal an inventor's powerful new explosive device. White was not without style: he enjoyed using groups of people moving in formal, geometrical fashion, and he quite ingeniously welds the old and new material. In one scene Charlie the kitchen boy throws a pail of garbage over a fence in sunny California, 1915; it lands on the other side, in wintry Chicago, 1918. The film was a travesty. Chaplin had learned his lesson, however, and this time did not seek legal remedy.

Essanay continued until 1922 to press their claim on account of the alleged revised agreement of July 1915. In 1921 Spoor brashly proposed that he would settle the case in exchange for distribution rights in *The Kid* – an arrangement which would have required Chaplin to break his current contract with First National. Sydney curtly answered, 'nothing doing'. Chaplin's initial dislike of Spoor seemed vindicated when Spoor threatened that if necessary he would start a scandal relating to poor Hannah, still in the care of the Peckham House nursing home. Spoor claimed that his brother in England had advanced money to Aunt Kate Mowbray to pay the Peckham House bills, and that the money had not been returned. Kate was dead by this time, and so could not deny Spoor's charges. Sydney wrote to his brother on 1 April 1922 to confirm that Kate had borrowed money from Spoor's brother, but that it had been returned and that he had receipts to prove it. The situation had arisen in May 1915, when payments to Peckham House became so overdue that the nursing home threatened to send Mrs Chaplin back to Cane Hill at the charge of the Board of Guardians. The Lambeth Settlement Examination Book recorded:

> Chaplin, Hannah Harriet, Widow. Has been Private Patient in Peckham House since 9th Sept 1912. Sent to Cane Hill by Lambeth 18th March 1905. 2 Sons, Sidney and Charles Chaplin were subsequently discovered earning large salaries as Music Hall Artists – with motor cars of their own &c.
>
> Owing to payments lapsing at Peckham House where the sons had their mother transferred as above, Peckham House apply under Sec 19 for the woman to be placed on Parish Class.
>
> Mrs Mowbray, sister, now of 4 Coram Street Bloomsbury states that possibly owing to the war and sons Charles and Sidney moving about America, they have not been able to send.
>
> These sons are now prominent Cinema Artists Charles earning about £70 per week with the Essanay and Keystone Producers and Sidney about £40 per week and no difficulty will be experienced if patient again sent to Cane Hill. Patient has expressed a wish to go there . . .[6]

The Peckham House receipts have survived and show that Hannah's sons were conscientious but irregular in remitting their weekly thirty shillings. The pressure of their work and the uncertain wartime mails across the Atlantic were contributory causes. So Kate, desperate to prevent her sister being sent back to Cane Hill, had sought the then willing help of the Spoors. She could hardly have foreseen the mean advantage Spoor would later seek from the incident.

Chaplin was, during this period, so tied up in his work at Essanay that he was almost the last to realize the extent of his phenomenal popularity. The year 1915 had seen the great Chaplin explosion. Every newspaper carried cartoons and poems about him. He became a character in comic strips and in a new Pat Sullivan animated cartoon series. There were Chaplin dolls, Chaplin toys, Chaplin books. In the revue *Watch Your Step* Lupino Lane sang 'That Charlie Chaplin Walk':

> Since Charlie Chaplin became all the craze,
> Ev'ryone copies his funny old ways;
> They copy his hat and the curl in his hair,
> His moustache is something you cannot compare!
> They copy the ways he makes love to the girls,
> His method is a treat;
> There's one thing about Charlie they never will get,
> And that is the shoes on his feet.

It doesn't matter anywhere you go
Watch 'em coming out of any cinema show,
Shuffling along, they're acting like a rabbit,
When you see Charlie Chaplin you can't help but get the habit.
First they stumble over both their feet,
Swing their sticks then look up and down the street,
Fathers, mothers, sisters, brothers,
All your wife's relations and a half dozen others,
In London, Paris or New York
Ev'rybody does that Charlie Chaplin Walk!

There was a 'new fox-trot song' of the same title, a 'Charlie Chaplin Glide', 'Charlie Chaplin – March Grotesque', 'Those Charlie Chaplin Feet', 'Charlie Chaplin, the Funniest of them All', and 'The Funniest Man in Pictures' with words by Marguerite Kendall:

He tips his hat and twirls his cane,
His moustache drives the girls insane . . .

In France there was a popular 'Charlot One-Step'.

By the autumn of 1915 Sydney had worked out his Keystone contract and now proposed to devote himself whole-time to the management of his brother's affairs. He persuaded Chaplin that they should themselves undertake the commercial exploitation of the various Chaplin by-products, and accordingly the Charles Chaplin Music Company and the Charles Chaplin Advertising Service Company were incorporated. Neither seems to have lasted very long: the administrative cost and problems of chasing royalties on ephemeral productions selling for a few cents proved uneconomic. In October 1915 James Pershing, who had been appointed to run the advertising service, reported to Sydney:

We find that things pertaining to royalties are in a very chaotic state. There seems to be hundreds of people making different things under the name of Charlie Chaplin. First we have to find out where they are, what they are making, and are notifying them as fast as possible to stop or arrange with us for royalties, which is about all we can do.

Sydney suggested that Aunt Kate would be an ideal English representative for the Advertising Service, and accordingly Mr Pershing wrote:

In regard to the English rights, we have attended to that by writing to your aunt, asking her to look us up an attorney and engage him on a commission basis, and are suggesting the various things that may be made over the name of Charlie and endeavouring to get her to place these rights herself, or have it done by some competent party. It is impossible for any of us to go over at the present time, although we realize that this should be done . . .

Evidently Aunt Kate entered into the arrangement with an enthusiasm worthy of her nephews, for a month later the President of the Advertising Service indignantly reported to Sydney:

Miss Kate Mowbray cabled that she had been appointed agent and insisted upon 25% royalties. We did not appoint her, as you know, and I hardly believed that you have assumed the authority. If you have, we are going to back you up, but we cannot, from our end, give her 25%. Let me hear from you in this connection so that we can write her intelligently.

Almost from the moment of Chaplin's arrival in the United States, there was a bizarre fascination with his racial origins. Even during the Karno tours, interviewers and reporters frequently reported that he was the child of Jewish vaudeville artists. Yet in the four generations that we can confidently trace back his ancestry – through the Chaplins, Hills, Terrys, and Hodges, and certainly through the gypsy Smiths – there is no positive evidence of Jewish blood. All these forbears seem to have regularly performed the family rituals within the Church of England, until Hannah sought solace with the Baptists in later years.

Chaplin's first recorded statement on the question dates from 1915, when a reporter asked him, if, as was supposed, he was Jewish. With the grace he so often mustered in the face of the press, Chaplin replied 'I have not that good fortune.' This was not an empty courtesy: throughout his life Chaplin would continue to express a profound admiration for the race (which in itself would certainly have led him to acknowledge any Jewish origins). On a boat returning from Europe in 1921 (see page 290) he told a small girl who was a fellow-passenger: "All great geniuses have Jewish blood in them. No, I am not Jewish . . . but I am sure there must be some somewhere in me. I hope so'. This feeling for the race did not imply uncritical approval of everything Jewish. He always suspected, for instance, that circumcision must be dangerous psychologically as well as undesirable aesthetically and physically.

A fragment of film in the Chaplin Archive, showing Sydney and the studio staff seeing Chaplin off on an east-bound train, provides charming and curious evidence of his own conviction that he was not, to his regret, Jewish. The family tradition was that Sydney's father, the putative Mr Hawkes, *was* Jewish – even though Sydney was baptized according to the rites of the Church of England. Fooling for the cameras, Chaplin puts his arm around Sydney and mimes, with beautiful clarity of expression: 'We're brothers. Aren't we alike?' He thereupon answers his own question in the negative, explaining the lack of familial resemblance by pointing a finger at Sydney and doing a stage-Jew impersonation, all shrugs and raised hands, to indicate that Sydney is Jewish and he is not. Another odd visual comment appears in a shot of Chaplin with Harry Lauder in 1918. Lauder draws a crude caricature of Chaplin on a blackboard. Chaplin pointedly alters the unmistakable hook nose of a caricature Jew.

Chaplin, the supposed Jew, was an early target for Nazi anti-Semitism. *The Gold Rush* was banned from the early years of the Third Reich, and Chaplin figured in a hideous publication attacking prominent international Jewish intellectuals. Along with Einstein, Mann, Reinhardt and others, Chaplin's portrait, crudely retouched to emphasize its 'Hebraic' features, was printed with an accompanying caption which dismissed him as 'a little Jewish acrobat, as disgusting as he is tedious'. Chaplin's riposte, in *The Great Dictator*, was to play an overtly Jewish character, and to say, 'I did this film for the Jews of the world.' By this time he was adamant in his refusal ever to contradict any statement that he was a Jew. He explained to Ivor Montagu, 'Anyone who denies this in respect of himself plays into the hands of the anti-Semites.'

6

Mutual

Chaplin only became aware of the extent of his fame in February 1916 when he took a train east to join Sydney in New York. To his astonishment, when they stopped at Amarillo, Texas, the station was hung with bunting, there was a civic deputation to greet him and a huge crowd mobbed the train. In Kansas City and Chicago the crowds were even greater and before they arrived in New York the Chief of Police requested him by cable to alight at 125th Street station instead of Grand Union to avoid trouble with the throng that had been assembling since early morning. News of his itinerary had been leaked to the press by the telegraphists who had relayed his telegram to Sydney announcing his time of arrival.

Sydney had gone ahead to canvas offers for Chaplin's future services. While relations were still tolerable, Spoor had gone from Chicago to Los Angeles with an offer of $350,000 for twelve two-reelers, but would not meet Chaplin's demand of a bonus on signature of $150,000. Chaplin knew his value, and Sydney was determined to get the right price. Sydney found himself wooed on all sides. Universal, Mutual, The Triangle, Famous Players, Fox and Vitagraph were all bidding optimistically; even Spoor and Anderson followed Charlie to New York in an effort to gain a new contract. In the end none of them could better the proposition of John R. Freuler, President of the Mutual Film Corporation, which had been incorporated only three years before by Freuler and Harry Aitken, and now set the seal on its success with the acquisition of the biggest star in motion pictures. Freuler agreed to pay Chaplin $10,000 a week, with a bonus of $150,000 on signing.

Mutual, as it happened, had just engaged the most gifted publicist in motion pictures, Terry Ramsaye (1885–1954) who a decade later was to write the first and classic history of the motion picture industry in the United States.* It was Ramsaye who wrote the account of the contract in Mutual's publicity magazine, *Reel Life* (4 March 1916):

> Charles Chaplin has signed a contract to appear exclusively in the releases of the Mutual Film Corporation.
>
> Chaplin will receive a salary of $670,000 for his first year's work under the contract. The total operation in forming the Chaplin producing company involved the sum of $1,530,000. This stands as the biggest operation centered about a single star in the history of the motion picture industry.

AN EXPRESSION OF POLICY

Following close on this announcement from President John R. Freuler of the Mutual, comes his declaration that the signing of Chaplin is but the beginning of a dominating policy on the part of the corporation and the suggestion that the expiration of certain contracts held by other famous stars now working for other concerns will result in further announcements rivaling that of the Mutual's achievement this week.

The game of 'button, button, who's got Chaplin?' which had been engaging the attention of the photoplay world so long was brought to an abrupt end in President Freuler's office late last Saturday night, at the close of the last of the weighty series of conferences and negotiations.

Next to the war in Europe Chaplin is the most expensive item in contemporaneous history.

Every hour that goes by brings Chaplin $77.55 and if he should need a nickel for a carfare it only takes two seconds to earn it.

COMPETITORS' GUESSES ALL TOO LOW

Mr Chaplin will be twenty-seven years old the 16th of April. He is doing reasonably well for his age.

The closing of the contract ends a war of negotiations involving unending conferences and diplomatic exchanges for weeks. In this time five or six motion picture concerns and promoters have claimed Chaplin and audibly whispered figures – with every guess too low. A week ago Mr Freuler put Chaplin under a tentative contract or option, pending the completion of arrangements for the organization of a special producing company. At that time the negotiations were entirely personal between President Freuler and Chaplin.

---

* *A Million and One Nights*, New York, 1926.

Saturday night the final conference was held and the ceremony of signing up with the Mutual proceeded, with all due array of attorneys, notaries, etc., including, of course, a battery of arc lamps and a motion picture camera, since the motion picture does its own reporting these days.

Charles Chaplin was accompanied as usual by his brother, Sidney Chaplin, who conducts the younger comedian's business affairs and salary negotiations.

The lawyers for everybody looked over all the papers for the last tedious time and announced that everything was correct. The ponderous seal was brought forth from a vault by a law clerk and placed with precise care on the president's mahogany office table.

FILM SIGNING FOR MUTUAL WEEKLY

The lights flared up under the pressure of 'more juice' and the office shimmered with the rippling glare of a studio.

Charles Chaplin was draped over the edge of the table in one of his characteristic off-stage attitudes, eyeing the proceedings with a casual air of shocking disinterestedness.

'What's the action in this scene?' he inquired of his brother, spreading the expensive [*sic*] Chaplin smile.

'Sign here and here,' explained Sid, indicating the neat and beckoning dotted lines on the last page of the ponderous twenty-thousand word contract evolved by the Mutual's astonishingly industrious legal department.

President Freuler handed over his pet fountain pen, with which all the stars sign. Sidney Chaplin called 'camera' and the action started.

In five minutes the deed was done and the camera man reported 'three hundred feet' as President Freuler handed Chaplin a check for $150,000 bonus payment.

Chaplin looked over the check critically, then with gingery fingers passed it on. 'Take it, Sidney, take it away from me please, my eyes hurt.'

In addition to the bonus paid Mr Chaplin on the signing of the contract, he receives a salary of $10,000 a week.

TO MAKE FILMS IN LOS ANGELES

The new Mutual Chaplins will be produced in studios now being equipped in Los Angeles, Cal., where the comedian will begin work March 20, or at an earlier date if conditions permit. One two-part comedy will be produced each month.

The Chaplin contract is one of the most ponderous and intricate documents ever evolved for the employment of a motion picture star. It contains something more than 20,000 words and provides conditions and clauses to cover anything that might happen and a lot of things that can not. An element of 'war risk' enters into the contract. Mr Chaplin is a British subject. It is stipulated that he shall not leave the United States within the life of the contract without the permission of the corporation. Incidentally, Mr Freuler has insured the costly comedian's life for $250,000.

'This contract,' observed Mr Freuler yesterday, 'is only a new token of the bigness of the motion picture and the motion picture industry, a combination of art, amusement and business. The figures are all business,' he added with a dry smile.

'We can afford to pay Mr Chaplin this large sum annually because the public wants Chaplin and will pay for him. I consider this contract a very pleasing bargain for everybody concerned – including this corporation, Mr Chaplin and the fun-loving American public.'

Chaplin himself made a skilful and disarming statement to the press:

A great many people are inclined to make wide eyes at what is called my salary. Honestly, it is a matter I do not spend much time thinking about.

Money and business are very serious matters and I have to keep my mind off of them. In fact I do not worry about money at all.

It would get in the way of my work. I do not think that life is all a joke to me, but I do enjoy working on the sunny side of it.

What this contract means is simply that I am in business with the worry left out and with the dividends guaranteed.

It means that I am left free to be just as funny as I dare, to do the best work that is in me and to spend my energies on the thing that the people want. I have felt for a long time that this would be my big year and this contract gives me my opportunity. There is inspiration in it. I am like an author with a big publisher to give him circulation.

The Chaplin contract was capitalized from a newly floated company, the Lone Star Film Corporation; and Mr Freuler was able to give his stockholders a rosy forecast of results from the Chaplin films. According to the President's calculations the average cost of the twelve features would be $10,000 each, or a total of $120,000, which when added to the comedian's salary made an overall outlay of $790,000. The revenue was calculated on an income of $25 a day for each copy of a two-reeler for a period of at least thirty days. The company aimed to make at least one hundred prints of each film, so that there would be a minimum daily income of $2500, or $75,000 a month. Multiplied by twelve months, at a film per month, the total came to $900,000 – already $110,000 over the outlay. The life of the prints, however, would in fact be considerably longer than thirty days: the 'sixties' and 'nineties' as the more used prints were known, could go on earning $20 and $10 per day in smaller cinemas. Freuler told his stockholders that his estimate of the potential profits was conservative: it did not take into account the possibility of distributing many more than one hundred prints of each subject, or the foreign sales which, even in war conditions, remained huge. Freuler was soon to discover how much even he had underestimated his prize. He would no doubt have been even more surprised to learn that films whose life expectancy he estimated at sixty days would still be entertaining millions (with no advantage to Mutual) sixty *years* later.

The press and the public were thrilled and even sceptical at the size of Chaplin's earnings. $670,000 a year meant $12,884 a week, $1840 a day, $76.70 an hour, $1.27 a minute. No person in the world other than a king or an emperor – unless perhaps Charlie Schwab of the US Steel Corporation – had ever received even half that salary. Mary Pickford was to ensure that Chaplin's record salary did not go unchallenged for long, but for the moment it was the topic of the day. On one hand it triumphantly realized the American dream of success; on the other it offended a puritan reverence for money. The Reverend Frederick E. Heath, preaching at the Warren Avenue Baptist Church in Boston, took as his text 'Charlie Chaplin's Half Million': 'Had Chaplin lived in the old Puritanical days they would have believed him a witch and taken his life . . . I believe in a good laugh . . . The great mistake in American life today is this wicked and immoral manner of throwing away money.'

Chaplin, as it happened, somewhat disappointed New York during his visit. For Easterners, the stars of motion pictures had already become a strange and exotic species, given to high living and reckless spending. Chaplin did not at all conform to this image. He was serious, quiet and retiring. Worse, he did not throw his money around. Memories of poverty were too close; and he was for long to consider, quite philosophically, the possibility that one day the public would tire of him. He respected money as those who have been without it must, but he was not mean: while he was in New York he gave a cheque for $1300 to Sam Goldfish's actors' fund – it was half the fee he had received for a personal appearance at a Sunday show at the Hippodrome. The myth of Chaplin's tightwaddedness however started from this time; notably in an interesting portrait of Chaplin at the age of twenty-six by Karl K. Kitchen:

> Charlie is enjoying his riches with becoming modesty. He spent a month in New York before he signed his contract, and it was a dizzy month, up and down and across Broadway, dining, wining, playgoing and dancing and having the time of his young life, but – keeping his bankroll exclusively to himself.
>
> For at the age of 26 and with an annual income of $670,000 Charlie Chaplin has the finance idea developed to 100 per cent efficiency. The only thing he spent on Broadway in a month of gay life was four weeks. Not since Harry Lauder astonished and then amused New York with his Scotch thrift, to use a pleasant word, has Broadway known such a frugal celebrity.

To be fair, the writer conceded, Chaplin had had no need to spend money. He was the most sought-after man in New York. With every motion picture magnate trying to get him under contract, 'he was fêted as no actor who ever visited New York was fêted before.' Innumerable dinners were given in his honour and he took back with him to California a trunk full of costly presents.

> His only extravagance is a 12-cylinder automobile. He does not even allow himself the luxury of a wife. Jewelry, slow horses and fast company, country homes, *objets d'art* and other expensive fads of the predatory rich do not appeal to this slender young movie actor, who has risen in less than five years from obscurity to the distinction of being the highest-paid employee in the world . . .
>
> His personal expenses last year were considerably less than $500 and there are no indications that his new contract has turned his head. If anything it has caused him to be even more tight-fisted. Chaplin's theory of life may not be plain living and high thinking – he is more interested in prize fights than art or literature – but the fact remains that he lives plainly – except when someone else foots the bill.
>
> Instead of a secretary he has his brother Sidney . . . to look after his social and business arrangements. He is without a valet for the reason that he has less than half a dozen suits of clothes. Unless he is specially requested to wear evening dress he appears at the theatre or even a more formal function in a tweed suit . . .
>
> In flesh he is entirely different from the gelatine. He is of surprisingly small stature – he weighs less than 125 pounds – and he possesses a perfectly ordinary face – a face that would not attract attention in a crowd of five, let alone 500. To be sure, he has black eyes of more than ordinary brilliance and a mass of coal black hair inclined to curl, but all

in all his appearance is absolutely undistinguished. His manner too is in striking contrast to his picture antics. For in private life he is unusually shy, quiet and reserved. When he talks, his cockney speech betrays his origin. Strangely enough, he speaks without gestures, a remarkable thing for an actor of any brand.[1]

Chaplin tried to explain his own position: 'No one realizes more than I do that my services may not be worth $100 a week five years from now. I'm simply making hay while the sun shines.'[2] Another interview statement was at once prophetic and an accurate self-analysis: 'I have been a worker all my life. It is true that I could quit the screen today if I wished and live the rest of my life in ease and comfort. I'm still a young man – just twenty-six years old but you will find me working just as hard fifty years from now. Money is not everything. One can find more happiness in work than in anything else I know of.'[3] As he anticipated, exactly fifty years from that time he was working on a new film, *A Countess from Hong Kong*. He also gave his views on marriage: 'When I wanted to marry I didn't have the money. Now that I have the money I don't care to marry. Besides, there's plenty of time for that sort of thing when I quit work.'[4]

For all that he had not been able to forget Hetty Kelly. He recalled half a century later that when he was in New York, believing that Hetty was living with her sister on Fifth Avenue, he had loitered near the house, hoping to meet her. It was a vain hope: Hetty was in England where, six months earlier, she had married Lieutenant Alan Horne, son of the MP for Guildford.

This was the first time since they had met almost a year before, that Chaplin and Edna had been apart. While Chaplin was in New York, Edna had gone home to her family in Lovelock, Nevada. Chaplin promised to write to her, but he was never a good correspondent, and Edna wrote to reproach him gently:

> I really don't know why you don't send me some word. Just one little telegram so unsatisfactory. Even a night letter would be better than nothing. You know 'Boodie' you promised faithfully to write. Is your time so taken up that you can't even think of me. Every night before I go to bed I send out little love thoughts wishing you all the success in the world and counting the minutes until you return. How much longer do you expect to stay. Please, Hon, don't forget your 'Modie' and hurry back. Have been home for over a week and believe me my feet are itching to get back.
>
> Have you seen Mable and the Bunch? I suppose so. Am so sorry that

you couldn't have taken me. Have you been true to me? I'm afraid not. Oh, well, do whatever you think is right. I really do trust you to that extent . . .

After 'Lots of love and kisses' Edna signs herself, charmingly, 'Yours faithfully'.

Chaplin, from his own account, passed a rather quiet time in New York, trying to avoid the crowds, and somewhat depressed by a sense of loneliness. He went to the opera and was induced against his better judgement to go backstage and meet Caruso. Slightly confused as to whether he was seeing *Carmen* or *Rigoletto*, blithely introduced as 'the Caruso of the moving pictures' and aware that Caruso was not particularly interested to meet him, Chaplin was triply mortified. The conversation, according to a contemporary news report, ran: 'Caruso: "I read you make gooda contract." Chaplin: "Yes, I've made a fine contract." Caruso: "That's gooda. I geta gooda contract too. I am very glada to meet you." And there the interview ended.' Afterwards Chaplin remarked, 'I'm sorry I didn't call him the Chaplin of opera. I intended to, but I lost my nerve.' He was to have happier encounters with other stars of the musical world. Later in the year Dame Nellie Melba visited him in his new studios during her Los Angeles season, and revealed promising gifts for comedy. Fooling for the camera, Chaplin walked down a flight of stairs with her and did a comic fall. Melba jerked him to his feet, slammed his hat on his head and said: 'Charlie, behave yourself. This is not a place of amusement.' Paderewski also visited the studio, watched Chaplin at work, clapped his hands in delight and exclaimed enigmatically: 'Bravo! What a grand piano player has the motion picture lost. What a great pie thrower has the music world gained in the fine Mr Chaplin.'

On 10 March the Chaplin brothers, in company with Henry P. Caulfield who had been appointed by Mutual as general manager of Chaplin's new studio, boarded the *Twentieth Century* for their return journey to the West coast. The party stopped off for a couple of days in Chicago. Chaplin was induced to do his funny walk outside a cinema where one of his films was playing, but the publicity stunt fell flat. No one recognized him and the cashier, bored to death with would-be Chaplin imitators, only sniffed haughtily. In the lobby of the Sherman Hotel, Chaplin gave an interview while Sydney strove to keep the curious onlookers at bay and to deal with the excited bellboys forever bringing more letters for the comedy king. He spoke of his plans for the forthcoming films:

One can be just as artistic in shoes that flap as in a dress suit. It isn't how one is dressed, but what one does and how. Slapstick comedy has as much artistic possibility as the best tailored efforts from the stage . . .

This year has a large inspiration . . . I'm going to make better pictures than I did last. I am doing my own scenarios and my own directing. We're to have a little bit more legitimate plots. I like a little story, with maybe an idea in it, not too much, not to teach anything, but some effect, like in *The Bank* for instance. I think *Police* (to be released in a few weeks by Essanay) is the best thing I've ever done. One must consider the kiddies, not to go over their heads, and remember the grown-ups too . . .

I'll keep the moustache, but won't stick so closely to the other clothes. It'll depend on what the circumstances demand. And it doesn't matter what one is funny in so [long as] one is funny. That's why I can't take things too seriously. This salary is just figures, figures to me. It doesn't mean anything. If I took things seriously I couldn't make pictures.

Some time, when they don't care about me in pictures any more, and I hope I know it in time before it happens . . . oh yes, some time that will happen. It won't be my fault, it will be the public's. It will get tired of seeing the same figure, you know. Well, then I hope to accomplish something bigger. Not that pictures aren't big, but I want to work on the stage a little, to feel my audience.[5]

Shortly after they returned to California, the Chaplin brothers learned that Aunt Kate, whose beauty and gaiety was one of the happiest memories of their boyhood, had died. She had died among strangers in her lodgings at 99 Gower Street; no one there even knew her real name, and her death was registered in her professional name of Kate Mowbray. Her death certificate, which gives her occupation as Actress, states that she died of cancer. She would no doubt have been delighted that they put down her age as thirty-five: in fact she was forty-one. The Hill sisters, whatever else befell them, kept their youthful looks. With Kate's death there was no near relative left to watch over Hannah, or to take action when the fees at Peckham House fell into arrears.

The new Lone Star Studio was opened on 27 March, only a week later than Mutual had hoped. Formerly the Climax Studios, the lot stood on the corner of Lillian Way and Eleanor Avenue in the Colegrave district of Los Angeles. In the centre of the property was the stage, said to be the largest of any single producing unit in California. It was open, but surrounded by canvas side walls, with linen diffusers draped overhead. There was plenty of space for the erection of large exterior sets like the street scene for *Easy Street*, and it was rarely necessary for the unit to go out on location except where water was needed. There were few administration buildings: the largest was the laboratory where all the studio's films were to be developed and printed. The offices were contained in a four-room bungalow with a projection room in an annexe. To the south and west there were twenty dressing rooms, also in bungalow style. Scene docks, property rooms and the scenic workshops adjoined the stage on the west side.

Caulfield was production manager; William C. Foster was chief cameraman, and Roland Totheroh became his assistant. Totheroh had left Essanay, and was without a job when Chaplin arrived back from New York.

> I went to see him. Charlie said, 'Sure we can use you.' He said we'd get started the next week. The cameraman was Bill Foster, later head cameraman at Universal. I met Bill and told him I'd been shooting comedies and everything else, and I knew about the speed. At that time they had no motors on the cameras and we changed the speed for chases. Foster had always shot dramas and things like that. We started together, Bill and I, as camera one and two. When it came to selecting scenes and that, pretty near all of my scenes were selected. When Charlie would do something like kick his feet, we had to be all prepared and crank.[6]

Foster left the Lone Star Studio after four films, leaving Totheroh as chief cameraman.

> Bill Foster had heard about some cameraman who was going to do a film at Fox, so he left to work over there. Now I was on my own. I did all the Mutuals, the First Nationals, and all the rest.[7]

With his first film, Chaplin built up his little stock company of players. Edna, naturally, remained his leading lady. From Essanay he brought Leo White (whose involvement in the *Carmen* affair seems not to have been held against him), Charlotte Mineau, Lloyd Bacon, John Rand, Frank J. Coleman, and James T. Kelley, an elderly Irish actor with a fine line in ruinous old men. Two invaluable Essanay colleagues, Bud Jamison and Billy Armstrong, had departed to pursue independent careers; in their place Chaplin engaged three new actors who would make a significant contribution to his future films. Albert Austin, born in Birmingham in 1885, was an old Karno trouper who had played in *Mumming Birds*. Lean and lugubrious, with a sort of bewildered irritability, he was the only player to appear alongside Chaplin in each of the twelve Mutual comedies. In Eric Stuart

Campbell, Chaplin found the ideal Goliath to his own David. Campbell looked much older than his thirty-seven years, and much more fearsome than he was in real life: he seems in fact to have been a jolly and sociable man. Six-foot-four and almost twenty stone, he made an even more striking contrast to Charlie's slight figure than Bud Jamison or Mack Swain.

Roland Totheroh described Chaplin's method of work at the time he moved to the Lone Star Studio:

> When Charlie was working on an idea, often he would call me in. There were always a lot of his own people around. He'd hit on a certain situation where there was something he was building on, and he'd want conversation more or less. If someone came up with an idea that sounded as if he could dovetail it and it would build up his situation, it would sink back in his head and he'd chew it over . . .
>
> He didn't have a script at the time, didn't have a script girl or anything like that, and he never checked whether the scene was in its right place or that continuity was followed. The script would develop as it went along. A lot of times after we saw the dailies the next morning, if it didn't warrant what he thought the expectation was, he'd put in some other sort of a sequence and work on that instead of going through with what he started out to do. We never had a continuity. He'd have an idea and he'd build up. He had sort of a synopsis laid out in his mind but nothing on paper. He'd talk it over and come in and do a sequence. In a lot of his old pictures, he'd make that separation by using titles about the time: 'next day' or 'the following day' or 'that night' – these would cover the script gaps in between.
>
> Every picture that he made always had one particular highlight, a good built-up spot to rock the house with it. Of course, everyone would contribute a little bit to the ideas and the script. But no one'd dare butt in and say, 'Oh, you should do this and you should do that.' I would never leave that camera when they were rehearsing, always right behind them, watching every move, everything that he did. When the scene was taken, if I saw something in there, I was around that camera in a wink. In a nice way I'd say, 'Gee, Charlie, you could do this,' or 'Aren't you going to do that?' and he'd agree to it. But you couldn't go out and say to him things like some of them did, like Albert Austin . . . he'd say something to Charlie, and then tell everybody all around the lot: 'I gave Charlie that gag.'
>
> Charlie would rehearse them. He'd rehearse everybody and even in silents, we had dialogue. It came to a little woman's part, and he'd go out there and he'd play it. He'd change his voice and he'd be in the character that he wanted the little old woman to play. He'd build their

lines up and rehearse them, even before he rehearsed himself in it. He rehearsed so many darn different ways with them that when he came in there, it'd be changed all around with what he put down. You had to be on the alert for him.

I never got away from that camera, looking through that lens. And all those rehearsals, I sat right there, watching every move he made. Then if he came along and something spontaneous hit him, you had to be ready there to take it and get it.

As a director, Mr Chaplin didn't have anything to say as far as exposures, things like that [were concerned]. Otherwise, I used to say, 'Take a look through here.' The idea of that was that if he was directing, he'd have to know the field that I was taking in. Of course, in the early days, the role of the cameraman was much bigger than it is now. It was up to the cameraman to decide what angle to shoot for lighting; or outside, which is the best angle on a building or whatever it is. Then you have to figure what time of the day it would be better to shoot that shot, whether you want back-light or cross-light or whatever on your set.

On a typical day, we'd shoot from around eight or nine in the morning right straight through till lunch. Of course, this was before unions. And a lot of times he'd want to shoot two hours after dinner. After we'd break for lunch or for dinner, we'd start up again. I could always tell my set-ups because I was smoking Bull Durhams and I used so many matches. You could see all those matches all over the floor.

While Charlie was working, rehearsing or filming or whatever, lots of his people would stand around and watch. He used to use their reactions to see how his stuff was going over. But later on he got so that if they stood there gawking at him, he'd stop and say, 'Get out of here! What are you standing there glaring at me for?' But prior to that, anything he'd do on location or anything, the crowds around, they'd laugh their heads off at his antics.

A lot of times we'd get through a sequence and run it maybe three or four days later. And he'd figure, 'No, that's not it.' So he'd go on to something else. Then if that was worthy of carrying on and adding and building to it, then he'd go and do it. He finished a lot of times a sequence and then he'd blame it on somebody else. He didn't want people to think that he didn't know what he was doing. He'd turn around and think overnight, 'Jesus Criminy, this is what I should have done. I didn't do it.' Now he'd dismissed all the people and had sets torn down. But it was his own money, so what the devil – 'Call the people back.' . . .

Lots of times he'd start building sets before he was really set on his story. Once they double-crossed him after he pulled this once or twice. He'd have an idea but it wasn't really set. Then for a stall, he'd say, 'I don't want the window in the back there or the door in this side.' So it would take a few couple of days to make that changeover. Then they got tired of that, and they put casters on the set . . .

Charlie was always so proud when he was building a set. We had the lousiest looking sets I ever saw, a side wall and a back wall. He'd build something with a little balcony or something and he'd get ahold of Doug Fairbanks or somebody and say, 'I want you to see this set I'm building.' He'd make his little sketches for these set guys . . . Fairbanks had the most spectacular sets of anybody. And Doug used to say, 'Oh, gee, that's swell, Charlie.' He always wanted to encourage Charlie in whatever he did.[8]

There is evidence of Chaplin's methods of work at this time far more detailed than exists for any other director of the silent films. Sydney, always provident, carefully kept and stored all the out-takes, every piece of film that Chaplin exposed in the course of making the Mutual films. Totheroh, who had the problem of accommodating all this material, was distinctly irritated:

Syd kept all the out-takes of Charlie's early films. He held those in reserve. He thought at the time when Charlie passed away that there'd be nobody to object: he had all sorts of cuttings from Mutual, but they didn't belong to Charlie – a lot of scenes and sequences we didn't use. I had them there in the vault, and Syd knew it. And he'd want to cut into them, and I'd say, 'Oh, no – that's not our property.' And he knew that I knew, too. I said, 'That belongs to Mutual.'[9]

Mutual in time vanished, but the out-takes were preserved. When Chaplin closed down his studio in 1952, Totheroh was ordered to destroy the great mass of material. He was no longer young, and not well and, perhaps fortunately, did not do the job very efficiently. Several hundred reels survived, and eventually came into the possession of the distributor Raymond Rohauer. In 1982 they were to provide the basis for a remarkable series of three television programmes, *Unknown Chaplin*, directed by Kevin Brownlow and David Gill. Brownlow and Gill demonstrated that the analysis of Chaplin's rushes, with a comparison of the shot numbers, provided an incomparable insight into his methods.

The out-takes reveal, first of all, that Chaplin rehearsed, practised, perfected and refined his gags in front of the camera. We can see him, for example, tentatively trying out and then developing the best ways to use a wonderful new prop he had had built for his first Mutual film, *The Floorwalker* – a moving staircase. Terry Ramsaye described the genesis of the film:

Firstly – Chaplin comedies are not made. They occur . . .

The comedian had only three weeks in which to decide upon the plot which would enable him to kick somebody in the addenda to the satisfaction of the expectant millions waiting, dime in hand, at the box office.

Two weeks and six days Mr Chaplin wandered about New York between breakfast at the Plaza and dinner all over town . . .

One day when time was desperately short he was walking up Sixth Avenue at Thirty-third Street when an unfortunate pedestrian slipped and skidded down the escalator serving the adjacent elevated station. Everybody but Chaplin laughed. But Mr Chaplin's eyes lit up. Also he lit out – for the studio in Los Angeles.

Thus was *The Floorwalker* born. Mr Chaplin did not care a whoop about the floorwalker person as a type – what he sought were the wonderful possibilities of the escalator as a vehicle upon which to have a lot of most amusing troubles. *The Floorwalker* was built about the escalator not the floorwalker.

This history of *The Floorwalker* is in a diagnostic sense typical of the building of a Chaplin comedy. Every one of them is built *around* something.[10]

Around this particular something Chaplin created a whole department store. On the ground floor are toiletries, travel goods, shoes and ladies' hosiery, all watched over by Albert Austin as a suspicious assistant. On the first floor are the offices where the manager, played by a heavily whiskered Eric Campbell, is planning large-scale embezzlement with the floorwalker (Lloyd Bacon). The store's customers are shop-lifters to a man, or woman, and much assisted by the concentration of Austin's baleful gaze upon the innocent Charlie. Ultimately pursued by Austin, Charlie flees upstairs and bumps into the floorwalker who happens to be his near double. The floorwalker, having just double-crossed his confederate, the manager, offers Charlie the chance to change places with him, to which Charlie, with innocent gratitude, agrees. When the manager comes to, his pursuit of Charlie culminates in a final, fade-out scrum.

The Floorwalker reverts to pure physical comedy, with little of the irony and none of the romance that had became increasingly evident in the Essanay films. Edna plays only a minor role as the manager's secretary. The gag sequences are developed with virtuosity. The pursuits on the escalator are miracuously timed and choreographed. Charlie's confrontation with the angry giant manager produces bizarre moments of comedy: Charlie suddenly breaks away, to divert him with a passage of classical ballet; later the manager picks Charlie up by his neck and carries him across the room. The elaborate mechanism to produce this effect – Chaplin was in fact suspended on a wire to make Campbell's support of him seem effortless – is entirely effaced by the dexterity of the execution. Chaplin also provides a virtuoso performance of an old music hall routine – already done in films by Max Linder. Entering the floorwalker's office, he sees in front of him a figure so like himself that he can only suppose it is a mirror. The two men continue so exactly to reproduce each other's actions that both continue in their illusion until Charlie suddenly notices that while he is holding a cane in his hand the floorwalker has a satchel (containing the embezzled funds).

An early scene in the toiletries department provides an extended sequence of character comedy. Charlie fills a mug with water from a drinking fountain and ambles with it to the counter, where he proceeds to borrow the goods on display to shave and perfume himself, all under the outraged eyes of Albert Austin. As he finishes with each of the expensive cosmetics, Charlie throws them back on the counter with the exaggerated disdain of a dissatisfied customer. In other scenes he works new variations on favourite themes. Serving in the shoe department, he arranges an electric fan to deflect the fumes from the clients' hot feet. The recurrent homosexual motif appears in the scene where he and the floorwalker begin to realize that they are looking at each other, and not into the mirror. The shopwalker stretches out a hand to stroke Charlie's cheek and Charlie, misunderstanding, responds to the supposed caress with an amiable kiss. Later he also plants a kiss upon the withered brow of James Kelley, playing the oldest lift-boy in the world.

Casting around for another everyday occupation that might be food for comedy, Chaplin next hit upon *The Fireman*. Again the film has pretensions to little but light-hearted slapstick. It is strung together with an anecdote rather like *Shanghaied* or a Keystone plot. Fireman Charlie and his brutish chief (Eric Campbell) are both in love with Edna. Edna's father promises the chief the girl, so long as he agrees not to bring the brigade when the old man burns down his house for the sake of the insurance. Unknowingly he sets fire to the house while his daughter is upstairs. In a thrilling finale Charlie climbs the ladder to rescue the girl, and win her hand and heart. A subsidiary intrigue has Leo White as an excitable man who is quite unable to interest the firemen in the conflagration of his house.

Invention was sacrificed to elaborate production. The film was shot in a real fire station and its stables where the magnificent engine-horses nervily watch the proceedings. Two condemned houses were burnt down to provide the spectacular conflagrations. The horsedrawn engine, with its inclination to strew firemen and parts of itself along the road, suggested possibilities for comic chases. Otherwise Chaplin's most characteristic gag constructions in this film are in the styles of transposition (the fire engine's boilers become a coffee urn, as Charlie draws coffee and cream from its taps) and disproportion, as when Charlie, cleaning up the firehouse, sets about the horses with a dainty feather duster. There is a touch of irony when the firemen arrive at the scene of the blaze and, before setting to work, perform their drill exercises rather in the style of a musical comedy chorus.

From these uncomplicated scenarios *The Vagabond* marks a huge leap forward. It is a well-turned miniature drama, in which Charlie's adoption of a friendless girl anticipates *The Circus*, *Modern Times*, *City Lights* and *Limelight*. Gag comedy is skilfully juxtaposed with a subtler comedy of character and with a sentimental theme which, though it may seem a trifle heavy to modern tastes, is handled with a delicacy and judgement superior to most dramatic cinema of the period.

Charlie is a street musician and we are able to see, if not to hear, his accomplishment as a left-handed violinist. Out in the country, he rescues a little blonde drudge from villainous gypsies. Their life together in a stolen caravan is a (very chaste) idyll until a handsome young artist chances along and wins the heart of the girl. The artist's portrait of her is exhibited and recognized (thanks to the inevitable birthmark) by her long-lost mother. The girl is whisked off to a new life, leaving Charlie alone and disconsolate, unable even to manage the usual recuperative flip of his heels.

For the release version of the film, Chaplin imposed an improbable happy ending, in which the girl turns back the car in which she is being driven away, to take Charlie along. The viewer is left to speculate on the little Tramp's chances of co-existence with rich Mama and handsome artist. There is a legend, unsubstantiated by any existing footage, that Chaplin shot an alternative ending, in which the despairing Charlie throws himself into a river. He is fished out by a passing maiden, but since the maiden proves to be the hatchet-faced Phyllis Allen, he plunges back into the water to face a kinder fate.

Chaplin's sentiment is invariably saved fom mawkishness by comedy and the belligerence that always underlies his despair. His jealousy as he watches the girl dancing with the artist is not entirely impotent: he maliciously flicks a fly in the man's direction, and later manages to drop an egg on his shoes. After the girl's elegant mother condescendingly shakes hands with him, he suspiciously sniffs the perfume left on his fingers. He uses his favourite trick of deflating his own dramatic despair with farce: in *The Vagabond* the anguish of a lover rejected is quite eclipsed by the agonies of the same man accidentally sitting on a stove.

One A.M. was a daring display of virtuosity – so daring that Chaplin afterwards confided to his collaborators: 'One more like that and it's goodbye Charlie.' It is a solo performance, played for most of its two reels in a single set. The tramp costume is abandoned for elegant evening dress, silk hat and opera cloak. This might be the inebriate returning home from *Mumming Birds*. An introductory scene shows the drunken swell arriving at his house in a taxi driven by Albert Austin, whose role is to sit in the cab displaying impervious lack of concern at the accidents which befall his vulnerable passenger as he endeavours to disentangle himself from the vehicle. After this Chaplin is alone on the screen, in what might be an elaborated vaudeville solo: in fact Billie Reeves had performed a very similar routine called 'The Clubman' not many months before. Unable to find his key, Charlie, with gravity and difficulty, enters through the window. Having made his way in, falling into a goldfish bowl *en route*, he discovers his key with delight and solemnly makes his way back through the window in order to enter with greater decorum through the door. The succeeding battles with the furnishings of a stylishly over-dressed house of the period become a comic nightmare, a series of variations of beautifully structured escalation.

Surviving out-takes from the film reveal Chaplin's pains to perfect some tiny and apparently simple piece of business like a slide on a slithery mat, and how many failures were sometimes necessary to achieve the perfect take. *One A.M.* is one of the best and most sustained film records of Chaplin's inebriate, who perfectly illustrates the principle set out in an article credited to Chaplin in *American Magazine* of November 1918:

> Even funnier than the man who has been made ridiculous . . . is the man who, having had something funny happen to him, refuses to admit that anything out of the way has happened, and attempts to maintain his

dignity. Perhaps the best example is the intoxicated man who, though his tongue and walk will give him away, attempts in a dignified manner to convince you that he is quite sober.

He is much funnier than the man who, wildly hilarious, is frankly drunk and doesn't care a whoop who knows it. Intoxicated characters on the stage are almost always 'slightly tipsy' with an attempt at dignity, because theatrical managers have learned that this attempt at dignity is funny.

A considerable quantity of out-takes from Chaplin's next film, *The Count*, have survived to reveal the way he constructed and developed his stories in the course of shooting. In its completed form, *The Count* opens with Charlie as assistant to an ill-tempered and grotesquely bearded tailor played, inevitably, by Eric Campbell. The tailor masquerades as a Count at a party given by Miss Moneybags (Edna) and here he again encounters his troublesome former assistant, who is competing with the local police force for the cook's affections. For a while they collaborate in imposture, but inevitably set to fighting for the favours of the lovely Miss Moneybags. The film ends in a general mêlée, a ferocious battle with shotgun and iced cake.

We know that at this time Chaplin, working without a written script, tried as nearly as possible to shoot his films in exact order of story sequence. So by examining the out-takes and comparing the shot numbers, we can make a fairly accurate guess at how his original plan for the film was modified in the course of shooting. The earliest shot numbers are all found on the kitchen scenes so it may have been that Chaplin started the film with the idea of making a comedy of below-stairs intrigue: both the butler and the policeman are promising characters who vanish after the present kitchen episode. The numbering progresses to show that Chaplin next intended to go into the fake Count plot that had already served, in rudimentary form, for *Caught in a Cabaret*, *Her Friend the Bandit* and *A Jitney Elopement*. The scenes in the tailor's shop, which established the prior relationship of Charlie and the tailor, appear to have been shot as an afterthought, when all the other scenes of the film had been completed. The out-takes include one attractive little scene shot for this sequence but in the end abandoned: Charlie sits cross-legged, industriously sewing a garment, only to discover that he has firmly attached it to his own trousers.

The Count was one of Chaplin's most elaborate productions of that time, with three quite ambitious settings for the shop, the kitchen and Miss Moneybags' opulent home, complete with ballroom. Chaplin seems to have spent a considerable amount of the production time on the brilliantly choreographed dance sequence, for which he hired an entire dance orchestra. Chester Courtney, an old music hall acquaintance who had been given a job at the studio and recalled his impressions in an article in *Film Weekly* in 1931, remembered that most of the time they played 'They Call it Dixieland'. Chaplin's routine is a masterpeice of eccentric dancing, involving a lot of splits, from one of which he retrieves himself by hooking his cane to the chandelier and pulling himself to his feet. A recurrently dislocating hip joint anticipates the leg-shortening gag in the vaudeville finale of *Limelight*. Another detail which looks forward to later years is the star-shaped hat which Edna wears for the party. Its form clearly stuck in Chaplin's strange memory for fifteen years, until he found a comic use for it in a party scene in *City Lights*, in which a rather tipsy Charlie mistakes a bald head framed in exactly such a hat for a pink blancmange on a frilly plate.

Of all Chaplin's films *The Pawnshop* is the richest in gag invention. The setting is a back-street pawnbroker establishment, and both it and its eccentric customers smack more of Chaplin's boyhood London than of California. Chaplin maintains constant hostilities with his fellow assistant (John Rand), asphyxiating him with dust, engulfing him in a snowstorm of feathers by absentmindedly dusting the electric fan with a feather duster, assaulting him with ladders, fists and the three balls of the shop sign. When he is dismissed by the fat old pawnbroker Charlie pleads, in a celebrated flash of mime, the plight of his large family. He is reinstated, and so is able to continue his courtship of the pawnbroker's pretty daughter, Edna. His claim to her hand is vindicated when his prompt and ingenious action accomplishes the capture of a burglar (Eric Campbell).

It is as if in this film Chaplin were exploring every possible use of the comedy of transposition which had appeared fairly frequently in his preceding work. Here every object seems to suggest some other thing and other use to his ingenious mind. In Edna's kitchen, her freshly baked doughnuts are wielded as if they were heavy dumb bells; a roll of dough becomes a leg and a ladle a Hawaiian guitar; cups and saucers, Charlie's own hands and eventually a wad of dough are briskly rolled through the mangle. Comic transposition is brought to its utmost refinement in the lengthy scene in which Charlie examines an alarm clock brought in by a dusty and dejected customer

174

(Albert Austin). Charlie becomes a doctor and the clock his patient as he sounds it with a stethoscope and tests its reflexes. Suddenly it is a rare piece of porcelain as he deftly rings it with his finger tips. He drills it like a safe. He opens it up with a can-opener and then dubiously smells the contents with a look that declares them putrid. Momentarily the clock becomes a clock again as Charlie unscrews the mouthpiece of the telephone and transforms *that* into a jeweller's eye-glass. Having oiled the springs, he produces a pair of forceps and becomes a dentist as he ferociously pulls out the contents. Extracting the spring, he measures it off like ribbon from nose to fingertip. He snips off lengths, then tips out the rest of the clock's contents onto the counter. When they start wriggling like a basket of worms he squirts them with oil. Having now demolished the alarm clock, he sweeps the contents back into the empty case and hands it back to the dazed Austin with a shake of the head and a look of grave distaste.

The pawnbroker was played by Henry Bergman, a new recruit who was to become an indispensable member of the Chaplin entourage for the next thirty years. Bergman was born in 1868 and claimed to be a third-generation Californian. His father was a horse-breeder and his mother a former Grand Opera singer, known in Europe as Aeolia. Henry inherited his mother's vocal talent, and studied in Italy and Germany, making his operatic debut in a small role in *Faust*. He told an interviewer in 1931:

> I got my histrionic training in Wagnerian roles. Twenty years ago I came into pictures. Before that I had been with Augustin Daly's company for nine years in New York. I was catapulted from stage to screen by a musical comedy flop. I had been rehearsing for it for many weeks without pay, and when it closed a few days after it opened I was disgusted. 'This is no business for me,' I said. One day I ran into a player I had known in Germany. When I asked him what he was doing he said, 'Shh. Don't let anybody know. I'm working in pictures. Doing pretty well too – making five dollars a day.' He suggested he might be able to fix me up at the studio . . . So I went to Pathé. There I got my first job with Pearl White in *The Perils of Pauline*. An introduction by Paul Panzer led to my association with Henry Lehrman, with whom I came to Hollywood with the L-Ko Company in 1914. We did a series of pictures, after which I went to Mr Chaplin to play with him. I had known Mr Chaplin personally. We used to be quite friendly at dinners etc, and when I mentioned to him that I was looking for a job he said, 'Why don't you come with me? You

can work with me when I start a company of my own.' That's the way it was.[11]

A bachelor, Bergman's single-minded, adoring dedication to Chaplin was to become his ruling passion. He assumed the role of assistant, confidant and indulgent aunt. Chaplin was happy to rely on an amanuensis, helper and foil as loyal as Henry, as well as using him as an actor in every one of his films up to *Modern Times*. Henry's pride in sharing Chaplin's confidences, and in his own ability to play any role, tended to spark jealousies among the rest of the studio staff. Totheroh, ordinarily a generous man, said: 'Some of the make-ups were terrible, especially Henry Bergman. He always thought he was a great make-up artist. He'd put on a beard and you'd see the glue sticking through it. He thought he was the greatest make-up man in the world. He used to brag about it.'[12] Edward Sutherland's view of Henry was: 'He was a great big fat actor who played in all of Charlie's pictures and revered and adored Charlie, to the extent that he was a detriment at times, because Charlie, like everybody else, made mistakes from time to time, and with Henry he could make no mistakes. Everything he did was great.'[13]

In *Behind the Screen* Henry was cast as a film director. This was Chaplin's fourth comedy set in a film studio. At Keystone he had made *A Film Johnnie* and *The Masquerader*, and at Essanay, *His New Job. Behind the Screen* is in fact merely a refinement of the same business. Charlie is the put-upon assistant of the idle, bullying property man (Eric Campbell), whose earnest efforts manage to disrupt all three of the productions being shot side by side. Edna plays a would-be actress who disguises herself as a boy and gets a job as a stage hand when the regular crew go on strike. (The strikers, and their plot to blow up the studio, are inherited from *Dough and Dynamite*.) Most of the business is unremarkable, some of it lifted almost directly from *His New Job*.

The surviving out-takes show that one gag whose ingenuity probably exceeded its comic effectiveness was cut out of the film altogether. It seems to have been a running joke: every time Charlie pushed his sack barrow past the set for the costume picture where a beheading was taking place, a heavy and evidently very sharp axe would crash to the ground within millimetres of his feet. Kevin Brownlow and David Gill, working on *Unknown Chaplin*, discovered that the effect was achieved by a camera trick: Totheroh *reversed* the camera,

Charlie went backwards, and the axe was heaved out of the floor and into the air. The number of takes of the scene shows that it was only achieved with much effort, yet the effect was convincing. Chaplin must nevertheless have estimated that it would not get the laugh that he wanted. Elsewhere, however, the out-takes show that though he was prepared to shoot a scene innumerable times to get it right, it was very rare for him to eliminate a scene or idea entirely, as he did in this case, and with the sewing scene in *The Count*. Film was cheap, but ideas came hard. (Chaplin often told his collaborators that 'film is cheap' when they marvelled at the number of times that he was prepared to shoot a scene. It was characteristic of his economic caprices, however, that he always insisted that Totheroh cut the shot exactly when told: film was not so cheap that he wanted to waste six inches at the shot-ends.)

In *Behind the Screen* Chaplin adds two more notable gags to his collection of comic transpositions. Doubled up beneath the weight of a dozen bentwood chairs, all looped around his person with their legs sticking into the air, he is metamorphosed into a porcupine. He becomes a coiffeur as he dresses a bearskin rug, combing it, sprinkling on tonic, applying a finger massage, parting the hair and finally applying hot towels to the face. Chaplin's preoccupation with nasty eaters and smelly food recurs in the lunch-hour scene in which he is seated beside Albert Austin who is devouring onions. Charlie uses a bellows to deflect the fumes, then puts on a helmet, stuffing his own food through the briefly-opened visor. He is not, however, too proud to steal an occasional bite from the end of Austin's meat-bone, clamping it between his own slices of bread.

The most surprising element in the film is a sequence that was to remain the most overt representation of a homosexual situation anywhere in the Anglo-Saxon commercial cinema before the 1950s. Edna has disguised herself in workman's overalls and a large cloth cap which conceals her hair. Charlie comes upon the 'boy' sitting playing a guitar (in the first takes Edna had a harp, but this was clearly discarded as being too obviously feminine). Charlie teases the 'boy' when he catches him powdering 'his' face. At that moment Bergman, who has split the seat of his trousers in a prior encounter with Charlie, enters and asks the 'boy' to sew them up for him. Edna promptly faints away and her cap falls off, releasing her hair. She comes to, begs Charlie not to expose her, and replaces her cap. The brutish property man (Campbell) enters just in time to catch them kissing. 'Oh you naughty boys!' he exclaims in a title; and teases them by doing a little 'fairy' dance, finally turning his back and offering his huge bottom – which Charlie obligingly kicks.

The Rink must have been suggested by the old Karno sketch *Skating*, though the resemblance remains fairly superficial. The *raison d'être* of the piece is the actual rink scene and Chaplin's spectacular and supremely graceful demonstration of his roller-skating skills. The opening sequence shows Charlie as a waiter, making up Eric Campbell's bills by checking off the stains on his lapels, and shaking a remarkable cocktail, topped with a carnation. There is a park-style amorous quadrangle with Mr Stout (Campbell) importuning Edna while Mrs Stout (Henry Bergman in the first of several amusing female impersonations) flirts with Edna's father (James T. Kelley). There is even an element of the bogus count theme, since Charlie makes a hit at the evening skating party by introducing himself as 'Sir Cecil Seltzer'.

The Rink occasioned some critical stir thanks to the terms in which Heywood Broun discussed it in his review in the *New York Tribune*, which was headed

NIETZSCHE HAS GRIP ON CHAPLIN
'The Rink' Strong Plea for Acceptance of Master Morality
FERMENT AT WORK ON POPULAR FILMS
Discussion of Education To Be Derived by Visit to Rialto

After summarizing the action, Broun concluded:

This is the play, barring a few diversions of no particular importance. It is interesting to note that Chaplin falls only twice during the picture, both times of his own volition, and that not once is he kicked. Is it not obvious, then, what ferment is at work in the philosophy of the Chaplin comedies? Gone is the old comedy of submission, as emphasized in *The Bank*, *The Tramp*, *Shanghaied* and others, and in its place there has grown up a comedy of aggression. One cannot overlook the influence of Nietzsche and the 'Will to Power' here.

Was it in 'Menschliches, Allzumenschliches' or in 'Also Sprach Zara-thustra' that the sage declared it was comic to kick, but never to be kicked? At any rate 'master morality' has set its mark upon Charlie Chaplin and his comedies. The old Chaplin of whom it was said, 'Here is the head upon which all the ends of the world are come and the eyelids are a little weary' is done. 'Welcome' has been erased from his shoulder-blades. The new Chaplin is a superman, and though the hordes of fat villains may rage against him, with pie and soup and siphons they shall not prevail.

Broun, we may take it, was not wholly serious; but a lot of his readers took him to be so. A day or two later the following anonymous poem appeared:

> TO CHARLIE CHAPLIN,
> AFTER READING THURSDAY'S TRIBUNE
>
> Triply distilled octessence of the vulgar,
> Puller of chairs from overweighty women,
> Hurler of pies into aged person's faces,
> Cinema lowbrow -
>
> Wreaker of wrongs that rouse the careless giggle,
> Skater that skateth but to lose his balance,
> Walking with steps unutterably comic,
> How I detest thee!
>
> How (though in years of profitless adventure
> Crowded with wasted afternoons and evenings
> Not even once – no, never – have I seen thee)
> Scornful I'm of thee!
>
> Scorn and contempt have I for all thine antics,
> Menace are they, say I, to little children
> Yet there is that which urges me to write thee
> Words of laudation.
>
> These are the words, then, Menace of the Movies,
> Thanks for thy coarse and pseudo-comic antics,
> For they produce those peerless things about thee
> Old Heywood Broun writes.[14]

Here was another detractor who boasted he had never actually seen the artist he was attacking.

The Rink was released on 4 December 1916, and was Chaplin's last film of the year. Chaplin had kept very nearly to the schedule of one film every four weeks he had agreed with Mutual. Only *Behind the Screen* had come out late, and the press reported that in this case Chaplin had telegraphed the company with the request 'It's the best idea I ever had. Give me two weeks more and I will make it the funniest comedy I ever produced.' *The Rink*, issued only three weeks later, caught up at least one week of the schedule. For the remaining films under the Mutual contract, however, Chaplin was to demand

and take more time: he would in fact take a total of ten months to make four two-reelers.

The year that was ending had brought some irritations, not the least of which was the book called *Charlie Chaplin's Own Story*. Despite Chaplin's strenuous efforts to suppress it, this spurious publication has continued to this day to confuse and falsify the record of Chaplin's career. It is useful to disentangle the story of this curious publication.

With the start of the great Chaplin mania in 1915 there was keen competition between publishers of books and periodicals to secure the biography of Charlie Chaplin. Unauthorized versions appeared in many less reputable journals. On 15 November 1915, the dismayed editor of the *Detroit News* telegraphed Chaplin at Essanay:

> WE ARE RUNNING YOUR LIFE STORY PURCHASED FROM THE DAVID SWING RICHES SYNDICATE. THE DETROIT JOURNAL HAS STARTED ANOTHER STORY VARYING GREATLY IN CHARACTER AND CLAIMING TO BE AUTHORIZED BY YOURSELF CAN YOU WIRE US OUR EXPENSE WHICH IS THE AUTHORIZED STORY OF YOUR LIFE.

In March or April 1915 Chaplin had given an interview to a representative of the *San Francisco Bulletin*, Rose Wilder Lane at the Niles Essanay studio. Subsequently to publication in the newspaper, Mrs Lane's manuscript was acquired by an entrepreneur called Guy Mayston. The original story was augmented with colourful invented detail. Mayston's agent interested the New York publishers, Bobbs Merrill, in the book, and they went ahead with publication. The only notification that reached Chaplin was a telegram so casual in tone that little note was taken of it in the studio office, though the photographs requested in it were duly supplied. The telegram was dated 10 July 1916:

> WE HAVE ACCEPTED AND SHALL PUBLISH AS QUICKLY AS POSSIBLE THE STORY OF YOUR LIFE CAN YOU SEND US PHOTOGRAPHS OF YOURSELVES AS A BOY YOUR FATHER MOTHER AND BROTHER ALSO OF THE STUDIO IN WHICH YOU ARE NOW WORKING ANY ASSISTANCE YOU WILL GIVE WILL BE APPRECIATED.

Within two months of this, and without any further word passing between publisher and alleged 'author', *Charlie Chaplin's Own Story* was printed and ready for publication. As early as 20 September however it was clear that Bobbs Merrill were girding themselves for some kind of trouble. An official of the company called D. L. Chambers telegraphed a colleague, Samuel Dorsey, in Los Angeles:

CONTRACT FOR CHARLIE CHAPLIN'S STORY WAS SIGNED BY GUY MAYSTON OF SAN FRANCISCO AS OWNER OF THE MANU-SCRIPT IT GUARANTEES US AGAINST ALL CLAIMS CURTIS BROWN MAYSTONE'S AGENT IN NEW YORK SAYS WE ARE FULLY PROTECTED IN OUR RIGHTS NOTICE OF AN ACCEPT-ANCE OF THE STORY AND INTENTION TO PUBLISH WAS WIRED CHARLIE CHAPLIN JULY 10TH.[15]

This might be thought a rather broad interpretation of the July telegram. Towards the end of September Chaplin came by a copy of the book, and both he and Sydney were outraged, not least by the plain untruths of the title page: 'The faithful recital of a romantic career, beginning with early recollections of boyhood in London and closing with the signing of his latest motion picture contract ... The subject of this biography takes great pleasure in expressing his obligations and his thanks to Mrs Rose Wilder Lane for invaluable editorial assistance.' The subject was anything but grateful, in fact. The book began with an account of Chaplin's birth in a small town in France. (It may be that in his early days in movies Chaplin himself had laid claim to a French birthplace to satisfy reporters who wanted something more romantic for their public than the hard realities of Kennington.) Mrs Chaplin was described kindly, but Charles Chaplin Senior was depicted as a drunken brute. Chaplin's early employers were as unjustly dealt with. The eminently respectable John William Jackson was transformed into a kind of Fagin, who pursued little Charlie with dogs when he ran away to London. *Casey's Court Circus* became 'fifteen ragged, hungry-looking, sallow-faced boys desperately being funny under the direction of a fat greasy-looking manager who smelt stongly of ale'. Presumably intended to represent poor Will Murray, he was named 'Mr Casey' (who, of course, had never existed). Inevitably the *Casey's Court Circus* company rehearsed in 'a very dirty dark room', and dressed in 'a dirty makeshift dressing room in a cheap East End music hall', where the audience threw vegetables. So much for the Moss and Thornton tour.

Karno, in his turn, became Carno; and Dr Walford Bodie, the toast of the halls, became

Doctor Body, a patent-medicine faker, who was drawing big crowds on the London street corners and selling a specific for all the ills of man and beast at a shilling a bottle. Watching him one afternoon I was seized with the great idea – I would let the manager rehearse me all he jolly well liked, but when the opening night came I would play Doctor Body as he really was – I would put on such a marvellous character delineation that even the lowest music-hall audience would recognize it as great acting and I would be rescued by some good manager and brought back to a West End theater . . .

The book is full of such romantic and misleading nonsense, which has nevertheless continued to supply and confuse gullible Chaplin historians for seven decades.

On 1 October Chaplin's New York lawyer, Nathan Burkan, wrote to Bobbs Merrill's lawyers, Lockwood and Jeffery, informing them that Chaplin had instructed him to institute proceedings

to prevent the publication and sale of this work on the grounds that it is not his autobiography, as the work is advertised, that it is purely a work of fiction, holding him to public ridicule and contempt, and that it reflects upon the memory of his late lamented father and is libel on several men of excellent reputation.

Mr Chaplin informs me that he has never authorized or consented to the use of his name, picture or portrait in connexion with this work and that he never acknowledged the publication thereof.

The same day Burkan wrote in a similar vein to Bobbs Merrill themselves, adding: 'Mr Chaplin's father, who was a lovable character and devoted husband and kind father, is depicted in the work as a drunken sot who brutalized and neglected his wife and family. Several characters represented as being employers of Mr Chaplin in his early days are purely fictitious and are not known to Mr Chaplin.' Burkan perhaps exaggerated the domestic virtues of the elder Charles Chaplin. He threatened an injunction to prevent publication but was evidently cautious, for he wrote to Sydney, also on 1 October:

Please ask Charlie to communicate to the best of his recollections what he told to the lady who called upon him in Niles for an interview.

Will you please get me a copy of the article that appeared in the *San Francisco Bulletin* purporting to be a biography of Charlie. You say this biography was syndicated to a number of papers as an autobiography of Charlie Chaplin. Will you get me a copy of this biography as it appeared in the Harmsworth papers?

On 6 October Mrs Lane herself reappeared in the affair, addressing a lengthy letter to Chaplin in a vein which suggests remarkable ingenuousness:

> It won't require any effort on your part to imagine that the news fell upon me like a thunderbolt, in one way at least . . . You were so very courteous in giving me a great deal of time, and all the information on which to base the story, while I was in Los Angeles, that I have been assuming that your attitude toward me was quite friendly . . .
>
> I'm sure you will feel, in recalling the information you gave me, that this is true, and that I made the best possible use of it in writing the story. Its appeal to the public was tremendous. It not only disposed of any number of wild rumors which, as you know, were afloat about you, but in addition the sympathetic interest of the public in the little boy who had such a hard time to get started in London was greater than that of any of the other successful men whose life stories I have written. Not even excepting Henry Ford or Art Smith, who was the idol of San Francisco during the Exposition.
>
> Your mother, too, made a wonderful appeal, as well as your brother. Truly, I don't believe you realize how very well that story was written, how real you and she and your brother were for the people who read it, and how much it increased your own interest in the eyes of the public here . . .
>
> Your present attitude of course puts me in a perfectly frightful position with the Bobbs Merrill people. I suppose I deserve it for not making sure that the arrangement would be all right with you . . .
>
> I suppose that your feeling is simply that you should have some money from the book if it should appear. It is natural enough to want money, but I wonder if you are not exaggerating the possible profits to be made from book publication? My own profits from it, even if it sold up to the very limit of our expectations, would be only a few hundred dollars – perhaps worth half a day of your time. As matters now stand, it appears that your action will result merely in my losing the amount – which I need not say would make much more of an impression on my bank account than on yours – and also in your losing publicity value of the book, a publicity which even Theodore Roosevelt in his palmiest days was glad to utilize.

Having, however unwittingly, added insult to the injuries committed, Mrs Lane goes on to a rather endearing assessment of her work:

> You've lived a life which makes a corking book. I have written the book – and really, it is no more than true to say that it is a book whose popular appeal is greater than that of a book any other hack writer is apt to write . . .

It is in the interest of both of us to have the book published. I admit it's more to my interest than yours . . . But it is to the interest of neither of us to stop the publication of the book. And if the situation is allowed to develop into a real scrap, we'll both be in the position of the two men who fought over a nut and brought the matter to a judge who ate the nut and divided the shell. I don't see a bit of use in the world in letting the lawyers have the nut, do you?

Yours very sincerely,
Rose Wilder Lane.

Chaplin, not surprisingly, was unmoved by Mrs Lane's appeal. Burkan had meanwhile received a reply from John L. Lockwood of Lockwood and Jeffery, saying that he was waiting for documentation but considered that since Bobbs Merrill had acted in good faith, believing that Chaplin had authorized what Mrs Lane wrote, the rights as sold by Mayston were good. It was Lockwood's view that the remarks about Charles Chaplin Senior were 'quite respectful'.

By the end of November, Bobbs Merrill were seeking a compromise. Burkan telegraphed to Sydney on the 29th:

BOBBS MERRILL WILL NOT PUBLISH CHARLIE CHAPLIN'S OWN STORY WITHOUT HIS WRITTEN CONSENT THEY ARE WILLING TO ELIMINATE HAWKINS AND [MARCUS] LOEW'S NAME AND PAY CHARLIE FIVE PER CENT OF THE RETAIL SELLING PRICE OF BOOK TO BE RAISED TO ONE DOLLAR FIFTY I PERSONALLY THINK IT BAD FORM FOR CHARLIE TO GIVE HIS PERMISSION TO PUBLISH BOOK ON ACCOUNT OF REFLECTION ON YOUR FATHER HOWEVER YOU AND CHARLIE ARE THE BEST JUDGES OF THAT PLEASE WIRE ME WHETHER I SHOULD GO AHEAD AND POSTPONE CONTRACT BOBBS MERRILL UNWILLING TO ACCEPT YOUR PROPOSITION FOR CHARLIE AND MISS WILDER [*sic*] TO COLLABORATE ON WRITING A NEW BOOK REGARDS TO CHARLIE.

The entrepreneur Mayston now attempted to act as go-between, but was as unsuccessful in his attempts to persuade Bobbs Merrill to undertake the cost of a completely new book as he was in persuading Chaplin to allow publication and split the royalties with himself. The matter was settled quite precipitately in mid-December. A New York police magistrate was awarded damages of $35,000 in a libel action against Bobbs Merrill. The firm saw no merit in risking trouble on other fronts, and Lockwood forthwith gave Burkan an undertaking that the book would not be sold without the prior consent of Chaplin.

Valueless as its content is, the book is now rated the greatest rarity in the Chaplin bibliography. The stock was suppressed but not before one or two copies had leaked out to be the bane of film historians. Stan Laurel possessed a copy, which he annotated with corrections and subsequently gave to a Chaplin biographer, John McCabe.

Chaplin still had not finished with the troubles brought by *Charlie Chaplin's Own Story*. As Burkan mentioned in his letter, syndication rights in Mrs Lane's original articles had been acquired by the Harmsworth press; plans for English newspaper publication were already advanced when Burkan stepped in to prevent it. The campaign which now began, to discredit Chaplin for failure to enlist in the British services, appears to have been stimulated by Lord Northcliffe's consequent personal pique. It is true that as early as March 1916 there had been adverse comment in the *Daily Mail* about the war risks clause in the Mutual contract, which specified that Chaplin should not return to Britain during the duration of hostilities and so run the risk of being mobilized in the British armed forces: 'We have received several letters protesting against the idea of Freuler or any other American making a profit on the exhibition in this country of a man who binds himself not to come home to fight for his native land.' In June 1917 Northcliffe went onto the offensive, with an editorial in the *Weekly Despatch*:

Charles Chaplin, although slightly built, is very firm on his feet, as is evidenced by his screen acrobatics. The way he is able to mount stairs suggests the alacrity with which he would go over the top when the whistle blew.

During the thirty-four months of the war it is estimated by Charlie's friends that he has earned well over £125,000. He is contracted for next year's pictures for a sum exceeding £1,000,000 with the First National Exhibitors, a newly formed and wealthy syndicate. Under the contract, Charlie will produce his own pictures and have his own company.

Cable messages have sought to show that Chaplin has invested £25,000 of his earnings in the British war loan, but this has not been confirmed. Chaplin can hardly refuse the British Nation both his money and his services.

If Charlie joined up, as is his duty, if he is fit, at least thirty other British cinema performers of military age who are now performing in the United States would have no excuse for withholding from the British Army . . .

Nobody would want Charlie Chaplin to join up if the Army doctors pronounced him unfit, but until he has undergone medical examination he is under the suspicion of regarding himself as specially privileged to escape the common responsibilities of British citizenship. This thought may not have occurred to the much-boomed film performer, and he will no doubt be thankful that an opportunity for reminding him has been presented by the course of events.

Charlie in khaki would be one of the most popular figures in the Army. He would compete in popularity even with Bairnsfather's 'Old Bill'. If his condition did not warrant him going into the trenches he could do admirable work by amusing troops in billets.

In any case, it is Charlie's duty to offer himself as a recruit and thus show himself proud of his British origin. It is his example which will count so very much, rather than the difference to the war that his joining up will make. We shall win without Charlie, but (his millions of admirers will say) we would rather win with him.

A *Daily Express* article in the same vein carried the headline:

FIGHTING – FOR MILLIONS
Charlie Chaplin Still Faces the Deadly Films.

Chaplin issued a statement to the press:

I am ready and willing to answer the call of my country to serve in any branch of the military service at whatever post the national authorities may consider I might do the most good. But, like thousands of other Britishers, I am awaiting word from the British Embassy in Washington. Meanwhile I have invested a quarter of a million dollars in the war activities of America and England . . .

I registered for the draft here, and asked no exemption or favours. Had I been drawn I would have gone to the front like any other patriotic citizen. As it is I shall wait for orders from the British Government through its Ambassador in Washington.

The British Embassy confirmed:

We would not consider Chaplin a slacker unless we received instructions to put the compulsory service law into effect in the United States and unless after that he refused to join the colours . . .

Chaplin could volunteer any day he wanted to, but he is of as much use to Great Britain now making big money and subscribing to war loans as he would be in the trenches, especially when the need for individual men is not extremely pressing.

There are various ways for one to do one's bit. Certainly the man who subscribes liberally to war loans and the Red Cross could not be said to be a slacker, especially when he follows his subscriptions with an announcement that he will serve in the trenches when called. Obviously, when the compulsory law is not in operation here, where Chaplin has made his home for a number of years, he could not be considered a slacker.

Such statements did not immediately put a stop to the 'slacker' charges. The Draft Board received anonymous reports that Sydney had falsified his age and was eligible for the draft. Sydney was in consequence called before the Board to satisfy them that he was, in fact, over thirty-one. The campaign finally abated when it was reported that Charlie had actually gone to a recruiting office but been turned down by the doctors because he was underweight. For years afterwards Chaplin continued to receive white feathers and anonymous invective for his failure to fight.

These attacks certainly did not come from servicemen. When Chaplin visited England in 1921, one ex-soldier wanted to give him his medals, because, he said, of all he had done for the men at war. 'Charlie is a prime favourite with our gallant soldiers and sailors,' wrote Essanay's English publicist, Langford Reed, 'who feel that the brightness and joy he has brought into their lives outweighs, a million times, any services he might have been able to render as an asthenic little castigator of Huns.'[16] In military hospitals special projectors were fitted up so that Chaplin's films could be projected onto the ceilings for patients unable to sit up. Dr Lewis Coleman Hall, attached to a US Army neurological unit in France, appealed to Chaplin for autographed pictures of himself: 'Please write your name on the photos, the idea being that nearly everyone has seen you in pictures. I will show your picture to a poor fellow and it may arrest his mind for a second. He may say, "Do you know Charlie?" and then begins the first ray of hope that the boy's mind can be saved.'[17] Miracle cures were attributed to the effect of Chaplin's image on the screen. Sam Leonard, General Manager of the United Picture Company of St Helens, Lancashire, wrote:

> Since the war it has been my greatest pleasure to entertain wounded soldiers at my hall. Last week I was showing a 'Charlie Chaplin', and a wounded soldier laughed so much he got up and walked to the end of the hall, and quite forgot he had left his crutches behind. My assistant went after him, and he said, 'That fellow Chaplin would make anyone forget his head. I never laughed so much in my life.'[18]

'If Chaplin had done what was expected of him and answered his country's call to the colours in August 1914, the chances of his surviving the war would have been slight. Chaplin would have been a footnote in film history,' commented Kevin Brownlow, sixty years after the end of the First World War.[19] The smears of Northcliffe and his followers in no way affected Chaplin's popularity with his audience, but they were to hurt him deeply and for many years.

Towards the end of 1916 Chaplin began to change his way of life. He hired a valet-secretary, Tom Harrington, who became, he said, 'the *sine qua non*' of my existence. Harrington was a New Yorker, who had been dresser and handyman to an English comedian, Bert Clark, who worked for a while at Keystone. In 1915 Clark became a partner in the short-lived Chaplin Music Corporation, and brought Harrington with him to take charge of the office. When the office was closed and Clark returned East, Harrington offered to stay on and work for Chaplin. Harrington is glimpsed once or twice in Chaplin films: he was a lean, solemn, ascetic-looking man, who proved not only the ideal gentleman's gentleman, but also helped Chaplin with his choice of reading. It was Harrington who introduced him, as he remembered, to Lafcadio Hearn, Frank Harris and James Boswell.

Sydney persuaded Chaplin that he should have another car, and at the beginning of December Chaplin bought a standard Locomobile tourer, with blue body and white wire wheels. Harrington engaged a chauffeur, a 28-year-old Japanese, Toraichi Kono. Kono came from a well-off middle-class family in Hiroshima, but had emigrated to the United States to avoid a career in the family business after several commercial ventures of his own failed. In the United States he had been dissuaded from a career as an aviator by his young wife, so reconciled himself to working as chauffeur. Kono's efficiency and discretion impressed Chaplin and gave him a preference for Japanese servants: there was to be a succession of them until the outbreak of hostilities with Japan in the Second World War, when the Chaplin domestic staff was interned. Kono himself remained with Chaplin for eighteen years and assumed the role of special confidant and emissary.

Along with the acquisition of a *ménage*, Chaplin's social life was changing. He had continued to be regarded as something of a solitary in Hollywood. Most evenings he would dine with Edna at the Los

Angeles Athletic Club, where he had set up a permanent residence. Occasionally everyone from the studio would go off to a fight after work was done. Totheroh remarked that the unit began to feel him growing away from them socially:

> In the evenings he'd go maybe to Levy's Café or some of those places. He always attended the prize fights, every Tuesday night at Doyle's out in Vernon. All the bunch got together and we used to meet there and afterwards we'd go some place for a glass of beer and a sandwich. He more or less mingled, went to the baseball games; he had the spirit of everybody around him and they did, too. But as soon as he got out of that character of the tramp, making these features, a big change came over him. He didn't mingle around with the bunch any more. He more or less entertained up at his house. And the people that he had associated with no doubt were people of reputation – authors and writers and maybe actors. But he had well-known columnists and different ones up at his house. He'd throw these parties up at his house because he was the center of attraction. He was a great entertainer and he had the floor. He'd entertain them and he just drifted away from the old bunch.
>
> When he went to fights, he had tickets set up. I didn't sit right with the bunch, but I sat a lot of times a couple of rows behind him. It was set up for three tickets: it was Albert Austin, Eric Campbell and Charlie; there might have been a fourth one, but Charlie was the center of attraction there, too. Especially among the fighters; he got to think the world of a bunch of these fighters. Before the fight would start, the first thing they'd go over there – they knew where he sat – and they'd reach out and shake hands with him. They all got to know who he was. Even at baseball games, they'd spot him and you'd see everybody looking down in the box seat – Charlie's there. He was one of the bunch, meeting down at Barney Oldfield's or any place where they all hung out after. Charlie coined a phrase, he'd say, 'How's the light, Rollie?' And I would say, 'Well, maybe we can shoot another scene, couple of scenes. I think the light is better down at Barney Oldfield's.' Meaning that the light beer is better. Maybe he might have been tired or he ran out of ideas, then he'd dismiss the crew.

Dining one evening at Levy's Café, Chaplin was thrilled to be invited to her table by Constance Collier, who had arrived in the United States to appear opposite Sir Herbert Tree in Triangle's film of *Macbeth*. Miss Collier had been one of Chaplin's boyhood heroines when she was Tree's leading lady at His Majesty's Theatre, and he, in his early teens, watched them from the gallery between his own modest theatrical engagements. They took to each other at once, and were to remain friends until Constance's death in 1955. It is possible that it was she who helped him improve his elocution during these early years in Hollywood. She recalled in her own memoirs that he dined with her very often,

> and we would talk about London, and the Lambeth Road, and Kennington, and all the places we had known in our youth. He was a strange, morbid, romantic creature, seemingly totally unconscious of the greatness that was in him. How he loved England! And yet the years he had spent there had been so bitter and full of poverty and sorrow. America had given him all, and his allegiance belonged to her, but in our talks one felt his longing, sometimes, to see the twisted streets and misty days and hear Big Ben chiming over London . . .
>
> Sometimes we would steal down to Los Angeles and have a meal at a cafeteria, and Charlie would wait on me, fetch my coffee and thick sandwiches, or bread and cheese, and we would talk for hours. He was happier this way. It was impossible to go to the big restaurants, as the minute he appeared he was mobbed. Besides, he said he couldn't bear the masses of knives and forks on the table, and the magnificence of the head waiters gave him a feeling of inferiority.
>
> He didn't like luxury in those days. He hated to drive in a car – he said it made him feel nervous – but I expect he has got used to it by this time.
>
> He remembered all the plays and every actor he had seen in England, and described to me how he used to sit in the gallery at His Majesty's whenever he could spare a shilling or two, and would give up his meal for his seat.
>
> He worshipped the theatre and had the same reverence for it as had that other great comedian I had once met – Dan Leno.
>
> One would never have thought of Charlie Chaplin as funny in those long, serious talks we had.
>
> Then – some nights – his mood would quite change, and he would be ridiculous and make me laugh until I was ill. He would pretend to be a German or a Frenchman or an Italian and invent an imaginary language, and keep it up so wonderfully that he really looked like the part he was assuming. He would keep up this mood for hours and insist on answering serious questions with that same absurd accent.[20]

Constance Collier took the young Chaplin's social life in hand, and introduced him to Tree and his young daughter Iris, both of whom initially awed him somewhat, though later they would all go off together on jaunts to Venice beach. Chaplin, noted Constance, 'had the greatest admiration for Herbert Tree, whose eccentricities in the unusual environment of the picture world were more marked than ever.' It was Constance, too, who insisted that he should meet another Triangle player, Douglas Fairbanks, who had just arrived in pictures after some success on the stage. 'They had never met, and one night I took Charles to dinner at Douglas Fairbanks' house. They were a bit shy and self-conscious during the early part of the evening, but from that day on their friendship never wavered.' Near the end of his life, Chaplin said that Fairbanks had been perhaps the only really close friend he had ever known. He was to be an intimate witness to the romance between Fairbanks and Mary Pickford – both at this time in the process of divorcing their previous partners – which resulted in 1920 in the most celebrated of all Hollywood marriages.

Another friendship at this time was with Julian Eltinge, who had come to stardom as a female impersonator and arrived in Hollywood in early 1917 to make three films for Jesse Lasky. Eltinge was amusing, cultured, and five years older than Chaplin, and seems also to have had some influence in broadening his social life.[21]

Chaplin's last four films for Mutual, all made in 1917, remain among his finest. Two, certainly, were masterworks. The first of these was *Easy Street* – 'an exquisite short comedy,' wrote Walter Kerr; 'humor encapsulated in the regular rhythms of light verse.'[22] At the impressive cost of $10,000 Chaplin built the first of those T-junction street sets that were to prove his ideal theatre. The setting has the unmistakable look of South London. Even today Methley Street, where Hannah Chaplin and her younger son lodged, between Hayward's pickle factory and the slaughterhouse, presents the same arrested vista, the cross-bar of the 'T' leading to the grimier mysteries on either side.

The story is a comic parody of Victorian 'reformation' melodramas. The vagrant Charlie wanders into a mission, where he is moved – less by the hymn-singing than by the charms of missionary Edna – to turn over a new leaf. Joining the police force, he is at once posted to the perilous beat of Easy Street, terrorized by the Herculean Eric Campbell. The most effective of Charlie's ploys to conquer the bully and restore peace to Easy Street results when Campbell proves his strength by bending a street lamp in two. Charlie seizes the opportunity thus offered to fit the lamp over the man's head, and operates the gas tap with the expertise of a dentist's anaesthetist.

The production was not without its troubles. On 16 December 1916 the prop lamppost prepared for Campbell's strong-man act buckled of its own accord and injured Chaplin's nose, preventing him from wearing make-up for several days. The Californian rains were particularly persistent that year. The least of the problems to be coped with was that the baby which Charlie nurses in the mission scene stole his moustache. By 1 February, Mutual were obliged to issue a statement explaining the postponed release:

> Owing to the unusual character of the latest Charlie Chaplin production, *Easy Street*, involving so many big scenes which, while they appear to be 'interiors' are 'exteriors', necessitating sun for their success, Mr Chaplin has been compelled to announce the postponement of release of No 9 of the Chaplin series from January 22 to February 5, preferring to delay completion of the comedy until conditions for its successful filming are perfect.
>
> With this announcement of the postponement, Mr Chaplin, while expressing regret at the delay, points out that it is his determination to permit nothing but the best to be released, and he would prefer producing nothing at all to assuming responsibility for poor photography. He remarks incidentally that 30,000 feet of negative have already been used in the effort to perfect 2000 feet of laughs.[23]

Just before the film's release, Chaplin published his reflections upon it:

> If there is one human type more than any other that the whole wide world has it in for, it is the policeman type. Of course the policeman isn't really to blame for the public prejudice against his uniform – it's just the natural human revulsion against any sort of authority – but just the same everybody loves to see the 'copper' get it where the chicken got the axe.
>
> So, to begin with, I make myself solid by letting my friends understand that I am not a real policeman except in the sense that I've been put on for a special job – that of manhandling a big bully. Of course I have my work cut out tackling a contract like that and the sympathy of the audience is with me, but I have also the element of suspense which is invaluable in a motion picture plot. The natural supposition is that the policeman is going to get the worst of it and there is an intense interest in how I am to come out of my apparently unequal combat with 'Bully' Campbell.
>
> There is further contrast between my comedy walk and general funny business and the popular conception of dignity that is supposed to hedge a uniformed police officer.[24]

For his next subject Chaplin settled on *The Cure*, for which he chose a setting similar to Sydney's old Karno hit, *The Hydro*. Chaplin warned the Mutual office, in the same terms as the press release for *Easy Street*, 'Owing to the incessant rains on the coast and because I do not care to risk the chance of a single Chaplin release being in any way below quality, it is impossible to complete *The Cure* according to schedule.'[25]

We can learn more about the genesis of *The Cure*, thanks to the survival of most of the rushes and out-takes, which were analyzed first by Kevin Brownlow and David Gill for the *Unknown Chaplin*. Take 1 shows Chaplin's first conception of the hydro. The forecourt is full of patients; in the centre is a fountain, all ready for future fun. The staff of this 'health' resort are a crumbling bunch, so decrepit that it takes four of them to lift a cane chair. The proprietor of the hydro, played by the diminutive Loyal Underwood, is a pathetic wreck with a hacking cough. By take 17 or earlier Chaplin has made his appearance, at this stage of the game dressed as a bellboy and pushing with difficulty a wheelchair containing Eric Campbell, his gouty foot bound up in a monstrous bandage.

By take 23 he has decided to shift the action originally planned in the forecourt of the hydro to the lobby. Fourteen takes later he has changed his own costume from a bellboy to that of a spa attendant in a white jacket; and the patient in the wheelchair from the volcanic Eric Campbell to a comatose Albert Austin. At this stage, too, Chaplin introduces a wonderful gag. Despairing at the confusion of wheelchairs being pushed all over the place, he sets himself up as a traffic cop, and imposes order on the chaos. At one moment he stops both streams of traffic to permit an excruciatingly decrepit bellhop (played by James T. Kelley, a specialist in such roles) to cross the 'road'.

By take 77 the whole set has been changed. The fountain in the forecourt has been replaced by a well, which clearly provides more comic perils for unwary walkers and in particular for a drunk, played by John Rand with very evident instruction from Chaplin himself. Only seven takes later, Chaplin has been unable to resist the drunk's part, and has taken over Rand's role and costume himself. By this time he has discovered one of those props which always stimulated his invention – a revolving door. One take in particular shows the part that chance could play in his comic creation. The take is spoiled when he inadvertently catches his cane in the revolving door, and jams it. Soon afterwards he begins to introduce the caught cane as a deliberate piece of business.

After the first hundred or so takes Chaplin is into his narrative stride, and the shooting follows very much the progression of the finished film. Charlie, the inebriate, arrives at the hydro and in no time at all has made an enemy of the gouty-legged Eric Campbell, following an encounter in the revolving door, and a friend of Edna, Eric's companion. While the staff interest themselves in Charlie's luggage, which consists of a cabin trunk exclusively stocked with liquor, Charlie unenthusiastically samples the amenities of the place – the massage parlour, the swimming pool and the sauna. Meanwhile the director has ordered his staff to get rid of Charlie's liquor store. It is emptied by accident into the pool, which considerably raises the spirits of the entire establishment.

The highest slate number on the surviving out-takes is 677 and since this shot, though it was never used, was evidently an intended fade-out for the film – Charlie falls into the pool and sinks amid a flurry of bubbles – it is most likely one of the final takes for the film. We can consequently assume that take 622 was made quite late in the shooting period, yet at this stage we find Chaplin once more trying the traffic cop gag. As one of his collaborators said, 'Chaplin had a mind like an attic. Everything was stored away in case it ever came in handy.' Clearly this was too good a piece of business to waste. This time he filmed it wearing his costume of white blazer, slacks and boater. As it survives in the out-takes it is a scene of great comic brilliance, but again it was rejected. As Brownlow and Gill speculate in their commentary to *Unknown Chaplin*, he must have recognized that it could never be in character for Charlie to create, rather than disrupt, order.

The production was held up when Chaplin caught a chill after shooting the swimming pool scenes, but was eventually ready for release on 16 April 1917. The following day's issue of *Photoplay News* declared,

> As the Chaplin specials are unfolded to the public gaze it becomes increasingly apparent that the great comedian is a master of innumerable arts. For instance it was not known until he produced *The Rink* that Charlie could skate like a professional, and it was not until he devised the swimming bath scene in *The Cure* that anyone realized what an expert swimmer he is. In that scene Chaplin dives under the vast bulk of Campbell with the speed and agility of an otter, circles him in the water, sits on his head and nearly drowns him and in other ways disports himself as an expert waterman.

Altogether *The Cure* is certain to enhance Chaplin's popularity for he has never produced anything funnier.

On 24 April Chaplin received a telegram:

CHARLES CHAPLIN,
LOS ANGELES ATHLETIC CLUB.

WE THE UNDERSIGNED BRING SUIT AGAINST YOU FOR SORE RIBS WE SAW THE CURE.
> MARY PICKFORD
> DOUGLAS FAIRBANKS
> MRS CHARLOTTE PICKFORD
> TED HAMMER

In the case of *The Immigrant*, the surviving out-takes enable us to follow in even greater detail the progression of Chaplin's conception. This comic masterpiece, whose qualities of irony and satire and pity survive intact after almost seventy years, took from start to finish a bare two months to make. *The Cure* had been released on Chaplin's twenty-eighth birthday, and he began his new film immediately in an effort to catch up on his production schedule. He had probably already begun production when he told an interviewer,

> I have also long been ambitious to produce a serio-comedy, the action of which is set in the Parisian *Quartier Latin*.
> This theme offers unbounded scope for the sentimental touch which somehow always creeps into my stories. But the trouble is to prevent that touch from smothering the comedy end. There's so much pathos back of the lives of all true bohemians that it is hard to lose sight of it even for a moment and the real spirit of that community is far too human and deeply respected by the world at large for me to even think of burlesquing it.[26]

The Immigrant clearly started out to be this film. Among the first few takes are some establishing scenes representing an artists' café populated by bizarre and extravagant types – men in cloaks and broad-brimmed hats, aquiline women in mannish suits. In a corner of the café, beside the arch that leads to the kitchens, is an unlikely guest, Charlie. He is sitting beside Albert Austin, who was always to be his favourite partner for eating scenes. In this case Austin is a well-dressed diner who is having some trouble with a plate of hot beans. Every time he puts the fork to his mouth he burns himself and starts violently, to the distress of the fastidious Charlie. By take 46, Edna has been introduced into the film and the bean-eating business.

At this time Chaplin averaged around twenty shots a day, so that we can assume that this was at the start of the third day of shooting. Edna was shot sitting alone and disconsolate at a table across the other side of the archway, then side by side with Charlie, having supplanted Albert Austin. The principal business on which they worked at this time involved Charlie's sharing his plate of beans with the apparently impecunious Edna. Edna was still eating beans more than a hundred takes later, and this was reckoned good for a publicity story, which appeared in the newspaper towards the end of production:

CONTINUOUS DIET OF BEANS CAUSES A REAL GAGGING

Edna Purviance Forced to Consume
This Viand in Latest Chaplin Comedy

Edna Purviance, Charlie Chaplin's vis-a-vis running mate, hopes something happens to the bean crop this year. The reason is this: the play on which they are now working opens in a cheap restaurant and shows her a famished orphan whom Charlie is regaling with copious plates of beans.

So far so good, but there were so many trying gags to be worked out that retake after retake was necessary and, as the days follow close upon each other without a cessation of the eternal bean diet, Miss Purviance began to experience difficulty in even getting the succulent Boston viand up to her mouth.

'It's no use, Charlie,' she announced. 'I simply can't swallow another one.'

'Great Scott!' exclaimed Charlie. 'How am I going to get my gagging over, then?'

'I give it up,' replied Edna. 'If you'd been gagging as much as I have for the past five days you wouldn't want to gag any more.'[27]

The out-takes reveal that Chaplin began shooting these scenes with James T. Kelley playing the decrepit waiter who served Charlie and Edna. By around the fourth day, however, he had devised some new comedy business which required a heavyweight, so he recast Henry Bergman in the role of waiter. The sequence involves Charlie's inability to pay his bill. He and Edna look on in alarm as a tipsy diner who has failed to pay his bill is set upon and mercilessly pummelled by the restaurant staff, led by Bergman. Charlie feels in his own pocket, and discovers in mounting panic that his one and only coin has slipped through a hole. By the time he spies it on the floor, the waiter has firmly planted his foot on it and is already writing out the bill. Charlie succeeds in retrieving his coin from the floor and grandly hands it to the waiter, who promptly bends it between his teeth to establish that it is a particularly pliable counterfeit.

Chaplin continued to shoot, re-shoot and vary these scenes for more than a week before he discovered what was wrong with them. Bergman clearly lacked the menace necessary to give the dramatic-comic motive for Charlie's fear. Chaplin scrapped all the previous material and recast Eric Campbell in the role, wearing his most diabolic false eyebrows. According to conventional standards and economies of film production in 1917 this kind of decision, the courage to scrap a week's work (when many producers were making entire two-reel comedies in that time) was without precedent. Indeed Chaplin's whole approach of making take after take until he was totally satisfied with the result was something new in Hollywood. For most directors, shots were only retaken if something had gone noticeably wrong. More than two years after *The Immigrant*, D. W. Griffith made his ambitious *Broken Blossoms* practically without a second take. For a director like Griffith to shoot any scene more than once would have been an admission of inadequate rehearsal and error. For Chaplin it was an assertion that it was always possible to do better.

Having cast Campbell as the waiter Chaplin discovered a new role for Bergman, as a flamboyant artist. This new character offered a perfect denouement to Charlie's drama of paying the bill. The artist notices Edna, is instantly taken by her beauty, and joins the couple at their table to ask if he may paint her portrait. Magnanimously he attempts to pay their bill along with his own, but Charlie declines the offer – politely and too insistently, since the artist takes him at his word and contents himself with paying his own bill. Charlie deftly solves the problem. The waiter brings a plate with the change, which the artist disdainfully pushes aside as a tip. Charlie niftily slips his bill under the coins and airily pushes it to the waiter, who is baffled to see his tip thus diminished to pennies. The scene neatly wrapped up the sequence, but the artists' café had not provided enough material for a full two-reeler.

Chaplin needed something else for his story, and evidently found it by asking himself where Edna has come from, and how it is that she and Charlie recognize each other in the restaurant. He found his answer: they are both migrants, and have met on an immigrant ship. The ship immediately set his comic imagination whirling. He revived the rocker idea he had used for *Shanghaied*, and created a convincing rolling deck and steerage-class mess room. Some scenes were actually taken on a boat at sea; for these Rollie Totheroh devised a pivot so that the camera could swing on the tripod, controlled by a heavy pendulum. The storm-tossed vessel was peopled by a weird and sorry lot of migrants: Albert Austin as a sea-sick Russian, Henry Bergman as a stout peasant woman and Loyal Underwood as her diminutive spouse, whom she dandles like a child and sticks over the side of the ship when he, too, is sick. Charlie also falls in with a murderous bunch of card-sharpers; the out-takes show that he originally intended a dice game, but changed his mind since the card game offers the opportunity for an amusing gag of high-speed shuffling which anticipates Monsieur Verdoux's dexterity in counting bank notes.

Among the passengers, Charlie meets Edna and her aged mother, played by Kitty Bradbury, a sweet-faced old character actress. Mother is robbed of all their savings while she is sleeping, but Charlie consoles the weeping Edna by stuffing into her purse all the money he has won at cards — all, that is, except for one note which he providently retrieves for his own needs. A passing purser, inevitably, sees him taking the note back, and threatens to put him in irons until Edna intercedes.

The café scenes represent takes numbers 1 to 384; the boat scenes numbers 385 to approximately 730. Knowing Chaplin's method of work in subsequent films, we can safely assume that there would have been a pause of a week or two between the two stages of the shooting, while he edited together the first sequence or 'faction', as the usage was on the Chaplin unit. There would have been a comparable break for editing after the complexity of the boat shooting. A final group of some thirty takes reveals Chaplin dexterously tying up his narrative into the beautifully structured two-act whole that *The Immigrant* was to become.

First (takes 737 *et seq.*) he films the exterior of the café, and Charlie finding a coin on the pavement. This provides an ideal transition between the ship and the city scenes, and motivates the hitherto broke Charlie's entrance into the café. Next (743 *et seq.*) he re-shoots the scene inside the café, where he first sees and recognizes Edna at the opposite table. He has added one detail: Charlie now observes that

Edna's handkerchief is edged with black. Nothing more is needed to tell us that since the boat trip Edna's mother has died. Chaplin also took the opportunity to temper sentiment with comedy: as Charlie gazes rapt and blissful into Edna's eyes, his beans fall from his knife into his coffee cup.

In a few takes around number 763 Chaplin invented a scene which was outrageous in its irony, and remains to this day astounding. As the sequence appears in the finished film, we see a distant view of the Statue of Liberty. A title announces 'Arrival in the Land of Liberty'. On the deck of the boat the huddled masses stand – and the immigration authorities suddenly arrive to throw a rope around them, as if they were so many cattle. (One of the out-takes for this last shot contains an unrehearsed moment: the extras are clearly not acting to order, and Charlie the Tramp is suddenly transformed into Chaplin the director, turning on them in sudden rage.)

After this there remained only a couple more shots to be made. In a charming little scene, Charlie drags the bashful Edna to the registry office. On the doorstep Charlie's ebullience provokes the unspoken rebuke of a solemn clerk, played by Chaplin's new valet, Tom Harrington.

At this time, at the beginning of June 1917, there were some changes at the Lone Star Studio. John Jasper succeeded Henry Caulfield as general manager, and in turn Jasper recruited Carlyle T. Robinson, whom he had known when they both worked at the Horsley Studios in 1915, as publicity director. Originally a journalist, Robinson was one of the first generation of Hollywood publicists. He was to remain with Chaplin for the next fourteen years. Before Robinson's appointment any publicity stories had been written by Fred Goodwins, an old English vaudeville acquaintance of Chaplin's who had some newspaper experience and appeared in several Essanay and Mutual films.

When Robinson reported for work at the Lone Star Studio he found that Chaplin was away for a few days while a new set was being built.

> This allowed me to familiarize myself meanwhile with my new job. One of the first things I discovered was that Chaplin was a very difficult person to meet, even within his own studio. I learned also that it was absolutely forbidden for strangers to penetrate into the studio, that the star did not

like journalists, and did not at all wish to be bothered by old friends, even those who had known Charlie Chaplin when he played in the English music halls.

I discovered that he liked to be called Charlie and hated to hear himself called 'Mr'. I discovered that his hours were very irregular, and most of his demands impossible to satisfy, that he had very strong likings and even stronger hatreds, that anyone whom he seemed to prefer among the studio employees was always the most disliked by the rest, that he had not the least idea of time, that although he was theoretically an employee his prestige was such that he had the real right to decide ultimately who would work or who would not work at the studio.[28]

Robinson was struck – as others were later to be – by the jealousies among the male members of the unit, and was surprised that Chaplin himself appeared unaware of them. He was also astounded by the daily ceremonial attending Chaplin's arrival at the studio, which began with the cry, 'He's here!'

Instantly everyone stopped whatever they were doing. Actors, stage-hands, electricians, everybody stood in line, at attention. Then Chaplin entered the studio gates.

All this comedy seemed to me quite absurd. They might just as well have blown a trumpet or fired a cannon, I thought.

He arrived in a big sports car with black coachwork, very luxurious. Two men were seated in front: one, tall and thin, jumped out of the car first. The other was a Japanese. The tall thin man ran round the car and opened the door. Chaplin stepped out, dressed in a long overcoat with an astrakhan collar. He was hatless. He slowly crossed the studio yard, with the tall man at his heels, while the Japanese chauffeur put the car away.[29]

Robinson asked the studio typist, Miss Roberts, if the same ceremony happened every day. 'Oh yes,' she told him, 'the whole gang does that for a gag. Charlie has no illusions, but he adores it!'[30]

The first day that Chaplin was back at the studio, Robinson was asked to join a screening of the 'Land of Liberty' scene from *The Immigrant* in the studio projection room.

I had a curious impression when I entered the room. From the people scattered around the screening room there emanated such an absence of friendliness that it verged on hostility. I was instantly aware of their dislike. There were two rows, each of half a dozen chairs. In one corner a man stood at a table with a pencil and paper.

I chose a chair near the door. No one introduced me to my new boss. I felt very embarrassed . . .

When the lights went on again, Charlie addressed me:

'What do you think of all that?' he asked me, with a pronounced Cockney accent.

'Very funny and very realistic,' I answered.

'Do you find anything shocking in it?'

'Not that I can recall.'

Chaplin thereupon turned to the man on his left, who spoke with a strong accent similar to his own. From his remarks I understood that he was the one who had criticized the scene. Charlie pointed to me: 'So you see, he didn't find anything wrong with it. It shocks you because you see too much in it. But I'm sure there will not be any difficulties with the public.'

Of course I had no idea what they were talking about. Later I learned that the one who had criticized Chaplin had claimed that the public would not like his showing the Statue of Liberty in this way. The scene was kept in the final version of the film, and there was never the least complaint.[31]

Robinson was to be embarrassed in the early days of his employment by his new boss's quirks. The same night as this screening Robinson saw Chaplin with Edna in a restaurant and greeted him amiably, only to be cut dead (much to his embarrassment since he had been boasting to his table companions of his prestigious new job). Some days later some English trades unionists were guests at the studio. One of them was whistling while Chaplin was trying to work, whereupon Chaplin turned angrily on Robinson, accusing *him* of being the whistler. Afterwards Robinson asked him if he really believed him to be the culprit. 'Oh, of course not. But I had to use that little trick. I couldn't tell off my guest myself, and that's why I made it your responsibility!'

Robinson hardened himself against such embarrassments, and at the same time developed a high regard for his employer's dedication:

I was only really able fully to appreciate the little man's energy after the final scene of *The Immigrant* had been shot. It was then a matter of eliminating the thousands of metres of excess film that had been exposed.

The Immigrant had to be reduced to a length of 1800 feet before being handed over to the distributors. Now he had shot more than 40,000 feet of film! For four days and four nights, wihout taking any rest, Chaplin cut the film. He would view the same scene fifty times in succession, cutting four inches here, a foot there! One collaborator assisted him, another simply watched. Rollie Totheroh, his cameraman, was the assistant, and I was the 'observer'.

By the time the film had been definitively brought to the requisite length, and was wholly approved by Chaplin, the great comedian's best friends would certainly not have recognized him. His beard had grown several centimetres. His hair was tangled. He was dirty, haggard and collarless. But his film was finished.[32]

The Immigrant was released on 17 June. Four months were to elapse before the next Chaplin release – the longest interval between pictures since the start of his film career. After completing *The Immigrant* Chaplin and Sydney went to San Francisco for a holiday. On their return the unit moved to location on the Sierra Madre coast, where most of the first two hundred takes of *The Adventurer* were made. Shooting there must have extended into August, since it was reported in the press that on 11 August Chaplin dived into the rough seas off Topango Canyon to save a seven-year-old girl from drowning. The child, Mildred Morrison, daughter of a stockbroker, had been swept off a rock by a wave whilst watching the Chaplin company at work. There was a more serious interruption to production a week or so later, when Edna was admitted to the Good Samaritan Hospital with an unspecified illness.

The scenes shot on the coast, which were to provide the opening sequence of the film, were of inspired comic virtuosity; a series of complex and beautiful variations as Charlie, in prison stripes, attempts to elude the pursuit of a troupe of prison warders. After this, and after Edna's recovery, Chaplin spent some weeks and more than 300 takes on a sequence of a party in a rich house where Charlie, now in elegant evening dress, flirts with the daughter of the house, Edna, under the angry eyes of her jealous suitor, Eric Campbell. To judge from the unavailing effort to work out a gag involving a seductive Spanish dancer, and another with a hot steam radiator – neither of which remain except as hints in the finished film – Chaplin was going through a period of comparative creative block.

One gag in this sequence is of particular interest since Chaplin himself analyzed it in detail in an article in *American Magazine* (most likely, to judge from the style, transcribed by his friend Rob Wagner from Chaplin's ideas):

> . . . all my pictures are built around the idea of getting me into trouble and so giving me the chance to be desperately serious in my attempt to

appear as a normal little gentleman. That is why, no matter how desperate the predicament is, I am always very much in earnest about clutching my cane, straightening my derby hat and fixing my tie, even though I have just landed on my head.

I am so sure of this point that I not only try to get myself into embarrassing situations, but I also incriminate the other characters in the picture. When I do this, I always aim for economy of means. By this I mean that when one incident can get two big, separate laughs, it is much better than two individual incidents. In *The Adventurer* I accomplished this by first placing myself on a balcony, eating ice cream with a girl. On the floor directly underneath the balcony, I put a stout, dignified, well-dressed woman at a table. Then, while eating the ice cream, I let a piece drop off my spoon, slip through my baggy trousers, and drop from the balcony onto this woman's neck.

The first laugh came at my embarrassment over my own predicament. The second, and the much greater one, came when the ice cream landed on the woman's neck and she shrieked and started to dance around. Only one incident had been used, but it had got two people into trouble and had also got two big laughs.

Simple as this trick seems, there were two real points of human nature involved in it. One was the delight the average person takes in seeing wealth and luxury in trouble. The other was the tendency of the human being to experience within himself the emotions he sees on the stage or screen.

One of the things most quickly learned in theatrical work is that people as a whole get satisfaction from seeing the rich get the worst of things. The reason for this, of course, lies in the fact that nine tenths of the people in the world are poor, and secretly resent the wealth of the other tenth.

If I had dropped the ice cream, for example, on a scrubwoman's neck, instead of getting laughs sympathy would have been aroused for the woman. Also, because a scrubwoman has no dignity to lose, that point would not have been funny. Dropping ice cream down a rich woman's neck, however, is, in the minds of the audience, just giving the rich what they deserve.

By saying that human beings experience the same emotions as the people in the incidents they witness, I mean that – taking ice cream as an example – when the rich woman shivered the audience shivered with her. A thing that puts a person in an embarrassing predicament must always be perfectly familiar to an audience, or else the people will miss the point entirely. Knowing that the ice cream is cold, the audience shivers. If something was used that the audience did not recognize at once, it would not be able to appreciate the point as well. On this same fact was based the throwing of custard pies in the early pictures. Everyone knew that custard pie is squashy and so was able to appreciate how the actor felt when one landed on him.

Chaplin completed shooting the material for his party sequence by take 550, and devoted the next 150 takes to filming a sequence in which, his imposture having been discovered, he is chased around the house by prison warders and eventually makes his escape. The sequence provided an exciting climactic finish to the film. As with *The Immigrant* Chaplin left to the end the problem of tying up the separate parts of the film – the opening chase and escape of Charlie the convict, and Charlie's subsequent appearance as an imposter in a grand house. His solution was a sequence in which Charlie, having swum around the coast to safety, comes upon a catastrophe at a jetty. Edna's mother has fallen into the sea. When the cowardly Campbell refuses to go in after her, Edna dives in. Charlie arrives at the opportune moment to rescue Edna and, with rather less enthusiasm, her mother. Campbell has meanwhile himself tumbled into the water, but when Charlie far too gallantly rescues him too, he brutally pushes Charlie under the water. Unconscious, Charlie is fished from under the jetty by Edna's Japanese chauffeur, who drives him back to Edna's house. Charlie wakes next morning in a luxurious bed, though he is momentarily alarmed to find himself wearing striped pyjamas and gazing through the bars of an iron bedstead.

The car used in the sequence was Chaplin's own new Locomobile, and the handsome young chauffeur was Kono. This was to be Kono's only appearance on the screen. When his wife saw the film she protested. To work as a chauffeur was one thing but to play the movie actor was altogether too demeaning for a Japanese of respectable family.

The out-takes from *The Adventurer* provide a lively glimpse of the way that, even on the Chaplin set, there were unforeseen hazards. A gag in the jetty scene involves the unconscious Campbell being placed on a stretcher laid with one end to the edge of the jetty. Charlie busily takes up the other end of the stretcher, unaware that he is precipitating Campbell over the edge and into the sea. They had reckoned without Campbell's massive belly, which wedged firmly beneath the lowest rail of the fence and refused to budge.

The Adventurer was to be the last screen appearance of Eric Campbell, who has taken his place in screen history as Chaplin's ideal heavy opponent. Campbell's life during the period of production had been eventful. On 9 July his wife died. While travelling to make arrangements for the funeral, the actor and his daughter Una were injured in a car accident – Campbell had a weakness for fast cars. On or about 1 August, Carlyle Robinson introduced him to a young woman called Pearl Gilman, whose sister Mabelle was a *Floradora* sextet girl and married to a millionaire steel magnate, W. E. Corey. After a five-day courtship, Campbell and Pearl were married at the home of Mrs Elsie Hardy.

The couple planned a honeymoon in Honolulu in December, following completion of *The Adventurer*, but a few weeks after the wedding Pearl was suing her husband for separation maintenance. On 20 December Campbell was driving with two girls in his car, allegedly at sixty miles an hour, when it collided with another vehicle at the corner of Wilshire Boulevard and Vermont Avenue. Campbell was killed instantly. Belying his looks, this massive, kindly, child-like Scot was only thirty-seven.

We have a revealing glimpse of Chaplin's personal life at this period in an article that was syndicated in the press at the time he was at work on *The Vagabond*. The article is unsigned, but it reveals a fairly privileged insight and was probably the work of Terry Ramsaye in his role as Mutual's press chief:

> What are his diversions, his hobbies, his amusements when he leaves the studio? If you were to drop into Chaplin's home in Los Angeles some evening, you might be surprised to find him playing a selection from *Carmen* or *La Bohème* on his violin. Not only is Chaplin an exceptionally good violinist, but he is a composer of music as well. A number of his pieces have already found favor with the music loving public, particularly the march song he composed especially for the benefit performance held some time ago at the Hippodrome in New York City.
>
> Off the screen Chaplin is a serious-minded young fellow, whose entire time is spent in seeking to better himself in other lines. He doesn't want to remain a funny man in the cinema all his life. He wants to make a name for himself in some other field that will win him just as much fame – and money – as he has earned on the screen. Chaplin is, to some extent, a dreamer.
>
> 'No man or woman,' said the Mutual comedian recently, 'should be satisfied with having won a fortune or fame in one particular line of endeavour. The field is large, and there are opportunities everywhere for the young man of today. But he must work if he expects to climb to the top. Otherwise I am afraid there is not much hope.

DAY BEGINS AT 6.30

Chaplin is just as busy a young man away from the studio as he is in it. He is what may be classed as a systematic worker and a systematic liver. His day begins promptly at 6.30 o'clock every morning. And every night at 10 o'clock, with an exception here and there, he turns off the electric light and gives himself into the hands of Morpheus.

While Chaplin's salary received from the Mutual Film Corporation aggregates $670,000 and his income from various other investments totals many additional thousands a year, he is by no means what may be termed a spender. He lives well but quietly, dresses well, owns several automobiles,* employs a chauffeur, valet and several secretaries. Chaplin believes in [getting] the best and most out of life.

As previously stated, Chaplin's day begins at 6.30 o'clock. At that hour his valet wakes him. Five minutes later he is in his bath. This over with, he places himself in the hands of his barber, sits down to breakfast, spends a half hour with the morning papers and then – a visit to his chiropodist!

HIS OWN CHIROPODIST

It is not generally known that Chaplin employs the service of a chiropodist. Nevertheless such is a fact. Violinists, pianists and others of similar professions have experts who care for their fingers and hands, so why shouldn't Chaplin, whose feet help earn him a princely income each year, have the services of a chiropodist?

This visit over, Chaplin takes a whirl through the Los Angeles park in his car, provided, of course, he has the time. He reaches the studio every morning when he is working, which is practically every day of the year, at 10 o'clock. Once in the studio, Chaplin confers with his studio manager, members of his company and other officials and then doffs his street clothes for his make-up.

A PROLIFIC WORKER

In the studio Chaplin is a prolific worker, for he directs as well as acts. Every set, regardless of its size, is placed under his personal direction. He is an expert in lighting effects and sees to it that everything in this respect is in proper shape before starting work. This completed, he summons his company, rehearses the scenes about to be staged and then becomes the busiest young man imaginable.

Chaplin's day at the studio comprises anywhere from eight to ten hours, depending on the importance of the production he is working on. In many respects Chaplin is a hard taskmaster. He is a great believer in

* This is the only indication that Chaplin had *several* cars at this time. In spring 1917, however, Sydney bought a car for his wife, Minnie – a Mitchell sedan 'which did not have a lot of complicated devices unknown and hard to operate by a woman'.

details and sees to it that every member of his company, from himself all the way down the line, do their parts and do them well.

His day at the studio generally ends about 4 o'clock. A half hour later he is again in his street clothes. But this does not mean that he rushes away from the studio to seek some amusement. Far from it. When the day has closed, so far as the actual work is concerned, Chaplin enters a little private office and lays out the routine for the following day.

Then he leaves for a short spin in his car, generally with his studio manager or some other intimate, and winds up at the Los Angeles Athletic Club, where he is domiciled during his stay in Los Angeles. Until time to dine, Chaplin lounges about the corridors, talking with friends or reading the afternoon papers. Dinner over, Chaplin goes immediately to his room, where he dons his 'gym' suit and repairs to the club's gymnasium. Here he spends an hour each evening boxing, wrestling, tussling with the weight machines and bag punching, followed by a plunge in the pool.

HUNDREDS OF LETTERS

Following this, unless he has an engagement to spend the evening with friends, at a theater, Chaplin remains in his suite, answering the mass of correspondence that reaches him every day from admirers in every section of the universe. Chaplin does not pay much attention to business for most of that is handled by one of his secretaries, whose duties consist of nothing else. Although the letters run into the hundreds on some occasions, Chaplin replies each day to as many as he possibly can.

A letter from a little boy far off in Australia, or from a little girl in equally far off Scotland, receives just as much consideration as does one from his personal representative in New York. If the writer asks for his photograph, Chaplin invariably sends it.*

Chaplin devotes almost two hours every night to his correspondence and the business affairs he must personally take care of, aside from those handled by one of his secretaries. Ten o'clock finds him ready for bed. His valet prepares his bath again and after a cold shower, Chaplin ducks in between the sheets. Within the space of a very few minutes he is fast asleep.**

* This is a surprising statement, since Chaplin was throughout his life a reluctant letter-writer, and very few letters in his hand have survived. However some rough drafts, apparently for letters to be subsequently worked up by a secretary, exist; this may have been the nature of his evening work on correspondence.

** This conflicts with reports that at this period he tended to suffer from insomnia. At the time he began producing for Mutual, he had already installed a dictaphone by his bed at the Athletic Club so that he could record any sudden inspiration in the night. He seems to have retained the dictaphone for many years. Luis Buñuel humorously reported that while preparing *City Lights* Chaplin awoke one morning to find that he had composed Padilla's 'La Violetera' (see page 418).

OUTDOOR RECREATIONS

Chaplin does not smoke nor drink. To be exact, he smoked but one time in his life. He never cared to make another attempt.

The comedian is an expert tennis player and an exceedingly clever dancer.

Of late he has taken up golf and is mastering the intricate points of the game. Motoring is one of his hobbies, but he prefers to let his chauffeur do the driving. Chaplin does not believe in speed – while motoring, of course – rather preferring to move along at a fair rate and drinking in plenty of fresh air. When opportunity permits, Chaplin likes nothing better than to steal off for an hour or so for a little walk by himself in the park.

Like all red-blooded young men, Chaplin delights in the latest of light fiction. He is not what one might call a heavy reader, rather preferring to read slowly and thoughtfully. He has read Shakespeare from beginning to end, is familiar with the works of George Eliot and other noted writers and is a stickler for poetry.

His chief hobby, however, is found in his violin. Every spare moment away from the studio is devoted to this instrument. He does not play from notes excepting in a very few instances. He can run through selections of popular operas by ear and if in the humor, can rattle off the famous Irish jig or some negro selection with the ease of a vaudeville entertainer.

Chaplin admits that as a violinst he is no Kubelik or Elman but he hopes, nevertheless, to play in concerts some day before very long.

The delicacy in omitting any mention of Chaplin's leading lady perhaps confirms that this account originated in Mutual's publicity department. Throughout the Mutual years the affair with Edna was conducted with the utmost discretion. While Chaplin lived at the Athletic Club, Edna stayed at the Engstrom Hotel. They were seen dining together most nights, and most mornings Chaplin would drive past her hotel and pick her up to take her to the studio. The relationship with Edna was the happiest of his early life. Although she was younger, she provided a protective, encouraging and maternal presence in his life. Years afterwards he remembered with affection how, when he was about to go in front of the camera for a scene, she would say to him, 'Go on. Be cute!' Partly out of total confidence in Edna's devotion and partly out of the constant need to test it, Chaplin often treated her in an inconsiderate manner. He later told a friend that she only rebelled once, but that the occasion was alarming. He had been rude to her on the set in some way, and she suddenly flew at him with such fury that he fled to his dressing room and locked himself in. Only after some time did he emerge and make his way apologetically to Edna's dressing room. She had forgotten her anger and only laughed.

At this period Chaplin would still go to a boxing matches or ball games with Totheroh, Bergman and others from the studio. Reporting the excitement of the crowd at the bout between Little Eddie Miller and Young Kitchell at Jack Doyle's, on 19 November 1916, one newspaper observed, 'Even Charlie Chaplin rose on top of his chair and advised the pugilists to "get together".'

In March 1917, too, he was a participant in a memorable ball game played in Washington Park, Los Angeles, beween the Tragics and the Comics. The Tragics were Wallace Reid, William Desmond, George Walsh, 'Gene (Eugene) Pallette, Antonio Moreno, Franklin Farnum, Jack Pickford, Hobart Bosworth and George Behan; the Comics, apart from Chaplin, were Eric Campbell, Charlie Murray, Slim Summerville, Bobby Dunn, Hank Mann, Lonesome Luke (better known in later years as Harold Lloyd), Ben Turpin and Chester Conklin. The umpires were the famous motor racer Barney Oldfield and James J. Jeffries.

The medium which Chaplin had made his own was still regarded as a pretty common and low-class thing. True, a few prestigious works like *La Reine Elisabeth* with Bernhardt, *Cabiria*, *Quo Vadis* and recently the D. W. Griffith epics *Birth of a Nation* and *Intolerance* had turned the attention of a more serious-minded audience to the moving pictures, but comedy was still for the people. On 6 May 1916, however, *Harper's Weekly* published an article that was to have far-reaching influence. Entitled 'The Art of Charles Chaplin' it was written by a distinguished stage actress of the day, Minnie Maddern Fiske:

> It will surprise numbers of well-meaning Americans to learn that a constantly increasing body of cultured, artistic people are beginning to regard the young English buffoon, Charles Chaplin, as an extraordinary artist, as well as a comic genius. To these Americans one may dare only to whisper that it is dangerous to condemn a great national figure thoughtlessly. First, let us realize that at the age of twenty-six Charles Chaplin (a boy with a serious, wistful face) has made the whole world laugh. This proves that his work possesses a quality more vital than mere clowning. Doubtless, before he came upon the scene there were many

'comedians' who expressed themselves in grotesque antics and grimaces, but where among them was there one who at twenty-six made his name a part of the common language of almost every country, and whose little, baggy-trousered figure became universally familiar? To the writer Charles Chaplin appears as a great comic artist, possessing inspirational powers and a technique as unfaltering as Réjane's. If it be treason to Art to say this, then let those exalted persons who allow culture to be defined only upon their own terms make the most of it.

Apart from the qualified critics, many thoughtful persons are beginning to analyze the Chaplin performances with a serious desire to discover his secret for making irresistible entertainment out of more or less worthless material. They seek the elusive quality that leavens the lump of the usually pointless burlesques in which he takes part. The critic knows his secret. It is the old, familiar secret of inexhaustible imagination, governed by the unfailing precision of a perfect technique.

Chaplin is vulgar. At the present stage of his career he is frankly a buffoon, and buffoonery is and always has been tinctured with the vulgar. Broad comedy all the way through history has never been able to keep entirely free from vulgarity. There is vulgarity in the comedies of Aristophanes, and in those of Plautus and Terence and the Elizabethans, not excluding Shakespeare. Rabelais is vulgar, Fielding and Smollett and Swift are vulgar. Among the great comedians there is vulgarity without end. Vulgarity and distinguished art can exist together . . .

Mrs Fiske returned some months later to the subject of Chaplin's art, when she rebuked a drama critic for speaking slightingly of the comedian. Not as well known as her earlier essay, her letter is no less eloquent:

Until I read your article in Sunday's paper I was unaware of the existence of anyone who failed to appreciate the art of Charlie Chaplin. Your passing depreciation is difficult to answer on account of its vagueness. And, of course, I feel the absurdity of my taking up cudgels in defense of an artist whose name and mannerisms are familiar to, and whose art is appreciated by, the people of every nation where moving pictures are shown. If it is true that the test of an artist's greatness is the width of his human appeal, then Charlie Chaplin must be entitled to a place amongst the foremost of all living artists. It is almost unprecedented that a comedian can appeal to the widely different senses of humor possessed by the Anglo-Saxon, Latin, Teutonic, Slavonic and Mongolian races.

Like all true artists, he is a master of light and shade, merriment and pathos, smiles and tears. The manner in which he approaches the object of his affections, realizing the futility of his devotion, is very pathetic. It reminds one of a mongrel who, half boldly, half diffidently, licks one's hand, hoping for a caress but fearing a kick. Nevertheless, Charlie Chaplin's is a brave, dauntless philosophy, for no matter what vicissitudes he may have undergone, he squares his shoulders and walks bravely into the future, ignoring his past troubles. Surely he serves a worthy cause who makes the world brighter and preaches optimism, and I am a unit of the vast multitude grateful for Charlie Chaplin.

In conclusion, let me beg you to reinstate yourself in the estimation of the playgoing public, which I trust you enjoyed before the publication of last Sunday's article. I would suggest, as a preliminary step, a speedy visit to the nearest picture house where a Chaplin picture is being shown. For, obviously, you have never seen him!

Hard on the heels of Mrs Fiske came the playwright Harvey O'Higgins with an article in *The New Republic* of 3 February 1917, entitled 'Charlie Chaplin's Art'. O'Higgins compared Chaplin to a great though little-known circus clown, Slivers, a comedian of 'a penetrating imagination':

He would see the shoelace as anything from an angleworm to a string of spaghetti, and see it and relate himself to it so convincingly that he made you see it as he did. Chaplin performs the same miracle with a walking stick. He will see it – outrageously – as a toothpick, but he will use it exactly as you see toothpicks used at a lunch counter, looking at you with an air of sad repletion, with a glazed eye from which all intelligence has withdrawn, inwardly, to brood over the internal satisfaction of digestive process – absurdly, but with unimpeachable realism. Or he is a clerk in a pawnshop, and a man brings in an alarm clock to pledge it. Chaplin has to decide how much it is worth. He sees it first as a patient to be examined diagnostically. He taps it, percusses it, puts his ear to its chest, listens to its heartbeat with a stethoscope, and, while he listens, fixes a thoughtful medical eye on space, looking inscrutably wise and professionally self-confident. He begins to operate on it – with a can-opener. And immediately the round tin clock becomes a round tin can whose contents are under suspicion. He cuts around the circular top of the can, bends back the flap of tin with a kitchen thumb gingerly, scrutinizes the contents gingerly, and then, gingerly approaching his nose to it, sniffs with the melancholy expression of an experienced housekeeper who believes the worst of the packing-houses. The imagination is accurate. The acting is restrained and naturalistic. The result is a scream.

And do not believe that such acting is a matter of crude and simple means. It is as subtle in its naturalness as the shades of intonation in a really tragic speech.

Chaplin, concluded O'Higgins,

> is on a stage where the slapstick, the 'knockabout', the gutta-percha
> hammer and the 'rough-house' are accepted as the necessary ingredients
> of comedy; and these things fight against the finer qualities of his art, yet
> he overcomes them. In his burlesque of Carmen he commits suicide with
> a collapsible dagger, and the moment of his death is as tragic as any of
> Bernhardt's. His work has become more and more delicate and finished
> as the medium of its reproduction has improved to admit of delicate and
> finished work. There is no doubt, as Mrs Fiske has said, that he is a great
> artist. And he is a great lesson and encouragement to anyone who loves
> an art or practises it, for he is an example of how the best can be the
> most successful, and of how a real talent can triumph over the most
> appalling limitations put upon its expression, and of how the popular eye
> can recognize such a talent without the aid of the pundits of culture and
> even in spite of their anathemas.

Chaplin had become and was to remain a name among the intelligentsia. Reviewing Dukas's *L'Apprenti Sorcier*, Edwin Stone, music critic of the *Los Angeles Times*, compared it complimentarily to Chaplin. So did Heywood Broun reviewing a production of *Gammer Gurton's Needle*, in the *New York Tribune*. Robert Benchley, already a widely syndicated journalist, devoted a humorous column to comparing Chaplin's Tramp with Falstaff. A writer in the *Kansas City Star*, in an article headed 'Have you the Chaplinitis? – Kansas City in the Throes of a Movie Mania Epidemic', attempted seriously to analyze Chaplin's appeal:

> Why should a comedian, whose work is of the broadest slapstick variety,
> attain such a vogue? Why should a film actor, without the aid of the
> comedian's chief asset, humorous lines, be able to send his audiences into
> near hysterics and draw those to the picture houses who will not look at
> other films? Why is Charlie Chaplin so funny to the great majority of the
> public?
> To which it must be answered first of all that he is a master of
> pantomime. Seldom, if ever, does he utter a word in the picture. Emotions,
> thoughts and lines are expressed by his universal power of facial and
> bodily expression. His feet are most eloquent of all.
> In addition to this, he uses every clown trick in the calendar. Every
> device developed by the funny men of the sawdust ring in the years since
> circuses began is employed by Chaplin at some time or other on the
> screen. This in connexion with the agility of an acrobat is another great
> help to his art of laugh creating.
> Another reason may be psychological. Chaplin is such a nonchalant,

happy-go-lucky fellow. His are the same sort of deeds, grotesque and somewhat distorted, maybe, that endear D'Artagnan and his fellow musketeers to the reader, that cause the tales of swashbuckling heroes to stir the blood; and that have fired the imagination and the sympathies since knights errant went forth in search of adventures with lances instead of a bamboo cane and plumed helmets instead of a battered derby.

Commentators of the time were not unanimous in enthusiasm. The *Yale Magazine* was inclined to blame Chaplin for the dearth of good men on the athletic field: 'It is in the upper classes that the lapses begin to occur and students equipped for serious competition for varsity teams are too often lured by that growing indoor sport, the motion-picture show. We find them lingering with Mr Chaplin in *Easy Street.*' Mrs Lillian W. Betts, executive secretary of the Brooklyn Parks and Playgrounds Committee, went further when she told the members of the Womens' Alliance of the Fourth Unitarian Church at Beverley Road, East 19th Street, that Charlie Chaplin was 'a moral menace. His is the low type of humor that appeals only to the lowest type of intellect. I cannot understand how any resident of Flatbush can go to see [him].' (Mrs Betts was at the time crusading for a municipal bath in Flatbush, 'not only for the health of those who need washing, but for the health of those who must necessarily at one time or another come in contact with them.')

Not all the efforts of such zealots could stop the spread of Chaplinitis. Costume balls were in great vogue in 1917 but magazine writers constantly complained that they were spoiled because most of the girls came as Annette Kellerman, and nine out of ten men as Charlie Chaplin. In February 1917 a Charlie Chaplin costume was used as a disguise by a hold-up man in Cincinnati.[33] About the same time the Boston Society for Psychical Research was investigating 'certain phenomena connected with the simultaneous paging of Mr Charles Chaplin, motion picture comedian, in more than 800 large hotels of the United States'. This surprising psycho-pathological phenomenon was supposed to have been observed on 12 November 1916 across the country from the Atlantic to the Pacific coasts, and from the Canadian boundary to the Gulf. Professor Bamfylde More Carew, a member of the society and author of the paper on the phenomenon, pointed out that Chaplin with his 'singular brand of humor' had become an American obsession, and that among young and active minds of the country, Chaplin was a subject of constantly recurrent thought – in fact, the inspiration of widely registered impulse waves plainly to be noted on charts of the society which are perfected from local charts submitted from widely separated localities.

We find beyond peradventure that on the date mentioned, November 12, there existed for some inexplicable reason a Chaplin impulse, which extended through the length and breadth of the continent. In more than 800 of the principal hotels Mr Chaplin was being paged at the same hour. In hundreds of smaller towns people were waiting at stations to see him disembark from trains upon which he was supposed to arrive.

There is no reason to doubt the correctness of scientific proof that constant reiteration of a certain fact or idea will or may precipitate precisely such a phenomenon as that which has resulted from the wide display of Chaplin absurdities in motion picture theatres – a sudden mental impulse manifesting itself simultaneously practically throughout the length and breadth of the land. It is therefore important though the incident in itself appears trivial, to establish the exact extent of the Chaplin wave and, so far as it may be traced, local causerie.[34]

We have two vivid glimpses of how audiences of the time received Chaplin's films. At Christmas 1916 an unprecedented experiment was undertaken at the New Jersey State Prison. A film – inevitably a Charlie Chaplin comedy – was shown to 1200 prisoners in the prison chapel.

Of course there were some among the more recent arrivals at the prison who were more or less familiar with Charlie and his movements and those who knew him only by reputation. There was a great number, however, to whom he was entirely an unknown personage, and for these the film held the largest measure of delight.

It is doubtful if merriment was ever before in the institution's history unloosed in such abundant stores within its grim walls. Men whose faces had become set and hardened through constant contact with the harsh phases of life gave way to smiles when Charlie and his million dollar feet and funny hat and cane ambled into their visions, and they made no effort to subdue their mirth . . .[35]

The *Memphis Tennessee Appeal* (17 June 1917) reported,

The boy or girl who has not picked his or her favourite of the film world is lost forever in the estimation of his friends. Mary Pickford and Charlie Chaplin are household companions. Boys speak to Charlie like he had for years been a companion in arms. It is interesting to hear the conversation carried on with Charlie at some of the suburban picture theatres. The boys call to him and express their approval over certain things that he does and their disapproval of the things that he does not do. They bid him goodnight as though he was present in person. His astral body does the same work on the screen that his physical personality is expected to do.

There was still more concrete evidence of Chaplin's unique appeal in *Photoplay News* on 3 March 1917: several cinema managements reported that after two weeks' run of Chaplin comedies it was necessary to tighten up the bolts in the theatre seats, since the audience laughed so hard that the vibration had loosened them.

A more irksome kind of flattery was the surge of Chaplin imitators at this time. They even included Chaplin's old Karno colleague Stan Jefferson (later Stan Laurel) who was touring the vaudeville circuits with an act called 'The Keystone Trio' in which he imitated Chaplin while two other old Karnoites impersonated Mabel Normand and Chester Conklin. Counterfeit Charlies in films were more damaging. The most persistent Chaplin imitator was the Russian-born Billy West (1883–1975) who made some fifty one- and two-reelers of quite competent quality.

Billy Ritchie (1879–1921) was an old Karno colleague who had originated the part of the drunk in *Mumming Birds* in 1903. Arriving in America in 1905, he continued to specialize in comedy drunk roles, and had a successful stage career for eight years. In July 1914, however, he had the ill luck to fall in with Chaplin's old Keystone enemy, Henry Lehrman, who had just seceded from Sennett to set up the L-Ko Motion Picture Company. Lehrman engaged Ritchie as principal comedian, and persuaded him to adopt a character which, though not an exact imitation of Chaplin, was undeniably Chaplin-esque. Ritchie defended his prior right to this character; a letter from his lawyers dated 2 January 1915 states: 'Ritchie in his statement says that he first used the present make-up (of which he affirms "I am the originator; also of this kind of comedy") in the year 1887.'[36]

The association with Lehrman was unfortunate. Ritchie twice received severe injuries while working on the lot (the second time he was attacked by an ostrich) and died as a result in 1921. He had trusted his financial affairs to Lehrman and had told his widow Winifred and his young daughter Wyn that they would be provided for when he died. In fact they found themselves penniless. Chaplin seems to have had no lasting animus against Ritchie as he had against his other imitators, and the comedian's dependents found a helpful friend in Alfred Reeves, who by the time of Ritchie's death was Chaplin's general manager. Winifred Ritchie supported herself by her skill in making costumes and was to work from time to time at the Chaplin Studio.

In November 1917 Chaplin found himself obliged to file a suit against a number of his imitators. His suit was decribed as 'the most sweeping known to motion picture circles'. Against the Otis Lithograph Company, the Motion Picture Film Company, the Big A Film Company and several individuals he sought a permanent injunction against Chaplin imitations, the suppression of pictures in which he supposedly appeared, and damages amounting to $250,000. Another action against the F.F.F. Amusement Corporation sought the suppression of a spurious Chaplin picture called *The Fall of the Rummy-Nuffs*. A third was directed against the New Apollo Feature Film Company and sought to restrain them from releasing *Charlie in a Harem* and *Charlie Chaplin in a Son of the Gods*. The injunctions were granted in all three cases.

> Chaplin's managers have found a new way to insure the authenticity of his pictures. He will be the first screen artist to sign his plays and his signature will appear at the start of each one.
>
> If Charlie gets his damages, and he certainly appears to deserve them, it will be rather a good thing for the motion picture industry. For where is the incentive for an actor to work and establish a type, if imitators can wait until the type is perfected and appropriate it for their own?[37]

While Chaplin was still at Mutual, there was a startling reminder of his boyhood. In the autumn of 1917, Edna received a letter from Hannah Chaplin's long-lost son by Leo Dryden:

Royal Opera House,
Bombay, INDIA.
September 8th 1917

Dear Miss Purviance,

Kindly excuse the liberty I take in writing to you, but I am sending you this letter in the hope that you will assist me in my hitherto futile attempts to obtain recognition and acknowledgement from my half-brother, Charles Chaplin, for whose Company I believe you are Leading Lady. Now do not throw this letter aside, but kindly read every word very carefully and pay attention to my story, which I will tell you as shortly as possible.

My father is Leo Dryden, the famous British Music Hall Star. I came out to India in January 1912 with his Vaudeville Company, and on his return to England I stayed in India and have been here, in Burma, China, Japan, Straits Settlements, Philippine Islands, Federated Malay States, etc. ever since, touring with various travelling theatrical companies. I am at present the Principal Comedian of the Charles Howitt and A. Phillips Dramatic and Comedy Repertoire Company, which position I have occupied for the last three years or thereabouts. When the Company was in Singapore (Straits Settlements) in September 1915, that is to say, two years ago, I heard from my father for the first time since his return to England from India, and in his letter he mentioned that my half-brother, Charlie Chaplin, had been making a great name for himself in Cinema work in America. Well, when I read this you can imagine my surprise, for my father had always kept the secret of my birth unknown to me, and had always evaded any questions on the subject that I had put to him when a boy. I immediately wrote to my Dad and asked him for further particulars of my birth and of my relationship to Charlie Chaplin, which he sent me in a letter received at Calcutta a few months later. He explained how my mother was a certain Lily Harley, an impersonator of Variety Artistes in her day, with whom he had lived as man and wife, and to whom I had been born, an illegitimate child! He told me how she had been the wife of Charles Chaplin (Senior) who was the father of the present Charlie Chaplin, and how she had lived with another man previously, a certain Sidney Hawke, who was the father of her other son, the eldest, who now calls himself Sid Chaplin! In this way you will see, Miss Purviance, Charlie Chaplin is my mother's only legitimate son, and that Sid and myself are both illegitimate. All this I have since had corroborated by my Aunts Jessie, Ada and Louie, and my Grandfather, who is still alive. They all remember my mother, and Charlie and Sid, so you see I am no imposter, Miss Purviance.

On receipt of Dad's letter I wrote a nice long letter to Charlie (he was with the Essanay Company in Chicago at the time) and sent him my photograph, and told him all about myself and what I was doing in India and the Far East, and of my work with the Howitt-Phillips Company, and congratulated him on his great success in America, and told him that it was not my fault that I had not acknowledged him years ago when he was a poorly paid Comedian in Fred Karno's Company in England, but that I had always been kept in ignorance of the circumstances of my birth, and that I hoped he would be glad to hear from me, but judge my surprise when I didn't get a reply from Charlie. I wrote again, and again, and again, from various places in the Far East when the Company was touring, but still failed to get any acknowledgement from him. Then I wrote to Sid and told him to explain to Charlie, what I had already explained to him time after time, and that was, that it was not my fault that I had not acknowledged him in the old days, and that I did not write to him now that he had made such a success because I wanted any of his money, but because I wanted his FRIENDSHIP and brotherly interest in my work. Sid did not reply either! This was curious, for I had previously heard from a friend of mine in London that when Sid had been playing at the Empress Theatre, Brixton, London, in one of Fred Karno's Companies, he had particularly asked after me, and had wondered where I was.

And so, Miss Purviance, this ridiculous farce has continued for two solid years! Neither Charlie or Sid will acknowledge me as their own flesh and blood! For Charlie there might be some excuse, for LEGALLY I am nothing to him, except an illegitimate half-brother. But I am surprised at Sid's conduct, for HE IS IN THE SAME POSITION AS REGARDS HIS RELATIONSHIP TO CHARLIE AS MYSELF! If Charlie has seen it fit to publicly acknowledge Sid as not only his half-brother, but his BROTHER, and allowed him to use his name too, then surely he can at least ACKNOWLEDGE me, his other half-brother? I don't want his money, I only want his friendship and brotherly interest and encouragement. Surely I am not asking much?

And so, Miss Purviance, I am asking you to intercede with Charlie on my behalf, and let me know what he says. I am sure that I have acted in a perfectly honourable and straightforward manner throughout the whole proceedings, and I am only asking for a little courteous treatment. I am enclosing you a couple of photographs of myself impersonating Charlie, in which you will see the striking family resemblance, although on account of my nose being rather longer than Charlie's, I am more like Sid in features, though not so stout, for I gauge that he is stout by some of his 'Keystone' pictures that I have seen. I also send you one of my private photos, which I hope you will accept with my very best wishes and sincere regards. All three of us have good teeth, you will notice, though Charlie's are better than Sid's and mine.

I celebrated the twenty-fifth anniversary of my birthday last month (August the thirty-first – last day) and begin to feel quite old and responsible. I am like my father in disposition, very ambitious and determined, and like him have made what little reputation I have amongst the theatrical world in India and the East, entirely on my own merits. My Dad is not ashamed to acknowledge that he started as a singer in the streets, and has had to work his way up to the top. Of course he is getting on in years now (fifty-four or thereabouts) and cannot command the high salary he once used to. No doubt you have heard some of his famous songs: The Miner's Dream of Home, which all Britishers sing on New Year's Eve throughout the world where the English language is spoken: India's Reply: Bravo! Dublin Fusiliers (written at the time of the Boer War); Josephine (written on the famous Napoleonic play 'A Royal Divorce');

The Skipper's Daughter; Mercia (written on the famous play 'The Sign of the Cross') and a host of others, most of his own writing and composition.

Well, My Dear Miss Purviance, I will not bore you further with my letter but leave myself entirely in your hands. Please do your best for me in your chat with Charlie. Explain things as I have explained them to you, and then write and tell me what he has to say on the matter.

Trusting to be favoured with your friendship,

Believe me,

Very Sincerely Yours,

Wheeler Dryden
(Son of the famous Leo Dryden and half-brother of
Charlie Chaplin).

P.S. Send your reply to:- c/o Thos. Cook & Son, Calcutta, India. It will be re-directed to where I am at the time.

It is unlikely that the gentle and generous Edna failed to respond to so touching an appeal. Certainly Chaplin and Sydney were eventually to recognize their long-lost half-brother. In the mid 1920s he visited Hollywood and was reunited with the mother from whom he had been snatched more than thirty years before. Subsequently he assisted Sydney on an abortive project to establish a production organization in England. In 1939 he was to become a regular member of the staff of the Chaplin Studio, where he remained until Chaplin's final departure from the USA.

It was about this time that Chaplin and Edna began to drift apart. They had been so close and dependent that it is hard to see what led Edna, apparently so loyal and loving, to be unfaithful. Was it perhaps that like other women after her she eventually succumbed to jealousy over the one insuperable rival, the ruling passion in Chaplin's life, his work; and wanted to retaliate? Reflecting on the matter in his autobiography, nearly half a century after the event, Chaplin recalled, 'I blamed myself for having neglected her at times.'

The autobiography makes clear the pain he felt at the break, and his forlorn hope of a reconciliation – difficult as that was with his need for exclusive and undivided love. Even so he could see an element of comedy in the circumstances in which he discovered Edna's infidelity. In 1917 they had begun to enter more into the social life of Hollywood, with the unavoidable dinners and galas in aid of the Red Cross and other war charities. Unused to this kind of gathering,

Edna tended to become jealous when other women monopolized Chaplin, and devised an innocent if eventually rather irritating ruse. She would disappear, stage a faint and on coming round ask for Chaplin. One night however, at a party given by the beautiful actress Fanny Ward, she asked instead for Thomas Meighan, a Hollywood actor just coming into vogue at that moment. Ten years older than Chaplin and married, Meighan had trained as a doctor, but then embarked on a long stage career before arriving in pictures. Chaplin was not unreasonably suspicious and jealous. There was a showdown (during which Edna hurt him by saying there was nothing that need prevent them from being 'good friends') and a reconciliation, but subsequently Chaplin found that Edna was still seeing Meighan. From this time the most fulfilling love of Chaplin's early life was at an end.

The loss was no less to Edna herself. The affair with Meighan, such as it was, was brief. Afterwards, though their working relationship apparently continued as cordial and fruitful as before, Edna never again sought to obtrude upon Chaplin's private life. Her devotion, though, undoubtedly revived and survived. She never married. To the end of her life she continued painstakingly to collect every newspaper item about Chaplin's activities, and this touching archive and testimony of affection, which also includes Wheeler's letter, survives in the collection of Inman Hunter.

Alphabeticature Self-portrait by Wheeler Dryden

7

Penalties and rewards of independence

The Adventurer concluded the contract with Mutual. Unlike the Essanay relationship, it ended amicably on both sides: the company had sagely remained patient through the increasingly lengthy delays between releases. Mutual in fact offered a million dollars for eight more films, but Chaplin realized that he needed still greater independence if he was to achieve the standards of which he knew he was capable. Sydney was again sent off shopping for a new contract. On the way to New York in April he stopped off in Chicago and spoke to the press:

All the big film companies are now negotiating with me for Charlie's services, and I am just waiting for the best offer. We are in no hurry but I hope to be able to sign him up before leaving New York this time.

The best offer we have had so far is $1,000,000 for eight pictures. We are also considering forming our own producing company, but haven't been able to arrange satisfactory releasing arrangements, so probably will not enter the field as producers for several months.

There is one thing that will be stipulated in the articles of all Charlie Chaplin contracts hereafter, and that is that Charlie be allowed all the time he needs and all the money for producing them the way he wants. No more of this sixty-mile-an-hour producing stuff will be seen in the Chaplin films from now on. Charlie has made enough money now so that he doesn't have to worry. He is able to either dictate his own terms or sit back and bide his time.

Hereafter the Chaplin pictures will take from two to three times longer to produce than they do now. The settings and stage properties will be the finest. It is quality, not quantity that we are after. After we have made a scene and it isn't up to the new Chaplin quality, it will be made over.

And then, if the whole reel doesn't satisfy Charlie, it will not be released, no matter what money is offered, but thrown into the discard where it belongs.

A close observer of late probably has noticed the increased quality of Chaplin pictures. Charlie has been bringing out more and more new stuff, and he has a great deal more to bring out. The new pictures will be surprises even for the most ardent Chaplin fans.

Also the films hereafter, instead of being just a series of comical stunts or humorous situations, will have a continuous story running through them, with a beginning gradually rising to a climax and winding up with the catastrophe.

We are in the field now for real scenarios. We want the best, and are now negotiating with some of the finest writers in the country to prepare them for us. We have the money to buy what we want, and will be most discriminating in selecting from what is offered.

The next Chaplin series will be wonders. They will be improved upon in every way from those that have gone before. The supporting casts will be greatly strengthened.

Either in this next series, or in those that we plan producing ourselves, I myself will play with Charlie. I have a great many things that are new and will go big, and the two of us, with a strong supporting cast, good stories and good directing and scenery, will be unbeatable.

Charlie and I talked it over before I left Los Angeles on this trip, and we concluded that it was up to us to make the name Chaplin stand for all that there is in true and wholesome comedy, no matter what some of the producing companies want. That is why I am going to take plenty of time before signing the next contract.[1]

Strategically, Sydney could not have chosen a better moment to go to New York. The film industry was on the point of a revolution, and Chaplin was to be a significant factor in it. The most influential figure in industry politics was, and was long to remain, Adolph Zukor. Zukor had arrived in the United States as an immigrant the year before Chaplin was born. He had gone into the fur trade, made a killing by inventing a patent clip for fox furs, and then early in the century entered the nickelodeon business. In 1973, on his hundredth birthday, he was still around to pass judgement on the movies: 'There is nothing wrong with Hollywood that good pictures will not cure.'

Zukor was the first to perceive that the key to domination of the industry lay with the stars. Having captured the unchallenged sweetheart of the box office, Mary Pickford, by the beginning of 1917 Zukor's Paramount Pictures Corporation was on the way to achieving a monopoly of the nation's first-run theatrical outlets. This would enable him to raise his rental rates without restraint. A group of prominent exhibitors, led by Thomas L. Tally and John D. Williamson, decided to fight Zukor by creating an organization to buy, or make, and distribute pictures of its own. The new organization, First National Exhibitors' Circuit, had its inaugural meeting in April 1917. The timing was perfect. Nothing could have given First National a finer send-off than the announcement two months later that they had captured Chaplin, and that their arrangement with him was of a kind likely to be much more attractive to other stars than any which Zukor's Paramount-Artcraft could offer.

Chaplin was to become his own producer, contracted to make for First National eight two-reel comedies a year. First National would advance $125,000 to produce each negative, with the star's salary included in the sum. If the films were longer than two reels, First National would advance $15,000 for each additional reel. First National were also to pay for positives, trade advertising and various other incidentals. The cost of distribution was set at thirty per cent of the total rentals, and after all costs were recouped, First National and Chaplin were to divide net profits equally.

The contract involved protracted negotiations between First National and Sydney, aided by Charlie's lawyer, Nathan Burkan, and was completed late in June. Sydney's doggedness in fighting for Charlie's advantage at this time was the more remarkable since he was having troubles of his own. His wife Minnie had undergone a dangerous operation in Sterns Hospital in New York. In the second month of pregnancy a growth was discovered in her stomach, and its removal involved the loss of the child. She was told that she would be able to have future pregnancies; in fact the couple were to remain childless. Moreover, Sydney was fighting to gain for Charlie an independence which privately made him nervous. Whatever he might say to the press about his brother's perfectionism, as long as they worked together he would be uneasy at Charlie's disregard of cost in his single-minded pursuit of the best.

On 3 July Sydney wrote:

> Well Charlie, I hope you were satisfied with the contract. Burkan and I tried to think of every little thing we could to put in, and I think everything of importance has been covered. During the discussion of the terms of the contract, the subject of a second negative came up. The other side were of opinion that you should include a second negative for the sum

arranged as only a limited number of prints could be obtained from the one negative, besides the risk of losing some in the event it would be necessary to ship it abroad. I tried to evade the provision of a second negative, but as they had been very lenient with all our other clauses in the contract and had raised very few objections I did not wish to appear too grabbing, so offered to provide a second negative if they would pay half the cost which they agreed to. I told them the cost of film and cameraman would be about $1000 per picture, but I very much doubt whether it will cost so much as that. Anyway they agreed to pay an extra $500 a picture, so under the circumstances, if you will take my advice, you will use three cameras on your pictures in the future. I certainly think it is worth the added cost to have a brand new negative locked away for the future, especially as the rights to the pictures revert to you after five years, and I feel sure they have a great future value.

There was one other point that was discussed strongly during the framing of the contract, and that was that instead of them paying you the $200,000 in advance, the money should be deposited in escrow until you had carried out your contract. Even Burkan agreed with them in this but I stood pat and insisted that the cash should be paid without any restrictions. I had mother's old saying well in mind, that 'possession is nine points of the law' so they eventually agreed after a long discussion. How did you like the clause about the extra reel? Getting that by pleased me more than anything. I was racking my brains all the way up in the train trying to think how I could raise the price of your pictures even more than I had agreed upon, and yet not break my word with them, when the thought occurred to me, why not make them pay for extra footage. I remembered how difficult it was for you to cut your picture down to footage, and how in doing so you were often compelled to sacrifice a lot of good business and sometimes whole factions.* Here was a chance to not only get them to accept a picture if by chance it should run over two thousand feet, but at the same time make them pay for it. Of course I did not tell them that you had great difficulty in cutting your pictures to two thousand feet. On the contrary I said that many a time you had a story that would make an excellent three-reel picture, but you were compelled to make it a mediocre two reeler, due to the restrictions of your past contracts, but I also impressed them strongly with the fact that by making a three reeler, it would naturally take a great deal more money and time, so with that I raised the price another fifteen thousand dollars per picture which should pay for the cost of your production, and if you are wise, every picture will run about 2500 feet.

---

* 'Faction' was a word that came into use (apparently exclusively) at the Chaplin Studio to indicate a complete story episode.

Well Charlie, everyone in town here seems to be remarking about the much better class work you are turning out now. I am glad to hear it and I hope you will keep it up and above all refrain from any vulgarity. We must try and frame up a bunch of good stories for the next year and above all, decide and know exactly what you are going to do before the sets are ordered. Have you decided where you are going for your holiday? Marcus Loew I think would be glad to take a trip with you somewhere . . .²

There is a hint of reproach in Sydney's remark about Charlie's need to make up his mind what he is going to do before building his sets, and an optimism that was quickly to be dashed in his hope that the films could be made at a cost within the supplementary advance for an extra reel. Though he never adopted Sydney's wily but somewhat impractical advice about shooting with three cameras, Charlie profited by First National's demand that he make two negatives. Throughout the rest of his career in silent films he always shot with two cameras. The wisdom of this precaution was proved when the second negative of *The Kid* was accidentally destroyed by fire in the late summer of 1938.

Marcus Loew did not have the pleasure of taking a trip with Chaplin. Having finished *The Adventurer* Charlie took off for Hawaii in company with Edna, his secretary-valet Tom Harrington, and Rob Wagner, who had become a regular member of the immediate entourage. A teacher of Greek and art, Wagner became fascinated by Chaplin, and on this trip hoped to write a biography. Instead he worked for a period as press representative, and wrote a number of very perceptive articles on Chaplin's art persona.

The party left in August, and stayed five weeks. The affair with Edna seems already to have ended, but perhaps there was some forlorn hope on one side or the other that the holiday might retrieve it. Chaplin, though, was eager to get back. Before he left he had approved the plans for his new studio, and was impatient to start the actual construction. The site was a five-acre plot which had been the home of a Mr R. S. McClennan, on the corner of Sunset Boulevard and La Brea Avenue. At the north side of the property stood a handsome ten-roomed house in colonial style, and initially Chaplin intended to make this his own residence. Instead Sydney and Minnie lived there for a time. The site was then a good mile away from the usual studio quarter, in one of Hollywood's best residential districts; and at first there was considerable local alarm at this encroachment by the movie folk. Film studios of that period tended to be no asset to a community: mostly they were dreadful agglomerations of tumble-down outhouses, corrugated iron, flapping canvas diffusers supported on crazy structures of girders, the whole protected by flimsy timber fences. Chaplin's Lone Star Studio had been one of the more presentable examples of the kind.

Chaplin's plans however completely won over the élite of La Brea and De Longpre Avenues. The exposed elevations were designed to look like a row of English cottages. The local aesthetes were bound to admit that the irruption of an Olde English village street on Sunset 'was not only conferring distinction on the neighborhood, but was considerably improving it'. The cottages served as offices, dressing rooms and work rooms, and the elevation that faced into the studio was more functionally designed in the style of Californian bungalows. The grounds were laid out with lawns and gardens, and there was a large swimming pool. The production facilities were the best that money could buy.

> The stage will be unusually large, and for months Mr Chaplin has been studying a new diffusing system which will dispense with the old coverings and at the same time will cope with all the climatic conditions of the Pacific coast.
> The site of the new studio was purchased for the sum of $30,500*, but Mr Chaplin plans the investment of $500,000 in beautifying his property.

Charlie and Sydney broke the first sod in November, with an informal and unpublicized ceremony witnessed by the permanent cast and unit. During the three months it took to build the studio Rollie Totheroh filmed a record of the progress. His shots of the daily growth of the cottage façades, when cut together as stop-action, provided an amusing effect of a magical mushroom growth. When everything was more or less ready, Chaplin shot more film to show off the facilities of the studio. He was filmed arriving in his car and going to his dressing room, to get into his costume and make-up. Tom Harrington is seen solemnly opening a safe and taking out the studio's 'most priceless possessions', Charlie's derby and boots, and then being reprimanded for failing to treat them with the proper reverence. The dreadful boots are delicately placed on a cushion. On the stage (at this time almost bare of sets or scenery) the company, including Henry Bergman, Albert Austin and the diminutive Loyal

---

* The freehold seems in fact to have cost $34,000.

Underwood, hide their playing cards and leap into suitably industrious attitudes. Chaplin takes a rehearsal, and delicately and repeatedly instructs a gigantic actor how to strangle Loyal Underwood. Other scenes show Chaplin attending to the hair-dressing of an actress, and fun and games at the pool.

At some point in the First National contract Chaplin seems to have had the idea of putting this material together as a two-reeler to be called *How To Make Movies*, but perhaps First National would not accept it as a substitute for regular comedy. Parts of the material were used by Chaplin as introduction to a later re-issue of a compilation of First National films, *The Chaplin Revue*. In 1982 Kevin Brownlow and David Gill edited the whole film together, using the continuity provided by a title list surviving in the Chaplin archives.

In January 1918 Alf Reeves arrived from England to join the studio staff. Since the start of the War he had been touring Britain with the Karno companies, 'thrashing the old horse *Mumming Birds* to pieces still'. He had kept up a fairly regular correspondence with the Chaplin brothers, giving them news of Karno and all their old colleagues, and reporting on the reception of Chaplin's new fame. In January 1916 he wrote to Chaplin, 'I always, as you know, expected big things of you, but never dreamed of the extent of the popularity you would enjoy.' In August 1917 he congratulated the brothers on Charlie's new contract: 'Everyone's breath is taken away.'

Alf's health had not been good, and he had nostalgic memories of California:

> I have to be careful, and these winters here are rather trying – you know the old digs – sitting room just warm as long as you keep around the fires – cold when you leave them, and as for the bedrooms – wow. I really miss the good old steam heat in those nice hotel rooms there, where the warmth is equable and distributed all over the house . . . The little hotel room with its bath, its running water, its elevator, and up to date comfort of it springs to my memory . . .

When Sydney suggested that there might be a job for him at the new studios Alf leapt at the chance:

> When you tell me there is a probability of Charlie embarking on his own account next year, and that he might think of a way to fix me up you fill me full of good hopes. There is nothing I should like more than a long sojourn in the land of Sun. Warm weather and I agree. Venice, Los Angeles, is one of my ideal spots on this earth. Your suggestion, even, of

the bungalow, with its car ride to town, is far too good to be true I am afraid – especially the Automobile part of it, but then, say I, what's the matter with the streetcar . . .?

So when you are again conversing with Charlie, and thoughts turn this far – if there is anything to suit me – you know about the extent of my humble qualifications – here we are all ready and willing – two of us. Amy is a good cook – Charlie knows – ask him . . . We used to indulge in beefsteak and kidney puddings, and used to do *some* scoffing . . . There are no bones in a beefsteak and kidney pudding. If there had been – I'm sure we would have eaten them. It was Charlie's favourite dinner.

At the end of August 1917 Chaplin offered Reeves a job at the studio, and he at once handed his resignation to Karno and set about making arrangements for sailing. Even though he was forty-eight and so well over military service, there was some difficulty in obtaining the necessary visas from the foreign office; but at last, just after Christmas 1917, Alf and Amy set sail. They arrived in time for Alf to appear before the cameras for *How To Make Movies*: he is seen alerting the company with the cry of 'He's here!' which was part of the daily ritual at the studio. He also made brief appearances in *A Dog's Life* and *Shoulder Arms*: after that Alf's brief acting career came to an end.

When the studio was completed Chaplin decided that it would be good for public relations to open it up to the public, and 2000 people signed the visitors' book in January 1918. A disagreeable incident which resulted from this undoubtedly contributed to Chaplin's secrecy and suspicion in later years. Two people who had represented themselves as journalists spent three days in the studio before they were detected, eavesdropping outside a production meeting. When they were searched they turned out to be in possession of a series of eight sketches of the completed sets for *A Dog's Life*, stenograph notes of story discussions, and descriptions of characters and costumes. In view of the extent to which Chaplin's films were improvised and altered until the very last day of production, his claim that it had cost an estimated $10,000 to scrap the material already planned must be regarded as exaggeration. However the incident was taken seriously enough for all visitors to be banned for the future.

Everything was ready for shooting to start on 15 January 1918. The first production was provisionally titled *I Should Worry*: only when it was completed did Chaplin decide on the title *A Dog's Life*. It remains one of his most perfect films. Louis Delluc called it 'the cinema's first total work of art'. It is as fast and prodigal of gags as a Karno sketch; its individual scenes cohere into a purposeful structure; at the same time it has a harder core of reality than any film that Chaplin had made before. It is about street life, low life, poverty and hunger, prostitution and exploitation. Without pretension and without sacrificing anything of its comic verve, Chaplin drives home the parallel between the existence of a stray dog, Scraps, and two human unfortunates – Charlie the Tramp and Edna, the bar singer. *A Dog's Life*, said *Photoplay* 'though only a grimy little backyard tableau, ranks with the year's few real achievements.'

Charlie's battle with other applicants for the few available jobs at the Employment Office is compared with Scraps' furious struggle over a bone with a horde of bigger and fiercer dogs. The two strays adopt each other and prove an effective partnership in filching a meal from Syd Chaplin's lunch-wagon. They chance into The Green Dragon, described by a critic of the day as 'a dance hall of the character for which Coney Island, New York's Bowery and the Tenderloin of Chicago were famous some twenty years ago, where the "celebrities" of the underworld gave and took fractured skulls as nightly souvenirs.' It is there that they meet Edna, and become rich by outwitting a couple of crooks who have stolen the wallet of a passing drunk.

A Dog's Life has a strange and charming little coda. The last image of Charlie's escape from the crooks ends on an iris-out. This is followed by an iris-in on a vast ploughed field. Charlie, in a big straw hat, astride a ridge between the furrows, waddles along, dibbing holes with his forefinger and planting a seed in each. He looks up and waves happily towards the camera and to Edna, awaiting him in their idyllic little cottage, all cretonne and Home Sweet Home. A cradle stands beside the fire, and the couple gaze into it with pride. The audience is permitted to jump to the obvious conclusion before the interior of the cradle is revealed: within lies a proud Scraps amongst a litter of puppies. The pride is not unjustified – in earlier scenes Scraps' male sex has been more than evident.

Charlie had perceived the comic possibilities of dogs at least as early as *The Champion* – and Sydney had introduced canine comedy into Karno's *Flats* sketch years earlier. More than a year before he began *A Dog's Life*, in December 1916, the newspapers were carrying the headline 'Chaplin Wants A Dog with Lots of Comedy Sense'. Chaplin told the reporters:

> For a long time I've been considering the idea that a good comedy dog would be an asset in some of my plays, and of course the first that was offered me was a dachshund. The long snaky piece of hose got on my nerves. I bought him from a fat man named Ehrmentraut, and when Sausages went back to his master I made no kick.
>
> The second was a Pomeranian picked up by Miss Purviance, who had him clipped where he ought to have worn hair and left him with whiskers where he didn't need 'em. I got sick of having 'Fluffy Ruffles' round me so I traded the 'Pom' for Helene Rosson's poodle. That moon-eyed snuffling little beast lasted two days.

After this he was reported to have tried a Boston bull terrier, and in March 1917 he was said to have been seen in the company of a pedigree English bulldog called Bandy, whose grandmother, appropriately, was Brixton Bess.

'What I really want,' he said, 'is a mongrel dog. The funniest "purps" I ever set eyes on were mongrels. These studio beasts are too well kept. What I want is a dog that can appreciate a bone and is hungry enough to be funny for his feed. I'm watching all the alleys and some day I'll come home with a comedy dog that will fill the bill.' If the news reports are to be believed, after starting work on *A Dog's Life* Chaplin had taken into the studio twenty-one dogs from the Los Angeles pound. In response to complaints from the neighbours, however, the city authorities insisted that he reduce the number to twelve. The studio petty cash accounts show entries for dogs' meat starting from the second week of production and continuing until the end of shooting. The star of the film, a charming little mongrel called Mut (or Mutt), certainly became resident and remained on staff until his untimely death.

Even at this critical early period of his career as an independent, Chaplin was apparently always ready for extemporization or distraction. He had to be, for his studio was to become a place of pilgrimage for the famous in all walks of life who chanced to be in Los Angeles. Harry Lauder, the great Scottish comedian who had rocketed to stardom in the British music hall about the time that Chaplin was touring with Eight Lancashire Lads, was playing the Empress Theatre. He came to call on 22 January. All work stopped while the two comedians fraternized. Over lunch they decided to make a short film together, there and then, in aid of the Million Pound War Fund to which Lauder had dedicated his efforts following the death of his son at the front in December 1916.*

In the afternoon the two cameras were set up and 745 feet of film (approximately eight and a half minutes) were exposed on each while the two comedians fooled before them. Lauder put on Chaplin's derby and twirled his cane, while Chaplin adopted Lauder's tam o'shanter and knobbly walking stick; each impersonated the other's characteristic comedy walk – Chaplin a good deal more successfully than Lauder. There was more business with a bottle of whisky and a blackboard on which they drew each other's caricature. The *pièce de résistance* was the old music hall 'William Tell' gag. Chaplin placed an apple on Lauder's head and then prepared to shoot it with a pistol. Each time Chaplin's back was turned, however, Lauder would take a great bite out of the apple, reducing it to an emaciated core before Chaplin had a chance to take aim. Each time Chaplin turned to throw a suspicious glance, Lauder's face would freeze into blank, immobile innocence. The two comedians optimistically told the press that they anticipated the film would raise a million dollars for the fund. In fact it was never released or even finished.

The T-shaped street set first seen in *Easy Street*, which, variously redressed to suit the current needs, was to remain for twenty years the central and essential location for Chaplin's comic world, was erected in the new studio. In *A Dog's Life* Chaplin fixes on this little plot of ground all the mean streets of every city in the world. Methley Street and all the other back ways of Kennington which he had wandered as a boy are clearly the originals, just as they were for *Easy Street*. Yet Chaplin discovers here something universal, in the mysterious doorways, the loitering bums, the loungers at corners, the sitters on doorsteps, the traders with their flimsy stalls only waiting for pilferers or for the small daily catastrophe which will upend them with avalanches of fruit and vegetables. The locale and atmosphere were to prove as recognizable to audiences in London as in Paris, Chicago, Rio or Manila. Yet it is not an abstraction: there is such a local reality in the setting that Chaplin was able to cut from studio shots to scenes filmed on location in the city (there was a day's

---

* The Harry Lauder Million Pound Fund For Maimed Men, Scottish Soldiers and Sailors, launched 17–18 September 1917. In April 1919 Lauder was knighted by George V for his fund-raising activities.

shooting of dog scenes in front of the Palace Market) without the difference being evident.

Little pre-planning was possible with the dog scenes. The animals and Charlie were set off on the run, and Rollie Totheroh and Jack Wilson, the resourceful cameramen, followed them as best they could. The canine extras were fearsome brutes, and things evidently became somewhat boisterous. After one or two days of work with the dogs, the studio prop people sent out for a large syringe and sixty-five cents' worth of ammonia to separate the dogs when they became too rough.

After a couple of weeks Chaplin suddenly became dissatisfied with the entire story. His staff had become too accustomed to these abrupt switches of mood to be unduly disconcerted by them. Returning to the studio on Monday morning, 11 February, he announced that they would start on an entirely new film to be called *Wiggle and Son*. He took a few shots, ordered the property department to buy ant paste, salts and half a dozen snails, for comic purposes which will never now be divined. The next day, however, *Wiggle and Son* was forgotten, and Chaplin returned with fresh enthusiasm to *I Should Worry*, as the film was still officially known.*

For the crowd scenes in the dance hall thirty extras were hired to supplement the stock company, and as usually happened on Chaplin productions, friends and studio staff were recruited from time to time. Alf Reeves and Rob Wagner may be glimpsed, and Sydney's wife, Minnie Chaplin, played a role. The tough proprietor of the dance hall was played by another new acquaintance of Chaplin's, Granville Redmond, a successful landscape painter. Redmond was a deaf-mute, but he and his director established a perfect pantomime communication, as his performances in *A Dog's Life* and *The Kid* testify.

Grace Kingsley, a keenly observant journalist of the day, visited the studio during the filming of the dance hall sequence, and recorded her impressions:

> It's coming to be quite the fad to visit the Chaplin Studio – that is, if you can get in. Of course nobody is allowed to visit there. Nobody, that is, except picture magnates and newspaper and magazine representatives and their friends, and fellow artists – of whom there are always some thousands in the city – and all the soldiers and sailors and–

* According to a contemporary report, however, (*The Bioscope*, Scottish edition, 18 April 1918) the final title was suggested by a remark of Harry Lauder's who told Chaplin, 'It's a dog's life you're leadin' these days, Charlie.'

The Keystone Studios around 1913.

Mack Sennett on the set, about the time that Chaplin joined the studio.

Left: The Essanay Studio at Niles, California, 1915.

Below left: The Majestic Studio (formerly the Bradbury Mansion) where *Work* was filmed.

Right: Mabel Normand.

Below: *Making a Living*, Chaplin's first film. The other actor is Henry 'Pathé' Lehrman, who also directed the film.

Right: Group of picture postcards issued in 1915, with scenes from Essanay films.

Essanay publicity, 1915.

RED LETTER PHOTOCARD.

RED LETTER PHOTOCARD.

"... Shanghaied."

(Charles Chaplin.) "I've come aboard, sir." (Shanghaied.)

RED LETTER PHOTOCARD.

(Charles Chaplin.) Spoons.

RED LETTER PHOTOCARD.

Charlie and the Bulldog. (Champion Charlie.)

RED LETTER PHOTOCARD.

Making Love to the Queen. (Charlie's New Job).

(Charles Chaplin).

LETTER PHOTOCARD.

(Charles Chaplin.) Charlie's Flirtation. (Charlie by the Sea.)

1   2   3   4   5   6   7   8   9   10   11   12   13   14   15   16   17   18

Panoramic group photograph of Chaplin's Essanay unit taken on the set of *The Bank*, 1915. Each person in the picture has signed the photograph, but many of the signatures are now illegible. A note at the foot of the picture says that the dotted cross indicates the British members of the unit. From left to right: 1 (unknown), 2 Chaplin, 3 Edna Purviance, 4 (unknown), 5 Charles Insley, 6 Leo White, 7 Billy Armstrong, 8 Carl Stockdale, 9 Fred Goodwins, 10 Lawrence A. Bowes, 11 Harold (?), 12 Paddy McQuire (*sic*), 13 John L. Crizer, 14 (?) Easterday, 15 Jack Roach, 16 (?) Stockdale, 17 (unknown), 18 George Cleethorpes, 19 Harry Ensign (cameraman), 20 (unknown), 21 (unknown), 22 Shortie Wilson, 23 (unknown), 24 (?) Charlie Gordon Jr, 25 (unknown), 26 (unknown), 27 (unknown), 28 George Green, 29 (unknown), 30 (unknown), 31 William Gorham, 32 Lee Hall, 33 Jesse Robbins. The set for the bank vault is clearly visible; to the left is part of the set of the manager's office. At the right of the picture are the dressing rooms and overhead are the muslin light diffusers.

Right: Detail showing Chaplin and Edna.

of "THE BANK."

21   22   23   24   25   26   27   28   29   30   31   32   33

Details showing Harry Ensign,
Chaplin's cameraman at Essanay
and Jesse Robbins, the producer

Below: Filming *The Vagabond*, 1916.

Left: Chaplin's first days at
the Lone Star Studios. Chaplin can
be seen at the front of the stage.
Around him are the uncompleted
sets for *The Floorwalker*, including
the escalator.

Right: Edna Purviance, 1918.
A previously unpublished photograph by
Jack Wilson, Chaplin's second cameraman.

Edna's star hat, *The Count*, 1916.

Above left: The old mansion in the grounds of the Chaplin Studio. Sydney Chaplin, Kono Toraichi and Wheeler Dryden lived here at various times. It was eventually demolished, and the site is now occupied by a Safeway supermarket.

Left: Chaplin and Sydney visit the site of the projected studio.

Above: Building the studio, 1918.

Right: *How to Make Movies:* Chaplin offers a lemon from the grove on the studio site.

1917 cartoon by the French artist Cami,
showing Chaplin in a German helmet.

Anticipation of *Shoulder Arms*:
'advertisement' for a putative film,
probably sketched by Chaplin
in April-May 1918.

Left: Aerial view of Chaplin Studio taken by Jack Wilson, 1918 and showing the extent of the citrus groves in Hollywood.

Below: Aerial views of studio during shooting of *A Woman of Paris* (1922-3) and *Modern Times* (1935-6) showing the urban encroachment. The film sets may be distinguished on the back lot.

A Dog's Life (1918).
The 'lady' at top right is Henry Bergman.

A Dog's Life: Chaplin with Mut.

Below: A rehearsal at the studio, posed for *How To Make Movies*, 1918. From left to right: (unknown), Loyal Underwood, Chaplin, Henry Bergman, Edna Purviance; standing: Jack Wilson.

Visitors to the studio. Above (1918): Helen Keller with Annie Sullivan. Miss Keller 'saw' *Shoulder Arms* on this occasion.

Below: Douglas Fairbanks and Harry Lauder. Sydney is on the left.

But that's enough to show you what one of Charlie's days must be like. And he's the most astonishing combination of busy artist and gracious, good-natured host . . .

Catch Charlie in the right mood and he'll do $10,000 worth of acting for you while you wait. So that, though following Charlie Chaplin around all day is as strenuous as following a soldier at drill, the similarity ends there.

After Charlie has drawn on his funny trousers and shoes and his old shirt, in the privacy of his luxurious dressing room, he finishes making up at a little dressing table on the stage, where he can keep an eye on the dressing of the sets. This happens around 9 o'clock, when the sun encourages photography.

'If I don't get this moustache on right, it's all off,' grinned Charlie as he carefully combed the crêpe and cut it, pasting it on his lip first as a big wad. 'Got to trim that down, or Chester Conklin will think I'm trying to steal his stuff!'

I'm only one of the many interviewers who call on Charlie, so he talks as he makes up: 'The day of sausage pictures is over,' he said. Then he made an important announcement. 'I shall never again bind myself to the making of two-reel comedies. You must have a story, and it's got to be a clear story. Otherwise quite naturally the public doesn't get it. Also you've got to have the gags and the jokes and the jazz. You've got to grab these out of the air as it were. You don't know just when or where the ideas come from – and sometimes they don't!'

Charlie's make-up being on straight by now and his hat on crooked, he took a peep in his glass and descrying over his shoulders a bunch of soldiers, of course, he had to go over and say 'Hello'. Some dear ladies of the Red Cross just then entered, and a candy company having contributed a whole shop full of chocolates for Charlie to auction off, he had to pause to be photographed before the collection with some of the Red Cross ladies.

I think Charlie gets most of his inspiration when he is 'kidding'. He wanted some special idea for that photograph, and he took a dozen different comical poses before, grasping a broom which lay on the set, he hit upon the right idea.

'The Chocolate Soldier!' he grinned, as he fell into a funny attitude with the broom as a gun.

Then the comedian went over to the dance hall set and called out to Miss Purviance and the other members of the company. He sat down beside the two cameras that are always ranged on the action, and he shut his eyes and put his fingers in his ears.

'That's the way he visualizes an idea,' explained Brother Sid. 'He sees it on the screen that way.'

233

A rehearsal – a long and careful rehearsal with Chaplin playing all the parts in turn – followed . . .

It was lunch time then. So we all went to lunch in Sid's beautiful house, Charlie and Edna Purviance still in their make-up. After lunch it was discovered that there was one of those awful – what Charlie calls 'brick walls' – a dead stop, until a minor snarl in the story and its action was straightened out. For this, Charlie called Charles Lapworth into consultation. Then out came Charlie and kidded around a bit – he does that while he's waiting for an idea to pop, kept everyone laughing, while in the back of his head all the while was that awful question – the brick wall. Presently it came, the longed-for idea.

He had just started once more for the stage when Carlyle Robinson, his publicity man, came forward, announcing in a fairly awe-struck whisper: 'The Earl of Dunmore!'

Of course one cannot overlook a real Earl on the busiest day, so Mr Chaplin paused and chatted a few moments. And though the Earl was an Earl, he realized that a comedian is a hard-working person, and so insisted Charlie should go back to work. Anyhow, Earl or no Earl he was probably dying, just like everybody else, to see Charlie at work. So Charlie hopped onto the stage, and, having at last got possession of the longed-for idea, and having escaped all visitors, he set briskly to work. Half an hour, an hour, two hours passed, with no let-up to the filming of scenes. Somebody brought him some mail, which, after opening, he dropped as carelessly as the hero of a motion picture does when thickening the plot with 'the papers'.

'He'll be working like this until he finishes all the scenes he has in mind,' said Brother Sid, 'until 6, 7, or even 8 o'clock. And when the cutting begins, he will work all night and all day too.'

You'd think to see him acting out there on the stage, that he was still kidding. Maybe he doesn't quite know himself, you think.

Charles Lapworth was an emigré English journalist who had arrived to interview Chaplin, and briefly found a niche in the studio. His own impressions of Chaplin in his dressing room and on the set fill out Grace Kingsley's description:

He will permit you to sit in his dressing room, and let you do the talking while he affixes the horsehair to make up his moustache. You will notice a violin near at hand, also a cello. And it will be unusual if Charlie does not pick up the fiddle and the bow, and accompany your remarks with an obligato from the classics, what time he will fix you with a far-away stare and keep you going with monosyllabic responses.

If you run out of remarks before the violinist has come back to earth, and you are curious enough to glance round the luxuriously furnished room, you may judge a little of Charlie's literary tastes by observing cheek by jowl with Thomas Burke's *Limehouse Nights*, Sigmund Freud's *Psychoneurosis* and Lafcadio Hearn's *Life and Literature*; not on the shelves, but lying around as if they are really being read. On the desk, perhaps, Mark Twain's *Mysterious Stranger*, an allegory that sometimes Charlie will get enthusiastic about; while in the bookcase one may notice that the man who first introduced custard pie into polite argument has not failed to acquaint himself with what the philosophers from way back down to Bergson have had to say about the underlying causes of laughter . . .

No matter how competent any member of his company may be, he has to acknowledge that when he responds to Charlie's direction he achieves better results. It is interesting, for instance, to watch him show the big heavy how to be 'tough', or a girl, obviously at the moral crossroads, how to look the part. His variety of facial gestures is amazing: he is a king of burlesque.

Sometimes, of course, he strikes a snag, and then he will just disappear off the 'lot'. The whole works are at a standstill, and there is a hue and cry around the neighboring orange groves. Perhaps two hours afterwards the comedian steals back to the studio, and his return is made known by the soul-stirring strains from his cello. A little later work is resumed, and Charlie will confess that after much prayerful wrestling he has ironed out the kinks . . .

He frequently interrupts the 'shooting' with an impromptu clog dance. He may close his eyes, and with his hands make weird passes of a geometrical character. But nobody gets alarmed. The chief is just inwardly visualizing the camera shots and when he has got the angles worked out to his own satisfaction he gives instructions for the necessary modifications of the set. Like as not he will order it burned; he has changed his mind, and the carpenters have to tear down an elaborate and costly set, unused.

Chaplin is at once the joy and despair of all managers. If he does not feel like work, he won't work. And he can always fall back on the public for support of his argument that the public are entitled to the best. If he does not feel he is doing his best, he quits and hang the expense. And the thousands of feet of film that he shoots go to waste. Again, that's nobody's business but his. He pays for it, and he will declare that if a picture costs him every penny he makes (it took him three months to make his last one), he is still determined to make it as perfect as he can. And, oh the travail of the cutting! Sometimes sixty thousand feet to get two thousand. Only a rewrite man on a newspaper knows what such a boiling down means. Yet Charlie, and Charlie alone, does the cutting. And he ruthlessly comdemns to the scrap-heap miles of excellent comedy that would make the fortunes of other comedians.[3]

For all Chaplin's extravagance in the pursuit of perfection, the book-keeping of this first independent production was meticulous; and the daily record of petty cash disbursements is often as amusing as revealing. Everything is detailed, down to the last five cents for 'beans', seemingly used by Charlie to represent seeds in the final sequence. A wastage of thirty-five feet of film stock (with a running time of about thirty seconds) calls for detailed explanation in the accounts. There are daily entries for dog meat and for gas and oil for the studio Ford (at nineteen cents a gallon). Prop food and drink – pies, sausages, rolls, 'tamalies', chewing gum, beer, near-beer and ginger-ale – figure large also. Henry Bergman played several roles in the film, but his favourite was clearly that of the stout, gum-chewing old lady in the dance hall, whose tears on hearing Edna's plaintive song drench Charlie. Entries for 'fur for Bergman – $2.34' and 'elastic for Bergman – 30¢' show that he started preparing his costume well ahead of time. On 26 February there is a disconcerting item: 'Whiskey (Mut) – 60¢'. The explanation is a scene in which Charlie and the dog sleep together on their plot of waste ground. Charlie uses the suspiciously compliant animal as a pillow, energetically plumping him into shape before settling down, and then agitatedly searching the immobile dog for fleas. ('There are strangers in our midst,' says one of the film's very few titles.) The item in the petty cash account reveals the secret of Mut's docility: he was dead drunk.

Shooting was completed on 22 March, when Chaplin used 1792 feet of film to round off one thousand takes and 35,887 feet of film exposed on each camera. This time Chaplin was forced to accept help with the editing. From 26 to 29 March he stayed night and day in the cutting room with Bergman, the two cameramen and two assistants, Brown and Depew to help him. Between times he had a last-minute inspiration and shot a charming little scene in which Charlie sits on the steps of a second-hand store and feeds the dog with milk from a near-empty bottle he has found there. When the dog cannot reach the milk with his tongue, Charlie obligingly dips Mut's tail into the bottle and gives it to him to suck like a dummy.

With a superhuman effort the cutting was completed late on 31 March, and Chaplin was ready to depart on a Liberty Bond tour the following day. The staff worked on to prepare the negatives. While Chaplin was off on the Bond tour, the staff were instructed to prepare ideas for submission on his return. Mut, sad to say, did not live to see Charlie's return to California. He had apparently grown so attached to his master that he pined during his absence, refused to eat, and died. He was buried in the studio ground under a little memorial composed of artistically arranged garbage, and with the epitaph: 'Mut, died April 29th – a broken heart'. His single film role had earned him his small piece of immortality.

The trip east was made in company with Douglas Fairbanks, Mary Pickford, and Rob Wagner. The plan was for the three stars to take part in the official launching of the Third Liberty Bond campaign in Washington, to go on together to New York, and then to split up, Doug and Mary taking on the northern states and Chaplin the southern. Chaplin slept during the first two days of the rail journey. Recovering from his exhaustion, he set to writing his speech and confided to the others his nervousness about making a serious address to a crowd. Doug suggested that he practised on the crowd that gathered around the train at a stop *en route* but, as the last speaker, he found the train moving off just as he got into his stride, enthusiastically addressing a rapidly receding audience.

In Washington the party made a triumphal progress through the streets to a football field where a vast crowd had come to hear them. Marie Dressler was on the platform as well, and when Chaplin was carried away by his own eloquence, and fell off the platform, he managed to take the ample Marie with him. They fell on top of the young Assistant Secretary of the Navy, Franklin D. Roosevelt. Later they were formally presented to President Wilson at the White House; Chaplin felt that he and the President were mutually unimpressed by the encounter.

In New York the excitement was even greater. Crowds began to gather at the junction of Broad and Wall Streets during the morning, and by the time the party arrived around noon, on 8 April 1918, it was estimated that between twenty and thirty thousand people were waiting, many clinging to the Morgan Building, the Stock Exchange and the pillars of the Sub-Treasury. Their speeches were greeted with applause, laughter and shouting; and the crowd went wild when Fairbanks lifted Chaplin onto his shoulders. Chaplin was wearing a wasp-waisted blue suit, light-top shoes and a black derby.

'Now listen –' he began, only to be interrupted by cheers and laughter from the thousands of bankers, brokers, office boys and stenographers. 'I never made a speech before in my life –' he continued, and was interrupted again, '— but I believe I can make one now!' The next few words were inaudible; then the crowd settled down, and most of the rest of his words, screamed through a megaphone, were heard:

> You people out there – I want you to forget all about percentages in this third Liberty Loan. Human life is at stake, and no one ought to worry about what rate of interest the bonds are going to bring or what he can make by purchasing them.
>
> Money is needed – money to support the great army and navy of Uncle Sam. This very minute the Germans occupy a position of advantage, and we have got to get the dollars. It ought to go over so that we can drive that old devil the Kaiser, out of France!

The cheers for this sentiment resounded through several blocks of the city. When he could again get silence, Chaplin concluded: 'How many of you men – how many of you boys, out there, have bought or are willing to buy Liberty Bonds?' The hand-stretching that followed, said the *Wall Street Journal*, 'suggested vividly the latter part of the seventh innings at the Polo Grounds during a world series'.

The New York trip brought one personal bonus. Marie Doro, the beautiful star of the London production of *Sherlock Holmes* thirteen years ago, was playing in *Barbara* at the Klaw Theatre, and Chaplin was able to arrange an intimate dinner with her. The impossible dream of the sixteen-year-old who played Billy the pageboy had come true.

Chaplin's tour began at Petersburg, Virginia, and took him through North Carolina, Kentucky, Tennessee and Mississippi. He arrived in New Orleans exhausted, and was forced to rest for a few days before completing the tour, and returning home via Texas.   In Memphis he found waiting for him a letter from his exasperated studio manager, John Jasper, resigning his post. Chaplin had departed California leaving Jasper's drawing account for running the studio three weeks in arrears. In reply to Jasper's protests, he had arranged by cable for a weekly payment of $2000, even though it was previously agreed that the minimum average budget was $3000. 'I expected of course that I would have the money every week,' wrote Jasper. 'The only way any Manager can ever give satisfaction in this job is to have a drawing account. Why don't you put sufficient funds in the Citizen's National Bank and stop all this confusion? It is not as if you did not have the money like so many others.'

		DAILY PRODUCTON REPORT		NUMBER OF DAYS ON PICTURE INCLUDING TO-DAY		
				IDLE	WORK	TOTAL
				1	11	12

DIRECTOR _____

CAMERAMAN _____

WORKING TITLE "I Should Worry"

DATE January 28th 191 8

PICTURE No. 1

NUMBER OF REELS _____

CAST	RATE	SCENES PLAYED IN	ARTICLE	AMOUNT	
			PETTY CASH EXPENDITURES		
CHARLIE CHAPLIN	*		BALANCE OF HAND	11	90
			Meat for Dogs		34
HENRY BERGMAN	STOCK		" " "		20
ALBERT AUSTIN	STOCK		" " "		36
FRED STARR	STOCK		Gasoline		20
TOM WILSON	STOCK		Fur for Bergman	2	34
SLIM COLE	STOCK		Rent of 2 Dogs	2	00
JAMES T. KELLEY	GUAR				
TED EDWARDS	GUAR				
				6	46
			STILLS TAKEN TO-DAY:		2
			NUMBER BROUGHT FORWARD		2
			TOTAL STILLS TO DATE		5

SCENES TAKEN TO-DAY					FILM USED		STARTED WORK	
NO.	FEET	SCENT NO.	FEET	SCENE NO	FEET	FOOTAGE	A. M.	P. M.
		FORWARD		FORWARD		TO-DAY	1200	10:30
						BAL FORWD	4877	
						TOTAL TO DATE	6077	

MEMO. Mr Chaplin arrived at 9:40 A M
Started shooting dog no tract kept of
scenes. Fight was unsatisfactory.

TOTAL	TOTAL	GRAND TOT.				

AUTO USED	STARTED TIME		FINISHED TIME		
	A. M.	P. M.	A. M.	P. M	

WEATHER { FAIR / CLOUDY / RAIN }

O.K. _John W Brown_   CLERK

1918 - Production report on
A Dog's Life (at first called
I Should Worry).

239

DAILY PRODUCTON REPORT

NUMBER OF DAYS ON PICTURE INCLUDING TO-DAY		
IDLE	WORK	TOTAL
1	18	19

DIRECTOR _____ DATE **February 4th** 191 **8**

CAMERAMAN _____ PICTURE No. **1**

WORKING TITLE _____ NUMBER OF REELS **2**

CAST	RATE		SCENES PLAYED IN	PETTY CASH EXPENDITURES		
				ARTICLE	AMOUNT	
CHARLIE CHAPLIN	*		Shot only dog scenes today	BALANCE OF HAND	6	38
HENRY BERGMAN	STOCK			Advanced	10	00
ALBERT AUSTIN	STOCK					
FRED STARR	STOCK			Gas & Oil		45
TOM WILSON	STOCK			Radiator Cap		50
SLIM COLE	STOCK			Sausage		75
JAMES KELLEY	GUAR			Rolls		12
TED EDWARDS	GUAR	Made up.		Sausage compound		50
LOUIS FITZROY	GUAR			Casters		90
THOMAS RILEY	GUAR			Pies & Eggs	1	22
DAVE ANDERSON	GUAR			Hot dogs		60
JANET SULLEY	GUAR					
MISS PITTS	STOCK					
JAMES McCORMICK	2 50					
GRACE WILSON	2 50					
MARGARET DRACUP	2 50					
OLIVER HALL	2 50				11	34
JERRY FARRAGAMA	2 50			STILLS TAKEN TO-DAY:		
LOYAL UNDERWOOD	2 50			NUMBER BROUGHT FORWARD		8
CHAS. GEE (Dog)	5 00			TOTAL STILLS TO DATE		

SCENES TAKEN TO-DAY					FILM USED		STARTED WORK	
NO.	FEET	SCENE NO.	FEET	SCENE NO	FEET	FOOTAGE	A. M.	P. M.
3	12	FORWARD	46	FORWARD	128	TO-DAY	1256	10:00
4	8	320	12	326	13	BAL FORWD	12837	
5	5	321	10	327	10	TOTAL TO DATE	13093	
6	8	322	12	328	7	MEMO. Shooting dogs in street scene.		
7	3	323	15	329	6			
8	3	324	15	330	62			
9	7	325	18	331	25			
TOTAL		TOTAL		GRAND TOT				

AUTO USED	STARTED TIME		FINISHED TIME				
	A. M.	P. M.	A.	P M		WEATHER	FAIR CLOUDY RAIN
—					O K *Mr. Brown*		
—						CLERK	

— Over —

1918 - Production report on
A Dog's Life (at first called
I Should Worry).

Chaplin appears not to have been gravely inconvenienced by the departure of Jasper. Alf Reeves was immediately appointed as his successor, and for the next twenty-eight years proved an ideal manager, seemingly never surprised or discomposed by his employer's caprices.

The world's two great comedians.

1917 - Spanish cartoon showing Chaplin with the Kaiser.

Chaplin was back in Hollywood in early May and by the end of the month was ready to start his new film, tentatively recorded as 'Production No 2. *Camouflage.* 2 reels'. The notion of Charlie at war was irresistible. From the time of the 'slacker' campaign against him, newspaper cartoonists in every country had delighted in speculating on the possibilities of a confrontation beween Charlie and the Kaiser. Late in 1917, Chaplin had amused himself by drawing on a post-card – still preserved in one of his scrap books – an advertisement for a putative film, *Private Chaplin U.S.A.*: 'Ladies and Gentlemen – Charlie in this picture lies down his cane and picks up the sword to fight for Democracy. Picture produced by Charlie Chaplin Film Corp. released through First National Exhibitors' Circuit.' Chaplin's collaborators and friends shook their heads about the wisdom of making comedy out of so dreadful an event as the War, whose full effect Americans had so recently begun to experience. Chaplin, however, always growing more aware of the proximity of comedy, drama and tragedy, was confident.

He seems to have begun the film with a more determined idea of its structure than was customary, though in the event this idea was to be modified. Originally he planned three acts. The first would show Charlie in civilian life, at the mercy of a virago wife and the father of several children. After a bridging sequence in the recruiting office, the film would show his adventures at the front. The third part was to be 'the banquet', with the crowned heads of Europe gratefully toasting Charlie for his gallant capture of the Kaiser. At the end, like Jimmy the Fearless or Charlie in *The Bank*, he would wake up to the cold reality of the training camp.

When his plans were as certain as this, Chaplin liked to shoot his stories in sequence. He began with the scenes of civilian life, using three child actors, True Boardman Jr, Frankie Lee and Marion Feducha. The angry wife was to remain off screen, her presence indicated only by the occasional flying plate, frying-pan or other missile. As finally assembled, the sequence shows Charlie coming along the street with his three sons. Without a sign he turns into the door of a saloon, leaving them to wait patiently outside. When he rejoins them they all troop home where he docilely sets about making soup for lunch amidst the bombardments of his unseen spouse. The arrival of the postman with his draft papers comes as a happy release.

The next sequence, which took two weeks to prepare and shoot, shows Charlie's arrival at the recruiting office for his medical examination. He is told to enter the office and disrobe. Partially stripped, he opens the wrong door and finds himself trapped in a maze of glass partitioned offices occupied by lady clerks. After much trouble Charlie evades the women and arrives at the office of 'Dr Frances'. The name makes him still more apprehensive; the doctor turns out to be no lady, however, but the lugubrious Albert Austin, heavily bearded. The examination is seen only in silhouette through the frosted glass panel of the office door. The doctor appears and sticks a gigantic probe into Charlie's throat, only to have it repeatedly and violently shot back at him. Eventually Charlie swallows the thing entirely, and the doctor is obliged to resort to a line and hook to retrieve it. No doubt suggested by memories of the Karno *Harlequinade* of Christmas 1910, in essence it is a hoary old routine of the vaudeville 'shadowgraphist'. Chaplin was a master at giving new life to old jokes, though, and when, sixty-five years on, the rediscovered sequence was included in the *Unknown Chaplin* television series, it proved to have lost none of its verve.

Yet Chaplin was to discard all that he had shot in this first month of work. Such rigorous self-censorship would seem remarkable at any time in the history of the cinema. In 1918, when a month was reckoned time enough to shoot a first-class feature film, it was astounding. Moreover, under the contract with First National, Chaplin bore all the production costs. It was his own money that he was prepared to throw away in the cause of perfection. Rightly, though, he knew that he could do better.

The first week of July was devoted to revising the story and building new sets. When shooting was resumed, Chaplin filmed from beginning to end, practically without the breaks to talk over and revise the story which had become and were to remain customary. The most substantial interruption to shooting came on 11 July when Marie Dressler visited the studio, accompanied by the actress Ina Claire. As usual, Chaplin abandoned work with surprising cheerfulness to entertain his old co-star. They posed together for photographs which show the formidable Marie in Hun-scaring mood in the trench set.

The trench and dug-out are a remarkable abstraction of the reality of the Western Front. When Chaplin reissued *Shoulder Arms* more than half a century later, he proudly prefaced it with actuality shots of the war, to show how well his set-builders had done. The trench scenes, showing Charlie, Sydney and their companions adapting to front-line conditions – vermin, bad food, homesickness, snipers, rain, mud, floods and fear – took four weeks to shoot. By this time it was high summer. One day the heat was so great that it was impossible to film at all. Chaplin spent four days of this heatwave sweating inside a camouflage tree. His discomfort was rewarded by one of the most deliriously surreal episodes of his work. Charlie scuttles around no-man's-land in his tree disguise, freezing into arborial immobility at the approach of a German patrol, and coping ingeniously with a great German soldier with an axe who is bent on chopping him down for firewood. In our last memorable vision of the Charlie-tree it is skipping and hopping off towards a distant horizon. The expanses of no-man's-land were provided, in those days of a still-rural Hollywood, by the back of Beverly Hills, while Wilshire Boulevard and the back of Sherman provided the forest. Back of Sherman, too, they found a half-buried pipe which suggested a piece of comic business. Charlie bolts, rabbit-like into the pipe; his German pursuers grab his legs, but capture only his boots and his disguise which he has shed like a snake-skin. Following this, rotund Henry Bergman, playing a German officer, gets stuck in the pipe as he goes after Charlie, and has to be broken out. It is not recorded if the Los Angeles sewage authorities ever discovered how their property came to be shattered.

Dedicated to his patriotic commitments, Chaplin had agreed to donate a short film to the Liberty Bond drive, and now realized that to deliver it on time he would have to interrupt production of *Camouflage*, which had inevitably already overrun its anticipated schedule. On 14 August the unit worked on until 1 a.m., to complete the scenes of Private Charlie's encounter with Edna, playing a French peasant, in her ruined home. The next day the studio was turned over to making what was identified only as 'propaganda film'. Eventually titled *The Bond*, it ran 685 feet (about ten minutes) and was completed in six working days. Sydney appeared as the Kaiser in the costume and make-up he used for *Camouflage*. Besides Chaplin the rest of the cast was made up of Edna, Albert Austin and a child called Dorothy Rosher. The film had four episodes, introduced by the title, 'There are different kind of Bonds: the Bond of Friendship; the Bond of Love; the Marriage Bond; and most important of all – the Liberty Bond.' The use of simple, stylized white properties against a plain black back-drop gave this curious little film a proto-Expressionist look. It was donated to the Government, and distributed without charge to all theatres in the United States in the Autumn of 1918.

With *The Bond* out of the way, Chaplin rapidly finished off *Camouflage*. By 16 September the film was cut and re-titled *Shoulder Arms*.

Chaplin, tired, dispirited and depressed by personal troubles, suddenly lost confidence in the film, and later claimed that he had seriously thought of scrapping it and was incredulous when Douglas Fairbanks, having demanded to see it, laughed till the tears ran down his cheeks. Better than any other clown in history, Chaplin was able to prove that comedy is never so rich as when it is poised on the edge of tragedy. He had metamorphosed the real-life horrors of war into a cause for laughter; and in the event there was no audience more appreciative of *Shoulder Arms* than the men who had seen and suffered the reality. Soldier Charlie includes in his kit a mousetrap and a grater which serves as a back-scratcher when the lice grow too assertive. His food parcel from home includes biscuits as hard as ration issue, and a Limburger cheese so high that he uses it like a grenade to bomb and gas the enemy. He takes advantage of passing bullets to open a bottle and light a cigarette. As a sniper, he chalks up his hits – then rubs out the last mark in acknowledgement of a return shot that clips his tin helmet. Even the nightmare of the flooded trenches of the Somme is turned into laughter: Charlie fishes out his submerged pillow to plump it up ineffectually before settling down for the night, and blows out the candle as it floats by on the flood water. One title became a classic joke of the First World War. Asked how he has captured thirteen Germans single-handed, Charlie replies simply and mystifyingly: 'I surrounded them.'

As memorable is the scene where Charlie is the only soldier to receive no letter or parcel in the mail delivery. With misguided pride he refuses an offer of cake from a luckier comrade, and wanders from the dugout into the trench. There a soldier on guard duty is reading a letter from home. Charlie reads over his shoulder, and echoes all the emotions that are passing over the soldier's face. Though he might make comedy from it, the folly and tragedy and waste of war were always to bewilder and torment Chaplin. One apparently light-hearted scene in *Shoulder Arms* already hints at a more serious drift of thought. Charlie, having 'surrounded' and captured his German prisoners, offers them cigarettes. The common soldiers accept them gratefully, but the diminutive Prussian officer takes a cigarette only to throw it away with contempt. Charlie instantly seizes the little man, lays him across his knee and spanks him soundly. The German soldiers delightedly gather round and applaud. There is a comradeship of ordinary men that transcends the warring of governments and armies.

Shoulder Arms was one of the greatest successes of Chaplin's career. His marriage to Mildred Harris was not. When he met Mildred at a party given by Samuel Goldwyn, probably in the early part of 1918, she was rising sixteen. Already established as a child actress before she was ten, she was at this time employed at Paramount under the direction of Lois Weber. She still radiated a child-like quality which charmed Chaplin: his feminine ideal had been definitively fixed, it seemed, by his first infatuation with the fifteen-year-old Hetty Kelly. For her part, Mildred seems to have made knowing use of her golden hair, blue eyes and flirtatious prattle. She was presumably not discouraged by her mother, who as wardrobe mistress at the Ince

Studios could not but be aware of Chaplin as the most eligible and the most handsome bachelor in Hollywood. Harriette Underhill described his appearance at this time: 'He talks humorously, he thinks seriously, he dresses quietly and he looks handsome. He has the whitest teeth we ever saw, the bluest eyes and the blackest eye-lashes . . .'

Soon both Chaplin and the Harrises were coyly fending off enquiries from the press, who were not however to be easily put off. On 25 June the *Los Angeles Times* reported rumours of an engagement, and the subsequent denials. The following day the *Los Angeles Examiner* had a fuller and more circumstantial report:

CHAPLIN MARRIAGE RUMOR IS DENIED

Despite rumors that will not die down to the effect that Mildred Harris, the dainty screen favorite, has won the heart of Charlie Chaplin and soon is to be his bride, both the petite actress and her mother Mrs A. F. Harris denied last night the last half of the double-barrelled allegation.

'No, Mr Chaplin and I are not engaged,' Miss Harris said last night when she returned to her quarters in the Wilshire Apartments after an evening at his studio. 'We're just very dear friends. Why, we've only known each other two months and we've only been going together a month or so. I'm sure, too, Mr Chaplin will deny the report. We have not discussed the rumor as we have not seen each other for about a week.'

Mrs Harris was much surprised by the report, she said, and added that her daughter was only seventeen years of age and too young to think of marrying.

According to the circulated report in motion picture circles, Chaplin recently conferred with Philip Smalley of the Lois Weber Studio, where Miss Harris is employed, and asked how her contract would be affected if they should be married. It was said, according to the report, that the marriage would not affect the contract.

Philip Smalley denied that this reported conference took place.

Mrs Harris stopped her denials shortly after the completion of *Shoulder Arms*, when Mildred announced that she was pregnant. Chaplin was trapped: he could not possibly risk the scandal of this kind of involvement with a seventeen-year-old. Tom Harrington, his valet, secretary, confidant and general factotum, was told to arrange a registry office marriage for 23 September 1918, after studio working hours. Harrington arranged the affair with the discretion for which Chaplin valued him, and Chaplin found himself, without any pleasure, a married man. Leaving the Los Angeles Athletic Club, which had been his home practically since he arrived in Hollywood, he rented a house at 2000 De Mille Drive. The lease was only for six months, but long tenancies were hardly appropriate to the marriage. His reaction on seeing the bride awaiting his arrival at the registry office was, to say the least, not promising: 'I felt a little sorry for her.'

Edna only knew about the marriage when she read the newspapers the following day, but she faced the fact with dignity and outward calm. Chaplin recalled that when he went to the studio the morning after, she appeared at the door of her dressing room. "Congratulations", she said softly. "Thank you," he replied, and went on his way to his dressing room. "Edna made me feel embarrassed.' Edna did not see *Shoulder Arms* in the studio projection room with Chaplin; but when he was about to embark for a week of honeymoon on Catalina Island, she wrote to him:

1918 - Letter written by Edna Purviance after seeing *Shoulder Arms*.

To her other qualities Edna added that of being a noble loser. Poor Mildred was, as Chaplin gently put it, 'no mental heavyweight'. She bored him, and in her turn resented the exclusive single-mindedness of his concentration when he was working. She was annoyed because he would not concern himself in her career, which enjoyed a brief stimulus from the celebrity of being Mildred Harris Chaplin. The worst irony for Chaplin was that the pregnancy which had shotgunned him into marriage turned out to be a false alarm.

Chaplin was convinced that the marriage debilitated his creative ability, and the acute difficulties he experienced with his next film, *Sunnyside*, begun under the working title *Jack of All Trades*, seemed to confirm his fears. Chaplin's ideas seemed much less clear than usual. He had decided on a rural subject, had turned the studio's regular street setting into the main thoroughfare of an old world village and built a set for the lobby of a seedy hotel, in which he himself was to play the man of all work who gave the film its (provisional) title. The first few days of shooting were spent on location at the Phelps ranch; and the petty cash disbursements that survive from this period are evocative of that far-off, rustic California. Mrs Phelps was paid $3 a day for the use of her ranch, a dollar a day for the hire of a cow, a dollar for repairs to a fence, and thirty cents a head for lunch for the unit in the ranch cook-house. Cowboys and horses were hired from a neighbouring rancher, Joe Florie.

Production began on 4 November, five weeks behind the scheduled starting date, but Chaplin's desperate lack of a guiding idea was evident from the number of days he took off to 'talk the story' with Bergman and the others, and his readiness to seize on any distraction which offered itself. Work was abandoned so that Charlie, Sydney and Minnie Chaplin could lunch with the Bishop of Birmingham, whose visit to the studio was duly filmed. Another day Chaplin reported to the studio but then went off motoring with Carter De Haven in a 'juvenile racer'. Later in the production the whole company took three days off to go to the air circus in San Diego, vaguely justifying the trip by shooting two thousand feet of film of the event, which was never used. In mid-December Chaplin cut together what he had already shot, but was so dispirited that he absented himself from the studio altogether. Christmas came but Chaplin did not. Neither he nor Edna was seen at the studio in the first weeks of the new year, and on 19 January 1919 the studio closed down altogether. In all Chaplin stayed away from the studio for six weeks. None of his colleagues had ever witnessed such a severe creative crisis in him.

Chaplin returned to the studio on 29 January, and announced that the 21,053 feet of film that had been exposed for *Jack of All Trades* was to be abandoned, and that he intended embarking on a new production to be called *Putting It Over*. Matters proceeded no better: and the situation was aggravated by a series of rainy days that prevented shooting. Chaplin tested some new actresses, hired a couple of cowboys and horses, a cow, a bull and a stunt man; then, after a few more days, he announced that they would after all resume work on *Jack of All Trades*, once more called *Sunnyside*.

The studio daily reports tell their own story:

February 21	Did not shoot. Mr Chaplin cutting
February 22	Did not shoot. Mr Chaplin cutting
February 23	Did not shoot. Mr Chaplin cutting
February 25	Did not shoot. Looking for locations
February 26	Did not shoot. Mr Chaplin not feeling well
February 27	Did not shoot. Mr Chaplin cutting
February 28	Did not shoot
March 1	Did not shoot. Filmed sunset, 100 feet.
March 2	Did not shoot. Talked story
March 4	Did not shoot. Talked story
March 5	Did not shoot. Mr Chaplin sick
March 6	Did not shoot. Mr Chaplin absent
March 7	Shot 376 feet
March 8	Did not shoot. Talked story

Suddenly, in the middle of March, Chaplin was seized either by desperation or by inspiration. He had by this time spent 150 days on the production, two thirds of them idle. Now however, for three weeks he shot day in and day out, filming well over a thousand feet of film most days, and putting together the elements of a rough and ready but cohesive story. He developed a love interest, between Edna and himself, and a rival in the shape of a dashing city slicker who arrives to turn her head with his natty clothes and gallant manners. (Was he turning life into art?)

Sunnyside betrays the strain that went into its completion, and Chaplin and his contemporaries regarded it as one of his least successful pictures. Certainly the comedy is neither so tightly structured nor so firmly motivated as in his other films of this period, but there are interesting departures fom Chaplin's usual manner, quite apart from the experiment of showing Charlie in a bucolic setting. He indulges a peculiarly macabre strain with his device to get rid of the village idiot, while he is courting Edna. Blindfolding the youth under the pretext of a game of hide-and-seek, he gently guides him to the middle of the road where the wretched creature stays for the rest of the film, threatened by on-rushing traffic. There is, too, Charlie's strange homage to *L'Après-midi d'un Faune*. The sequence begins with the cattle chase through the village after cowherd Charlie has allowed his charges to stray. He is tossed by the most ferocious of the beasts, lands on her back and is borne out of the village to be thrown, unconscious, into a ditch beside a little bridge.

He dreams that he is awakened by four nymphs, who draw him into an arcadian dance with them. Charlie's ballet becomes decidedly more animated after he has fallen backwards on a cactus. A brilliant if eccentric dancer, as he was often to demonstrate, Chaplin had been fascinated by the Ballets Russes on their recent appearances in Los Angeles, and flattered by the dancers' admiration of his own mimetic gifts. Nijinsky and his company visited the studios, and when Chaplin went to see them in the theatre, the great dancer – who had recently left Diaghilev and was himself experiencing the problems of independence – kept the audience waiting for half an hour while he chatted to Chaplin in the interval.

The ending is more enigmatic than any other in Chaplin's films. Seeing that he has lost Edna to the city slicker, he places himself deliberately in the path of an on-coming car. Abruptly the scene cuts to a swift and happy dénouement, in which a truculent Charlie sends the city slicker packing in his automobile, and wins back his Edna. In sixty-five years, critics have failed to agree whether it is the suicide itself which is the dream, or whether the happy end is itself the wish-dream of the dying suicide. *Sunnyside* was finished, to Chaplin's intense relief, on 15 April 1919, and premièred two months later.

There were other causes for Chaplin's anxiety besides his cheerless marriage. As early as 1917 Sydney had been making efforts to bring Hannah to California. Since Aunt Kate's death, Aubrey Chaplin, Charlie's cousin, had kept an eye on Hannah in Peckham House. It seemed an ideal opportunity to bring Hannah to America when Alf Reeves came over in the autumn of 1917, and Sydney cabled him: 'Have obtained American Government permission for my mother's admission here for special treatment. Can you bring her over with two special nurses? See Aubrey Chaplin 47 Hereford Road Bayswater he has full particulars. If satisfactory will cable money for fare, clothes.'

Aubrey found however that the necessary permits were not forthcoming at the English end, and poor Hannah remained in the home. In March 1919, however, Aubrey was able to write to Chaplin that he hoped that arrangements for her journey would be completed by mid-May. Plagued by his marriage and his creative crisis, Chaplin suddenly realized that he could not at this time face the pain of seeing his mother in her current condition. On 21 April he cabled Sydney, who was at the Claridge Hotel, New York: 'SECOND THOUGHTS CONSIDER WILL BE BEST MOTHER REMAIN IN ENGLAND SOME GOOD SEASIDE RESORT. AFRAID PRESENCE HERE MIGHT DEPRESS AND AFFECT MY WORK. GOOD MAY COME ALONE.' Loyal Aubrey set about finding a suitable haven on the coast, and suggested she might be settled, preferably under an assumed name, at Margate, with a nurse and a companion; but for the time being she continued at Peckham House, her dull days varied by occasional rides out and visits from an old friend, Marie Thorne.

After a month's break, Chaplin started on a new production – and the trouble began all over again. The title, *Charlie's Picnic* suggested all sorts of gag possibilities. Chaplin tried out a number of children and chose five, True Boardman Jr, Marion Feducha, Raymond Lee, Bob Kelly and Dixie Doll, who were kept on the payroll for the next four weeks. During the whole time Chaplin managed only to shoot a few desultory scenes on two days. A sweltering summer was not conducive to inspiration. One day the studio clerk recorded 'Hot as the devil'. On 16 June Chaplin gave up, dismissed the children and went out riding with Clement Shorter. A fortnight later he tried again. For four days at the beginning of July he struggled to film something – anything. He dragged in Kono, his chauffeur, to drive his car, and put Alf Reeves and a friend, Elmer Ellsworth, into a scene. Then the studio relapsed into inactivity. One day all the studio clerk could find to enter on his daily report sheet was 'Note: Willard took a nap today'. History has left no clue to the identity of Willard – perhaps he was the studio cat – but the comment indicates the general desperation in face of the inactivity at Sunset and La Brea.

Not the least of Chaplin's problems were domestic worries. Mildred was now really pregnant, and on 7 July gave birth to a malformed boy. Three days later, on 10 July 1919 the studio report loconically records, 'Norman Spencer Chaplin passed on today – 4 p.m.' and the next day: '11 July. Cast all absent . . . Did not shoot. Norman Spencer Chaplin buried today 3 p.m. Inglewood Cemetery.' It was Mildred's idea to inscribe on his gravestone 'The Little Mouse'. Many years later Mildred recalled, 'Charlie took it hard . . . that's the only thing I can remember about Charlie . . . that he cried when the baby died.' Chaplin told a friend bitterly that the undertakers had manipulated a prop smile on the tiny dead face, though the baby had never smiled in life.

It would be presumptuous to trace connexions between this emotional shock and the sudden startling resurgence of creativity in Chaplin that followed it; or between the death of his first child and the subject of the film he was about to make, and which for many remains his greatest work. Ten days after Norman Chaplin's death, Charlie was auditioning babies at the studio. He had meanwhile already found a co-star. In the depressed period which followed the completion of *Sunnyside* he had gone to the Orpheum, and seen there an eccentric dance act, Jack Coogan. For the finish of his act Coogan brought on his four-year-old son who took a bow, gave an impersonation of his father's dancing, and made his exit with an energetic shimmy. Chaplin was delighted – perhaps it reminded him of his own first appearance on the stage when he was not much older than Jackie Coogan.

A night or two later, Chaplin met Jackie for the first time. He entered the dining room of the Alexandria Hotel with Sid Grauman, just as Jackie and his parents were leaving. They stopped and spoke: Grauman had known both Coogan parents in vaudeville, when he was managing theatres for his father; Mrs Coogan had toured the circuit as a child performer known as Baby Lillian. While Grauman and the Coogans were talking, Chaplin sat down beside Jackie so that he was on his level, and began to talk to him. Then he asked Mrs Coogan if he could borrow him for a few moments. Mrs Coogan was surprised, but Charlie Chaplin was Charlie Chaplin. As she later remembered, for an hour and forty-five minutes Chaplin and Coogan played together in the corner of the lobby on the Alexandria's famous 'million-dollar carpet' (so called because of all the movie deals that had been made on it).

Eventually Chaplin brought the child back, and said, 'This is the most amazing person I ever met in my life.' The moment of enchantment for Chaplin, it appeared, was when he asked Jackie what he did, and Jackie serenely replied: 'I am a prestidigitator who works in a world of legerdemain.' The phrase must have been one of the brilliant little mimic's show pieces, but it could not fail to touch Chaplin with his own keen delight in words. Charmed as he was, however, Chaplin had still no thought of using Jackie in a picture.

During the period of sitting around in the studio, waiting for inspiration for *Charlie's Picnic*, Chaplin began to talk about the Coogan act. Somebody in the unit said that he had heard that Roscoe Arbuckle had just signed up Coogan. At once Chaplin kicked himself for not having the idea of putting the boy into films himself. Wretchedly he began to think of all the gags he might have done with the child. The publicity man, Carlyle Robinson, made the happy discovery that it was the father and not the son who had been signed up by Arbuckle. The studio secretary, Mr Biby, was sent to see Jack Coogan, who agreed to let his son work for Chaplin. 'Of course you can have the little punk,' he said.

On 30 July Chaplin happily laid aside the 6570 feet of film he had already shot for *Charlie's Picnic*, decided that the best of the infant aspirants he had auditioned was Baby Hathaway, and started to work on *The Waif*. Now he seemed inspired. Throughout August and September he worked in a fury of enthusiasm. There were no absences from the studio, no days off to 'talk the story' or to make outings to San Diego. Some days the unit would shoot more than four thousand feet of film, the footage of two two-reelers.

As usual Chaplin filmed the story in continuity; and the scenes he shot during these prolific weeks were to appear almost without revision in the definitive version of *The Kid*. Edna is seen leaving the charity hospital, a child in her arms, under the scornful gaze of a nurse and a gateman: in the completed film a title succinctly explains her situation: 'The woman – whose sin was motherhood'. Edna – probably intending suicide – leaves the baby in the back of an opulent car,* with a note asking the finder to protect and care for him. Ironically the car is thereupon stolen by two murderous-looking crooks. Finding the baby in the back, they roughly dump him in an alley.

In the studio Charles D. Hall had created the attic setting which indelibly defines our vision of *The Kid*. It might be an illustration to *Oliver Twist*, with its sloping ceiling under the eaves, its peeling walls, bare boards, maimed furniture and a door giving onto a precipice of

---

* The car used for the scene belonged to D. W. Griffith.

stairs. It might – must – also be a recollection of the attic at 3 Pownall Terrace, where Charlie had bumped his head on the ceiling when he sat up in bed.

Here, in four days of shooting, Chaplin created the memorable sequence with Baby Hathaway, in which the Tramp, having unwillingly become the guardian of Edna's mislaid child, teaches himself the crafts of child care. He improvises a hammock-cradle, a feeding bottle made from an old coffee pot and (when with some concern he feels the moist underside of the hammock) a handy device consisting of a chair with a hole cut in the seat and a cuspidor placed beneath it. These homely details caused offence to a few more puritanical spectators of the period, but the audience at large loved them.

Chaplin moved on to the scenes in the same attic supposed to take place some five years later, when the baby has grown into Jackie Coogan. Jackie proved such a natural actor and apt pupil that most of this sequence was shot within a week. One or other of the Coogan parents was always on the set – Mrs Coogan during the early period while Jack Senior was still under contract to Arbuckle; later Jack Senior himself. They watched with delighted fascination Chaplin's relationship with their son. It was a very real and close friendship. The two of them would disappear together to walk and play in the orange groves. They might spend hours watching ants at work, and Chaplin would enjoy explaining to Jackie the marvels of nature. For his part Jackie was not really aware of Chaplin's importance: he simply regarded him as the most remarkable man he had ever met.

Mrs Coogan, as she explained much later to her grandson, Anthony Coogan, felt that the relationship was one of great complexity. On one level Chaplin, in Jackie's company, became a child. A large part of his gift, and of the character of the Tramp, was his ability to see life from a child-like viewpoint. In his association with Jackie he was able to exhibit and extend this child-like behaviour. On another level Chaplin, off screen as well as on, adopted a paternal role to Jackie. It was impossible for people at the studio to resist the feeling that Jackie represented the child that he had just lost.

Above all Jackie provided Chaplin with the most perfect actor with whom he was ever to work. For Chaplin, the complete protean, actors were necessary tools. Ideally he would have played every part in his films himself. Because he could not, he needed actors who could reproduce his own performances. What he looked for in his actors was a perfect imitation of the looks and gestures and, later, intonations he would show them. This was why more independently creative players were often irked; and why in some of the best performances we seem to be seeing Chaplin himself in someone else's skin – it could be man or woman.

Jackie's genius was as a mimic. When Chaplin showed him something, he could do it. Three or four rehearsals were usually enough; and Chaplin said he was a one-take player. He could undertake scenes of complexity that might defeat grown-ups. 'The mechanics,' Chaplin noted, 'induced the emotion.' It cannot have invariably gone so easily but, as Lita Grey remembered, 'his patience was limitless with the child, even when Jackie muffed one take after another. "We've plenty of time," he said, soothing the confused child. "The most difficult scenes are the simplest to do. The simplest bits of business are usually the hardest ..."[4] No child actor, whether in silent or in sound pictures, has ever surpassed Jackie Coogan's performance as The Kid, in its truthfulness and range of sentiment.

Little could stem Chaplin's tremendous creative surge, though there were interruptions. One day in that very different Hollywood, the smoke from a nearby forest fire spoilt the pictures. There was a day of rain; and one day Jackie disgraced himself by going missing. The incident is tersely recorded in the daily report for 17 September: 'Jackie Coogan – lost and licked'.* At the end of September, however, the surge ended. Chaplin moved into a new set, and a dead end. The scene was a dosshouse, for which he was later to find the right use in *The Kid*. For the moment though he was evidently unclear how best to use it. He spent three days and upwards of seven thousand feet of film for an elaborate gag about a flea circus and the inconveniences attendant on the escape of artistes. This footage was later to play a part in one of the more intriguing mysteries of Chaplin's creative life. For the moment it was abandoned. Then work on *The Waif* came to a halt.

One reason was that Chaplin had realized that *The Waif* was going to prove much bigger than anything he had previously attempted, and was likely to take many months to complete. First National, however, were impatient for a new release. The only way to gain the breathing space necessary to work at his own pace on *The Waif* was

---

* This minimizes the anxiety of the event. Jackie had fallen asleep behind some scenery. When he woke up he stayed in his hiding place watching with detached curiosity the hue and cry for him, as a nearby lake was dragged. It was Jack Coogan Senior who administered the ultimate licking.

to knock out a film as fast as possible. He had, after all, made two-reelers in a month for Mutual and in a week at Keystone.

With such a strong incentive to produce a film, Chaplin had little trouble with his 'quickie'. The material with the cars and the children already shot for *Charlie's Picnic* was reconsidered. It cut together well enough, and the title was changed to *The Ford Story*. Chaplin hired a featured comedienne, ample Babe London (enthusiastically described on the daily studio reports as 'great'), along with fifteen extras and four coloured musicians. The whole unit was bussed to San Pedro, where a pleasure boat, the *Ace*, was rented from the San Pedro Transportation Company for $5 an hour. The boat was the kind of prop that had never failed to ignite his imagintion in the old Mutual days, and he set to inventing variations on the themes of dancing, sea-sickness, collapsing deckchairs, jealous husbands and the perils of storm-tossed boats. In seven consecutive working days he had shot some twenty-five thousand feet of film. The editing was finished in a fortnight, and the film, now called *A Day's Pleasure* was shipped to First National on 3 November.

The film was a cheerful throw-back to Mutual days and earlier. As Chaplin originally planned the editing, it would have been even more like the old style of Essanay and Mutual two-act two-reeler than in the event it turned out. His first idea was simply to precede the boat sequence with the motor car material, involving Charlie's efforts to start his temperamental Ford, and his encounters on the road with angry fellow-motorists, hostile speed cops and newly-spread tar. In the end, however, the car material was divided to provide neat framing sequences for the central boat material. The film now ends with a title, 'The end of a perfect day', as Charlie's car shimmies off towards the horizon amidst clouds of smoke.

Chaplin was quite aware that the film was a makeshift, and neither audiences nor reviewers of the time concealed their disappointment with *A Day's Pleasure*, as with *Sunnyside*. Chaplin was confident enough in his current project to ignore criticisms. On 14 November he resumed work on the film which was now definitively re-titled *The Kid*. The next sequence on which he embarked was destined to be removed from the film, on the grounds of its excessive sentimentality, when Chaplin re-edited the film and added a musical accompaniment, fifty years later. As it appeared in the original release version of the film, the scene followed Edna's discharge from the charity hospital and a brief sequence introducing the father of her child, an artist.

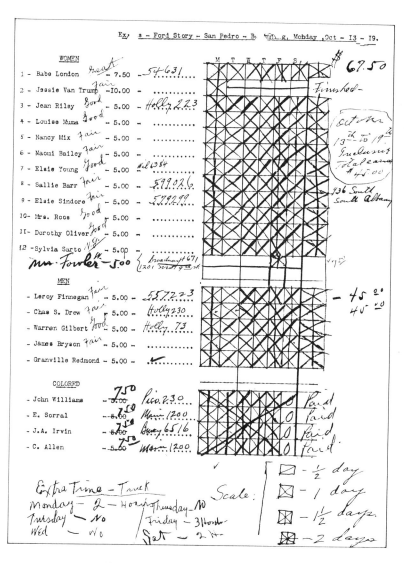

1919 - Record of employment
and payment of actors while shooting
the boat scenes of *A Day's Pleasure.*

Edna arrives at a church where a marriage is being celebrated. As she pauses by a window to watch, the bride's corsage falls to the ground and is accidentally crushed under the feet of the elderly bridegroom. A reflection in the window appears momentarily like a halo around Edna's head. The scene preceded that of the mother abandoning her child in the limousine.

One incident during the filming of this sequence is a reminder that these were still very much the infant days of the film industry. One of the extras hired was a man called Edgar Sherrod, so much a specialist in playing priests that he brought along his own vestments. There was an ugly scene over this, however. The studio paysheet records:

> Edgar Sherrod and vestments. Paid $25. Paid under protest. Note: After being established in picture at rate of $12.50, Edgar Sherrod held out for $25.00. Reported to M.P.P.S for Black List.

For Christmas 1919 Chaplin asked Jackie what he would like as a present. The boy told him that most of all he would like to visit his grandmother in San Francisco. To make this possible, Chaplin closed the studio for a week – perhaps the most singular mark of his feeling for his small co-star. With only this interruption, the whole of December and the first week of the New Year were spent on the sequence which remains the most extraordinary in the film, and indeed one of the most memorable in the whole history of the cinema. The Kid falls sick, and the Tramp calls in a curmudgeonly old physician. When the doctor asks if he is the boy's father, the Tramp inadvisedly shows the note that was attached to the foundling, and which he now keeps carefully preserved between the pages of a worn and dusty copy of the *Police Gazette*. The doctor says that the child needs proper care and attention. Proper care and attention soon arrive – in the form of a self-important representative of the orphan asylum and his toadying aide. Despite the heroic struggles of the Tramp and the Kid – armed with a hammer as big as himself – the child is carried off and thrown, like a stray dog, into the back of a wagon. With a fierce cop in hot pursuit, the Tramp blunders across the slum roof-tops to intercept the wagon, hurls the orphanage official into the road, and rescues the Kid. This astonishing scene never loses its impact, however often it is seen. There is passion, despair, madness in the Tramp's desperate trajectory across the roofs, and the absurd, waddling little figure is elevated to heroic pathos. Few screen embraces are as affecting as the kiss which the Tramp plants on the quivering lips of the terrified child.

The ebullient Jackie was not too easily subdued to the emotional temper of the scene. Chaplin could not bear to make Jackie cry himself. The direction of Jackie in this scene was left to his father. Jack Senior quite simply whispered to Jackie that if he did not cry to order he would be taken off the film and sent to a real workhouse. Jackie was no fool. He cried so hard that Chaplin was alarmed and anxiously reassured him that nobody would take him away. 'I knew Daddy was fooling,' he replied, conspiratorially. Jack Coogan Senior was a useful man to have about the set. He played several roles in the film: the skid row bum who picks the Tramp's pocket, the Devil, and a guest at the artists' party at which Edna, now become a famous opera star, meets again the father of her child. Chaplin removed this scene from his 1970 re-issue of *The Kid*.

At this stage of production, Chaplin's domestic troubles began to obtrude once more. After the lease on their first home expired, Chaplin had moved the household – it now included Mildred's mother, which did not help matters – to 674 South Oxford Drive, Beverly Hills. In the months of creative exaltation Chaplin had been able to forget the frustrations and irritations of his marriage but Mildred did not relish being forgotten. The estrangement which now occurred was inevitable. Chaplin moved back to the Los Angeles Athletic Club. Mildred retained the house.

At first the separation was fairly amicable and dignified. Then the press latched on to the story and provoked the talkative Mildred into attacks on her estranged husband. Irritation and anxiety made it more and more difficult for Chaplin to concentrate. Towards the end of February 1920 the pace of work at the studio began to slow down and Chaplin was increasingly absent. From 15 March filming stopped completely, and two days later the newspapers across the country published the news that Mrs Chaplin was filing a suit for divorce. The announcement followed very soon after the news that Douglas Fairbanks and Mary Pickford, Chaplin's friends and peers as million dollar stars, were divorcing their respective partners. At first Mildred merely accused her husband of desertion, said she still 'loved him to death' and that she did not want a divorce or money. A day or two later, on 22 March 1920, her lawyers had changed the charges to cruelty, and Mildred now announced that she proposed to 'tell everything. I shall let the world know how he failed to provide for me and how he sent an employee to my house and took away certain of my private papers. He humiliated me before the servants. Isn't that cruelty?' Chaplin replied with a brief press statement:

> On account of my reputation, which I have spent eighteen years in building up, I am compelled to refute Mrs Chaplin's statement as to non-support, for I have over $50,000 in cancelled cheques which have been paid out during our short married life on her behalf. And this has been spent in addition to her own salary which is $1000 a week. Until this outbreak of hers I have not refused payment of one solitary request or bill which she has presented to me. With reference to legal proceedings I wish to remain absolutely silent. I have tried to be gentlemanly and to act with dignity under the unfortunate circumstances, and have nothing further to say.

The circumstances of Hollywood made it hard to remain dignified, however, and on 7 April 1920 Chaplin was involved in one of the scandals which thrilled the motion picture fans and were throughout his life deeply repugnant to his naturally reserved temper. He was dining at the Alexandria Hotel with some friends; Louis B. Mayer, who had Mildred Harris under contract, was with a party at a neighbouring table. Notes were exchanged (Roland Totheroh alleged however that Mayer's supposed note, which sparked the affair, was in fact fabricated as a prank by one of Chaplin's own party, Jack Pickford). Chaplin was still resentful of Mayer for having rushed Mildred into a contract immediately following the marriage and the attendant publicity, against Chaplin's advice. Now Chaplin told Mayer to take off his glasses, and aimed a punch at him. Mayer, after a youth spent in the scrap metal business, was no weakling and hit back. Both men fell, the hotel staff intervened, Chaplin was escorted to his room and Mayer left the hotel.

Mildred at the time was dancing fox-trots with the Prince of Wales and Lord Louis Mountbatten at a dance given by the Mayor of San Diego at Coronado Beach, eight hundred miles from Hollywood. When told by eager reporters what had occurred, she showed only mild concern and was keener to tell them that 'The Prince is a nice, clean-cut boy, and he is certainly a clever dancer. I enjoyed every minute of our dance together.'

Work at the studio had briefly resumed soon after this, on 17 April, but only to pose some stills of Christ bearing the cross (they were shot on Eagle Rock Hill) which were eventually to be inserted in the opening scenes of the film as a commentary upon the sufferings of the unwed mother. An additional factor in the break-down of production may have been difficulties with Edna. During the shooting of the film, she had begun to drink, 'not heavily', said Lita Grey, who worked on the film, 'but enough to displease Chaplin, who viewed drinking during working hours as unprofessional and therefore intolerable.' However the difficulties, whatever they were, were smoothed over, and Edna remained in the film.

Eventually Chaplin sought distraction from private annoyances in a return to work. He made tests for the last sequence of the film, reshot some of the attic material and in May had the dosshouse set rebuilt. Now he had a narrative purpose for it: Tramp and Kid seek refuge there from the orphanage officials, but are betrayed by the housekeeper (Henry Bergman). The dosshouse scenes were finished by the end of May, and the next two months were spent on the last major sequence of the film – one of the most elaborate and certainly the strangest of the many dream sequences in Chaplin's films. Alone, wretched and locked out, the Tramp falls asleep on the doorstep and dreams that the alley is transformed into paradise. All the characters of the film – even the Bully, the Cop and the orphanage officials – become genial winged angels. He is reunited with the Kid; but when all seems bliss, Sin creeps in. The Devil tempts the Tramp with a pretty girl, which arouses the jealousy of her boyfriend, the Bully. He takes out a gun and shoots the Tramp. The Kid cries over his bleeding and lifeless body . . . at which point the Tramp is wakened by the Cop.

The dream puzzled contemporary spectators and critics; Chaplin was disappointed when Sir James Barrie, king of whimsy, accused him of being too whimsical and said the sequence was a mistake. Francis Hackett in *The New Republic* was more perceptive:

> The dream of Heaven I thought highly amusing. What amused me was its limitedness, its meagreness. It was like a simple man's version of the Big Change, made up from the few properties with which a simple man would be likely to be acquainted. The lack of inventiveness seemed to me to be its best point. Others tell me that it was a failure of inventiveness. Mayhap. But after suffering the success of movie-inventiveness so many times, with the whole apparatus of the factory employed to turn out some sort of slick statement or other, I rejoice over this bit of thin and faltering fantasy. And I venture to believe that it represents exactly what Chaplin intended. It was the simplified Heaven of the antic sprite whom Chaplin

has created and whose inner whimsicality is here so amusingly indulged.

Not the least intriguing aspect of the dream sequence in *The Kid* is the casting. One of the children who appears in it is Esther Ralston, who was to become a major star in the later 1920s. The minx who vamps and tempts the Tramp was a twelve-year-old called Lillita McMurray who had been introduced to the studio by Chaplin's assistant, Chuck Riesner, a neighbour of the child's mother and grandparents. Her prettiness intrigued Chaplin, and he put her under contract. Lillita believed that the dream sequence in the film was actually inspired by her arrival at the studio. Four years later Lillita, as Lita Grey, was to become the second Mrs Chaplin, a marriage that was to bring more bitterness to Chaplin's life even than his time with Mildred.

Mildred, however, was giving her husband a great deal of trouble, spurred on, rather unexpectedly, by Chaplin's business associates at First National. Chaplin was in dispute with the company over the way they intended to deal with him over *The Kid*. They were determined to pay him for its seven reels on the basis of three two-reelers. Having expended $500,000 and eighteen months of his life on the film, he was asking for a special arrangement which would give him something more than the $405,000 this would have produced. When Mildred suddenly reneged on her previous agreement to a divorce settlement of $100,000 Chaplin realized that First National was behind her, meaning to make use of her divorce suit to attach his business assets – which included the negative of *The Kid*.

Chaplin had in fact been aware of such a danger for several months. As early as 9 April he had telegraphed to Sydney in New York: 'IMPENDING TROUBLE WILL I SHIP NEGATIVE TO YOU FOR SAFETY WIRE ADVISE IMMEDIATELY.' For the moment, however, no such precaution had seemed necessary. At the beginning of August 1920 Totheroh was awakened at three o'clock one morning by Alf Reeves, who told him that they had to get out of town. In turn Totheroh got hold of his assistant, Jack Wilson, and the studio carpenter and together they worked to pack the negative – it amounted to some 400,000 feet – in twelve crates. Inside the crates the film was in 200-foot rolls, enclosed for safety in coffee tins. At Santa Fe railroad depot they were met by Chaplin and his secretary Tom Harrington, with the tickets. There was a moment of thoroughly

Chaplinesque comedy: Chaplin was confident that no one would recognize him behind his dark glasses, but no sooner had they entered the station restaurant than a small boy began to shriek 'Charlie Chaplin! Charlie Chaplin!'[5]

The conspirators arrived at Salt Lake City, and put up at a hotel where they turned a bedroom into an improvised cutting room. Handling the highly inflammable nitrate film in a public place of this sort was against all regulations, but somehow they managed to keep their operations and the vast quantities of film secret. When the editing was completed, they risked a trial preview in a local cinema. Chaplin was greatly reassured by the enthusiasm of the audience. With the cut negative, they took the train to New York and found a vacant studio in New Jersey to complete the editing and laboratory work. To evade awkward inquiries they erected a notice outside the place saying 'Blue Moon Film Company'.

Chaplin moved into the Ritz where he stayed in hiding for fear of process servers. He was bored, however, and badly wanted to meet the writer Frank Harris, so borrowed a dress, hat and veil from Minnie Chaplin and swept through the Ritz lobby in drag. He was rewarded: he and Harris got on famously, and Chaplin stayed until the small hours after which, having resumed his own clothes, he did not dare to return to the Ritz. Unable to find a hotel, he was obliged to stay in the home of a sympathetic taxi driver. During the evening Chaplin acted out for Harris his own version of the divorce settlement negotiations, as Harris later described:

> Every morning in the paper a fresh appeal appeared from Mildred Chaplin: the injured lady wept, protested, cajoled, threatened all in a breath. One morning a change: she published the following:
>
> 'My final statement: Mr Chaplin is not a Socialist. He is a great artist, a very serious personality, and a real intellectual.' Yes, those are her very words; and she continues: 'The world will be amazed at the intensity of his mind.' What can have happened? I ask myself. Has Charlie weakened and paid without counting?
>
> I read on: 'I have no desire to obtain half of his fortune. (No?) I will not hinder the sale of his latest moving picture.' (Whew, the wind sets in that quarter, does it?)
>
> And then: 'I am entitled to a settlement. (Eh?) I am too ill, physically and mentally, to work at present, and this notoriety and exposition of my personal affairs is very disagreeable to me.' (Really? You needn't indulge in it, Madame, unless you want to.)
>
> Finally: 'He is a great artist, a brilliant man, plays the violin, 'cello,

piano, and so forth . . . I have already filed papers against him.' Well, well, and again well.

Here is Charlie's story of talks with his wife on the 'phone about their divorce.

'Is that you, Charlie? It's me. Mildred. I'm ill and have no money. Won't you give me fifty thousand dollars, and settle all this disagreeable law business? You will? You're a dear; I knew a great artist like you couldn't be mean. If you knew how I hate to quarrel and dispute. Let us meet at my lawyer's in an hour, eh? Goodbye till then.'

Quarter of an hour later:

'Is that you, Charlie? Oh, I'm so sorry, but my lawyer won't let me take fifty thousand; he says it's ridiculous. Won't you give me a hundred thousand, and I can satisfy him? Please; I'm so nervous and ill. You will? Oh you –! Well, you're just you – the one man in the world. I can't say more. Now for that dreadful lawyer, and then we'll meet and just sign. How are you? Well! Oh, I'm so glad. In half an hour, dear.'

Quarter of an hour later:

'Charlie! What can I say? I'm just heart-broken, and I've such a headache. That lawyer says I mustn't settle for a hundred thousand. His fee is goodness knows how much. I must have at least a hundred and fifty thousand. What am I to do? Mamma says – You will? Oh, my! I'm so glad. I don't know how to thank you. It's the last word, you say? All right, Charlie, I'm satisfied. In half an hour, then.'

Ten minutes later:

'It's no good, Charlie. I can't settle for that; it's really too little. You see, Charlie! Charlie! Did you ring off? Or is it the filthy exchange? Oh, dear! Damn!'

Charlie Chaplin is a master of comedy in life, as he is on the stage; an artist in refined humour, he can laugh even at himself and his own emotions. On the point of leaving Pasadena for a trip to New York, he rang his wife up.

'Mildred, it's me, Charlie. Will you take half a million dollars, and settle this ridiculous claim? You will? No, I'm not a darling; but meet me at my lawyer's in an hour, and we can sign.'

A quarter of an hour later:

'Mildred, dear, I'm sorry, but my lawyer won't let me give half a million; he says a year's earnings for a week's marriage is too much. He says a hundred thousand is more than generous. Will I listen to you? Of course I will. Talk away . . .'

A woman's voice, high pitched: 'You're no man. Again you've let me down, and made a fool of me. You've no character. I'll teach you . . .' (Left talking).

Charlie Chaplin strolls away from the 'phone with a smile on his lips and a little sub-acid contempt for human, and especially for feminine, nature.[6]

The divorce suit commenced in August. Chaplin's lawyer announced that he would not contest it provided that Mildred's lawyers withdrew an order restraining him from selling *The Kid*. The divorce was granted on 19 November: Mildred was awarded $100,000 and a share of community property.

Chaplin was now free to negotiate *The Kid* with First National. Emboldened by the enthusiasm at the first showing in Salt Lake City, he asked them for an advance of $1,500,000, and 50 per cent of the net after the company had recovered the advance. The company demurred, and affected an insulting lack of enthusiasm when Chaplin showed them the film, but he stuck out until even the executives of First National recognized that in *The Kid* he had an untrumpable card. The film finally opened in New York on 6 January 1921 to instant and huge success. Within the next three years *The Kid* was distributed in some fifty countries across the world from Norway to Malaya, Egypt to Australia. By 1924 the Soviet Union, Yugoslavia and Colombia were practically the only places where it had not been shown. Everywhere its reception was as enthusiastic.

The Kid made little Jackie Coogan into a world figure. Chaplin himself was among those who felt that the vast, universal response to Jackie's image was in part due to his function as a symbol of all the orphans of the recent war. Jackie provided something that the world needed, as he himself had done. He also saw that they could not continue to work together. He told the Coogans, 'I am not going to hold him back,' and gave them the option he held on Jackie's services.

Jackie went on to make a score of feature films for First National and Metro. One or two, like *Peck's Bad Boy* and *Oliver Twist*, caught something of the great child actor of *The Kid*; but for the most part the rest suffered from sentimental scripts and insensitive direction. By 1927 Jackie's film career had virtually finished. 'Senility,' it was said in Hollywood, 'hit him at thirteen.' In the half dozen years of his fame, however, he had mixed with great celebrities of the world. In 1924 he undertook a World Crusade in aid of Near East Relief. It raised more than a million dollars' worth of food and clothing: the Coogan family would accept no fees or expenses. The crusade became a royal progress. Jackie met Mussolini and was decorated by the Pope in special audience. Only Clemenceau declined to meet him, cabling his regret to Jackie's father that, 'I am not celebrity enough to meet your illustrious son.' Jackie received the adoration of the public everywhere he went, and somehow managed to stay natural, unspoilt, the perfect child.

His parents had meanwhile become estranged, though their Catholicism and concern for their son's career kept them from making the matter public. Jack Coogan Senior devoted himself to the management of Jackie's business affairs, and Jackie confidently believed that the $4 million he had earned in the good years were held in trust for him and would be his when he reached his majority. Five months before Jackie's twenty-first birthday, however, his father was killed when the car in which they were driving crashed. His father's estate went to his mother, who was subsequently to deny the existence of a trust fund and to assert, on the contrary, the legal right of parents to all moneys earned by their children while minors. In 1938 Jackie brought a suit against his mother and his former business manager, Arthur L. Bernstein, whom she had by this time married.

The suit dragged on until most of the fortune was eaten away. Finally, in March 1939 a settlement was agreed.* Not long afterwards Jackie was reconciled with his mother, who clearly had exerted a dominating influence over him and would continue to do so until her death. At the time of the suit, he was married to Betty Grable. It was to be the first of a number of somewhat turbulent marriages. He served in the United States forces during the war, and afterwards had an uneven career as entertainer and actor. There was a special irony in the most celebrated role of his later career – as Uncle Fester in the television series *The Addams Family*. The most wonderful child in the world had become the nastiest of all old men. The older Coogan took pleasure in this kind of irony: at the end of his life he drove a car whose registration plate carried the letters K-I-D, but with the order reversed.

Chaplin had little contact with his child friend in later years: he appears not even to have included him on his Christmas card list.

---

* The single positive outcome of the Coogan case was that it led to the passage of the Child Actor's Bill (4 May 1939), which has always since been known as The Coogan Act. This provides that the guardian of a child artist shall set aside half the earnings for a trust fund or equivalent form of savings for the child's benefit, and account to the court for the remainder of the earnings.

When Jackie in a moment of particular financial crisis asked him for assistance, however, Chaplin handed him $1,000 without hesitation.

After his disillusion with First National over *The Kid*, Chaplin was eager to be done with the contract as quickly as possible. His partners in a new distribution venture were also impatient. In January 1919 United Artists had been incorporated with Douglas Fairbanks, Mary Pickford, D. W. Griffith and Chaplin as partners. The seeds of the plan had been sown in the course of the Liberty Bond tours, when Chaplin, Fairbanks and Pickford had met Oscar Price, press agent of William Gibbs McAdoo, Secretary of the Treasury, in Washington. 'Why,' Price asked them, 'don't you folks get together and distribute your own pictures?' They began to consider the idea more seriously at the end of 1918, when their suspicions were aroused by the behaviour of their various employers. First National were adamant in their refusal to better Chaplin's existing contract; Paramount showed no interest at all in renewing the contracts of Pickford and Fairbanks, which were due to expire. The three stars got together with Griffith and William S. Hart, the stone-faced western hero, and speculated that the film companies were planning a strategy to put a stop to the astronomical salaries that the major stars were commanding. The idea, they rightly guessed, was to organize a great merger of the producing companies and a monopoly of distribution outlets, and in this way bring the stars to heel once more. The producers' move was imminent: during the first week in January the heads of the industry met for a convention in the Alexandria Hotel.

Fairbanks and Chaplin decided to hire private detectives to spy on the delegates to the convention. The reports of Pinkertons' Operator 5 and Operator 8 read like operetta, as they describe their ruses of paging and shadowing Adolph Zukor, Sam Goldfish (later Goldwyn) and the rest of the boardroom *dramatis personae*. Operator 8 was an attractive young woman, and used her charms to advantage:

> While gentleman was waiting for 'Jim' to return he looked at me and smiled. I did not return the smile but looked at said gentleman at different times.
>
> Later, after this gentleman had left Parlor A. and sent downstairs, he sent me a card asking me to call him at 8 p.m. in Room 1157. Later, at 4.30 p.m. gentleman met me on the mezzanine and asked me my room number, which I gave him. At 5 p.m. this gentleman knocked on my

door. I answered door and was rather surprised to find said gentleman. He stated his name was Mr Harry, and that he would try and see me later in the p.m. Within five hours, 10 p.m., this gentleman came to my door, stating he had to go up to the twelfth floor to see Mr Zukor and that Clara Kimball Young was up there, but that he would be back in a few minutes. At 10.35 he returned and sat in a chair and smoked. He asked if my home was in Los Angeles. I told him no, that I was from Kentucky, but that I came from San Francisco here. He then asked me if I was interested in the pictures. I said no, but that I always enjoyed looking at a good picture. He then stated he was here from Detroit, Mich., and that they were holding a meeting in regard to the releasing of pictures. He then asked me who my favourite actress was. I told him Clara Kimball Young and Norma Talmadge. He asked me if I liked Mary Pickford. I told him yes and I liked Clara. He asked me if I knew how much Mary made. I told him no. He said that she got the biggest salary of any moving picture actress or actor. I remarked that I had heard that Charlie Chaplin received the highest salary, and he said no indeed. I then said that I did not think it right for Mary and Charlie to receive such salary when there were others that are just as good. He said, 'That's so, too, and their salary will have to be cut for we picture men cannot pay the price that is being asked for the releasing of their pictures. I then asked if that was the reason he came to Los Angeles and he said yes. I asked if he thought they would succeed and he said, 'Surely they will have to come to our terms.' About this time the House Officer came to my door. I went to door and he stated he was sorry but that the house would not allow any lady that's alone to have company in her room. Officer said he realized there was no harm done but that it was the rules of the house. I told the officer that I was sorry. Gentleman assured Officer that there was no harm meant. Officer said that he could see that, but it was merely the rules of the house. Gentleman left, saying he would call me the next day in the p.m.[7]

Despite this frustrating interruption at the most exciting part of her Mata Hari effort, Operator 8 managed more meetings with 'Mr Harry', and used her charms (precisely how we shall never know) to extract from him the information that Fairbanks and Chaplin needed. Fairbanks, Pickford, Hart and Chaplin made sure that the moguls were aware of their presence around the Alexandria Hotel, and on 15 January 1919 called a press conference to announce their intention of setting up a company to distribute their own independent productions, which they would call United Artists. Now committed to their idea, they drew up contracts of incorporation for the company on 5 February (by this time Hart had withdrawn from the scheme).

Certificates of incorporation were filed in Delaware on 17 April. At once they were besieged by offers from prominent producers – including Zukor himself – who wanted to resign their jobs to run United Artists. The Artists however invited McAdoo to be President. He declined, but said that if they appointed Oscar Price, the first begetter of the idea, he would help them organize and act as general counsel. Hiram Abrams, a former President of Paramount who had seceded from Zukor after disagreements, became General Manager. (Benjamin B. Hampton's authoritative *History of the American Film Industry* credits Abrams and his colleague Benjamin P. Schulberg with the original concept of United Artists. Abrams remained General Manager until his death in 1928.)

The corporation operated as a distributor for films which the four partners – and other film makers who wished to join in the plan – produced independently. The arrangement was revolutionary. Until this time producers and distributors – with the exception of First National – had been employers, and the stars salaried employees. Now the stars became their own employers. They were their own financiers, and they received the profits that had hitherto gone to their employers. Each in addition received his share of the profits of the distributing organization.

Fairbanks and Pickford built a fine modern studio on Santa Monica Boulevard to make their pictures for United Artists' Release. Fairbanks had already released five films through United Artists, including the spectacular *Robin Hood*. Griffith brought *Broken Blossoms* (which he bought back from Paramount for $250,000) and *Way Down East*. Pickford's *Dorothy Vernon of Haddon Hall* was less successful with the public. Chaplin meanwhile was stuck with First National: at the time of the formation of United Artists he was still entangled with *Sunnyside*, with four films to go after that.

Now, at the start of 1921, he had still three films to deliver, and his partners were understandably impatient. *The Idle Class*, though it took five months to complete, gave him few problems. Although much more opulent in its production, it was a story simple enough for an Essanay or early Mutual film: some elements recall the early 'bogus Count' stories. Ironically, the story centres upon an unhappy marriage. Chaplin plays a dual role: as Edna's inebriate and neglectful husband; and as Charlie the Tramp, his double, who is mistaken for her husband by Edna, her father and friends. Completed at the end of June, *The Idle Class* was not released until 25 September.

Chaplin now felt that he could face the strain of having his mother near him, and fresh application for a visa was made to the State Department. On 3 March 1921 the State Department informed the Justice Deparment, 'Referring to your desire to have Mrs Hannah Chaplin, mother of Charles Chaplin, come to this country from England, you are informed that telegraphic authorization is now being sent to the American Consul General at London to grant a visa to the above-mentioned person.' Mr Hughes of the Solicitor General's office passed on the message to Charles and Sydney, expressing his hope that 'the matter has been satisfactorily adjusted and that the old lady will soon be on her way over.'

Tom Harrington was sent to England to bring her back to California. Hannah was astonished and delighted when Harrington, with

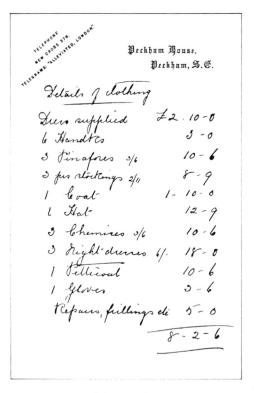

1920 - Bill from Peckham House
for Hannah Chaplin's clothing.

the help of Aubrey Chaplin and his wife, spent more than £100 on a new wardrobe for her, including hats, coats, a dressing gown and a toilet case. On the journey she behaved quite normally, but on her arrival in New York there was a slight contretemps when she mistook an immigration official for Jesus Christ. Harrington smoothed over the incident. Hannah was settled in a bungalow with a pleasant garden near the sea, with a couple to keep house and a trained nurse, Mrs Carey. Chaplin found it painful to visit her too often, but Sydney and Minnie, Amy Reeves and (during the period of her marriage with Chaplin) Lita Grey were among her visitors. They remembered that she would seem perfectly normal for long periods, and entertain them with stories and songs from the music hall days. Sometimes she would talk affectionately about her husband, and would discuss the Zeppelin raids on London. (The Chaplin publicity office announced that her health had been affected by the air raids.) People noticed that she was more subdued and quiet when she was with her son; and Chaplin was sometimes startled by enigmatic insights. 'If you weren't so diffident, I might be able to give you a little advice,' she told him at the time of his marital problems; and then said no more.

She enjoyed sewing, and playing draughts – which she always won. She also liked to go out in her car on shopping expeditions. Konrad Bercovici recounted how on one such spree she came back with hundreds of yards of coloured silk, costing some thousands of dollars. Chaplin was about to send the silk back, but suddenly said, 'Let her have all that and more, and all that she wants of the frippery. The poor soul has been longing for such things all her life.' Only occasionally did her whims, like handing ice cream to startled passers-by, result in embarrassment.

Sometimes she seemed indifferent to her sons' prosperity; at other times she was puzzled and embarrassed by it. Chaplin once or twice brought her to the studio to try to make her understand what his work consisted of. Edward Sutherland was there on one such occasion.

> I remember we were making tests one day, I think for *The Gold Rush*, and we were shooting indoors. In the old days, we had Cooper-Hewitt lighting, the grandfather of the neon light. This was a kind of ghastly blue which washed all the colour out of one's face – the lips were green or purplish. Klieg lights were carbon arc lights . . . These were hard lights encased. Mrs Chaplin, Charlie's mother, came in to the lot. Charlie was made up in character. She said, 'Charlie, I have to get you a new suit.'

He said, 'Now look, Mother. You've seen me in character a million times. You've seen me in pictures. I don't need a new suit.'

She said, 'I've got to get you a new suit – and you have a ghastly colour. You ought to go out in the sunlight.'

He took her out in the sunlight and said, 'Now look, Mother, this is the part I play. This is the character I play.' But he couldn't get it through to her; this day, it wouldn't penetrate to her intelligence. I don't know that he was particularly devoted to her: he felt under obligation to her. I don't think Charlie is what I would call devoted to anybody.[8]

The people chosen to visit Mrs Chaplin in her house in the valley were family friends whose discretion could be relied upon. Winifred Ritchie often went with Alf or Amy Reeves, and sometimes took young Wyn, their daughter.

I was only a schoolgirl, but they knew I wouldn't talk about such things. I never did speak of my visits to Nan till after she died and after Charlie died. She had a very nice house in the valley, with a companion and a nurse. We would go out with Amy and have lunch or dinner with Nan. Sometimes she was brilliant. She would do old songs and sketches. She was like Charlie. She would do wonderful imitations. She could do whole plays from beginning to end. And then all of a sudden, she wouldn't be right.

One day I was sitting beside her at lunch, and I noticed a mark on her arm. And innocently I said, 'Nan, what's that?' And immediately she drew her arm away and hid it; and then started putting bits of bread all about herself, and on her head. The nurse, Mrs Carey, said 'Come with me, Nan,' and took her off into another room. When Mrs Carey came back she said that the mark was a tattoo from the workhouse. She said it brought back the days when they had not had enough to eat; and she was putting the bread away for Sydney and Charlie.[9]

During her days in Hollywood, Hannah was at last reunited with her youngest son, Wheeler Dryden, whom she had not seen since he was snatched away by his father, Leo Dryden, at the age of six months. Wheeler, given to histrionic postures, staged his entrance and asked her dramatically, 'Do you know who I am?' 'Of course I do,' Hannah replied pleasantly. 'You're my son. Sit down and have a cup of tea.'

8

Escape

After finishing *The Idle Class* Chaplin started directly into a new picture, which was provisionally called *Come Seven*, and was to feature himself and Mack Swain as a pair of rich plumbers given to arriving at their work in a chauffeur-driven limousine. He spent the latter part of July at Catalina with Edward Knoblock and Carlyle Robinson working on ideas for the scenario, and returned to the studio at the beginning of August to start work. Sets were built, locations were found and the cast was assembled: Edna, Sydney, Mack Swain, Henry Bergman, Loyal Underwood, John Rand and two bit players, Pete Griffin and Jos Kedian. On 22 August Chaplin began to shoot. But after only 348 feet of film had been exposed he took a sudden decision to go to Europe. Carlyle Robinson was told to make the arrangements and five days later* Chaplin, accompanied by Robinson and Tom Harrington, was seen off at the Los Angeles railway depot by 'most of Hollywood . . . and . . . their sisters and their cousins and their aunts'. As the train pulled out, Sydney called to Robinson, 'For God's sake don't let him get married.' 'It gave the crowd a laugh and me a scare,' Chaplin commented.

A number of circumstances had led to this apparently capricious decision. A bout of influenza and the symptomatic depression had brought home to Chaplin how tired he was after seven years of almost continuous work, during which he made seventy-one films. Growing nostalgia for England had crystallized when Montague Glass, the

---

* In his own account of the 1921 trip, *My Trip Abroad* (in the English edition *My Wonderful Visit*) Chaplin says that he stopped work one day and left for New York the next. This was dramatic licence.

author of *Potash and Perlmutter*, had invited him to dinner and served a very English steak-and-kidney pie. He had started a correspondence with H. G. Wells after Wells had written solicitously to him on reading a much exaggerated account of burns he had suffered while filming *The Idle Class*, and was curious to meet an author whom he much admired. *The Kid* was about to open in London, and he wanted for the first time to be present at a première of his own and enjoy the applause. 'I wanted to grab it while it was good. Perhaps *The Kid* might be my last picture. Maybe there would never be another chance for me to bask in the spotlight . . .'[1] He had still the feeling that one day, like Jimmy the Fearless, he would have to wake up.

England, too, meant Hetty Kelly. The slim gazelle with the oval face and bewitching mouth still haunted his memory. He had seen her once since the parting at her home in Camberwell Road. She was seventeen, and was just about to leave for America to join her sister.

He had found her silly and coquettish, and the charm had faded for the moment. In his new bachelorhood, however, he found his curiosity stirring. In August 1915 Hetty, then twenty-one, had married Lieutenant Alan Edgar Horne, serving with the Surrey Yeomanry. His father was the MP for Guildford, subsequently Sir William Edgar Horne, Bt. Hetty by this time called herself Henriette, and was described on the marriage certificate as 'Spinster, of Independent means'. After the marriage the couple moved into Alan Horne's home at 5 Tilney Street, Mayfair.

One day in July 1918, out of the blue, Chaplin received a letter from Hetty. We do not know what it contained, except that it began, 'Do you remember a silly young girl . . .?' Chaplin's reply to Hetty, however, dated 18 July 1918, has survived. It is a mixture of enthusiasm and reserve, pleasure and embarrassment:

Dear Hetty,

It is always the unexpected that happens, both in moving pictures and in real life. You can imagine what an unexpected pleasure it was for me when I discovered your letter on my desk this morning. At first, when I caught sight of the envelope, my pulse quickened, then there was the recognition of a familiar 'E' I had not seen for a number of years. Something in my subconscious mind said 'Hetty'. I quickly tore open the envelope and – Lo and Behold! – it was from you. *You*, above all people, to hear from and after so many years! I was certainly thrilled, and yet I half expected you would write some time or other because of the interesting events that have taken place in our lives; and, after all, to hear from one's old friends is a great pleasure.

Well, Hetty, you have not changed a particle. By that I mean your personality – it is manifest on every page of your letter. Of course, environment and association may have improved your viewpoint, but your charming personality is evident – which, to my way of thinking, is one's biggest asset. In your letter you ask how I am, etc., etc., Well, physically I am perfect; morally? – well, I am all that could be desired for a young man of twenty-nine years. I am still a bachelor, but that is not my fault. And now, philosophically – like yourself, my environment has given me a particular outlook on life. I suppose I have arrived at the pessimistic age of youth, but still there is hope, for I have that priceless quality of being curious about life and things which keeps up my enthusiasm.

Do you remember, Hetty, I once told you that money and success were not everything. At the time I had not had the experience of either, but I felt it was so, and now I have experienced both. I find that the pursuit of happiness can only be had from within ourselves and the interest of others.

But enough of this philosophy. How about yourself? I sincerely hope you have fully recovered by now, and are in the pink of condition. You must take greater care of yourself. Don't forget to remember me to Sonney [*sic*] and give Edie my best wishes. As for yourself – I shall be anxiously counting the days until I hear from you, so please write and let me know that you are well and smiling again.

Yours ever,
Charlie

Chaplin rarely wrote letters. Carlyle Robinson marvelled that the man who received more letters than anyone else wrote so few. He estimated that in his whole life Chaplin had written no more than a dozen. This one was obviously composed with great care; and the literary style of *My Autobiography* is already quite recognizable. It was evidently typed by a secretary, since it reveals none of the persistent idiosyncrasies of Chaplin's orthography: he always wrote 'ect' for 'etc', for instance.

He seems to have received no reply. It is possible that Hetty never read it, for transatlantic mails in the last year of the war could be delayed for weeks, and on 4 November 1918, a week before the Armistice, Henriette Florence Horne, née Hetty Kelly, died.

The concern for her health which Chaplin expresses in his letter suggests that she had already been ill, perhaps following the birth of her only child, a daughter. On 18 October she fell ill with the influenza then epidemic in Europe. On the 27th the sickness was complicated by pneumonia, and only a week afterwards, Hetty died.

Chaplin knew nothing of this when he set out on his European trip more than three years after he had written to Hetty. He, Robinson and Harrington amused themselves on the train journey with solitaire, and stopped for a night in Chicago, where Chaplin was a judge in a scenario competition and where he attempted to meet Carl Sandburg. It was there, too, that he had his first taste of the reporters who were going to dog him throughout the trip. Their questions, he found, varied little wherever he met them:

'Mr Chaplin, why are you going to Europe?'
'Just for a vacation!'
'Are you going to make pictures while you are there?'
'No.'
'What do you do with your old moustaches?'
'Throw them away.'
'What do you do with your old canes?'
'Throw them away.'
'What do you do with your old shoes?'
'Throw them away.'
That lad did well. He got in all those questions before he was shouldered aside and two black eyes boring through lenses surrounded by tortoise-shell frames claimed an innings. I restored the 'prop grin' which I had decided was effective for interviews.
'Mr Chaplin, have you your cane and shoes with you?'
'No.'
'Why not?'
'I don't think I'll need them.'
'Are you going to get married while you are in Europe?'
'No ...'
'Mr Chaplin, do you ever expect to get married?'
'Yes.'
'To whom?'
'I don't know.'
'Do you want to play Hamlet?'
'Why, I don't know. I haven't thought much about it, but if you think there are any reasons why –'
But she was gone. Another district attorney had the floor.
'Mr Chaplin, are you a Bolshevik?'
'No.'
'Then why are you going to Europe?'

'For a holiday?'

'What holiday?'

'Pardon me, folks, but I did not sleep well on the train and I must go to bed.'

In New York he was met by Douglas Fairbanks and Mary Pickford who were there for the première of *The Three Musketeers*. Before the première they screened the film for him, as well as Mary's *Little Lord Fauntleroy*, and solemnly asked for his criticisms and suggestions. He gave them as solemnly, knowing that they would be politely heard and ignored. The première was a nightmare: Fairbanks and Pickford managed to enter the theatre unscathed, but Chaplin lost his hat and tie in the crowd, had a piece cut from his trousers by a lady souvenir-hunter, and was repeatedly pummelled and punched in the face by policemen. Eventually he was handed in, over the heads of the crowds, and felt that his companions were shocked by his sartorial disarray.

Chaplin shared his time in New York between his lawyer, Nathan Burkan, and new and old friends among the East Coast intelligentsia – Alexander Woollcott, Heywood Broun, the radical Max Eastman, Edward Knoblock, Harrison Rhodes and Madame Maurice Maeterlinck. Eastman gave a party for Chaplin, at which he met a young IWW worker on parole from a twenty-year prison sentence because of ill health, who made a great impression on him. Chaplin in turn gave a dinner party, at which they played games and did turns of various kinds:

I acted with Mme Maeterlinck. We played a burlesque on the great dying scene of *Camille*. But we gave it a touch that Dumas overlooked.

When she coughed, I got the disease immediately, and was soon taken with convulsions and died instead of Camille.

He went to see *Liliom* and afterwards met Joseph Schildkraut and Eva le Gallienne who were starring in it; and suddenly had an uncharacteristic yearning to go back on the stage. Despite the crowds and the reporters, New York society was a great relief after California:

No one asked me to walk funny, no one asked me to twirl a cane. If I wanted to do a tragic bit, I did, and so did everyone else. You were a creature of the present, not a production of the past, not a promise of the future. You were accepted as is, *sans* 'Who's Who' labels and income-tax records.

The trio left New York on the *Olympic* on the morning of 3 September. Edward Knoblock was also travelling to England on the ship. Many friends, including Fairbanks and Pickford, came to see them off, but

> Somehow I don't seem interested in them very much . . . I am trying to make a conversation, but am more interested in the people and the boat and those who are going to travel with me.
>
> Many of the passengers on the boat are bringing their children that I may be introduced . . .
>
> I find myself smiling at them graciously and pleasantly, especially the children.
>
> I doubt if I am really sincere in this, as it is too early in the morning. Despite the fact that I love children, I find them difficult to meet. I feel rather inferior to them. Most of them have assurance, have not yet been cursed with self-consciousness.
>
> And one has to be very much on his best behaviour with children because they detect our insincerity . . .

Chaplin's account of the visit is disarmingly frank and self-critical. It is as if this unaccustomed experience of relaxation permitted him to stand back and take a detached, amused view of his reactions to every experience. The days on board ship were a mixture of excitements and annoyances. He enjoyed the luxury. ('There is nothing like money. It does make life so easy.') He was both annoyed and flattered by the people who forced their attentions and their opinions on him. After a conversation with some of them he decided, 'I am, indeed, a narrow-minded little pinhead.' Inhibited about speaking to Marguerite Namara, the opera singer and wife of the dramatist Guy Bolton, he decided, 'I just do not know how to meet people.' He was uncertain as to which members of the crew he ought to tip.

There is an odd discrepancy about an incident on the voyage. Carlyle Robinson claimed that Chaplin declined to appear in a ship's concert, and was as a result insulted by the chairman, Herman Metz, who told the audience that Chaplin had refused to appear (it was in aid of a seamen's charity) but that it hardly mattered since they could see him on the screen for a nickel any time they pleased. Guy Bolton, however, recalled that

> at the ship's concert Marguerite sang and Chaplin did a pantomime act in which he portrayed an out-of-work actor applying for a job. As the manager, played by Knoblock, described each aspect of the character, Chaplin became successively humble, aggressive, charming, ultra-

aristocratic. Told he was too short for the role, he seemingly grew several inches taller. Questioned as to his romantic qualification, he hurled himself into the manager's lap. Finally he is asked to run through a scene in which he is supposed to come home and find his wife in the arms of his best friend. In a frenzy of jealous rage he is called on to kill his betrayer. The manager shakes his head and says he fears Charlie can never be sufficiently convincing in the scene, whereupon the actor, determined to win the coveted role, seizes the manager by the throat. When he at last relaxes his grip and turns away to get his hat and stick, the manager is a corpse on the floor. Charlie, turning back with an ingratiating smile to receive his applause, was Chaplin at his best. His surprise on seeing the empty chair, his consternation on discovering the body that has slipped down under the desk were done as only Chaplin can do it. And then his famous shuffling exit, looking back over his shoulder and raising his hat to the corpse. It made a perfect finish.

Daily bulletins on the ship's noticeboard reported the excitement already being echoed in the British press. Long before his departure the newspapers had begun to sustain a running commentary on his Eastward progress. Now cables from correspondents aboard the *Olympic* described in detail his life aboard:

Charlie rests in his suite on the promenade deck until eleven, when he takes his breakfast, consisting of a glass of hot water with a pinch of salt. He then starts at a brisk walk round the deck in the company of one or two friends. Four laps on the deck equal one mile. His next occupation is a further spell of rest in a steamer chair, reading or watching games of volley ball, deck tennis, shuffleboard or quoits. Occasionally he joins the children in the gymnasium on the boat deck, delightedly romping with them in their games. He is a great favourite with the children, although they listen, wide-eyed with amazement, when you tell them that this

DAPPER YOUNG MAN

who so successfully plays uncle is Charlie Chaplin. Noon finds Charlie in the gymnasium beginning a bout of systematic exercise. Then to the Turkish bath and the swimming pool. Luncheon follows.

In the afternoon he watches the card games – but does not play himself – until it is time for a second turn round the deck. Towards evening he will be found on the forward deck playing cricket with the deck hands. Later he often appears in the smoke room listening to the bids at the auction pool on the ship's daily run. The passengers have identified their unassuming young fellow voyager.[2]

The *Olympic* was due at Cherbourg at 1 p.m. on 9 September but fog delayed the arrival until 5 p.m. Fifty or more newsmen, cameramen and network photographers instantly invaded the ship and ran Chaplin to earth behind the navigator's bridge. 'This is far, far worse than New York,' he said, and in reply to the barrage of questions – this time mostly in French – he made an impromptu speech:

> This is my first holiday for years, and there is only one place to spend a holiday, long overdue, and that is at home. That is why I intend to go to London. I want to walk the streets, see all the many changes, and feel the good old London atmosphere again.
>
> My trip across has been the result of a last-minute decision the day before the *Olympic* sailed [*sic*]. I felt I had to come home and here I am. After England I mean to go to Paris and then Russia.
>
> 'Why Russia?' you say. Because I am immensely interested in that great country and its efforts towards social reconstruciton after chaos. After Russia I have plans for seeing Spain. There is a great desire in my heart for the romance of Seville, and besides, I want to see a bullfight.
>
> I mean to enjoy myself thoroughly, and to go to all the old corners that I knew when I was a boy. I want to be a Londoner among Londoners, not a sort of comic hero to be stared at.[3]

To the inevitable 'Are you a Bolshevik?' he replied, 'I am an artist, not a politician.' Asked whether he thought Lenin or Lloyd George the greater man he answered mischievously and enigmatically, 'One works, the other plays.' Such moments were anxious for Robinson as his press representative. After this, somewhat to the surprise of the reporters, Chaplin vanished through a handy doorway.

The ship crawled through the fog to Southampton, where they had been warned there would be a civic reception. Chaplin was unreasonably nervous at the prospect of making a speech of thanks, sat up half the night drafting it, and then left his notes behind in the confusion. In the event it was considered he gave a better performance than the flustered Mayor. Chaplin confessed to slight disappointment that the crowds in Southmpton were not larger. It was explained that this was because of their delayed arrival. 'This explanation relieves me tremendously, though it is not so much for myself that I feel this, but for my companions and my friends, who expect so much. I feel that the whole thing should go off with a bang for their sake. Yes I do.' He was relieved to find familiar faces to greet him: Tom Geraghty, Fairbanks's sometime script writer, Donald Crisp, the Scottish-born actor who had played Battling Burrows in Griffith's *Broken Blossoms*,

Abe Breman, the London representative of United Artists, and Hetty's brother, Arthur Kelly, known as 'Sonny', who had independently found his way into the film business.* There was also Chaplin's cousin Aubrey, Uncle Spencer Chaplin's son, who had helped care for Hannah during her stay in Peckham House. 'I feel that Aubrey is a nice, simple soul and quite desirous of taking me in hand.' He found himself wanting to pose a little in front of Aubrey, 'I want to shock him; no, not exactly shock him, but surprise him . . . I shall have a long talk with Aubrey later and explain everything . . .'

On the train journey to London he found everything different and irresistibly beautiful: the girls, the countryside – despite the parching and the new buildings – the crowds that waited to see his train pass

Charlie's Rest Cure

1921 – Low's comment on Chaplin's
visit to London.

* Edith Kelly, sister of Hetty and Arthur, had married Frank Jay Gould, the American millionaire. When Gould added films to his many business interests, Arthur was found a post in his New York office. Arthur was subsequently to work in United Artists as Chaplin's representative. Later he became Vice President of the company. It was at this meeting with Kelly that Chaplin first learned of Hetty's death, almost three years before.

at every station. As it drew towards Waterloo, it passed through the streets of his boyhood: he could even glimpse Uncle Spencer's old pub, the Queen's Head in Broad Street, Lambeth. The scenes that awaited him in London were astonishing. His homecoming was a triumph hardly paralleled in the twentieth century outside a few great royal or national events.

From Waterloo to the Ritz the streets were thronged with people all waiting for a glimpse of their idol and a chance to cheer.

> I feel like doing something big. What an opportunity for a politician to say something and do something big!
>
> Then, as we approach, the tide comes in towards the gates of the hotel. They have been kept locked to prevent the crowd from demolishing the building. I can see one intrepid motion-picture camera man at the door as the crowd starts to swarm. He begins to edge in, and starts grinding his camera frantically as he is lifted into the whirlpool of humanity. But he keeps turning, and his camera and himself are gradually turned up to the sky, and his lens is registering nothing but clouds as he goes down turning – the most honorable fall a camera man can have, to go down grinding. I wonder if he really got any pictures.
>
> In some way my body has been pushed, carried, lifted, and projected into the hotel. I can assure you that through no action of mine was that accomplished.

The crowd insisted on his showing himself at the window of his suite, but the management of the Ritz asked him to desist from throwing flowers to the people below for fear of causing a riot.

Chaplin now felt a desperate urge to see the places of his youth without delay. With Geraghty and Crisp he managed to make his way out of the service entrance of the hotel. Then he left his companions, to go alone in a taxi to Kennington. From his own description there seems to have been a real passion of hunger in this search for the scenes and impressions remembered from his childhood. Much remained: an old, blind, Bible-reading beggar under the arches by the Canterbury Music Hall; Christchurch, where Hannah worshipped when religion took her; Baxter Hall, 'where we used to see magic lantern shows for a penny . . . You could get a cup of coffee and a piece of cake there and see the Crucifixion of Christ all at the same time'; Kennington Police Station; Kennington Baths, 'reason for many a day's hookey'; Kennington Cross. In Chester Street he recognized the shop where he had once worked as lather boy, though the barber had gone, and an old tub where he himself once used to wash in the morning. He saw himself in the children who played in the street. He thought them lovely, and was thrilled to hear them speak: 'They seem to talk from their souls.' Proceeding to Lambeth Walk he met a girl who had been the servant in a cheap lodging house where he had once stayed, and whom he remembered losing her job, because she had 'fallen'.

His clothes made him conspicuous in Lambeth Walk. He was recognized, and a crowd began to follow him, though at a respectful distance. He felt ashamed after he asked a policeman for help and the policeman reassured him, 'That's all right, Charlie. These people won't hurt you.' They called 'Goodbye, Charlie. God bless you!' as he drove off in his taxi. He drove to Kennington Gate, where he had had his rendezvous with Hetty, to the Horns, and to Kennington Cross, where he had heard the clarinettist play 'The Honeysuckle and the Bee', and 'music first entered my soul'. He reflected that he was seeing all this 'through other eyes. Age trying to look back through the eyes of youth.' Yet, after all, he was only thirty-two.

A couple of nights later he decided to return to Lambeth, this time in the company of Robinson, Geraghty, Crisp and Kelly. He noticed Sharps the photographers in Westminster Bridge Road, and went in and asked if he could buy prints of some photographs they took of him when he was with *Casey's Court Circus*. The assistant replied that the negatives would have been destroyed long ago. He pointed out that they had still a photograph of Dan Leno, who had died seventeen years before, in the window.

> 'Have you destroyed Mr Leno's negative?' I asked him.
> 'No,' was the reply, 'but Mr Leno is a famous comedian.'
> Such is fame.

There were other landmarks he remembered: an old bottle-nosed tomato seller, ten years more decrepit; the coffee stall at Elephant and Castle which was the focus of the nightlife of the neighbouring streets, and where Chaplin noticed among the loungers a number of men maimed by the war. Then Chaplin took his friends to 3 Pownall Terrace. Mrs Reynolds, the aging war widow who now lived in the Chaplins' former garret, was astonished to be got out of bed at 10.30 p.m. by the celebrity of the moment, but not nonplussed:

> The place was in darkness ... and when I heard a scuffling outside, I shouted, 'Who is there!'
> 'It is Charlie Chaplin,' I heard a voice say.

Never dreaming it was really Mr Chaplin, I shouted from the bed, 'Oh, don't you try and play any jokes on me. Charlie won't come at this hour.'

But the knocking went on, so I got out of bed. I had to take a picture away before I could open the door, as it has no key and I have to wedge it up.

Then I saw four gentlemen on the stairs, and one of them, slightly built and wearing a grey lounge suit said in a gentle voice, 'I really am Charlie Chaplin. Were you asleep?' he asked, and I said, 'No' as I had been listening to the [news] boys calling the results of the great fight.

'Oh,' said Charlie, 'I was supposed to be there.'

Then he looked round the room – I was glad that the sheets on the bed were clean . . . and said, 'This is my old room. I have bumped my head many times on that ceiling' – pointing to the slope above the bed – 'and got thrashed for it. I should like to sleep here again for a night.'

I said, 'It's not like your hotel,' and he answered merrily, 'Never you mind about my hotel. This is my old room, and I am much more interested in that than my hotel!'

Having had their fill of drabness for the night, the friends went back to Park Lane to visit the American film director George Fitzmaurice. There Chaplin quarrelled with another guest, an American actor who had gone sightseeing in Limehouse in search of the tough and highly coloured world of Thomas Burke's *Limehouse Nights*, and was disappointed that nobody there wanted to pick a fight.

That was enough. It annoyed.

I told him that it was very fine for well-fed, overpaid actors flaunting toughness at these deprived people, who are gentle and nice and, if ever tough, only so because of environment. I asked him just how tough he would be if he were living the life that some of these unfortunate families must live. How easy for him with five meals a day beneath that thrust-out chest with his muscles trained and perfect, trying to start something with these people. Of course they were not tough, but when it comes to four years of war, when it comes to losing an arm or a leg, then they are tough. But they are not going around looking for fights unless there is a reason.

It rather broke up the party, but I was feeling so disgusted that I did not care.

On the way back to the Ritz they fell into conversation with three very young prostitutes; Chaplin was rather sad that having gaily hailed them, 'Hello, boys', as soon as they recognized him they became solemn and respectful and called him 'Mr Chaplin'. They helped a driver, on his way to Covent Garden with a load of apples, to push his wagon up a slippery street, and Chaplin was touched that the man 'did not belay the tired animal with a whip and curse and swear at him in his helplessness. He saw the animal was up against it, and instead of beating him he got out and put his shoulder to the wheel, never for the moment doubting that the horse was doing his best.'

The derelicts huddled at night under the arches of the Ritz, the newest and most glamorous hotel in London at that time, seemed to symbolize the two poles of Chaplin's life: the privations of boyhood and the triumph of this homecoming. Chaplin woke the sleepers to give them money. He never ceased observing behaviour: 'There was an old woman about seventy. I gave her something. She woke up, or stirred in her sleep, took the money without a word of thanks – took it as though it was her ration from the bread line and no thanks were expected, huddled herself up in a tighter knot than before, and continued her slumber. The inertia of poverty had long since claimed her.'

Chaplin's search for his past, at first so urgent, seems now to have been satisfied – though to the end of his life he was to return to Kennington and Lambeth and regret the disappearance of the places he had known. Now he was quite content to be a celebrity, an immortal among (as he called them) the immortals. Knoblock took him to meet Bernard Shaw, but at the door of Shaw's flat at 10 Adelphi Terrace held back. Every visiting movie actor called on Shaw and he did not want to be like the rest. He was not to meet Shaw until ten years later. E. V. Lucas gave a dinner in his honour at the Garrick, where he sat between Sir James Barrie, who told him he would like him to play Peter Pan, and Sir Squire Bancroft. Sir Squire, then in his eightieth year, had broken his rule that day and gone to the pictures to see *Shoulder Arms*. Chaplin was overjoyed when he praised the letter-reading scene. He disputed Barrie's criticism that the Heaven scene in *The Kid* was 'entirely unnecessary', but generally felt that he was not making sufficient contribution to the conversation of the party which also included the extrovert Edwin Lutyens (whom Chaplin thought rather common), George Frampton, Harry Graham and Knoblock. Afterwards Chaplin and Knoblock went with Barrie to his flat in Robert Street, Adelphi, close to Shaw's, and there met Gerald du Maurier who had come from playing in *Bulldog Drummond* at Wyndham's Theatre.

The most significant encounters in London were H. G. Wells and Thomas Burke. Chaplin had come to London with the intention of meeting Wells, but their first meeting was engineered by the publicists of the Stoll Picture Corporation, who got each man to a screening of a new film of *Kipps* by telling him that the other wished to meet him there. George K. Arthur, who made his film début in the title role,

1921 – Will Owen on Chaplin's
visit to London.

was at the showing, and Chaplin was impressed by Wells's kindliness when he whispered to him, 'Say something nice to the boy,' even though he knew Wells was not impressed by the film. (Some years later Arthur would be instrumental in bringing together Chaplin and Josef von Sternberg – a meeting which resulted in the ill-fated *Sea*

Gulls.) Later they had a pleasant dinner at which Rebecca West was present. Wells complimented him on his turn of phrase when, a bit for the sake of effect, Chaplin apostrophized 'The indecent moon!' He was obliged to confess that the phrase was not original, but was Knoblock's. A quarter of a century later he used it again, in *Monsieur Verdoux*, but without acknowledgement to the originator.

Later in the trip, after his return from Paris and Berlin, Chaplin spent a weekend at Wells's house in the country. It was a carefree visit. Chaplin relaxed and slept a lot and they talked and played games with Wells's two young sons. St John Ervine came to visit and talked about the possibility of talking pictures. Chaplin told him that he didn't think the voice was necessary, that it would spoil the art as much as painting statuary. 'I would as soon rouge marble cheeks. Pictures are pantomimic art. We might as well have the stage. There would be nothing left to the imagination.' Even when he was most comfortable with people, Chaplin still questioned his relationship with them: 'As I speed into town I am wondering if Wells wants to know me or whether he wants me to know him.'

Chaplin found an immediate sympathy with Thomas Burke, who had had a great success with his stories of the darker aspects of East London. A small, silent man, Burke accompanied him on a tour of the places that provided the settings for his books, speaking little but pointing things out with his walking stick. Burke was later to write perhaps the most perceptive analysis of Chaplin's character. The source of their understanding came from their similar backgrounds. As Burke described it:

> He didn't know then, nor did I, that when he was young, and I was young, we were walking the same side-streets of Kennington, living a similar shabby, makeshift kind of life, and loathing it with equal intensity. He was mixed up with red-nose comedians of the minor music halls; I was mixed up with futile clerks. But our backgrounds were much the same. We grew and played in the same streets; we knew the same experiences in the same settings, and took them through a common temperament. In our teens each of us was recoiling from the drab, draggled Kennington in which we lived; each of us, in a crude, undirected way, was yearning towards the things of decency and the things of the mind, and each of us was hopeless of ever attaining them. I discovered literature by picking up a copy of *T.P.'s Weekly* in a tea-shop; he discovered the inwardness of music on hearing a man playing a clarinet outside a Kennington pub – playing *The Honeysuckle and the Bee!*[4]

Impetuously Chaplin decided to go to France, taking Robinson with him. The boat trip was one of his own *mal de mer* gags in real life. He had just decided to take advantage of the offer of a charming young woman to teach him French when he was immobilized by seasickness. On the train to Paris he was impressed by the service and the cheapness of the lunch, but on arrival in Paris to find rain and reporters awaiting him, nausea struck again.

He was eager to meet the caricaturist Cami, with whom he had been in a correspondence – or rather an exchange of drawings and photographs – since Cami had written him a fan letter in 1914. It came as a shock to find that the two, reckoning themselves friends, had no common language. Cami's account is charming, though perhaps over-coloured; Chaplin's own account however in part confirms it. When they met they at first chattered to each other in their own languages, not troubling too much that the other could not understand. Then, when they were having lunch together in Chaplin's hotel, Chaplin suddenly became depressed and left the table with tears in his eyes. The English hotel manager explained to Cami, 'He is overcome by the thought that there is a greater barrier than the ocean between you – the barrier of language.' Later, Cami said, they developed a deaf-and-dumb pantomime, and got on well enough. The went together to the Folies Bergères, which Chaplin found grubbier and less glamorous than when he had played there with the Karno troupe. He dealt with the French-speaking reporters as best he could, and among the Americans and British in Paris met Dudley Field Malone, Waldo Frank, Lady Astor and Sir Philip Sassoon, Lloyd George's private secretary, who invited him for the weekend when he returned to England, and was to become and remain a friend for many years. Of the local celebrities he met Georges Carpentier and Jacques Copeau, and had supper with the Copeau Company. He was excited by the ambience and the performers of the Quartier Latin, and was clearly storing up impressions which would later be useful when he came to make *A Woman of Paris*.

Chaplin and Robinson next took the train to Berlin. Chaplin's films had not been shown in Germany, so his face was unknown. At first he enjoyed relief from the crowds and the reporters; later he began to feel mildly resentful, missing the celebrity treatment and finding himself placed at the worst tables in restaurants. Things looked up when he met the spectacular star Pola Negri, who showed an immediate and lively interest in him. Negri was born Apolonia Chalupiec in

Yanowa, near Lipnia in Poland. She was a dancer at the Imperial Theatre in St Petersburg, and acted on stage and screen in Poland before being invited to Berlin by Max Reinhardt to play in *Sumurun*.

Pola Negri is really beautiful. She is Polish and really true to the type. Beautiful jet-black hair, white, even teeth and wonderful coloring. I think it such a pity that such coloring does not register on the screen.

She is the centre of attraction here. I am introduced. What a voice she has! Her mouth speaks so prettily the German language. Her voice has a soft, mellow quality, with charming inflection. Offered a drink, she clinks my glass and offers her only English words, 'Jazz boy Charlie.'

Returning briefly to Paris, Chaplin was impressed by a young Russian emigrée called Moussia Sodskaya whom he saw singing in a Montmartre restaurant, and talked of putting her into pictures. The following day he flew from Le Bourget. In those less formal days of passenger transport, the pilot obligingly put him off at Lympne in Kent, where he was to attend Sir Philip Sassoon's garden party. The next day they attended the unveiling of a war memorial in the local school, and Chaplin was embarrassed and upset to find that he, rather than the ceremony, was the centre of attention. 'I wished I hadn't come.' Sassoon also took him to a hospital for the war wounded, and he was greatly shocked and depressed by what he saw. 'What is to become of them?' he asked. 'That is up to you and me.'

Then followed his weekend with Wells, after which he intrepidly flew back to Paris for a charity première of *The Kid* at the Trocadero. He had been persuaded to attend by the daughter of J. P. Morgan, with the promise of an award. In the outcome the award itself was not very impressive – Officier de l'Instruction Publique – but the event was. The audience included Prince George of Greece and Princess Xenia, an assortment of dukes, duchesses, marquis, marquises, Stuyvesants and Vanderbilts. There were also Elsa Maxwell, Georges Carpentier, Cecile Sorel and Henri Letellier, a prominent Parisian publisher who was to provide the original for the character of Pierre Revel in *A Woman of Paris*. Chaplin dined with Carpentier and Letellier the following evening.

With an appointment for lunch with Sassoon to meet Lloyd George and other celebrities, Chaplin decided to fly back to London, but the plane was lost in the fog and the cross-channel journey took seven hours. He missed Lloyd George and was disappointed. 'I love to meet interesting personages. I would love to meet Lenin, Trotsky and the Kaiser.'

Despite this, Chaplin refused Wells's invitation to dinner with Chaliapin, since he had promised to spend his last evening in England with cousin Aubrey. Uncharacteristically, and despite Aubrey's own objections, Chaplin insisted on visiting Aubrey's pub and behaving flamboyantly because, 'I must get him more custom.' He stayed with Aubrey until four in the morning, learning about his Chaplin forbears; then hitched a lift back to the Ritz in a Ford truck driven by an ex-officer who was now in the grocery business, and on his way from Bayswater to Covent Garden. Chaplin revelled in those casual encounters.

It was now the second week in October, and Chaplin set off for Southampton 'dejected and sad'. He felt that he was going to miss the crowds more than the friends who had come to see him off, like Arthur Kelly, who brought him a picture of Hetty. He even forgave reporters – 'After all, it's their job to ask questions and they have been merely doing their job with me.' On the boat back to America he struck up a pleasant friendship with an eight-year-old girl. He describes a fragment of their conversation:

'You like smashing windows? You must be Spanish,' I tell her.
'Oh! no, not Spanish; I'm Jewish,' she answers.
'That accounts for your genius.'
'Oh, do you think Jewish people are clever?' she asks eagerly.
'Of course. All great geniuses have Jewish blood in them. No, I am not Jewish,' as she is about to put that question, 'but I am sure there must be some somewhere in me. I hope so.'

On the boat he also befriended the English producer-director Cecil Hepworth and his star Alma Taylor who were making their first visit to the States. On their arrival he took them to dinner with Sam Goldwyn, and invited them to his home.

In New York he met Claude McKay, the negro poet, and the educationalist Marguerite Naumberg. Frank Harris took him to Sing Sing where he met the Irish nationalist and labour leader Jim Larkin, was appalled by the death chamber, and made an impromptu speech which went down well:

Brother criminals and fellow sinners: Christ said, 'Let him who is without sin cast the first stone.' I cannot cast the stone, though. I have compromised and thrown many a pie. But I cannot cast the first stone.

'Some got it,' he remarked, 'others never will.'
Chaplin's record of the trip was mostly written in the course of the

train journey back to California, and was taken down at his dictation by a young newspaper man, Monta Bell, who was subsequently to be an assistant on *A Woman of Paris* and to go on to become a very competent director in his own right. Some Chaplin biographers have suggested that the text was 'ghosted' by Bell, but the style is too distinctive and the analysis of Chaplin's reactions and sensations far too personal for that. The account originally appeared as a series of articles in *Photoplay* before publication in book form as *My Trip Abroad* (*My Wonderful Visit*, for the English edition). 'Going over it all,' Chaplin's account concluded,

> it has all been worth while and the job ahead of me looks worth while. If I can bring smiles to the tired eyes in Kennington and Whitechapel, if I have absorbed and understood the virtues and problems of those simpler people I have met, and if I have gathered the least bit of inspiration from those greater personages who were kind to me, then this has been a wonderful trip, and somehow I am eager to get back to work and begin paying for it.

He was not to return to work instantly, however. He arrived back in Los Angeles at noon on 31 October, and that evening dined with some friends, Mr and Mrs Abraham Lehr. There was only one other guest, Clare Sheridan, the sculptor, painter, traveller and writer. She and Chaplin struck up an instant friendship. Mrs Sheridan was a niece of Winston Churchill. Her husband had been killed in France, leaving her with a daughter and a small son, Dick, who was in California with her. She had been commissioned by the Soviet Government to make portrait busts of Lenin, Trotsky, Dzerzhinsky and other Bolshevik leaders, and her subsequent articles and interviews had created a furore. Americans, Chaplin pointed out in his autobiography, were confused by the phenomenon of an English aristocrat writing pro-Bolshevik articles. Chaplin was fascinated by all she had to tell him about the Soviet Union; she was interested in his impressions of Britain. 'A good country to belong to, we agreed, but not a country to live in – not for the creative artist, and he advised me to remain where I am.'

Mrs Sheridan said that in the United States she was becoming a writer rather than a sculptor because American men were self-conscious about being portrayed in sculpture. 'I'm vain, thank goodness,' said Chaplin; and there and then they decided that she would make his bust. As he accompanied her back to the Hollywood Hotel they had an argument about marriage, and Chaplin put her in mind of Francis Thompson's essay on Shelley in which he said that Shelley tired not so much of a woman's arms as of her mind. 'It seemed to me that it is more spiritual than a physical companionship that Charlie is subconsciously searching for in his heart.'

Two days later on Monday 2 November they met again, this time with little Dick. At noon they went to the studio where Chaplin showed them *The Kid*. In the pathetic parts he would tiptoe to the harmonium in the screening room and play an acompaniment. Dick sobbed so hysterically that Chaplin was alarmed and kept reassuring him, 'It's only a play, Dick! It will come right in the end.' They lunched at Chaplin's home. He was somewhat apologetic about his rented house on Beechwood Drive and Argyle, 'the tortuous unsimplicity' of whose Moorish architecture greatly disturbed him though he liked the panoramic view of the city below. After lunch they went for a walk and talked about art and the satisfaction it gives, suicide and immortality. Chaplin became quite carried away:

> There is nothing so beautiful that it will make people forget their eggs and bacon for breakfast – as for admiration of the world – it's not worth anything – there is in the end but oneself to please: – you make something because it means something to you. You work – because you have a superabundance of vital energy. You find that not only can you make children but you can express yourself in other ways. In the end it is you – all you – your work, your thought, your conception of the beautiful, yours the happiness, yours the satisfaction. Be brave enough to face the veil and lift it, and see and know the void it hides, and stand before that void and know that within yourself is your world . . .[5]

Then they laughed at themselves for being so serious. After tea they took Dick home and then Chaplin and Mrs Sheridan dined and danced at the Ambassador Hotel, where most of the other guests knew Chaplin and hurried to welcome him back and to speculate about Mrs Sheridan.

The following day they began work on the bust. Chaplin insisted it must be finished by Saturday because he wanted to go to Catalina to fish. Mrs Sheridan found it an amusing and productive day. Chaplin started the morning in a brown silk dressing gown and was serious. After a while he seized his violin and walked about the room playing it. Then, clearly in a gayer mood, he disappeared to change into an orange and primrose robe. Occasionally they would stop for tea. Chaplin 'would either philosophize or impersonate'; or he might put on a gramophone record and conduct an imaginary band. Between times he confided that when he was a young man in London he longed to know people, but that now he knew many, he felt lonelier than ever.

The bust was finished in three days. Friends were amazed that Chaplin had stayed patient so long; and Mrs Sheridan congratulated herself on her foresight in making it in his own home and specifying that he should be bare-throated. 'A man in his dressing gown does not suddenly get a notion to order his motor car and go off to some place. I had him fairly anchored. Nevertheless he has been difficult to do. There is so much subtlety in the face, and sensitiveness, and varying personality.'

Chaplin was pleased with it, said it might be the head of a criminal, and at once concocted a theory that criminals and artists were psychologically akin, that 'on reflection we all have a flame, a burning flame of impulse, a vision, a sidetracked mind, a deep sense of unlawfulness.' Jean de Limur arrived as the bust was finished and commented slyly: 'I see it is Pan . . . *on ne peut jamais tromper une femme.*'

Chaplin changed his mind about Catalina, since he had discovered that the fishing season had closed on 1 November. He decided instead that he and the Sheridans would go camping on Sunday morning. They set off in Chaplin's car, followed by a van with the tents and paraphernalia and a Ford containing the chef. The Sunday roads were thick with cars and exhaust fumes, and they began to despair of finding a camping site. Eventually they struck off across country and found an idyllic seaside spot, designated with a sign 'Private Property. No trespassing. No camping. No hunting'. For Charlie Chaplin, however, the owner made an exception.

> Late into the night I sat with him over the camp fire. A sea mist rose and little veils of sea mist swept like gossamer over the dunes and the naked, shiny eucalyptus stems cast black shadows. Mingling with the nightbird cries, the rhythmical sound of the sea and the shore.
>
> One by one the lanterns in the camp flickered and went out. Charlie sat huddled up before the flame, an elfin, elemental creature with gleaming eyes and tousled hair, his little nervous hands raking the embers with a stick. His voice was very deep, the voice of a much bigger man. He ruminated moodily. He said it was 'Too much – too great – too beautiful – there are no words –'[6]

They stayed in the camp through the week. Chaplin played with Dick, and entertained them with imitations of Nijinsky and Pavlova which he did so well and so gracefully that Mrs Sheridan did not know whether to 'laugh or silently appreciate'. On Friday the seaside idyll was broken with the arrival of five motors full of children wanting to see him, and two reporters. They returned to Hollywood. Back at the house, taking tea, Mrs Sheridan wrote,

> We found ourselves making conversation to one another with difficulty. He looked at me as strangely as I looked at him, and then he said:
> 'You know what's the matter – we don't know each other.'
> And it was true. I was talking not with the elemental, wild-haired Charlie of the camp fire, nor yet with Charlie Chaplin of the films, but with a neatly dressed, smooth-haired young man I didn't even know by sight. Civilization and its trappings had changed us both. The past seemed tinged with unreality. 'I think it has all been a dream,' I said.[7]

This stimulating friendship ended rather abruptly. The newspapers were eager to sniff out a love affair, and Carlyle Robinson emphasized his denial by adding rather tactlessly 'Mrs Sheridan is old enough to be Mr Chaplin's mother.' The Sheridans thereupon returned to New York. Dick Sheridan was to die at the age of nineteen, and his mother spent her later years in North Africa. Her powerful bust portrait of Chaplin still stands in the Manoir de Ban at Corsier sur Vevey.

Since the divorce the Hollywood gossip columns had eagerly watched every feminine social liaison. The names of Thelma Morgan Converse, Lila Lee and Anna Q. Nilsson were from time to time connected with Chaplin's. Rumours of an engagement to a New York actress, May Collins, were admitted, then denied. Enthusiasm for a beautiful film actress, Claire Windsor, waned after she pulled the kind of stunt which always offended Chaplin's sense of dignity and propriety: she staged a 'disappearance'. Chaplin joined in the search in the nearby hills, and offered a reward for the discovery of Miss Windsor whom the headlines now described as his 'fiancée'. She was found apparently unconscious: Robinson was the first to notice how clean her riding boots were. When a young couple claimed the reward, there was closer investigation into the 'disappearance', and the hoax was exposed.

His picnic over, Chaplin was soon back in the studio and working with a will to finish the two films still due under the First National contract. *Pay Day* and *The Pilgrim* were completed in eight months.

Pay Day took thirty working days; *The Pilgrim*, in four reels, took forty-two and was by far the most economically made of all Chaplin's feature productions. *Pay Day* was to be the last Chaplin two-reeler released. Visually it marks a considerable advance. During Chaplin's absence, Totheroh seems to have been experimenting with the new lights installed in the studio, and the night scenes with rain are lit with sophistication.

Chaplin is cast as a working man and hen-pecked husband, and the comedy is derived from the ordinary frustrations of daily life. The opening section of the film has Charlie at work as a labourer on a building site; the middle section shows the effects of an inebriate night out as Charlie endeavours to make his way home – eventually strap-hanging in a lunch-wagon under the mistaken impression that it is a moving bus. In the last sequence he returns home, oiling his boots in a vain hope of creeping to bed unobserved by his virago wife who sleeps with a rolling pin at her side. He ends the night seeking repose in the bath – as in *A Night Out* and *One A.M.* Too late he finds the bath is full of cold water. There is a notably articulate piece of mime in the payday scene. Charlie is seen arguing with some person off-screen, pleading that he has been underpaid. As he calculates on his fingers, his mime betrays the gradual realization that he has in fact been paid too much.

There was only one pause during shooting for story preparation, which indicates that Chaplin had begun the film with a more fully developed scenario than was his usual habit. This degree of pre-planning was no doubt the reason why he was able to depart from his normal practice up to this time of shooting in narrative continuity. The second part of *Pay Day*, filmed in the studio, was shot first, during the last five days of November and most of December. Chaplin was ill with a cold in the first week of the New Year; when he returned he shot in the space of four working weeks the first part of the film, on the building site. Material filmed on location at La Brea and De Longpre where a large new building was in construction, was matched with studio material shot 'by natural light', as the studio records now specify, indicating the growing adoption of artificial lighting.

Pay Day was despatched to First National on 23 February 1922, and Chaplin began to prepare the story that was to be *The Pilgrim*. By the time shooting began on 10 April, the narrative continuity seems to have been largely worked out. Monta Bell, having finished his work on *My Trip Abroad*, was taken on as a general assistant and bit player. It is possible that his advent introduced a new method for the preparation of the Chaplin pictures. *The Pilgrim* is the first film for which there survives a quantity of written scenario and gag notes. It is possible, though not likely, that this kind of preparatory writing did take place on earlier films, but has simply not survived. The reduction of the periods during which production was halted for 'working on story' and the extent of these notes would seem rather to indicate that Chaplin was moving away from his earlier method of creating and improvising on the set and even on film, towards a greater degree of advance planning on paper.

The film was originally intended as a Western comedy – it would have had some similarities to *The Gold Rush* – and for a first working title was simply designated *Western*.* The earliest scenario was clearly modified because it would at that time have been judged too sophisticated and ironic for a comic subject; aspects of it look directly forward to *Monsieur Verdoux*.

Charlie was to have been one of four desperate escaped convicts who waylay a minister and steal his clothes. Disguised as a man of the cloth, Charlie arrives in the Wild West town of Hell's Hinges, a sink of immorality. He is taken for the new young reformer sent to replace the town's old minister, helpless in the face of the immorality of the place:

> Show a Chinaman or two shot down by the rough element in casual fashion . . . Show scene in saloon which is also combination gambling house, lunchroom and dance hall. Men rough with women. Gold dust for dance hall girls. Card game that ends in a fight and there is gun play.

With the same kind of fortuity that made him master of Easy Street, Charlie overcomes the town bullies and falls in love with Edna, the Minister's beautiful daughter. His programme for reform is to replace the church organ with a jazz band, to perform the hymns in ragtime and to introduce other attractions such as motion pictures and dice games for the collection. As a result the saloon empties while the church fills up.

> Charlie begins to preach a peculiar sort of preaching based on common sense rather than religion. He goes through all sorts of gestures. He is a lousy talker and they go to sleep on him in spots. But when they do he

---

* When shooting began the working title became *The Tail End*, a jocular reference to the anticipated conclusion of the First National contract.

waves for the band and with the jazz they awaken and listen as Charlie goes on . . .

At the end of the service, Charlie amiably shakes hands with his congregation, finally holding out his hands absently to a sheriff who immediately claps a pair of handcuffs on him. The congregation

> demand that Charlie be released and threaten sheriff. With eloquent gesture Charlie bids them do no violence. Tells them to stick by the church and the old man. He shakes old man's hand and bids him build new church. There are tears in girl's eyes as he bids her goodbye and with the crowd shouting his praise she goes up the aisle and out with the sheriff into fadeout.

This curious moral fable was never made: the eventual film was in more conventional comedy style, with the Wild West element replaced by lightly satirical treatment of the manners and hypocrisies of small-town religion. Charlie is still an escaped convict. Stealing the clothes of a bathing parson, he arrives thus disguised in the town of Dead Man's Gulch, where he is mistaken for the new minister. Called upon to deliver a sermon, he pantomimes the story of David and Goliath. He experiences such hazards of the clerical life as a parochial tea party where he is tormented by a horrid spoilt child. Having fallen in love with his landlady's beautiful daughter, he foils the attempt of a former cell-mate to rob the women.

The local sheriff realizes his identity and reluctantly arrests him. Touched by his gallantry and the girl's pleas, he takes him to the Mexican border to give him a chance to escape. He orders Charlie to pick some flowers on the other side of the border and – unable to take the hint – Charlie obediently returns with a bouquet. The exasperated sheriff is finally obliged to kick him over the border to freedom. On the Mexican side however a bunch of bandits spring out of the bushes, wildly shooting at one another. Caught between two hostile countries, Charlie waddles off into the distance with one foot in Mexico and one in the United States. It is an image open to any number of symbolic interpretations.

One of the most polished and charming of the films of Chaplin's middle period, and with admirable scenes of sustained comedy such as the tea party, *The Pilgrim* seems to have been shot with few problems. Chaplin made extensive use of locations for the shooting, and there are evocative scenes of still-rural Saugus, Sawtella, Newhall, Rosoc, South Pasadena, Ventura Road and Eagle Rock.

Dinky Dean, who played the horrid little boy in the tea party scene, was in real life not at all horrid. He was the son of Chuck Riesner; sixty years later as Dean Riesner, a prominent Hollywood scriptwriter, he recalled how difficult it had been for him to pummel two men whom he knew as Uncle Sydney and Uncle Charlie. He was finally persuaded to do it only when Charles and Sydney spent some time slapping each other and laughing wildly to prove to the sceptical child that it really was fun after all.

In some quarters *The Pilgrim* ran into trouble with censors and church authorities. In Atlanta the Evangelical Ministers' Association demanded its withdrawal as 'an insult to the Gospel'. In South Carolina the Daniel Morgan Klan of the Knights of the Ku Klux Klan protested at the showing of the film on the grounds that it held the Protestant ministry up to ridicule. The Pennsylvania Board of Censors eliminated so many scenes that it virtually constituted a ban on the film. Elsewhere, however, churchmen as well as laity agreed with P. W. Gallico, writing in the *New York Daily News*:

> Now Mr Chaplin's picture is not without satire. But the shaft is not directed at the clergy. It is aimed at the narrow mind, the bigot, the person who can see no farther than the written word. In fact it seems to travel on dead line and smite the very people who in this case had the power to condemn, to shut off from others, laughter which might be directed at them.

Arrangements for the distribution of *The Pilgrim* were the source of much acrimony between Chaplin and First National. Chaplin was already roused to fury at the beginning of September, when he was still cutting the film, by an article in the *Exhibitor's Herald* which quoted Harry Schwalbe of First National accusing him of not fulfilling his contracts over *The Kid*. 'I INTEND SUING SCHWALBE AND FIRST NATIONAL FOR TEN MILLION DOLLARS,' Chaplin cabled Sydney; but the affair was smoothed over. Chaplin had no intention of letting First National have *The Pilgrim* under the terms applying to a normal two-reeler supplied under the contract. Like *The Kid* it was a feature of altogether more ambitious scope than had been anticipated by the original agreement with the distributors. Sydney was sent to New York to negotiate with Schwalbe, and was given a memorandum on the matter by Alf Reeves:

IDEA

The idea is, Chief wishes to deliver No. 8 'Pilgrim' as a feature four reeler to terminate the contract. He thinks to let them have it on a 70–30 basis same as 'Kid'. This for U.S., Canada and all Foreign Countries, with a guarantee from them of $400,000.00 in advance of his share, payable $200,000.00 on delivery of the two negatives and one Positive print, and a note for $200,000.00 due in three or six months, at their convenience . . .

Failing their acceptance of these terms, it is proposed you will deliver picture No. 8 as per contract, a two-reeler entitled 'The Professor' for which he has received full contract price.

Before delivery to First National of either, Mr Burkan and yourself will see that his interests are protected in regard to any question that may arise in the future.

Before exhibiting 'Pilgrim' or 'Professor' to First National (there being no compulsion on our part to give them a preview) they should agree that if they do not come to terms for 'Pilgrim' as a feature, they are to accept 'The Professor' as picture No. 8 in full termination of all Chief's obligations to them under the Contract.

The remarkable aspect of this document is its discussion of *The Professor*. No Chaplin film of this title was ever shown or released, and nowhere in the comprehensive daily records of the Chaplin studio is there any reference to its producion. Yet the subsequent correspondence between Chaplin in Los Angeles and Sydney in New York seems to establish beyond doubt that such a film actually existed in 1922. On 13 November Sydney sent a long telegram to Chaplin reporting the results of a meeting with Harry Schwalbe. Schwalbe, he said, was very friendly, sympathetic to the Chaplin proposition and eager to conclude the contract amicably. Schwalbe felt however that it would be easier to negotiate if his executive committee could see the films. He further suggested that Chaplin should offer First National both films: *The Professor* could conclude the contract, and *The Pilgrim* could be handled as an independent producton, though he insisted that Chaplin's 70–30 proposition left no profit for the company.

Sydney recommended that Chaplin permit him to show both pictures to First National without getting a written release in advance; and that he increase the distribution allowance to the distributors for release of *The Pilgrim*.

Chaplin replied the following day that he would on no account allow First National to have both films. He waived his objection to showing them *The Pilgrim* but not in the case of the two-reeler. He was willing to modify the distribution arrangement to 65–35, but in other respects the contract had to be the same as for *The Kid*. 'IN THE EVENT FIRST NATIONAL DO NOT WANT PILGRIM AFTER VIEWING SAME, THEN DELIVER TWO-REELER AS PER CONTRACT.' First National, via Sydney, made a counter-proposal of 50 per cent of the gross over $280,000 for *The Pilgrim*. Chaplin wired back on November 21st: PROPOSITION RIDICULOUS STOP DELIVER TWO REELER AND MAKE IMMEDIATE ARRANGE-MENTS WITH ABRAMS* TO DISTRIBUTE PILGRIM. He confirmed these instructions in a further telegram sent both to Sydney and to Burkan on 7 December:

> FIRST NATIONAL EXECUTIVES HAVING FAILED TO OFFER SUIT-ABLE CONDITIONS FOR PRODUCTION OF SPECIAL FOUR REEL FEATURE PILGRIM IT NOW OK COURSE FOR YOU AND MR BURKAN TO DELIVER TWO REELS PROFESSOR IN ACCORD-ANCE WITH CONTRACTS AND THEIR ACCEPTANCE OF THIS AS NUMBER EIGHT TERMINATES THE SERIES STOP REGARDS.

On 15 December Chaplin cabled Sydney:

> WILL ACCEPT THEIR PROPOSITIONS AS OUTLINED IN YOUR TELEGRAM OF DECEMBER THIRTEEN PROVIDING THEIR GUARANTEE FURTHER SEVENTY-FIVE THOUSAND DOLLARS CASH IN SIX MONTHS STOP USE YOUR JUDGMENT IF YOU CAN GET ANY BETTER TERMS BY JUDICIOUS APPROACH STOP HAVING NEGATIVE PILGRIM HERE WILL DELIVER WHEN FIRST CASH PAYMENT IS MADE STOP ON NO ACCOUNT RELEASE TWO REEL PROFESSOR STOP REGARDS.

After a few more telegrams of indignation, conciliation and threats to let United Artists distribute *The Pilgrim* after all, amicable arrangements were finally concluded with First National. *The Professor* was never mentioned again and for the moment remains the major mystery in the Chaplin canon. The film must have existed, unless we predicate some outlandish bluff between the two brothers to convince the telegraph operators between California and New York of the existence of a purely imaginary film. A partial solution was suggested when Kevin Brownlow and David Gill, preparing their *Unknown*

* of United Artists

Chaplin, found in the Chaplin archives a complete and cut five-minute sequence in a can labelled *The Professor*. The sequence begins in a slum street, down which waddles Chaplin in a quite unfamilar costume and make-up. He wears a heavy and dejected moustache and is dressed in a long coat and battered silk hat. He carries a suitcase labelled 'PROFESSOR BOSCO. FLEA CIRCUS'. Bosco enters a dosshouse, and before retiring to sleep inspects his fleas. Chaplin's mime creates a whole world of the busy but invisible creatures (the act was to be recreated in *Limelight*, thirty years later*). While Bosco sleeps, a dog of disgustingly mangy appearance wanders into the dormitory and knocks over the box of fleas. The dog starts to scratch desperately. So, very shortly, do the other inmates of the dormitory. Bosco wakes up and desperately runs about the place, retrieving his pets from the whiskers of his neighbours. He takes his case and leaves the doss house and the sequence ends with him trotting down the road where we first saw him.

The sequence gives all the appearance of a section cut out of a completed film. Among the out-takes which Brownlow and Gill examined is a series of shots taken in the same dosshouse set, but with Chaplin costumed as a very shabby bellboy who goes about the now empty dormitory, preparing the beds with all the aplomb and dexterity of an employee of the Ritz. The dosshouse set is the same in both the cut sequence and the out-takes, but is quite different from the dosshouse scenes in both *Police* and *The Kid*. Three years earlier, however, when he reached a block with *The Kid* Chaplin spent three days, 30 September and 1–2 October 1919, shooting some 7500 feet of film merely described in the daily shooting reports as 'Flophouse set – Flea bus.' or 'Trained fleas – bunkhouse bus.' Two snapshots taken at the time by Jack Wilson** (see plates in section 3) confirm that this is the material found by Brownlow and Gill. But of what did the rest of *The Professor* consist, if a two-reel version really existed? Had Chaplin or his cutter in fact assembled a new film out of rejected scenes, perhaps from the Mutual as well as the First National series? There is no one living who can give us the answer, and unless the film itself one day comes to light, the mystery of *The Professor* will remain unsolved.

---

* Chaplin clearly had a particular affection for this flea circus gag. Before managing to use it in *Limelight* he had tried to work it into both *The Circus* and *The Great Dictator*.

** Discovered in London in 1984.

9

A WOMAN OF PARIS

With the completion of *The Pilgrim*, Chaplin was at last free to make his first film for the United Artists. This was a considerable relief to his partners Douglas Fairbanks, Mary Pickford and D. W. Griffith who were fretting because Chaplin had not yet made any contribution to the profits of the corporation. As it turned out, his first United Artists picture was, in this respect at least, to prove a disappointment.

Chaplin decided that he would use his new independence to fulfil an old ambition. He would make a serious dramatic film. He had already moved in that direction with *The Kid*, of course, and the unfinished Essanay picture *Work* was clearly a good deal more sombre than the general run of comedy at that time. In 1917 he had made another move towards drama when he attempted to buy the film rights to Hall Caine's play *The Prodigal Son*, in which he saw a serious role for himself.

He was moreover concerned to launch Edna in an independent starring role. Even though they had remained, as he put it, 'emotionally estranged', he retained an affectionate concern for her. She was no longer an ideal comic partner. Totheroh remembered that 'by this time Edna was getting pretty heavy but her little face still had charm in it. And she got to drinking pretty heavy. One day we were looking at rushes and Charlie could see it.' Chaplin tried to think of suitably mature roles. He considered an adaptation of *The Trojan Women*, then considered casting Edna as Josephine to his own Napoleon – a role which would continue to fascinate him. The idea for *A Woman of Paris* came to him as a result of his meetings with the notorious

Peggy Hopkins Joyce. The term 'gold digger' was coined in honour of Peggy around 1920. Born Margaret Upton in Virginia, she arrived in Chicago at the time of the First World War, changed her name to Hopkins, and landed her first millionaire husband, Stanley Joyce. Divorced and with a million-dollar settlement, she became a Ziegfeld girl, from which strategic launching she went on to net four more millionaire husbands in rapid succession. In 1922 she arrived in Hollywood, bent on a film career.

Marshall Neilan found himself threatened with the prospect of directing Peggy's first picture. Neilan was a colourful and erratic Hollywood figure. Born in 1891, he had left school at eleven, drifted into films as an actor, and seen service at Biograph Studios as D. W. Griffith's chauffeur. He graduated to directing and by the age of twenty-six he was Mary Pickford's favourite director. In addition Neilan was one of Hollywood's most colourful playboys: his high-living and marathon drinking bouts cut short his career. Temperamentally he was no doubt well matched to Peggy; professionally he probably saw the hazards of trying to turn her into an actress. It may not have been without some ulterior motive that he brought her on a visit to the Chaplin studios one afternoon in the high summer of 1922.

Peggy was at all times a flamboyant dresser and that afternoon she was weighed down with jewels and exuded costly and exotic perfumes. Faced with a new and highly eligible millionaire divorcé, she determined to impress, and played the lady with a fine excess of airs and graces. Chaplin was amused, not least when the *noblesse oblige* role collapsed rather suddenly. After an hour or so of liquid hospitality Neilan said he thought they should be going, and emphasized the fact by playfully slapping Peggy's bottom. Her dignity thus assaulted, Peggy turned on him with an impressive tirade of profanities. Chaplin was intrigued by this former country girl and self-made woman of the world. For a couple of weeks they were inseparable. They took a trip together to Catalina Island, and Hollywood gossip marked Chaplin as Peggy's sixth conquest.

Peggy was soon to recognize that Chaplin was not to be one of her more profitable ventures, and moved on to more promising quarry in the shape of the young Irving Thalberg. It was Chaplin who gained from the liaison, which he was to describe as 'bizarre but brief'. Peggy had given him the idea for his next film. During their meetings she had regaled Chaplin with her colourful reminiscences. She had described her affair with the rich and famous Parisian publisher and man-about-town, Henri Letellier, whom Chaplin had met during his European trip the previous year. She told him also about a young man who had committed suicide out of desperate love for her, giving her the excuse for some very stylish mourning outfits. He was no less amused by her protestations that she was really a simple girl at heart, and desired only a home and babies.

A story based on Peggy's Parisian encounters had the added attraction of the setting. Paris had intrigued Chaplin since he first went there with the Karno company. Even at Mutual he had talked of a story set in the Bohemian quarter of Paris: *The Immigrant*, as we have seen, was begun as such. For weeks Chaplin wrestled with the story, for which he chose the working title *Destiny*. Many pages of notes survive from this stage, ranging from sketchy memoranda scribbled on the backs of Western Union telegraph forms to elaborate directions for the sets that would be required. These notes reveal the way that Chaplin built his story, elaborating and eliminating, inventing and refining, developing complex emotional situations and then analyzing them in order to isolate an essence that could be expressed by visual means. *A Woman of Paris* was to represent a very conscious stage in his development. Through eight years of film work he had discovered and developed his ability to reveal the inner workings of the mind and heart through external signs. In his new film he wanted to explore the limits of that expressiveness – the range, subtlety and sophistication of the sentiments and motives that could be revealed in pictures.

In the earliest stages of the story development the characters are called Peggy and Letellier, and it seems likely that some incidents in the first versions of the plot are just as Peggy related them. As the characters become more and more Chaplin's own creatures, though, they acquire fictional names – at first Marie Arnette and Poiret; later, and definitively, Marie St Clair and Pierre Revel. It is interesting however that much later, as the identification of the role and the character becomes more important, the notes frequently refer to them by the players' names, Edna and [Adolphe] Menjou.

Chaplin possessed the gift of just selection. Here, as always in the preparatory stages of his films, the notes show him exploring a great mass of ideas and incidents, and then eliminating and paring them away to arrive at a story progression.

Although at this stage the plot remained unclear the tone of irony that would characterize the film was already marked, as suggestions for incidents and details show:

> Peggy wants marriage and kids. Let. gives her elaborate doll . . .
> Mentions fact, 'If we were only married.' He laughs at it . . .
> Girl tells Let. she is going to leave him – He laughs at it – But humours her – Tells her that she will be back – She emotional about 'Goodbyes' – Goes home starts to send back jewelry. Then keeps it.

In outline the final plot could serve any old melodrama, and in other hands it might well have been no more. Marie lives with her tyrannical father in a little French village. Her boyfriend Jean helps her escape from the house for an evening, but on their return her father will not let her in. Nor will Jean's father allow her to remain in his house. Marie and Jean decide to elope to Paris, but Jean fails to arrive for the *rendezvous* at the station: his father has died suddenly of a stroke. Marie sets off for Paris alone . . .

A year later Marie St Clair is the glittering but discontented mistress of a rich man-about-town, Pierre Revel. By chance she once more meets Jean, who has come to Paris with his mother and is now a struggling artist. Marie commissions him to paint her portrait. They fall in love once again, and Jean proposes marriage. Marie decides to leave Pierre but then overhears the weak-willed Jean reassuring his possessive mother that his proposal of marriage is not serious. Marie returns to Pierre, and refuses to see the now distraught and remorseful Jean. In despair, he shoots himself. His mother sets out with his gun to avenge herself on Marie, but is touched when she finds the disconsolate girl weeping over the body of Jean. The two women are reconciled.

Chaplin agonized week after week before he found the right ending, eventually an ironic anti-climax. Marie and the mother of Jean have together found redemption and consolation in the service of others – raising orphans in a country home. In the final shot Marie is cheerfully riding with her charges on the back of a haycart. A limousine flashes by. Inside it, Pierre Revel's secretary asks him, 'By the way, whatever happened to Marie St Clair?' Pierre shrugs with indifference.

Chaplin's directions for sets to his designer, Arthur Stibolt, show that even when this story line was worked out he had ideas for elaborations and other scenes that were not finally to be filmed. He asked for a race track, for an art gallery and a jewellery store. He

proposed that they should rent facilities at Universal Studios for
scenes of a church and church bazaar, and a poor hotel. A whole
group of Canadian settings relates to one of several alternative ends
proposed for the film. He asked Stibolt to provide exteriors of a
Canadian street, a railway station, a hospital and a preacher's house,
and interiors of the same preacher's house.

Chaplin's instructions to Stibolt show his concern for the sets and
their relationship to the characters. Edna's Parisian apartment must
be 'elaborate and costly looking'. Letellier's house 'must be beautiful
. . . every means must be taken to make this set very elaborate and
still in good taste.' The café was 'supposed to be the most expensive
café in Paris'. Of the boy's Parisian studio apartment: 'while it is not
a "poor" set it should get over the atmosphere of the Latin Quarter
. . . It must be artistically furnished, so make preparations for this in
your construction . . . this set is not elaborate but must be comfortable
and suggest the home of an artist in Paris who is fairly successful.'
(In the outcome, Jean was shown as being poor.) The jewellery
store, Chaplin suggested, might be shot on actual location, perhaps
Nordlingers. At this point his idea was to match up the studio sets
with locations which he would film in Paris:

FRENCH EXTERIORS

> Entrance to First Café
> Driving away to Theatre
> Driving to Jazz Café
> Driving home in front of church
> In front of Edna's Apt.
> Front of Boy's Studio
> Front of Menjou Home
> Front of Menjou Office
> Along Seine (Boy's Scene)
> Streets for driving

For *A Woman of Paris*, Chaplin hired four young assistants, each of
whom was soon afterwards to become a capable director in his own
right. Edward Sutherland already knew Chaplin socially, and had
just written off his chances of making good as an actor when he met
Chaplin in a restaurant.

> He said, 'What are you doing, Eddie?'
> I said, 'Well, I just changed my life.'
> He said, 'What are you going to do?'

I said, 'I'm going to be your assistant.'

He said, 'You are?'

I said, 'Yes, I want to be your assistant, Charlie.'

He said, 'Why?'

I said, 'Well, I admire you greatly, and I want to be a director, and I think the best way I can do that is to study under you.'

He said, 'Well, we might be able to fix it. How much money are you getting?'

I told him the largest amount, $500.

He said, 'Oh, I couldn't pay anything like that.'

I said, 'I don't care what you pay me as long as I get the job.'

Charlie was very frugal. He had a geat fear of poverty.[1]

Sutherland, who was briefly married to Louise Brooks, was later to have a successful career as a director: he was responsible for two of the best early W. C. Fields films, *It's The Old Army Game* and *Poppy*. A second American assistant, Monta Bell, who had helped Chaplin with his book *My Trip Abroad*, was to become a prolific director and supervisor of Paramount's sound studios in New York. Among his most notable films was *The Torrent*, Garbo's first American picture.

Two young Frenchmen were engaged as research assistants, to ensure correct Parisian atmosphere. Comte Jean de Limur had arrived in Hollywood, after war service as a flyer, to try his luck as an actor, and played in Fairbanks' *The Three Musketeers*. After *A Woman of Paris* he worked as assistant to De Mille and Rex Ingram before becoming a director in his own right. Two early sound films in which he directed Jeanne Eagels, *The Letter* and *Jealousy*, were supervised by Monta Bell: there was clearly a camaraderie of Chaplin alumni. Returning to France, de Limur's work included co-direction with G. W. Pabst on *Don Quixote*.

Henri d'Abbadie d'Arrast was born in Argentina in 1897 and trained as an architect. For many years after *A Woman of Paris* he retained the friendship of Chaplin, who was attracted by his sharp intelligence and amused by his volatile and irascible temperament. Irascibility in the end limited his career as a director in Hollywood, which was a pity because he made a group of films distinguished by wit that still glitters after more than half a century; they include two of Adolphe Menjou's best silent films, *Service for Ladies* and *A Gentleman of Paris*.

These two young experts competed fiercely to establish who was the more expert on taste and other matters Parisian. They seldom agreed on anything, as Menjou recalled:

> One day Chaplin decided that he wanted some rare dish to be served and discussed in a dinner scene. The technical experts racked their minds to remember some of the exotic and expensive dishes served in Parisian restaurants. Finally one of them had an inspiration – truffle soup with champagne! The second expert refused to sanction such a dish. He had eaten at the best restaurants in Paris but never once had he been served such a *potage* as truffle soup!
>
> But expert number one only curled his lip. 'You have probably failed to dine at the finest restaurant of all,' he replied. 'It is a very small place where a very select clientèle is allowed to dine by invitation only. It is called *La Truffe d'Or* and it is the one place in the world where they serve truffle soup with champagne.'
>
> Expert number two was sure he was being out-experted by sheer imagination, but despite his protests, Chaplin decided that he liked the idea of truffle soup with champagne and ordered the prop man to prepare such a dish. The prop man was stumped. He didn't even know what a truffle was. He refused to admit his ignorance, however, and called up several chefs in the town's best restaurants to try to get a special order of truffle soup. But there were no truffles in all Los Angeles nor was there a chef who would attempt to make imitation truffle soup.
>
> Prop men are always ingenious, however, so we ended up with a horrible concoction that looked like clear soup with several withered objects floating in it. They might even have been truffles, but they were probably some sort of deadly fungi grown in the shade of a *nux vomica* tree. No one ever had nerve enough to taste the truffle soup with champagne, but it was in the picture.[2]

Edward Sutherland remembered that Jim Tully* was already employed at the Chaplin studio:

> Jim always thought of himself as kind of an American Gorki. He was an awfully nice man, but having taken an awful beating in his youth, never quite got over the inferiority that this gave him, in spite of the fact that he wrote powerfully. It has been said, I think with some degree of truth, that his subject matter was never up to his talent. He was having an awful time, and Charlie gave him fifty bucks a week so he could eat, and gave him an office at the studio, really to do nothing, just to give him a chance to write . . . There were always people coming in and out, on jobs. Charlie was supposed to be very tough with a buck, but he was always befriending anybody who was really in trouble.[3]

* Tully became a celebrity in the 1920s as the 'hobo' author of *Beggars of Life*, which was filmed in 1928. He also acted in *Way for a Sailor* (1930).

The entourage for *A Woman of Paris* included an artist who was kept on the payroll for most of the film simply to provide the painting of Edna which was to figure in the plot, but he never actually came up with a usable likeness.

The film was not, in the end, to make a great star of Edna; in fact it virtually marked the end of her career. Her role as sophisticated woman of the world destroyed her old image for the public without giving her a new one. It was, however a milestone for Adolphe Menjou, whom Chaplin chose for the role of Pierre Revel. The son of a French-born restaurateur and his Irish wife, Menjou had been acting in films since 1912, but it was only after his return from the war that he began to establish himself as a character actor. He played Louis XIII in Fairbanks' *The Three Musketeers*, the confidant of Rudolph Valentino in *The Sheik*, and was undergoing the colourful experience of playing alongside Pola Negri in *Bella Donna*, when he heard rumours that Chaplin was preparing *A Woman of Paris*. He seemed destined for the part. During Chaplin's brief liaison with Peggy Hopkins Joyce, Peggy had pointed Menjou out to him in a restaurant as having the Parisian style of Henri Letellier. Menjou was friendly with both Sutherland and Bell, both of whom recommended him to Chaplin. For his own part, Menjou was especially attracted to the job after Bell told him that the character 'goes all through the story, and you know what that means on a Chaplin picture. You will have a steady job for months and months.'

Bell warned Menjou that there were other candidates for the part but Menjou determined to have it, and prepared his strategy with care. He discovered that Chaplin was in the habit of lunching on Hollywood Boulevard, at Armstrong-Carlton's or at Musso and Frank's. Menjou made a point of arriving for lunch at the same restaurant and the same time as Chaplin, always wearing an elegant outfit he reckoned would give the impression of a *boulevardier* – morning suit, cutaway, hunting tweeds with Alpine hat, white flannels, white tie and tails. This in itself did not surprise anyone: Hollywood restaurants at lunchtime were regularly filled with movie actors in make-up and costume. It was more conspicuous when he asked a nonplussed waiter, loud enough for Chaplin to hear, for fresh *escargots* in white wine sauce. Either this play-acting or a reel of a Menjou film which Sutherland showed him persuaded Chaplin to interview Menjou. This in itself was unusual: Chaplin usually hated to interview actors because he felt so bad afterwards if he could not give them the job. He found Menjou perfect for the part but was somewhat startled by his salary demands, as Sutherland recalled:

> Chaplin had never paid more than $250 a week in his life, but Mr Menjou insisted on $500 or no contract, and he would not budge an inch, and Charlie finally, reluctantly, gave in. It nearly killed all of us.
>
> We were supposed to start this on a certain date, and time marched on. I had given Menjou a starting date three months hence – perfectly safe to my opinion or anybody's opinion – but we didn't start for another month after that. Menjou came around and said, 'I'm ready,' and I said, 'Well, we're not.'
>
> He said, 'I've got to have my money.'
>
> 'Oh, no, no . . .'
>
> Not an inch would he budge. He had the courage of a lion. We had to pay him, and it's a good thing we did, because it got us started eventually.[4]

Menjou also remembered the incident vividly:

> When I think of it now, my brassiness frightens me. There I was quibbling about a week's salary and my career was hanging in the balance. But Sutherland went to Chaplin and told him what I had said. According to Eddie, Chaplin called me some very unpleasant names, but finally ordered a voucher sent through for my salary. Every week I went down and drew my pay cheque, even though I was not called to work until January 11.[5]

It was still quite usual at that time for actors to provide their own wardrobe, so Menjou spent the interim with his tailors. Chaplin was still planning a scene on a racecourse, so Menjou ordered an expensive grey cutaway and topper. He was greatly irked when it was not used, and three years later had a racetrack scene written into one of his pictures so that he could use the outfit. He also spent half of one week's salary on an opera cloak which was not in the end required.

Shooting began on 27 November 1922 and continued for seven months. Even in this elaborate feature Chaplin worked without a script, a fact which surprised commentators at the time. In fact, by the time he came to shoot the film the scenario, worked out over the preceding months in masses of notes, was so precise in Chaplin's mind that a normal screenplay would have been superfluous, even a distraction. This method of working demanded a very careful documentation of the shooting continuity, and this has survived. It shows that Chaplin, once on the set, worked with confidence and precision. There was nothing tentative or improvisational about the shooting. In a few scenes he shot variants of the action, so that in editing he could select the most effective version. Though he made many takes to get any particular shot right, there was very little outright wastage: only three minor scenes were actually shot but not used. 'Charlie shot pictures as we went along,' said Sutherland.

> We had a basic idea of the story, then we would do the incident every day. We'd shoot for three or four days, then lay off for two weeks and rewrite and perfect it and rehearse it and rarify it. Charlie had the patience of Job. Nothing is too much trouble. A real perfectionist.
>
> With this basis of working, it took us about a year to shoot the picture, because Charlie had another theory that he really believed. He said, 'I shoot a sequence and if I'm not completely happy with it, I shoot it over the next day. That only puts me one day behind schedule. Well, he didn't figure it put him one day behind schedule every day. That's the way he worked and that's the way he did good pictures, because he could afford to and he was a great perfectionist.[6]

On one occasion after watching the daily rushes Chaplin expressed himself satisfied with one of Menjou's scenes but asked the actor how he liked it. 'I think I can do better,' Menjou replied. 'Great!' said Chaplin. 'Let's go!' and the rest of the day was spent reshooting the scene.

Chaplin's method involved shooting his film in the exact order of the story. It was a method as singular (because so costly) in 1922 as it would be now. Thus the very first shot filmed is the opening shot of the finished film: a long-shot of the house in the little French village where Edna lives, and Edna herself looking out of the window of the bedroom where her stern father has locked her to prevent her seeing her boyfriend Jean.

The brief sequence in the railway station, which has a major place in film history, was filmed between 11 p.m. and 6 a.m. on the night of 29/30 November. The innovation which aroused so much admiring comment when the film appeared was in fact dictated by economy. The scene required Marie to stand on the station as the fateful train for Paris arrives. In order to save the trouble and expense of simulating a French train, Rollie Totheroh simply cut apertures to represent the windows of a train in a ten-foot piece of board, then drew it across the front of a powerful spotlight. The light cast upon Marie's face appeared like the reflection from the lights of a moving train. The effect was done in eight takes.

In this scene Chaplin made a brief appearance as a clumsy porter.

He was not listed as an actor on the credit titles of the film, and in fact he prefaced the film with a title emphasizing that he did not appear. He was heavily disguised and muffled up. Nevertheless audiences found the scene so funny, according to Menjou, that it was necessary to abbreviate it so as not to destroy the mood of the film. Even in its cut form, one reviewer of the time picked it out:

> People laugh at an incident which may occupy three seconds. A baggage smasher enters with a trunk, drops it, and goes out. It is the simplest, unexaggerated incident of a station platform. Its effectiveness is so great as to suggest that the comedian himself was the baggage smasher, although he announces that he took no part in the play. Possibly not, but he knew how to get that baggage smasher to drop a trunk, get a laugh, and be out of it in three seconds.[7]

For four more months the work went on, creating the story, scene after scene, in the exact order in which it would appear on the screen. As the plot progressed to deal with the relationship between Revel and Marie, Chaplin demanded an altogether new style of acting from his players. Adolphe Menjou was never to forget what he learnt from Chaplin at that time:

> Not until we started shooting did I begin to realize that we were making a novel and exciting picture. It was Chaplin's genius that transformed the very ordinary story. Aside from his own great talent as an actor he had the ability to inspire other actors to perform their best. Within a few days I realized that I was going to learn more about acting from Chaplin than I had ever learned from any director. He had one wonderful, unforgettable line that he kept repeating over and over throughout the picture. 'Don't sell it!' he would say. 'Remember, they're peeking at you.'
>
> It was a colourful and concise way to sum up the difference between the legitimate stage and the movies – a reminder that in pictures, when one has an important emotion or thought to express, the camera moves up to his face and there he is on the screen with a head that measures six feet from brow to chin. The audience is peeking at him under a microscope, so he can't start playing to the gallery 200 feet away, because there is no gallery in a movie theatre; the audience is sitting in his lap.
>
> From my early days in movies I had been schooled in the exaggerated gestures and reactions that were thought necessary to tell a story in pantomime. But when I, or any other actor, would give out with one of those big takes, Chaplin would just shake his head and say, 'They're peeking at you.' That did it. I knew that I had just cut myself a large slice of ham and had tossed the scene out of the window.

Since then I have never played a scene before a camera without thinking to myself, 'They're peeking at you; don't sock it.'

Another pet line of Chaplin's was, 'Think the scene! I don't care what you do with your hands or your feet. If you think the scene, it will get over.'

And we had to keep shooting every scene until we *were* thinking it – until we believed it and were playing it with our brains and not just with our hands or our feet or our eyebrows.[8]

The novel style and the expressive restraint which Chaplin sought from his actors was not achieved without pain. Two days and ninety takes were necessary to get the right reactions in a tiny scene, in which Marie, bored, throws down her cigarette and says she will not go out.

Menjou also remembered with mixed feelings shooting a scene with Edna in which they were required to kiss. Menjou had to express passion and yet make it clear that he was not in love with Marie; Edna had to show that the kiss was not objectionable to her, but that she was unhappy and bored. 'It was like engraving the Constitution on the head of a pin – much to be told in a very confined space. To achieve this required so many takes that affectionate proximity to Edna had lost all its charm.' Yet 'it was remarkable how much Chaplin made us tell with just a look, a gesture, a lifted eyebrow.'[9]

Sometimes things went easily. Seen today, the finest moment of Edna's impeccable performance is a scene in which her girlfriends, too gleefully, show her a magazine with an announcement that Revel is to marry a rich heiress. She laughs it off and only the nervy irregularity with which she taps her cigarette indicates the emotion she is repressing. This scene, which seems as remarkable on every re-viewing, was swiftly shot in half a dozen takes at the end of a February afternoon.

The new style of acting which Chaplin demanded was easier for the younger artists than for older and more seasoned performers. For the role of Jean's mother Chaplin cast Lydia Knott who, though she was at the time only forty-eight years old, had made a speciality of playing sweet old ladies ever since her entry into films in 1917. She remained a very busy character player in the 1930s.

She was a beautiful Madonna-faced old lady with a will of steel. We had a scene where she found out that Carl Miller, her son, was killed, and the Sûreté was asking her the normal questions: 'What was his name?', 'Age?' etc. We wanted a complete, dead, no-reaction from her – wanted the audience to supply the emotion, not the actress. I can't tell you how many times we shot it, and she would always do it feeling sorry for herself and smiling sweetly. I don't know how many times we shot it, then finally Charlie determined to get it the way he wanted it – and we were all with him – and he shot it 110 times, and then said 'You shoot it for a while' so I shot it about 100 times, and finally the old lady got so angry that she swore at us and just went through this scene in such a temper that we got it. And I venture to say we shot that scene 500 times. I don't know how many days it took us, about a week, to get that one reaction. I would think that took the record for retakes. In dollars and cents I don't know whether that pays off, but certainly in quality it did.[10]

Unfortunately for legend, Sutherland considerably exaggerates the number of takes. In fact Charlie shot the scene thirty-nine times on Friday 4 May, then brought Miss Knott back on Saturday morning for forty-one more takes. For a single brief shot, however, eighty takes is a lot. Chaplin was not satisfied even then: fifty years later he still shuddered at Lydia Knott's over-acting whenever he saw *A Woman of Paris*.

Non-professional actors could be much more malleable. One of the most memorable figures in *A Woman of Paris* is the stony-faced lady who gives Edna a massage, as Edna's *demi-mondaine* friends (played by Betty Morrissey and Malvina Polo) discuss the latest gossip with her. The camera rises to the face and upper half of the masseuse. From the movement of her arms we can sense which portion of Edna's voluptuous body is receiving attention: her face is set in perpetual disapproval, impassive yet all too evidently soaking in the gossip like blotting paper. The lady was not an actress at all but the studio secretary, Nellie Bly Baker, yet the set of her features and every move is exactly Chaplin; he had schooled her to a perfect imitation. Like little Jackie Coogan, Nellie Bly Baker, as a perfect mimic, provided Chaplin with the acting material most ideal for his purposes: bodies through whom he could convey his own performance. Nellie's performance made such an impression that she left her work at the studio to become a character actress in a few films for other directors.

Chaplin's comedy had always been built upon visual suggestion, metaphor, simile. In the comedies an alarm clock could become a can of gone-off fish, a cow's tail a pump handle, or a man a bird. Adolphe Menjou described how he extended his range of visual symbolism to meet the needs of drama.

Because of the censorship boards in various states Chaplin had to indicate [the relationship between Pierre Revel and Marie] in a way that would not be obvious or offensive. He accomplished it in a manner that was, at that time, amazingly subtle.

This is the way the scene was developed: Revel came to the girl's luxurious apartment and was admitted by a maid. The audience had no idea who or what this man was in her life. Apparently he was just an admirer calling to take her out to dinner. Chaplin wanted to find some casual piece of business that would suddenly reveal that Revel was a frequent and privileged caller. A good many devices were discussed. First Chaplin had me pick up a pipe from the table and light it, but that was no good because Revel was not the pipe-smoking type. Then he considered having the maid bring me a pair of slippers, but that was out of key because I had called to take Marie out to dinner.

Finally Chaplin thought of the handkerchief business, which solved the problem. I went to a liquor cabinet, took out a bottle of sherry and poured a drink, then sipped it. But when I started to take a handkerchief from my pocket I discovered that I had none, so I turned casually and walked into the bedroom. Edna was at her dressing table, fully dressed but still fussing with her coiffure. I didn't look at her and she paid no attention to me as I crossed to a chiffonier. There I opened a top drawer and took out a large gentleman's handkerchief, put it in my pocket, and walked out. Immediately the relationship was established: we were living together and had been for some time.

It happened that when Chaplin thought of this piece of busines, the property man had not dressed the drawers of the chiffonier because he didn't know that they would be used. So I went to my dressing room and brought back several handkerchiefs and one of my dress collars and it fell out of the drawer. This gave Charlie an idea for a later scene in which the maid accidentally dropped a collar and thus disclosed to the girl's former sweetheart that she was living with Revel.

Little touches like this gave the picture a flavour that was new to picturemaking.[11]

Right up until the beginning of June 1923, Chaplin was still puzzled as to how to end the film. He considered letting Marie marry Revel, or alternatively having her return to the village to nurse her now widowed and failing mother. There are notes for a version in which she emigrates to America, and for another where she goes to Canada and devotes herself to Christian works. He considered a railway accident which would give Marie the opportunity to redeem herself by heroism. Both Sutherland and Menjou remembered with unseemly glee a day when Chaplin arrived at the studio with a new solution:

Marie should give up Revel to consecrate herself to a life of penance as a nurse in a leper colony. Chaplin all too accurately sensed the adverse reactions of Bell, Sutherland, Menjou and others of his entourage. Huffily he left the studio and stayed away for several days. When he returned the leper colony was forgotten.

Even without the mute distaste of his collaborators, Chaplin with his gift for selection, rejection, simplification would undoubtedly have quickly seen the faults of his solution. It is illuminating to see how the eventual swift, ironic ending of the film was refined out of a much more elaborate sequence in which Revel was to seek out Marie in her country retreat. Revel was to propose marriage; Marie was to refuse; then,

> 'You know where you can find me. I shall always love you. Goodbye'. They shake hands and look into each other's eyes and the souls of both of them are in that look. Menjou then gets into the car and drives off in the direction he had come passing on the way a rustic looking farm cart carrying several workers from the fields one of them playing an accordion and the rest singing a homely folk song to the accompaniment.
>
> Edna looks after Menjou's car and as the farm cart comes abreast the kiddie begs to ride back to the picnic grounds. The workers also urge it and Edna lifting the kid on the cart, gets on it herself and they drive down the road to the tune of the worker's song as Menjou and his fancy car pass out of the picture in the other direction.[12]

By avoiding a sentimental reunion of Marie and Pierre in favour of a scene in which two very different vehicles carry the pair to their separate destinies, Chaplin arrived at the essence.

Unusually intelligent and perceptive men themselves, both Sutherland and Menjou were impressed by Chaplin's talent for selection:

> Chaplin listened to everybody's ideas and evaluated them with an unerring instinct for those that were good. He had no academic knowledge of proper dramatic structure, only an innate comprehension of good theatre and how to portray either simple or complex ideas in pantomime without the aid of dialogue or subtitles. I remember hearing him say in an argument about a certain scene, 'I don't know why I'm right about the scene. I just know I'm right.' And it was true.[13]

'While Chaplin is supposed to be a great intellectual', said Sutherland, '(this will make him furious if he ever hears it) I think that Charlie's intellect is mostly emotion. I think his instincts are magnificent, and

I think his knowledge is perception, feeling, rather than anything else . . .'[14]

The daily studio staff conferences, with their interchange of ideas, were important to Chaplin's creative activity. They were not always fruitful. On one occasion they sat for hours trying to decide whether the better title for the gigolo scene would be 'Who is it?' or 'Who is he?' When everyone was beginning to think that perfectionism can be carried too far, the conference was brought to an end by an Airedale dog which Chaplin kept at the studio and which wandered into the room, listened for a while with its head cocked on one side, and then vomited on the floor.

Nor was Chaplin always right, particularly towards the end of shooting when nerves became frayed. One day the unit was shooting exteriors near Westlake Park (of Keystone days) when it was recognized that in shooting a scene of two actors walking past a building Chaplin was breaking the basic, practical rule that you must never cut to a reverse shot of an actor or group of actors crossing the screen, since it reverses the direction of the action, changes the background and generally confuses the viewer. Sutherland pointed out the error to Chaplin, who was embarrassed to be corrected in front of bystanders and rebuked his critic so forcefully that Sutherland instantly threatened to quit. Next day the rushes revealed the mistake all too clearly, and the chagrined Chaplin had to go out and take the scenes again. On another occasion even the gentle Rollie rebelled when Chaplin, in a mood of irritation, insisted that some shots were out of focus when they quite clearly were not. 'Well, if you can say that is lousy, you'd better get yourself another boy,' Rollie told him. 'I will,' replied Chaplin, and Rollie stormed off.

The next morning I was sitting on the bench and instead of Charlie driving in through the gates the way he always did, he came into his office through the screen door and I was sitting on the bench outside. He motioned me to come down to him and he turned around and put his behind up in the air and said, 'Kick me in the ass, Rollie.' And I did. And he said, 'You know, I wanted to take that shot over anyhow.'[15]

His moods were a byword. The regular studio staff insisted that they knew his mood at once from the colour of the suit he was wearing, and would telephone his home to find out from the valet what clothes he had put on that morning. His green suit was notorious. 'Every time he wore it all hell broke loose,' said Sutherland. The blue suit with pin stripes portended a jovial, productive day. The grey suit was in between, 'so we would feel our way for a while until a definite mood developed.' As Menjou remarked:

> One or two of the staff had this suit-to-match-the-mood theory developed to a very fine degree. I think they were exaggerating; the only thing I noticed about Charlie's wardrobe was that it was deplorable. His clothes did not fit properly and there was no style to the way he wore them. I inquired one day who his tailor was, thinking that I would take great pains to avoid the fellow. To my horror Charlie confessed that he had no tailor, that he hated tailors. He had never had a tailored suit in his life![16]

Chaplin explained that he could not bear to waste time being fitted, so just walked into a good men's store and ordered half a dozen ready-made suits for convenience. 'I believe him. He looked terrible in his clothes. That was a long time ago. Since then he has outgrown this attitude.'[17]

The final scene of the film, with Revel and his secretary speeding down the country road, was shot on Monday 25 June. The editing was completed one year, one month and fourteen days after Chaplin had first begun work on the scenario. He had shot a total of 3,862 takes, amounting to 130,115 feet, which were reduced in the finished film to 7,557 feet. The total cost of the production was $351,853.

In the course of production the title had changed from *Destiny* to *Public Opinion*. Alternative titles considered before the choice eventually fell on *A Woman of Paris* included *Melody of Life*, *The Joy Route*, *Social Customs*, *Human Nature*, *Love*, *Ladies and Life* and *The Stars Incline*. Chaplin prefaced the film with a title which might have been the motto of many of his films: 'The world is not composed of heroes and villains, but of men and women with all the passions that God has given them. The ignorant condemn but the wise pity.'

The première on 26 September 1923 was the opening attraction of the Criterion Theatre on Grand Avenue and 7th Street in Hollywood. 'The most aristocratic showplace in Hollywood', the theatre had been decorated and furnished without regard to cost. 'The inside resembles a Byzantine jewel box. Walls of antique stone in colours of gray and silver, with bolder hues like mellow sunlight caught without.' The première was one of the most glittering occasions of the era. The guests included Fairbanks, Pickford, Irving Thalberg, the De Milles, Will Rogers and most of the other ruling stars of Hollywood as well as the Mayor, fire chief and civic dignitaries of Los Angeles. Old acquaintances of the star included Mack Sennett, Mabel Normand, Jackie Coogan and Mildred Harris. The musical accompaniment was conducted by Adolf Tandler, former director of the Los Angeles Symphony Orchestra; and Chaplin had himself devised a special live mimed prologue entitled *Nocturne*. Menjou was convinced of the film's success when he heard loud stage whispers of 'Wonderful! Terrific!' from the Irish-born director Herbert Brenon, and when outside the theatre Harold Lloyd, whom he had never met, clasped his hands above his head in a congratulatory handshake and grinned his compliments across the heads of the crowd that separated them.

Chaplin and Edna did not attend the première: they were already on the train for New York where the film was to be premièred at the Lyric Theatre on 1 October. For that show Chaplin had written a special programme note which revealed his growing anxiety about the public's reaction to the film: it was certainly not his usual style to ask for comments from his audiences:

No doubt while you are waiting I can have a little heart to heart talk with you. I've been thinking that the public wants a little more realism in pictures, whereby a story is pursued to the logical ending. I would like to get your ideas on the subject, for I am sure that those of us who are producing pictures do not know – we only guess.

In my first serious drama, *A Woman of Paris*, I've striven for realism, true to life. What you will see is life as I personally see it – the beauty – the sadness – the touches – the gaiety, all of which are necessary to make life interesting. However, it is not for me to say that I am right. My first thoughts have been to entertain you. The story is intimate, simple and human, presenting a problem as old as the ages – showing it with as much truth as I am allowed to put into it – giving it a treatment as near realism as I have been able to devise.

I do not wish that *A Woman of Paris* should appear as a preachment, or am I expounding a sort of philosophy, unless it be an appeal for a better understanding of human frailties.

After all, you are the judge, and your taste must be served. To some it may look as though I have not taken full advantage of dramatic possibilities, while others may see good taste in the strength of repression, and by your reception will I guide myself in the future.

I was over seven months making *A Woman of Paris* and I enjoyed every moment of the time. However, if I have failed in my effort to

319

entertain you, I feel it will be my loss. Nevertheless I enjoyed making it, and sincerely hope you will enjoy seeing it.

Sincerely,
CHARLES CHAPLIN

Few films have ever enjoyed such unanimous enthusiasm from the press. Chaplin was freely compared to Hardy, to de Maupassant and to Ibsen, though generally they thought him a good deal better than Ibsen because, having long demonstrated that comedy is never far removed from tragedy, Chaplin now showed that tragedy could have its share of gaiety. Robert Sherwood in the *New York Herald* wrote:

> There is more real genius in Charles Chaplin's *A Woman of Paris* than in any picture I have ever seen ... Charles Chaplin has proved many times that he understands humanity; he has leavened his hilariously broad comedy with elements of poignant tragedy. He has caught and conveyed the contrast between joy and sorrow which makes existence on this terrestrial ball as interesting as it is.

The critic of *Exceptional Photoplays* wrote that

> Mr Chaplin ... has not done anything radical or anything esoteric. He has merely used his intelligence in the highest degree, an act which has ceased to be expected of motion picture people for many years. He has written and directed a story in which all the characters act upon motives which the spectator immediately recognizes as natural and sincere, and therefore *A Woman of Paris* breathes an atmosphere of reality, and thereby holds the attention of any perceptive audience in thrall ...
>
> *A Woman of Paris* has the one quality almost every other motion picture that has been made to date lacks – restraint. The acting is moving without ever being fierce, the story is simple and realistic without ever being inane, the settings are pleasing and adequate without ever being colossally stupid. The result is a picture of dignity and intelligence and the effect is startling because it is so unusual.

When the film reached Britain, the critic of the *Manchester Guardian* called it 'the greatest modern story that the screen has yet seen ...

> He has had the courage to throw the sum total of screen convention on the scrap heap.'

As most critics pointed out, there was nothing very new about the plot: when Chaplin first recounted it to Menjou, he thought it 'a trite bit of schmaltz'. What made it so startling for audiences of its own time was the novelty of its characters, who observed none of the rules of screen drama. The heroine was no better than she should be; the villain was likeable, charming, generous and considerate; the hero was a mother-dominated weakling; and all the tragedy was precipitated by the folly, blindness and selfishness of parents – who as a class the screen had hitherto held in superstitious reverence.

After sixty years it is difficult to appreciate the first surprise of Chaplin's new methods of story telling, new style of acting and new sophistication of the expressive means of pantomime; his innovations were all rapidly assimilated to become part of the common practice of film craft. Chaplin's own approach to his discoveries, too, had been so simple in its logic: 'As I have noticed life in its dramatic climaxes,' he told an interviewer in New York, 'men and women try to hide their emotions rather than seek to express them. And that is the method I have pursued in an endeavour to become as realistic as possible.'

Inaugurating a whole new style of comedy of manners, *A Woman of Paris* opened the way for the director Ernst Lubitsch, who confessed himself overwhelmed by the film, which he saw just as he was embarking on his own satirical masterpiece, *The Marriage Circle*. Every film maker studied Chaplin's discoveries: the future work of Sutherland, Bell, de Limur and d'Arrast all bears the clear mark of their experience with Chaplin. Menjou summed up his own impressions:

> To him motion pictures were a new art form and required the painstaking care that any art requires. Of course he happened also to be an artist. Everyone who has worked with Chaplin the actor or with Chaplin the director seems to agree on that point, regardless of what he may think of him personally.
>
> The word 'genius' is used very carelessly in Hollywood, but when it is said of Chaplin, it is always with a special note of sincerity. If Hollywood has ever produced a genius, Chaplin is certainly first choice.[18]

The éclat of the New York première made up for missing the Hollywood gala. Two days afterwards Chaplin made his first radio broadcast, from L. Bamberger's WOR Studio in Newark, under the sponsorship of the *Morning Telegraph*. 'My friends,' he began, 'this is all way beyond me. I'm glad you can't see me – I am nervous as a witch.' In the course of the broadcast, which lasted half an hour, he told the listeners that he was experimenting with the possibilities of voice on the air. He then played the violin and saxophone and did some impersonations.

On 5 October he went to hear Lloyd George speak at City Hall, and was deeply embarrassed when his own presence completely stole the audience's attention from the great British politician. He even stole the thunder of three bandits who robbed the jewellery store at the Ritz Carlton where he was staying: just because he happened to walk through the lobby a few minutes after the crime, it was Chaplin who made the headlines in all the newspaper reports. On the way back he stopped at Detroit. Again poor Herbert Hoover, who was on the same train, was upstaged and even found difficulty getting someone to carry his bags, so taken up was everyone with the excitement of seeing Chaplin.

Later Chaplin went on the platform with Hoover and the President of the Rockefeller Foundation at the first Annual General Meeting of the American Child Health Association, and gave a message to the children of the nation: 'Brush your teeth every day so that you'll always be proud to laugh. And remember that as long as you can laugh you're happy and happiness means much towards good health.' The two hundred children in the audience needed some convincing that he really was Chaplin, since they did not recognize him without his moustache and big boots. He received a visit from Henry and Edsel Ford. 'I have come twenty miles from Dearborn to see you,' grunted Ford. 'That's nothing,' Chaplin told him, 'I came all the way from Los Angeles to see you.'[19]

The euphoria of the premières, the press and this royal progress was soon to be dashed. The Hollywood run of *A Woman of Paris* ended after only four weeks. After the first few days, Chaplin's film proved to be a failure at the box office. The New York run actually lost money. In Hollywood and London the film barely covered its guarantee. Such a thing had never happened to a Chaplin film before. Ironically, it was probably the enthusiasm of the press that had killed the film. The critics told the public that the picture was great art, but Chaplin's audience were not interested in him as a great artist: they liked him because he was funny. Moreover, they were clearly not disposed to pay money to see a Chaplin film in which he didn't appear, except heavily disguised in a walk-on part of two or three seconds. Chaplin's disappointment was intense and lasting. As soon as he was able, he withdrew the picture from circulation and hid it in his vaults, unseen, for more than half a century. He loved *A Woman of Paris* and was proud of it, and was not inclined to expose himself again to this snub from his public.

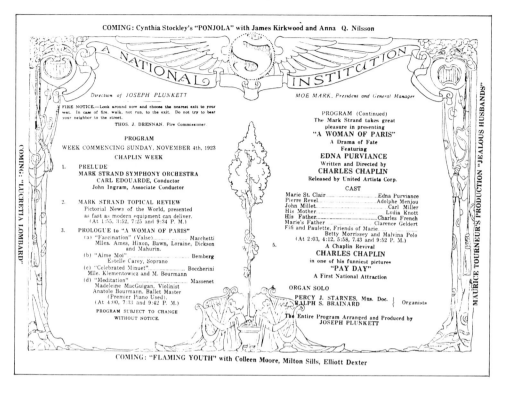

COMING: Cynthia Stockley's "PONJOLA" with James Kirkwood and Anna Q. Nilsson

A NATIONAL INSTITUTION

Direction of JOSEPH PLUNKETT

MOE MARK, *President and General Manager*

FIRE NOTICE—Look around now and choose the nearest exit to your seat. In case of fire, walk, not run, to the exit. Do not try to beat your neighbor to the street.

THOS. J. DRENNAN, Fire Commissioner.

PROGRAM

WEEK COMMENCING SUNDAY, NOVEMBER 4th, 1923

CHAPLIN WEEK

1. PRELUDE
MARK STRAND SYMPHONY ORCHESTRA
CARL EDOUARDE, Conductor
John Ingram, Associate Conductor

2. MARK STRAND TOPICAL REVIEW
Pictorial News of the World, presented as fast as modern equipment can deliver.
(At 1:55, 3:52, 7:25 and 9:34 P. M.)

3. PROLOGUE to "A WOMAN OF PARIS"
(a) "Fascination" (Valse).......... Marchetti
Mlles. Ames, Hixon, Bawn, Loraine, Dickson and Mahurin.
(b) "Aime Moi".......... Bemberg
Estelle Carey, Soprano
(c) "Celebrated Minuet".......... Boccherini
Mlle. Klementowicz and M. Bourmann
(d) "Meditation".......... Massenet
Madeleine MacGuigan, Violinist
Anatole Bourmann, Ballet Master
(Premier Piano Used).
(At 4:00, 7:33 and 9:42 P. M.)

PROGRAM SUBJECT TO CHANGE
WITHOUT NOTICE.

PROGRAM (Continued)
The Mark Strand takes great pleasure in presenting
"A WOMAN OF PARIS"
A Drama of Fate
Featuring
EDNA PURVIANCE
Written and Directed by
CHARLES CHAPLIN
Released by United Artists Corp.

CAST

Marie St. Clair..........Edna Purviance
Pierre Revel..........Adolphe Menjou
John Millet..........Carl Miller
His Mother..........Lydia Knott
His Father..........Charles French
Marie's Father..........Clarence Geldert
Fifi and Paulette, Friends of Marie.
Betty Morrissey and Malvina Polo
(At 2:03, 4:12, 5:58, 7.43 and 9:52 P. M.)

5. A Chaplin Revival
CHARLES CHAPLIN
in one of his funniest pictures
"PAY DAY"
A First National Attraction

ORGAN SOLO

PERCY J. STARNES, Mus. Doc. }
RALPH S. BRAINARD } Organists

The Entire Program Arranged and Produced by
JOSEPH PLUNKETT

COMING: "FLAMING YOUTH" with Colleen Moore, Milton Sills, Elliott Dexter

1923 - Programme for *A Woman of Paris.*

To exacerbate the pain there was the activity of the official guardians of the nation's morals. New York's Board of Censors approved the film without changes, but in Kansas, where cigarette smoking was regarded with the same horror as Dreiser's novels and bootleg liquor, all scenes that showed people smoking were excised. The Pennsylvania censors, who had a not unreasonable aversion to firearms, cut out the scene of Jean's suicide, thus confusing the plot somewhat. Ohio achieved most notoriety, as a result of the action taken by the State Director of Education and Head of the Board of Censors, a Vernon M. Riegel. Mr Riegel admitted the artistic merits of the film but regretted that the leading characters behaved in a fashion so unacceptable. He therefore set about making them conduct themselves 'as a lady and gentleman should conduct themselves toward one another', by cutting out a number of scenes and adding a title to explain that Marie's opulent style of living in Paris was made possible only by a bequest from a wealthy aunt. Maryland took up the idea, restoring Marie's respectability by attributing her luxurious accessories to her earnings as a popular actress.

Work on a film ordinarily left Chaplin no time for private life, but the period of *A Woman of Paris* was exceptional, thanks to the irruption into Hollywood of Pola Negri. Her screen career had flourished in Germany thanks to her association with the director Ernst Lubitsch. Lubitsch's *Madame Dubarry* – retitled for America *Passion* – brought international celebrity and offers from Hollywood. Paramount won her, and she arrived in September 1922 to begin work. Immediately she informed the press of her eagerness to be reunited with 'Sharlee', whom she had met briefly in Berlin the previous year. As Negri was to remember:

> We spent four delightful days together in Berlin on the occasion of his first visit to Germany.
>
> I was completely captivated by his gaiety, but as he did not speak more than three words of German and at that time I did not speak more than three words of English, our conversation was rather limited. In fact, I don't think we thought of love.
>
> But now, as I look back on our meeting, I know that my love for him began on that fateful night at the Palais Heinroth.[20]

Chaplin too admitted:

> It began in Berlin, a year and a half ago. I fell in love with Pola the instant I met her and the only reason I didn't tell her so was because I was too bashful to confess it. I did tell her she was the loveliest lady I had ever met and I'm sure she must have guessed the secret of my heart.
>
> But for nearly a year an ocean separated us – and an ocean is an awful bar to a successful love affair.[21]

Despite such touching protestations, Chaplin managed to avoid meeting Pola during her first weeks in Hollywood. Later he explained gallantly: 'I have purposely avoided her when she first arrived in Hollywood for I felt that it would result exactly as it has. Isn't it strange how we instinctively feel the fate that is about to overtake us?'[22]

The fateful meeting eventually could be postponed no longer: it took place at the Actors' Fund Pageant at the Hollywood Ball in October 1922. Pola was playing Cleopatra and Chaplin was conducting the orchestra. Even at this stage he must have been putting off the moment, because Pola recalled,

> Strangely enough we missed each other at rehearsals – it was not until the actual performance that I saw him wielding his baton. And as I walked toward him I looked into his face.
>
> It was then that I realized that I had been in love with him for more than a year – without being aware of it. I could hardly wait until the pageant was over to see him. And later he confided to me that he had experienced the same feeling at exactly the same time.
>
> Of course, after the performance we met. The following day he called at my home and since then, except when business or social duties prevented, we have been inseparable.
>
> We understand each other perfectly, and I am sure we will be happy. For my Charlie is not only the dearest boy in the world, but the cleverest. He is a genius.[23]

Chaplin, with not much alternative, corroborated Pola's story:

> ... when I saw Pola in all her glorious beauty as she swept toward me that fateful day of the great pageant I could not resist her any longer. Something I can't describe surged all over inside of me. I felt like a drowning man – yet excited as I had never been before.
>
> And it was not long before I confessed my love, and, to my happiness and surprise, I learned that Pola felt the same way about me.[24]

From this time the two stars were inseparable and for the next nine months news and rumours of the on-and-off romance were to delight American newspaper readers and embarrass poor Chaplin. By the end of November the press were asking him to confirm whether they were going to marry. 'I can't say yes,' he replied cagily; 'any such announcement must of necessity come from her. Neither can I say no: think of the position that would put her in.' On 25 January 1923 Jesse Lasky, on behalf of Paramount Studios, announced that there was nothing in Pola's contract which presented any obstacle to her marrying Chaplin. He did not add that such a marriage would be exceedingly advantageous for the star's publicity. Three days later, on 28 January, Chaplin and Pola invited the press to the Del Monte Lodge suite of the Countess Domaska – Pola's title by a marriage just ended by special Vatican dispensation. Chaplin was reported to be looking rather ill when he arrived by train, but Pola was pronounced 'exquisite . . . exotic . . . Her paleness, comparable only to the creamy texture of the leaf of a camellia blossom, contrasted sharply with the vivid crimson of her lips. Happiness burned in her expressive eyes of greenish gray. She was clad in a simple black velvet suit with a vestee of old lace and a black velvet tam.'

When the press were admitted to Pola's drawing room, they found her snuggling on the shoulder of Chaplin, whom they described as 'squirming' with embarrassment and confusion. He was tongue-tied, but Pola's volubility made up for that:

> I am a European woman. I do not understand zee custom but I am – we are – what you say? – Mr Chaplin and I are engaged. We are to be married.
>
> In these words, Pola, in hesitant and dulcet words, for the first time officially announced the engagement.
>
> Charlie blushed, swallowed hard and affirmed the marriage compact in answer to a little shake and Pola's question:
>
> 'Eez zat not so, Sharlie?'
>
> 'Sharlie' gulped. A bridegroom blush swept up to his gray temples. He opened his lips. He was speechless. Another gulp.
>
> 'Yes,' was his sole historical utterance.
>
> Then Pola buried her face on his shoulder. 'Sharlie's' arm stole protectively about her. The gorgeous diamond on Pola's ring finger sparkled happily . . .[25]

Pola kept on talking. When the press men asked Chaplin when the happy event would take place, he referred the question to his fiancée:

> We are to marry – when I do not know. Perhaps after my contract has feenished. Perhaps before. We do not know and have not decided . . .
>
> We have been engaged for a long time, but we decided to say nossing about it. We felt it was our affair and not zee world's. But newspaper men have been so-o-o persistent, and since we wanted this one day together without being haunted we decided to tell you so that you could all tell zee people.[26]

Rumour and speculation only increased after the announcement. It was said that the couple had actually married a year before in Europe, and that Pola had signed a telegram 'Pola Negri Chaplin'. The rumours were denied. Five weeks later zee people read that the engagement was broken off and that Pola was prostrate with grief. The cause was a newspaper report that Chaplin had said that he was 'too poor to marry just now. This is a workaday world and we've all got to stay busy and keep away from the climaxes of sentiment' – which seemed a rather apt description of Pola. Pola countered with much-photographed tears and a typewritten statement declaring that she was 'too poor to marry Charles Chaplin; he needs a wealthy woman.' Orally she added, 'There were a thousand things. It was another experience. I have learned. Now I will live only for my work. As for the rest, the happy days are dead for me. It is all over.'

Six hours afterwards it was all on again. Chaplin denied that he had said anything of the sort and drove to Pola for a conference of reconciliation. Afterwards, in the small hours of 2 March, Pola told newsmen that she was 'too happy to sleep' and that Chaplin had told her 'he loved me and could not live without me'.

Chaplin corroborated his repentance in an interview with one of the best Hollywood reporters, Karl K. Kitchen. His assessment of Pola's matrimonial assets and likely domestic virtues might seem, given all the evidence, a trifle exaggerated. His statement is more interesting for his very realistic view of his own ambitions and potential shortcomings as a husband:

> I have always wanted to be married, to have a real home, with children. I have wanted this more than anything in the world. And for years I had hoped that I would meet the right woman – a woman with sympathy, understanding, affection and at the same time possessed of beauty, charm and intelligence.
>
> Until I met Pola this ideal woman remained a dream. Today she is a reality.
>
> I can understand my love for Pola, for she is everything I have ever dreamed of. But why she should love me is something I will never understand. I lack the physique, the physical strength that a beautiful woman admires. However, perhaps it is best that I do not question the gifts of the gods.
>
> I will be a difficult husband to live with – for when I am at work I give every ounce of myself to my task. My wife will have to show great understanding – great sympathy. And my wife must trust me – there must be mutual trust, mutual freedom from suspicion, or there can be no happiness. Understanding – that's the great thing in married life. And that is what Pola and I have in common.[27]

Chaplin's assessment of the desiderata and difficulties of marriage might be ideally applied to his last and brilliantly successful union. It is fascinating however to find it stated at this period of his life and strange to find it applied to Pola, who seems not to have been the marrying kind, as Chaplin was to recognize in the course of the succeeding months.

The next disruption in the relationship came with the Marina Varga affair. Marina was a somewhat disturbed young Mexican woman with a desire to go into pictures and an excessive fan-worship of Chaplin. Having run away from her husband in Vera Cruz and crossed the border without papers, disguised as a boy, she presented herself at the studio, where she was sent off by Kono. The same night, however, she managed somehow to make her way to Chaplin's bedroom and to enter not only his bed but also his pyjamas. She was discovered by Kono while Chaplin and Pola were dining downstairs with Chaplin's friends and neighbours, Dr and Mrs Reynolds. (Dr Reynolds was a good conversationalist, a poor amateur actor and a brain surgeon. It was a standing joke that there was not much material in Hollywood for him to work on in this professional capacity.) Kono persuaded Marina to dress, with the promise that Chaplin would then speak to her; after Chaplin had talked kindly to her under the unfriendly gaze of Pola, Marina was persuaded to leave the house.

Next day Marina was again seen around the Chaplin grounds. According to her own account, she subsequently despaired of winning her idol, went to a neighbouring drug store, asked for arsenic, and swallowed whatever it was the store clerk gave her. She then took herself to Chaplin's garden to lie down and die, having first scattered an offering of roses around the front steps. She was discovered and carried into a laundry room where Dr Reynolds examined her and concluded that her distressed state was due to hysteria rather than poison. Chaplin and Pola again met her. This time however Chaplin's rival admirers, volatile Mexican and temperamental Pole, started an altercation. It quickly became so ferocious that Chaplin (so it was said) had to cool them down with a pail of cold water. Marina was removed to the Receiving Hospital where the physicians could discover no symptoms of poisoning. At the Alexandria Hotel, where she was staying, her luggage was found to consist of little more than copies of telegrams to the Mexican Secretary of War and the Inspector General of Police asking them for financial aid. On being discharged from the hospital, Marina went directly to the offices of the *Los Angeles Examiner*, where she co-operatively posed for photographs. She was rewarded next day with front-page headlines: 'GIRL TRIES TO DIE FOR LOVE IN CHARLIE CHAPLIN'S HOUSE'.

Chaplin addressing a Bond rally in Wall Street, 1918.

Chaplin at a Bond rally in Washington, 1918.
Also in the group are Franklin D. Roosevelt,
Secretary of the Navy, Douglas Fairbanks and
Mary Pickford, and (next to Chaplin), Marie Dressler.

Above: *Shoulder Arms*: Set for
the abandoned prologue.

Centre: *Shoulder Arms*: Set for
the abandoned epilogue,
'The Banquet'.

Right: *Shoulder Arms*: Chaplin
getting into his tree costume.

Chaplin with Dorothy Rosher during the making of *The Bond*.

Right: *The Bond* (1918): Chaplin and Edna. This shot shows particularly clearly the remarkable Expressionist style of the decors.

A break during filming of *The Bond*. In the foreground Henry Bergman, as John Bull, is chatting to Sydney, as the Kaiser.

An impetuous visitor: Douglas Fairbanks vaults the gate of the Chaplin Studio.

Below left: Tea break during shooting of *Sunnyside*.

Mildred Harris Chaplin, 1918.

A Day's Pleasure: Edna sits on the pavement outside the studio chatting to the children in the cast. At this point she had no role in the film: the part of Chaplin's wife was to be played by Tom Wood, who can be glimpsed wearing a woman's straw hat, behind Chaplin.

The Kid: Chaplin, with wings, practices flying.

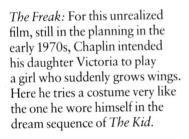

The Freak: For this unrealized film, still in the planning in the early 1970s, Chaplin intended his daughter Victoria to play a girl who suddenly grows wings. Here he tries a costume very like the one he wore himself in the dream sequence of *The Kid*.

The Professor: Hitherto unknown photographs taken during the shooting of the dosshouse scene.

The Kid: Chaplin with Jackie Coogan, Edith Wilson
and her baby. Edith Wilson was the wife of Jack Wilson,
the second cameraman, who wrote on the back of this
photograph: 'Charlie thanking Edith for taking part
in his picture. She was paid $15 for 4 hours work.
Not bad, eh?'

Handing over the negative of *The Kid*: left to right:
A First National executive; Sol Lesser; Alf Reeves,
with cheque; Chaplin; another First National executive;
Sydney. The First National men show every sign of having
come off worse in the financial negotiations.

Chaplin was not always at ease with the first-class
passengers on the *Olympic*, and took the opportunity
to chat with the stokers when they came up on deck.
Once they put on an impromptu entertainment for him and,
in return, he demonstrated his 'funny walk' and
led them round the deck in a conga.

Chaplin leaving the *Olympic* at Southampton.
He was mobbed by crowds as he arrived.

Portrait of Max Linder
dedicated by Linder to
'The King of All Directors'.

Chaplin directs Lord Louis
Mountbatten in an improvised
film – *Nice and Friendly*.

Chaplin in his cutting
room, c. 1920.

Lady Mountbatten in
Nice and Friendly.

Pola Negri

Above right: *A Woman of Paris* (1923): A Bohemian party.

Right: *A Woman of Paris* (1923): Lydia Knott, Carl Miller, Edna Purviance.

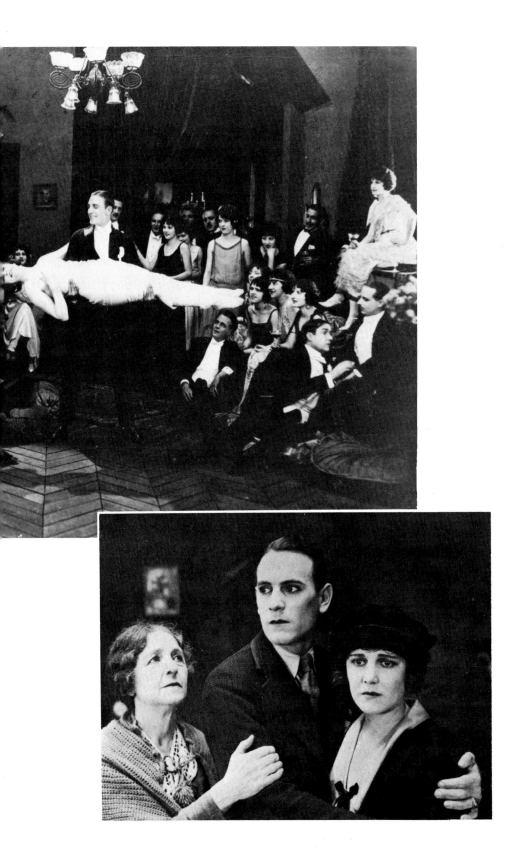

The United Artists: Douglas Fairbanks, Mary Pickford, Chaplin and D.W. Griffith with Mr Price.

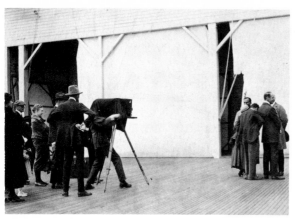

Jack Wilson photographs the four United Artists (Chaplin, Fairbanks, Pickford and Griffith). Mr Biby, the studio manager, is beside the camera; Edna in shawl behind.

Below: Chaplin rehearsing for a recording with Abe Lyman's orchestra, 1925.

Pola was highly displeased with the whole incident. There were clearly other rifts in the harmony. As Rodney Ackland wrote years later. 'She had a blind and uncritical admiration of her own genius in the blaze of which her sense of humour evaporated like a dew-drop on a million-watt arc lamp.' Chaplin's sense of humour however was not to be quenched. Menjou, a generally reliable witness, described an incident which cannot have furthered the romance, given the temperaments involved. At a party Pola, overcome by some passing emotion, swooned decorously. The rest of the guests ran for water to revive her but Chaplin, not to be upstaged, lay down on the hearth rug and calmly swooned beside her. Pola, reviving swiftly, did not appreciate it.

On 28 July the comedy was officially pronounced ended. A night or two before, at the reopening of the Ambassador's Coconut Grove, Chaplin and Pola had sat at separate tables. He was with the young actress Leonore Ulrich; she was with the tennis star William Tilden. They did not acknowledge each other. The loyal *Examiner* interviewed Pola:

'I realized five weeks ago that it was an impossibility. He's a charming fellow. We're still friends. I say "hello" to him but I realize now I could never have married him – he is too temperamental – as changing as the wind – he dramatizes everything – he experiments in love.

'In my opinion Mr Chaplin should never marry. He has not any quality for matrimony. I am glad it is over for it was interfering with my life, my work. I have great ambitions and I am sure that I could not be a great actress as Mrs Chaplin.

'I am glad it is over and I have profited by the experience.'

Here she wrote 'finis' on Mr Chaplin, her 'Sharlie' of other days, by assailing a peach. It takes perfect self control for a screen star to attack a juicy peach when she has her make-up on, but she did it daintily. Actresses, especially Europeans, are great two-handed eaters, but here Pola excels them as well. She disposed of each peach as surely, as completely as she had disposed of Charlie Chaplin.

For the newspapers and their readers the Chaplin–Negri romance had been a delectable farce. The statements of the principals, however, at moments seem to intimate genuine feeling and genuine pain. We can now never know how much love there was between these two exceptional and certainly irreconcilable temperaments. They were, after all, the King of Comedy and the Tragedy Queen. In later years both monarchs tended to disclaim their own role in the affair. Negri, in her memoirs, said that the persistence was all on Chaplin's side: she was not really attracted to him, though she enjoyed his conversation. Chaplin said that the party most interested in the match was the Paramount publicity department, who pressed him to marry her because the bad publicity of broken engagements might be injurious to the company's investment in her. Chaplin drily replied that since he held no Paramount stock, he saw no reason why he should marry her. Though she charged Chaplin with not being the marrying kind, Negri herself was destined never to remarry. She retired to San Antonio with a Texan heiress, and caused some scandal by threatening to sue when her friend married. Happily the lady shortly afterwards divorced and returned to San Antonio and Pola.

The colourful and comic Negri affair was a singular episode in Chaplin's life. It was the only time that he was voluntarily involved in a relationship that attracted to his private life the kind of publicity he ordinarily abhorred; and it was the only time in his career that he permitted himself to be simultaneously engaged in the production of a film and the entanglements of a dramatic romance. Since there is no doubt about Chaplin's concern with and concentration on *A Woman of Paris* during this period, an attractive possibility suggests itself to explain Chaplin's susceptibility to the distractions of Pola. Perhaps they were not in fact distractions. Whether Chaplin was conscious of it or not, Pola may have served to provide the atmosphere of 'contintental' sophistication which he needed for his film, which he certainly achieved in it and which could not have been supplied by Peggy Hopkins Joyce, the country girl from Virginia. It would not have been the only time an artist combined or confused romance and research.

During the period of their romance, Pola had taken a keen interest in the preparations of Chaplin's new house on Summit Drive, no doubt anticipating the day when she would be its mistress. Chaplin had finally yielded to the pleas of Douglas Fairbanks and Mary Pickford that he should build a permanent home after eight years of living in hotels and rented houses. The site he chose, with their help, was a six-and-a-half-acre plot on the hillside immediately below Pickfair. Below it again lay Harold Lloyd's house. Beside these mansions, Chaplin's fourteen-room house was comparatively modest, though it shared their view of the Pacific Ocean, with Catalina Island just visible on a clear day. On the lower side the lawns sloped away to a tennis court and swimming pool. Behind the house were the

---

POLA DROPS "SHARLIE"

Tennis Champion Ace-High Now

Celebrated Actress Asserts Chaplin "Got the Gate" Five Weeks Ago

---

She Still Says "Hello" to Him, but Thinks He's Too Temperamental

---

BY H. B. K. WILLIS

The king is dead! Long live the king!

The tennis racket has supplanted the mask of comedy as the omen of domestic bliss in Pola Negri's demesne. Yesterday the gorgeous tragedy queen, with a laugh on her lips, admitted that Charlie Chaplin, clowndom's king, received his congé five weeks ago, thus ending the match which has kept kings and caddies on the qui vive for almost a year.

---

green slopes of the Santa Monica Mountains. Pola made one lasting contribution by supervising the planting of fir, cedar, pine, spruce and hemlock on three sides of the house. Today these trees, a memorial to a long-ago and short-lived Hollywood sensation, hide the house from the road.

Pola's interest tended somewhat to complicate the building of the house. Chaplin had designed it himself in what he jokingly called 'Californian Gothic'. He had originally planned huge windows looking towards the ocean but Pola persuaded him to reduce their size. After Pola's reign was over, Mary Pickford persuaded him to revert to the large windows.

Inside, a large hall extended the full length and height of the house, with a balustraded balcony at first floor level. In a high arched vestibule to the left of the hall, Chaplin installed a massive pipe organ.

331

The vestibule also served as a projection room, with a screen which dropped down in front of the organ. Down the hall was the living room which, until a study was added in the corner of the house, gave onto terraced lawns at the back. In the 1920s the living room was cosy, cluttered with books and mementoes and containing a rather heterogeneous collection of furniture, mostly in the English style, which Chaplin had gradually acquired in his previous residences. It had an open fire, a Steinway grand and, as Charles Chaplin Junior remembered 'close by was the big Webster dictionary, which Dad consulted so often, and the table he used when he worked downstairs.' Across the hall was the dining room, which also gave on to the lawns and which made greater concessions to modernity and design in its planning. Beyond it lay the kitchen and staff quarters.

The stairs were at the front of the hall. Some years later, Charles Chaplin Junior remembered that an oriental gong stood on the bend. 'There seemed to be a secret rapport between Dad and that gong. Sometimes when he was passing by deep in thought he would turn and lightly tap it with one finger and then wait quietly to hear the muted tone come softly back to him as though in reply to some question he had asked.'

Upstairs were three bedrooms, each with its bathroom. Chaplin's son remembered that his father's bathroom seemed 'always permeated with the odor of Mitsouko, my father's favourite cologne'. (This was in the 1930s. Chaplin was evidently already using the perfume in 1922, since it was one of Peggy Hopkins Joyce's more annoying quirks, during her friendship with him, to sprinkle his Mitsouko around the house on Beechwood Drive to improve the atmosphere. Kono was outraged both by the extravagance and by the resulting spots on the upholstery.) His bedroom was a large, bright room with a fine fireplace that was never used, but it was simply furnished with a writing table and chair, twin beds and night stands, and another Webster dictionary. However worn and disreputable it became Chaplin would never part with the Persian rug on the floor, which he was sure brought him luck.

> My father usually slept in the far bed, the one by the windows. I recall the pulp detective magazines that were always stacked by this bed. My father might read Spengler and Schopenhauer and Kant for edification, but for sheer relaxation he chose murder mysteries. Tired from a hard day's work, he liked to read them in bed for they put him to sleep.
>
> In the drawer of the night stand beside his bed, my father kept a

thirty-eight caliber automatic with its bullets. He would sometimes show it to Syd and me, though we never saw him fire it.[28]

Two more things in their father's room were to delight and intrigue his sons in their boyhood. One was the little closet that led off the bedroom and which contained the pipes of the organ below: 'It took a lot of work to get them all in there. A lot of work,' Chaplin would tell them proudly. The other was a powerful telescope which he had installed to study the heavens. His sons noticed, though, that he was far more interested in watching what went on on the earth below. It is hard to know whether he was consciously passing on the childhood lessons in observation he had learned from Hannah, looking out at the Kennington streets, when he would train a telescope on some far-off pedestrian and say to his sons, 'You see that man? He must be going home after a day's work. Look at his gait, so slow, so tired. His head's bent. Something's on his mind. What could it be?'[29]

10

THE GOLD RUSH

Chaplin was now to embark upon the film by which, he often said, he would most like to be remembered; and a marriage which for the rest of his life he would try vainly to forget. Chaplin recalled very clearly the moment when the inspiration for *The Gold Rush* had come to him. One Sunday morning in September or October 1923 he had been invited to breakfast by Douglas Fairbanks and Mary Pickford who, as his partners in United Artists, were anxious to see him start on a new film. After breakfast he amused himself looking at stereograms and was particularly struck by one showing an endless line of prospectors in the 1898 Klondike gold rush, toiling up the Chilkoot Pass. A caption on the back described the hardships the men suffered in their search for gold.

His imagination was further stimulated by reading a book about the disasters which befell a party of immigrants – twenty-nine men, eighteen women and forty-three children – on the trail to California in 1846. Led by George Donner, their misfortunes multiplied, until eventually they found themselves snowbound in the Sierra Nevada. Of a party of ten men and five women who set out to cross the mountains to bring help, eight men died and the rest survived by eating their bodies. Before relief could be brought to those who had remained in camp, many of them also had died, and the survivors had resorted to eating the corpses of their comrades, as well as dogs, cowhides and, it was said, their own moccasins.

Out of this unlikely material Chaplin was to create one of the cinema's great comedies. 'It is paradoxical,' he wrote, 'that tragedy stimulates the spirit of ridicule . . . ridicule, I suppose, is an attitude of defiance; we must laugh in the face of our helplessness against the forces of nature – or go insane.'[1] Although he was as usual to work without a conventional script, improvising and developing new incidents as the shooting progressed, Chaplin seems to have had a much clearer sense of the eventual story line than at the start of most of his previous films. He worked fast on the first draft story, and on 3 December 1923 – only two months after the première of *A Woman of Paris*, he was able to deposit for copyright a 'play in two scenes' provisionally entitled *The Lucky Strike*.

Throughout December and January Chaplin whipped along activity in the studio in preparation for what they now called 'the northern story'. Chaplin continued to tinker with the scenario while his assistants – Eddie Sutherland, Henri d'Abbadie d'Arrast and Chuck Riesner, as well as the indispensable Henry Bergman – compiled research data about Alaska. Props and costumes were meanwhile prepared; dog-sleighs and fur coats were not readily come by in southern California. Danny Hall's staff were feverishly building the elaborate sets required for the opening scenes of the film. Chaplin asked for a huge scenic cyclorama of a mountain background with a 'snowfield' of salt and flour in front of it. Hall also built the prospectors' hut, arranged on a pivoted rocker and operated by an elaborate system of pulleys, for the scene in which it is supposed to have slid to the edge of a ravine where it teeters perilously with each movement of the men within. The cameramen were, as usual, to be Rollie Totheroh and Jack Wilson.

The first actor engaged was Fred Karno Junior. The only players on regular contract were Henry Bergman and Edna, but it soon became evident that Edna was not to be Chaplin's leading lady. Even before *A Woman of Paris* Chaplin had observed that she had grown too 'matronly' for comedy roles. Her drinking had made her weight unpredictable and her acting unreliable. Josef von Sternberg, who was to direct her last American film a couple of years later, said that she 'was still charming, though she had not appeared in pictures for a number of years and had become unbelievably timid and unable to act in even the simplest scene without great difficulty.' Moreover, just as work was starting on *The Gold Rush* Edna was involved in one of the scandals that shadowed Hollywood's brightest years like nightmares.

By coincidence the scandal also involved Chaplin's previous leading lady, the unhappy Mabel Normand. The incident was never wholly explained. On New Year's Day 1924 Edna was the guest of an oil magnate, Courtland Dines. She had spent the day in his apartment. In the afternoon they were joined by Mabel Normand and some time later Mabel's chauffeur arrived, apparently to take her home. There was an altercation between Dines and the chauffeur, who produced a revolver belonging to Mabel and fired. Dines was not killed, but Edna's reputation was. All the parties claimed to recall nothing of the events: Dines, who at the time was wearing only an undershirt and knee-length silk dressing gown, said he had been drinking all night and day. After inconclusive courtroom hearings a number of cities banned *A Woman of Paris*, and Edna withdrew from the limelight to her little apartment on the outskirts of the city.

Though there was no longer a deep emotional involvement, Chaplin retained his affection for Edna and his concern for her career. Certainly he was too loyal, too gallant, and too scornful of Hollywood gossip to let the scandal affect his decision not to use her. But the incident cannot have helped Edna's failing confidence and competence. When it was announced that he would choose a new leading lady, Chaplin emphasized in his press statements that there was no truth in rumours that Edna was no longer associated with his studios, and no long-term significance in her absence from the cast of *The Gold Rush*. 'Miss Purviance is still under contract and receives her weekly salary as though she were actively engaged in production . . . Miss Purviance will again appear under the Chaplin banner, in a dramatic production supervised by Charles Spencer Chaplin.'

Chaplin now had to find a replacement for his leading lady. The news reached the ears of Lillita McMurray, the Angel of Temptation in *The Kid*. Lillita was now fifteen years and nine months old. On Saturday 3 February 1924 she presented herself in the studio reception office accompanied by her best friend, Merna Kennedy, who was five months younger but had acquired a store of worldly wisdom as child dancer in touring vaudeville. They asked to see Chuck Riesner, who had been a neighbour of the McMurrays, and Riesner allowed them to go on to the set and watch Chaplin doing tests of himself and Mack Swain in the rocking cabin. Lillita no doubt made sure that Chaplin noticed her and Chaplin was impressed with the way her looks had matured since the expiry of her original one-year contract to the studio. He invited her to make a screen test, which Alf Reeves arranged at some point during the subsequent four weeks.

After satisfying himself with tests of the moving hut and the wind machines which were to provide the blizzard effects, Chaplin began to shoot *The Gold Rush* on 8 February. The first scenes were for the sequence where Charlie, lost in the white wilderness, chances into the hut, is menaced by the villainous Black Larson but is unable to obey Larson's orders to leave the hut as he is coninually blown back inside by the blizzard. Larson was played with great energy by Tom Murray, a vaudevillian who had long toured throughout the English-speaking world with a blackface song-and-dance-act, Gillihan and Murray. When the scenes were completed and cut, Chaplin prepared to embark on a preliminary reconnaissance of Truckee, near the Donner Pass, where the location scenes were to be shot. He took with him Riesner, Totheroh and Hall.

Truckee stands beside Lake Tahoe high in the Sierra Nevada, almost four hundred miles north of Hollywood and just over twenty miles from Reno. At that time it boasted only one hotel, of awful modesty – Lita Grey noted that the appointments of the room she later shared with her mother there included one chamber pot and three cuspidors. The winter climate was bitterly cold; Chaplin could rely on all the snow he needed until the end of April.

Chaplin and his reconnaissance party stayed at Truckee from 20 to 24 February. When they returned to the studio the following week, there was a new addition to the cast – a large and sleek brown bear accompanied by its keeper, Bud White. The studio began to look like a menagerie when a Mr Niemayer and ten husky dogs were signed up a couple of days later. The bear had the privilege of two scenes with Chaplin. In the opening sequence of the film he pads silently after Charlie who, unaware, makes his way along a precarious cliff path. In the hut scene Charlie, blinded by a blanket that has become entangled about his head, grapples with the bear under the impression that it is big Mack Swain in his bearskin coat.

Meanwhile Chaplin had run Lillita McMurray's tests a number of times. Rollie Totheroh and Jim Tully – who was engaged to work on the script and on publicity copywriting, were bold enough to express their dismay. Lita was a big-boned, heavy-faced girl – cheerful enough but hardly sparkling. Chaplin disregarded his colleagues' adverse views, and on 2 March Lillita McMurray signed a contract to appear as leading lady of *The Gold Rush* at $75 per week. It was agreed that she should adopt the professional name of Lita Grey. Whatever his misgivings about her talent, Tully did a valiant job on the press. During the succeeding weeks American newspaper readers were constantly regaled with Lita's slightly squinting portrait and fulsome stories of her beauty, talent, charm, innocence and aristocratic lineage.

Her talent [runs a typical example, in the florid prose of the popular press of the time] is as yet in its formative period. Chaplin claims, however, that a rare spark is there and that with training she will develop a splendid talent. Of Lita personally there is little to say, for she knows so much less of life than does the average jazzy, effervescent flapper.

No love affairs have ever brought a quick beating to her heart, a flush to her cheeks. She idolizes Chaplin, but much as a child feels for some much older man who has shown her a great kindness. Romances constitute her favorite reading – and the glamorous deeds of yesterday's heroes who walk across the pages of her history books.

One is conscious of an awakened something in her, as though some glow were breathing back of her large brown eyes, lurking upon her half-curved lips. She is so quiet, with that Spanish slumberous quality seeming to hold back her fires of expression until some moment of great feeling will liberate them to flame, one imagines, into beauty. Even her sports – swimming, horseback riding, tennis – she enjoys in leisurely fashion until that inherent dominant streak makes itself felt through her languor and gives her an animated grace.

It is as if she expresses two forces – the slumberous calm of her Spanish heritage that suggests dreamy, sunlit days of unhurried beauty, and a vitality that quivers beneath her tranquillity. Perhaps it is the spirit of those gallant Dons who braved the dangers of the new world for the glory of conquest, perhaps merely modern feminine independence struggling beneath the placid ivory loveliness of her. Whatever its origin, I have an idea that it is likely some day to make itself felt, to establish her as one of the unique personalities of the shadow-screen.

She dreams with her capabilities not yet fully awakened. When she speaks of the possibilities ahead, her eyes grow luminous and there is fire in them, and her pale face becomes mobile with her thoughts and feelings. She has a charming voice, of soft, musical cadence, rising in inflection when she becomes keenly interested, vibrant with what she is saying . . .[2]

When she signed her contract, it was reported, Lillita–Lita jumped up and down, clapping her hands and crying 'Goody, goody.' The view of another journalist, Jack Junsmeyer, reveals a little more:

Schooling in the dance and the arts, supplemented by business college education and dramatic training has occupied the four-year interval following her only [*sic*] appearance on the screen in *The Kid.*

338

'I have held firm to my ambition to go into pictures,' says Miss Grey, 'but I felt that I didn't want to work with anyone except Mr Chaplin. Patience has its reward.'

Her first interview at the Chaplin studio revealed the new leading lady as a peculiarly shy, reticent and far from loquacious girl. She seemed phlegmatic.

But a few minutes later, in the presence of Chaplin on the set where his Alaska gold rush comedy is under way, the girl underwent a remarkable transformation. She bloomed with animation. She became galvanic.

Observation indicated that Chaplin wields a powerful professional sway over his new protégée – that almost hypnotic influence which the more masterful directors exert upon sensitive players before the camera.[3]

Every newspaper report said that Lita was nineteen. Clearly the studio publicity department felt it prudent not to publicize the employment of a minor as the star of the film. Lita was sufficiently well-developed to make the subterfuge convincing.

During her first fortnight at the studio, Lita had nothing to do but watch. Chaplin moved on to his scenes in the cabin with Mack Swain as Big Jim McKay. The two men are snow-bound and starving. Jim, takes it badly, in old-time melodrama style, clutching his head and declaiming 'Food! I must have food!' Charlie, with the flair of a Brillat-Savarin, stews his boot but it proves a less than satisfying meal and Big Jim, suffering hallucinations from hunger, imagines that Charlie is a plump hen and almost eats him. Shooting the scenes of cooking and eating the boot took three shooting days and sixty-three takes. Chaplin was as usual constantly refining and elaborating his business during this time. Only on the afternoon of the third day of shooting, for instance, did he arrive at two of his most memorable transposition gags. Charlie's dainty handling of the sole of the boot – he has graciously given Big Jim the more tender upper – transforms it into a *filet*; then, coming upon a bent nail, he crooks it on his little finger and invites Jim to break it with him as if it were a wishbone. The boots and laces used for the scene were made from liquorice and it is said that both actors experienced its inconvenient laxative effects.

The scene of Charlie's metamorphosis, under Mack's crazed eyes, into a chicken, was similarly evolved during shooting. For several days the unit shot a version of the scene in which Mack simply sees the vision of a fine fat turkey sitting on the cabin table. When he grabs for it, it disappears only to reappear in Charlie's person, whereupon Mack chases him around the hut with a knife. When Mack comes to himself a little, Charlie gives him a book to take his mind off food. On the Saturday however (15 March 1924) Chaplin had a better idea; and when work resumed the following Monday the costume department had provided him with a man-size chicken costume. Now Big Jim would not imagine that he saw a turkey, but that Charlie actually became a chicken.

The film cameramen of those days had to be resourceful. Their cameras were technically excellent, but had few refinements compared to present-day apparatus. Much effects-work, like fades, dissolves or irises which in later years were done in the laboratories, had still to be achieved in the camera. So it was with the chicken transformations in *The Gold Rush*. Chaplin would start the scene in his ordinary costume. At a given moment the camera would be faded out and stopped. The scene and camera position would be kept unchanged while Chaplin rapidly changed into his chicken costume. At the same time the camera was wound back to the start of the fade, the place where the transformation was to begin. While the camera started up and faded in, Chaplin would precisely retrace the action he had just filmed. In this way the two images of Charlie and the chicken, would be exactly superimposed so that the two figures would seem to dissolve into one another. Precisely the same technique was needed to turn the chicken back into Charlie. During the pause for the costume change Mack Swain, who was also in the scene, had to stay absolutely motionless. To help him, he was seated at a table with his head firmly supported on his elbows. The precision and faultless matching of the effect is a remarkable tribute to the technicians* as well as to the actors. The whole thing is made to seem quite effortless. As Chaplin would have wished, the magic remains intact.

The peculiar genius for perceiving in any object the properties of another object, which was the basis of a life-time of 'transposition' gags, is here seen at its most developed as Chaplin discovers the chickenish properties in his own person. The 'dissolve' is not only in the camera but in his own mind and physique. He discerns, in the manner that Charlie flaps his arms and in his toes-out waddle, those characteristics which exactly coincide with the movements of the chicken. Eddie Sutherland recalled that for another scene, another

---

* The elaborate technical feat had to be accomplished, of course, by *two* cameras, simultaneously.

actor was substituted in the chicken costume. It did not work. Chaplin had to take over. The actor was only able to be a man in a chicken costume. Chaplin, at will, could *be* a chicken.

For use in the publicity matter of the film, Jim Tully wrote a description of Chaplin at work on the starvation scenes in the cabin:*

There are present neither mobs nor megaphones. There is a minimum of noise. The cameramen, property men, electricians all speak amongst themselves in hushed whispers when they speak at all. For the most part they look into the center of the set in much the same way as the Sunday flock looks at its pastor. For there gesticulates Charlie Chaplin.

'Great! Now just one more for luck . . .'

Only three scenes were taken in the entire afternoon, but the proof that Mr Chaplin is without doubt the hardest working individual in Hollywood is that each scene is shot at least twenty times. Any one of the twenty would transport almost any director other than Charlie; he does them over and over again, seeking just the shade to blend with the mood. And his moods are even more numerous than his scenes.

'Just once more – we'll get it this time!' It is his continual cry, ceaseless as the waves of the sea. And each additional 'take' means just three times as much work for him as for anyone else.

Perhaps in the middle of a scene when everything seems to be superlative, he will stop the action with a gesture, 'Cut' – he walks over to a little stool beside one of the cameras and leans his head upon the tripod. The cameramen stand silently beside their cranks; everyone virtually holds his breath until Charlie jumps up with an enthusiastic yell:

'I've got it, Mack; you should cry: "Food! Food! I I must have food!" You're starving and you are going to pieces. See – like this!'**

Mr Swain, a veteran trooper, watches intently as Charlie goes through every detail of the action.

'Let's take it!' Charlie suddenly exclaims. 'What do you say, Mack?'

'Sure,' answers Mack.

And again the scene is re-enacted and recorded by the tireless cameras.[4]

---

* In the publicity brochure for the film the article appears as 'On the Set with Charlie' by Sid Grauman. (Grauman was the Hollywood showman who built Grauman's Chinese and Grauman's Egyptian Theatres.) In the Chaplin archives, however, there is a typescript of the article, with a manuscript note discussing who might be the most suitable person to whom to attribute authorship.

** The continuity reports show that Mack Swain actually spoke these words on the set. In the original version of the film they appeared as a sub-title. When Chaplin made a version with synchronized soundtrack, he retained them in his own commentary.

Now, finally, it was time to shoot Lita's first scene. It was in fact to be the only scene for *The Gold Rush* which she shot in the studio. Chaplin seemed sometimes to have an eerie gift of presentiment. In *The Kid* Lita had appeared in a dream sequence, as the Angel of Temptation whose blandishments (in his dream) bring about his death. In *The Gold Rush*, too, she was to appear in a dream. As first conceived, the scene had Charlie sleeping in the cabin. He dreams that he is awakened by a beautiful girl (Lita) who brings him a great plate of roast turkey.

The scene, the setting for which was a dream kitchen, was begun on Saturday 22 March. When he returned to the studio on the following Monday, however, Chaplin had quite a new idea. The turkey was replaced by a big, beautiful strawberry shortcake. The new action is described in the day's continuity reports. The final take, completed at 6.30 p.m., was thus:

> Scene 14: Close-up. Dissolve. C. asleep in kitchen on couch. Lita stand-
> ing over him with cake – wakens him – he sits up – she sits
> down beside him – smiles – takes berry – gives it to him –
> he turns forward – eats it – smiles – she takes another berry
> – starts to give it to him. She says: Close your eyes and open
> your mouth. He does so and she throws whole cake in his
> face and laughs. C. takes cake off – face all smeared with
> cream – Fade out and fade into close-up in cabin with C.
> asleep in cot – blanket over body but not on head – snow
> on neck and face – snow drops down from roof five times –
> he wakes up then sits up – and looks around room – brushes
> snow off – gets up – comes forward left of camera. O.K.

The scene, which was never to reach the screen, was to prove a vivid metaphor for the sad story of Charlie's future relationship with Lita.

The succeeding fortnight was spent in cutting and re-shooting the cabin scenes with Mack Swain: it was probably at this time that Tully wrote the description of Chaplin at work just quoted. Now preparations began for the great trek to Truckee to shoot the scenes on the locations already selected by the February advance party. The first party, consisting of Eddie Sutherland, Danny Hall, seven carpenters, four electricians and Mr Wood the painter, left on 9 April. The following day the camera crew and a Mexican labourer, Frank Antunez, followed. A week later they were joined by the main party: Chaplin attended by Kono, Lita chaperoned by her mother Mrs Spicer, Henri d'Arrast, Jim Tully, Tom Murray, Mack Swain, Della

Steele (the clerk who made up the daily continuity reports) several assistants and handymen, and Bud White and his bear. The journey, though long, was not uncomfortable: the party travelled in private cars, with drawing rooms and dining rooms. Despite (or perhaps because of) Mrs Spicer's watchful presence, Lita sensed a growing mutual interest between herself and her employer that was more than professional.

Eddie Sutherland had efficiently prepared everything so that the morning after his arrival Chaplin could direct the opening scene of the film, which remains one of the most memorable visions in the whole of cinema. Again, Tully has left a colourful description of the occasion:

> . . . To make the pass, a pathway of 2300 feet long was cut through the snows, rising to an ascent of 1000 feet at an elevation of 9850 feet. Winding through a narrow defile to the top of Mount Lincoln, the pass was only made possible because of the drifts of eternal snow against the mountainside. The exact location of this feat was accomplished in a narrow basin, a natural formation known as the 'Sugar Bowl'.
>
> To reach this spot, trail was broken through the big trees and deep snows, a distance of nine miles from the railroad, and all paraphernalia was hauled through the immense fir forest. There a construction camp was laid for the building of the pioneers' city. To make possible the cutting out of the pass, a club of young men, professional ski-jumpers, were employed to dig steps in the frozen snows, at the topmost point, as there the pass is perpendicular and the ascent was made only after strenuous effort.
>
> With the building of the mining camp, and the pass completed, special agents of the Southern Pacific Railway were asked to round up 2500 men for this scene . . . On two days a great gathering of derelicts had assembled. They came with their own blanket packs on their backs, the frayed wanderers of the western nation. It was beggardom on holiday.
>
> A more rugged and picturesque gathering of men could hardly be imagined. They arrived at the improvised scene of Chilkoot Pass in special trains; and, what is more, special trains of dining cars went ahead of them. It was thought best to keep the diners in full view of the derelicts . . .
>
> They trudged through the heavy snows of the narrow pass as if gold were actually to be their reward, and not just a day's pay. To them what mattered [was]: they were to be seen in a picture with Chaplin, the mightiest vagrant of them all. It would be a red-letter day in their lives, the day they went over Chilkoot Pass with Charlie Chaplin.[5]

343

Tully is guilty here of some exaggeration. The studio records show that 600 men were brought from Sacramento, not the 2500 he claims. They were supplemented by every member of the unit not otherwise occupied. Both Sutherland and Lita joined the trail.

Chaplin was very concerned to sustain morale in the discomfort, bitter cold and tedium of Truckee. On Monday he shot one scene of the cabin sliding down the mountainside. Then, while the carpenters were making changes to the cabin set, he joined the unit in bob-sledding and ski racing. As a result, the following day he was confined to bed with a chill. Two feet of snow had fallen in the night, and the snowstorm continued. The storm was an opportunity too good to be missed, so in Chaplin's absence Eddie Sutherland shot some effective scenes of Tom Murray as Black Larson, battling through the blizzard with his sledge.

Chaplin was up and about again next day: he was eager not to prolong the costly and uncomfortable stay in Truckee. Material was shot for some action that was not to figure in the final film, involving Tom Murray's partner, played by Eddie Sutherland. In one scene they were filmed together outside the cabin; in another they rescue Lita from the assault of a villainous prospector played by Joseph Van Meter, for many years a general assistant at the Chaplin studios and blessed with a mean face which came in handy whenever Chaplin needed an extra for a criminal role. Other scenes shot in the Truckee snow showed Charlie finding a grave marked 'Here lies Jim Sourdough'; Bud White's bear prowling around the cabin; and Big Jim chasing the Charlie-chicken across the snowy wastes. Mack Swain had by this time succumbed to 'flu, so Sid Swaney stood in for him in these scenes. The last day of location shooting was 28 April. The four cameras were again used for a shot of Charlie sliding down 'Chilkoot Pass'. Then Chaplin, with Kono, Bergman, d'Arrast and Mack Swain entrained for Los Angeles via San Francisco. The unit stayed behind to tear down the sets: on the evening of the 29th what remained was burned after dark and Sutherland filmed the conflagration in case it came in handy. That night Lita and her mother,* the camera crew, Danny Hall and some others boarded the train home. Everyone was back by 2 May.

---

* In her own account, *My Life With Chaplin*, Lita described conversations with Chaplin on this return journey. The transportation records show that her memory is at fault.

Having captured his snow, Chaplin shot nothing more throughout May and June, and the company grew restive. While Chaplin worked over script and gag material with Bergman, d'Arrast and Tully, and Lita was photographed for stills in different costumes and coiffures, the scenic department were occupied in recreating Alaska in the studio during a California summer. Even though extra labour was brought in (Tully's publicity claimed that 500 scenic craftsmen had been employed) they were hard pressed to complete the sets in the eight or nine weeks allotted to them. A small-scale mountain range was built. Its 'snow'-capped peaks, glistening in the sun, were visible miles off, and brought hundreds of curious sightseers for a closer view. Tully published some statistics on the making of the mountains. The framework required 239,577 feet of timber, which was covered with 22,750 linear feet of chicken wire, and over that 22,000 feet of burlap. The artificial ice and snow required 200 tons of plaster, 285 tons of salt and one hundred barrels of flour. The blizzard scenes called for an additional four cart-loads of confetti.

Other miscellaneous items from the hardware bills on *The Gold Rush* included 300 picks and shovels, 2000 feet of garden hose, 7000 feet of rope, four tons of steel, five tons of coke, four tons of asbestos, thirty-five tons of cement, 400 kegs of nails, 3000 bolts and several tons of smaller items.

Shooting resumed on 1 July, with more scenes of Chaplin and Mack Swain hungry in the cabin. A pleasant gag sequence which was ultimately rejected had the two of them playing cards. Mack falls asleep over the game, but with his elbow too firmly planted on his own cards to permit Charlie to take advantage with a little cheating. Instead, Charlie constructs a toy windmill, and playfully powers it with Mack's windy snores. These scenes finished, he moved on to the sequence in which the cabin slides to the edge of the chasm where it delicately balances, responding to every move and cough of the two men inside. This required work with miniature models. In the early 1920s there were as yet no special effects firms in Hollywood to entrust with this kind of work; all depended on the skills of cameramen, production designers, set builders and property men. The miniature work in *The Gold Rush* is exemplary. The cuts from the full-size hut to the model are barely perceptible: sometimes when the viewer thinks he has detected the model, he is suddenly made aware of his error. The continuity reports of the shots made with models suggest that Chaplin contemplated a scene – anticipating the opening of *The*

Wizard of Oz – in which the hut and its occupants would whirl
through the blizzard:

> Scene 2175: L.S. camera on moving platform – l. to r. – trees in foreground
> moving l. to r. – backgound storm effect – panorama for
> insert where C.C. looks out window house going 90 m.p.h.

In the last days of September 1924 Chaplin shot a few more scenes
of the cabin in the snowstorm, but by the end of the month all work
had come to a halt. Chaplin was to shoot nothing in his studio for
the rest of that year. He had been stopped dead in his tracks by the
bombshell delivered by Lita. Some time in the last days of September
she announced that she was pregnant. She had a mother aflame with
outrage, a grandfather who literally toted a shotgun and an uncle
who was a lawyer in San Francisco. Where minors were concerned,
the Californian law afforded a charter to shotgun weddings: for a
man to have relations with an under-age girl constituted, *de facto*,
rape, carrying penalties of up to thirty years in gaol. The McMurrays
held the trump card and would hear of no solution but an immediate
marriage. Chaplin had again trapped himself with a hopelessly incom-
patible partner.

The press for once suspected nothing. Chaplin and his young
leading lady had been seen in public a good deal, but always chaperoned by Lita's mother or by Thelma Morgan Converse, the sister
of Gloria Vanderbilt, whom the gossips had decided was Chaplin's
secret fiancée. At this moment too they were off following another
scent. On 16 November Grace Kingsley, the columnist of the *New
York Daily News* commented : 'Charlie Chaplin continues to pay
ardent attention to Marion Davies. He spent the evening at Montmartre dining and dancing with the fair Marion the other night.
There was a lovely young dancer entertaining that evening. And
Charlie applauded but with with his back turned. He never took his
eyes off Marion's blonde beauty.'

This kind of item in a publication of a rival newspaper group was
not likely to please William Randolph Hearst, who by this time had
been for almost nine years Marion Davies' devoted and jealously
possessive lover. Both Hearst and his wife had known and admired
Chaplin for several years, and Hearst can not have been unaware
that the friendship between Chaplin and Marion was closer than with
most of the men with whom she flirted. Marion was shooting a circus
story, *Zander the Great*, at the same time as Chaplin was making

The Gold Rush, and he would often pick her up after he had finished the day's work. Marion's biographer, Fred Laurence Guiles', view is that 'All of the cast and crew of *Zander* were aware that something was going on, but Marion was far too much like Chaplin for it to have been a meaningful affair. In the presence of others, they clowned together like an affectionate brother and sister, and it is difficult to imagine them being very different when they were alone together.'

Hearst was nevertheless, in Guiles' words, 'wounded in spirit and fretting what he should do'. In fact he returned to California from New York and on 18 November – two days after the appearance of Grace Kingsley's squib – set off on a trip on his yacht the *Oneida* with a party of invited guests. Principal among these was the producer Thomas Harper Ince, whom Hearst was attempting to persuade to become an active producer for his own Cosmopolitan Pictures. Others on board, apart from Hearst and Marion, were the columnist Louella Parsons, the actress Seena Owen, the dancer Theodore Kosloff, the writer Elinor Glyn, Hearst's secretary Joseph Willicombe, a publisher, Frank Barham with his wife, Marion's sisters Ethel and Reine and her niece Pepi, and Hearst's studio manager, Dr Daniel Goodman. According to Hollywood mythology, Chaplin also was on the boat. In Guiles' account, 'Hearst also invited Chaplin. Perhaps he thought that it was safe to do so, if he believed that he had broken up the romance; or he may have wanted to clarify Marion's status a bit with Chaplin, since Chaplin seemed to have some doubts about it.'

What happened next is one of the great unsolved mysteries of Hollywood. On 19 November Ince was carried unconscious from the yacht at San Diego, and died a few hours afterwards. The official story was that Ince died of a heart attack brought on by ptomaine poison or acute indigestion. The persistent rumour was that Hearst had discovered Ince and Marion together in the dimly lit lower galley and had pulled out a pistol and shot Ince. The question is whether or not the shooting (if it actually happened) was a case of mistaken identity: Ince was a small man with similar head shape and hair colour to Chaplin from the back view.

With time the rumour might have died but for the startling contradictions in the evidence of all those concerned. With blatant untruth, the Hearst press at first gave out a story that Ince was taken ill at his ranch. Marion said that there were no firearms aboard. Hearst's biographer, John Tebbel, recorded that Hearst kept a gun aboard to pot the occasional seagull. There is great doubt as to whether or not Ince's girlfriend, the actress Margaret Livingstone, was aboard. Chaplin consistently declared to his intimates that he was not aboard the yacht, and in his autobiography is so hazy about the chronology that he asserts Ince survived for three more weeks, and received a visit from Hearst, Marion and Chaplin. (There exist, however, photographs of Chaplin at Ince's cremation, which took place forty-eight hours after the death.) Kono, according to Eleanor Boardman, then Mrs King Vidor, said that when he was meeting the boat, he saw Ince being carried off with a bullet wound in his head. Others said that the blood that was visible had been vomited from a perforated ulcer.

Elinor Glyn told Eleanor Boardman that everyone aboard the yacht had been sworn to secrecy, which would hardly have seemed necessary if poor Ince had died of natural causes. There was no inquest to settle the matter, though the San Diego District Attorney, the Los Angeles Homicide Chief and the proprietor of the mortuary where Ince's body was taken all declared themselves satisfied that there had been no foul play. Sixty years after the events, there is little hope that we shall ever satisfactorily explain the mystery which remains, casting a shadow on all those who were, however remotely, concerned.

Three days after attending Ince's funeral, Chaplin sent Lita and her mother off to Guaymas, Mexico. He had decided that the wedding, if there must be one, should at least be discreet. He devised an elaborate cover to avoid publicity, and left the ingenious Kono to mastermind the details. A nucleus of the *Gold Rush* unit was marshalled, and on 25 November entrained for Guaymas. Two newsmen, sensing a story, boarded the train and quizzed Chaplin, who successfully fobbed them off with the implausible story that he was setting some of the scenes of *The Gold Rush* in Mexico. 'I'm very odd when I make pictures,' he told them humorously. The following day, to lend conviction to his story, he hired a fishing boat and sent the camera crew out in it to shoot sea scenes. (The 1600 feet of film they shot that day still survive.) That evening Chaplin, Riesner, Lita and her mother drove to neighbouring Empalme, a dismal railway junction with sea on one side and desert on the other, on the edge of Yaqui Indian territory. There the marriage ceremony was performed by a stout civil magistrate in his shabby parlour. Afterwards they returned to the little hotel in Guaymas. That night Chaplin left the bridal suite to Lita and her mother.

Returning to Los Angeles next day, Chaplin planned to avoid the reporters. It was arranged that while the main part of the unit would travel back to the Southern Pacific station, he and Lita, accompanied by Kono, would get off at the little whistle-stop station of Shorb, near Alhambra, where they would be met by the Japanese chauffeur, Frank Kawa.

Turning up his overcoat and pulling a derby hat over his ears, Chaplin, surrounded by a few close friends, helped his bride from the rear platform of the private car in which they travelled on their return from Empalme, Mexico, where they were married last Tuesday [*sic*].

Everything, it appeared, was working to a carefully scheduled plan whereby Chaplin was to return to his home in Beverly Hills with a degree of privacy rarely sought by film stars.

The comedian and his bride skirted a fence, looking for their limousine and Japanese driver. Just as they rounded a corner, they met 'the press'. A movie camera, to which Charlie owes so much of his fame, commenced grinding away. Chaplin displayed impatience.

'Can't a man have a little privacy? I've been trying to avoid this. It's awful!' was the actor's only comment to the reporters, who immediately began firing questions at him.

The limousine was sighted about a block away and Chaplin's Japanese secretary was despatched to summon it. Meanwhile the comedian only turned up his overcoat further and with his bride tried to avoid facing the battery of cameras which were trained on him, and grumbled loudly at the fact that his Japanese chauffeur had apparently not understood his directions to run his machine as close to the tracks as possible.

'Home,' said Chaplin, and as a parting farewell to the newspaper men who had paid him so much attention, 'I don't want any publicity.'

A large group of studio friends, of the mistaken opinion that a royal welcome would please the comedian, had gathered at the Southern Pacific station, but were disappointed to find only the lesser lights of the Chaplin party who had remained aboard the private car as a supposed decoy for the newspaper men who were aboard the train.

After the newlyweds reached Chaplin's new home in Beverly Hills, they were seen no more during the day.[6]

To reach the door of their home they had to run the gauntlet of a siege party at the gates of the house.

A leading article in the *New York Daily News* offered peculiarly wry congratulations to the newlyweds:

SPOILING A GOOD CLOWN

One of Charlie Chaplin's screen comedies ended with the comedian doing a wild dash among the cactuses (or cacti) along the Mexican border.

Then he was uncertain upon which side of the boundary lay safety. Now he has made a decision, but whether he considered safety in making it is a question.

The other day the comedian dashed across the border into Mexico aboard a train. His destination was Guaymas and his purpose was to wed Lita Grey, his leading lady. Marrying leading ladies seems to be a weakness among male screen and stage stars. Why, we don't know.

But the practice seems to give weight to the old saying that 'while absence makes the heart grow fonder, presence is a darned sight more effective'. Leading ladies are usually present – and unusually effective.

We hope Charlie finds what he is supposed to be looking for – happiness. But he and his leading lady are about to tackle the toughest cross word puzzle of the ages – married life. So often there are more cross words than there are solutions; and frequently a synonym of four letters meaning 'love' is set down on the matrimonial patchwork as 'bunk'.

We wish Mr Chaplin and Miss Grey the conventional quota of joy. But if they have to give up the puzzle we have this consolation. The best clowns have broken hearts. And no tragedy could be as great as spoiling the best clown of the screen by making him too happy.

The liaison threatened no such danger. One of the incidental compensations of the marriage was that Chaplin threw himself feverishly back into work at the studio – no doubt to avoid spending time at home with his child bride, who forlornly realized that her position in her husband's house was that of an unwanted guest. It may have been comforting to her when her mother moved in with them a few weeks after the marriage, though it cannot have made life easier for Chaplin. He remained impeccably courteous in his dealings with his wife's family, however.

Lita's pregnancy also gave Chaplin an excuse to find a new leading lady for *The Gold Rush*, the production of which was clearly likely to go on for several more months. For the moment the press were necessarily kept in ignorance of Lita's condition. Tully imaginatively told the press that the former Miss Lita Grey had given up her role as the dance hall girl because now that she was married she wished 'to devote every moment of her time to her husband.'

Just before Christmas it was announced that the actress who would replace Lita was Georgia Hale, still quite unknown to the public. She was eighteen. Born into a working class family in St Joseph, Missouri, she had spent most of her life in Chicago. A striking, delicate beauty, at sixteen she won the title of Miss Chicago, which brought with it a cash prize and a chance to compete in the Miss America contest in

Atlantic City. She was knocked out of the competition, but her prize money enabled her to reach Hollywood in July 1923. Her hopes of work as a dancer were dashed by a fall in which she badly sprained her ankle; when her money ran out she settled for work as an extra. One of her first jobs was in a film directed by Roy William Neill, called *By Divine Right*. The star, by chance, was Mildred Harris. The writer and assistant director was the young Josef von Sternberg, who was greatly impressed when he discovered the girl reading his own translation of Karl Adolph's novel *Daughters of Vienna*, and much more impressed to notice that she had dropped a mascara-stained tear on the page. A few months later when von Sternberg embarked on his own first film, a shoe-string experiment in an expressionist manner, *The Salvation Hunters*, he remembered Georgia Hale and cast her in the lead, paying her the same as her daily salary as an extra.

Von Sternberg's partner and leading man, the English actor George K. Arthur, somehow succeeded in getting Chaplin to see the film (Sternberg claimed that he had bribed Kono to smuggle it into the projection box of the screening room at Chaplin's home).

> George K. Arthur was a little devil. You couldn't understand him: he had such a funny accent from some place in England [*sic*: Arthur was born in Aberdeen]. He was so cute. He was a promoter. He got Kono to put it on. Charlie fell in love with that picture. He thought it was a little gem. Von Sternberg was not a genius, but he had talent.[7]

Chaplin at once called up the Fairbankses, who came from next door to see the picture the same night. A day or two later he showed the film to Nazimova, and it was at this showing that he first met Georgia.

> We met in the screening room at FBO Studios. He wanted Joe and me to be there for the show. I sat behind him and Nazimova. After the screening Joe said, 'This is Georgia, the girl.' He said, 'Oh, I'm so happy to meet you.' And then he lost interest in Nazimova and everyone else, and wanted to take me for tea. He asked me what I was doing, and I said I was doing fine. I had a regular daily understanding with Sennett. If I didn't have anything else I could work there any day. He said, 'Keep that up. That's fine. But I want to keep in touch. I like your work.'
>
> Then Douglas Fairbanks signed me to play the Queen in *Don Q, Son of Zorro*. I'd done a test and it turned out fine. All the costumes were ready, but then Charlie went to Doug and said: 'You've signed the girl I need. I want her for *The Gold Rush*.' However, they got together and agreed, and Douglas Fairbanks released me.

Now, he'd tested lots of people for the part. Everybody tested. One of them was Jean Peters – she became Carole Lombard. He invited me to see the tests, and I said to him, 'But *they're* wonderful!' Because I thought I was terrible. In my test I just stood there looking mad and doing nothing. And they were all laughing and such. And he said, 'That's what I want. That's the quality.'[8]

For Georgia it was a dream come true. She had idolized Chaplin long before she thought of Hollywood. As a child and adolescent in Chicago, psychologically bruised by her father's insensitive discouragement of all her ambitions, she had discovered reassurance in the Tramp's defiant resilience and had convinced herself of some mystical affinity with him. Working with him in no way disillusioned her.

> You just knew you were working with a genius. He's the greatest genius of all times for motion picture business. He was so wonderful to work with. You didn't mind that he told you what to do all the time, every little thing. He was infinitely patient with actors – kind. He knew exactly what to say and what to do to get what he wanted.
>
> One thing was that everything in his pictures was for real. Take the scene where I slap the boy [Malcolm Waite]. That slap was really for real. Charlie had had us doing that scene, and him pawing me, for so long, that I got really mad with him. I really did slap him – good and hard. And of course that was what Charlie wanted.[9]

The change of leading lady was not too disruptive since the character of the dance hall girl does not appear until half-way through the film – it is one of the odd aspects of its structure, but in the outcome perfectly satisfactory. Since Chaplin was as usual shooting in story continuity, he had not yet arrived at the heroine's scenes. The brief sequences which he had already shot with Lita were possibly intended as tests, and in the end had no place in the story. The rest of December was spent reworking the story, testing and costuming Georgia and organizing her publicity and photographs. Meanwhile Danny Hall and his staff were building the big dance hall and bar where Charlie first meets Georgia.

The bar room scenes were difficult and costly, involving paying – and worse, keeping under control – as many as a hundred extras, who included Mexicans, Indians and, the pride of the unit, a proven centenarian, 'Daddy' Taylor, who was already over forty when he saw service in the Civil War. Chaplin was so delighted by the old man's energy as a dancer, that he gave him a brief scene of his own in the New Year party scene. Extra rates had gone up since First

National days. The base rate was now $7.50 a day, while some received as much as twice that sum. 'Tiny' Sanford, as the barman, was paid $20 a day. The highest daily rate on the unit, however, was paid to the dog which appears with Chaplin in the dance hall scene – seizing a handy length of rope to support his sinking trousers, Charlie fails to notice that it is attached to the collar of this heavy-weight but docile animal. The dog was on hire from the Hal Roach studios and cost $35 a day.

Perhaps it was the celebrations of New Year 1925 that suggested to Chaplin setting the Tramp's most poignant scenes on New Year's Eve, when everyone else is celebrating, leaving the lonely prospector lonelier than ever. The dance hall scenes were finished on 19 January, when Chaplin filmed the comic-pathetic moment where the Tramp retrieves a torn and discarded picture of Georgia from the floor under the disconcerting gaze of a prospector of somewhat demented mien.

By the beginning of February the set-builders had completed the cabin supposed to be in the same township as the dance hall, where Charlie finds a home with the kindly engineer Hank Curtis (played by Henry Bergman). This was to be the setting for the New Year party which Charlie, with his meagre savings, prepares for Georgia and her friends. The girls forget all about him and fail to turn up. Waiting for them, Charlie falls asleep and dreams that the dinner party is a brilliant social success. The English music hall artist Wee Georgie Wood, who knew Chaplin both in England and the United States, said that the scene was suggested by an incident in the young Chaplin's days on tour when he invited the members of another juvenile troupe, working another theatre, to tea. The manager of the troupe would not let them go, but nobody informed Chaplin, who vainly waited for his guests.

Chaplin seems to have been conscious that this sequence had to be something out of the ordinary. At most other studios in the silent period it was customary to employ instrumental groups, even small orchestras, to inspire the actors with mood music. At the Chaplin studios this was not considered necessary. For these hut scenes, however, musicians were employed on the set. The first week or so it was the Hollywood String Quartet, at $50 a day; after that the studio replaced them with Abe Lyman and a trio of players who did the job for $37.50 plus overtime. The famous 'Dance of the Rolls' which is the climax of the sequence was clearly filmed to music; every one of the eleven takes Chaplin made of the sequence was uniform

353

in length, and when he subsequently added a music track to the film the turn synchronized perfectly to 'The Oceana Roll'.

Famous though it was, this was not the first time that the 'Dance of the Rolls' had been filmed. In *The Cook*, made in 1918, Roscoe Arbuckle also speared two bread rolls with forks and made the miniature booted legs thus formed perform a little dance. Quite possibly Arbuckle had picked up the gag from Chaplin during their days together at Sennett. With Arbuckle it is an ingenious gag; with Chaplin it is touched with genius, in the dexterity, the timing, the expressiveness and reality of the dancing legs. The bread-roll feet become a living extension, their every move reflected in the face above them. The scene was initially shot quite casually, in the middle of a miscellaneous series of takes made late in the afternoon of 19 February:

> Scene 3653: Great close-up – C.C. at head of table – doing dance with rolls on forks.
>
> Scene 3655: Retake
> Scene 3656: Retake

Chaplin evidently liked the rushes, and the following day did eight retakes of the scene.

After more than a year, the end of shooting was in sight. The last big set to be constructed was the street of the mining town. The cheerful scene in which Charlie earns money for Georgia's party by clearing snow, ensuring continued custom by shifting it from one door to the next, was finished in two swift days of shooting. On 10 April Chaplin, Georgia and Mack Swain left for San Diego with a camera crew to film the final scenes with Big Jim and Charlie, now millionaires as a result of Jim's lucky strike, on the boat returning home. The scenes were shot on a boat called *The Lark* while it plied its regular route between San Diego, Los Angeles and San Francisco. Chaplin was clearly feeling relaxed; Georgia recalls, 'Coming back, we went to a nightclub. When we went in they started to play "Charlie, My Boy". Then the band started to play a tango, and we danced, and everybody else got off the floor. He really loved that. You'd have thought it would have made him a million dollars, he was so pleased.'[10]

The last scene (apart from some retakes on the miniatures) was shot on 14–15 May 1925. This was to be one of the most spectacular and surprising moments in the film – the end of the villainous Black

Larson, when a chasm opens up in the ice and snow and he plummets to his death. Partly it was done with miniatures, though how the shots done to full scale and with the actor Tom Murray were made, has never been explained. The collapse of a huge cliff-edge of snow and ice may have been arranged in connexion with the dismantling of the mountain sets.

For nine weeks, from 20 April almost to the day of the première on 26 June, Chaplin was cutting the film. Meanwhile his domestic affairs were again impinging. The couple had put a brave public face on their marriage. Cornered by the correspondent of the London *People*, Chaplin said, 'I am the happiest married man in the whole world, and but for these malignant rumours, quite content.' Asked about stories of a marriage settlement Chaplin replied, 'The marriage settlement is just a wedding present to my wife, a present any man would give to the woman he loved.' Lita in her turn said that she was 'as happy as the day is long', and that she had given up her role as leading lady to become the mistress of the nursery. She denied a rumour that Chaplin had moved back to his old quarters in the Los Angeles Athletic Club.

On 5 May 1925 Lita gave birth to a boy. Chaplin's concern over the final stages of her pregnancy and his pride in the baby seemed to achieve a temporary rapprochement. He even reconsidered his earlier objection to naming a son Charles: hitherto he had declared that to give a child the name of a famous parent was to give it a cross to bear. In order to give no ammunition to Hollywood gossips, it was thought prudent to keep the child's birth a secret for a while; it was still less than six months since the marriage in Mexico. So Lita, with her baby and her mother, remained hidden, at first in a cabin in the San Bernardino Mountains belonging to the doctor who attended the birth and now (for a monetary consideration) falsified the birth registration. Subsequently they moved to a house at Manhattan Beach rented for them by Alf Reeves, whose wife Amy helped care for Lita when she suffered a post-natal illness. It was agreed that the baby's official birthday should be 28 June – two days after the Los Angeles première of *The Gold Rush*.

While Lita fretted because he had no time to visit his first son, Chaplin laboured in the cutting room. In a shooting period that had spread over a year and three months, with 170 days of actual filming, he had shot 231,505 feet of film. From this mass he edited a finished film of 8555 feet. The longest comedy he had yet made, *The Gold*

Rush was edited with unchecked narrative fluidity. The harmony of the scenes and the images betrayed nothing of the interruptions, the irritations, the technical effort. When Chaplin came to reissue the film with a sound track seventeen years later, the only significant (and inexplicable) change he made, apart from leaving out the titles, was to the ending. The original version ended with Charlie and Georgia in a long and loving embrace. In the reissue Chaplin substituted a more chaste fade-out, with the two simply walking out of view.

'A Chaplin première,' said the *Los Angeles Evening Herald*, the day after the gala showing of *The Gold Rush* on 26 June 1925, 'is always an outstanding event. Other stars and pictures attract great throngs, but a certain significance which attaches to the first presentations of films bearing the comedian's hallmark makes his première just a little more important or, at least, it would seem so judging by the avidity shown by profession as well as public. There was not a vacant seat at the opening. If any ticket-holder preferred to stay away, he could have disposed of his coupons at a fancy figure . . .'

The court in front of Grauman's Egyptian Theatre was 'a veritable fairyland of color and light. The most skilled decorators in the realm of make-believe had been at work for a week dressing the enclosure for the occasion.' Inside, the celebrities were announced as they entered the auditorium by a stentorian voice, and each was applauded according to his or her degree of popularity. 'The house rang with applause as favorites sauntered along behind attentive ushers.' These announcements were an innovation, as was the chilled punch served by pretty usherettes in the interval. The film was preceded by a prologue 'of matchless beauty . . . Grauman has actually outdone himself in this achievement and *The Gold Rush* première probably never will be surpassed. If it is, only a genius like Grauman can do it.' The curtain rose on a panorama of the frozen north, revealing a school of seals mounting a jagged crag of ice. The seals were quickly joined by a group of Eskimo dancing girls. They were followed by a series of 'impressively artistic dances by fascinatingly pretty young women wearing astoundingly rich and beautiful gowns all blending with the Arctic atmosphere and bespeaking the moods of the barren white country.' The numbers which followed included ice skating, a balloon act presented by Miss Lillian Powell and a Monte Carlo dance hall scene.

After the film, the director-star was led down to the stage. 'He was too emotional, he explained, to make much of a speech and then, characteristically, he proceeded to deliver a fairly good one.' Georgia noted that this was one of the rare occasions when Chaplin had no self-doubts about his work: 'He was confident about that. He really felt it was the greatest picture he had made. He was quite satisfied.'[11]

Chaplin spent the next week refining the cutting of the film, and then a fortnight after that preparing a new musical score. Once there was no more work to be done, he was clearly eager to get away from

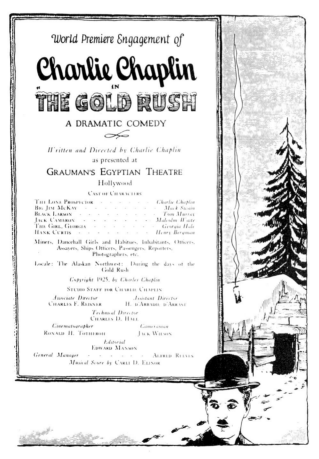

1925 - Première programme for
The Gold Rush.

Los Angeles and the house and on 29 July left for New York by train with Kono and Henri d'Arrast, though the New York première was not until 16 August. Edna, who was on the way to Europe, joined Chaplin briefly in New York between 17 August and her sailing for Cherbourg on 22 August.

In the big cities *The Gold Rush* was an instant success, but business was slower in the sticks. In January Arthur Kelly of United Artists wrote to Sydney that *The Gold Rush* had 'proved to be a flop in all the small cities. In fact it is rather disastrous to some of the exhibitors. Apparently they do not want to see Charlie in any dramatic work, which is proved by analyzing his gross receipts. On every engagement the opening broke all records, but immediately flopped on the second and subsequent days, proving that they had all made up their minds to go for a big laugh in which they were disappointed, and naturally a reaction set in. Perhaps this will be a tip to you on your future productions . . .' Kelly's fears proved unjustified. *The Gold Rush* had cost Chaplin $923,886.45; in time it would gross more than six million dollars.

In Britain *The Gold Rush* opened at the Tivoli, Strand, which Chaplin had known as a music hall and which had recently been converted into a luxury cinema. It made broadcasting history, or at least a rather bizarre fragment of it:

> Next Saturday at 7.30 an attempt will be made to broadcast the laughter of the audience at the Tivoli Theatre during the ten most uproariously funny minutes of the new Charlie Chaplin film *The Gold Rush*. I hear that a preliminary experiment has been successful, but the BBC will not guarantee good results on the night itself, for this sort of transmission is a difficult and uncertain business.[12]

Evidently all went off well, however:

> What so far has been the most original experiment in radio work was carried out by the British Broadcasting Company on Saturday evening last (26 September) when there was broadcasted to every station throughout the British Isles what was announced badly [?baldly] enough in every newspaper in the United Kingdom thus:
>
> '7.30 p.m. Interlude of Laughter. Ten Minutes with Charlie
> Chaplin and his audience at the Tivoli.'
>
> 'Uncle Rex', the broadcasting announcer, prefaced the item by stating that the B.B.C. were trying a unique experiment – that of broadcasting 'a storm of uncontrolled laughter, inspired by the only man in the world

who could make people laugh continually for the space of five minutes, viz., Charlie Chaplin!' The episode chosen was that which forms the climactic scene of *The Gold Rush* when Charlie and his partner awake to discover their log cabin is resting perilously on the edge of a precipice.

This experiment, as reported by one listener-in, proved highly successful. The first outburst of laughter from the audience sounded like big crested waves breaking in fury against huge butting crags, and slowly dissolving in a thousand ripples and cascades that dropped like sea-pearls in an angry sea.

This was succeeded by a sound that echoed like the rolling of jam jars in an express train. Followed sounds of vague, whimsical crescendoes of delirious delight, which culminated in torrential laughter that finally broke out into a terrific uproar – a perfect storm of uncontrollable guffaws. Then shrieks of shrill but helpless laughter – and above them all the piercing silver-toned laugh of a woman which overtopped the thousand and one outbursts.

The climax came when one mighty outburst of laughter broke out in fullest fury, and sounding like salvoes of a thousand guns making the Royal salute. Gradually the laughter died away with sounds like an exhaust-valve, stuttering away its strength into thin air.

So ended what may be regarded as a historic event in film history – ten minutes of laughter with Charlie Chaplin at the Tivoli, London.[13]

The film's première at the Capitol in Berlin was distinguished by the perhaps unique occurrence of an encore within a film. At the Dance of the Rolls the audience went wild with enthusiasm. The manager of the theatre, with admirable presence of mind, rushed up to the projection box and instructed the projectionist to roll the film back and play the scene again. The orchestra picked up their cue and the *reprise* was greeted with even more tumultuous applause.[14]

THE CIRCUS

California and the house on Summit Drive now held little attraction, and Chaplin remained more than two months in New York after the première of *The Gold Rush*. He eventually returned on 15 October 1925, and was very soon at work on *The Circus*. It was to be a production dogged by persistent misfortune. The most surprising aspect of the film is not that it is as good as it is, but that it was ever completed at all.

After *The Gold Rush*, Chaplin considered a version of Stevenson's *The Suicide Club* and *The Dandy*. He was always toying with an idea for a Napoleon film. In March Sydney had cabled him from New York:

SHERWOOD OF LIFE WRITTEN MOVIE STORY CALLED SKY-SCRAPER FOR BUSTER KEATON STOP KEATON CONSIDERS STORY GOOD BUT HAS NOT AS YET DEFINITELY PURCHASED IT STOP HAVE READ IT AND THINK IT OKAY SHERWOOD WRITING ANOTHER ONE SUITABLE FOR YOU STOP WIRE ME IF YOU WANT ME TO TRY AND CLOSE THE DEAL FOR YOU.

Sherwood was one of Chaplin's most appreciative critics, but Chaplin seems not to have responded to the proposition.

Henry Bergman, a modest man who recorded few impressions of his many years with Chaplin, described the genesis of the new film:

Before he had made *The Circus* he said to me one night, 'Henry, I have an idea I would like to do a gag placing me in a position I can't get away from for some reason. I'm on a high place troubled by something else, monkeys or things that come to me and I can't get away from them.' He was mulling around in his head a vaudeville story. I said to him, 'Charlie, you can't do anything like that on a stage. The audience would be uncomfortable craning their necks to watch a vaudeville actor. It would be unnatural. Why not develop your idea in a circus tent on a tightrope. I'll teach you to walk a rope.'[1]

Clearly there were other arguments against setting a film in a vaudeville theatre so soon after E. A. Dupont's German production *Variety* which was currently the talk of the film world.

'Many of his ideas are built on one gag,' Bergman added. Nightmare has often been the essence of comedy. Harold Lloyd's most famous film *Safety Last* is centred on his perils on the top of a skyscraper. James Agee described a sequence in a Laurel and Hardy film 'simple and real . . . as a nightmare. Laurel and Hardy are trying to move a piano across a narrow suspension bridge. The bridge is slung over a sickening chasm, between a couple of Alps. Midway they meet a gorilla.'[2]

The nightmare that Chaplin invented – to what extent might it have been an unconscious metaphor for his troubles? – was to place himself on a tightrope, high above the ring of a circus. He has no net. His safety harness comes loose. He is attacked by monkeys. They rip off his trousers. He has forgotten to put on his tights.,

The story which eventually grew around this climactic incident of farcical horror is a neat comic-romantic melodrama. Charlie the Tramp chances upon a travelling circus which is doing bad business. He is chased into the ring by police, and his accidents there prove a tremendous hit with the audience. He is consequently taken on as a clown: the problem is that he is funny only when he does not intend to be. He falls in love with the daughter of the proprietor, and defends her from her father's cruelties. The idyll is ended when a new star, Rex the High Wire Walker, arrives in the show and steals the girl's heart. It is in consequence of his efforts to emulate his rival that he finds himself in the disastrous predicament on the tightrope. He finally faces defeat, helps the couple to elope, and at the end is left alone in the ring of trodden grass which is all that remains of the circus.

Chaplin had a new assistant, who was also eventually to be chosen to play the part of Rex. Harry Crocker was a new favourite in the San Simeon set, and it was through Hearst and Marion Davies that Chaplin first met him. Crocker at this time was thirty years old, slightly over six feet tall and conventionally handsome. He came from a prominent San Francisco banking family, had been through Yale and had started his working life in the brokerage business. Yearning for something more glamorous he had thrown brokerage up in the autumn of 1924 to come to Hollywood, where his good looks and taste for practical jokes attracted Marion Davies. Having acted with the Los Angeles Playhouse Company and done a bit part as a soldier in *The Big Parade*, he was given a leading role by Marion in her film *Tillie the Toiler*. Since then he had landed three other film roles, and when Chaplin suggested he might work with him had just begun work as an extra in King Vidor's *La Bohème*. Chaplin told Crocker to make the necessary arrangements with Alf Reeves; but when Crocker reported to Reeves' office, the latter knew nothing about it. 'Don't let that bother you,' he said. 'He is very vague.'[3] When Eddie Sutherland heard that Crocker had joined Chaplin in his own former capacity as assistant director, he advised him: 'If you're smart you enter Chaplin on your books as a son-of-a-bitch. He isn't always one, but he can be one on occasion. I thought it better to start off with that appellation of him in mind, then when he behaves badly it doesn't come as quite the shock it might otherwise be, and all his good behaviour comes as quite a pleasant surprise.'

Another former Chaplin assistant, Henri d'Abbadie d'Arrast, also warned him, 'Charlie has a sadistic streak in him. Even if he's very fond of you he'll try and lick you mentally, to cow you, to get your goat. He can't help it. You'll be surprised how many friends he's alienated through that one trait.' Crocker's experiences of Chaplin were happier, and his affection and admiration lasted through the years, even though on occasion their fights could be bitter, and a disagreement led to his departure from *City Lights*. On *The Circus* he found he had been engaged as assistant, writer-actor and companion. His first job was to work with Chaplin on story ideas, which essentially meant acting as sounding board and stenographer. Chaplin and Crocker took off for ten days (9–18 November 1925) to Del Monte to work on the story, leaving the studio staff, under the supervision of Danny Hall, to start building a circus tent and menagerie on the studio lot. The trip provided a further escape from the household at Summit Drive. It was also necessary to get away from the now regular distractions of evenings in the company of Hearst and Marion.

Chaplin's chauffeur, Frank Kawa, drove them in the black Locomobile, with Kono following in his own car. Crocker later recalled his bewilderment at the variety of Chaplin's conversation on the leisurely journey. He outlined a scheme for taxing industry by a kind of 25 per cent tithe on its products; he talked of his horror at working conditions in factories and the pressure to succeed exerted upon employees by American business; about customs of breakfast time gastronomy; about time and space and light.

A lot of their thinking was done in the course of long walks around Del Monte. Crocker recalled how Chaplin, oblivious of the surrounding traffic, suddenly acted out a piece of business he had thought up himself. The spieler in front of a side show would point at the banners advertising a giant and a midget. Charlie would pause on his way out of the door of the tent, reach up to shake hands with the unseen giant, then turn to the other side and stoop to say goodbye to the midget.

When these creative sessions had gone well Chaplin would sing music hall songs on the way back to Pearl Lodge, where they stayed, or launch upon discussions of international finance or the transmigration of souls. Then he might suddenly propose games of betting on the length of each straight stretch of road to the next curve. One night in the Lodge, Crocker recalled, they competed to make bad puns, after which Chaplin performed all the parts in a performance of the third and fourth acts of *Sherlock Holmes*.

The notes which they brought back from their scenario trip still exist and clearly illustrate Chaplin's method of starting the construction of a film by assembling a disparate mass of potential gags, scenes or hazy notions. He collected together a mass of fabrics; only later did he settle upon the pattern of the material and cut of the garment. At this time Chaplin was still undecided as to whether to call the film *The Circus* or *The Traveller*. The notes are presented as a series of 'suggestions'. Some are for whole sequences:

Suggestion: Charlie notices the dog trainer is ill-treating animals – one dog especially. He takes trainer to task and fight ensues. As the 2 men are struggling, the dog that Charlie has tried to save comes into the fight and bites Charlie. Charlie finally flees. He is angered at dog, but dog sits up and begs. Charlie forgives him and goes to pat him and dog almost bites his hand off.

The last is a parable of ingratitude worthy of Luis Buñuel. Chaplin had a characteristic afterthought:

Suggestion: At end of episode with cruel trainer, have Charlie present him with whip to replace one he has broken.

This sequence, like others, was to be rejected. Other 'suggestions' remained intact in the eventual scenario:

Suggestion: Charlie mistaken for pickpocket. Cop chases him through funhouse. Charlie takes place on outside of fun house beside dummies, imitating their wooden action. Maybe introduce crook – also in fight with police – hiding as dummy when Charlie socks him as part of act – crook being forced to take it as cop is watching.

Some 'suggestions' are for individual gags:

Suggestions: Charlie is standing near camel. Tactlessly he asks fellow workman for a 'Lucky Strike'* and the incensed camel bites him.

Suggestion: Charlie at work with hose, accidentally hits boss, blames it on elephant and spanks elephant's trunk. Tells elephant 'Put that away.'

Often in this kind of preliminary work on a film we find Chaplin reverting to ideas which seem almost obsessive with him, but then – perhaps recognizing a too persistent preoccupation – rejecting them. The lurking fear of the audience – particularly an audience in a live theatre – which was to be most completely expressed in *Limelight*, is ever present:

Suggestion: During the efforts of Charlie to be funny as clown, there is a tough guy in the audience who fails to appreciate his efforts, making it exceedingly difficult for Charlie to work.

One gag idea echoes, whether consciously or not, Chaplin's current efforts to keep his domestic worries from a suspicious and prying press:

Suggestion: An acrobat fights violently with wife or partner off-stage and is very suave and loving on.

Chaplin's first idea for the beginning was never used: his eventual solution was certainly much neater. It nevertheless showed his reluctance ever to waste a good idea, for here once more was the stuff of the abandoned film, *The Professor*:

Suggestion for opening: Under the archway of a bridge is a jungle of hoboes. Some asleep – some sitting around – one stirring food in a can over the fire. Charlie comes into camp. He looks around fastidiously –

---

* 'Lucky Strike' and 'Camel' were rival brands of cigarettes.

takes out a handkerchief – dusts off a rock and sits down. One bum looks up and inquires: 'What's your line?' Charlie answers: 'I am a circus man.' Bum looks at him incredulously. He notices look and takes from under his arm a small box labelled 'Flea Circus'. Business ad lib with fleas.

In putting fleas away for night, Charlie discovers one gone – goes over to bum with long beard – picks up flea from beard, regards it and puts it back. It is evidently not one of the circus.

All asleep. In movements in sleep, flea circus is overturned and fleas escape. Scratching commences among bums but fleas concentrate on dog. Dog finally gets up in agony and whines, waking Charlie. He notices overturned flea circus – watches dog and jumps at the right conclusion. Pursuit of dog which goes into the lake, drowning circus. Charlie in despair.

The surviving sequence of *The Professor* also ends with the Professor giving chase to the dog. The tragic finale indicated in his 'suggestion' perhaps tells us how the sequence might have ended in the earlier film. The idea for the opening of *The Circus* continues with a wonderful gag which was unfortunately never used – by Chaplin or any other comedian:

Next morning bums prepare to board train. They will ride brakebeams. Charlie spies mail-sack in brackets – removes same and stands in brackets – is caught in arm of mail-car. Mail clerk is asleep. Charlie rides at ease, enjoying view, while bums gaze enviously from underneath car. Passenger in car in front of Charlie throws cigarette out of window. Charlie catches same and smokes it – dropping butt with gesture to one of the bums underneath car. Arrives in town to discover circus in progress.

Although much would be changed in the course of the lengthy production of *The Circus* there was plenty for the unit to work on when Chaplin and Crocker returned from Del Monte on 18 November.

Henry Bergman carried out his promise to teach Chaplin to walk the tightrope: it is not clear at what point in his career this man of so many parts had learned a skill not evidently suited to a man of his large girth. 'I taught Charlie to walk a rope in one week ... We stretched the rope this high from the floor [he indicated a foot high to the interviewer] then raised it as high as the ceiling with a net under it, but Charlie never fell. He walked it all day long. You didn't see anything in the picture of what he did on that rope.' Crocker, for the role of Rex, also had to learn to walk the rope convincingly, and day after day, right up to Christmas, he and Chaplin practised for hours while below and around them the sets were decorated and the costumes prepared. They were only briefly interrupted by the first of the catastrophes which hit the production. The tent was almost ready when, on Sunday 6 December, an exceptionally rough storm of wind and rain badly damaged it.

As the use of her name in the story suggestions indicates, Georgia Hale was expected to be Chaplin's leading lady once more. Her contract however came to an end on 31 December. It is not certain why it was not renewed. Her work in *The Gold Rush* had been good and Chaplin seems to have been genuinely fond of her; their friendship continued intermittently for years after the film. Perhaps Georgia was impatient for a faster-moving career. As it was she had appeared in five films before *The Circus* eventually emerged. She made half a dozen more films by 1928 and then retired from the screen: her voice and diction were not as pleasing as her looks and her career was doomed by talking pictures. Her most memorable performances were those in *The Salvation Hunters*, *The Gold Rush* and *The Last Moment*, directed by the gifted Paul Fejös – apparently confirming von Sternberg's view that Georgia Hale was an actress whose on-screen qualities depended to a great extent upon the gifts of her directors.

Chaplin's new leading lady was Merna Kennedy, the childhood friend of Lita Grey who had accompanied her to the studio on the day she secured her test for *The Gold Rush*. The studio publicity for the release of the film related how Merna got the part:

> . . . Charlie was about to make *The Circus*. He was to walk a tightrope and frolic about in the sideshows and seek to win the fluff-skirted girl who rides the circling white Arabian in the middle ring. Who was to be the girl?
> 'Merna Kennedy is playing in a musical show at the Mason Opera House here in Los Angeles.'
> 'Let's look at her tonight,' was the answer.
> So Charlie Chaplin went to the Mason and saw the musical show *All For You*.
> Merna Kennedy was picked. Screen tests followed, of course, and the vivaciousness and charm of the red-haired lady with the screen eyes registered with Charlie. He chose a leading lady whom none knew, whom none had seen on the screen.[4]

Merna Kennedy had in fact been suggested for the role by her childhood friend Lita, who had met Merna again after more than a year, while Chaplin was in New York. Chaplin appears initially to have been less enthusiastic about the suggestion than the press story suggests, but he was persuaded. Lita herself came to regret her initiative: she had already been jealous of Georgia Hale and came to realize that her husband was more attentive to the leading lady she had proposed than he was to herself. Merna Kennedy's contract was dated to start on 2 January 1926. There was little other casting to be done. Chaplin wanted Henry Bergman to be Merna's step-father, the mean circus proprietor, 'but I said, "No, Charlie, I'm a roly-poly kind-faced man, not the dirty heavy who would beat a girl." So I was cast as the fat old clown.' Instead Allan Garcia, making his first appearance in a major role, was put under contract to play the part.

Shooting began on Monday 11 January. The first two weeks were spent on the scenes on the tightrope. This was contrary to Chaplin's usual method of shooting in story sequence, but he was in training, and in any case this was the one scene of the film which was so far fully worked out in his head. On 17 January – a Sunday, which showed that Chaplin was particularly engrossed in the scene – he began work with the monkeys. On 27 January he steeled himself to shooting material of the audience in the circus tent. He was never happy with crowd scenes, and the cost – even in 1926 – was worrying if crowd shooting went on too long. For the circus audience the studio hired 185 extras at $5 for the day, 114 at $7.50, seventy-seven at $10, and one at $15. Chaplin made eighteen long takes with the crowd to be subsequently cut up for inserts, and ensured that the crowd shots were finished that day. Three days later there was a more costly extra on the lot – an elephant whose day's hire was $150, with $15 for its trainer.

The first week in February, no doubt somewhat depressed by a cold, Chaplin edited the scenes already shot on the tightrope and decided he wanted to retake them, which took up the rest of the week. The following week he and Crocker shot the scenes in which they rode the bicycle on the tightrope, with Charlie making his 'ride for life'. Thereupon catastrophe struck again. The unit realized that the rushes they had seen so far were marred by scratches. Faults or errors were discovered in the studio laboratory. There is no record of precisely what happened, but it is not hard to guess Chaplin's reaction. The laboratory staff was changed, but Chaplin had to face the fact that all the work of the past month would have to be redone. Throughout the week of 16 February he was back on the tightrope again. By the time he had finished, he had done more than 700 takes on the wire. It is hardly surprising that he was, as Crocker remembered, often exhausted. 'Nobody has ever noticed that my legs doubled for Charlie's when he needed a rest.' The retakes were completed by the end of February and the first week in March Merna Kennedy was put to work. She apparently worked well under Chaplin's tutelage: the daily shooting records indicate few problems with her scenes.

Work on the film was a welcome distraction from the wretchedness of Summit Drive. In the autumn of 1925 Lita discovered that she was again pregnant. Chaplin was furious to find he had created yet another snare for himself (or so he felt) and the pregnancy led, if it were possible, to further deterioration of relations between the couple. Lita found it impossible to please her husband and was wretchedly jealous of his attentions to Marion Davies, Merna Kennedy and Georgia Hale. Chaplin for his part was tormented by the situation; he began to suffer from acute insomnia, and would prowl the house at night with a shotgun, fearing intruders. He would bathe or shower a dozen times a day. He had the studio electricians fix bugging devices in Lita's room, but there was nothing to hear and the equipment was in any case technically inadequate. Even efforts at conciliation went wrong. Chaplin acceded to Lita's pleas to meet people of her own age, and paid for her to give a party for eight of her young friends in a restaurant. Rashly, Lita took them home to Summit Drive afterwards. When Chaplin returned unexpectedly he flew into a rage and threw the guests out of the house. The incident was to be cited by both parties in the subsequent divorce action. In this fraught atmosphere Lita's second child, Sydney Earle Chaplin, was born five weeks prematurely, on 30 March 1926. Lita's single consolation was that the birth, unlike that of her first son, was easy.

Certainly the new child did nothing to improve the unhappy marriage. Again the choice of name was a matter of dispute but Lita agreed to name the boy after her brother-in-law. After the break-up of the marriage, Lita called the boy 'Tommy'. There was disagreement over baptism: Chaplin always believed that children should be allowed to choose their own religion when they reached a sufficiently mature age.

Home life was merely a distraction, with work on *The Circus* resuming at full tilt. The day after the birth Chaplin was rehearsing the mirror maze, which required some ingenious camera placement by Totheroh. The exteriors of the carnival were shot at Venice Beach, not far from the spot where *Kid Auto Races* had been filmed. The location scenes, which involved up to thirty extras and a bus to take them to the shooting, were shot in the mornings, before the regular crowds arrived. Among the scenes filmed in the studio in the afternoons was the business where the hungry Charlie eats a hot dog clutched by a babe in arms, solicitously wiping the child's mouth when its father turns round. The incident was perhaps suggested by a favourite yarn of Fred Karno, who related how he and some young friends from the circus stole jam sandwiches from school children when they had no money to buy breakfast.

Throughout the succeeding five months work continued steadily. There was a brief but notable interruption on 16 June when Raquel Meller visited the set. Chaplin had conceived great enthusiasm for the petite and colourful Spanish actress and *chanteuse*. For a while he felt that he had at last found the ideal Josephine for the Napoleon film that continued to obsess him. On 7 September the studio was closed for the day to mark the funeral of Rudolph Valentino. Chaplin, who was one of the Great Screen Lover's pall-bearers, said graciously that his death was 'one of the greatest tragedies that has occurred in the history of the motion picture industry'.

The work with the lions caused concern. Two animals were hired (at a cost of $150 a day, including the trainer). One was docile, but the other was a spirited creature. In at least one scene that appears in the finished film, as Chaplin would unashamedly point out in later years, the fear on his face was not pretence. Despite the risk, Chaplin went back into the cage day after day. By the time the sequence was completed he had made more than 200 takes with the lions.

One of the inconveniences of working with the lions was that the unit had to fit in with their meal hours, and the lions preferred to eat around three in the afternoon. Between the nervous strain and the change of routine, Chaplin suffered from indigestion, and the doctor prescribed Epsom salts taken in regular small doses in hot water for two or three days. Crocker recalled how he would pace the floor in story conferences, interspersing his oratory with belches, each of which would be followed by a relieved sigh of 'Ah! That's better.' Crocker remembered a typical example: 'Now, what I want in this story is not only love and romance, but magic. There must be *magic*. The audience must be enthralled – burp – ah, that's better!'

Apart from gas on the director's heart, all seemed for the moment to be going well. Then, on 28 September a fire suddenly broke out, sweeping through the closed stage. Before it could be brought under control, the set had been completely destroyed. Props and equipment were damaged by fire and water. Thousands of panes of glass in the roof and walls were broken. The electrical equipment was put out of action. The stills photographer captured a few shots of Chaplin, still in his costume, gazing in dismay at the wreckage. These unposed shots are some of the most poignant images of the Tramp. Totheroh was as resourceful, and filmed 250 feet of the catastrophe and his bemused boss. It was slight compensation that this piece of impromptu film could be exploited as pre-publicity for *The Circus*.

The studio was rapidly put back into partial operation; and in only ten working days, between 3 and 14 October, Chaplin had completed a lengthy and complicated sequence in the café set. For reasons known only to himself, he was not to use the sequence in the film, though it is a faultlessly constructed and self-contained comic sketch. Charlie, his nose much out of joint, reluctantly accompanies Rex and Merna to the café. At a neighbouring table sit two prize fighters, twin brothers. (Both 'twins' are played by the same actor, 'Doc' Stone: Totheroh and his fellow cameramen performed the magic with double exposure.) One of the two brothers amuses himself by insulting and annoying Charlie. This gives Charlie an idea for winning back Merna's admiration. He takes the fighter aside, and pays him $5 to pretend to be beaten in a fight. The ruse works successfully, and Rex and Merna see Charlie with fresh eyes – until the fighter's twin, who had earlier left the restaurant, returns to take his brother's place. Charlie, expecting to repeat his earlier performance, attacks him, but is dismayed when the fighter starts hitting back. Only a happy accident with a clock saves the day and knocks out Charlie's opponent. As the party departs from the restaurant, Charlie leaves Rex and Merna for a moment to retrieve $5 from the pocket of the opponent whom he believes to have reneged on the contract.

In early November Chaplin shot an amusing sequence to lead in to this café episode. It was filmed on Sunset Boulevard, which still retained a pleasantly rural look. Charlie is proudly walking Merna out, despite the tiresome attentions of a stray dog which snaps about his ankles. To his chagrin however they meet Rex, who joins them in their walk. Merna is touched by Rex's gallantry when he picks up the purse a lady has dropped. Charlie determines to show himself as gallant, but unhappily the distressed damsel who falls to his lot is a stalwart woman laden with indequately wrapped parcels of fish. Charlie attempts to pick up a single fish she has dropped but his efforts only result in an endless scaly avalanche, as he struggles desperately to rewrap them. The lady becomes more and more angry and Charlie more and more helpless until he retreats with the embarrassed hint of a shrug.

At the end of November, while Chaplin was rehearsing a new roller-skating routine, Lita walked out of the house on Summit Drive, taking their two children with her. Life can have been no easier for the unwelcome child bride than for her exasperated husband. Lita was jealous and fearful of the more sophisticated, beautiful and intelligent women who, she felt, exerted a much more powerful attraction than she herself could ever do. She must have understood, however, that the single rival with which she could never compete was Chaplin's work. Chaplin knew also that this was where he was most vulnerable. He remembered the adventures involved in spiriting *The Kid* to safety, a mere five years ago; as soon as Lita's lawyers began to gather (her lawyer uncle, Edwin McMurray, moved from San Francisco to an office in Los Angeles so that he could be near the case), Chaplin took action to protect *The Circus* in the event of trouble. On 3 December stock was taken of the film already shot; nine reels of cut positive and thirteen reels of essential uncut scenes were carefully packed into two boxes ready for removal to safety. On Sunday 5 December notice was posted that studio operations were temporarily suspended. The studio staff was cut down to the minimum. All the actors were laid off, with the exception of Merna Kennedy, Henry Bergman, Harry Crocker and Allan Garcia. As if all this were not enough, the US Government chose this moment to decide that Chaplin's income tax for the preceding years was underpaid by $1,113,000.

It was at about this time that Robert Florey, a French idolater of Chaplin who was later to become a director in his own right and was to be Chaplin's assistant on *Monsieur Verdoux*, wrote a haunting pen portrait of his hero:

> Often in the evening, around eleven, when I go to Henry's, the actors' restaurant in Hollywood run by the excellent Henry Bergman (whom you have seen in all Chaplin's films) I meet, walking alone or sometimes with his devoted assistant Harry Crocker, the popular Charlie, the great Charles Spencer Chaplin, unrecognizable beneath his big, shapeless felt hat. To protect himself against the evening mists – the night can be

perilous in California – he wraps himself in a big grey overcoat, and his trousers, quite wide, according to the current fashion, hide his tiny feet, shod in buttoned boots with beige cloth tops. So it was that one night last December, coming out of Grauman's Egyptian, I was striding the short distance between the theatre and our favourite restaurant when I recognized, a few steps ahead of me, the familiar outline of Charlie. Instinctively I slowed my pace, and I cannot express what melancholy overwhelmed me in recognizing the total solitude of the most popular man in the world. He was walking slowly, close to the darkened shop windows; the fog was thick, and Charlie, his hands in the pockets of his raglan, was making a slight, regular movement of his elbows. His footsteps made no sound; his collar was turned up, and he was so slight in his big coat that he might have been taken for a child dressed up in his father's clothes. This man whose cinematic masterpieces had been shown that very night on screens all across the world, this man who had made people laugh that night in all the continents, was there, walking in front of me in the fog. There was infinite sadness in the spectacle of Charlie, alone in the night. A man whom the smartest *salons* in the world would have fought to entertain, was quietly walking, alone in the shadows, his hands in his pockets and the brim of his hat pulled down over his eyes. It is true that the life of artists in Hollywood, especially in the evening, when the day's work is finished, cannot be compared to existence in Paris or London, but to see Charlie Chaplin, alone on the boulevard, like some little extra without a job or a place to live, wrung my heart.

At the corner of Cherokee Street an important event occurred – important for Charlie at least . . . he met a dog. A fat, common, mongrel who was sitting waiting for who knew what. And Charlie stopped, abruptly. He had found someone to talk to. And he started to question the dog, who probably recognized in him a comrade, because it offered him its paw. I couldn't hear Charlie's words, but as I caught up with him he said to me: 'Are you going to Henry's? Let's go together.' Two minutes later we arrived at the café-restaurant. But instead of entering the front door on Hollywood Boulevard, he went through the kitchen, because Charlie had a guest with him – the fat dog, who had followed him. Charlie ordered a copious dinner for his friend from the Filipino cook, and the dog, once more offered his paw to be shaken. We left the kitchen, and as we were going into the restaurant Charlie said, 'That dog knows me. He often waits on the corner of Cherokee, and I realized tonight that he hadn't eaten again . . . so you see I couldn't do anything else but invite him!' And that sweet, large-hearted little man talked of other things.[5]

On 10 January 1927, a day after Chaplin had left for New York, Lita's lawyers filed the divorce complaint. It was an exceptional document of its kind. In the first place Chaplin was joined as defendant with his studio, his company, Kono, Reeves, the National Bank of Los Angeles, the Bank of Italy, and various other banks and corporations. Again, it was unprecedented among divorce complaints for its length. Normally such complaints run to three or four pages: this one had fifty-two. For the most part it was the awful tittle-tattle of who said

Charlie and 'the Kid'- BY HUNGERFORD

1927 - A cartoonist's view of
the Chaplin - Grey divorce.

and did what, a wretched reprise of the abuses and recriminations of a marriage fast repented. Then there was an innuendo of infidelity with 'a certain prominent film actress'. The lawyers' biggest gun, though, was their demonstration that things which are done in the dark privacy of the bedroom take on a lurid and shocking aspect in the light of print and the spotlight of the courtroom. They had moreover discovered an obscure corner of the Californian Statute

373

Book – a certain section 288a – which whimsically forbade areas of commonplace sexual practice.

The style of the complaint made clear its dual purpose. The joining of Chaplin's business associates and interests indicated the lawyers' intention of securing as large a proportion of his material goods as possible. The grubbing detail of the rest was intended, quite simply, to destroy his reputation in the eyes of the public. The Fatty Arbuckle and William Desmond Taylor scandals were still recent in memory. Arbuckle had been acquitted of the manslaughter of Virginia Rappe, but the associations of the trials were enough to ruin him and end his career. The lawyers must have been confident that so much innuendo would ensure Chaplin's fall.

The document was demeaning and humiliating to everyone concerned. What pain it must have caused to a man who so prized his privacy and public dignity can hardly be imagined. Chaplin was reported to be in a state of nervous breakdown in New York, where he was with his lawyer, Nathan Burkan. It would hardly have been surprising. Meanwhile pirated copies of the divorce complaint became best sellers in the shadier areas of the book trade: the paperback was titled: *The Complaint of Lita*. The reporters were insatiable and the Chaplin case supplanted Teapot Dome, the American landings in Nicaragua, Aimée Semple McPherson and the Hall-Mills murder case in the headlines.

Chaplin's foresight in removing *The Circus* to safety was swiftly vindicated. Lita's lawyers asked for, and were granted, the exceptional remedy of a temporary restraining order to secure not only the community property but also his personal assets, pending litigation. On 12 January the receivers put the studio under guard: in charge of the operation were an attorney, W. I. Gilbert, and a real-estate agent, Herman Spitzel. Alfred Reeves had conveniently taken leave of absence, taking the keys with him, but on 18 January, for no very evident purpose, the receivers opened up the safe and vault. Chaplin talked vaguely of continuing work on *The Circus* in New York but even he must have had fears that it would never be completed.

Almost more degrading than the complaint was the wrangling over money that now commenced. The court awarded Lita temporary occupation of the house and provisional alimony of $3000 a month. The house brought her little joy: the servants had left it; the cost of upkeep was enormous; and since the Federal Tax Authorities had placed a lien on Chaplin's financial assets, the temporary alimony payments were not forthcoming.

Chaplin's Californian lawyers, with a very poor sense of public relations, proposed a permanent settlement of $25 a week for Lita and the children. Uncle Edwin made nation-wide propaganda with this: one women's club started a milk fund for the Chaplin babies before the Chaplin lawyers agreed to the adjudicated temporary alimony.

> Suddenly [Robert Florey recorded] Charlie disappeared ... Overnight, *Charlie's house is empty.*
>
> The other day, when I was working with Douglas in his Beverly Hills drawing room, I was surprised to see the interpreter of *Zorro* stop abruptly in front of the window and gaze at something which, from where I sat, I could not see. I didn't interrupt his meditation, thinking that he was working out some idea for his new film ... but after a few moments of silence, Doug exclaimed:
>
> 'Look at the house with the blind windows!'
>
> And, in my turn, I looked and saw the sad spectacle of Charlie's house, two hundred yards away, standing in the misty first light of the Californian December; Charlie had been gone two months and all that remained were thirty-eight big black eyes. The house was deserted, no light, no curtains at the windows; thirty-eight blind eyes which wept for the sentimental and lamentable existence of the greatest of screen comedians ... And Douglas added: 'How well that house reflects the existence of the great Chaplin.'
>
> The house with thirty-eight blind windows was truly melancholy, surrounded by its pines and cypresses.[6]

Contrary to the expectations of Lita's lawyers, the complaint did not ruin Chaplin; though it would have ruined almost any other man in America. Neither the lawyers nor anyone else could have conceived how deep was the love the public held for him, or that it would survive even smears so black. Some women's clubs agitated for the boycott of Chaplin's films, and in a few backwoods cities and states they succeeded. News of these boycotts produced a strong counter-reaction, which greatly heartened Chaplin, in the form of a protest signed by French intellectuals including Louis Aragon, René Clair, Germaine Dulac and (French by adoption) Man Ray. When Chaplin began to emerge from his seclusion, East Coast society, as if in demonstration, courted and entertained him. He was invited to the Old Timers' Night of the New York Newspaper Club, and delighted them by performing a pantomime about an ill-fated toreador. It was no waste of effort to win over an influential section of the Eastern press in this way.

Among the innumerable letters of encouragement and support from friends and collaborators, one of the most touching was from the un-named, plain-faced woman who had worked with him for a day on a scene with tumbling fish, just before the studio close-down:

> All I can say is I think you are wonderful and don't let them break your heart.

Even in the letter, she did not reveal her name: she signed herself simply: 'Your Fishwoman'.

Sydney was in California and keeping an eye on the studio; careful about money as he was, he was troubled to see that there were still 'several people walking around the studio – such as publicity men etc., and I am wondering if you know they are still on salary and if you want to keep up this big expense as your future actions are so indefinite.' His letter to Chaplin is full of fraternal concern and anxiety:

Dear Charlie:

> Because I have not written to you is not that I lack sympathy – you are continually in my thoughts. I hate to imagine how you must have felt when you were on that train, alone, and the news broke. It was like a bomb-shell to me. I did not believe that she could be so vindictive as to actually try to ruin you. She was cutting her own throat. I only just learned the result of the last conference Wright* had with her attorneys – I certainly would not pay her a million nor for that matter make any settlement until the government suit was out of the way. Certainly if worse comes to worse the government will take so much there will be nothing left for her any way. She would have a tough time collecting, especially if you go to England for your future work. The more I think of England the more I believe it will be the best thing.
>
> It all seems to me that some one must have a personal grudge against you – I have heard from several people that there has been considerable talk about your socialist tendencies – and as this is a capitalistic government it does not help under the circumstances. I do hate to paint GLOOM but it does seem to me that we should be prepared to go to the other side if things do not shape themselves to our satisfaction . . .

Thoughts of England touchingly stirred old memories:

* Loyd Wright, Chaplin's lawyer.

Do not get too despondent, Charlie, remember there is more in life than great wealth – as long as you know you are comfortably fixed for the future and your health is good it would help to maintain a philosophical attitude toward your troubles. When I am feeling sort of worried, myself, I always think of the great joy, happiness and elated feeling I had when I signed on the dotted line for Fred Karno – just think, the great sum of three pounds a week – why I ran all the way to Kennington Road to send you the glad news. So it seems, after all, that happiness is a matter of comparison and dependent upon our own viewpoint or way of thinking. So CHEER UP OLD KID it will be interesting reading in your biography.

In this, Sydney was mistaken. Almost forty years afterwards, when Chaplin did finally write his memoirs, the recollection of these desolate times was still too painful to touch on beyond a bare mention: 'For two years we were married and tried to make a go of it, but it was hopeless and ended in a great deal of bitterness.'

On 2 June Chaplin's lawyers filed an answer to the complaint. In general this was simply a denial of the charges. It was admitted that the defendant had not visited the plaintiff on occasions when she had left home to holiday in Coronado, but that 'the plaintiff well knew that, because of the fact that at that time the defendant had from two hundred to three hundred people actually working, it would be impossible for this defendant to leave his work and go to Coronado.'

One charge evokes special sympathy for the defendant:

3(h) That on several occasions during the past year, defendant had said to plaintiff: 'Go away some place for a while; I can't work or create when you are here. You are ruining my career.' That on one such occasion plaintiff replied to defendant: 'Why, Charlie, I don't understand how I interfere with your work. I never see you or annoy you.' And he replied in a tone of exasperation; 'That isn't it. It is just the fact that you are here, and I am supposed to give the usual attention to a home and family. It annoys me, and irritates me, and I cannot work.'

The answer specifically denied this charge, but added significantly in this connexion:

this defendant alleges that during said time, the plaintiff well knew that the defendant was busily engaged in the work of his profession and she at all times well knew of the demands and requirements made upon this defendant, and of the necessity of his devoting his undivided attention to the work of his profession; that the plaintiff was aware that in order for this defendant successfully to produce a good picture, that it was necessary and important that he concentrate upon his work and devote his every attention to it. That during said time this defendant explained to the plaintiff that it was vitally important that he give his undivided attention to his motion picture production.

One week after the answer was filed, the guards were removed from the studio and the receivers left. In August Lita's lawyers decided to precipitate matters by announcing that they were ready to name 'five prominent women' with whom, they would allege, Chaplin had been intimate during the period of his marriage. Rightly, they estimated that Chaplin was not the man to allow other people's careers to be ruined as, in the prevailing temper, they certainly would be. To make quite sure, however, Lita herself went to Marion Davies to tell her that she was at the top of the list (the others were Merna Kennedy, Edna Purviance, Claire Windsor and either Pola Negri or Peggy Hopkins Joyce). Marion, fearful of the possible effect the incident would have upon Hearst, conveyed her terror to Chaplin. The Chaplin lawyers agreed on a cash settlement and the case was settled with a brief, anti-climactic court hearing on 22 August 1927. The judge declined to hear all the unseemly stuff of the complaint. Lita withdrew her charges and asked for an interlocutory decree on the single charge of cruelty. She was awarded a settlement of $600,000, with a trust fund of $100,000 for each child. It was the largest such settlement in American legal history to that time. Chaplin was granted access to his sons. His legal costs amounted to almost one million dollars.

Lita was to find a generous portion of her settlement going to her lawyers, and the case they made for her would in the end ricochet harmfully on her own reputation. The last unsporting gesture of smearing the five women had not helped. Chaplin's popularity on the contrary seemed almost unaffected. One of many similar leading articles in the daily press stated:

CHARLIE IS A REAL HERO

Charlie Chaplin, who has entertained millions on the screen, has never been as satisfying as when he declines to entertain the thrill seekers by refusing to fight the divorce suit of his 'girl wife'. Charlie 'stands and delivers' to the tune of nearly a million dollars, thus depriving his public of another opportunity to determine whether where a film star lives is a home or a night club.

There have been enough lurid stories to last for a while . . . Whether

Charlie was actuated by good taste or good business sense is beside the point. His popularity, which is his capital, might seriously have been impaired had Lita been granted the opportunity to 'tell all' on the stand. The 'unnamed actresses' whom Lita was to have named are as well left in the obscurity of the screen as to the publicity of the printed page. We prefer to see them on the silver sheet showing high emotion by feverish undulation of the diaphragm, to placing them in the witness box to 'deny the allegation' with real tears.

It is also a coincidence that Fatty Arbuckle, trying a comeback from a scandal years old, is denied a hearing in Washington, which would have none of him even at this late date. There has been enough washing of movie dirty linen in public to have a depressing effect on more than one reputation which lost its earning capacity.

Whatever the reason, a rising vote of thanks to Charlie for sparing us the minute details of life, liberty, and the pursuit of happiness with the little woman.

The great comedian Will Rogers was as usual more succinct: 'Good joke on me. I left Hollywood to keep from being named in the Chaplin trial and now they go and name nobody. Not a name was mentioned but Charlie's bank. Charlie is not what I would call a devoted husband, but he certainly is worth marrying.'

The Circus was almost finished at the time of the suspension, and the material shot in the few weeks after work was resumed was mostly to fill out what had already been shot. Further scenes were taken in the circus ring, again entailing bringing back extras – about 250 of them this time – for two days' work. The fates had not quite done with *The Circus*. Months before, a location (a squat one-storeyed store on the corner of Lankersheim and Hill, in Sawtelle) had been selected for the scene where Charlie is shot right out of the circus tent after his ride for life from the tightrope. One day in early October the crew was loaded into seven cars and set out for the location to shoot retakes. Unfortunately Sawtelle was a mushrooming suburb. In the long months since the spot had been selected, the one-storey building had been replaced by an ornate new hotel. A witness of Chaplin's reaction noted: 'A crowd of the curious surge about the big blue car and Charlie is somewhat embarrassed. The tramp atmosphere disappears as a soft English voice remonstrates: "You see, things like this are responsible for the delay." The Lankersheim and Hill scene, with its grocery store, was faithfully reconstructed on the studio lot.

At the beginning of October, Chaplin and Crocker were searching Glendale for a suitably deserted and melancholy location for the final scenes of the film. The same reporter described the scene in the small hours of 10 October 1927:

Perspiring men rush about the Chaplin studio. Carpenters, painters, electricians, technical minds, laborers. Charlie must not be held up. A caravan of circus wagons are hitched on behind four huge motor trucks. They start for Cahuenga Pass. A long and hard pull to Glendale. The location is flooded with light. It comes from all directions. The dynamo wagon hums. So the men work through the night.

Daylight breaks. The morning is cold. Crackings echo from a dozen fires. It is an unusual Californian crispness. Cars begin to arrive. The roar of exhausts signals their coming. There is an extra-loud rumbling. The big blue limousine comes to a stop. *The Circus* must be finished. Everyone is on time. Cameras are set up. Now the sun is holding things up. Why doesn't it hurry and come up over the mountains? It is long shadows the Tramp wants.

Six o'clock and half the morning wasted. The edge of the circus ring is too dark. It doesn't look natural. The tramp refuses to work artificially. Men start to perspire again. Thirty minutes later the soft voice speaks, 'Fine! That's fine! Let's shoot!'

Cameras grind. Circus wagons move across the vast stretch of open space. There is a beautiful haze in the background. The horses and the wagon wheels cause clouds of dust. The picture is gorgeous. No artist would be believed should he paint it. Twenty times the scene is taken.

The cameras move in close to the ring. Carefully the operators measure the distance. From the lens to the tramp. He is alone in the center of the ring.

He rehearses. Then action for camera. Eighty feet. The business is done again. And again! And again! Fifty persons are looking on. All members of the company. There are few eyes that are not moist. Most of them know the story. They knew the meaning of this final 'shot'.

'How was that?' came inquiring from the Tramp. Fifty heads nodded in affirmation. 'Then we'll take it again; just once more,' spoke the man in the baggy pants and derby hat and misfit coat and dreadnought shoes. The sun was getting high. The long shadows became shorter and shorter. 'Call it a day,' said the Tramp, 'we'll be here again tomorrow at four.'

At three the following morning Chaplin was watching the day's rushes:

The little fellow in the big black leather chair was no longer the Tramp. But he was watching him on the screen. Charlie Chaplin was passing judgement. 'He should do that much better.' 'He doesn't ring true.' 'He has his derby down too far over his eyes.' 'They have burned his face up with those silver reflectors.' A severe critic, this Chaplin. The Tramp doesn't please him. The stuff must be retaken. A leap from the leather chair. Speed, dust, location.

Now followed the last of the misfortunes of *The Circus*. In the night the wagons had disappeared. The sheriff had his deputies on the job, but there was to be no shooting that day: all that the company could do was to rehearse for retakes, should the wagons ever be recovered.

They were, that night. They had been taken by some students who planned to burn them at their fire celebration. An entire freshman class was arrested, but Chaplin declined to prosecute: anything to avoid a further delay. The retakes were made on 14 October.

Even those who worked for years with Chaplin were often mystified by his constant retakes. He might rebuke Totheroh if he heard the camera crank a couple of turns after he had called 'Cut', but he would use hundreds of feet retaking some apparently insignificant piece of business. It was sometimes suggested by his colleagues that when he was stuck for an idea as to what to do next, he would just go on retaking the last thing to hide his indecision. Yet that could not explain the retakes of such a scene as this, taken at the end of a shooting session, when time and light were pressing. The answer must be sought elsewhere. Charlie Chaplin had a compulsion to seek perfection, and equally a conviction that he could never achieve it. He just went on trying.

So much of the film had been cut as the work went along that the final cutting and titling took barely a fortnight. On 28 October the working print of the film was previewed at the Alexandra Theatre, Glendale. (The audience must have been delighted to glimpse the Glendale courthouse used as the scene of the marriage of Rex and Merna.) It was well received, but the reactions suggested some cuts and retakes. For four days Chaplin and Crocker were back on the tightrope for retakes. The close-ups presented some difficulties when it came to matching shots made almost two years before. The anguish of the divorce had left its mark on Chaplin's features. At the height of the troubles with Lita his hair had gone white overnight: Henry Bergman remembered the shock when the changed Chaplin arrived at the studio one morning. When he began the film his naturally black hair was touched with silver. Now it had to be dyed for the screen.

The revised print was previewed again at Bard & West Adams

Theatre on West Adams and Crenshaw, and Miss Steele recorded in the daily studio reports that it 'went over great'. Chaplin could at last relax. He went on a fishing trip with Harry Crocker.

In the 1920s, even in a small independent organization like Chaplin's, all the work towards the release and exploitation of films was done within the studio. There were as yet no independent outside laboratories and publicity organizations to undertake the work. So the period between the completion and release of a film was one of the busiest for the staff. The cameramen under Totheroh had to cut two negatives, made on two cameras, for domestic and European release. The laboratory then had to make the release prints – fifteen copies of the film were required for the initial release of *The Circus*. The press department had to prepare press books, programmes, releases and to supervise the distribution of the stills that were printed in great numbers by the stills department. Meanwhile the last sets had to be struck and cleared, the costumes, properties and electrical equipment carefully renovated, and the studio made ready for the next production.

Chaplin had more than once declared his views on the importance of the musical accompaniment to films. The preview of *The Circus* had been accompanied by stock themes chosen *ad hoc* by the theatre's musical arrangers. For the première performances, however, Arthur Kay was commissioned to compile a special score. Chaplin worked closely with Kay in the final stages.

The world première was held on 6 January 1928 at the Strand Theatre, New York: perhaps Chaplin felt that he owed that city a debt for the refuge it had provided during the troubles of the preceding year. The Los Angeles opening was three weeks later, on 27 January, at Grauman's Chinese. Sid Grauman provided a spectacular showcase for his friend's picture. Patrons were greeted on the forecourt of the theatre by a full-scale menagerie and sideshows including Alice from Dallas, the 503-pound fat girl and Major Mite and Lady Ruth, respectively twenty-five inches tall and twenty-one pounds, and thirty-two inches tall and fifty-two pounds. On the stage a live Prologue starred Poodles Hannaford, the Ace of Riding Clowns and his troupe, Pallenberg's Performing Bears on their bicycles, a lion tamer, and Samaroff and Sona's performing dogs.

Chaplin had no cause to be dissatisfied with his press: the reviews were hardly less enthusiastic than for *The Gold Rush*. Some critics indeed welcomed a film in which, they felt, the drama and pathos did not eclipse the slapstick element. The Lita affair seemed all but forgotten, barely six months later. Only the ever-faithful Alexander Woollcott touched on it with irony: the film, he said, was overdue 'because it was interrupted in the making. I now only vaguely recall the circumstances, but I believe it was because thanks to the witless clumsiness of the machinery of our civilization, someone (a wife I think it was, or something like that) was actually permitted to have the law on Chaplin as though he were a mere person and not such a bearer of healing laughter as the world had never known.' Woollcott's uncritical devotion was a byword among his contemporaries, though this romantic move to place the artist above the law might well have invited scepticism. The thought, though, was kind.

It was while working on *The Circus* that Chaplin embarked for the first and last time on the adventure of producing a film by another director. The most likely reason for this venture was to launch Edna – for whom he evidently no longer saw a place in his own studio – on a new phase of her career, as a dramatic actress. He had been immoderately enthusiastic over Josef von Sternberg's shoe-string production *The Salvation Hunters* and even more enthusiastic about its star Georgia Hale. Now he invited von Sternberg to direct a film tentatively titled *Sea Gulls*. 'This was quite a distinction' wrote von Sternberg forty years later in his autobiography, *Fun in a Chinese Laundry*:

> as he had never honored another director in this fashion, but it only resulted in an unpleasant experience for me.
> The film was to revolve around Edna Purviance, a former star of his, with whom, among other notable films, he had made the impressive *Woman of Paris*. She was still charming, though she had not appeared in pictures for a number of years and had become unbelievably timid and unable to act in even the simplest scene without great difficulty. Aware of this, Mr Chaplin credited me with sufficient skill to overcome such handicaps, and in the completed film she actually seemed at ease.
> The tentative title of the film was *The Sea-Gull* [sic] (no relation to the Anton Chekhov tragedy) and it was based on a story of mine about some fishermen on the Californian coast. When the filming had ended I showed it exactly once at one theatre, then titled *A Woman of the Sea* and that was the end of that. The film was promptly returned to Mr Chaplin's vaults and no one has ever seen it again. We spent many idle hours with each other, before, during, and after the making of this film, but not once was this work of mine discussed, nor have I ever broached the subject of

its fate to him. He charged off its cost against his formidable income tax, and I charged it off to experience.

Though it did me a great deal of harm at the time, I bore Mr Chaplin no ill will for repressing my work. I have always been fond of him though for a few hours his arbitrary action placed a great strain on my affection.

Chaplin did not even mention the film in his own autobiography, and the story of *Sea Gulls* has hitherto been shrouded in myth and mystery. Neither the film itself nor any scenario survives; but the daily shooting records and the title list still preserved in the Chaplin archive enable us to recreate something of its history.

There seems no foundation for the often repeated assertion that the story of the film was Chaplin's: the credit titles clearly stated 'written and directed by Josef von Sternberg'. It was in essence a commonplace melodrama about the two daughters of a fisherman: Edna played Joan, the good sister; Eve Southern was Magdalen, the bad one. Magdalen abandons Peter, her simple fisherman fiancé to go off to the big city with a playboy novelist. Years later, when Joan and Peter are happily married, Magdalen returns to trifle once more with Peter's affections and disrupt the marriage. Peter and Joan are finally reconciled however, and the mischievous Magdalen gets her just deserts.

Work on the film began in January 1926, almost simultaneously with *The Circus* and continued without break until the end of shooting on 2 June. Cutting was completed three weeks later. The story that Chaplin ordered some retakes is not borne out by the shooting records. Certainly there can be no truth in the frequent assertion that Chaplin himself shot some material on the film, since throughout the production period he was working full out and every day on *The Circus*.

The production – part of which took place on location at Carmel and Monterey – may well have been fraught with difficulties. Von Sternberg seems frequently to have returned to scenes with which he was apparently dissatisfied. When work began the photographer was Edward Gheller, who had filmed *The Salvation Hunters*, but on 26 April he was replaced by the 25-year-old, Russian-born Paul Ivano, who had previously co-directed *Seven Years' Bad Luck* with Max Linder, acted as technical director on *The Four Horsemen of the Apocalypse* and shot the chariot race in *Ben Hur*. Ivano was to be the credited cinematographer, though the bulk of the film was shot by Gheller.

Von Sternberg's statements about Edna's condition seem to be confirmed by the daily shooting records. For the most part he was shooting with considerable economy, generally printing the second or third take of a shot. Scenes which demanded work of the slightest complication from Edna, however, seem often to have required nine, ten or more takes. It was said that Sternberg endeavoured to assist her by having two kettle-drums on the set to establish a rhythm for the performance.

Speculation about Chaplin's reasons for suppressing the film have included the notion – less than likely, given Chaplin's commercial sense – that he was jealous because von Sternberg had directed Edna so successfully; and, alternatively and ever so slightly more possibly, that he was distressed by the quality of Edna's performance. Privately Chaplin himself said later that the film was simply not good enough to release. Von Sternberg was a man of strong opinions, and the mild tone of his protests might well be taken to imply his own sense of the film's shortcomings.

John Grierson claimed to have seen the film, and as a good journalist made a good story out of this exclusive privilege; but his rather misleading references to the narrative cast some doubt on the rest of his evidence:

> The story was Chaplin's, and humanist to a degree; with fishermen that toiled, and sweated, and lived and loved as proletarians do. Introspective as before, Sternberg could not see it like Chaplin. Instead, he played with the symbolism of the sea* till the fishermen and the fish were forgotten. It would have meant something just as fine in its different way as Chaplin's version, but he went on to doubt himself. He wanted to be a success, and here plainly and pessimistically was the one way to be unsuccessful. The film was as a result neither Chaplin's nor Sternberg's. It was a strangely beautiful and empty affair – possibly the most beautiful I have ever seen – of net patterns, sea patterns and hair in the wind. When a director dies he becomes a photographer.

---

* The last title in the film runs: 'And the sea – made of all the useless tears that have ever been shed – grows neither less nor more.' Compared with Chaplin's films, *A Woman of the Sea* made excessive use of titles – more than 160 of them in seven reels.

The only person now living* who saw *A Woman of the Sea* – as *Sea Gulls* was eventually retitled – is Georgia Hale; and her opinion corroborates Chaplin's view that the film was commercially unshowable. It was, she said, wonderfully beautiful to look at;** but the narrative was incomprehensible. Nor does she feel that von Sternberg had wholly overcome the problems of Edna's nervous state. The eventual fate of *A Woman of the Sea* is dealt with in Chapter 14.

* Paul Ivano died on 20 April 1984.

** The shooting records suggest that there was no stills photographer on the production; and no stills of *A Woman of the Sea* were known until several photographs turned up in Edna Purviance's private archive, now in the possession of Inman Hunter, by whose courtesy four are reprinted for the first time in this volume.

12

CITY LIGHTS

Even before the Los Angeles première of *The Circus*, Chaplin was already at work on a new scenario – in part spurred on, no doubt, by the financial demands of the divorce and the Federal Tax Authorities. During the two years that *The Circus* had been in production, the sound film had not only arrived, but made clear its intention of staying. It is a hitherto unknown curiosity of film history that Chaplin could have been the one to effect the revolution, almost a decade earlier. On 9 December 1918, when Chaplin was working on *Sunny-side*, Eugène Augustin Lauste, the pioneer of sound-on-film recording, wrote to him from New York:

To Mr Charlie Chaplin
California Studio.

Dear Sir,

I have just returned from England, on at my arrival I heard that you have started a new moving pictures studio on your own, for which I am very pleased to congratulate you as a wonder artist who by your cleverness and your ingenuity you have been able to conquer the whole world. I am myself one of your admirer at the time that you have been engaged with Fred. Karno. Since that time, you have rapidly progressed with enormous success, so, let me take the liberty to present to you my most hearty congratulations for the great achievement you have already done in the history of the cinematograph.

My self, I am an inventor, I was first working with Mr T. A. Edison, at his private laboratory at Orange N.J. for many years. Then in 1894, I had design, build, and exhibited the first projecting moving pictures machine, called the (Eidoloscope) so I claim that I was the first one who bring out this great invention, which is not my last one. However, I am very please to say that my invention has been favorable to you, and my other one, if you are interested in it, would bring to you an enormous fortune . . .

Referring to my invention, kindly allow me few seconds of your attention to explain the great future of it. As you know, the present machines will in a short time, come at end. For years and years, the public want to see the realism, that means the real talking pictures which up to now has never been accomplished practically and commercially. Many inventors they have already tried to synchronize the gramophone or phonograph in connection with the cinematograph, which has been a failure, and always will be. The only way which that could be done satisfactory, is my own principle on which I have working on, for over 25 years.

I do not want that you think I come to you and bring to you an invention which is an imaginary or dreaming idea which is in the air, but the truth. So before I will engage myself with a party which I have in view, I like to give you the opportunity to take in your hands this wonderful discovery which I believe you will be surprise to hear that a such machine was in existence. The fact, that I had giving in London, several demonstrations to the press, and also to scientists experts, which their opinions was very satisfactory from the reports which I will prove to you by the originals.

In few words, I will explain the principle of my invention, which after his completion will certainly revolutionize the cinematograph industry. The idea which has already accomplished, is to photograph pictures and sounds simultaneously on the same film, and in one operation, and reproduce same without any contact on the film, or the use of a gramophone or phonograph. The sounds is absolutely clear, no scratching whatever or distortion in the voice or music, I am certain that you will be very surprise to hear it.

However, if you think you will be interested, let me know as soon as possible, then I will send to you more particular regarding same, and also a copies of the reports and documents . . .

Notwithstanding the strong French accent in Monsieur Lauste's letter, Chaplin was clearly intrigued by the idea, and Sydney replied on his behalf: 'Regarding your invention, it sounds very interesting to Mr Chaplin and he would be glad to receive further details concerning same if you will be so good as to send them on.' Lauste seems never have to have replied, and Chaplin was too taken up with his current productions to follow the matter up. Lauste's claims were not exaggerated: Merritt Crawford, an authority on Lauste's work on sound films, considers that but for war conditions and lack of capital he would have brought forward the sound era by a decade.

The chance slipped by in 1918. Warners presented their first Vitaphone programme, featuring John Barrymore and Mary Astor in *Don Juan*, on 6 August 1926: it was Hannah Chaplin's sixty-first birthday, and Chaplin was just then flinching in the lions' cage. The feature in the second Vitaphone show, at Christmas 1926, was *The Better 'Ole*. Since the star of the film was Sydney Chaplin himself, the Chaplin brothers must have been keenly aware of the new technique and its implications. A year later, on 6 October 1927, *The Jazz Singer* had demonstrated voice synchronization; and by 8 July 1928, when Chaplin was still in the preparatory stages for *City Lights*, Warner Brothers had shown the first all-talking picture *Lights of New York*.

Hollywood for the most part was on the defensive. Like everyone else, Chaplin was very conscious of the technical shortcomings of the first sound films and – in the early stages – of the unimaginative and inartistic use of the new medium. As late as 1931 he was still declaring: 'I'll give the talkies three years, that's all.' He may not have believed this, but he knew how much he had to lose if he were forced into talking pictures. Chaplin had made the silent pantomime into an international language. He had proved that the gestures, the expressions, the quirks, the thoughts, the feelings of his little Tramp were as readily comprehensible to Japanese, Chinese, Bantu tribesmen or Uzbekhs as to the great cinema audiences of America or Europe. Speech would instantly rob the figure of this universality. In any case, how would he speak? What kind of voice and accent could be conceived to suit the Tramp? This was a conundrum that was still puzzling him more than thirty years after he parted from the character.

Chaplin had no doubt that he must continue to make silent films; even so, the decision left him in a state of anxiety which, as his unit was well aware, stayed with him throughout the new production. Chaplin and Harry Crocker started work on the story in Chaplin's bungalow at the studio. Chaplin's first notion was for another circus story: a clown has lost his sight in an accident but is obliged to conceal the fact from his frail and nervous little daughter. The pathos and comedy would have come from the clown's efforts to pretend that his errors and stumbles are done for fun. He also thought of having two rich men conduct the experiment of giving a wretched tramp a night of luxury and pleasure and then dumping him back on the Embankment where they found him. He was thinking on other lines also: 'How would people like to see me with a companion?' he asked Crocker. 'Would they laugh to see me, a character laughed at by the world, discover someone of even less education, someone over whom I could lord it, someone to whom I would be a great person. I can see lots of fun in that idea.'

'Given the germ of an idea,' commented Crocker,

> from it a dozen stories will grow. Charlie does not concern himself at once with concrete action, the story merely grows as he goes along. If fifty different people were to inquire about his story, he tells fifty different stories. The underlying feeling is always the same, but he emphasizes the particular sequence which happens to be uppermost in his mind at the moment as the main theme of the current story. Thus Chaplin and I launched into the writing of *City Lights* and it was to bring to the screen another facet of the Chaplin genius. Our personal relationship was as close during the preparation of *City Lights* and its shooting [as on *The Circus*].[1]

Many years later, Chaplin was to describe the process of constructing a film as like being in a labyrinth, challenged to find the way out: 'I've got into the proposition, how do I get out?' Again his working notes illustrate the process, and how Chaplin threaded this particular labyrinth to arrive, from an unlikely starting point, at the story of *City Lights*. The brevity and simplicity with which the eventual plot can be told is a mark of its structural excellence.

A tramp, wandering a large and hostile city, meets a fellow waif, a blind flower girl. He also makes the acquaintance of an eccentric millionaire when he saves him from suicide in a moment of alcoholic depression. When drunk the millionaire entertains and treats him lavishly. When sober he has no recollection of him and turns him out of the house.

The Tramp learns that the girl's sight can be cured if she goes to Vienna for an operation. He tries various methods – as street cleaner and prize fighter – to earn the money for her trip; but then chances on the millionaire, in expansive mood, once more. Unfortunately the millionaire's gift of money coincides with a burglary of his house. Sobered up, he forgets his gift and the Tramp (having meanwhile given the money to the girl) is suspected of the theft and gaoled.

The Tramp comes out of prison a sorrier creature than before but the flower girl, now cured, has a flower shop of her own. She longs to meet the benefactor whom she never saw, and whom she imagines must be rich and handsome. The Tramp chances on her shop and gazes with joy at the cured girl. When she approaches him – to give him a coin and a flower, out of pity – he attempts to flee, however, ashamed and afraid to speak to her. But she touches his hand – and recognizes it. They gaze at each other. 'You?' she asks. He nods. 'You can see now?'

Although Chaplin abandoned the idea of the blind clown as too sticky with sentiment, the possibilities of blindness as a theme caught his imagination, and he decided almost from the start to place the blind flower girl at the centre of his story. The city, at this stage, was to be Paris. After juggling with various ideas for scenes, characters and gags, they were still far from having a real story to work on; but about this time, Chaplin hit upon the ending for the film which was to prove the key to the whole:

Charlie meets blind girl trying to cross street.

Punctuate story with his buying flowers. Eventually she is cured and Charlie finds her in little shop. As she laughs at him, Charlie does not dare disclose identity. Girl finally recognizes him – takes him by hand and leads him into flower shop.

From the moment of this discovery, Chaplin's invention seemed to be liberated. Now pages are covered with propositions, suggestions, plot devices, gags. Most of the ideas focus on the theme of blindness which provided possibilities both for pathos and for gags about Charlie's discomfiture and the scope for irony in the contrasts between what the blind girl imagines and the reality. So false would be the poor girl's illusions about her tramp friend that she would know him as 'the Duke'. The essence of their relationship at this time was that

the two of them are driven towards each other – she by her physical disability – he by his being ridiculed by all but her. She may fall wildly in love with him as the Duke, and refuses to believe other stories and descriptions of him.

Already Chaplin had the germ of the scene of their first meeting:

Might have first meeting with girl in helping her across the street. Might have her fixing flowers under parasol and hail him. 'Flower, sir?' He thinks quickly how to get coin for flower and comes back to get one. Plays he is wealthy person. 'Nice day,' he remarks as she puts flower in his buttonhole. Slams automobile door as taxi drives off, to make her believe that it is his.

```
                        Thursday, Oct. 23, 1930.
                             Time 1 P.M.
                              of C.C.
Scene 4537. -  Exterior. Ext. Closeup/ New Flower shop. A retake of finish of picture.
Focus 6'       (C.C. with collar turned up, no collar, tie or shirt, derby on,
Speed 18.      coat buttoned top button and ragged trousers, no cane)  C.C. standing
               with rose in right hand and biting finger of same hand - looks
               at (Virginia - partly in shot as she holds his left hand in hers
               and then runs right hand up his coat sleeve and to coat lapel as
               she recognises him) C.C. nods as she asks if he is the duke - smiles
               then points to right eye and says: "You can see now?" - tries to
               smile, bites finger nervously and looks at her.              O.K.-44

Scene 4538. -  Retake. Fade out.
Focus 6'
Speed 18.                                                                   O.K.-44

Scene 4539. -  Retake. Fade out.
6'
Speed 18.                                                                   O.K.-41

Scene 4540. -  Retake. Fade out.
6'
Speed 18.                                                                   O.K.-38

Scene 4541. -  Retake. Fade out. C.C. has both buttons on coat buttoned and
6'             large safety pin in trousers.
Speed 18.                                                                   O.K.-41

Scene 4542. -  Retake. Fade out.
6'
Speed 18.                                                                   O.K.-40

Scene 4543. -  Retake. Fade out.
6'
Speed 18.                                                                   O.K.-44

                           Time 1:30 P.M.
```

1930 - Shooting continuity for
final scene of *City Lights*.

There is also the germ of that part of the plot which involves the girl's need of money:

> On one occasion the Duke passes the girl's stand and sees the sign 'For Rent' which indicates to him that the girl is in desperate straits. On another occasion the Duke makes his visit to the flower girl's stand and finds the place in possession of an elderly woman and after his inquiry as to the whereabouts of the blind girl, he learns that she no longer has the stand because she was unable to meet the cost of her licence.

He had still not wholly solved the problem of integrating the story of the millionaire:

> The desire [to see] the blind flower girl prosper causes him to bring her in contact with the millionaire, while the latter is having one of his orgies and it so develops that thereafter the millionaire, when under the influence

392

of drink, craves both the companionship of the Tramp and the flower girl. The Tramp gains the knowledge of the millionaire's devotion for the flower girl when the two men are out on one of their sprees and it is because of this knowledge that the Tramp realizes that now that the girl has regained her sight and because of everything the millionaire is in a position to offer her, he sees that it would be futile for him to make known his identity to the girl.

The rich man calls Charlie 'the Duke' and sells that idea to the girl.

An ending in which the girl went off with the millionaire would, however, have interfered with the last scene of which Chaplin had now an even clearer conception.

Ext. of Flower Shop. It is late afternoon. In front of the shop there is a mass of flowers and the flower girl with several others are trimming and watering the various plants. As they throw some of the withered flowers into the gutter the Tramp comes into view. He stops to bend down and pick up a flower and as he places it in his coat lapel, the girls laugh at him. He fixes his eyes on the flower girl and smiles at her. With a gesture of laughter, she turns to the other girls and remarks, 'He's flirting with us,' and they all laugh.

She is unaware of the Tramp's identity but he is of the knowledge that she had dreamed of the day of his return as her ideal. She suddenly plucks a beautiful rose and with extended hand offers it to him while she is still amused at his ridiculous appearance. The Tramp still continues to smile and his gaze is fixed on her and he slowly moves toward her and takes the flower from her hand without turning his gaze from her and places it in his buttonhole and slowly walks away, looking back smiling as though through tears while the flower girl and the others are shown in a hearty laugh.

Chaplin had rarely before begun a film with an idea of how it would end. Certainly never before had he described a final scene in such detail, almost like a shooting script, long before he had begun to shoot. But he knew already that this scene was to be the climax, perhaps the very *raison d'être* of *City Lights*.

There was a host of ideas for additional elaborations and complications of the plot. Perhaps the Tramp could take a room in the same lodging house as the girl, and perhaps the girl and the other lodgers could take him for a rich and well-known author who is reported to be living in disguise in a poor quarter to get material for a novel. Or perhaps he could be mistaken for a kidnapper when he accidentally picks up a package of ransom money that has been thrown from a passing car. Perhaps the girl might have a ne'er-do-well brother who takes her money for crap games, and a sick little sister. Several pages are filled with possible schemes to exploit the comedy, irony and pathos in the girl's illusions about her friend and benefactor:

> When Charlie calls for girl, her friends are hiding to get a peek at him. 'He doesn't like to meet people,' she confides to them, 'but, my, he's grand.' When they see him they roar then one girl weeps. 'We should tell her,' they say. 'Don't laugh, it's tragic,' says weeping girl. 'And don't tell her, it would break her heart.' Charlie overhears the friends discussing him as a comic figure and looks disconsolately at his big feet. Charlie overhears Virginia [the flower girl] inquire from her friends what he looks like. He waits tensely for the girl's answer. 'Oh, he's wonderful,' says Virginia's friend. Charlie relaxes and two tears come into his eyes.
>
> There is a child in neighbourhood who laughs at Charlie at every appearance. 'Why are they laughing?' she asks Charlie. Charlie is invariably laughed at in street scenes with girl. Girl gradually notices that people all laugh.

The girl's blindness could also provoke gags of inappropriate reaction. The couple could go out boating: when Charlie is knocked out by a low bridge, the girl comments dreamily, 'It's so nice here.' There might be a complex variation on the shame gag-nightmares: Charlie could lose his trousers, but then realize that there is no cause for shame since the girl cannot see. One characteristic piece of business involving the abrupt termination of sentiment was to reach the finished film, with some variation, to provide one of the most memorable moments:

> Another time Virginia comes home with Charlie. Charlie looks back and sees her watering the plants in the window – sneaks back and gets water in face. Sneaks away . . .

The old nightmares of thirty years before also briefly recur:

> Blind girl's living room – The Tramp has departed on an errand for the girl. At his departure the landlady enters and confronts the girl with a demand for her back rent. When it is not forthcoming the landlady suggests that the girl give herself over to an institution for the blind and that she send her younger sister to the almshouse . . .

Chaplin seems already at this stage to have anticipated the addition of a synchronized track of some sort:

The blind girl shall own a phonograph which she operates at her flower stand. Her favorite record shall be 'Bright Eyes' or some other semi-jazzy number. The Duke becomes haunted by the melody and whistles the tune as he strolls. In a penny arcade he seeks the number and listens to it through the old-fashioned ear receivers and his mannerisms attract attention by onlookers. This means is also suggested for a love-making scene between the Duke and the girl through his answering her song with another of significance. The Duke also buys or gets in some manner new records for the girl.

Jean Cocteau said that when they met in the course of Chaplin's 1936 world tour, Chaplin told him that he felt a film was like a tree: you shook it, and all that was loose and unnecessary fell away, leaving only the essential form.[2] In Chaplin's case most of his elimination took place at the story stage. Even though he might shoot fifty times the quantity of raw film that appeared in the finished picture, he rarely filmed material for any scene that was not eventually used in the final film. There would, however, be two such discarded sequences in *City Lights*.

By the beginning of May Chaplin was sure enough of his story to set the studio staff to work on sets and props and to order costumes. Still given to sudden enthusiasms for interesting people, he had taken up an Australian artist, Henry Clive, and invited Clive to prepare sketches for the sets and costumes. Clive was working on these sketches throughout June, July and August, though eventually Danny Hall was to take responsibility. Then Chaplin decided that Clive would be ideal for the role of the millionaire, and he was recruited as the first member of the supporting cast.

Robert Sherwood was later to write about the mythical city which eventually became the setting for *City Lights*, 'It is a weird city, with confusing resemblances to London, Los Angeles, Naples, Paris, Tangier and Cancel Bluffs. It is no city on earth and it is also all cities.' Practically everything was shot within the studio. At the rear of the open stage, a high concrete wall was built, and on it the scenic men painted a cyclorama of huge buildings. A T-shaped set in front of this followed the old plan of the intersecting streets that had done service in so many of the two-reelers. On one side of the T was the entrance to a theatre and a cabaret; opposite were one or two shops, including an art store, and just round the corner from them the flower shop. The monument to 'Peace and Prosperity' which figures in the opening scene of the film, stood at the crossing of the T. On a corner a park was planted up, with a railing surrounding it. On the outside of this stood the blind girl's flower stand. The inside served as the garden of the millionaire's house. The sets for the millionaire's house were erected on the closed stage. From these elements Chaplin created his own mythical city.

On 28 August 1928 Hannah Chaplin died. Chaplin had continued to find frequent visits to his mother distressing but when, a week or so before her death, she was taken into Glendale Hospital suffering from an infected gall-bladder, he visited her every day, and forced himself to joke with her: the day before she died nurses at the hospital heard them laughing together. A few hours before the end she fell into a coma, and Chaplin was advised not to see her. He drove away from the hospital, but then turned back. He decided to go to her after all. She momentarily recovered consciousness, and took his hand. When he tried to reassure her that she would get well, she wearily murmured 'Perhaps', and lapsed into unconsciousness.

Chaplin was at work at the studio the following day when a message came that she had died. Harry Crocker went with him to the hospital and waited outside while Chaplin went into the room, with the sunlight filtering through the half-drawn curtains. It was the first time he had seen someone close to him in death. Twenty-seven years before he had been taken to see his dead father but 'I couldn't see my father in his coffin. I shrugged, I turned away, frightened like a child . . .' With his mother it was different, 'because it was natural. She wasn't incarcerated in a coffin. I didn't see her in a coffin. I couldn't. Afterwards at the burial they wanted me to see her before they put the lid on. I said no: I couldn't . . . on the bed there was . . . relief. You see, she'd been in pain, and there was a relief. Before she had looked puzzled, as though . . . and then there was a release. You could see that she suffered no more . . . I suppose when life tortures, death is very welcome. She was still in hospital on a bed. I had seen her the day before and she was in agony. But then the following day, suddenly seeing somebody beloved and small, you think of all the events of life . . . It's really moving . . . I couldn't . . . I couldn't touch her. No, I couldn't touch her.'[3] He remembered that as he looked at the little figure he thought of the battles she had fought in her life, and wept. Afterwards he drove home in silence with Crocker. Chaplin sent telegrams to Sydney, who was ill in Europe, and to Wheeler Dryden in New York. Hannah was buried in the Hollywood Cemetery. Her simple gravestone lies in the shadow of the great mausoleum erected for Marion Davies and the rest of her family, and close to the graves of Henry Lehrman and his wife Virginia Rappe. Lita arrived at the funeral with the two children, but to the relief of Chaplin's friends he was too upset to notice her. Friends said that it was several weeks before he overcame his distress at his mother's death. Throughout her lifetime, Hannah had consistently subtracted a few years from her age. She might have been pleased that her gravestone gives the year of her birth as 1866 instead of 1865.

A note dated 10 September 1928 shows that Chaplin was then still far from the final narrative form of *City Lights*. A negro newsboy still figured prominently in the incidents planned – apparently the character which Chaplin had discussed with Crocker: 'someone of even less education, someone over whom I could lord it, someone to whom I would be a great person.' Their adventures together would have produced chaos in a theatre and a public library.

Since *The Bank* a recurrent motif had been the dream of bliss and the subsequent awakening to cold reality. Most likely this owed more to childhood escape dreams when he was away from home in institutions than to *Jimmy the Fearless*. At this period of his work on *City Lights* Chaplin was determined to open the film with a dream, from which the Tramp would be rudely awakened. In the dream he would have been a prince, wooing and winning a princess. The princess 'seizes and kisses him madly' but he awakes to find himself still a tramp, and being licked by a stray dog. Stills survive showing Chaplin wearing the resplendent white uniform intended for the prince role. A variant of the scene was set in Venice, so that the prince could arrive by gondola for his rendezvous with the princess.

An alternative dream opening had Charlie the Tramp being summoned into a house by a mysterious femme fatale:

Charlie enters and finds woman on settee. She holds out her arms toward him and as music sounds she says: 'My adorable one, come to me.' Charlie at once gives her a passionate kiss and as he kisses the woman's hand, grasps and crushes an orange. As they stand and continue their kiss, the curtains are thrown back and the butler brings in a feast – a turkey and champagne. As Charlie continues to press the lips of the woman, he swings her around so that his hungry eyes can follow the feast to its destination. As he releases her he makes gracious gesture towards the table and says: 'Shall we eat?' The woman, swooning from his kiss, says: 'One more – one more.'

Charlie kisses her beside the table and as she puts her head forward on his shoulder he picks up a drumstick from the table and eats it, then kisses her again. A conflict between his desire for love and food has put him in a quandary. As he is again kissing her passionately, we lap dissolve into the dog licking his face and the police, who chase him off the bench.

Chaplin seems to have been very much taken by this theme of the competing claims of love and hunger. Other comedy business contemplated included the confusion of two chicken drumsticks and two roses, and a moment in which Chaplin passionately bends the woman back over the table – so that he can reach the salt.

When shooting finally began on 27 December 1928, Chaplin had been working for almost a year on the story, and was still far from the eventual structure. He had found a leading lady, however. There is some disagreement over how Chaplin first encountered Virginia Cherrill. The contemporary publicity for the film said that during the summer of 1928 Virginia, then just twenty, 'ventured to Hollywood. Her mission was to tour California and spend some time with friends.' In fact she was recuperating from her first divorce, from Irving Adler. Chaplin, having interviewed applicants for the role of the flower girl all day, noticed her one night when they were both in ringside seats for a prizefight at the Hollywood American Legion Stadium. He instantly saw in her something of the young Edna Purviance. She was invited to the studios, where she took a screen test the following day. In his autobiography, however, Chaplin said that he had met her previously, having noticed her when she was working with a film company on Santa Monica beach, wearing a blue bathing suit. He called her for a screen test, he said, 'out of sheer desperation'. Virginia was beautiful, photographed well, and had no acting experience, which in the past Chaplin had already proved could be a considerable advantage. The decisive factor was that she was the only actress he tested who could 'look blind without being offensive, repulsive – the others all turned their eyes up to show the whites.' Chaplin, with his gift for giving his actors the right instruction, simply advised her to look at him but 'to look inwardly and not to see me'. Virginia's family, who belonged to the Chicago social set, were not at first happy about a career for her in the movies. Her contract was signed, however, to run from 1 November 1928, and Mrs Cherrill moved to Los Angeles to set up house in the Hancock Park district and to watch over her daughter.

Chaplin still liked to surround himself with known and trusted people. Allan Garcia had done good work as the proprietor in *The Circus*. With no very clear idea for a part for him as yet, Chaplin hired him as casting director of the new film: in time Garcia would play two roles in the picture. As Christmas passed, with the sets more or less ready, Chaplin felt forced to make some effort to start shooting, though he was aware he had not yet properly worked out the story. Work during the first three weeks was desultory, general shots establishing Charlie about the city streets. The week of 21 January Chaplin left with Crocker and the new favourite, Henry Clive, for San Simeon – ostensibly to do more work on the story, though Hearst's pleasure-dome can hardly have been conducive to concentration. Before he left he gave orders to call extras for 28 February. Two scenes were firmly fixed in his plans: the first meeting of Charlie and the flower girl, and the closing scene. The closing scene was too difficult to begin with an untried actress, so he settled to start on the flower stand.

As it turned out this was to give him more trouble than any other sequence he had attempted. From the start he began to have doubts about Virginia. It has become legendary how Chaplin spent shot after shot, hour after hour, day after day, trying to get her to hand a flower with the line and rhythm he wanted, and to speak to his satisfaction a line – 'Flower, sir?' – which was never to be heard. The fault was not all Virginia's inexperience. One problem, undoubtedly was that for the first time Chaplin was working with a leading lady with whom he felt no personal contact of affection or even liking. 'I never liked Charlie and he never liked me,' said Virginia more than half a century later.[4] He never met her outside the studio or invited her to his home. Many years later, when he wrote his autobiography, Chaplin admitted it was not Virginia's fault, but 'partly my own, for I had worked myself into a neurotic state of wanting perfection'. His state was aggravated no doubt by his anxiety over the arrival of sound films. He was bothered too by the necessary presence of the extras when he was working on a scene requiring such delicate handling. His friend the artist and cartoonist Ralph Barton recorded some moments of the work with a 16mm camera, and captured a moment of sudden fearsome anger as Chaplin rounds on an assistant who is apparently responsible for the extras.

Along with his 'neurotic state of wanting perfection', Chaplin had a very clear idea of what he wanted from this scene, as he described, almost forty years later, to Richard Meryman:

Everything I do is a dance. I think in terms of dance. I think more so in *City Lights*. The blind girl – beautiful dance there. I call it a dance. Just purely pantomime. The girl extends her hand. And the Tramp doesn't know she's blind. And he says, 'I'll take this one.' 'Which one?' He looks incredulous – what a stupid girl . . . Then the flower falls to the ground; and she goes to feel for where it is. I pick it up and hold it there for a moment. And then she says, 'Have you found it sir?' And then he looks, and realizes. He holds it in front of her eyes – just makes a gesture. Not much. That is completely dancing . . . It took a long time. We took this day after day after day . . .

She'd be doing something which wasn't right. Lines. A line. A contour hurts me if it's not right. And she'd say, 'Flower, sir?' I'd say, 'Look at that! Nobody says "flower" like that.' She was an amateur . . .

I'd know in a minute when she wasn't there, when she'd be searching, or looking up just too much or too soon . . . Or she waited a second. I'd know in a minute.[5]

The minutes went by, and the days, from 29 January to 14 February. On 20 February they tried again, changing the action of the scene. Then on 25 February Chaplin fell ill, apparently with ptomaine poisoning, though acute anxiety may have had something to do with it. The stomach infection passed into influenza, and Chaplin did not return to the studio, except for a couple of conferences with the staff, during the whole of March. He returned on 1 April determined to start the flower stand scene all over again. After ten days he was still not satisfied, but decided to set it aside and start on another sequence.

By this time he had decided – it was to prove a stroke of genius – to open the film with a scene which, in a single stroke of comic irony, sums up the economic and social inequalities of modern urban life. In its completed form the scene opens on a large crowd assembled for the unveiling of a monument, 'Peace and Prosperity'. A stout civic dignitary and a hawk-like club woman make speeches, and the monument is unveiled. There, cradled in the lap of the central female figure, is the disreputable and calmly sleeping figure of the Tramp. When ordered to descend by the angry and embarrassed officials, he does his best, but manages to get the sword of Peace (!) entangled in his trousers. Thus suspended he loyally attempts to maintain a position of attention throughout the playing of the national anthem. The sequence ends with a mêlée and the Tramp's retreat.

This elaborate scene was finished, apart from some of Chaplin's close-ups, in a week: the presence and cost of a crowd of extras (one day 380 people were called for this sequence) was always an effective goad to Chaplin. Alf Reeves, who as manager of the studios saw his role as being to worry quietly, wrote to Sydney Chaplin with some satisfaction on 28 April:

> Charlie is working on his picture as usual but of course sound effects, if required, can be added afterwards.
>
> He is just in the midst of a sequence which looks to me as if it will be one of the greatest moments in motion picture comedy when it is finally cut. We are using four hundred extras in the scene.

The scene did, indeed, benefit from one of Chaplin's happiest aural gags, asserting right at the start of the film his hostility to sound films. The speeches of the dignitary and the lady were rendered by jabbering saxophones which burlesqued the metallic tones of early talkie voices. Adept lip-readers, however, are able to observe that Henry Bergman conscientiously mouths an actual speech:

> Ladies and Gentlemen – It is with great pleasure and admiration that I introduce these charming ladies who have done so much to make this moment possible. Miss-ess Fill-ber-nut! Also Miss-ess Oscar Beedell-Bottom. And last, but not least, Miss-ess Putt. Ladies and Gentlemen, I am only too happy to be able to do anything for this occasion, but I am sure you will know who is really responsible for this great moment. It is the artist himself, Mr Hugo Frothingham-Grimthorpe-Shafe-Shaferkee . . .

Poor Chaplin's already frayed nerves were not helped by major structural work that had now to be done on the studio. The city authorities had decided as part of a modernization scheme to widen La Brea Avenue, which meant that the studio buildings on that side, including office accommodation, dressing rooms and laboratories, had to be bodily moved back fifteen feet. Chaplin was at least able to move his shooting as far as possible from the building work, to the studio swimming pool where the suicide sequence was to be filmed. This was the sort of knockabout with which he anticipated no problems. The sequence had been fully worked out a month before: a note dated 24 May described the action:

> . . . At midnight we find Charlie wandering along the embankment searching for a place to sleep. As he is about to curl up in the darkness, we see the drunk arriving in evening dress clothes in a taxi-cab. He gets out with a large, heavy bundle under his arm – tosses a roll of bills to the taxi-cab driver – and staggers with his parcel to the edge of the river. From the package he takes a large stone with a rope tied round it. As he

commences to knot the rope around his neck, Charlie rushes out to stop him from suicide. In the argument Charlie gets the rope around his own neck and as the drunk heaves the stone into the river to take his own life, Charlie is thrown in. The drunk rescues him and takes him home where he confides to Charlie as he is feeding the latter brandy in front of a fire that he is bored with life. He points to a photograph of a beautiful woman and indicates that he is bored with her. To show how little anything means to him he throws a roll of bills into the fire . . .

Henry Clive, as the millionaire, did his scenes admirably; but on the third day of shooting, when it was his turn to fall into the water, he demurred. He explained he had bronchial trouble and had not been well recently, and asked if they could wait until the sun had been on the water for a while. Chaplin left the set in a fury and Carl Robinson was sent back to tell Clive that he was dismissed. The friendship ended then and there. Four days later Chaplin resumed work with a new actor, Harry Myers, in the role. Myers was a veteran who had started his career in vaudeville and joined the Biograph Company about the same time as Mack Sennett. Since then he had played leading roles in over fifty films (including *Up in Mabel's Room* and *Getting Gertie's Garter*), and was too much the professional to be bothered by a little cold water, or even a pool-full. After the conclusion of the water-suicide scene and a few location exteriors shot at Pasadena Bridge in the small hours of 11 July, the building operations at the studio, added to the extreme heat of the summer of 1929, brought work to a total halt.

Not until the middle of August was the laboratory reconstructed and the other buildings that had suffered from the removal redecorated and refurnished. The enforced lay-off had at least given Chaplin leisure to work out an entirely new piece of business, which he now spent seven days shooting. This seven-minute sequence is one of the most fascinating creations of Chaplin's *oeuvre*, not least because it was in the end never used. As a series of variations, escalating in absurdity, on a single theme, it might have been a Karno sketch; but Chaplin makes it one of the great peaks of his comic invention and execution.

All that happens is that the Tramp, walking past the window of a dress shop, spies a piece of wood wedged between the bars of a grating in the pavement. Idly he prods it with his stick to try to release it, but it only pivots in position and stays there. He becomes intrigued, engrossed, and involves the spectator in his mounting frustration. A crowd gathers and the inevitable cop has to disperse them, with accusatory glances at Charlie, who pretends of course that he has nothing to do with it. When he returns to the problem of the stick, innocent bystanders become involved. A messenger boy of dim and soporific mien which gives the lie to the message 'EXPRESS' emblazoned on his cap, stops to gaze with contempt. He is chewing an orange and absently spits his peel at Charlie, whose natural fastidiousness is affronted. The boy is paid out next moment when he squirts himself in the eye with juice. When he has passed on, two women stop to look in the window. Charlie is far too engrossed to notice the interruption, and with his stick fumbles between the stouter lady's feet, below her skirts. The ladies walk on in understandable huff. Then a display artist in the shop window (Harry Crocker) involves himself, mouthing and signalling his increasingly testy advice through the sound-barrier of the plate glass window. Inattention brings troubles for him too: he absently sticks a price tag not onto the dummy as intended, but onto the rear of a stout manageress. The sketch ends with a fine anti-climactic dénouement when the stick, unnoticed by Charlie and the entourage he has collected, simply slips away.

The messenger boy – a haunting figure whose malevolent, wooden-faced idiocy gives him the look of a distant and mentally retarded cousin of Buster Keaton – was played by Charles Lederer, Marion Davies's favourite nephew, the son of her sister Reine Douras. Eighteen or thereabouts at this time, he was already a favourite – even with Hearst himself – at San Simeon, for his intelligence, wit and outrageous pranks. In later years he was to become a successful Hollywood writer and less successful director. He was also co-writer, with Luther Davis, of the stage musical *Kismet*. No doubt Marion Davies or Harry Crocker – often Lederer's co-conspirator in practical jokes – had recommended him to Chaplin; or Chaplin may have met him and been taken with him, like the rest of the circle at San Simeon.

Almost forty years later, when Richard Meryman interviewed him, Chaplin recalled the sequence with enormous pleasure: 'a beautiful sequence . . . It was marvellous.' He remembered it all and could still act it out, and thought that Lederer's messenger boy was 'very well acted'. The decision in the end not to use it shows that however prolix Chaplin's invention in the stages of inventing a story, his rigour in eliminating the inessential or distracting – 'shaking the tree' – was extreme. The sequence – as Chaplin said, 'a whole story in itself' – was not seen publicly for more than fifty years, until it was included by Kevin Brownlow and David Gill in their *Unknown Chaplin*.

Chaplin went on to film a solo gag that does remain in the final film. The Tramp pauses in front of the window of an art store, in the centre of which is a voluptuous nude statuette. He legitimizes his interest by affecting the poses of a connoisseur, sizing up the art works with a fine critical detachment. As he steps backwards and forwards for the sake of better perspective, he does not notice an elevator in the pavement which is moving constantly up and down, its arrival at ground level always luckily coinciding with the moment he chooses to step upon it. When, finally, he takes too sudden a step and almost falls into the hole, he upbraids the workman whose head alone is seen protruding from the hole. The elevator rises and rises, gradually revealing the full seven feet (as it seems) of the powerful figure. Charlie's indignation is somewhat tempered by the revelation of his opponent's stature.

The trick with the elevator was simply done, by having the camera in the shop window looking out, and someone behind the camera keeping watch on the elevator and signalling to Chaplin its position. He rehearsed the effect on film, wearing smart everyday clothes, and the rehearsal scene still survives (it is also included in *Unknown Chaplin*). The comparison between the graceful gymnastics of the handsome, elegant man in white flannels and sweater and the comical cuts of the little Tramp are perhaps the most vivid illustration we have of the way the costume and make-up wholly metamorphosed the personality of the man within.

Chaplin's moods remained very erratic. One morning early in September 1929, when he had just begun rehearsing the scene in which the millionaire takes the Tramp to a night club, he telephoned Alf Reeves from his home and told him, 'I will not set foot in the studio as long as Crocker stays there.' He then hung up. Reeves found Crocker preparing the day's schedule, and passed on the message.

'What does that mean?' asked Crocker.

'I don't know,' replied Reeves, 'but in your place I would hand in my resignation.'[6]

Crocker did so. The reasons for the rift must have been extremely personal, since neither Chaplin nor Crocker spoke of them, and no one else at the studio could guess at them. Henry Bergman and Carlyle Robinson were no doubt delighted to be reinstated to the roles of Chaplin's confidants: they had felt somewhat eclipsed by the friendships with Clive and Crocker.

The next month went by calmly enough, with rehearsals and the filming of the night club scene, in which the drunken millionaire and a tipsy Charlie introduce a touch of chaos with cigars, matches, seltzer water, and spaghetti that gets mixed up with the party streamers. Charlie has unfortunate encounters with a stout lady dancer, an over-loaded waiter and an apache floorshow act.

Chaplin now prepared to resume work with Virginia Cherrill. Though she had reported daily to the studio, she had not been required in front of the cameras for more than six months. During that time Chaplin's feelings towards her had not improved. The other members of the unit were puzzled by his evident coolness, but perhaps it was not so surprising. Virginia was not, and could not be, a worker in the sense that Chaplin understood the term. She was not a career actress, nor dependent upon her job at the studio. She probably showed clearly that she was bored with the months of inactivity. She went to parties at night, and showed the effects of tiredness the day after. Chaplin throughout his career desperately needed collaborators who could share in his enthusiasm.

Many years later Chaplin explained to Richard Meryman how the essential impetus of his creation was enthusiasm: 'An idea will generate enthusiasm, and then you're off! The enthusiasm only lasts for a little while, and then you wait for another day. It replenishes itself, and you start again. If something is right, and I think it is right, then it will generate enthusiasm.' The problem was that enthusiasm was vulnerable to the mood of those around. 'If I get an idea and someone tries to dampen my enthusiasm, then I'm lost. That's what it is. It's a fact that my enthusiasm is the thing that makes me mad and everything else.' Virginia's inability to reflect his enthusiasm undoubtedly made him mad. She went before the cameras again on Monday 4 November 1929. He worked her in with an easy scene, then he wanted to attempt the crucial final scene of the film. By Saturday they were ready to try a few close-ups and Chaplin announced that they would continue the scene on the following Monday. It is not quite certain what happened on that day: the version related by Chaplin's son Sydney is that just when his father was keyed up for this most emotional and difficult scene, Virginia innocently if tactlessly asked if she could leave early because she had a hair appointment. Chaplin, who always needed an intermediary for such unpleasant jobs, instructed Carlyle Robinson to tell Virginia that she would not be required for work in the near future. Georgia Hale, who had not worked in films for more than a year, was called in that same day, and was overjoyed to be put on the payroll. Two days later Chaplin began to test Georgia in the role of the girl, in the last scene of the film. Every writer on Chaplin has marvelled at the recklessness of his decision to replace his leading lady after almost a year's shooting. In fact during that time he had used Virginia in only two sequences, neither of which had been completed to his satisfaction. Similarly the replacement of Henry Clive had represented only three lost shooting days. Many directors – including Chaplin himself – were often more prodigal.

Those tests of Georgia survive. She would have been a very beautiful flower girl, and her work on *The Gold Rush* proved that she could be tender as well as crisply gay. She loved the part and longed to play it:

> Oh, that *City Lights*. That's what I would have loved to do. And I had it, you know. We went to dinner at the Double Eagle on Sunset afterwards and he told me 'You've got the part. You're going to do it. Now I'll get what I want.'[7]

The following morning Chaplin ran the tests. The others in the projection room all agreed that she could do the part, but Carlyle Robinson, who appears to have liked Virginia more than the others, was highly critical. He told Chaplin that Georgia could no more do this part than Virginia could have played the dance hall girl in *The Gold Rush*. Chaplin was disturbed and annoyed, but Robinson followed up this attack skilfully. Knowing Chaplin's sensitivity in this area, he warned him that Georgia would certainly sue him if he did not give her the part. It was always a weakness of the Chaplin brothers that suspicion once planted in their minds rapidly grew to seem reality. Chaplin was persuaded. Next time he met Georgia he was chilly.

> Then he told me what a terrible person I was, and he raved and raved and raved. He only calmed down when he realized I had no idea what he was talking about. Then he said, 'But I thought you were going to sue me.' Oh, I wanted to do that part. I loved that part so.[8]

Chaplin, however, was not to change his mind again.

Next he tested a beautiful and clever sixteen-year-old blonde called Violet Krauth, who had taken the professional name of Marilyn

Morgan, and arrived at the studio with her mother. Chaplin was enthusiastic at her tests, and decided to draw up a contract there and then. Reeves and Robinson, however, knew his indecisive state of mind at the time, and moreover felt nervous at the arrival of yet another sixteen-year-old with a mother in tow. It was late in the afternoon: Reeves and Robinson tactically sent the secretary home, so that they were obliged to tell Chaplin that the contract could not be prepared that night as there was no one to type it. As they had anticipated, Chaplin's enthusiasm had faded somewhat the next morning, and Robinson was instructed to break it gently to Miss Morgan and her mother that he had changed his mind. The girl accepted the rejection with good grace which considerably impressed the two conspirators, Robinson and Reeves. Under a new name of Marion Marsh she went on to enjoy a small but bright career as a leading lady of the 1930s; among other films she starred in Josef von Sternberg's *Crime and Punishment*.

A week after she had left, Virginia was asked to return to the studio. As she remembers the events, she had in the meantime discussed the business with Marion Davies. On Marion's advice, she now told Chaplin that she would not come back unless he doubled her previous salary of $75 a week. Chaplin protested, but she pointed out that their agreement had been signed when she was under age and so had never been legally valid. Chaplin, says Virginia, gave in. While he probably felt that insult was added to injury, it may be that this show of spirit, or even spite, on Virginia's part actually raised her in his estimation. According to Carlyle Robinson, when Virginia returned to the studio Chaplin sent for her to go to his dressing room, and she emerged after an hour's interview chastened and tearful. From this time on, Chaplin seems to have had no serious difficulties in working with her. Perhaps he began to realize that a professional Hollywood actress could not have done the part better. Perhaps precisely because she *was* so phlegmatic about her work, her interpretation wholly resists all the obvious pitfalls of sentimentality. After fifty years the performance that resulted from the eventual mutual patience (or forbearance) of director and actress remains pure and charming.

For the role of the girl's mother (when the film was finished the role was re-named as her grandmother) Chaplin hired an experienced old character actress, Florence D. Lee, who gave none of the problems of the stage-trained matriarch, Lydia Knott, in *A Woman of Paris*. For five weeks Chaplin worked with Virginia and Mrs Lee on the uncomplicated scenes in their home. In the final days of 1929 he took the plunge and started out again on the flower stand sequence. None of the material he had shot before satisfied him: for the new takes he even decided on a different costume for Virginia. This time, in only six days' shooting he seems to have achieved his 'dance': except for one or two minor retakes, this troublesome, marvellous scene was done at last. After all the agonies, it would, as Alistair Cooke remarked of it, flow as easily as water over pebbles.

The reinstatement of Virginia Cherrill and the successful completion of the flower stand scene were a turning point in the film. The shooting had gone on for over a year and there were still nine months to go but after this, though Chaplin must often have been exhausted, his anxieties had dissipated. There is no more record of quarrels and sackings. Virgina had three more months of idleness – her job must have seemed quite boring sometimes – while Chaplin went back to work with Harry Myers on the millionaire scenes. Allan Garcia was cast as the millionaire's butler, required to act, straight-faced, according to the whims of his master as he now clutches the tramp to his bosom, now orders him to be thrown out. The 'whoopee party' in the millionaire's house at which a tipsy Charlie commits various faux-pas like mistaking an old gentleman's bald head for a blancmange, and swallowing a whistle which chirps as he hiccups, involved thirty extras and an orchestra which cost $80 a day. Sometimes Chaplin could indulge in extravagance. The singer whose soulful ballad is constantly interrupted by the cheeps of Charlie's whistle was not just another extra, but a *real* singer, whose fee was $50 a day, even though his voice would not be heard from the screen. No doubt Chaplin felt that an extra could not convincingly mime the style of the professional performer.

Throughout most of March and April Chaplin was working on the various sequences that take place in the millionaire's house. When he needed an exterior for this he found it on location, at Town House, Wilshire Boulevard. In the roles of the burglars who break into the house he cast Joe Van Meter and Albert Austin – the last time that an old Karno colleague would appear in a Chaplin film.

Only one major comedy sequence now remained to be shot. Chaplin had left the prize-fight scenes to the end. The speed and concentration with which they were filmed reveals that they represented one of Chaplin's greatest bursts of 'enthusiasm'. To the end of his life the sequence continued to give him immense pleasure and satisfaction.

For his opponent he engaged the hang-dog giant Hank Mann, with whom he had worked in his third Keystone film and often afterwards, and who had since made a considerable career in Hollywood. The dignified referee was Eddie Baker, an actor who had been seen in only one of two small parts. A dozen extras had sufficed for a previous Chaplin bout in *The Champion*. For the fight scenes in *City Lights* more than a hundred extras were hired for the audience. The fight was rehearsed in four days and shot in six, and proved the apogee of Chaplin's 'dance' in slapstick mode.

By the end of July 1930 the shooting of *City Lights* was all but finished, but for six weeks more Chaplin nervously continued with innumerable retakes before the various artists' engagements should come to an end. On 25 August he shot some scenes in which two cheeky newsboys on a street corner mock the Tramp. They were to appear twice – once at the beginning of the film where the Tramp affects a contemptuous insouciance in reply to their mockery; the second time immediately before the final scene, where, in his wretchedness after a jail sentence, he is as miserably vulnerable as a mangy stray. Chaplin seems to have worked easily with children, perhaps because they were simply required to copy his own actions; and the shots required only half a day. One of the newsboys, a pretty, round-faced, insolent child, was Robert Parrish, who in time would become a prominent Hollywood editor and director. In his memoirs he recalled:

> He would blow a pea [from Parrish's peashooter] and then run over and pretend to be hit by it, then back to blow another pea. He became a kind of dervish, playing all the parts, using all the props, seeing and cane-twisting as the Tramp, not seeing and grateful as the blind girl, peashooting as the newsboys. Austin [the other boy actor] and I and Miss Cherrill watched while Charlie did his show. Finally, he had it all worked out and reluctantly gave us back our parts. I felt that he would much rather have played all of them himself.[9]

Chaplin had left to the end the retakes on the final scene. He spent six days on the general action inside and outside the flower shop, then on 22 September 1930 once more attempted the critical final close-ups with Virginia. This time there were no problems, no anxieties, no hair appointments. They worked from 2.30 to 5.30 that afternoon, and made seventeen takes. Whatever it was – enthusiasm, inspiration, magic – this time it worked, as Chaplin remembered four decades later:

Sometimes it comes through with a great deal of that magic. I've had that once or twice ... I had one close-up once, in *City Lights*, just the last scene. One could have gone overboard ... I was looking more at her and interested in her, and I detached myself in a way that gives a beautiful sensation. I'm not acting ... almost apologetic, standing outside myself and looking, studying her reactions and being slightly embarrassed about it. And it came off. It's a beautiful scene, beautiful; and because it isn't over-acted.[10]

Richard Meryman said to Chaplin that he thought the ending of *City Lights* was one of the greatest moments in films ever. Chaplin replied simply: 'Well, I know it was *right*.' James Agee, less restrained, wrote that 'It is enough to shrivel the heart to see, and it is the greatest piece of acting and the highest moment in movies.'[11]

Among the pick-up shots that were all that now remained to be done, Chaplin had a pleasant afterthought, and devised a piece of slapstick nonsense to play with Albert Austin, a nostalgic tribute to their many adventures together with Karno, Essanay and Mutual. A corner of the public market at Vine and Melrose did service as the public street-cleaners' yard, and Chaplin and Austin, as sweepers, sat down to one of the odorous and onion-scented packed lunches that had so often figured in the early shorts. In this case Charlie, blinded by suds as he is washing his face, seizes poor Austin's cheese in mistake for the soap, while myopic Austin takes a hearty bite from a soap sandwich. The sequence ends with Austin attempting to bawl out Charlie, but only managing to erupt in clouds of soap bubbles. It was the last appearance before the cameras of this loyal old collaborator.

The cutting and titling of *City Lights* took from mid-October to mid-December. The film was finished, but it was a *silent* film. By this time, however, after *Broadway Melody*, *All Quiet on the Western Front*, *Hallelujah!*, *Sous les Toits de Paris* and *The Blue Angel*, the silent cinema was an anachronism. Chaplin, though he may still have hoped, had evidently foreseen the possibility: such gags as the swallowed whistle and the incidents that ensue from it must have been conceived in anticipation of sound synchronization. In April 1929, as we have seen, Alf Reeves had written to Sydney that 'sound effects, if required, can be added afterwards'. On 16 May 1930 he wrote again, confirming: '... he intends to synchronize it for sound and music ... no dialogue.'

Chaplin was to surprise his collaborators, and all Hollywood into the bargain. Other directors, having completed their films, simply handed them over to the musical arrangers who had descended upon Hollywood since 1927 – many of them former directors of cinema orchestras whose jobs had been taken from them by the advent of synchronized films. Chaplin, who since *A Woman of Paris* had taken a keen interest in the musical accompaniments for his silent films, determined that he would create his own musical accompaniment.

Chaplin had no musical training, but he had an irrepressible musical gift. In 1915 his Aunt Kate considered that

> If Charles Chaplin remains a picture actor, the musical world will be a genius less ... As a baby, he would stop playing with his toys the instant he heard music of any description, and would beat time with his tiny hand and nod his head until the music ceased. In later years I have seen him sit for hours at the piano, composing as he went along.
>
> The 'cello was the instrument I think he loved best, 'because it was so plaintive', he said. I took a delight in watching his changing expression and his small hand quivering as he touched the chords. It was almost a caress.
>
> It was only when he caught my eyes glistening that he would laugh, and suddenly do some funny little movement or dash off a gay air. This would immediately change my sad mood to one scream of laughter ...

In 1921, seeing Kennington Cross again had awakened strange memories for Charlie:

> It was here that I first discovered music, or where I first learned its rare beauty, a beauty that has gladdened and haunted me from that moment. It all happened one night when I was there, about midnight. I recall the whole thing so distinctly.
>
> I was just a boy, and its beauty was like some sweet mystery. I did not understand. I only knew that I loved it and I became reverent as the sounds carried themselves through my brain *via* my heart.
>
> I suddenly became aware of a harmonica and a clarinet playing a weird, harmonious message. I learned later that it was 'The Honeysuckle and the Bee'. It was played with such feeling that I became conscious for the first time of what melody really was. My first awakening to music.
>
> I remembered how thrilled I was as the sweet sounds pealed into the night. I learned the words the next day. How I ... would love to hear it now, that same tune, that same way!
>
> Kennington Cross, where music first entered my soul. Trivial, perhaps, but it was the first time.[12]

Chaplin acquired his 'cello and violin when he was about sixteen, and painstakingly heaved them about on his various tours, taking

lessons from the musical directors of the theatres where he played
and practising from four to six hours a day. He played left-handed,
which meant that his violin had to be strung with the bass bar and
sounding post reversed from normal mode. He would improvise for
hours on the piano, and when he built his own home, installed a
costly pipe organ. In 1916 he started the Charles Chaplin Music
Corporation which was short-lived but published three of his compositions, 'There's Always One You Can't Forget', 'Oh, That 'Cello'
and 'The Peace Patrol'. He conducted Sousa's Band in a performance
of the last of these, along with the 'Poet and Peasant' overture at a
benefit concert at the New York Hippodrome on 20 February 1916.
In 1921 he composed special themes for *The Kid* and *The Idle Class*;
and in 1925 published two more compositions, 'Sing a Song' and
'With You Dear in Bombay' of which he also made a recording with
Abe Lyman's orchestra.

Something of the universal appeal of Chaplin's screen character
emerged in his composition also: the themes of *Modern Times* and
Limelight were to win a place among perennial favourites of popular
music. In method (the use of recurrent *leitmotifs* and strong emotional
themes) and power, Chaplin's film scores were akin to the musical
accompaniments of nineteenth-century drama which still occasionally
lingered in his boyhood. It cannot be without significance that among
Chaplin's working papers for the score to accompany *A Woman of
Paris* was a copy of André Wormser's music for *L'Enfant Prodigue*,
the most famous nineteenth-century mime play. It was revived several
times during Chaplin's youth, and it seems unlikely, with his already
conscious interest in pantomime, that he would have failed to see it.

After the première of *City Lights*, Chaplin told a reporter from the
New York Telegram: 'I really didn't write it down. I la-laed and
Arthur Johnson wrote it down, and I wish you would give him credit,
because he did a very good job. It is all simple music, you know, in
keeping with my character.'

Chaplin's work on the score with Arthur Johnson lasted six weeks.
The score had almost a hundred musical cues: the principal original
themes created by Chaplin included a trumpet fanfare, a kind of fate
theme which introduced the film and various subsequent sequences,
a 'cello theme for the Tramp, a mixture of operatic burlesque and Al
Jolson laughing-through-tears melodies for the suicide scenes, a jazz
motif for the nightclub, and a combination of comic tango and 'hurry'
music for the boxing match. The blind girl had several variant themes,

though the principal motif was Padilla's 'La Violetera', which had made a great impression on Chaplin when he had first heard it sung by Raquel Meller in 1926. Other musical quotations used for comic effect included a snatch of *Scheherezade*, 'I Hear You Calling Me' and 'How Dry Am I'. Chaplin always had difficulties with arrangers who wanted to make the music funny. 'I wanted no competition. I wanted the music to be a counterpoint of grace and charm . . . I tried to compose elegant and romantic music to frame my comedies . . .' In the same way he disliked the 'mickey-mousing' technique of directly pointing gags with sound effects and snare drums. In *City Lights* the effects are sparingly used: mainly for the whistle gag, for the saxophone voices of the officials at the unveiling, for pistol shots and the bells in the boxing ring.

The music was recorded over a period of five days under the direction of Alfred Newman, United Artists' musical director, and Ted Reed, who was in charge of sound and recording. Only Henry Bergman, with his musical background, was deeply disappointed in the results: 'It is interesting, the terrible deficiencies of the medium are too apparent. I don't think they will ever overcome them. Thirty-five of the very finest artists played the score for *City Lights* so beautifully on the set. Through the mechanics of the microphone it became something else.'

Chaplin was deeply depressed by the preview at the Tower Theatre, Los Angeles. The theatre was only half full and the audience, who had gone expecting to see the adventure drama which had been billed, was apathetic. As a result of the reactions he trimmed the film a little, though re-cutting, which had been a regular practice in silent films, was not so cheap or easy with sound. The notices which appeared on the day of the première, following the previous day's press show, were distinctly more heartening. A veteran critic on the *Los Angeles Examiner* recalled happily that 'not since I reviewed the first Chaplin comedy way back in the two-reel days has Charlie given us such an orgy of laughs.' *The Record* said:

Nobody in the world but Charlie Chaplin could have done it. He is the only person that has that peculiar something called 'audience appeal' in sufficient quantity to defy the popular penchant for pictures that talk. *City Lights*, though it was received with whole-hearted delight and punctuated with innumerable bursts of applause from the audience, is no menace for the talkies. It is the exception that proves the rule. It is sure to be an immense box-office attraction. He has made a picture that the world will want to see. Charlie Chaplin is an institution.

Even institutions have first-night nerves. Henry Bergman remembered that on the afternoon of the première, 'I was just leaving the studio in my car when Charlie drove up. At once he came to me and said in all seriousness, "Henry, I don't know so much about that picture. I'm not sure." And I said to him, "I'm telling you Charlie, I've never failed you yet, have I? If this isn't right, you'll quit the business and go to live abroad on what you've got. Nobody could do what you've done."'

The première, on 30 January 1931, went down to legend as the greatest Hollywood had ever seen – though it was not in fact held in Hollywood. Until this time premières had always been held in the handful of Hollywood picture palaces; but Chaplin decided to show *City Lights* in the brand new Los Angeles Theatre on Broadway, between 6th and 7th Streets. It was equipped with restaurant, soda fountain, art gallery, 'crying-room' for mothers with babies, ballroom, shoeshine parlour, broadcasting room, playroom, French cosmetics room and practically anything else the Californian heart might yearn for. From early afternoon the Los Angeles police were out to try to control the crowds that congested the city centre in the hope of glimpsing some small flash of the evening's glamour. The traffic was halted, and department store windows broken by the sheer pressure of the crowds. At one point the police threatened to use tear gas. The guests who made their slow progress through the crush included the aristocracy of Hollywood – the Vidors, the De Milles, the Zanucks, the Schenks, the John Barrymores, the Jack Warners, Hedda Hopper, Gloria Swanson. The press were also pleased to point out the present of Marion Davies, Claire Windsor, Merna Kennedy and Georgia Hale. Chaplin's personal guests were Professor and Mrs Albert Einstein, in whose honour the entire house rose. The Einsteins were still rather too overcome at battling their way through the crowds fully to appreciate the gesture.

Chaplin was accompanied to the première by Georgia. 'Going down in the car, all the way he was like a little mouse. "I don't think it's going to go over," he said. "I don't think they're going to like it . . . No, I just feel it." He was like a shy little kid. He was always that way about his work.'

From the first shot the audience were delighted. All went well until the end of the third reel, when the film was stopped, the houselights turned on, and a bland voice announced that the show would be interrupted so that the audience could admire the beautiful features of the new theatre. The glittering audience forgot decorum and started to boo and whistle. Their indignation was as nothing compared to Chaplin's fury as he charged off in search of the management. The film was resumed; the audience was instantly recaptured. The ovation at the end vindicated all the months of work and anxiety.

The next day Chaplin left to make preparations for the New York opening. This resulted in a major row with United Artists. Chaplin found that pre-publicity in the East was negligible, while United Artists questioned his policy of raising seat prices to $1.50 (15¢ over the normal top price) for a film which they no doubt now regarded as out-dated. Moreover they were outraged by his demand for a rental of 50 per cent of the gross. Chaplin decided to exhibit his picture independently, and took whole-page advertisements in the trade press to announce the fact. The première took place in the old George M. Cohan Theatre, somewhat off the beaten track of major moving picture theatres. Chaplin's gamble paid off well: in its twelve weeks at the Cohan, the film grossed $400,000. Two months later, while Chaplin was in Europe, Alf Reeves was despatched to New York to inform Arthur Kelly, who had represented Chaplin's interests in United Artists, that his services were no longer needed.

The years of *City Lights* had left Chaplin with little time or inclination for social life. When shooting he worked a six- and sometimes seven-day week; evenings and Sundays were for rest and recuperation. In 1968 he recalled, with feeling, 'I had to correct and act and write and produce a film, cut it . . . and I did it all, which very few in my day did, you know. They didn't do it all, you see . . . And that's why I was so exhausted.' He told Richard Meryman: 'The evening is rather a lonesome place, you know, in California, especially Hollywood.'[13]

It was a measure of the quiet social life that Chaplin was leading at this time that during the entire production of *City Lights*, and indeed since the divorce, the gossip columnists had failed to sniff out or invent any romantic liaisons for him. At this period his most constant companion was Georgia Hale, loyal, worshipping and undemanding. Sometimes in the evening he would still stop in at Henry's restaurant, where he liked the lentil soup and coleslaw. Ivor Montagu, who met Chaplin about this time, greatly admired Georgia's qualities of character:

> She was a fine person, and, I firmly believe, one of the few women in Charlie's early life who cared for him frankly and unselfishly.
>
> One evening, returning from the Hollywood Bowl with a girlfriend she went for a late bite to Henry's . . . Henry Bergman came over to their table and they grew sentimental together.
>
> 'Ah,' said Georgia, 'three hearts that beat as one – yours, mine and Charlie's.'
>
> 'Yes,' replied Henry, 'and they're all thinking of the same thing, Charlie.'
>
> When we retold the tale to Charlie in Georgia's presence, Charlie considered, then admitted: 'Yes, it's true.'[14]

Montagu was in Hollywood with Sergei Eisenstein and Grigori Alexandrov who were there studying American sound techniques and hoping to set up productions of their own. When finally they reached Chaplin, thanks to Montagu's letters of introduction from Shaw and Wells, he was warm in his hospitality. 'Charlie's house and garden became our second home. We would always ring up and ask Kono before dropping in, but Kono who, when he wished, could be an impenetrable wall, treated inquiry from us as a polite formality. Sometimes we would be rung up and asked over.' The party was especially welcome because they played tennis – Montagu well, Alexandrov conscientiously.

> Even Sergei Mikhailovich [Eisenstein] bought ducks and tried pursuing the ball with a sort of savage spite. He spoiled all by wearing braces and scarlet ones at that, as well as a belt for security. When I told him this was improper he was downcast, but reassured when I added that braces for tennis were a practice of the late Lord Birkenhead.[15]

Since Georgia had introduced Chaplin to tennis in the late 1920s, the game had become a passion. He developed unusual skill and always liked to challenge professionals. He told Konrad Bercovici – who was astonished at the rejuvenation it had produced in Chaplin – that he played tennis for several hours every day, and found that it exorcized his prime fears. He loved its form and grace; it was not important, he said, if you hit the ball or not, provided that you moved gracefully and 'in form'. (This was not strictly true: he was distinctly displeased to lose at any time.) It was for him not only recreation but an experience of beauty. Other friends too remarked on the therapeutic value the game had for him. He continued to play with pleasure and skill until late in his life. As soon as the Chaplins had settled down in their Swiss home in 1953 a tennis court was built.

Sunday tennis parties broadened Chaplin's social life. In the ordinary way he had never much cared for big parties: he preferred the intimacy of small dinners. The absence of an official hostess at the Summit Drive house gave him the excuse to do little formal entertaining. 'It wasn't that he was stingy,' Georgia recalls, 'but it wasn't easy for him. He wasn't at ease. Sometimes though he would do a big party, to pay back all the people who had entertained him.' The Montagu-Eisenstein troupe's first visit was to a rather formal, English-style garden party at the house:

> Chaplin afterwards confessed to us that this was an 'occasional garden party' when enough people had piled up to whom he owed hospitality. From time to time he would nerve himself to hold one and rid himself of all the accumulated obligations in one fell swoop.[16]

Generally he allowed Mary Pickford and Douglas Fairbanks to organize his social life for him. He was an indispensable guest when there were distinguished visitors at Pickfair. Fairbanks' fondness for fellow-celebrities, particularly if they had a European title, was a byword. One day Chaplin asked him, 'How's the Duke, Doug?' 'What Duke?' asked Fairbanks, puzzled. 'Oh, any Duke,' replied Chaplin.

There were other foreign visitors to the Chaplin home in the summer of 1930. One day when Eisenstein and Ivor Montagu were at the house, two young Spaniards, Luis Buñuel and the writer Eduardo Ugarte were deposited there by a mutual friend. Buñuel, having achieved notoriety with the Surrealist masterpieces *Un Chien Andalou* and *L'Age d'Or*, had been whimsically offered a kind of traineeship by Metro Goldwyn Mayer, and as whimsically accepted it. The conversation when they arrived at the house was an embarrassed struggle in sign language: too late did Montagu and Eisenstein discover that Buñuel's French was faultless. Buñuel became a visitor at the house, and recalled in his autobiography how Chaplin had obligingly arranged an 'orgy' for him and two of his compatriots. Alas, 'when the three ravishing young women arrived from Pasadena, they immediately got into a tremendous argument over which one was going to get Chaplin, and in the end all three left in a huff.'

At Christmas 1930, Chaplin and Georgia were invited to a dinner party given by some of the Spanish colony. Buñuel, Ugarte and an actor named Pena decided to liven things up with a Surrealist incident, and leapt up from the dinner table to set about hacking down the Christmas tree. Buñuel admitted that 'it's not easy to dismember a Christmas tree. In fact, we got a great many scratches for some rather pathetic results, so we resigned ourselves to throwing the presents on the floor and stomping on them.' The other guests were shocked. Nevertheless Chaplin ('a forgiving man') invited the Spaniards to his New Year's Eve party. They arrived to find an enormous Christmas tree. Chaplin took Buñuel aside before dinner and said, 'Since you're so fond of tearing up trees, Buñuel, why don't you get it over with now, so we won't be disturbed during dinner?'

'I replied,' said Buñuel, 'that I really had nothing against trees . . .'[17]

Buñuel remembered other visits to Chaplin's home. Several times he screened *Un Chien Andalou*: the first time Kono, who was running the projector, fainted away when he saw the opening scene of a razor blade slicing an eye. Years later Buñuel was delighted to learn from Carlos Saura that according to Geraldine Chaplin her father used to frighten the children by describing scenes from Buñuel's films.[18]

One day Buñuel was invited to see some rushes from *City Lights* with the writer Edgar Neville, who seems to have been officially attached to the unit for a while. Buñuel was too timid to declare his opinion, but Neville suggested that the scene with the swallowed whistle went on too long. Chaplin later cut it. 'Curiously, he seemed to lack self-confidence and had a good deal of trouble making decisions.' Georgia remarked the same when she watched rushes with Chaplin. 'He was real humble about some things. At rushes he'd ask, "Which one did you like?" And I'd tell him; and he would consider it. Then I got that I didn't want to see the rushes. It disturbed me seeing it out of continuity. When he *directed* you the continuity was there, because he would tell you before all that had happened up to that moment.'[19]

One of Buñuel's stories is engaging but inaccurate in detail: 'He also had strange work habits, which included composing the music for his films while sleeping. He'd set up a complicated recording device at his bedside and used to wake up partway, hum a few bars, and go back to sleep. He composed the entire score of "La Violetera" that way, a plagiarism that earned him a very costly trial.'[20] Although Chaplin may have re-composed the piece in his dreams, he was never in any doubt about its origins in his waking hours. Although there was some costly wrangling over copyright fees, there was certainly no plagiarism suit.

13

Away from it all

When Chaplin left Hollywood the day following the première of *City Lights*, neither he nor any of his entourage and friends could have guessed that it would be a year and four months before he returned. His immediate plans were to attend the New York and London premières of the film, and thereafter take a brief European holiday, perhaps of the duration of the 1921 trip. Writing just after his return Chaplin himself explained, 'The disillusion of love, fame and fortune left me somewhat apathetic . . . I needed emotional stimulus . . . like all egocentrics I turn to myself. I want to live in my youth again.'[1]

After two disastrous marriages and a succession of inconclusive love affairs, he was without doubt emotionally unsettled. Some of those nearest to him suspected that he was at this time eager to evade the perilous affections of Marion Davies, who by 1931 was a great deal more interested in Chaplin than Chaplin was in her. Certainly he felt disoriented professionally. Four years after the definitive establishment of sound films, he had got away with making what was virtually a silent film; but could he do it again? 'I was obsessed by a depressing fear of being old-fashioned,' he later admitted.

No doubt the holiday was a matter of playing for time and a search for new roles in his private life. 'He is,' wrote Thomas Burke, who by intuition probably knew Chaplin better than anyone else,

> first and last an actor, possessed by this, that or the other. He lives only in a role, and without it he is lost . . . He can be anything you expect him to be, and anything you don't expect him to be, and he can maintain the role for weeks . . .
>
> From time to time this imagined life changes. When he was in England

ten years ago, he was with every conviction the sad, remote Byronic figure – the friend of unseen millions and the loneliest man in the world. That period has passed. On his last visit to England* his role was that of the playboy, the Tyl Eulenspiegel of today.

In New York he was met by the usual crowd of reporters. Among the interviews he granted was one by transatlantic telephone to London. He much regretted this ordeal and adamantly refused to do the same for an Australian newspaper. It was at this time too that he refused an offer of $670,000 for twenty-six weekly radio broadcasts – which would have been the highest fee paid to any broadcaster up to that time. Apart from that his brief time in New York was taken up in social engagements on Fifth or Park Avenue, arrangements for the independent exhibition of *City Lights*, and a visit to Sing Sing, where he showed his new film to an audience of inmates, and was deeply touched by their enthusiasm. Carlyle Robinson had received a tip-off which made him fear an impending kidnap attempt, and he and Arthur Kelly arranged for Chaplin to be shadowed by two hefty detectives.

It had been decided that Robinson and Kono would accompany Chaplin to Europe, and Robinson was as usual entrusted with the arrangements. Unfortunately by this period Chaplin had conceived a growing dislike of Robinson, which was to come to a head during the impending trip and result in Robinson's dismissal after fourteen years' service. The explanation may have been that Robinson had by this time become more opinionated than Chaplin liked the people around him to be. Robinson was accustomed to joke that his job was less often that of 'press agent' than of 'sup-press agent'; and his constant anxiety to anticipate, forestall or cover up any indiscretions, *faux pas* or unintentional discourtesies on Chaplin's part threw him into a nannyish role which cannot have made relations with his boss especially easy.

It may have been partly to avoid being thrown too much upon Robinson's companionship that Chaplin at the last moment recruited an extra member of the touring entourage. This was his friend Ralph Barton, a well-known cartoonist and illustrator. Chaplin invited him along in the hope that it might allay the acute depression which had already resulted in one suicide attempt. Eccentric and hypersensitive, Barton was in deep despair after being deserted by the actress Carlotta

---

* i.e. 1931.

Monterey, who had left him to live with the playwright Eugene O'Neill. O'Neill was to become, a dozen years later, Chaplin's unwilling father-in-law. Coincidence always played a large role in Chaplin's life.

This last-minute change of plan caused Robinson some embarrassment. Having already negotiated special rates for three berths on the *Mauretania*, less than an hour before sailing he was now obliged to plead for an extra place on the ship, which was in theory fully booked. The problem was solved only by a shipping line official agreeing to share his cabin with Robinson, so that Barton could take Robinson's place in Chaplin's personal suite. During the voyage Chaplin finally yielded to the exhaustion that followed the years of work on *City Lights*. He rarely left his cabin, except for midnight walks on deck with Barton. Out of the mass of radiograms conveying good wishes and pressing invitations which he received, he responded only to three: from Lady Astor, Sir Phillip Sassoon and Alistair MacDonald, son of the Prime Minister, Ramsay MacDonald.

The *Mauretania* docked at Portsmouth, and Chaplin was delighted to find a private coach had been provided for the journey to Paddington. The rest of the train was full of journalists, but Chaplin pleaded tiredness and left Robinson to deal with them. Robinson was surprised therefore when the train made an unscheduled stop at a wayside station, and Chaplin energetically set to signing autographs for the large crowd of locals who had collected merely in the hope of seeing his train pass by. 'Weren't they nice people!' he murmured placidly as the train drew away again. At Paddington the crowds were as vast and enthusiastic as they had been at Waterloo ten years before, but the police were better prepared to deal with them; Chaplin obligingly mounted the roof of his car and waved his hat and stick, to the general delight.

An enormous suite had been reserved at the Carlton to accommodate Chaplin, Barton, Robinson and Kono; and Chaplin himself was impressed with its splendour: 'The saddest thing I can imagine is to get used to luxury. Each day I stepped into the Carlton was like entering a golden paradise. Being rich in London made life an exciting adventure every moment. The world was an entertainment. The performance started first thing in the morning.'

The performance involved a heady social whirl among the intellectual and political élite of London, mainly organized for him by Sassoon, Lady Astor and his old friend Edward Knoblock. At lunch

CARLTON HOTEL
LONDON, S.W. 1
Feb· 2 8·· 1931·

MR. CHARLES CHAPLIN begs to
acknowledge the receipt of your communication. Because of the enormous volume of
mail received by him, it is impossible at
this time to undertake to be more thorough
in writing Will you therefore kindly
accept this means of acknowledgment in
place of a personal letter.

1931 - Form of acknowledgement sent
to correspondents during Chaplin's
stay in London.

at Lady Astor's he had a lively debate on the world economy with
Maynard Keynes, and met Bernard Shaw for the first time. Initially
somewhat awed by Shaw, Chaplin decided after an argument or two
on the nature of art that he was 'just a benign old gentleman with a
great mind who uses his piercing intellect to hide his Irish sentiment'.
He frequently met H. G. Wells, who was now an established friend.
He was invited to Chartwell for the weekend by Winston Churchill,
whom he was to continue to admire deeply despite their apparent
political polarity. (Paradoxical and unpredictable as he was in this
respect, he even took the platform at one of Lady Astor's meetings
at the October 1931 election, though he had some difficulty in
explaining both to himself and his auditors this support for a Tory
candidate.) As guest of honour at a dinner party at Lady Astor's
home at Cliveden, Chaplin startled the guests – a carefully chosen

political spectrum, including Lloyd George – with an after-dinner speech in which he launched into a diatribe against complacent acceptance of the growth of the machine age. They could hardly have known that they were witnesses to the genesis of *Modern Times*.

Despite efforts to keep it from the press, Chaplin's visit to Chequers was much publicized. He seems to have been somewhat disappointed in the dour Labour premier, Ramsay MacDonald. A private meeting with Lloyd George arranged by Sassoon, who had served Lloyd George as secretary during his premiership, appears to have been at least more lively, with Chaplin enthusiastically developing a plan for clearance of the London slums.

Chaplin steeled himself to do something he had not brought himself to do in 1921: he visited the Hanwell Schools, where he had spent the loneliest months of his boyhood. Carlyle Robinson believed that he took Ralph Barton with him, but contemporary news reports suggest that he arrived alone and without any announcement. As soon as his arrival was known, however, the excitement in the school was intense.

> . . . He entered the dining hall, where four hundred boys and girls cheered their heads off at the sight of him – and he entered in style.
>
> He made to raise his hat, and it jumped magically into the air! He swung his cane and hit himself in the leg! He turned out his feet and hopped along inimitably. It was Charlie! Yells! Shrieks of joy! More yells!
>
> And he was enjoying himself as much as the children.
>
> He mounted the dais and announced solemnly that he would give an imitation of an old man inspecting some pictures. He turned his back and moved along, peering at the wall. Marvel of marvels – as he moved the old man grew visibly! A foot, two feet! A giant of an old man!
>
> The secret was plain if you faced him. His arms were stretched above his head; his overcoat was supported on his fingertips; his hat was balanced on the coat-collar.
>
> He saw the 'babies' bathed and in their night attire, sitting for a final warming round the fire, and the babies gave him another ovation, and he laughed like a baby.
>
> The children will never forget his visit.[2]

The experience seems to have made a great impression on Chaplin. Robinson alleged that Chaplin wept when he returned to the Carlton. A day or so later, however, Chaplin told Thomas Burke that it had been 'the greatest emotional experience of his life . . . He said excitedly that it *had* been fearful, but that he liked being hurt, and I

The Gold Rush: Lita Grey (Lillita McMurray) with Chaplin at the signing of her contract. Chaplin on the set (below); evidently things are not going quite right.

The Gold Rush: On location at Truckee (above). The 'sourdoughs' prepare for the great trek.

Left: Chaplin, out of costume, performs the Dance of the Rolls.

Above right: Preparing to film an elaborate travelling shot for a sequence which was never used. The scene was to have shown the hut being whirled at 100 miles an hour through the storm.

Right: Between takes on location. Chaplin as a chicken, with Mack Swain and Kono Toraichi.

The Gold Rush: Lita Grey (below) as leading lady and Georgia Hale (right) as leading lady.

Chaplin's first Hollywood home (above)
and his house on Summit Drive (below).

The Circus: Merna Kennedy (right).

Below: Chaplin succumbs to exhaustion. A photograph taken by Jack Wilson.

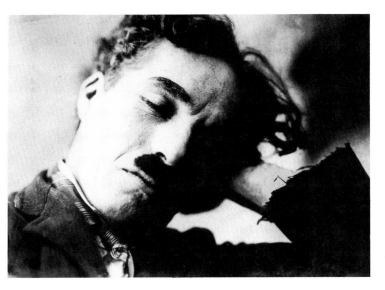

Left: The Lita Grey divorce. Lita takes the oath in court.

Right: After the studio fire.

Edna Purviance in two scenes from Josef von Sternberg's
Sea Gulls (*A Woman of the Sea*)

Sea Gulls (*A Woman of the Sea*): The cast and crew
on location (left). Flanking Edna Purviance are
the director Josef von Sternberg (on rock) and Gayne
Whitman. Standing behind Whitman is Eve Southern, and
to the right of her, Raymond Bloomer and Charles French.

Below: Edna Purviance and Gayne Whitman.

City Lights: Chaplin at the camera (left) and (right) on the set, with Ralph Barton by the fountain. When the film was finished, Barton accompanied Chaplin on the first stage of his world tour, but returned to New York and committed suicide.

Below: The studio back lot during the shooting of *City Lights*. The *trompe l'oeil* painted buildings can be clearly seen in the background. Chaplin can be seen at left of centre.

City Lights: Chaplin (above) in the costume of the Duke
for the projected dream sequence.
Below: Al Jolson, an important force in launching 'talkies',
visits Chaplin, the last director to resist them.

Above: Hannah Chaplin in 1921, while still in the nursing home in Peckham.

Right: Hannah in Hollywood, playing checkers with Amy Reeves.

Below: Hannah's grave in the Hollywood Cemetary, photographed in 1983.

Above right: Chaplin's sons, Sydney and Charles Jr, c. 1930.
Right: Chaplin, the bachelor, at home, c.1930.

The première of *City Lights*: Chaplin stands between
Mr and Mrs Albert Einstein

realized that his cold-blooded nature was interested in the throbbing of the neuralgia and the effects of the throbbing. He loves studying himself.'[3]

Chaplin told Burke,

I wouldn't have missed it for all I possess. It's what I've been wanting. God, you feel like the dead returning to earth. To smell the smell of the dining hall, and to remember that was where *you* sat, and that scratch on the pillar was made by *you*. Only it wasn't you. It was you in another life – your soul-mate – something you were and something you aren't now. Like a snake that sheds its skin every now and then. It's one of the skins you've shed, but it's still got your odour about it. O-o-oh, it was wonderful. When I got there, I knew it was what I'd been wanting for years. Everything had been leading up to it, and I was ripe for it. My return to London in 1921, and my return this year, were wonderful enough, but they were nothing to that. Being among those buildings and connecting with everything – with the misery and something that wasn't misery . . . The shock of it, too. You see, I never really believed that it'd be *there*. It was thirty years ago when I was there, and thirty years – why, nothing in America lasts that long. I wanted it to be, Oh God, how I wanted it to be, but I felt it couldn't be.

Well, I got a taxi, and told him the direction, and we started out for it. And when we got near the place it was all streets – and shops – and houses. And I guessed it was gone. I don't know what I'd have done if it was gone. I reckon I'd have gone right back to Hollywood. Because it was what I'd come for. I told the driver to go on, though I didn't think it was any good, because I'd always remembered that the place was in the country, with fields all round it. And then the taxi stopped . . . and then turned off the main road into something that looked like country fields and bushes. And then, all of a sudden, *th-ere* it was. O-o-oh, it was there – just as I'd left it. I've never had a moment like that in my life. I was almost physically sick with emotion.[4]

Burke chided him for his sentimentality in trying to recapture the past he had forever left behind. 'But one can pick it up and look at it,' he replied. 'One can think that one was happy once, or intensely miserable – perhaps it's the same thing as long as it's intense – and one can get something by looking at the setting where it happened . . . And anyway,' he added, 'I like being morbid. It does me good, I thrive on it.'

Moved as he was by their excitement, Chaplin promised the children that he would come back and see them, and bring them a cinema projector as a gift. Robinson was instructed to procure, with the help of United Artists, the most suitable equipment. For each child a present was prepared, consisting of a bag of sweets, an orange and a new shilling in an envelope inscribed 'A Present from Charlie Chaplin'.

On the day planned for his visit, however, Chaplin lunched with Lady Astor instead. Either the emotional effect of the first visit had proved too powerful, or it had worn off: in either event, no pleas from Robinson could persuade Chaplin to abandon the luncheon. Robinson and Kono were obliged to deliver the gifts, greatly embarrassed to find themselves driving in a limousine through huge crowds who had gathered for a glimpse of their idol. The press, who had also turned out in numbers, did not fail to point out the echoes of *The Gold Rush* in the tea table set out in the school dining hall for the guest who did not arrive.

The incident attracted the first less than favourable publicity which Chaplin had received since his arrival in England, but for the moment he was too busy with arrangements for the première of *City Lights* to worry. The show took place at the Dominion, Tottenham Court Road on 27 February. The vast crowds who assembled outside the theatre in pouring rain hoping for a sight of the star were disappointed: Chaplin and Robinson had been smuggled into the theatre during the afternoon before the show. There had been great competition for seats near Chaplin. In the event he was flanked by Lady Astor and Bernard Shaw and he was somewhat nervous in anticipation of Shaw's reaction to the film. Shaw, however, laughed and cried with the rest. Later a reporter asked him what he thought of the idea of Chaplin playing Hamlet. 'Why not?' he replied. 'Long before Mr Chaplin became famous, and had got no further than throwing bricks or having them thrown at him, I was struck with his haunting, tragic expression, remarkably like Henry Irving's, and Irving made a tremendous success as Hamlet – or rather of an invention of his own which he called Hamlet.'

Chaplin had planned a small private supper party after the show; but the invitation list rapidly expanded to more than two hundred, and the affair became the social event of the season. Thomas Burke who, like Wells and Barrie, cautiously declined to attend, remarked that 'Tyl Eulenspiegel himself never achieved so superb a prank as Charles did when he set the whole Mayfair mob struggling for invitations to his *City Lights* supper party, and made them give him all the amusement that his films gave them.' Titles and talent, the great, the good, and the gifted of London met; and Chaplin broke the ice with an endearing faux pas when he referred to Churchill, in the course of his speech as "the *late* Chancellor of the Exchequer".'

From this evening Chaplin threw himself energetically into the role of playboy, which it was to amuse him to fill for the next year or so. As if in reaction to the lonely years of work on *City Lights*, from the moment that the film was launched he embarked with almost adolescent enthusiasm on a series of flirtations and adventures. Contrary to his usual distaste for personal publicity, he appeared to welcome the attention as the world's press delightedly photographed him in the company of a succession of beautiful women, and speculated recklessly on future marriages and leading ladies. The first of the series was Sari Maritsa, who with her friend Vivian Gaye (later Mrs Ernst Lubitsch) had gone to the première and party as Carlyle Robinson's guests. Chaplin intimated his interest, was delighted to find that Miss Maritsa was an accomplished dancer, and thrilled his guests by performing a stylish tango with her. During the rest of this British visit Sari (whose real name seems to have been Patricia Deterring, and who was later to have a brief Hollywood career) was constantly in Chaplin's company. Robinson, in his role of 'sup-press agent', attempted to put reporters off the track by claiming that Sari was in fact his own girlfriend; but it did not prevent the British newspapers speculating that she would be the star of Chaplin's next film.

Both in Britain and abroad the press now began to assert confidently that Ramsay MacDonald had recommended Chaplin for a knighthood. Several papers published cartoons celebrating the forthcoming honour; a headline in the Boise (Idaho) *Statesman* trumpeted inelegantly, 'Charlie will get Cracked on Dome with King's Sword'. Suddenly, however, the press declared that the honour would not after all be accorded. The general opinion, openly published, was that the knighthood had been vetoed by the personal intervention of Queen Mary herself, who felt that the Royal Family would be party to some kind of publicity stunt in honouring a motion picture comedian.

More than forty years later, when Chaplin finally received his knighthood from the granddaughter of George V and Queen Mary, a press leak from the Prime Minister's office revealed that the only explanation for withholding the honour recorded in 1931 was the unfavourable publicity generated by the Northcliffe press during the

First World War. Ramsay MacDonald may not have been encouraged by Chaplin's last-minute refusal of an invitation to a dinner the Prime Minister had arranged in his honour at the House of Commons, to meet a select party of Members. Chaplin, who had clearly not taken to MacDonald, became less and less enthusiastic over the idea; and finally decided that it was imperative that he travel to Berlin the day

Knighthood proposed for Chaplin (News Item)

before the appointment. The Premier's son Alistair MacDonald and Chaplin's own entourage were additionally embarrassed by Chaplin's refusal to telephone his apologies. He would prefer to write, he said; and then, predictably, did not write either. Finally Sir Philip Sassoon was obliged to follow the party to Europe in order to draft a suitable letter to extricate all concerned from grave embarrassment. The embarrassment was indeed almost compounded at the very moment of Chaplin's departure, when Sari endeavoured to persuade him to stay in London rather than face the rigours of a stormy channel crossing. Realizing the affront to the Prime Minister that would be committed if Chaplin remained in London after having declined the invitation, his friends hurried him unwillingly off to Liverpool Street, where they had taken the precaution of arranging for the train to be delayed for fifteen minutes.

Barton had meanwhile left the group. Having arrived in apparently high spirits, he had declined once more into acute depression. After the first week or so he could not be persuaded to leave the hotel, but wandered the suite and the public corridors. On one occasion Robinson found him fingering a revolver, and was terrified that he might take Chaplin's life along with his own. Chaplin was alarmed and irritated to discover that Barton had cut the wires on the electric clocks, for reasons known only to himself. The party at the Carlton were positively relieved when Barton announced his intention to return home. Robinson booked him a passage on the *Europa* to New York and Chaplin gave him £25 for his expenses, since he was by this time penniless. Two or three weeks after his return, Ralph Barton shot himself in the head in his New York apartment.

In the decade since his last visit, Chaplin's fame had become as great in Germany as in the rest of the world, and the usual dense crowds lined the route from the railway station – where he was met by Marlene Dietrich – to the Hotel Adlon. He was entertained by members of the Reichstag and given a guided tour of Potsdam (which he did not like, but he never approved of palaces) by Prince Henry of Prussia. He visited the Einsteins and was much impressed by the modesty of their apartment and delighted when Einstein concluded a lively debate on world economics with the compliment, 'You are not a comedian, Charlie, but an economist.'

Even at this time the political atmosphere in Germany was ominous. The Nazi press railed against the Berlin populace for losing its head over a 'Jewish' comedian from America. Then, on a day when Chaplin had an audience with Chancellor Wirth, ten men claiming to represent unemployed cinema workers arrived at the Adlon demanding an interview with Chaplin. Robinson said that it was useless for them to see him, but they threatened a 10,000-strong demonstration outside the hotel if they did not. Finally three of them were admitted, and Chaplin told them that he was very sorry for their plight but that

To Ralph

From the author
of this dastardly crime.
Charlie Chaplin

1931 - Ralph Barton, caricatured
by Chaplin.

there were 75,000 unemployed in Hollywood also. An hour later, the Berlin Communist daily newspaper was out with a report that Chaplin had received a delegation of its editors and had expressed deep sympathy with the young Communist cause. The incident clearly annoyed and embarrassed Wirth at the subsequent audience.

Chaplin had the consolation of further romantic encounters, with the Viennese dancer La Jana and the American-born actress Betty Amann. Delightful as these flesh and blood acquaintances were, he was more permanently impressed by his first sight of Nefertiti in the Pergamon Museum. He at once ordered a facsimile of the bust by the artist who had made a copy for the museum at Munich, and it was to retain a permanent place of honour in his homes.

The party next moved on to Vienna, where the crowds which greeted his arrival were perhaps the most astounding of either of his

European trips. Fortunately news film of the event still survives, showing Chaplin being carried over the heads of the crowd, as he was all the way from the railway station to the Hotel Imperial. On this occasion, too, Chaplin spoke his first words before a sound film camera, five years before *Modern Times*. They consisted only of '*Gute tag! Gute tag!*' repeated rather nervously as he clung tightly to his hat and cane lest they be lost in the sea of faces on which he floated. The romantic encounters of Berlin were forgotten as he discovered shared artistic enthusiasms with the pianist Jennie Rothenstein. The ebullience of the beautiful operetta star Irene Palasthy proved too much for him, however, and he decided not to travel on to Budapest, fearing that the city's much vaunted female beauties might all prove as demonstrative.

Chaplin and his party then moved to Venice, which made a deep impression upon him although he found it too melancholy to spend more than a couple of days sightseeing there. He arrived somewhat fearful that Marion Davies might have arrived there on one of her European tours. In fact she descended on Venice a couple of months later when Chaplin was elsewhere and able thankfully to decline an invitation to a sumptuous party at her palazzo.

From Venice Chaplin travelled by train to Paris, where he was to lunch with Aristide Briand, and to receive the Légion d'Honneur. Unknown to Chaplin the decision to make the award was the outcome of representations by a group of his French admirers, led by his first and most faithful Parisian friend, the cartoonist Cami. Cami had in fact come to London during Chaplin's stay at the Carlton; but Chaplin had been too busy to do more than shake his hand hurriedly as he left the hotel for Liverpool Street on the final night of his stay.

As the train approached Paris the French police came aboard to warn Chaplin that because of the huge crowds he would be advised to leave the train before it arrived at the terminus. They had taken it upon themselves to change his hotel reservation to the Crillon in order to avoid the worst of the mob. Chaplin was irritated by this interference with his plans, and refused to leave the train before the terminus, though he agreed to the change of hotel. Despite the crowds and the twelve-strong police guard put around Chaplin, Cami somehow managed to reach his side. This however irritated rather than pleased Chaplin, who became positively furious when he suspected that Cami was involved in a plot to make him speak into a microphone that was thrust before him. (Cami had only been guilty of yelling in his ear that it would please the mob if he said something like '*Bonjour Paris*'.) Cami accompanied the Chaplin party to the Crillon, but Chaplin, still angry, insisted on his being ejected. This was, so far as can be discovered, the last time the two men met, though the sentimental Cami never wavered in his adoration of his youthful idol.

Apart from the Briand lunch, there were two memorable social occasions in France. For a rather uneasy audience with King Albert of the Belgians, Chaplin was seated on a very low chair while the tall King occupied a much higher one. The incident later gave Chaplin the idea for the meeting of the rival heads of state in *The Great Dictator*.

On the train to Venice, Chaplin had met the Duke and Duchess of Westminster and had unwisely accepted their invitation to a boar hunt at their estate at Saint-Saëns in Normandy. The rigours of the ride left him in need of days of massage. Moreover, ordinarily so careful of his appearance, Chaplin was chagrined to be photographed by press men while wearing an unbecoming hunting outfit made up of items borrowed from the Duke and various guests of assorted sizes. There was to be a memory of this, too, in the 'animal trainer' costume in *Limelight*.

It was now the end of March, and Chaplin decided to move on to the South of France. Sydney had been settled in Nice for six months: when a variety of causes, both financial and personal, frustrated his plans to set up production in England, he decided that he was sufficiently well off to retire to a life of leisure. Sydney's apartment was too small for guests, and Chaplin gratefully accepted the invitation of the American millionaire Frank Jay Gould to stay at the Majestic Hotel in Nice, which he owned along with the Casino. Gould had formerly been married to Edith Kelly, sister of Hetty and of Arthur Kelly, who had arranged the invitation.

Chaplin quickly realized that Gould's eagerness to have him as a guest was not entirely disinterested. Chaplin's presence at the Majestic and Gould's other Nice hotel, the Palais de la Méditerranée, was a big draw to the rich and curious local clientèle. On the evening of Chaplin's arrival Gould gave a dinner party in his honour at the Palais, and introduced an admission charge of five francs to the *terrasse*, from which guests could have a view of Chaplin. The charm of the latest Mrs Gould (there was even talk of Chaplin making her into an actress) dissuaded Chaplin from giving vent to his anger, but a number of social activities which Gould had optimistically planned for him were promptly cancelled. Both Charles and Sydney however seem to have been taken by Gould's busy press agent, an engaging, mischievous White Russian called Boris Evelinoff, who combined his work for Gould with a job as correspondent for *Le Soir*. Evelinoff became a regular member of the Chaplin entourage on the Riviera, and after Chaplin's return to America was for a while his official representative in Paris until it became evident that the size of his expense accounts somewhat outweighed the value of his services. Apart from the Gould circle, Chaplin mingled with the Riviera set, including Elsa Maxwell, Mary Garden and the Duke of Connaught. He was especially delighted to meet Emil Ludwig, the biographer of Napoleon, in whom Chaplin always envisioned an ideal part for himself.

The most significant Riviera encounter was with May Reeves, alias Mizzi Muller, who was to remain for eleven months the exclusive romantic involvement in his life and, more durably, was to provide much of the inspiration for the character of Natascha in the script *Stowaway*, eventually to become *A Countess from Hong Kong*. May's past was somewhat shadowy. She appears to have been Czech, and had won prizes in national beauty contests in Czechoslovakia. Arriving on the Riviera she had won a dancing contest, and had made the acquaintance of Sydney.

Robinson, since the arrival of the party in the South of France, had been overwhelmed by the bulk of Chaplin's correspondence, a large part of which was in languages he could not read. He asked Sydney if he could help him find a multi-lingual secretary and one evening at the Casino Sydney presented May as an ideal candidate for the job, since she spoke six languages fluently. Elegant and beautiful, with the look of a sophisticated adventuress, May did not give the appearance of the perfect secretary that night. Robinson was pleasantly surprised however the following morning when she arrived on the stroke of nine and buckled to to sort the letters and inscribe them with neat little *précis* translations.

He enjoyed the perfect secretary for a mere three hours, however. The moment that Chaplin set eyes on May he was struck by her beauty and charm. The same night she was invited to dinner with Chaplin, Sydney and Robinson and from that moment was Chaplin's inseparable companion. Chaplin seemed positively stimulated by the intense disapproval of the liaison evinced by everyone around him apart from Kono, who took warmly to the young woman, particularly after she nursed him capably through a severe bout of ptomaine poisoning. The Goulds were outraged that Chaplin should be seen in their establishment with this *déclassée* person; Sydney and Minnie were terrified that a new Lita Grey situation would ensue; Robinson gritted his teeth in his role of 'sup-press' agent.

Chaplin and his hosts both realized that it was time they parted company, but neither found it easy to make the first move. Mrs Gould found the most courteous way out of the impasse: one morning she arrived at Chaplin's suite, presented him with an exquisite pair of platinum cufflinks, and said graciously how lovely it had been having him there. Chaplin blithely announced that the party, including May and Sydney, would travel to Algeria. He was with difficulty persuaded that it would be better if May travelled on a different boat.

Such ruses did not entirely put the press off the scent, and articles continued to proliferate about Chaplin and 'the mysterious Mary' as May was for some reason generally identified. Back at the studios, Alf Reeves did his best to keep the Californian press happy. He told Kathlyn Hayden, whom the studio had trusted slightly more than most journalists:

> Charlie has fallen madly in love ... but it's not what you think! He managed to withstand the charms of all the beautiful ladies of London, Berlin, Paris and Vienna – only to succumb to the allure of – Algiers. And Algiers it is which will be Charlie's habitat for the next two or three years – or however long it may take him to complete his next film, which will be made *entirely* in that country.
>
> I understand that reports have been circulated in English and European newspapers to the effect that Charlie's next film will be made either in London, Paris or Berlin – but the truth is that every scene in the new picture will be shot in Algiers.
>
> Charlie is now at work developing the story. From the sketchy outline which he has cabled me I gather that he will repeat a trick which made a great hit in two of his earlier films – completely altering his appearance at some stage in the story for purposes of disguise. In *The Pilgrim* old-timers will remember that he dressed up as a clergyman, and in a still earlier film he donned a wig and woman's clothes. Of course, in the new film, he will be the same little tramp that he always has been, but at some stage of the action circumstances will compel him to disguise himself in the flowing robes of a sheik!

Nothing more was ever heard of Chaplin's sheik film. There can be little doubt however that one of the Chaplin brothers had given this information to Reeves, who was notoriously cautious in statements to the press. To squash other rumours that had filtered back from Europe, Reeves emphasized to Miss Hayden:

Charlie's leading lady in the new film will most assuredly *not* be any of the fair ones of London, Berlin and Paris whose names have been mentioned in this connection. She will definitely come from Hollywood.

Bored with inactivity, Sydney now began to take an interest once more in his brother's business affairs, and succeeded in convincing Chaplin that distribution arrangements both in America and France should be more closely overseen. This gave Chaplin an excuse to rid himself temporarily of the irksome Robinson, who was despatched to New York with a list of embarrassing investigatory instructions. On Robinson's return he and Sydney went together to Paris to look into the distribution arrangements of *City Lights* there. No sooner had they arrived than they began to receive a stream of letters from Minnie Chaplin in Nice, gravely alarmed by the mounting publicity being given to the May Reeves affair. Sydney despatched Robinson back to the South of the France with unequivocal instructions to put a stop to the affair, even though it meant telling Chaplin that Sydney had had an affair with the girl himself: he was acutely aware of his brother's need for monopoly in matters of the heart.

Apprehensively but dutifully, Robinson carried out his commission. He arrived in Marseilles in time to meet the boat bringing Chaplin and May from Algiers. Rushing onto the vessel ahead of the reporters, he managed to persuade the couple to leave the vessel separately, escorting May himself so that there were no compromising newspaper pictures. The results of his subsequent efforts to disillusion Chaplin with May were predictable. The relationship of the couple was no doubt impaired, but Robinson's relationship with Chaplin was ended, permanently and bitterly. Already irritated by Robinson's constant presence, Chaplin became furious over the wretched part he was now playing. So, in his turn, did Sydney when he discovered that Robinson had taken him at his word in revealing his own relationship with May.

Robinson was swiftly despatched to New York, where he was appointed the studio's East Coast representative. At the end of the year Robinson received a letter from Alf Reeves explaining that his services would no longer be required since work on *City Lights* contracts had more or less finished and Chaplin's future production plans remained vague. He was given a fortnight's notice. Robinson was subsequently to publish an embittered but verifiable account of his fifteen years as a Chaplin employee.

Robinson left France at the end of May 1931, and, despite some periods of separation, May remained close to Chaplin. She had fallen deeply in love with him. It is impossible to know what were his feelings for her after the first infatuation had worn off, but there seems no doubt that she was a jolly, affectionate, undemanding holiday companion. From Nice they moved on to Juan-les-Pins which was at the height of fashion at that time. It was there that Kono had his severe attack of ptomaine poisoning, to the great alarm of Chaplin who was sure that his indispensable attendant was about to die. Henri d'Abbadie d'Arrast, the former assistant on *A Woman of Paris*, devised motor trips to Paris and to his own family home. On one of the trips they were involved in an accident, but Chaplin was unharmed. D'Arrast next persuaded Chaplin to move to Biarritz, where he was entertained to lunch by Winston Churchill. In Biarritz, too, he first met Edward, Prince of Wales, through the introduction of Lady Furness, the former Thelma Morgan Converse. Lady Furness (who had done service as chaperone in the early Lita Grey days) was evidently important in arranging the Prince's social affairs: it was she who first introduced him to Mrs Wallis Simpson. From Biarritz it was a short trip to Spain, where Chaplin witnessed a bullfight. He was observed to flinch when the bull attacked the horse. Asked afterwards if he had enjoyed the fight he answered cautiously, 'I would rather not say anything.' In later years, following the rise of Franco, Chaplin was adamant in his refusal to return to Spain, even though his daughter Geraldine made her home there.

At the end of August Chaplin returned through Paris to spend the autumn in London. He was both relieved and disturbed to find his reception cooler than the previous winter. It was partly a case of novelty wearing off, but without the protection of a press agent, Chaplin had begun to attract some unfavourable notice in the English newspapers. A lady called May Shepherd, who had been hired by Robinson to remain in England to deal with the continuing avalanche of correspondence, demanded an increase of the weekly £5 to which she had originally agreed, since the job proved much more onerous than originally anticipated. United Artists and Chaplin's immediate friends and advisers urged him to agree to her request but he stood firm, regarding it as a matter of principle to hold her to the original agreement. Only after weeks of anxiety for everyone, considerable legal expenses and a good deal of press furore did Chaplin abruptly agree to settle with Miss Shepherd in full.

The newspapers took more malicious delight in the Royal Variety Performance fracas. While Chaplin was in Juan-les-Pins, he received a telegram from George Black inviting him to take part in the Royal Variety Performance the following month. There are two different versions of what happened next. One is that, lacking a secretary to deal with his correspondence, Chaplin simply overlooked the invitation. Most papers however reported that he had declined to appear, saying that he never appeared on the stage. (In one interview he said that it would be 'bad taste' for him to do so.) Instead he sent a donation of $1000 with the rather acid comment that this represented his earnings in his last two years of residence in England.

The popular press, perversely ignoring the fact that the Variety Performance is a Royal, but not a Royal Command performance, represented Chaplin's refusal as an insult to the King. Chaplin was, quite reasonably, incensed. Unfortunately he compounded his problems by pouring out his indignation to a young man he met on the tennis court in Juan, without being aware that he was a reporter – he was missing his 'sup-press' agent:

> They say I have a duty to England. I wonder just what that duty is. No one wanted me or cared for me in England seventeen years ago. I had to go to America for my chance and I got it there.
>
> . . . Then down here (at Juan-les-Pins) I sat one night patiently waiting for the Prince of Monaco, and it appears that I was insulting the Duke of Connaught.
>
> Why are people bothering their heads about me? I am only a movie comedian and they have made a politician out of me.

He went on to express some forthright opinions on the subject of patriotism:

> Patriotism is the greatest insanity the world has ever suffered. I have been all over Europe in the past few months. Patriotism is rampant everywhere, and the result is going to be another war. I hope they send the old men to the front the next time, for it is the old men who are the real criminals in Europe today.

More than thirty years afterwards Chaplin had found no reason to modify his views: 'How can one tolerate patriotism, when six million

Jews were murdered in its name?' Prescient as his opinion was, however, it was far from fashionable in the England of 1931.

The fickleness of the press had no effect upon Chaplin's social life in England. He saw the Prince of Wales several times, and was invited for the weekend to Fort Belvedere. This opened up to him a good many more doors than he cared to enter. Among the celebrated London hostesses who entertained him were Margot Asquith, Lady Oxford, Sibyl Lady Colefax and Lady Cunard. Late in September there was a much publicized meeting with Gandhi who was then visiting England and lodging in a modest house in East India Dock Road. The interview had a special piquancy since Gandhi was one of the very small handful of people in the world who did not know who Charlie Chaplin was, and had certainly never seen one of his films. The Mahatma was affable and gracious however, and politely exchanged economic ideas with his guest before inviting him to stay and watch him at prayers. Chaplin left with the impression of 'a realistic, virile-minded visionary with a will of iron'.

Chaplin also witnessed the autumn election, which resulted in a Conservative landslide, and accompanied some of his politician friends to election meetings. He made a sentimental journey to Lancashire in search of scenes he remembered from days on tour with *Sherlock Holmes* and in variety. He found Manchester on a Sunday 'cataleptic' and so drove on to Blackburn, which had been one of his favourite towns on tour. He found the pub where he used to lodge for fourteen shillings a week, and had a drink in the bar, unrecognized.

He was now ready to return to the United States, but the holiday was to be prolonged. Douglas Fairbanks invited him to join him in St Moritz. Chaplin went there in company with Lady Cholmondeley. In Switzerland they were joined by May Reeves and Sydney. Having hitherto always expressed an aversion to mountains in general and Switzerland in particular, Chaplin stayed on throughout January and February, until the season was coming to an end and Syd, Douglas and Lady Cholmondeley had all returned home. Chaplin now decided to prolong the holiday still further with a visit to Japan, a country in which his interest had been excited two years earlier when he had become enthusiastic over the visit of the Japanese Kengeki theatre to California.

Chaplin wired an invitation to Sydney who had meanwhile returned to Nice, and it was arranged that they would meet in Naples. Chaplin, Kono and May travelled through Italy via Milan and Rome, where a planned audience with Mussolini failed to take place. On the quayside at Naples Chaplin bade his final farewell to the devoted May. His last sight of her as the ship pulled out was on the dock, bravely attempting to smile and doing an imitation of his tramp walk.

When two great prophets meet!

1931 – Gandhi and Chaplin.

Sydney, fiercely protective of his brother and constitutionally suspicious of the rest of the world, continued to worry that there would be some bad aftermath to the affair. His fears became more acute a year later when it became necessary to dispense with the services of Boris Evelinoff as Paris representative. Sydney confided to Alf Reeves his fears that Evilinoff might have entered into some sort of league with May:

I would not be surprised if a story broke in the *Paris Midi* relating the whole history of that affair, although Robinson has taken the edge off.

439

The reason I mention this is because Evelinoff came to Cannes and hit upon a story of a girl who had been the mistress of a certain Balkan king. I met the girl and heard the proposition made to her to spew up all she knows. The king having given her up, she agreed to do so, and now the story is appearing in the *Paris Midi* under the glaring headlines 'From the Folies Bergère to the Throne'. At the time Evelinoff was arranging this, May was living in the same hotel as Boris at exceptionally low terms arranged by him. She left Cannes about the same time as he did. The other day in Paris Minnie phoned Boris at his house, the secretary anwered, and Minnie feels sure it was May's voice, so perhaps she is also writing her life story.

Poor Sydney must have felt his nightmares were to be realized in 1935 when May actually published her recollections of those eventful months in book form, as *Charlie Chaplin Intime*, edited by Claire Goll. Any such fears were unfounded. May's memoirs proved that she was no sophisticated and scheming adventuress but the cheerful, somewhat naïve young woman who had provided the ideal Riviera playmate. Her book was a touching, tedious declaration of affection, forgiveness and regret.

Chaplin and Sydney embarked on the *Suwa Maru* on 12 March 1932. Their first stop was Singapore, where they were delayed by Chaplin succumbing to a fever. When he recovered they moved on to Bali whose people and culture thrilled and astonished Chaplin. The brothers shot some 400 metres of film on the island, and were rather proud of it: unfortunately the best parts were lost through some rather dubious activity on the part of a Dutch cameraman, Hank Alsem, whom they entrusted with the editing.

In the second week of May they arrived in Tokyo to crowds and a welcome as spectacular as they were accustomed to encounter in Europe. Chaplin responded with enthusiasm and excitement to every aspect of Japanese culture – the geishas, the tea ceremony, wood-block prints and drama. The visit was shadowed however by a series of sinister events connected with the activities of an ultra-rightist group, the Black Dragon Society, which for a moment considered Chaplin as a likely assassination target. There were vague and not so vague menaces, of which poor Kono, as interpreter, bore the brunt. Then one night while the party was in the company of the young son of the Premier, Tsuyoshi Inugai, the Premier himself was murdered by six extremists.

Finally, on 2 June 1932, Chaplin with Kono set sail on the *Hikawa*

Maru from Yokohama to Seattle. The day before they sailed, Sydney, who was to make his separate way to Nice, wrote to Alf Reeves, 'Charlie is returning home with the solution to the world's problems, which he hopes to have put before the League of Nations. He has been working very hard on this solution and I must say that he has hit upon an exceptionally good idea.'

During the homeward voyage Chaplin continued to work on his economic theory as well, apparently, as on some preliminary notes for *Modern Times*. Perhaps this contemplation of the world's problems provided distractions from the problems of his own studio, which he had so soon now to face. Since the completion of *City Lights* the establishment on La Brea and Sunset had had its share of the general depression in the film industry. Knowing Chaplin's life-long habit of delegating to others any unpleasant or graceless duties, it is possible to suppose that one factor in his prolonged absence was the desire not to witness or to be seen as responsible for the current situation at the studio. On 23 April 1931 Alf Reeves had reported to Carl Robinson, who was then in Paris,

> You can tell the Chief the staff here is reduced to the minimum. Rollie, Mark, Morgan, Ted Miner, Anderson and Val Lane are all gone. I have retained Jack Wilson as a librarian and laboratory man. The carpenters, electric and paint shops are closed. The small staff we have here is very busy, and we have plenty to do. Most of the people who have left are out and things look pretty bad. The stock market is all to pieces but we are hoping for the best.
>
> P.S. General conditions are still bad here. The picture business is going down generally.

Henry Bergman seems to have been kept on a retainer, because in August 1932 it was widely reported in the press that he had declined to accept his weekly salary of $75 any longer, unless the studio was in active production. Bergman at that time had an income from his restaurant. For the others laid off, life could be difficult. Rollie Totheroh's son Jack remembers having to take along food and other necessities for his father; Rollie himself published a couple of cartoons urging Chaplin to get back to work so that the studio might reopen.

These were hard times for everyone. Since leaving the studio, Edna had resolutely refrained from asking for any help from Chaplin apart from the monthly retainer she was paid, and remained anxious not to impinge in any way upon his life. During the period of his holiday, however, things had become so difficult for her that she was finally forced to seek assistance, in a poignant letter:

Dear Charlie,

Fearing I might bother you and trouble you, I have hesitated writing, but finding it absolutely necessary I am doing so, hoping you will not be angry and misconstrue my real thoughts toward you, as they are constantly for you and with you on your so long and interesting travels. However you said many years ago (perhaps you have forgotten) what you were going to do, have been doing and are doing, and though you may not know I have been [watching] very silently and with the greatest pride your most every act.

Am just recuperating from severe illness, which almost terminated with the *final* rest. But to my great joy and gladness am feeling better than ever before in my life. On [*illegible*] 29 I was stricken with a perforated ulcer ... which caused haemorrhage in my stomach and was rushed to hospital. The first day four doctors worked constantly on me with the result of no result what-so-ever. Being unconscious but with apparently subconscious determination I rallied with the aid of every known heart stimulant and one good doctor. Saline was administered into the blood stream for one week as I was unable to take any other form of nourishment. I was in a run down condition to begin with from a bad cold. So to add to all I almost had pneumonia. All told it was a battle ...

The same night I was stricken, my father died, but I was too ill to be told of it. He was 84 years old, and of course not able to support himself for years. I have been sending him a small check every month to live on. So when friends notified us of his death, they wanted me to send the money for burial expenses. My mother in desperation went to see Alf Reeves and asked if he could lend the financial aid needed, as I only had about $300 in cash in the bank at the time, and money was needed every day at the hospital, so she knew we could not send that for burial purposes. I like others lost $2300 in the Fidelity Loan and Trust Co. So perhaps you can see why I was and am short of money. Mother again appealed to Alf, and he kindly let her have $750.00 – $350 for burial of my father and the rest for hospital and nurses. On top of this my Drs bill is $700 and $50 for heart specialist. So all in all I am in a most difficult and needy situation.

Charlie *I know* it is bothersome and a dam nuisance to have to read of or listen to anyone's troubles, and I feel that you know well enough *I would not* take up your time, not even for a second, unless I simply had to. Please forgive me.

Will be so happy to see you back here, But I wonder how long you will be interested enough to stay?

All my love,
Edna

April 3 1932

P.S. Saw by the papers that Minnie was here – Am going to telephone her.

In 1932 Chaplin was nearing the mid-point of both his actual and his professional life. We are fortunate to possess from this moment the most searching and perceptive portrait ever written of him. It is an essay under the title 'A Comedian' in Thomas Burke's *City of Encounters,* published in 1933. Burke's life started at the same period, in the same social background and the same part of London and Chaplin. They had first met in 1921 (Chaplin had been very excited by reading Burke's *Nights in Town*), kept up their acquaintance over the years, and met again during Chaplin's 1931 holiday. Chaplin invited him to take the unhappy Barton's place as his travelling companion on the trips to Berlin and Spain, but Burke refused: 'I knew that a fortnight of proximity to that million-voltage battery would have left me a cinder.'

Burke loved Chaplin without idolatry (he called him 'this hard, bright, icy creature') and understood him perhaps better than any other man in his lifetime. Burke's fifty-page essay is essential to the discovery of Chaplin. He compares his character to that of Dickens:

a man of querulous outlook, self-centred, moody, and vaguely dissatisfied with life. That is the kind of man he is.

Or nearly. For to get at him is not easy. It is impossible to see him straight. He dazzles everybody – the intellectual, the simple, the cunning, and even those who meet him every day. At no stage can one make a firm sketch and say: 'This is Charles Chaplin.' One can only say: 'This is Charles Chaplin, wasn't it?' He's like a brilliant, flashing now from this facet and now from that – blue, green, yellow, crimson by turns. A brilliant is the apt simile; he's as hard and bright as that, and his lustre is as erratic. And if you split him you would find, as with the brilliant, and as with Charles Dickens, that there was no personal source of those charging lights; they were only the flashings of genius. It is almost impossible to locate him. I doubt if he can locate himself; genius seldom can . . .

Burke attempts it, nonetheless:

> For the rest he is all this and that. He is often as kind and tender as any man could be, and often inconsiderate. He shrinks from the limelight, but misses it if it isn't turned upon him. He is intensely shy, yet loves to be the centre of attention. A born solitary, he knows the fascination of the crowd. He is really and truly modest, but very much aware that there is nobody quite like Charles Chaplin. He expects to get his own way in everything, and usually gets it. Life hampers him; he wants wings. He wants to eat his cake and have it. He wants a *peau de chagrin* for the granting of all his wishes, but the *peau de chagrin* must not diminish. He makes excessive demands upon life and upon people, and because these demands cannot always be answered he is perplexed and irritated. He commands the loyalty of friends while being casual himself. He takes their continuing friendship for granted. He likes to enjoy the best of the current social system, while at heart he is the reddest of Reds. Full of impulsive generosities, he is also capable of sudden changes to the opposite . . . He takes himself seriously, but he has a sharp sense of humour about himself and his doings. He has a genuine humility about the position he has won, but, like most other really humble artists, he doesn't always like you to take the humility as justified. For two hours he will be the sweetest fellow you have ever sat with; then, without apparent cause, he will be all petulance and asperity. Like a child, his interest is quickly caught and he is quickly bored. In essence he is still a Cockney, but he is no longer English – if he ever was. In moments of excitement, and in all his work, the Cockney appears. At other times he is, in manners, speech and attitude, American. He is not at all in sympathy with the reserved English character, and he cares little for England and English things.
>
> . . . He is by no means contemptuous of money, but the possession of a very large sum means little to him. It represents economic safety, nothing else. He likes plain bourgeois foods – on his visit to England he was babbling to me of kippers, bloaters, tripe, sheep's heart – and, although he has a large wardrobe, he prefers old clothes and no fuss. Drink doesn't interest him, and he smokes one or none to my twenty.
>
> He is one of the most honest of men. If you ask his opinion on anything or anybody you get it straight and clear. Most of us have some touch of humbug about us, but Charles has none. You can accept anything he says for the truth as he sees it. A point of his honesty is his selfishness. Most of us are selfish, in one way or another, but are annoyed if people bring the accusation . . . Yet selfish people are usually the more agreeable. By pleasing themselves they maintain a cheerful demeanour to those about them. Charles lives as most of us would if we had the necessary nerve to face ourselves as we really are – however disturbing the 'really' might be to our self-esteem. He will only do what he wants to do. If any engagement

is in opposition to his mood of the moment he breaks it, and if asked why he didn't keep it he will blandly answer – Because he didn't want to. In whatever company he may be, he is simple and spontaneous. He may be always living in a part, but he never poses; he has a hatred of sham . . .

His life at home, despite the Japanese valets and cooks and chauffeurs, is not the glamorous, crowded affair that some people imagine it to be. He told me that he leads almost as humdrum a life as a London clerk. He is not over-popular in that lunatic asylum – one could hardly expect Hollywood to know what to make of a poet – and they leave him pretty much to himself . . .

His mind is extraordinarily quick and receptive; retentive, too. He reads very little, but with a few elementary facts on a highly technical subject, his mind can so work upon them that he can talk with an expert on that subject in such a way as to make the expert think. He thus appears a very well-read and cultivated man when, in fact, his acquaintance with books is slight. With little interest in people, he yet has a swifter and acuter eye than any novelist I know for their oddities and their carefully hidden secrets. It is useless to pose before him; he can call your bluff in the moment of being introduced . . .

He is now (1931) forty-two in years, but he cannot live up to that age, and never will. His attitude and his interest are always towards youth and young things. He takes no concern in the historical past; his spiritual home is his own period. He is intensely a child of these times, and his mind finds nothing to engage it farther back than his own boyhood. 'I always feel such a kid,' he told me once, 'among grown-ups . . .'

14

MODERN TIMES

Chaplin arrived back in Hollywood on 10 June 1932. He had left on the last day of January 1931. Returning, he felt confused, disorientated and above all lonely. The house on Summit Drive was empty except for the servants. The first person he called was Georgia, and they spent the evening of his return together, but it was not a success. They dined by the fire. Chaplin had brought back two trunks full of souvenirs of the trip for Georgia. Late in the evening, as they ate cornflakes in the kitchen, she told him rather forcefully that all his presents did not make up for seventeen months without a word or a postcard. She refused his presents and left, telling him he need not trouble to telephone. He did not, and they were not to meet again for ten years. Like Edna, Georgia gave Chaplin disinterested friendship, loyalty and affection. There were incompatibilities between them. Georgia had her own mind and opinions. She was also religious. 'He used to say to me "Don't start talking to me about God."' He was more than half in earnest.[1]

Chaplin no longer felt at home in Hollywood. The place had changed since the age of golden silence, which was coming to an end when he began *City Lights*. During his absence, Douglas Fairbanks and Mary Pickford had separated, 'so that world was no more'.[2] There were new people and new techniques, and a new streamlined industrialization had supplanted artisan methods and pioneering enthusiasm. Chaplin was in no mood to take up battle with the talkies. In the empty moments of his return, he thought of selling up everything, retiring and going to live in China. (He never made clear why this was his choice.)

446

In his memoirs he admitted that he had had a vague hope of meeting someone in Europe who might orient his life. He did not, but there was soon to be a meeting on his doorstep in Hollywood. In July 1932, Joseph Schenck invited Chaplin for a weekend on his yacht. Schenck was accustomed to decorate his parties with pretty girls, and on this occasion they included Paulette Goddard. Paulette had been born in New York, most likely in 1911. Her real name was Pauline Levy. At fourteen she was a Ziegfeld girl, then appeared in the chorus of *No Foolin'* and *Rio Rita*, and landed a small part in Archie Selwyn's *The Conquering Male*. At sixteen she married a rich playboy, Edgar James, but divorced him in the same year, whereupon she made her way to Hollywood. By the time she met Chaplin she had played bit parts in *The Girl Habit*, *The Mouthpiece* and *The Kid From Spain*, and had signed a contract with the Hal Roach studio.

Paulette was beautiful, radiant, vivacious, ambitious and uncomplicated. She and Chaplin enjoyed an immediate rapport. There were similarities in their backgrounds – Paulette too came from a broken home and was the family breadwinner while still a child. They were both alone. Chaplin was delighted at this first meeting to give Paulette some financial counsel. She was still naïve enough in Hollywood ways to be contemplating 'investing' $50,000 of her alimony in a dubious film project. Chaplin was just in time to prevent her signing the documents.

Soon they were seeing a great deal of each other. Chaplin persuaded Paulette to revert from platinum blonde to her natural dark hair; he also bought up her Roach contract. The press were soon hard on their heels, describing Paulette as a 'mysterious blonde'. She did not long remain mysterious. When Chaplin saw her off on the plane to New York on 19 September – he had stayed up with her all night at Glendale Airport – their farewell kiss made headlines across the continent. Both denied rumours of an engagement. The kiss was only friendly, said Paulette, adding that she was to be his next leading lady.

Meanwhile there were irritating reminders that Chaplin was still, in a way, a family man. In the years immediately following the divorce he had made little effort to contact his sons. They were still babies, and the associations were still too painful. Now, however, Charles was seven and Sydney six. Before his departure he appears to have seen them a few times, mostly on the initiative of Lita's grandmother. With their upbringing left largely to Lita's mother, since Lita was trying to make a career for herself as a singer, they had grown into irresistibly attractive children. Ida Zeitlin, one of the most intelligent and perceptive of the great generation of Hollywood 'sob-sisters', interviewed them for *Screenland* in the summer of 1932 and her shrewd assessment of their contrasting personalities might serve, with very little change, to characterize them in their maturer years:

> Tommy [i.e. Sydney] is lively and venturesome, where Charlie is reflective and reserved. With Tommy, to have an idea is to act on it, but Charlie will think twice before he moves. Tommy is restless, turbulent, independent – Charlie is sensitive, high-strung and craves affection. Nothing is safe with Tommy – his toys have a habit of breaking apart in his hands. Charlie's clothes are always folded at night and his small shoes placed carefully side by side. Tommy would sleep sweetly, says his grandmother, through an explosion, but there aren't many nights when she isn't awakened by an apprehensive little voice from Charlie's bed: 'Are you there, Nana?' And only on being reassured does Charlie fall asleep again. Charlie has his father's troubled temperament – Tommy, like his mother, is equable; and if signs mean anything, life is going to be considerably harder on Charlie than on his little brother Tommy.[3]

Miss Zeitlin cannot have known how accurate a prophet time would prove her.

While their father was away on his travels, Sydney and Charlie had also been in Europe. They had spent almost a year in and around Nice, where their still youthful grandmother had a gentleman friend, and where the boys learned French (they already spoke Spanish fluently, as well as English). Although they must often have been very near their father on the Côte d'Azur, there appears to have been no contact. In France, however, the children discovered with delight that being Chaplin's sons made them, too, celebrities. Charlie learned that he could infallibly gain attention by imitating his father's screen walk – a feat which Sydney, slightly pigeon-toed, could not master.

A week or so before Chaplin arrived back in America, Lita summoned the boys and Nana home: she had fixed up a film contract with David Butler to appear together with her sons in *The Little Teacher*. In New York the children were met by a battery of cameramen and reporters, but they were by this time professionals with the press. Charlie modestly told them that he was going to be a great actor and would like to play cowboys. Sydney said that he was going to be Mickey Mouse. 'I am wondering,' speculated Louella Parsons with evident glee, 'just how Charles Chaplin Senior will react to this.'

She was soon to discover. On 25 August, Loyd Wright, Chaplin's attorney, filed a petition objecting to the boys working in motion pictures. Chaplin apeared in court on 27 August, but a further hearing was set for 2 September. On this occasion Alf Reeves represented Chaplin. When Lita refused to accept Judge H. Parker Wood's decision in Chaplin's favour, a new hearing was set for the following day. Again Reeves represented Chaplin. Judge Wood's decision was upheld. Lita announced she would appeal.

Lita's persistence showed bad judgement in public relations. Opinion was unanimously with Chaplin. 'A good mother,' said the *Boston Globe*, 'prefers a normal childhood for her children.' Support for Chaplin came from unexpected quarters. Mildred Harris, who had now a six-year-old son of her own, Johnny McGovern, told the press:

> I can understand Lita Grey Chaplin's reluctance to decline a $65,000 contract which she probably reasons would mean a geat deal to her boys' future.
>
> But I'd rather my child didn't do anything till he's old enough to know what he wants to do. I've been on the screen since I was eight. Child actors don't have a hard life. It isn't that. Quite the contrary. The danger is that they will be spoiled.[4]

The boys cried in understandable disappointment; but their father explained:

> If you're really in earnest about wanting to act, going into it now would be the worst thing in the world for you boys. You'd be typed as child actors. When you reached the gawky stage they'd drop you. Then you would have to make a complete comeback and you'd have a hard time of it, because everyone would remember you as those cute little juveniles. But if after you've grown up you still want to act, then I won't interfere.[5]

In later years they appreciated his wisdom. At the time they were less convinced, partly because their playmates included Shirley Temple.

On 15 September a new hearing was granted, and Lita wrote a ten-page letter to Chaplin appealing for his permission to allow the boys to work. Her letter reveals how keenly aware she was of the backlash of all the publicity. She said she had taken up a theatrical career 'in the hope that I might by such a contact with the public be able to remove the impression that I was coarse, vulgar and uneducated.'[6]

One happy outcome of the business was that Chaplin had begun to see much more of his sons. From now on he tried to arrange some meeting or trip every Saturday. On 15 October he called for them as usual, but on entering the house was served with a subpoena to appear in court on 26 October: Lita's lawyers were still a little short on delicacy. The case was again and finally decided in Chaplin's favour. In court he found himself face to face with Lita's lawyer uncle, Edwin T. McMurray, who asked him 'What do you mean by the word exploitation?' Chaplin had no hesitation in his reply: 'You exploit something when you sell it, and you're trying to sell the services of these little children. I want them to lead a natural existence of normal play.'[7] Chaplin knew well enough, from memories of his own childhood, what the alternatives could be.

The former husband and wife were to be in conflict once more the following February when Chaplin questioned the administration of the boys' trust fund. He insisted that a weekly savings account be set up for them – an arrangement for which they were duly grateful when they grew up and reaped the benefits. After this there was little contact between the couple except through the boys. Lita made a brief career as a vaudeville singer ('She must like work, for it is four-a-day at the least,' wrote Alf Reeves to Sydney) and drifted into an alcoholic breakdown, from which she was happily to recover. In 1936 she was playing at the Café de Paris in London at the same time as Mildred Harris, now an acute alcoholic, was singing in a bottle club. For some reason she decided to go and see Mildred in the club; for the first and only time these two former wives of Chaplin faced each other. Lita remembered Mildred's last words to her: 'Go home, Lady; go do your slumming some place else.'[8]

Chaplin had come back to other troubles. The national economic situation had led to a general tightening up of taxation and the federal tax authorities were taking a keen interest in Chaplin's affairs. They had estimated his taxable assets as the highest in the country, with taxable securities assessed at $7,687,570. Chaplin countered that the real value was only $1,657,316, and that the assessors' investigators had used old values instead of actual prices. 'They even charged me with $25,000 worth of old machinery which isn't worth $500 today and film paraphernalia that they list at $25,000 would bring about $558.'[9] The hearing was set for 14 July 1932. Sydney, in the South of France, was much concerned over his brother's troubles and characteristically worried that not all possible economies were being made in the studios.

Alf tried to reassure him but they were unlucky in having been alloted a ferret-like, relentlessly probing inspector. Alf had to break it to Sydney that he had started inquiries about a transaction in which some prop furniture had been written off the books and shipped to Sydney for use in his home. The inspector was charging that not only was the furniture improperly written off, but that it had been shipped under false declarations to avoid payment of French duty. The inspector was further demanding why no rental had been charged on the Chaplin home – reckoned as a studio asset – during his eighteen-month absence in Europe. 'And to add one more they are questioning Edna Purviance's place on the corporation payroll and want to make it a personal charge.'

The Federal inspectors were pushing the studios hard. Some stocks were sold on poor terms – Alf reckoned a $200,000 loss – but stock losses were no longer admissible. They sought relief on the losses incurred in 1926 on the production of *Sea Gulls*. The condition on which the inspectors allowed this were that the film must be shown, by destruction, to be utterly devoid of possible future value. Hence on 21 June 1933 the 'original and only negative' of von Sternberg's film was destroyed by fire in the presence of Alf Reeves, Jack Wilson, Sylvia Sobol, Lois G. Watt and Charles Bigelow, of Consolidated Film Inc., each of whom signed the affidavit to that effect.

Sydney was also worried because Chaplin showed no signs of settling down to make a new film. He was for the moment otherwise occupied. Willa Roberts, the managing editor of *Woman's Home Companion*, had trailed him to Europe and persuaded him to write a 50,000-word serialization of his European adventures for a fee of the same number of dollars. Chaplin was certainly more tempted by the challenge of writing than by the fee: he had after all just turned down the offer of $670,000 from the Blaine-Thompson advertising agency for a series of twenty-six fifteen-minute radio programmes which he would be free to use in any way he liked. At that time the highest fee ever paid for a broadcast was $15,000, paid to Heifetz for a one-hour recital. Theodore Huff, in his 1951 biography of Chaplin, said that the 'article' (*sic*) was 'ghost-written by his secretary, Catherine Hunter'; and the statement has been uncritically accepted by subsequent writers. It was quite inaccurate: Chaplin was too proud and too perfectionist to allow someone else to write under his name. It is true that in the early days Rob Wagner may have shaped his thoughts on comedy into literary form, but there is a consistency of

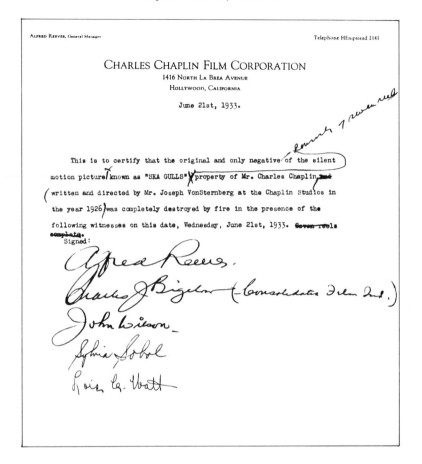

Alfred Reeves, General Manager

Telephone HEmpstead 2141

CHARLES CHAPLIN FILM CORPORATION
1416 North La Brea Avenue
Hollywood, California

June 21st, 1933.

This is to certify that the original and only negative of the silent
motion picture known as "SEA GULLS" property of Mr. Charles Chaplin, and
written and directed by Mr. Joseph VonSternberg at the Chaplin Studios in
the year 1926 was completely destroyed by fire in the presence of the
following witnesses on this date, Wednesday, June 21st, 1933. Seven reels
complete.
Signed:

1933 - Certificate of destruction
of *Sea Gulls*.

style, phrasing and vocabulary from *My Wonderful Visit (My Trip Abroad)* through *A Comedian Sees the World* – the title given to the *Woman's Home Companion* series – to *My Autobiography*.

Chaplin found writing laborious – which is why he practically never wrote personal letters – and remained cavalier about spelling. But he loved words and was fascinated by them. In his youth he had made a practice of learning one new word from the dictionary every day, and in both his speech and writing he used words vividly and with the freshness of new discovery. When Richard Meryman interviewed him, at the age of seventy-five, he had grown attached to the word 'atavistic'. Meryman asked him what it meant and Chaplin explained, adding disarmingly: 'I do like big words sometimes.'

His method was the same whether writing conventional prose or his later scripts. He would first write everything out in longhand, and then dictate it to his secretary. Afterwards he would work over the typescript, and successive secretaries were astonished at how he would labour over a word, trying different positions or variations. The typing and correcting process could be repeated many times: he was as tireless in writing as in making films. He worked solidly on the *Woman's Home Companion* articles from his return in July 1932 until late February 1933. Sydney, down in Nice, was exasperated, and Alf Reeves attempted to reassure him:

> Just a few remarks without the aid of the typist. Of course I understand your intent in commenting on time taken by C. in writing up his story – but you (*knowing him as well as you do*) realize that while he works hard – he works spasmodically – and all work and no play not being good for the health, he naturally plays quite a bit – possibly being in no great hurry in view of everything to make the government a present of the fruits of his labors whilst they are just sitting on the receiving end and making it hard for him at that – as far as they can. We know he could earn more by picturemaking and that the price he gets for the book whilst a lot in some people's ideas is nothing compared to what he commands as an actor.

Despite the attentions of the Federal tax agents, this was one of the happiest periods Chaplin had yet experienced in his private life. He saw his sons regularly, and they delighted him as much as he delighted them. 'Oh, those wonderful weekends,' Charlie Junior reminisced:

> That wonderful magical house on the hill, with the man who lived there, the man who was so many men in one. We were to see them all now: the strict disciplinarian, the priceless entertainer, the taciturn, moody dreamer, the wild man of Borneo with his flashes of volcanic temper. The beloved chameleon shape was to weave itself subtly through all my boyhood and was never to stop fascinating me.[10]

Paulette was essential to it all and the boys fell in love with her the moment their father introduced her:

> We lost our hearts at once, never to regain them through all the golden years of our childhood. Have you ever realized, Paulette, how much you

meant to us? You were like a mother, a sister, a friend all in one. You lightened our father's spells of sombre moodiness and you turned the big house on the hill into a real home. We thought you were the loveliest creature in the whole world. And somehow I feel, looking back today, that we meant as much to you, that we satisfied some need in your life too.[11]

Alf Reeves, who had watched Chaplin falling in and out of love for more than twenty years, was a trifle less romantic in his approval. 'Charlie,' he informed Sydney, 'is still quite "chummy" with Paulette, who is a nice little "cutie".' Some time later, about the time that *Modern Times* was being finished, Reeves wrote to Sydney:

I spent a day with Charlie on a recent trip I made to the coast. It was a Sunday and the two boys were there. I have never seen such attractive kids in my life, and Charlie is positively fascinated by them. They are terribly fond of Paulette and in her shorts she looks like a little girl and the boys look upon her as a sister and expect her to come out and play with them. I am afraid they have the adventurous spirit of one Sydney Chaplin.

When I was there they were on the roof of the house, exploring the innermost parts under the roof. Young Syd is turning out to be an artist and Charlie is a musician. Daddy Charlie gave Charlie Jr his first accordion on which he has been practising and he does quite well; and it would have made you very happy to see Daddy Charlie playing the accordion and young Charlie's expression totally fascinated by his daddy's movements over the notes and of course the minor tones that Charlie drags out of that instrument. You would be happy to see your namesake. They are lovely boys and I was terribly thrilled because it was the first time I had the opportunity of seeing Charlie *au famille*.

We had a regular English Tea with muffins and crumpets and cake and to make it thoroughly English, Paulette had a little drop of rum in her tea. I missed both you and Minnie. With you it would have made one grand happy family.

Charlie Junior remembered this Sunday tea (with marmalade on the crumpets) as an unchanging ritual. '"It's four o'clock, boys," he [their father] would religiously inform us on the weekends we spent with him. "Time for tea and crumpets as it's done in England just at this hour."'

That spring of 1933 Chaplin acquired a new toy, which was for years to provide him with therapeutic recreation. Disregarding financial stringencies, he ordered from Chris-Craft a 1932 model

38-foot commuting cruiser, with an 8-cylinder, 250 h.p. motor and a speed of 26 knots. It slept four, would ride twenty people, and had a one-man crew – Andy Anderson, a one-time Keystone Kop. It had luxurious cabin, galley and dining quarters and, provided with bedding, linen, stove, refrigerator and cooking utensils cost $13,950 at the Michigan factory. Sydney, between his usual advice about contracts and investments, wrote to Alf Reeves: 'I hear he has bought a yacht. Tom Harrington sent me a photograph of it. It is certainly a good looking boat, and he must be having a great time. It is a good place to concentrate on a story, provided he has not too many distractions aboard.' For the first few weeks of course the boat was nothing but distraction. On 25 March the two boys were taken to Wilmington to see it for the first time; after that Chaplin and Paulette spent every free moment in it, with trips to Catalina, Santa Cruz and Santa Barbara. Chaplin called the boat *Panacea*.

Sydney was right that a boat was a good place for writing; almost as soon as he had acquired it, Chaplin set to work on the scenario that was to become *Modern Times*.

It was in the 1930s that Chaplin's critics – often the best-disposed of them – began to complain that he was getting above his station. The clown was setting himself up as a philosopher and statesman. He had mingled so much with world leaders (they said) that he had begun to think of himself as one. They regretted the lost, innocent purity of the old slapstick and shook their heads at the arrogance, conceit and self-importance of the man. If this had been true, it would have been less surprising than that Chaplin had remained as human and as conscious of reality as he did. No one before or since had ever had such a burden of idolatry thrust upon him. It was not he or his critics, but the crowds that mobbed him everywhere on his world tour that cast him in the role of symbol of all the little men of the world. To survive this, still sane and human, was something of a miracle. Chaplin felt the burden and the responsibility deeply. In a sudden outburst, in 1931, he told Thomas Burke:

> But, Tommy, isn't it pathetic, isn't it awful that these people should hang around me and shout 'God bless you Charlie!' and want to touch my overcoat, and laugh and even shed tears. I've seen 'em do that – if they can touch my hand. And why? Why? Simply because I cheered 'em up. God, Tommy, what kind of a filthy world is this – that makes people lead such wretched lives that if anybody makes 'em laugh they want to kneel down and touch his overcoat, as though he was Jesus Christ raising

'em from the dead. There's a comment on life. There's a pretty world to live in. When those crowds come round me like that – sweet as it is to me personally – it makes me sick spiritually, because I know what's behind it. Such drabness, such ugliness, such utter misery, that simply because someone makes 'em laugh and helps 'em to forget, they ask God to bless him.[12]

Burke felt that Chaplin had failed to understand. It was not the world that was wrong ;

It's Charlie himself. He asks too much. If only he could be as tolerant as 'Charlie' he would be happier. A little melting of that icy detachment; a little something that helped him see the world clearly as a world, instead of through his own temperament, a view of that world as a place not entirely given over to the breaking of the noble and the beautiful, and he would come to that understanding by which men as acutely sensitive as himself manage to live happily in this pigstye. Much of the trouble in his private life, and he has had a lot, has arisen from this very lack of patience with human nature. With a wide experience of life, he seems not to have profited by it. He knows people and is a quick judge of character, but he cannot adjust his ideals to meet them. He has intellectual perception, but it is unwarmed by the rays of tolerance, and is therefore sterile. But whatever he is, generous, cold, capricious, he calls out all my affection as a man and all my admiration as an artist . . .[13]

If, from time to time, Chaplin felt impelled to set down his views on the state of the world and the path it should take, it was not from any overwhelming self-importance, but because he felt it was somehow his due to those billions who had appointed him their idol and their symbolic representative. He was a reasoning, reading, pensive man. He was realistically aware of his ability to gain a swift, superficial understanding of practically any subject. As a man in command of considerable personal wealth, he was particularly fascinated by economics. He had read Major H. Douglas's *Social Credit* and was so impressed by its theory of the direct relationship of unemployment to failure of profit and capital, that – taking warning from growing unemployment in the United States – he had in 1928 turned his stocks and bonds into liquid capital, and so been spared at the time of the Wall Street crash. Douglas's theory was enshrined in the opinions Chaplin gave forth to Flora Merrill of the *New York World* when she interviewed him in New York in February 1931, on the first stage of his world tour:

If America is to have sustained prosperity, the American people must have sustained ability to spend. If we continue to view the present condition as inevitable, the whole structure of our civilization may crumble. The present deplorable conditions certainly cannot be charged against the five million men out of work, ready to work, anxious to work, and yet unable to get jobs. If capital represents the genius of America it would seem obvious that for its own sake the present conditions should not continue or ever again be repeated. While crossing the continent I have been talking to all sorts of men – railroad men, workers, fellow travellers – and I heard that times are even harder than before the end of the old year. The country is talking about prohibition which, as Will Rogers says, you cannot feed to the hungry. Unemployment is the vital question, not prohibition. Machinery should benefit mankind. It should not spell tragedy and throw it out of work.

Labor-saving devices and other modern inventions were not really made for profit, but to help humanity in the pursuit of happiness. If there is to be any hope for the future it seems to me that there must be some radical change to cope with these conditions. Some people who are sitting comfortable do not want the present state of affairs changed. This is hardly the way to stave off bolshevistic or communistic ideas which may become prevalent.

Something is wrong. Things have been badly managed when five million men are out of work in the richest country in the world. I don't think you can dismiss this very shocking fact with the old-time argument that these are the inevitable hard times which are the reaction of prosperity. Nor do I think the present economic conditions should be blamed on current events. I personally doubt it. I think there is something wrong with our methods of production and systems of credit. Of course I speak as a layman, like many thousands of others who are anxious at this very serious state of affairs.

I am not in a position to go into world economics, but it seems to me that the question is not whether the country is wet or dry, but whether the country is starved or fed. Also, it doesn't seem to me that there is any doubt but that a shorter working day would take care of the unemployed. Mr Ford has urged for shorter hours for labor and innovations in our credit system. I think such changes might avert serious future national catastrophes.

Miss Merrill asked him what changes he most wanted to see. He replied:

Shorter hours for the working man, and a minimum wage for both skilled and unskilled labor, which will guarantee every man over the age of twenty-one a salary that will enable him to live decently.

457

Chaplin spent the whole of the first week after his return home working on the Economic Solution he had begun in Japan. As it finally emerged, it was an ingenious scheme to promote the movement of money in Europe, and to keep purchasing power abreast of production potential. It involved creating a new international currency, in which the former Allies would pay themselves the money owed them in war reparations, but which Germany was not in a position to pay. Each of the Allies would put up a bond to guarantee the currency. 'It only remains for the Allies to ratify this currency as having the value of gold, and it shall have the value of gold.' Whether Chaplin's Economic Solution could ever have been practical or not, it serves to illustrate the range and ingenuity of his intellectual effort. In political terms it probably represents capitalist utopianism rather than the socialism with which he was so regularly charged. Chaplin was full of enthusiasm for Roosevelt (who like himself was charged with dangerous socialist ideas) and the New Deal. He was delighted to make a broadcast on 23 October 1933 on station KHJ of the Columbia Broadcasting System in support of the National Recovery Act.

Undoubtedly these concerns and preoccupations underlay Chaplin's thinking on *Modern Times*, but it was not his concern now or at any other time to make a didactic or satirical film – a fact which, unreasonably perhaps, disappointed many critics of the picture. He told Miss Merrill in her February 1931 interview:

> I leave humanity to humanity. Achievement is more than propaganda. I am always suspicious of a picture with a message. Don't say that I'm a propagandist. The world at the moment is in such a turmoil of change that there are no signs of stability anywhere on which to speculate sensibly concerning the future, but I am sure it will be a good enough world to want to live in for a while. I want to live for ever. I find that life is very interesting, not from the point of view of success but from the changing conditions, if only people would meet them and accept them and go along with them. It is so much better to go with the change, I think, than to go against. As I grow older I find it is better to go with the tide.

Modern Times is an emotional response, based always in comedy, to the circumstances of the times. In the Keystone and Essanay films the Tramp was knocked around in a pre-war society of underprivilege among the other immigrants and vagrants and petty miscreants. In *Modern Times* he is one of the millions coping with poverty, unemployment, strikes and strike-breakers, and the tyranny of the machine.

A remarkable and revealing note by Chaplin on the characterization in *Modern Times* shows that he did not intend the Tramp and the Waif – 'the Gamin' as she was called, though in later years Chaplin was inclined to correct this to 'Gamine' – as either rebels or victims. They were rather spiritual escapees from a world in which he saw no other hope:

> The only two live spirits in a world of automatons. They really live. Both have an eternal spirit of youth and are absolutely unmoral.
>
> Alive because we are children with no sense of responsibility, whereas the rest of humanity is weighted down with duty.
>
> We are spiritually free.
>
> There is no romance in the relationship, really two playmates – partners in crime, comrades, babes in the woods.
>
> We beg, borrow or steal for a living. Two joyous spirits living by their wits.

The Tramp, then, is finally a self-confessed anarchist.

Modern Times has not the integrated and organic structure of Chaplin's previous features. The critic Otis Ferguson, not unjustly, said that it was really a collection of two-reelers which might have been called *The Shop*, *The Jailbird*, *The Watchman* and *The Singing Waiter*. The unifying theme is the battle for survival, ultimately a joint battle waged by the two main characters. The scenes of the Gamin's troubles before her meeting with the Tramp are among the very rare instances in Chaplin's films (another is Edna's scenes in *The Kid*) where there is an independent secondary and parallel line of action running alongside the narrative of the Tramp's misadventures.

The finished film opens with a symbolic juxtaposition of sheep being herded and workers streaming out of a factory. Charlie is seen at work on a conveyor belt in a great factory. He is caught up in the cogs of a giant machine, is used as guinea pig for an automatic feeder, and finally runs amok. Released from the mental hospital, he quickly lands in prison on a charge of being a Red agitator (he has merely helpfully picked up a red flag that has fallen off a lorry). After he inadvertently prevents a gaol-break, life in prison becomes so pleasant that he is heartbroken to be pardoned. He does his best to get arrested again, but changes his mind after he meets the Gamin, a gutsy little orphan on the run from the juvenile officers. They set up home together in a waterfront shack, where Charlie sleeps in the doghouse outside.

Now that he values freedom, Charlie is soon sent back to prison after some of his former prison friends burgle the department store where he works as night-watchman. On his release, he finds the Gamin working as a dancer in a low cabaret, where she finds him a job as a singing waiter. Called upon to substitute for the romantic tenor, Charlie writes the words on his cuffs, which inconveniently fly off at his first dramatic gesture. He retrieves the situation by performing the song in a make-believe jabberwock language. Before he can take his bow, however, the juvenile officers arrive to carry off the Gamin. The pair make a quick escape. On a country road, they jerk themselves out of their dejection. 'We'll get along,' says the title. Arm in arm they go off towards the horizon.

As usual, Chaplin's ideas went through many metamorphoses and permutations before the story took its final form. An early series of notes suggests a possible opening:

> Large city – early morning rush of commerce – showing subway street traffic – newspaper printing office – factory whistles – ferry boats – ambulance, fire engine – motor traffic – introducing a comedian in complete contrast – calm, nothing to do – business crossing the road – klaxon – policeman belching – mistaken for klaxon – stick business and grating outside store window – search for work – different jobs and fired from each . . .

It is interesting to find the stick business cut out of *City Lights* figuring here; later the notes also suggest, 'work the twin fighter gag in a café'. Chaplin never wasted anything. There are suggestions for nice ironic gags. The factory boss, nursing his ulcers on clear soup, crackers and pills looks out of his window and sees his workers gobbling huge lunches while listening to an agitator lamenting that the poor working man must starve while the bosses live on the fat of the land. The infuriated boss empties his soup out of the window onto the orator's head. Two tramps on a park bench solemnly discuss the world crisis and their fears of going off the gold standard: 'This means the end of our prosperity – we shall have to economize.' They replace their cigarette butts in their tins and one puts his lighted match into his pocket. The tone is ribald:

Second tramp: 'Are you carrying anything?' First tramp: 'Yes, I am loaded up with consolidated gas but I am afraid I shall have to let it go.' Second tramp, gives him look of concern: 'I would try and hold onto it for a while if I were you.'

Another idea is for a factory where heavy machinery is developed for such trivial tasks as cracking nuts or knocking the ash off cigars. After this the story takes off on a quite different tack as the Tramp or tramps stow away on a ship and land up in a series of Crusoe-like gag adventures on a tropical island – adventures evidently inspired as much by the possibility of parodying *King Kong* and *Tarzan* as by Chaplin's own recent oriental sightseeing.

Alf Reeves, who rarely sought to make a contribution to the creative side of the studio work, was this time responsible for a good idea, very similar to one used much later by Woody Allen in *Sleeper* (1973). Charlie would find his way into the locked room where the factory's management are experimenting with a robot which can fly an aircraft. Surprised by the bosses, Charlie is obliged to disguise himself as the robot, and must then go through the robot's actions, including flying the plane. 'If more thrills were required,' wrote Reeves enthusiastically in his memorandum, 'it could be worked up with the effects mechanism they use now and it should be an incident which could be worked up for a big gag.' The suggestion was never taken up, however. Chaplin was rejecting and refining his ideas, and at the next stage wrote out a list of the gag suggestions he now felt germane:

> Stomach rumbling
> Steam shovel
> Kidnapping
> City environment
> Museum and public gallery
> Dry goods store
> Street fair
> Docks
> Dives
> Cabarets
> Band parade
> Street fire
> Police raid
> Street riots
> Strikes
> Telephone wire repairing
> Dock working

461

Baggage staircase
Labor exchange
Bread line . . .

The earliest scenario draft which is clearly identifable as the proto-type for *Modern Times* has the title *Commonwealth*. The episodes are more numerous and less closely linked than in the finished film, though the relationship of Charlie and the Gamin and the general progression in search of work are already defined. Some incidents of the finished film are already present: the red flag, the accidental launch of a liner, the gaol-break, Charlie's efforts to get himself newly arrested, the meeting with the Gamin in the police wagon and subsequent escape. The factory is in part developed, with a world of push-button gadgets for the boss. Charlie's conveyor-belt mental breakdown is now the motive for pathos.

Among the sequences that were to be rejected was a long scene of slapstick action when Charlie pretends he is a qualified steam shovel operator in order to get a job. In another sequence Charlie and the Gamin take shelter in an empty house, unaware that it is in the process of being demolished. Chaplin's politico-economic preoccupations surface in a scene in which Charlie and the girl are punished for eating eggs which are being dumped in the sea as surplus. There is an echo of *The Kid* in one of their ruses to make a little money: the Gamin steals purses and wallets, which Charlie then politely returns hoping for (but not demanding) a reward from the grateful owners. The café sequence in this draft is very different: it is Charlie who first gets a job as waiter, and in turn gets a place for the girl – in blissful innocence that the place is also used as a bawdy house.

The major divergence, however, is the ending of the film. At this stage Chaplin was evidently looking for something to surpass *City Lights* in pathos. Following a breakdown brought on by nut-tightening, Charlie is put in hospital. As he is recuperating, he is told he has a visitor: it is the Gamin, who has become a nun. They part with sad smiles.

The 'nun' ending was fully elaborated:

The full moon has changed to a crescent, and from a crescent to a full moon again.
The scene changes to the hospital. Fully recovered, the Tramp, who is about to be discharged, is informed that a visitor is waiting to see him in the reception room. He makes his way, laboriously, towards it. When he

arrives there, to his surprise, he finds the Gamin, attired as a nun. She is standing, and beside her is a Mother Superior. The Gamin greets him, smiling wistfully. The Tramp looks bewildered. Somehow a barrier has risen up between them. He tries to speak but can say nothing. Smiling sympathetically, she takes his hand. 'You have been very ill,' she says, 'and now you are going out into the world again. Do take care of yourself, and remember I shall always like to hear from you.'

He tries to speak again but, with a gesture, gives it up. As she smiles, tears well up in her eyes while she holds his hand and he becomes embarrassed; then she stands [*sic*] as a final gesture that they must part.

The Mother Superior leads them to the door and at the entrance of the hospital she says her last 'goodbye', while the Mother Superior waits in the reception room.

He releases his hand and walks slowly down the hospital steps, she gazing after him. He turns and waves a last farewell and goes towards the city's skyline. She stands immobile, watching him as he fades away.

There is something inscrutable in her expression, something of resignation and regret. She stands as though lost in a dream, watching after him and her spirit goes with him, for out of herself the ghost of the Gamin appears and runs rampant down the hospital steps, dancing and bounding after him, calling and beckoning as she runs toward him. Along that lonely road she catches up to him, dancing and circling around him, but he does not see her, he walks alone.

She is standing on the hospital steps. She is awakened from her revelry [reverie?] by a light touch, the hand of the Mother Superior. She starts, then turns and smiles wistfully at the kindly old face and together they depart into the portals of the hospital again. FADE OUT

During the year that the story was in preparation, life went on practically without incident. At the studio the stages were repaired and made ready for the moment that Chaplin chose to start production, and a bathroom was added to the dressing room that was to be Paulette's. In September 1933 Carter De Haven was taken on to the staff, to be a general assistant to Chaplin, and in particular to help on the story. At the beginning of January 1934 Henry Bergman was put back on the payroll. De Haven and Henry sat in on most of Chaplin's script sessions. Chaplin had decided to keep the eventual title of the film secret. In November 1933 a sealed envelope containing the title was sent by registered mail to Will H. Hays, President of the Motion Picture Producers' and Distributors' Association in New York, with instructions not to open it but to register the unknown title as of 11 November 1933, and to place the envelope in safekeeping until publication should be announced.

At the house, too, life followed its routine, with trips on the boat when the weather was good and regular outings or visits for the boys. In April their father took them to the circus, and they were thrilled to be photographed with Poodles Hannaford and Chaplin's old Keystone colleague, Charlie Murray. Chaplin went to a party and to a drill demonstration at the Black-Foxe Military Academy where the boys had been enrolled. Charles Junior remembered 'that I marched straighter, that I was more alert, that I saluted with a snappier gesture and clicked my heels more sharply when I saw those ice-blue eyes upon me.'[14]

There was one major domestic revolution during this period. Kono, who had served Chaplin with discreet devotion for eighteen years, first as chauffeur, later as private secretary and major domo, announced his intention of leaving. Paulette was not content to be a guest at Summit Drive as Mildred and Lita had been, and as she gave more and more attention to the running of the house, Kono felt he was being gradually usurped. Chaplin and Paulette both ridiculed his fears, but he was adamant and resigned. Chaplin was distressed but arranged a job for Kono with the United Artists exchange in Tokyo, and sent him and his wife on their way with a present of $1000 each. Kono found no consolation in the job and made no better success when, his United Artists contract having run out, he tried distributing the Chaplin films in Japan. He returned to California but never rejoined the Chaplin staff.

By the end of August Chaplin was satisfied with his story. According to the studio records he spent a week or so at Lake Arrowhead with De Haven, Bergman and Miss Steele, the secretary, 'to put story into script form'. If there ever were a script in conventional form, however, no copy has survived; this note may be a reference to a dialogue script, which will be discussed later. Throughout September and the early part of October the studio went into full operation. Danny Hall had been preparing sketches for some time and now set his construction crew to build the factory sets in the studio. The films had outgrown the old studio street, and four acres of land at Wilmington were rented on which to build a big street set. The Chaplin studio was one of the last in Hollywood still to have a stage open to the sky, and preparations were finally begun to enclose it and bring it up to modern, sound-era standards. On 4 September Paulette signed her contract. On 20 September Alf Reeves wrote to Sydney: 'Looks like shooting next week. Some factory interiors are being built on the stage, and he has found some splendid locations. In view of the fact that he has practically eliminated the worry during production of thinking out his story, he expects to have the picture finished by January. However, this, as you know, is not definite.' Alf's doubts about the January finish were reasonable and justified: the final shot of the picture was not taken until 30 August 1935. Even so, the shooting period of ten and a half months was the shortest for a Chaplin film since *A Woman of Paris*.

Shooting finally began on 11 October with a scene in the office of the factory boss, played by Allan Garcia. The next sequence was set in the dynamo room, and on 15 October the unit worked through the night from 7.30 p.m. to 4.45 a.m. This seemed like prescience because the following evening, just as they were coming to the end of work on the sequence, a heavy rainstorm penetrated the tarpaulins laid over the set on the still open stage, and severely damaged it.

The rest of the factory scenes were shot in six weeks, uninterrupted except for a day in December when Douglas Fairbanks brought Lady Edwina Mountbatten and her party to visit the set. Working hours now tended to be longer than in silent days, when frequently no shooting began before lunch. Now Chaplin was generally at the studio by 10.30, although on days when he was playing alone he still preferred a shorter, afternoon session of work, perhaps to avoid exhaustion.

Even at this stage Chaplin remained undecided about sound. In public statements on the matter he was unequivocal. Early in 1931 he had made several statements to the press: 'I give the talkies six months more. At the most a year. Then they're done.' Three months later, in May 1931, he had modified his opinion slightly: 'Dialogue may or may not have a place in comedy ... What I merely said was that dialogue does not have a place in the sort of comedies I make ... For myself I know that I cannot use dialogue.' The interviewer asked him if he had tried:

> I never tried jumping off the monument in Trafalgar Square, but I have a definite idea that it would be unhealthful ... For years I have specialized in one type of comedy – strictly pantomime. I have measured it, gauged it, studied. I have been able to establish exact principles to govern its reactions on audiences. It has a certain pace and tempo. Dialogue, to my way of thinking, always slows action, because action must wait upon words.

However firm his public statements on the issue, in the privacy of his studio Chaplin was clearly less convinced. At the end of November he and Paulette did sound tests: since both had pleasant voices which recorded well, it is unlikely Chaplin was dissatisfied with them. It is now clear that Chaplin at this time had steeled himself to shoot the film, including his own scenes with dialogue. A dialogue script was prepared for all scenes up to and including the department store sequence, and still survives.

The dialogue which Chaplin gives to the Tramp is staccato, quippy, touched with nonsense; in the Dream House fantasy sequence it is remarkably similar to the cross-talk act between Calvero (Chaplin) and Terry (Claire Bloom), as Tramp and Pretty Girl, in Calvero's dream in *Limelight*.

GAMIN:	'What's your name?'
TRAMP:	'Me? oh, mine's a silly name. You wouldn't like it. It begins with an "X".'
GAMIN:	'Begins with an "X"?'
TRAMP:	'See if you can guess.'
GAMIN:	'Not eczema?'
TRAMP:	'Oh, worse than that – just call me Charlie.'
GAMIN:	'Charlie! There's no "X" in that!'
TRAMP:	'No – oh, well, where d'ya live?'
GAMIN:	'No place – here – there – anywhere.'
TRAMP:	'Anywhere? That's near where I live.'

The first dialogue which Chaplin began to rehearse was for the scenes in the gaol and warden's office. Much of the dialogue was concerned with confusions over the name of the curate and his wife – Stumbleglutz, Stumblerutz, Glumblestutz, Rumbleglutz. Stumblestutz and, as the inevitable climax, Grumblegutz. Chaplin was evidently deeply dissatisfied with the results. The unit had been told that the Dream House sequence would be shot the following day with sound. In fact no more dialogue scenes were to be shot for *Modern Times*.

Chaplin did proceed with sound effects, however, and used the recording apparatus set up to create the stomach rumbles for the scene. He created the noise himself by blowing bubbles into a pail of water. As Totheroh warned him, the noises were much too explosive;

eventually they were re-shot. The fact that Chaplin was sufficiently keen to create the effects personally indicates the extent to which he was intrigued by sound problems at this time. A memorandum about possible musical effects notes: 'Natural sounds part of composition, i.e. Auto horns, sirens, and cowbells worked into the music.'

Chester Conklin, who had worked with Chaplin so many times since *Making a Living*, was engaged for three weeks' work as the walrus-moustached old workman who gets caught up in the cog wheels of a gigantic machine of doubtful purpose. When he becomes completely stuck, Charlie considerately feeds lunch to his protruding head. Two other reliable old allies from two-reeler days – Hank Mann and an escalator – were introduced for the department store scenes which, including retakes, took five weeks to shoot. Eight working days of this time were taken up by Chaplin's brilliant roller-skating routine: the skating was quickly shot but time was needed to prepare the trick 'glass shots' to give the illusion that he was skating at the edge of a high balcony with no balustrade.

Charlie was still intent on ending the film with the Gamin as a nun. The sentiment was perilous, but Chaplin had attempted perilous things before: the ending of *City Lights*, seen set down on paper, could be cause for nerviness. He also planned to prepare for the ending with a recurrent theme of a kindly nun, and her effect upon the Gamin.

THEME

1. On one of our adventures we come into contact with a nun. It's just a momentary feeling or sense of beauty and the Gamin is moved by it.

Gamin: 'She makes me want to cry.'

The nun is always very tender and nice to the Gamin – a pat on the head, etc.

2. We encounter her in the street again. The Gamin imitates her headgear and admires it. Each time the Gamin sees her she stops short in the midst of the comedy and her eyes fill and she says:

Gamin: 'She makes me feel wicked.'

3. We are in the street and the Gamin has just pinched something. The nun comes around the corner and the Gamin puts it back.

Charlot:* 'What in blazes is wrong with you?'
Gamin: (Gulp) 'I dunno.'

The nun sequence was shot in late May and early June. On Friday 25 July 1935 Chaplin and his assistants ran the film and, noted the studio secretary at the time, discussed a new ending. No one concerned has left any account of the discussion, so we shall never know if the decision to change was spontaneously Chaplin's or whether, as sometimes happened, he made his judgement from watching the reactions of his colleagues. Whatever the temper of the meeting, Chaplin went off on his yacht the following day for the weekend.

The final sequence to be shot on *Modern Times* was the café scene. It took twelve days, and involved a large number of extras: 250 were called for the day when Chaplin shot the business of carrying a roast duck across the jam-packed dance floor. This was to be the historic scene in which the Tramp, for the first and only time, found his voice on the screen. When the Tramp opened his mouth and sang it was in a language of his own invention, expressive of everything and nothing:

> Se bella piu satore, je notre so catore,
> Je notre qui cavore, je la qu', la qui, la quai!
> Le spinash or le busho, cigaretto toto bello,
> Ce rakish spagoletto, si la tu, la tu, la tua!
> Senora pelafima, voulez-vous le taximeter,
> La zionta sur le tita, tu le tu le tu le wa!

and so on, for several more verses. The accompanying pantomime elaborates a tale of a seducer and a coyly yielding maiden.

At some point during late July or early August, the decision was finally taken to change the ending. The last shots taken on the café set, on 20 August, were those involving the detectives who arrive at the café to take the Gamin away. Since this action, and the subsequent getaway of Charlie and the Gamin, provide the link with the present ending of the film, the clear assumption is that the decision was made during the shooting of the café scenes.

The last retakes were taken on 30 August, and after the Labour Day holiday Chaplin began cutting. On 10 September the film was

---

* A curious aspect of this series of story notes is the alternation of 'Charlie' and 'Charlot' in referring to the Tramp character. Elsewhere in the same notes Chaplin, exceptionally, refers to his character in the first person, styling Tramp and Gamin as 'We'.

in a sufficiently assembled form for Chaplin to run it for two of his most valued critics: Charles Junior and Sydney, who had just arrived back after three months with their mother in New York. At ten years old, Charles Junior observed with astonishment the extent of the physical and emotional strain to which Chaplin submitted himself in the course of making a picture. After the day's work, during which he would astound and irritate his staff with his apparent inexhaustibility, he would arrive home, still in make-up and costume, already half asleep and so tired that he had to be helped from his car. The exhaustion, young Charles remembered years later, was worse when the day had not gone well. Chaplin's therapy for his weariness was in itself punishing. He would shut himself in his steam room for three quarters of an hour, after which he might well emerge sufficiently restored to go out for dinner. Sometimes, though, he would simply retire to bed for the evening, and have his meal sent up.

In the last stages of shooting *Modern Times* he had worked with such concentration that he had actually lived at the studio, and brought George, the Japanese cook, there to see to his meals. Paulette, like Chaplin's previous wives, discovered that at such critical times Chaplin's work left no room for personal life, even his most precious relationships. More easily than the previous women she ultimately acknowledged this insuperable rival. When she was seen around the town without Chaplin, however, there was speculation about a break-up; though what was to be broken up was unclear, since Chaplin and Paulette, with admirable disdain for the gossips, refused to clarify their marital or non-marital status merely to satisfy other people's curiosity.

Work on the music began in August 1935. Alfred Newman, whose collaboration on *City Lights* had given Chaplin great satisfaction, was again to be musical director, and Edward Powell was engaged as orchestrator. Powell wired to the East Coast to invite a talented colleague from his days with the music publishers Harms, David Raksin, to join him. Raksin, who has vividly and sensitively recorded his impressions of working with Chaplin,[*] recalls that Powell's telegram arrived on 8 August 1935, four days after his twenty-third birthday. Chaplin, having been promised a musician who was 'brilliant, experienced, a composer, orchestrator and arranger with several big shows in his arranging cap' confided that he was somewhat

[*] *Quarterly Journal of the Library of Congress*, Summer, 1983.

disconcerted when 'this infant shows up'. Raksin for his part was captivated by Chaplin, loved *Modern Times* and laughed at it so hard that Chaplin for a time wondered whether he was exaggerating for his benefit. After only a week and a half, however, Raksin was summarily fired:

> Like many self-made autocrats, Chaplin demanded unquestioning obedience from his associates; years of instant deference to his point of view had persuaded him that it was the only one that mattered. And he seemed unable, or unwilling, to understand the paradox that this imposition of will over his studio had been achieved in a manner akin to that which he professed to deplore in *Modern Times*. I, on the other hand, have never accepted the notion that it is my job merely to echo the ideas of those who employ me; and I had no fear of opposing him when necessary, because I believed he would recognize the value of an independent mind close at hand.
>
> When I think of it now, it strikes me as appallingly arrogant to have argued with a man like Chaplin about the appropriateness of the thematic material he proposed to use in his own picture. But the problem was real. There is a specific kind of genius that traces its ancestry back to the magpie family, and Charlie was one of those. He had accumulated a veritable attic full of memories and scraps of ideas, which he converted to his own purposes with great style and individuality. This can be perceived in the subject matter, as well as the execution of his story lines and sequences. In the area of music, the influence of the English music hall was very strong, and since I felt that nothing but the best would do for this remarkable film, when I thought his approach was a bit vulgar, I would say 'I think we can do better than that.' To Charlie this was insubordination, pure and simple – and the culprit had to go.

Raksin was heartbroken, but Newman told him, 'I've been looking at your sketches, and they're marvellous – what you're doing with Charlie's little tunes. He'd be crazy to fire you.' As Raksin was packing to leave, Alf Reeves called him and asked him to come back. Raksin agreed, after first explaining to Chaplin that he could always hire a musical secretary if that was what he wanted, 'but if he needed someone who loved his picture and was prepared to risk getting fired every day to make sure that the music was as good as it could possibly be, then I would love to work with him again.' This was the beginning of 'four and a half months of work and some of the happiest days of my life.'

Raksin feels that previous commentators have given at once too much and too little credit to Chaplin's musical abilities.

Charlie and I worked hand in hand. Sometimes the initial phrases were several phrases long, and sometimes they consisted of only a few notes, which Charlie would whistle, or hum, or pick out on the piano ... I remained in the projection room, where Charlie and I worked together to extend and develop the musical ideas to fit what was on the screen. When you have only a few notes or a short phrase with which to cover a scene of some length, there must ensue considerable development and variation – what is called for is the application of the techniques of composition to shape and extend the themes to the desired proportions. (That so few people understand this, even those who may otherwise be well informed, makes possible the common delusion that composing consists of getting some kind of microflash of an idea, and that the rest of it is mere artisanry; it is this misconception that has enabled a whole generation of hummers and strummers to masquerade as composers.)

Theodore Huff and others to the contrary, no informed person has claimed that Charlie had any of the essential techniques. But neither did he feed me a little tune and say, 'You take it from there.' On the contrary: we spent hours, days, months in that projection room running scenes and bits of action over and over, and we had a marvellous time shaping the music until it was exactly the way we wanted it. By the time we were through with a sequence we had run it so often that we were certain the music was in perfect sync. Very few composers work this way ... the usual procedure is to work from timing sheets, with a stop clock, to coordinate image and music ...

Chaplin had picked up an assortment of tricks of our trade and some of the jargon and took pleasure in telling me that some phrase should be played 'vrubato', which I embraced as a real improvement upon the intended Italian word, which was much the poorer for having been deprived of the *v*. Yet, very little escaped his eye or ear, and he had suggestions not only about themes and their appropriateness, but also about the way in which the music should develop ...

Sometimes in the course of our work, when the need for a new piece of thematic material arose, Charlie might say, 'A bit of "Gershwin" might be nice there.' He meant that the Gershwin style would be appropriate for that scene. And indeed there is one phrase that makes a very clear genuflection toward one of the themes in *Rhapsody in Blue*. Another instance would be the tune that later became a pop song called 'Smile'. Here, Charlie said something like, 'What we need here is one of those "Puccini" melodies.' Listen to the result, and you will hear that although the notes are not Puccini's, the style and feeling are.

The ten-year-old Charles Chaplin Junior observed that 'if the people in his own studio had suffered from Dad's perfectionist drive, the musicians ... endured pure torture.'

471

Dad wore them all out. Edward Powell concentrated so hard writing the music down that he almost lost his eyesight and had to go to a specialist to save it. David Raksin, working an average of twenty hours a day, lost twenty-five pounds and sometimes was so exhausted that he couldn't find strength to go home but would sleep on the studio floor. Al Newman saw him one day in the studio street walking along with tears running down his cheeks.

Chaplin would work with Raksin on the transcription of his compositions night after night until long after midnight, and did not even spare him at the weekends, though on one of these there was the consolation of working on the *Panacea* while Paulette took the children to Palm Springs to keep them out of their busy father's way. Raksin recalls not only the killing round-the-clock work, but also the gags and jokes and high spirits. Unfortunately it was to end unhappily. Newman liked to work in the small hours of the night. At one of these nocturnal sessions on 4 December, when Raksin was taking a night off at Chaplin's suggestion, Chaplin and the volatile Newman had a fierce argument. After a bad take, Chaplin accused the musicians of 'dogging it' (lying down on the job). Newman exploded, hurled his baton across the studio, addressed a string of curses to Chaplin and stalked off to his suite to revive himself with a whiskey before calling Sam Goldwyn to tell him that on no account would he ever work again with Chaplin. Nor did he. From loyalty to Newman, Raksin would not take over the conducting, and the outcome was an estrangement from Chaplin that lasted for many years. Powell was coerced on the strength of his contract to conduct. 'With Eddie conducting, I did most of the remaining orchestration, and the recordings concluded in a rather sad and indeterminate spirit.' The music was finally completed on 22 December 1935. Years later the former cordiality between Chaplin and Raksin was resumed: the musician last visited the studio the day before Chaplin's final departure from America in 1952.

To add to his anxieties, Chaplin had a distinguished house guest: H. G. Wells arrived in Hollywood on 27 November for a four-week stay; and the evening of the Newman row, he and Chaplin were guests of honour at a Motion Picture Academy dinner. With Paulette's help Wells was somehow entertained. Alf Reeves wrote to Sydney that he had not even seen the great man during his visit, because Chaplin only brought him to the studio at nights. With the music finished, however, his host at least had time to see Wells off on his flight back to the East.

Chaplin finally previewed *Modern Times*, with great secrecy ahead of the show, in San Francisco. Alf Reeves was able to report to Sydney the following day: 'audience applauded "Titine" (and "encored" it!) and cheered at the end.' Chaplin nevertheless decided on a few cuts and there were more after a second preview at the Alexander Theatre, Glendale. Generally the launching of this film was effected more quietly than that of *City Lights*. The film opened at the Rivoli, New York to capacity business on 5 February 1936, and at the Tivoli, London on 11 February. The following day there was a gala première at Grauman's Chinese Theatre in Hollywood, but it was a quieter event. Perhaps Chaplin was more confident this time. Certainly the public reaction was all he could have hoped for. The press was mixed. One section disapproved because he had attempted socio-political satire; another part regretted that he had not, though he seemed to promise it with the opening title of the film: 'the story of industry, of individual enterprise – humanity crusading in the pursuit of happiness'.

Private matters from time to time obtruded upon Chaplin's concentration. The Lindbergh case was still very much in people's minds in autumn 1934, and there were kidnap threats against the Chaplin children. Chaplin announced to the press that he had hired bodyguards and armed the house and studio; a few weeks earlier he had given his opinions on the possibility of his own kidnap. 'Not one cent for ransom! I've given positive orders to my associates that under no condition is one cent to be paid anyone trying to extort money from me. If I should be kidnapped – and I'm not worrying any that it's going to happen – I'd fight at the first opportunity. They'd either have to let me go or do murder.'

In April 1935 Minnie Chaplin became seriously ill in the South of France. She was operated upon but shortly afterwards died. The telegram of sympathy which Chaplin sent to his brother during Minnie's last illness vividly illustrates how even genuine fraternal concern could not supersede his preoccupation with work. He advises Sydney to be 'philosophical' and to 'buck up':

I HAVE BEEN WORKING HARD ON THE PICTURE WHICH WILL BE READY FOR FALL RELEASE AND FROM ALL INDICATIONS WE SHALL HAVE A SENSATIONAL SUCCESS STOP IN TREATMENT IT WILL BE SIMILAR TO CITY LIGHTS WITH SOUND EFFECTS AND AUDIBLE TITLES SPOKEN BY ONE PERSON HOW-

EVER WE ARE GOING TO EXPERIMENT WITH THIS IDEA STOP
I INTEND TO WORK RIGHT ON AFTER FINISHING THIS PICTURE
AS I FEEL I AM IN MY STRIDE AND INTEND TO MAKE HAY
WHILE THE SUN SHINES STOP WHAT YOU NEED IS A CHANGE
YOU SHOULD COME HERE WHERE YOUR ABILITY WOULD BE
OF GREAT SERVICE AND VALUE STOP WHEN MINNIE GETS
WELL YOU MIGHT CONSIDER COMING TO HOLLYWOOD IT
WOULD DO YOU BOTH GOOD STOP.

No doubt between his personal troubles Sydney was both cheered and sceptical about Chaplin's intentions to go straight back to work. Perhaps Chaplin had in mind a project which he had somehow found time to continue preparing during the whole production period of *Modern Times* – apparently the only time that he worked on another feature project when he was already occupied with a film. Chaplin commentators with a psychoanalytical bent have made much of his persistent ambition to make a film about Napoleon. His interest is probably quite simply explained. Napoleon offers a uniquely rich role for an actor of small stature. Chaplin had been fascinated by the character ever since childhood, when his mother had told him that his father resembled the Emperor. In 1922, when looking for a vehicle to launch Edna Purviance as a dramatic actress (the eventual choice was *A Woman of Paris*) he had thought of a story to team the two of them as Napoleon and Josephine. When he first showed an interest in Lita Grey he spoke of creating the role of Josephine for her. Chaplin and Lita went to a fancy dress party given by Marion Davies costumed as Napoleon and Josephine. Subsequently Lita began to worry when she found that he had offered the role in turn to Merna Kennedy. In 1926, much impressed by the Spanish singer Raquel Meller, Chaplin had spoken of working with her in a Napoleon film; but a year later the appearance of Abel Gance's spectacular *Napoleon* temporarily discouraged him, even though it was shown in the United States only in a version cut by Metro Goldwyn Mayer from the original six hours to little more than sixty minutes.

The idea of a Napoleon film became serious again soon after the completion of *City Lights*. In the course of his 1931 world tour, Chaplin met Comte Jean de Limur, who had been one of his young assistants on *A Woman of Paris*, and who recommended to him Jean Weber's novel *La Vie Secrète de Napoleon Ier*. Negotiations for the film rights began but foundered when Weber tried to impose restrictive conditions upon the adaptation .

Word of Chaplin's plans reached Sydney in Nice after his brother's return to Hollywood. His letter reflects his relief at the idea of a subject not likely to pose such problems and expense as *City Lights*:

There has been considerable publicity over here concerning your next picture. They say you are thinking of doing a Napoleonic story. Of course I know that this publicity has broken before but if you are really serious in the matter I think that a dramatic picture coming from you would be a great box-office attraction at this time, as so many millions of people are waiting to hear you in the talkies. Then again it might be a great advantage from the cost point of view as the scenario of the dramatic production would have to be almost complete in detail before you started to shoot, in which case the shooting would not take you so very long. It is also a great idea because it would leave your present character in its present pantomimic form. If you do decide upon this subject I would certainly advise that you make it more the domestic side of Napoleon's life as this offers great possibilities with good human comedy, and a side of Napoleon which so far, I think, has not been presented. Besides, it would save a tremendous outlay of money which would be required in portraying the spectacular or militaristic side of the Napoleonic period ... In any case whatever you decide to do I would strongly advise that you do not gamble too much of your fortune in your next picture as conditions are very unsettled and the film business is trending [*sic*] towards large combines with the small independent exhibitors being frozen out. This will make the booking situation a little more difficult ...

Back in California after his tour, Chaplin continued to ponder the project, but for the time being was too occupied with his *Woman's Home Companion* articles and the legal wrangles over the employment of Charles Junior and Sydney Junior. In the summer of 1933, however, Chaplin met Alistair Cooke. Cooke was then twenty-five and in the United States on a Commonwealth Fund Fellowship. When he arrived at the studio to interview Chaplin for the *Manchester Guardian* Chaplin was immediately taken by the attractive, intelligent and witty young Englishman. Invitations to dinner and then to the yacht followed. In the winter of 1933, after Cooke had returned to the East, Chaplin wrote to suggest that he might like to return to Hollywood the following summer to help him research and write a *Napoleon* script.

Cooke duly returned in the early summer of 1934 and began with historical research in the public library, using Las Cases' *Memorial of St Helena* as the principal source. The research notes still survive in the Chaplin archive, though nothing of the script remains. Cooke recalls long working sessions generally with Henry Bergman in attendance, and sometimes with Carter De Haven who was meanwhile working with Chaplin on *Modern Times*. Chaplin at the outset explained his method: 'We look for some little incident, some vignette that fixes the other characters. With them the audience must never be in any doubt. We have to fix them on sight. Nobody cares about *their* troubles. They stay the same. You know them every time they appear. This is no different from the characters who surround "the little fellow". *He's* the one we develop.'

The script sessions continued into August 1934 and Cooke thought they 'were coming along well' when Chaplin abruptly informed him that it was a beautiful idea, but for somebody else. Cooke married (Chaplin agreed to be best man, but since Cooke tactlessly failed to invite Paulette, did not make an appearance), declined Chaplin's offer to put him into *Modern Times* as a light comedian, and returned to London to be the BBC's film critic.

In fact, however, even though he was now hard at work on *Modern Times*, Chaplin had by no means abandoned the Napoleon project. In 1934 negotiations for the rights of *La Vie Secrète de Napoleon Ier* were reopened. Sydney now took an active interest, and was very suspicious of de Limur's procrastination in the affair. Weber, the author, was now more amenable – partly because he was having alimony problems. After a good deal of haggling and back-tracking by Weber and his agent, a price of 78,650 francs was agreed, though Weber, on account of his marital problems, requested that any publicity given to the arrangement should declare the sum as no more than 30,000 francs.

The Chaplin Film Corporation acquired rights to the book in December 1935 for a period of eight years; in January 1936 Jean de Limur delivered a film treatment based on the novel. The treatment had a fatal weakness: it did not provide a suitably prominent part for Paulette. Chaplin had meanwhile been working on an independent treatment of the Napoleon subject. In July 1935 John Strachey stayed with Chaplin and Paulette at their Beverly Hills house. It is not certain when or how they first met, though it was most likely during the 1931 European holiday.

Strachey was a sympathetic spirit. At thirty-four, he was already one of the most prominent left-wing intellectuals in Britain, and had recently published *The Coming Struggle for Power* and *The Nature of Capitalist Crisis.* Since breaking away from Oswald Mosley's New Party in 1931, he had become increasingly drawn to Communism, though he was never to become a member of the Communist Party. Like Chaplin, he admired both Roosevelt and Keynes. Here was someone with whom Chaplin could enjoy sympathetic discussion of his own newly-formulated Economic Solution and his pacifism. Strachey was amusing and charming as well as intelligent. Moreover, though he was tall and somewhat ungainly, he was an enthusiastic tennis player.

Together Chaplin and Strachey developed their ideas for a new scenario, and Strachey returned to England to write it. The script was completed early in 1936 and registered for copyright on 9 April as

NAPOLEON'S RETURN FROM ST HELENA,*

written by Charles Chaplin of Great Britain, domiciled in United States, at Los Angeles, California, in collaboration with John Strachey of Great Britain.

The Chaplin–Strachey script, which possibly incorporated the work already done with Cooke, was in several ways an advance on the de Limur treatment. There is a much stronger political and pacifist moral, it has more action and, most important, there is a well-tailored role for Paulette. The only significant element retained from the Weber novel is the initial premise of Napoleon's escape from St Helena with the help of a self-sacrificing double who takes his place. The script has many typical Chaplin elements, in particular a sustained tone of irony and the theme of love between an older man and a young girl which is frustrated by her romantic illusions. Chaplin also intended to develop some of his own notions on peace and politics through Napoleon. A draft annotated in Chaplin's handwriting sketches a discussion between Napoleon and Montholon at St Helena:

NAPOLEON: There is something wrong with the whole political structure of Europe ... Governments and Constitutions are old-fashioned, obsolete ... mechanical science is running away with us ... steamboats, railroads, iron barges ... all these things spell revolution and we must prepare for the future ... The man of the future will be a scientist ... Future Governments will realize that the religious and moral prin-

---

* Alternative titles suggested were *The Return*, *The Return From St Helena*, *The Return of the Emperor*, *Napoleon's Return* and *The Return of Napoleon*.

ciples are problems for the individual, but the economic problems of the individual are the business of the State, and the Governments of the future will separate these two factors . . . Countries will combine forces for the protection of their trades . . . The statesman of the future will be the Nation's book keeper, not a dispenser of moral principles, and politics will become mathematics . . . Montholon, one hears words like 'Socius' . . .

MONTHOLON: You have me swimming . . . I don't know what it is all about.

NAPOLEON: I mean the day of war and aggression will be a thing of the past . . . One can accomplish more by treaties, friendship, commercial understanding . . . If I could live my life again, I'd use the power of my victories to unite all nations of Europe into one solid State . . . Evolution tends towards these things . . .

This was only a first sketch of course – with much like it the audience would have been swimming along with poor Montholon. Still, in the Napoleon of 1936, with his prophecies of the EEC, we can already sense something of the final speech of *The Great Dictator* and anticipate the diatribes of young Macabee in *A King in New York*.

A device in the script concerning the theft of a treaty was suggested by a notorious adventure of Marion Davies which had occurred a few years earlier. In the summer of 1928 William Randolph Hearst, Marion and their entourage – including Harry Crocker – were touring in Europe and were entertained to lunch by the French Foreign Minister, Aristide Briand. Shortly afterwards Hearst's suite at the Crillon was searched and he was ordered to leave the country within an hour. Someone had stolen from the Ministry a pact concerning Anglo-French naval deployments, and Hearst was the prime suspect since the theft had occurred at the time of the lunch. Despite the search, Hearst, it seems, successfully concealed the document on his person when he left for London.

Subsequently, after a number of arrests in Paris, considerable diplomatic embarrassment and maximum use of the document's headline value in the Hearst press, Marion regaled her friends with a story that was tall even by her standards in an effort to exculpate Hearst. Her version was that during the dinner she excused herself to go to the ladies' room, and on the way noticed a half-open door to a room inside which there stood an unlocked safe. Unable to resist her curiosity, she had opened the safe, and merely out of mischief removed a document which she had stuck into the elastic of her 'sissy-britches'. This last detail makes all the less credible her claim that she then forgot about the deed – a document in one's underclothes is not exactly comfortable – until she was taking her bath, whereupon she confessed what she had done to the suitably shocked Hearst. Few people believed Marion's version of the story, but it clearly amused Chaplin sufficiently for him to adapt it for his Napoleon plot.

At some point Chaplin had still photographs made of himself in the role of Napoleon, with Harry Crocker as (presumably) Las Cases. His own costume is the one in which he attended Marion Davies' fancy-dress ball. Since Crocker already looks slightly older and heavier than he appeared in *The Circus*, the stills may have been taken some years after the party, and before Crocker's departure from the studio during the shooting of *City Lights*. The project of a Napoleon film seems to have been finally abandoned almost as soon as the Strachey script was finished, having remained a preoccupation with Chaplin for at least fourteen years. By the time *Napoleon's Return from St Helena* was registered for copyright, Chaplin and Paulette had embarked on a tour of the Far East, and were to return full of new ideas.

On Monday 17 February, five days after the gala première of *Modern Times* at Grauman's Chinese Theatre in Hollywood, Chaplin, together with Paulette, her mother and his valet, Frank Yonamori, sailed from Wilmington on the SS *Coolidge* for a holiday in Honolulu. Frank had previously made reservations at the Royal Hawaiian Hotel, but when the ship arrived in Honolulu the Chaplin party stayed aboard. Having noticed that the cargo was labelled for Hong Kong, Chaplin impetuously decided that he would take Paulette to the Far East. She protested that she was unprepared and had nothing suitable to wear for the trip, but he told her that they would buy anything they needed *en route*. The decision taken, Chaplin wired Alf Reeves, 'PLANNING TO BE ON "COOLIDGE" TO HONG KONG – WILL BE AWAY THREE MONTHS.' Alf had learned to accept Chaplin's caprices with equanimity.

Another passenger on the *Coolidge* was Jean Cocteau who, as a form of convalescence from illness, was retracing the steps of Phileas Fogg in company with his Moroccan lover, Marcel Khill. In his published account of the journey Cocteau coyly called Marcel his

'Passepartout'; Chaplin discreetly described him as Cocteau's 'secretary'. It is fascinating to compare Chaplin's account of their meetings with Cocteau's. Chaplin describes how the enthusiasm of their first encounter and a stirring philosophical conversation interpreted by Marcel, which went on far into the night, was quickly dispelled by the barrier and embarrassments of language. According to his version the rest of the journey was spent in dodging each other and diligently missing appointments. When they found they were both to make the return trip on the *Coolidge*, 'we became resigned, making no further attempts at enthusiasm.'

This is markedly different from Cocteau's account. The explanation of the disparity may be that Chaplin was too shy and in a certain sense too modest to believe that a stranger could feel so enthusiastic an affection for him as did Cocteau. 'My meeting with Charlie Chaplin,' the latter recalled, 'remains the delightful miracle of this voyage.' When he discovered Chaplin was on board, Cocteau with diffidence sent a note to his cabin. At dinner that night Chaplin showed no sign of recognition, and Cocteau reluctantly decided that he wished to remain incognito and undisturbed. Later that evening, however, as Cocteau was undressing for bed, Chaplin and Paulette knocked at Cocteau's door: they had only received his note after dinner, and had then cautiously checked with the purser to make sure it was not an imposture.

Cocteau felt none of Chaplin's embarrassment over their means of communication:

> I do not speak English; Chaplin does not speak French. Yet we talked without the slightest difficulty. What is happening? What is this language? It is *living* language, the most living of all and springs from the will to communicate at all costs in the language of mime, the language of poets, the language of the heart. Chaplin detaches every word, stands it on the table as it were on a plinth, walks back a step, turns it where it will catch the best light. The words he uses for my benefit are easily transported from one language to the other. Sometimes the gesture precedes the words and escorts them. He announces each word first before pronouncing it and comments on it afterwards. No slowness, or only the apparent slowness of balls when a juggler is juggling with them. He never confuses them, you can follow their flight in the air.[15]

Cocteau was delighted by Paulette's intelligence in refusing to intervene as interpreter, which she was equipped to do: 'If I help them they will lose themselves in details. Left to their own devices, they only say the essentials.'

Chaplin spoke to Cocteau with enthusiasm about his future projects. He was thinking of making a film in Bali, and seriously proposed that Marcel might play a part in it. (Marcel was thrilled, but Cocteau said he could not spare him.) His own next role, he said, was to be that of a clown torn between the contrasts of real life and the theatre – a foreshadowing, perhaps, of *Limelight*. Cocteau wished that he would one day play Prince Myshkin. They talked of *The Gold Rush* and Chaplin complained: 'The dance of the bread rolls. That's what they all congratulate me on. It is a mere cog in the machine. A detail. If that was what they specially noticed, they must have been blind to the rest!'[16] Of his most recent film Chaplin told Cocteau, 'I worked too long on *Modern Times*. When I had worked a scene up to perfection, it seemed to fall from the tree. I shook the branches and sacrificed the best episodes. They existed in their own right. I could show them separately, one by one, like my early two-reelers.'[17] Chaplin thereupon mimed two of his favourite cut scenes: the scene of the stick in the grating from *City Lights* and a street-crossing scene from *Modern Times*.

Cocteau was fascinated by Chaplin. Although, according to his account, 'we joined forces, shared our meals and the journey alike; to such an extent did we form the habit of living together that we found it painful to part company in San Francisco,' Cocteau nevertheless recognized Chaplin's shyness and withdrawal. 'Even friendship is suspect; the duties and inconveniences it entails. His instant taking to me was, it seems, unique, and it produced a kind of panic in him. I felt him withdraw into himself again, and close up after his expansiveness.'[18] Most of all he was delighted to observe Chaplin's relationship with Paulette:

> Paulette went off for a few minutes. Charlie bent over and whispered in a mysterious voice, 'And then I feel such pity.' What? Pity for this thousand-spiked cactus, this little lioness with her mane and superb claws, this great sports Rolls with its shining leatherwork and metal? The whole of Chaplin is in that remark: that is what his heart is like.
>
> Pity for himself, the tramp, pity for us, pity for her – the poor waif whom he drags after him to make her eat because she is hungry, put her to bed because she is sleepy, snatch her away from the snares of city life because she is pure, and suddenly I no longer see a Hollywood star in her silver satin page-boy outfit nor the rich impresario with his white curls

481

and salt and pepper tweeds – but a pale little man, curly-haired, with his comic cane, dragging away a victim of the ogre of capital cities and police-traps, as he stumbles along through the world on one leg.

I find it extremely difficult to fit the two pictures together. The florid-complexioned man who is talking to me and the pale little ghost who is his multiple angel whom he can divide up like quicksilver. I gradually succeed in superimposing the two Chaplins. A grimace, a wrinkle, a gesture, a wink and the two silhouettes coincide, that of the fool of the Bible, the little saint in a bowler hat who tugs at his cuffs and straightens his shoulders as he enters paradise, and that of the impresario pulling his own strings.[19]

Cocteau reported that Chaplin was working energetically during the course of the trip, 'shut up in his cabin . . . unshaved, in a suit which is too tight, his hair untidy, he stands fidgeting his glasses in those very small hands of his, setting in order sheets of paper covered in writing.' He may have been working on the Bali script that he mentioned to Cocteau, but Shanghai gave him a completely new idea. A party from the ship including Cocteau, Chaplin and Paulette went slumming to a dance hall called the 'Venus', where they watched American sailors dancing with 'taxi-girls'. Out of this and certain memories of May Reeves came the idea for *Stowaway*. By the time he arrived back in California on 11 June 1936 Chaplin was able to report that he had already written ten thousand words of a story with a Far Eastern setting for Paulette.

The story told of a White Russian countess, now earning her living as a Shanghai taxi-girl, who stows away in the cabin of an American millionaire diplomat. Chaplin continued to work energetically at the script for the next four months and by the end of October had completed a fairly polished draft. At this point, like the *Napoleon* idea, it was shelved. Unlike *Napoleon*, however, it was to be revived more than thirty years later and, with comparatively little revision apart from geographical relocation, to serve as the scenario for *A Countess From Hong Kong*.

In August work began on an alternative project. The London office of United Artists had purchased on behalf of the Chaplin Film Corporation film rights in D. L. Murray's period novel *Regency*, and a writer, Major Ronald Bodley, was hired to work on it. Bodley prepared a synopsis and treatment, and from October to February Chaplin also worked on the script, making copious manuscript emendations and notes. In March 1937 Major Bodley's engagement with the studio came to an end, and on 26 May, while dictating an introduction to Gilbert Seldes' book *Movies for the Millions*, Chaplin informed his secretary, Catherine Hunter, that *Regency* had been laid aside in favour of the contemporary story on which he was already working.

It is now rather unclear what recommended D. L. Murray's costume romance about the adventures of a high spirited and unconventional young girl of aristocratic blood in Regency England. True, it offered a lively part for Paulette. Moreover Chaplin gave it a political tinge by having the girl, Regency, torn between loyalty to the hedonist Regent and to a young highwayman of radical tendency. Chaplin's manuscript notes show a fascination with the central character; perhaps he saw in Regency something of Paulette herself.

> Regency has a dominant will. It manifests itself at a very early age . . . She was not popular among her own sex, but certain men, even young men, were irresistibly drawn to her . . . When men fell in love with her, they were so completely under her domination that she lost interest in them. On the other hand, anyone that tried to dominate her she immediately repelled. So long as no man stood in the path of her will, she was a friend to him. What stood out uppermost in her character was her firm sense of justice.

Years later Chaplin revealed that he and Paulette had been married in Canton during the course of their Far Eastern holiday. Although he maintained a genuine and loyal concern for Paulette's career, their professional and personal lives were by now already beginning to drift irresistibly apart. Paulette was too ambitious and impatient to wait for the next Chaplin project. Along with every other Hollywood leading lady, she longed for the role of Scarlett O'Hara in *Gone With The Wind*. Chaplin helped her in every way he could to equip herself for the role. He even arranged special tuition with his friend Constance Collier, the distinguished British stage actress. No one at the studio liked to tell him that Paulette was inclined to cut the lessons short in favour of other current interests. She eventually took her screen test on 1 October 1937. She did not get the part, though whether for want of tuition or too much of it, will never be known.

15

THE GREAT DICTATOR

Quite apart from any particular merits of the film, *The Great Dictator* remains an unparalleled phenomenon, an epic incident in the history of mankind. The greatest clown and best-loved personality of his age directly challenged the man who had instigated more evil and human misery than any other in modern history.

There was, to begin with, something uncanny in the resemblance between Chaplin and Hitler, representing opposite poles of humanity. On 21 April 1939, a year and a half before the release of *The Great Dictator*, an unsigned article in the *Spectator* noted:

> Providence was in an ironical mood when, fifty years ago this week, it was ordained that Charles Chaplin and Adolf Hitler should make their entry into the world within four days of each other . . . Each in his own way has expressed the ideas, sentiments, aspirations of the millions of struggling citizens ground between the upper and the lower millstone of society; the date of their birth and the identical little moustache (grotesque intentionally in Mr Chaplin) they well might have been fixed by nature to betray the common origin of their genius. For genius each of them undeniably possesses. Each has mirrored the same reality – the predicament of the 'little man' in modern society. Each is a distorting mirror, the one for good, the other for untold evil. In Chaplin the little man is a clown, timid, incompetent, infinitely resourceful yet bewildered by a world that has no place for him. The apple he bites has a worm in it; his trousers, remnants of gentility, trip him up; his cane pretends to a dignity his position is far from justifying; when he pulls a lever it is the wrong one and disaster follows. He is a heroic figure, but heroic only in the patience and resource with which he receives the blows that fall upon his bowler. In his actions and loves he emulates the angels. But in Herr Hitler

the angel has become a devil. The soleless boots have become *Reitstieffeln*; the shapeless trousers, riding breeches; the cane, a riding crop; the bowler, a forage cap. The Tramp has become a storm trooper; only the moustache is the same.

There were even those who believed that Hitler had at first adopted the moustache in a deliberate attempt to suggest a resemblance to the man who had attracted so much love and loyalty in the world.

Konrad Bercovici brought a plagiarism suit against Chaplin, claiming that he had first proposed that Chaplin should play Hitler in the mid-1930s. A good many newspaper cartoonists, notably David Low, might equally have claimed the idea as their own; after all, it was inevitable. Much later Chaplin admitted, 'Had I known of the actual horrors of the German concentration camps, I could not have made *The Great Dictator*; I could not have made fun of the homicidal insanity of the Nazis.'[1] Hitler, true, turned out to be no laughing matter; but there was nothing light-hearted in Chaplin's deeper intentions in making the film. He suffered very real and acute pain and revulsion at the horrors and omens of world politics in the 1930s. We have seen, in his 1931 diatribe against the myth of patriotism, that he already foresaw with dread another war. His recent Far Eastern tour had made him more alert than most to the perils of the China Incident of July 1937 and the escalation of the Sino–Japanese conflict.

He was no less disturbed by events in Spain. In April 1938 the French film magazine *Cinémonde* published a translation of a remark-

able short story by Chaplin himself, entitled 'Rhythme'.* It describes
the execution of a Spanish Loyalist, a popular humorous writer. The
officer in charge of the firing squad was formerly a friend of the
condemned man; 'their divergent views were then friendly, but they
had finally provoked the unhappiness and disruption of the whole of
Spain.' Both the officer and the six men of the firing squad privately
hope that a reprieve may still come. Finally, though, the officer must
give the rhythmic orders: 'Attention! . . . Shoulder arms! . . . Present
arms! . . . Fire!' The officer gives the first three orders. Hurried
footsteps are heard: all realize that it is the reprieve. The officer calls
out 'Stop!' to his firing squad, but,

> Six men each held a gun. Six men had been trained through rhythm. Six
> men, hearing the shout 'Stop!' fired.

The story at once embodies those fears of seeing men turned into
machines which Chaplin had expressed in *Modern Times*, and looks
forward to some grim, ironic gags in *The Great Dictator*.[2]

There is more evidence of Chaplin's feelings about Spain in a poem
which he scribbled in a folio notebook among some memoranda on
the development of *Regency*, presumably in the winter of 1936–7.
The poem was quite clearly never meant for publication, or even for
other eyes. It was a private attempt to express his sentiments.

> To a dead Loyalist soldier
> on the battlefields of Spain
>
> Prone, mangled form,
> Your silence speaks your deathless cause,
> Of freedom's dauntless march.
> Though treachery befell you on this day
> And built its barricades of fear and hate
> Triumphant death has cleared the way
> Beyond the scrambling of human life
> Beyond the pale of imprisoning spears
> To let you pass.

There was, he said euphemistically, 'a good deal of bad behaviour in
the world'. Feeling as deeply as he did, he felt impelled to do whatever
he could to correct it, or at least to focus attention upon it. His only
weapon, as he knew, was comedy.

In the latter part of the 1930s Chaplin was very friendly with the

* No original English text for the story has been traced.

director King Vidor and his family, and it was through the Vidors, some time in 1938, that he met Tim Durant. Like Harry Crocker, Durant was a tall, good-looking, patrician, university-educated young man: Chaplin seemed to have a penchant for the type among his friends and assistants. Durant had the added merits of being sympathetic, amusing, discreet, and very good at tennis. Through Durant he was introduced into the society of Pebble Beach and Carmel, one hundred miles south of San Francisco. Chaplin called Pebble Beach 'the abode of lost souls'. He was fascinated, charmed and attracted by the collection of Californian millionaires who still made their homes there, and no less by the abandoned mansions that now lay in decay. The more Bohemian colony at nearby Carmel, a section of coast much favoured by artists and writers, had a different but potent attraction. He was especially pleased by his meetings there with the famous Californian poet Robinson Jeffers.

Tim Durant remembered that at first Chaplin was reluctant to become involved with the Pebble Beach set:

> I knew a girl who was married to one of the Crockers in San Francisco, and she heard I was there and called me up and asked me to come over for dinner and bring Charlie. But Charlie said to me, 'Listen, Tim, I don't want to get into this group at all . . .' I said, 'Look, Charlie, will you do this just as a personal favour – I don't ask you to do anything. Will you just go over and have dinner with them, and we can say honestly that we have to get back and do some work, and you can leave immediately.'
>
> He said, 'All right, Tim; but get me out of there, remember; don't let me spend the evening there.'
>
> So we went over there. We walked in and everybody congregated around him, you know, and he was a hero. He had an audience, and he couldn't leave – wanted to stay until three o'clock in the morning. After that he wanted to go out every night, because they accepted him as a great artist and a wonderful person. They loved him and he entertained them, and we went out all the time. He wrote many stories – I took notes of stories about the characters there. He had an idea of making a story about the people there.[3]

One of his hosts was D. L. James, who lived in a Spanish-style mansion perched on the cliff-edge at Carmel, one of northern California's architectural monuments. (James's parents actually had him baptized 'D.L.' with the idea that he could choose names to suit the initials when he grew up. In fact he remained simply 'D.L.' though occasionally he intimated that he might consider 'Dan' as a first name.) At the James house Chaplin met D.L.'s son Dan, who was then twenty-six, an aspiring writer and ardent Marxist, and rather unsettled: 'My writing was getting nowhere; I was separating from my wife; and I was just then thinking of going to New York.' They met on several occasions and Dan would hold forth on films and about the war against Fascism. Chaplin in turn outlined his ideas for a Hitler film.

When Chaplin returned from Pebble Beach to Hollywood at the end of the summer, Dan James took a chance and wrote to him saying that he was enthusiastic about the idea of the Hitler film, and would be very happy to be able to work on it in any capacity. 'I went on packing my bags for the East, though.' Somewhat to his surprise a telephone call came from the Chaplin studio a few days later, and he was invited to call and see Alf Reeves. Reeves warned him that Chaplin was very 'changeable', but that he liked him and was prepared to employ him on a salary of $80 a week, and to put him up at the Beverly Hills Hotel until he could find somewhere to live. 'My first evening he took me to Ciro's Trocadero Oyster bar; then we dined and he told me the outline of the story. The next day I went up and started to make notes . . . I think Charlie took me on because of my height, because my family had a castle out here, and because he knew pretty quickly I was a declared Communist, so that my background and political preoccupations would keep me from selling him out for money.'

This was presumably at the end of September 1938. The James knew John Steinbeck, whom Chaplin was eager to meet; Dan James made the necessary arrangements. On 1 October Dan accompanied Chaplin for a weekend at Steinbeck's ranch at Los Gatos. He was impressed by Chaplin's perspicuity: 'Even then he said, "There's a lot that's phoney in Steinbeck," and I think time has proved him right.'

For three months James reported daily to the house in Beverly Hills, where he would make notes as Chaplin discussed ideas for the plot and gags. From time to time James would go to the studio to dictate the notes to Kathleen Pryor: the first of these dictation sessions seems to have taken place on 26 October 1938. During these three months James was able to assess Chaplin's own political thinking:

He did not read deeply, but he *felt* deeply everything that happened. The end of *Modern Times*, for instance, reflected perfectly the optimism of the New Deal period: already by 1934 and 1935 he had a sense of that. He had probably never read Marx, but his conception of the millionaire in *City Lights* is an exact image for Marx's conception of the business cycle. Marx wrote of the madness of the business cycle once it began to roll, the veering from one extreme to another. Chaplin presents a magnificent metaphor. Whether he was aware of the social meaning of this I do not know, but *he got it.*

He had a sixth sense about a lot of things. In 1927 and 1928, for instance, he began to feel that the stock market was going mad, and he took everything he had and put it into Canadian gold.

Charlie called himself an anarchist. He was always fascinated with people of the left. One of the people he wanted to meet was Harry Bridges of the Longshoremen's Union. I fixed up a meeting, and they took to each other immediately. Chaplin talked about the beauty of labor, and described how in the islands he had heard the fishermen sing as they went out in their boats. Harry said, 'I think you would have found that it was the old men on the shore, the ones who had given up going to sea, who did the singing.'[4]

Whatever his exact politics, Charlie had a position of revolt against wealth and stuffiness. He had a real feeling for the underdog . . . He was certainly a libertarian. He saw Stalin as a dangerous dictator very early, and Bob [Meltzer] and I had difficulty getting him to leave Stalin out of the last speech in *The Great Dictator*. He was horrified by the Soviet–German pact.

His description of himself as an anarchist is as good as any. He believed in human freedom and human dignity. He hated and suspected the machine, even though it was the motion picture machine that gave him his life. I would say that he was anti-capitalist, anti-organization. And dammit, that's the way people ought to be.

When it came to Hitler it is easy to say, with hindsight, that Chaplin made too light of him. You have to remember that the film was conceived before Munich, and that Chaplin had undoubtedly had it in his head a couple of years before that. And the thought then was that this monster was not so awe-inspiring as he appeared. He was a big phoney, and had to be shown up as such. Of course by the time the film appeared, France had fallen and we knew much more; so that a lot of the comedy had lost its point.

The Great Dictator marked an inevitable revolution in Chaplin's working methods. This was to be his first dialogue film, and for the first time he was to begin a picture with a complete script. The old method had been to work out each sequence in turn, alternating periods of story preparation with shooting – changing, selecting and discarding ideas as the work proceeded. Now these processes had to be transferred to the preparatory period, the work on a definitive script. The notes which Dan James periodically dictated to Miss Pryor reveal the metamorphoses through which the story progressed during his preparatory work.

The original and basic premise was the physical resemblance of the Dictator and the little Jew. All the early treatments of the story begin with the return of Jewish soldiers, many maimed, from the war to the ghetto. They are all welcomed back by wives and families, except 'the little Jew' (clearly returning from service in *Shoulder Arms*). He 'is alone walking down the ghetto street. In his hunger for companionship he embraces a lamppost.'

One early idea was for a flophouse sequence which

> can be used for the setting of our inflation material. The little Jew will return to pay his bill. The sign will read, 'Beds, $1,000,000 a night – baths $500,000 extra.' Someone will send out for a package of cigarettes: 'You'll have to carry the money yourself,' or perhaps the little Jew goes out balancing a huge basket of currency on his head. $10,000,000 for cigars. The tobacco dealer insists that the money be counted. It is all in $1.00 bills.

Never willing to waste a good comedy idea, Chaplin planned to use the flea circus business, just as it appears in *The Professor*, for this scene. It stayed in through several successive treatments, but was finally abandoned. Having been frustrated in his efforts to introduce the business into *The Circus* and *The Great Dictator*, Chaplin would eventually manage to squeeze it into *Limelight*.

Chaplin early conceived the idea of two rival dictators competing to upstage one another. He was to abandon an idea for the Great Dictator's wife, a role intended for the famous Jewish comedienne Fanny Brice. A scene sketched out, with a lot of revision in Dan James's handwriting, indicates the kind of relationship Chaplin had in mind, and suggests that it might have encountered serious problems with the Breen Office and other censorship groups:

> SCENE: Mrs Hinkle alone – boredom and sex starvation with Freudian fruit symbols. Enter Hinkle from speech. She's mad at him – orders him about. He's preoccupied about matters of State.
>
> MRS: I'm a woman. I need affection, and all you think about is the State! THE STATE! What kind of state do you think I'm in?

HINKLE: You've made me come to myself. I'm not getting any younger. Sometimes I wonder. (good old melo)

MRS: Life is so short and these moments are so rare . . . Remember, Hinkle, I did everything for you. I even had an operation . . . on my nose. If you don't pay more attention to me I'll tell the whole world I'm Jewish!

HINKLE: Shhh!

FANNY: [*sic*] And I'm not so sure you aren't Jewish, too. We're having gefüllte fish for dinner.

HINKLE: Quiet! Quiet!

FANNY: Last night I dreamt about blimps.

HINKLE: Blimps?

FANNY: Yes, I dreamt we captured Paris in a big blimp and we went right through the Arc de Triomphe. And then I dreamed about a city all full of Washington monuments.

(She presses grapes in his mouth, plays with a banana)

By 13 December 1938 Chaplin had decided on much of the story, including the idea of the ending. Charlie and the father of the Girl from the ghetto with whom he has fallen in love are put in a concentration camp. They escape, and on the road run into Hinkle's troops, preparing to invade the neighbouring country of Ostrich. The general in command mistakes Charlie for Hinkle. Hinkle himself, out shooting ducks while trying to make up his mind about the invasion, is meanwhile mistaken for Charlie and thrown into prison.

Charlie and the Girl's father are carried along on the invasion of Ostrich and finally find themselves in the palace square of Vanilla, the capital:

Hinkle's soldiers are drawn up before the platform from which the conqueror is about to speak. Charlie walks out on it. He can't say a word. The Girl's father is at his shoulder. 'You've got to talk now! It's our only chance! For God's sake, say something.' Herring (Hinkle's Prime Minister) first addresses the crowd – and through microphones the whole world, which is listening in. He calls for an end to democracies. He introduces Hinkle, the new conqueror who must be obeyed or else. In the crowd we show dozens of Ostrich patriots ready to kill Hinkle. Charlie steps forward. He begins slowly – scared to death. But his words give him power. As he goes on, the clown turns into the prophet.

491

By the middle of January 1939 Chaplin clearly felt confident with his story, though it was to undergo much subsequent revision. Dan James was set to adapt it into a dramatic composition in five acts and an epilogue, in order to register it for copyright. Copyright was also sought in the title *The Dictator*, but it was discovered that Paramount Pictures and the estate of Richard Harding Davies already owned the title and were unwilling to relinquish it. In June therefore the title *The Great Dictator* was registered, but Chaplin was not entirely convinced that it was right: having already registered *Ptomania*, he subsequently registered as alternatives *The Two Dictators*, *Dicta-mania* and *Dictator of Ptomania*.

After 16 January Dan James no longer went to the Beverly Hills house, since Chaplin now worked at the studio, where he could supervise preparations for shooting. The stage was being sound-proofed; there were contracts to be negotiated with outside organi-zations like RCA who were to be responsible for the sound; and work was already in hand on miniatures for special effects. Now the daily script conferences took place in Chaplin's bungalow on the lot. On 21 January Sydney returned to work at the studio for the first time in almost twenty years: with conditions in Europe as they were, he and his new French wife, Gypsy, had decided that they were likely to be safer in America. The daily script conferences were now aug-mented, as Sydney and Henry Bergman joined Chaplin and Dan James, who recalled:

> I don't remember Henry contributing anything to the meetings except enthusiasm and laughter – and that was very important. Sydney, though, was immensely ingenious with gags. Very few of them had any relevance to what we were doing, but that didn't matter. It was stimulating. A bad gag is always a challenge to do better . . .
>
> Sydney was always asking me to remind Charlie how much it was all costing, and that we didn't need all those extras and things, and that it wasn't necessary to do so much overtime. He was very much the older brother. You would never have taken them for brothers though – they seemed so different. I think Charlie had outgrown Sydney. Sydney would rarely go to Charlie's parties, with all his smart intellectual friends . . . If you saw Sydney you would never even have taken him for an actor . . .

By the late summer of 1939 when the script was finished and Chaplin was ready to start shooting, he was able to reassure Sydney: 'This time, Syd, I have the script totally visualized. I know where every close-up comes.' 'Of course,' said Dan James, 'it didn't work out quite like that.'

During the weeks of preparation, Chaplin ran films for the staff in the studio projection room, among them *Shoulder Arms* and the mysterious *The Professor*. He also screened all the newsreels of Hitler on which he could lay hands. He later returned often to a particular sequence showing Hitler at the signing of the French surrender. As Hitler left the railway carriage, he seemed to do a little dance. Chaplin would watch the scene with fascination, exclaiming, 'Oh, you bastard, you son-of-a-bitch, you swine. I know what's in your mind.' According to Tim Durant, 'He said, "this guy is one of the greatest actors I've ever seen . . . Charlie admired his acting. He really did.' Dan James commented forty-five years later, 'Of course he had in himself some of the qualities that Hitler had. He dominated his world. He created his world. And Chaplin's world was not a democracy either. Charlie was the dictator of all those things.'

The script, which was completed by 1 September, remains one of the most elaborate ever made for a Hollywood film. It runs to the extraordinary length of almost 300 pages (the average feature film script varies from 100 to 150 pages). It was divided into twenty-five sections, each designated by a letter of the alphabet and separately paginated; throughout shooting every take was identified by the letter and number of the relevant script page. Despite the doubt Dan James casts on Chaplin's assertion that everything was visualized, the system seems, to judge from the shooting records, to have served pretty well in the 168 days of a very complicated production.

Throughout the spring and early summer of 1939 Chaplin was collecting his crew around him. Henry Bergman was nominated 'co-ordinator'. Dan James was joined by two more assistant directors. One was Chaplin's half-brother Wheeler Dryden, who arrived at La Brea in March, overjoyed to be given a job on Chaplin's permanent studio staff. Wheeler had continued to pick up a living as an actor and in 1923 had had a play, *Suspicion*, co-written with George Appell, produced at the Egan Theatre in Los Angeles.* He was to remain at the studio until Chaplin's departure from the United States in 1952. A slight man, Wheeler retained the air and diction of an old-style stage actor. Though he adored Chaplin, Wheeler could

---

* In the late 1920s Sydney expressed a high regard for Wheeler and proposed taking him on as an assistant in his abortive British production venture.

sometimes madden him as well as the rest of the studio staff with his finicky attention to detail.

The amusing and devil-may-care Robert Meltzer, like James an avowed Communist, was in striking contrast to the solemn and nervy Wheeler. He had also been recruited in Pebble Beach. During the summer there the gossip writers had linked Chaplin's name with several women, notably the sugar heiress Geraldine Spreckels and a striking young red-headed actress called Dorothy Comingore, whom Chaplin saw on stage in Carmel. Dorothy Comingore was then living with Bob Meltzer, and when Chaplin convinced her that she should try her luck in Los Angeles, Meltzer came too. In the end it was Meltzer who worked for Chaplin and not Miss Comingore, who joined Orson Welles' Mercury Theatre and made her most striking impact as Susan Alexander – the role transparently based on Marion Davies – in *Citizen Kane*. After *The Great Dictator* Meltzer himself was to work briefly with Welles. With the outbreak of hostilities in 1941 he volunteered for service with the paratroops and died (exclaiming 'This is the best darn' football match I ever had') in the Battle of Normandy. Meltzer wanted to be a writer but Dan James recalls that 'nothing he wrote ever quite came off. He was witty, funny – but nothing much ended up on paper.'

Chaplin's staff were astonished when Chaplin engaged Karl Struss as director of photography. After twenty-three years as Chaplin's senior cameraman this was a cruel blow to Rollie Totheroh, who could never afterwards completely forgive his beloved boss. Chaplin had grown dissatisfied with Rollie's camerawork for reasons which were never quite clear. According to Dan James,

> He was having a great war with all the technical people . . . He wasn't satisfied with what Rollie had been giving him; but then he felt that Karl wasn't giving him enough light. He was getting in tree branches and things, to achieve 'mood'. It might have been 'mood', but it wasn't what Chaplin wanted.

The problem for a director making only one film every four or five years was that in the interval conditions in Hollywood had changed. Each time that Chaplin made a film he found himself bedevilled by new technical people whom he neither understood nor needed. He had a running feud with the script girl – a personage hitherto unknown on a Chaplin film.

He was always fighting against what he called 'chi-chi' – over-attention to detail of make-up, costumes and such. The script girl would stop him in a scene and say, 'But Mr Chaplin, last time you held your arm this way.' He would yell, and say '****! Who *cares*? If they're going to watch my hand we might as well throw the whole thing out of the window.'

Then one day in the cutting room he noticed that Paulette entered a door and came through the other side wearing a completely different dress. He was triumphant. So much for the script girl!

The Great Dictator was to make particular demands on the wardrobe department, and Chaplin engaged Paul (Ted) Tetrick, who had been around Hollywood since the 1920s working at various times in movies, real estate and the clothing business, to deal with it. Tetrick, useful in all sorts of aspects of production, was to work on both Chaplin's subsequent American films. Winifred Ritchie, the widow of Billie Ritchie, who had learned her skill in making trick costumes back in the Karno days and had long been indispensable during Chaplin productions, was again employed on *The Great Dictator*.

The role of Hannah was intended for Paulette, who reported for work at the studio on 29 July. She and Chaplin had spent a good deal of the previous year apart. While he went to Pebble Beach in the early half of 1938, Paulette flew to Florida, and during most of the rest of the year she was at work in Hollywood, while he stayed away from the studio. Already in March, while hardly finished with marriage rumours, the newspapers talked of impending divorce. Paulette's contract with the studio expired on 31 March 1938, and she had sought an earlier release to sign with the Myron Selznick agency. She was hired for *The Great Dictator* at $2500 a week; Chaplin was furious when she brought her agent (probably Selznick himself) to demand bigger billing.

She and Chaplin continued to live together in the Summit Drive house throughout the production of the film. As Chaplin nicely expressed it, 'Although we were somewhat estranged we were friends and still married.' To the Chaplin sons, now mischievous early teenagers, and to casual acquaintances, their relationship seemed much as before. At the studio, the staff were however aware of the change. Dan James remembers, 'You belonged to the Paulette faction or to the Charlie faction. You couldn't be both.' Sometimes, he felt, the strain showed when Chaplin and Paulette were working together.

'There was some anger on both sides. But he worked very hard with her. Sometimes he would make twenty-five or thirty takes. He would stand in her place on the set and try and give her the tone and the gestures. It was a method he had been able to use in silent films: it could not work so well with a talking picture.'

The final stencilled copies of the script were completed on Sunday 3 September 1939 – the day that Britain declared war on Germany. Three days later Chaplin began to rehearse and on 9 September shooting began on the first ghetto sequence. Filming was to continue with hardly a day's break apart from (most weeks) Sundays until the end of March 1940. By that time Chaplin would have shot most of the 477,440 feet of film which were eventually to be exposed. The length of the finished picture was 11,625 feet.

It is interesting, but perhaps not too surprising, to discover that Chaplin kept the shooting of his two roles quite distinct. First, until the end of October, he worked on the scenes of the ghetto, in the character of the barber. With the bulk of those completed, November was spent on more complicated action and location scenes, like the war scenes, particularly those involving Reginald Gardiner and the crashed 'plane. Chaplin had devised some very funny business with the aeroplane. Taking over the controls, Charlie manages to turn it upside down without either himself or his companion (Gardiner) being aware of it. They only notice with some concern that the sun is shining up from below them, that a watch released from a pocket leaps (apparently) into the air and sways there on its taut chain, and that they are passed by flocks of upside-down seagulls. Reginald Gardiner suffered much more than Chaplin from the experience of being strapped upside down, and only managed his lines and air of insouciance with great difficulty.

There were interludes and distractions in the work at the studio that November. Not all were welcome: a plagiarism suit brought by Michael Kustoff on account of *Modern Times* came to trial before Federal Judge McCormick, and kept Reeves busy. Chaplin himself was in court on 18 November when the case was decided in his favour.

More welcome was the arrival of another of Chaplin's English relatives. Betty Chaplin was the elder daughter of Cousin Aubrey. She had kept in touch with Sydney during her childhood. She was not happy in England; her marriage had broken down and she welcomed the chance to leave England, just then in the period of the 'phoney war'. She was lucky to get onto the last passenger ship to leave for America, with no clothes, money or passport, but with a diplomatic visa obtained from Joseph Kennedy, then Ambassador in London.

She arrived on 11 November. That day the Kustoff hearings were in progress; Chaplin had decided to change the entire set and lighting for the roof-top escape scene, and no one from the studio had time to meet Betty off the Superchief. Hal Roach's daughter Maggie stepped in to collect her from the railway station but on arrival at the studio, already nervous, she was advised that Chaplin was in a very difficult mood. She was heartened to find Wyn Ritchie, whom she knew from earlier visits to Hollywood, having a cup of coffee with Ted Tetrick, whom she introduced as 'the breaker of all the hearts of Hollywood'.

Betty was to marry Tetrick eight years later. Chaplin, taking a serious view of his responsibility for his young half-cousin, regularly complained because the marriage was so long delayed. He also continued to urge Betty to take American citizenship. When she countered that he had never done so, he would only reply that he was too old. (Betty became an American citizen on 9 December 1949.) Betty broke her own share of hearts among the studio staff, but her first and final choice was Ted Tetrick.

On 15 November 1939 Douglas Fairbanks and his new wife Sylvia, the former Lady Ashley, visited the location in Laurel Canyon where Chaplin was filming. Chaplin thought he looked older and stouter, though he was still as full of enthusiasm. He had always been Chaplin's favourite audience, and as so many times before, Chaplin showed Fairbanks his sets and expounded his plans. Although he was filming in the Barber's concentration camp costume, Chaplin put on his Hynkel* uniform to show his visitors, and, wearing it, was photographed with them. They all lunched together.

It was the last time he saw the man whom he later said had been his only close friend. At four o'clock in the morning of 12 December, Douglas Fairbanks Junior telephoned Chaplin to tell him that his father had died just over three hours earlier, in his sleep. There was no shooting at the Chaplin studio on the day of his funeral, 15

---

* In the final script the spelling was changed from Hinkle to Hynkel.

December. 'It was a terrible shock,' wrote Chaplin, 'for he belonged so much to life . . . I have missed his delightful friendship.'

As December came Chaplin began his Hynkel scenes. The supreme actor, Chaplin always became totally subsumed into the role he was playing, as colleagues throughout his career have testified. When, for the first time, he adopted the uniform and role of an autocratic and villainous character, even he was momentarily disconcerted by the effect. Reginald Gardiner remembered that when Chaplin first appeared on the set ready to shoot in his Hynkel uniform, he was noticeably more cool and abrupt than when he had been playing the Jewish barber. Gardiner recalled further that when he was driving with Chaplin – already in uniform – to a new location, Chaplin suddenly became uncharacteristically abusive about the driver of a car that was obstructing them. He quickly recovered himself, and recalled with laughter an earlier discussion about the false sense of superiority a uniform can produce. 'Just because I'm dressed up in this darned thing I go and do a thing like that.'

Although work on *The Great Dictator* proceeded on a much tighter schedule and pre-set plan than any previous Chaplin film, there was no fixed daily routine in the studio. Much, of course, depended upon Chaplin's own somewhat unpredictable time of arrival, although for the first time he appears to have delegated considerable responsibility for preparation and in some cases shooting to his assistants. Two daily reports from December give some idea of the way the day might go at the Chaplin studios during this period.

December 16

Rehearsals 9 a.m. on stage 1. Hynkel's office with Gilbert, Daniell, 3 girls, 2 guards. Rehearsed all scenes in office – mapped out new business. Lunch 12.45–1.45. Lining up on set till 3 p.m. when C.C. arrived on set. He then asked for a secretary to work in F5 (which was not according to plan in a.m.). Then rehearsed until 4 p.m. Male secretary arrived on set 4.15 ready. C.C. decided to continue to use guard, 1st shot 4 p.m. Finished at 7.10 p.m.

In the final three hours of this day, 2780 feet of film (about thirty minutes' running time) were exposed. Scene F was the first scene in Hynkel's palace.

December 30
Rushes 8.20 a.m. Shooting 9.30 a.m. C.C. came on set made minor changes. Returned on set made up at 11 a.m. 1st shot 11.55 a.m . Lunch 1.20–2.20. 1st shot 3 p.m. Continued scenes in Banquet Room till 7.20 p.m. when company finished.

That day 3570 feet of film (almost forty minutes' running time) were shot.

Dan James recalls going on location in the San Fernando Valley to film the rally scenes in which Chaplin, spouting wild Teutonic gibberish, miraculously caricatures Hitler's oratorical style. The inspired concoction of sibilants and gutturals seems to have been improvised; there is hardly a hint in the script of the sounds Chaplin would produce.

> We must have gone back to that scene a dozen times. The first time was in San Fernando Valley, with all the extras standing there in front of him. He said, 'Just keep the cameras rolling.' He would keep up that gibberish talk for 700 feet of film.
>
> The temperatures were over 100, but he would go on interminably, it seemed, and then in between he would amuse the extras by doing scenes from *Sherlock Holmes* or demonstrating pratfalls. At the end of the day he would be deadly gray, sweating, exhausted, with a towel wrapped around his neck. He would collapse into his car, and you would think, 'My God, he'll never be back tomorrow.' But he was.
>
> In the end we reshot most of the scene in the studio, and then it wasn't possible to match the light quality, so I think that what we used was mostly the studio stuff. But some of the shots made on that outdoor lot were breathtaking.

Just before Christmas Chaplin shot the scene which remains the most haunting and the most inspired of the film: Hynkel's ballet with the terrestrial globe. The first hint of a symbolic scene of this sort is a random story note dating from 15 February 1939:

> SCENE WITH MAP: cutting it up to suit himself, cutting off bits of countries with a pair of scissors.

The dance with the globe was to go far beyond this elementary notion. While the gibberish speech appears so precise and planned that it is surprising to discover that it was improvised, the dance with the globe seems to soar so freely in its inspiration that it is hard to imagine that it could be written down. Yet it was. In the complete version of the script, the description of Chaplin's *pas seul* occupies four pages, opening,

> HYNKEL GOES TO THE GLOBE – and caresses it – trance-like. Soft strains of Peer Gynt* waft into the room. Hynkel picks up the globe, bumps it into the air with his left wrist. It floats like a balloon and drops back into his hands. He bumps it with his right wrist and catches it. He dominates the world – kicks it viciously away. Sees himself in the mirror – plays God! Beckons, the world floats into his hand. Then he bumps it high in the air with his right wrist. He leaps up (on wire), catches the globe and brings it down . . .

Chaplin continued to develop his ideas for the scene, and by December a new version of the libretto had been substituted in the script. It is now actually headed 'Dance Routine', and is arranged in ten movements.

> I. Hynkel moves hypnotically toward the globe (one hand on hip – one outstretched). He lifts it from its stand. There is a moment of magical concentration. The globe becomes a balloon. Hynkel bounces it from wrist to wrist and off the top of his head. He finds he can do what he likes with it. The world is his oyster. He laughs ecstatically as he plays with it with nonchalance.
>
> II. Now he shows his power. He grips the globe, taps his foot. He changes his grip so that his right hand is above – his left hand underneath.
>
> III. Then he gets a transition – becomes sensuous about the world. It nearly gets away from him.
>
> IV. In revenge he grabs it angrily, kicks it away viciously.
>
> V. It returns to him. Gratified by his manifest power over it, Hynkel plays nonchalantly with the globe again – with silly gestures. Kicks it away with a comedy kick.
>
> VI. He catches the globe – authoritatively taps it from wrist to wrist as he stands before his desk.
>
> VII. Gracefully he leans back over the desk and gets very Greek about the whole thing. He bounces the globe from toe to head to rear. He's carried away with the beauty of it.
>
> VIII. He gets to his feet on the far side of the desk – becomes mystic about the world, tosses it high in the air, leaps after it to the desk top where he catches it.
>
> IX. Again he tosses it up, leaps from the desk to get it (slow motion).

---

* In the outcome the Prelude to *Lohengrin* proved more appropriate.

x. He catches it roughly (anger business). Laughs demoniacally. The globe pops. He picks up the skin forlornly and bursts into tears.

The particular attention that Chaplin was to give to the balloon dance indicates that he was well aware that it would remain one of his great virtuoso scenes. He spent three days (21, 22 and 23 December) on the main shooting, and then made some retakes on 6 January. The first three days of February 1940 seem to have been entirely taken up with running and rerunning the material, and on 6 February and again on 15 February Chaplin did further retakes.

Carter De Haven, who plays the Ambassador in the film, was later to attempt to get into the plagiarism game by claiming the ballet with the globe as his idea. Any doubt, however, was finally put to rest when Kevin Brownlow and David Gill, preparing their *Unknown Chaplin* film series, unearthed some forgotten home movies of a party at Pickfair somewhere in the early 1920s. Chaplin, in classical Grecian costume and crowned with a laurel wreath, performs a dance with a balloon which is the unmistakable prototype for *The Great Dictator*. No doubt Chaplin was remembering his party trick of nearly twenty years ago when he noted in the script description of the globe ballet, 'Then he slides to the table top to perform a series of Greek postures' (first version) and 'Gracefully he leans back over the desk and gets very Greek about the whole thing.'

In January 1940 Jack Oakie joined the cast to play Benzino Napaloni, the Dictator of Bacteria. When Chaplin first proposed the role to him, Oakie questioned the suitability of casting an Irish–Scottish American in a caricature of Mussolini. What, asked Chaplin, would be funny about an Italian playing Mussolini? Chaplin did perceive a problem however when he discovered that Oakie was at the time dieting to lose weight. According to Charles Chaplin Junior, Chaplin brought his own cook, George, to the studio and had him tempt Oakie with the richest and most fattening dishes he could devise. When he found his strategy was succeeding, and that Oakie was increasingly growing to resemble Mussolini in stature, he cheerfully nicknamed him 'Muscles'.[5]

Charles Junior considered that 'one of the pleasantest things about the new film was the affable relationship between Dad and Jack Oakie. Jack has a tough hide and was able to take Dad's drive in stride. Dad, on his part, has always had great admiration for Jack.' Others on the set observed that working in his scenes with Oakie brought out a certain competitive spirit in Chaplin. It was not jealousy: rationally Chaplin knew that his supremacy was unassailable. Rather it was Chaplin's legacy from the Karno and Keystone training: the essential and driving motive for a comedian must always be to outdo the rest. Chaplin's own script for *The Great Dictator* often gave the better comedy business to Oakie. Chaplin's professional instinct still drove him to top it with his own comedy. He would sense the reaction of the unit, and he played the comic game with the same intensity as he played tennis. As with tennis, he did not like to lose: finishing a scene in which he felt that Oakie had scored the biggest laughs from the bystanders, he could hardly conceal his irritation. Charles Junior, a very reliable witness, despite his youth at the time, recalled one day when Oakie had tried every trick he knew to do the impossible and steal a scene from Chaplin. In the middle of the scene, Chaplin grinned and offered advice: 'If you really want to steal a scene from me, you son-of-a-bitch, just look straight into the camera. That'll do it every time.'[6]

Chaplin undoubtedly found these duels of comedy nostalgic and stimulating. He was less happy with some of his actors from the legitimate theatre. In particular he found it very hard to work against Henry Daniell's measured timing. 'He developed a hatred for Daniell,' recalls Dan James. 'He really thought Daniell was trying to sabotage him. The trouble was that he had a respect for Daniell because he was a real stage actor, and couldn't bring himself to explain what was wrong. Poor Daniell knew that Chaplin was not pleased with him, but he never understood why. On the other hand he was crazy about Reggie Gardiner, though once he had got him, he never really gave Reggie any funny stuff.'

By the middle of February practically all the studio scenes had been shot, and Chaplin moved out onto location to shoot the First World War scenes for the opening of the film and the scene of Hynkel being arrested while out duck shooting, filmed at Malibu Lake. The war scenes involved the series of gags with Chaplin and the enormous Big Bertha gun, and for one day's shooting the Chaplin children were taken to watch. Fourteen-year-old Sydney was so overcome with mirth at his father's antics following the explosion of the gun that he laughed aloud. When he discovered who had wrecked the sound take, Chaplin flew at him in fury, saying 'Do you know your laugh just cost me fifteen thousand dollars?'

'In a twinkling, from being the funniest man alive, Dad had become the most furious.' The two boys feared some awful retribution; but then Chaplin began to laugh, and proudly called out to the crew, 'Even my own son thinks I'm funny.' To Sydney he added, 'Well, it was fifteen thousand dollars' worth of laugh, but if you appreciated it that much, it's all right . . . Just don't let it happen again, son.'[7]

One series of scenes shot during this period was destined never to be seen. Chaplin's first idea for the final scene of the speech, in which (in the words of the early treatment) 'the clown turns into the prophet' was extremely ambitious. He intended the speech to be laid over scenes supposed to take place in Spain, China, a German street and a Jewish ghetto in Germany. As Chaplin's speech came into their consciousness, a Spanish firing squad would throw down their arms; a Japanese bomber pilot would be overcome by wonder, and instead of bombs, toys on parachutes would rain down on the Chinese children below; a parade of goose-stepping German soldiers would break into waltz-time; and a Nazi storm-trooper would risk his life to save a little Jewish girl from an oncoming car. A couple of days were actually spent in shooting material for the sequence, but it was discarded.

By the end of March 1940, the main shooting was all finished, the labourers were already beginning to clear the studio, and Chaplin had a rough-cut of the film ready to show to a few friends such as Constance Collier in early April. The climactic scene, the final speech made by the little barber who has been mistaken for the Great Dictator, remained to be shot. Moreover Chaplin was to polish and tinker with the film more than with any other that he made. During the next six months he would suddenly decide to put up a set again; and he was still doing retakes of the ghetto scenes in late September, after he had already previewed the film. Redubbing of the sound went on practically until the première on 15 October 1940.

From April to June Chaplin laboured over the text of his big speech, between working on the editing of the film. His two young Marxist assistants were of no help to him: 'Bob and I said to him, "Couldn't you just say some simple little thing?" But Charlie wanted to make some great statement to the world. When he finally came to shoot it, we were exiled from the set. He said, "I can't do it with you two there. I can feel your hostility."'[8] The utopian idealism and unashamed emotionalism of the speech evidently offended their Communist orthodoxy. Others were anxious about the speech on more pragmatic grounds. Tim Durant remembered,

He made a speech about humanity, and there was a great argument about
that . . . that it did not belong . . . in the picture. It was unaesthetic. It
was wrong to have Charlie go out there and propagandize . . . The film
salesmen said, 'You'll lose a million dollars . . . for doing that' and he
said, 'Well I don't care if it's five million. I'm gonna do it.' So he did, you
know, and of course it did cost him quite a bit.[9]

Chaplin's judgement was not swayed. On 24 June he recorded the
speech, which in its final screen form runs six minutes. It has remained
one of the most controversial passages in all his works, but today
Chaplin's judgement seems to us correct. Simply and succinctly the
speech sums up his fears and his hopes for a world in the throes of its
most terrible war:

> The way of life can be free and beautiful, but we have lost the way. Greed
> has poisoned men's souls – has barricaded the world with hate – has
> goose-stepped us into misery and bloodshed. We have developed speed,
> but we have shut ourselves in. Machinery that gives abundance has left
> us in want. Our knowledge has made us cynical; our cleverness, hard and
> unkind. We think too much and feel too little. More than machinery we
> need humanity. More than cleverness we need kindness and gentleness.
> Without these qualities, life will be violent and all will be lost.

Chaplin's critics, from left and right, accused him of cliché and truism.
The most striking aspect of the speech, though, is that more than
forty years afterwards, not one phrase of it has dated or lost its force,
even if the optimism of the final lines ('We are coming out of the
darkness into the light! We are coming into a new world . . .!') can
hardly be said to have been fulfilled.

Music played a less important role in *The Great Dictator* than in
Chaplin's previous sound films; the score was completed in a bare
three weeks. On this occasion Chaplin's musical collaborator was
Meredith Willson. Many of the music sessions took place at the
Chaplin house, and Charles Junior was an interested observer. The
musicians, he noted, were really musical secretaries, working to
Chaplin's dictation. He would hum a tune or play it on the piano,
and the musicians would take it down and play it back for his
approval. It might take several tries before the tune gave him complete
satisfaction. He had very clear ideas on the scoring, and liked to
describe what he wanted by reference to a composer or an instrumental label: 'We should make this Wagnerian,' he would say, or,

'This part should be more Chopin. Let's make this light and airy, a lot of violins. I think we could use an oboe effect in this passage.'[10] Often the musicians were startled by the unorthodox timing Chaplin would demand to suit a special piece of action, but

> Dad's dramatic instinct as it related to music was brilliant . . . The musicians turned gray and were on the verge of nervous breakdown by the time it was over, but whatever they suffered they couldn't say that working with Dad was ever dull. He gave them a free performance at every session, because he didn't just hum or sing, or knock out a tune on the piano. He couldn't stay quiet that long. He would start gesturing with the music, acting out the parts of the various people in the scene he was working on, but caricaturing their movements to evoke a total response in himself. At those times his acting was closer than ever to ballet.[11]

Many more weeks of retakes, cutting and recutting, recording and re-recording, predubbing, dubbing and redubbing followed, until finally on 1 September a complete print of the picture was ready. The first audience that Sunday afternoon consisted of Paulette, Mr and Mrs King Vidor, Mr and Mrs Lewis Milestone, the three assistants, James, Meltzer and Wheeler Dryden, and Steve Pallos, who was invited as Alexander Korda's representative. Three days later, after further changes (mainly restoration of the conspiracy sequence, which he had previously decided to cut) the picture was shown to the United Artists people. Joseph Breen, the film industry censor, also saw the film: subsequently he was to ask for the deletion of the word 'lousy' from the dialogue.

Still anxious, Chaplin decided on a series of sneak previews. The first was at the Riverside Theatre on 5 September, attended by most of the staff. Noting the reaction, Chaplin set to recutting to speed up the picture, and ordered rebuilding of the ghetto street set for some retakes. Wheeler Dryden had by this time taken over the job of writing the daily studio reports. One day he notes, 'The music of the newly edited "Conspiracy" sequence was a difficult task, but Mr Chaplin stuck to it all day.' His no less characteristic comment on a second sneak preview at the UA Theatre, Long Beach on 20 September runs, 'The reaction accorded to the production showed unmistakably that the changes Mr Chaplin has made since the first "Sneak Preview" have improved the picture immeasurably.' All the same Chaplin decided on more retakes, and next day poor Wheeler writes, 'Wheeler Dryden spent whole day and several hours after dinner locating actors needed.'

Not until the end of September was Chaplin sufficiently satisfied to order the final dubbing of the picture. On the evening of 3 October he invited a select group of guests to see the finished work. They were James Roosevelt, Patricia Morrison, Gene Tierney, Mrs Rockwell Kent, Anita Loos, the Aldous Huxleys, the John Steinbecks and the Lewis Milestones. Tim Durant, Dan James and Robert Meltzer also attended.

Between this showing and the press previews, which took place eleven days later at the Carthay Circle Theatre, Los Angeles and the Astor Theatre, New York, Chaplin made still further changes to the sound. They were, Wheeler noted, 'just minor changes, but important ones'.

For the first time since work began on the film, Chaplin permitted himself to relax. Wheeler's painstaking notes sometimes recorded social occasions:

September 25

4.30. Countess of Jersey (Virginia Cherrill) visited C.C. in cutting room, looked at some scenes and drove him home from studio at 6.08.

October 1

At 6.45 p.m. Tim Durant, a friend of Mr Chaplin's arrived at stu'o. Shortly after Mr C. left the sound stage, dressed in clothes brought from his home by his valet, and at 7.30 p.m. Mr C. was driven from studio to attend social engagement. He drove out of studio in Tim Durant's car.

October 2

Lunch was called at 1.15 p.m., after which, at 3.43 p.m., Mr C. was driven by Jack Kneymeyer, in the latter's automobile, to Mr C.'s residence, where he and Kneymeyer played a game of tennis.

October 3

Heard remainder of dubbed tracks; gave instructions for few changes. *Afternoon*: tennis with Jack Kneymeyer.

Chaplin was understandably nervous about the reception of *The Great Dictator*. The rest of Hollywood had discreetly avoided making overt anti-Nazi films. A Gallup poll at the time of the outbreak of war in Europe showed 96 per cent opposition to America's entry into the war. Since the Depression a fiercely isolationist spirit had developed. Moreover the quantity of threatening letters Chaplin received testified to the strength of pro-Fascist feeling in the United States. He seriously discussed with Harry Bridges of the Longshoremen's Union having some of his men at the opening in case of a pro-Nazi demonstration.

Chaplin gambled that he was likely to get a more sympathetic press in New York than on the West Coast. He therefore decided to have the world première in New York on 15 October, with simultaneous press previews in New York and Los Angeles the day before. Favouring the East in this way was to rebound badly. When he eventually returned to Hollywood after an absence of almost four months in the East, he invited a group of the local press people to a conference at the house. He quickly realized how mortal was the offence he had committed: the press men refused a drink. 'You left here ignoring the press,' they told him, 'and we don't like it.' They were subsequently to punish him for it.

The American critics were on the whole guarded. Generally they admired the audacity of the undertaking and the sustained brilliance of the comedy, though Paul Goodman qualified a genuinely enthusiastic view with asides on 'calamitous music (Meredith Willson's)', 'feeble dialogue' and 'persistent lapses in style'. Most however had an uneasy sense that things had gone beyond the point where Hitler could be made a simple buffoon and his storm-troopers, Keystone Kops. On the other hand Paul Goodman found 'the invective against Hynkel is to my taste all-powerful: disgust expressed by the basic tricks of low vaudeville, gibberish, belching, dirty words and radio static. You will not find the like outside of Juvenal . . . On the other hand the personal Hynkel is not the political Hitler.' Goodman concluded that the film was 'something different, and something better, than the "grandiose failure" of the worried reviewers.' Unlike them, he did not find the last speech in any way out of character, for 'if this isn't meant from the heart, we have been deceived for twenty-five years.'

Another reviewer of special perception was Rudolph Arnheim, who wrote with the awareness of a recent refugee from Hitler's Germany:

> Charles Chaplin is the only artist who holds the secret weapon of mortal laughter. Not the laugh of superficial gibing that self-complacently underrates the enemy and ignores the danger, but rather the profound laughter of the sage who despises physical violence, even the threat of death, because behind it he has discovered the spiritual weakness, stupidity, and falseness of his antagonist. Chaplin could have opened the eyes of a world enchained by the spell of force and material success. But instead of

unmasking the common enemy, fascism, Chaplin unmasked a single man, 'The Great Dictator'. And that is why I feel that this good film should have been better.[12]

In London *The Great Dictator* opened on 16 December 1940, at the height of the Blitz, when Hitler was a very real and present enemy. The British seemed to delight in Chaplin's ridicule, with none of the reserve felt by the Americans. The British above all loved the prime joke of the physical resemblance of Old Adolf and the funniest man in the world. The critic of the *New Statesman and Nation* called the film 'the best heartener we could have, with war standing still or going for or against us'; and in the *Spectator* Basil Wright found in it 'undeniable greatness, both in its pure comedy and its bold contrast between the small people of the ghetto or the slums and the big people of the Fascist chancelleries, equating both in terms of fantasy and in terms of the adored Chaplin himself.'

The final speech, which the political right felt smacked of Communism and the left suspected of sentimentality, seemed not to embarrass the larger audience. It was widely quoted and reprinted. Chaplin's old friend Rob Wagner devoted a page to it in the 16 November issue of his magazine *Rob Wagner's Script*; Archie Mayo, mainly remembered as the director of *The Petrified Forest*, used it as his Christmas card for 1940, comparing it to Lincoln's Gettysburg address; and in England the Communist Party put it out as a special pamphlet.

16

MONSIEUR VERDOUX

The whole of Chaplin's life had been marked by dramatic contrasts. The decade which followed the release of *The Great Dictator* was to see both the most bitter period of his public and professional career and the achievement in his personal life of the happiness and success that hitherto persistently eluded him. Chaplin thrilled the audience at the première of *The Great Dictator* by introducing Paulette as 'my wife'. This delayed admission of the marriage made news across the world, yet it was oddly timed, since both partners were by then aware that the marriage had already run its course. For two years they had been drifting apart, apparently without great acrimony. They had even arrived separately in New York – Chaplin from California with Tim Durant, Paulette from Mexico where she had been visiting a new friend, Diego Rivera. Charles Junior suggested, realistically, that Chaplin calculated that a clarification in Paulette's status would disarm the club women of America, whose moral disapprobation could be harmful to the box office success of the new picture. He also believed Chaplin may have hoped that this public announcement might help to patch up the marriage.

It did not. After the première Paulette returned to Hollywood to perform her last duties as hostess at the Summit Drive house, entertaining H. G. Wells, who was on a lecture tour, for two weeks. Chaplin stayed on in New York for four months, until February 1941. In December he heard from Alf Reeves that Paulette had left the house and moved into a beach house lent to her by her agent, Myron Selznick.

Paulette was to get a divorce in Mexico in 1942 on the grounds of incompatibility and separation for more than a year. Chaplin seems to have had grudging admiration for Paulette's shrewdness over the settlement she won from him. It was rumoured to be in the region of one million, but was probably one third of that. Paulette also got the *Panacea*. The divorce proceedings (heard *in absentia* before Judge Javier Rosas Seballas in the Civil Court at Juarez) corroborated that the marriage had taken place in Canton in 1936.

Paulette's career as a Paramount contract star flourished for most of the next decade: her craving for independence was undoubtedly one of the main causes of the split with Chaplin. She had met Burgess Meredith while co-starring with Fred Astaire in *Second Chorus* (1940) and married him in 1944. That marriage ended with another Mexican divorce in June 1949, and in 1958 she married Erich Maria Remarque. Relations between Chaplin and Paulette remained quite cordial after the split, and the Chaplin sons continued to see her from time to time. They felt particularly keenly the loss of Paulette's vivid and cheering presence in the household. 'It's just one of those sad things, son,' Chaplin would tell Charles Junior. 'That's life for you.'

Quite apart from the separation, the year 1941 began badly. The very mixed critical and public reception of his film revealed, to Chaplin's growing distress, the extent of pro-Nazi feeling in the United States. In January he was delighted to accompany a Hollywood delegation to the inauguration of President Roosevelt, whom he had first met as Secretary to the Navy during the First World War, and whom he had since come to regard as the greatest president in United States history. Roosevelt's reception was cool however, and his only comment on *The Great Dictator* was to complain at the difficulties it had caused with pro-Axis countries in Latin America. As part of the celebrations Chaplin was to broadcast the final speech from *The Great Dictator* to a radio audience of sixty million. In the middle of it, perhaps from nerves, his throat went dry and his voice broke; it was two minutes before anyone could find some water in a folded sheet of paper so that he could continue. He carried it off triumphantly, and the audience filled the hiatus with applause; but it was the kind of nightmare of embarrassment that always haunted him.

On his return to Hollywood in February 1941 Chaplin had to concern himself not only with the Kustoff suit against *Modern Times*, but also with two insubstantial but irritating suits relating to *The Great Dictator*.

He remained a favourite target of the Federal tax authorities. This time their claim for a large supplementary payment was thrown out of court, while Chaplin was upheld in his contention that he had overpaid by $24,938. The court victory did not lessen the irritation or prevent unfavourable publicity: in 1947 the vituperative Westbrook Pegler, in his syndicated column 'Fair Enough' (*sic*) would interpret the judgement as showing Chaplin 'caught in the act of cheating the Government of an enormous debt for taxes'. It was hardly surprising that Chaplin willingly returned to New York on 26 March 1941, to appear as a character witness for Joseph M. Schenck who was being sued for income tax evasion. This time Chaplin remained in New York a month. His son Charles believed that he stayed on because he was considering a story about immigrants in New York which he thought of filming there, with Paulette as his leading lady. Charles Junior considered that this idea was the nucleus of *A King in New York*, though nothing seems to have been written at this time either on this story, or on another idea about the love of a drunken has-been star for a little chorus girl who doesn't even know he exists – perhaps the prototype for *Limelight*.

He returned to California on 30 April, but for the next six weeks stayed away from the studio. He was lonely, dispirited, and given to expressing dissatisfaction with his achievements. He enjoyed the companionship of his sons more than at any other time in his life. They were often taken along as chaperons when he dined with actresses who were often nearer their age than their father's. One date at this time was the 22-year-old Carole Landis, who had just arrived at stardom but was to commit suicide in 1948 at the age of twenty-nine. Another was the Viennese-born actress Hedy Lamarr, who had just co-starred with Clark Gable in two films. Although they could never have been regarded as 'dating', Chaplin and Garbo had a high mutual regard: she laughed with abandon at his jokes and impersonations; he regularly proposed films that they should do together – wonderful fantasies with which she played along happily if sceptically.

Chaplin seems at this period to have become unusually gregarious, largely as a result of his passion for tennis. His old Sunday ritual of quiet English teas was now supplanted by weekly tennis parties which grew larger and larger, as friends brought friends, and became a *rendezvous* for the Hollywood élite. The most welcome guests were the great professional players of the time, Budge, Perry, Tilden,

Pauline Betz and Helen Wills. Most of the domestic staff had Sunday free, but the entertainment always included tea and coffee, chicken sandwiches and the indispensable crumpets. Among the guests in this early summer of 1941 was Joan Barry.

At this time she was twenty-two. As Joan Berry she had arrived in Hollywood from Brooklyn in 1940, badly screen-struck but with no prospects. She was working as a waitress when she had her break, and was picked out by J. Paul Getty, the oil millionaire, as pretty enough to form part of the female entourage to accompany him to Mexico for the inauguration of Avila Camacho. In Mexico she caught the attention of a veteran film executive, A. C. Blumenthal, who gave her a letter of introduction to Tim Durant. Durant invited her and another girl to dine with himself and Chaplin. Chaplin thought her cheerful and pleasant, but attached no importance to the encounter. Next Sunday Durant brought her to the weekly tennis party. Chaplin invited them to dinner at Romanoffs; after that Joan Barry pursued him with a persistence which, although her eagerness made him uneasy, eventually won through. She was by no means unattractive, and Chaplin found himself involved in an affair with her.

His uneasiness about the girl was dissipated when he discovered, as he thought, that she had acting talent. Sinclair Lewis and Sir Cedric Hardwicke, who had played the leading role of Canon Skerritt in the New York production, drew his attention to Paul Vincent Carroll's play *Shadow and Substance*, and Chaplin decided it would make a good film subject. One evening Joan Barry read the part of Brigid to him with such effect that he at once made screen tests of her. Having bought the screen rights of the play for $20,000, at the end of June he put Joan Barry under a year's contract. Chaplin remembered that she was paid $250 a week; but though his memory was rarely at fault in matters of money the sum seems rather high. The salary of $75 rising to $100, which Charles Junior remembered, seems more in accordance with Chaplin studio scales.

There is no question about Chaplin's sincerity in believing that he could make Joan Barry into an actress. He had certainly neither the need nor the temperament to waste money wooing girls with contracts, even had there been any cause to woo Barry, who so determinedly threw herself at him. He said, and no doubt meant it, that she had 'all the qualities of a new Maude Adams' and told his sons, 'She has a quality, an ethereal something that's truly marvellous . . . a talent as great as any I've seen in my whole life . . .' Chaplin sent

Barry to Max Reinhardt's drama school, paid for elaborate dental work for her, and showed off her talents in Shakespearean snippets at parties.

Durant and other friends became alarmed at signs of Barry's mental instability before Chaplin himself apparently noticed it. By the spring of 1942 the signs could not be ignored. She began to drive up to the house, very drunk, in the small hours, and on one occasion crashed her Cadillac in the drive. On at least one occasion she began smashing windows when Chaplin refused to open up to her. Abhorring drunkenness, Chaplin was particularly anxious that, as an employee of the studios, her escapades should not become public. He discovered that she had not been attending the Reinhardt classes for weeks.

By mutual agreement the contract was cancelled on 22 May 1942 (it was due to expire on 25 July). As part of the settlement, Chaplin paid off $5000 of Barry's debts, and provided one-way tickets for her and her mother to return to New York, which they did on 5 October. Chaplin hoped and believed that he was at last rid of this unfortunate and troublesome girl.

In June 1941 Chaplin returned to work at the studio for the first time since the completion of *The Great Dictator*. Much of the rest of that year was taken up in preparing a sound re-issue of *The Gold Rush*. Chaplin wrote a new musical accompaniment, which was recorded under the direction of Max Terr; the titles were replaced by a commentary spoken by Chaplin himself. The words of the commentary were largely similar to the original titles: throughout the film Chaplin calls the hero 'The Little Fellow'. Chaplin brought in an editor, Harold McGhean, and trimmed the film slightly, excluding, besides the sub-titles, fifty-seven feet (thirty-eight seconds at normal sound speed of twenty-four frames per second) from the original length. The major change was the lingering fade-out kiss between Chaplin and Georgia Hale, modified to a chaster ending in which they simply walk off hand in hand.

Throughout 1942, and even after the departure of Barry, he continued to work on the script of *Shadow and Substance*. In Chaplin's hands Paul Vincent Carroll's play could have been a fascinating film subject. Written in 1934, the play was produced at the Abbey Theatre, Dublin in January 1937. It is the story of Brigid, a simple Irish girl who sees visions of her namesake, the holy Saint Brigid, and who works in the household of the Reverend Canon Thomas Skerritt. The Canon's two assistant priests represent the poles of rational and superstitious faith. A riot in the local town over the same conflict of belief results in Brigid's death, and leads the Canon to question his own faith and his sinful pride.

Chaplin's adaptation as completed late in 1942 is excellent, though he is much less interested in the issues of Catholicism than in the human and humanist content of the play. Clearly, sympathetic chords were touched in him by lines like 'Every year scores of decent Christians in America sprinkle negroes with petrol and burn them because they love God and his justice.' The film script retains the main dramatic line, while reducing the dialogue by at least one third, and reorganizing a number of the minor characters.

It concludes with a song, which seems to be Chaplin's own addition to the text:

> Ecce homo
> Ecce homo
> His crown
> Just a barren wreath of thorns
> There in the darkness
> He wore
> Just a barren wreath of thorns
>
> But in the starlight
> I saw
> A rose
> So red
> Blooming on his crown of thorns.
>
> Glory
> Glory
> A rose
> So red a rose
> Blooming on his crown of thorns.

On the back of this last page of the script, Chaplin has added some manuscript notes, including reflections on humour. It is not clear if they are notes for additional dialogue or simply *aides-mémoire*:

> Tensions are vital to life. One should never completely relax unless one wants to feel the poetry of slowly dying.
>
> Nonsense is not the proper word for humour. Fun is more appropriate . . .

Wisdom is the seed of humour.

Humour is the gauge that indicates excess in statement, action, attitude or manner.

On 7 December 1941 the Japanese attacked Pearl Harbour and America entered the war on the Allied side. This caused Chaplin domestic disruption since the Japanese servants were immediately interned. The house was re-staffed with English, whom Chaplin found tiresomely slow after more than twenty years of the swift, efficient, intuitive attentions of the Japanese. Spiritually the war affected Chaplin deeply, and both his sons were soon to be drafted for service. He was particularly chagrined by the widespread anti-Soviet feeling among many Americans who were happy to watch the mounting Russian casualties on the Eastern Front on the principle that in time it would produce the mutual destruction of both Nazis and Communists. Chaplin was eager to contribute his own war effort.

His opportunity came in May 1942. He received a telephone call from the American Committee for Russian War Relief asking if he could stand in for Ambassador Davies, who was ill, at a mass meeting in San Francisco the following day. He agreed, but as the time for his performance approached was overtaken by his old stage-fright at the prospect of facing an audience. He was not reassured by learning that he was expected to hold the platform for an hour. He was helped however by a couple of glasses of champagne and by the irritation he felt at the timidity of the preceding speakers, careful not to appear too enthusiastic about the Soviet ally. When it came to his turn, Chaplin startled his audience of between eight and ten thousand people by addressing them as 'Comrades!' and then going on to explain, 'I assume there are many Russians here tonight, and the way your countrymen are fighting and dying at this very moment, it is an honour and a privilege to call you comrades.' The enthusiasm of the audience spurred him on to an excited Shakespearean paraphrase:

I am not a Communist. I am a human being, and I think I know the reactions of human beings. The Communists are no different from anyone else; whether they lose an arm or a leg, they suffer as all of us do, and die as all of us die. And the Communist mother is the same as any other mother. When she receives the tragic news that her sons will not return, she weeps as other mothers weep. I do not have to be a Communist to know that. And at this moment Russian mothers are doing a lot of weeping and their sons a lot of dying . . .

The excitement of both speaker and audience escalated, and as a finale Chaplin called upon the enthusiastic multitude to send ten thousand telegrams to the President demanding the opening of a second front in Europe: 'Stalin wants it, Roosevelt has called for it – so let's all call for it – let's open a second front now!' Chaplin's fears that he might have gone too far – even without considering the dubious military implications of a second front at that juncture – were not dispelled by John Garfield's wondering remark at a dinner party after the event: 'You have a lot of courage!'

Dan James and his wife Lilith were present that night, and Lilith recalls that after the speech, 'everyone was scared of him, so they handed him over to us. It was a tremendous speech. It was a very bold political stand to take at that time.'

The experience seems to have given Chaplin a new taste for public speaking. Even he was not clear to what extent he was inspired by idealism or by the rediscovery of the heady and fearsome stimulus of applause. (In *Limelight*, when Terry challenges Calvero's assertion that he hates the theatre he replies: 'I hate the sight of blood, but I still have it in my veins.') Two months after the San Francisco speech he was asked to address a mass meeting in Madison Square by radio-telephone. The rally had been organized by the Council of the Congress of Industrial Organizations and was attended by sixty thousand trades unionists and others. Chaplin spent the whole of the previous day (21 July) preparing his speech, which lasted fourteen minutes and was heard with rapt attention. Again he called for a second front.

> Let us aim for victory in the spring. You in the factories, you in the fields, you in uniforms, you citizens of the world, let us work and fight towards that end. You, official Washington, and you, official London, let us make this our aim – victory in the spring!

'As usual,' commented Charles Junior, 'his enthusiasm ran away with him.' Despite (or perhaps, Chaplin felt, because of) Jack Warner's advice to refuse, he accepted an invitation to speak at a rally in Carnegie Hall organized by the Artists' Front to Win the War, even at that time regarded as a dangerously leftist organization. However, the platform was shared with such politically respectable celebrities as Orson Welles, Pearl Buck and Rockwell Kent. Chaplin arrived in New York on 15 October, the day before the rally, accompanied by Tim Durant and Edward Chaney, his new English valet. In New York he was met by Charles Junior, who recalled his father's habitual pre-performance nerves and nausea. There was also an amiable reunion with Paulette, whose divorce had become effective on 4 June.

Chaplin's platform appearance was the usual sucess. On returning to the Waldorf-Astoria he discovered that Joan Barry had been telephoning repeatedly. She called again, and when later she arrived at the hotel Chaplin took care that Durant stayed with them throughout the visit which he later recalled as lasting no more than half an hour. Barry told them that she had now moved into the Pierre Hotel, owned by J. Paul Getty.

Chaplin stayed on in New York for ten days after the rally, though he sensed that since his Second Front speeches he was no longer welcome at the homes of some of his former hosts. Speaking invitations continued to come, and to be accepted; conscientious as he was, Chaplin began to spend more time on the preparation of each successive speech. He spent much of the previous week dictating an address for a 'Salute to Our Russian Ally' meeting held at Orchestra Hall Chicago on 25 November. From Chicago he went on to New York to speak at an 'Arts for Russia' dinner at the Hotel Pennsylvania on 3 December. This brief but in the long run highly significant phase of Chaplin's activitities was rounded off early in 1943. In February he prepared a speech to be recorded at the office of the Soviet consul for subsequent broadcast in Russia. On Sunday 7 March he made a speech which was transmitted to Britain from the Los Angeles studio of CBS. It was presented as a Transatlantic Call to Lambeth, and painted a vivid picture of the London that Chaplin remembered from his boyhood. He concluded: 'I remember the Lambeth streets, the New Cut and the Lambeth Walk, Vauxhall Road. They were hard streets, and one couldn't say they were paved with gold. Nevertheless, the people who lived there are made of pretty good metal.'

Now Joan Barry returned to Hollywood, apparently using $300 Chaplin had given her at the Waldorf-Astoria to pay the fare. After pestering him with telephone calls, on the night of 23 December Barry used a ladder to break into Chaplin's house, where she produced a gun and threatened to kill herself. Chaplin's distress was aggravated when his two sons arrived at the house in the middle of the affair. Unwilling to involve them, he asked them to go to their rooms and only told them the following morning what had occurred. Barry was later to assert that intimacy had taken place on this occasion. Chaplin's version, that he locked the door between his room and the bathroom which lay between the rooms they occupied, seems, in the circumstances, more credible. She left the following morning when Chaplin gave her some money. A week or so later she was back, and this time Chaplin was obliged to call the police. She was given a ninety-day suspended sentence and ordered to leave town. An employee of the Chaplin studios handed her a railroad ticket and $100. In May 1943, six months pregnant, she was back again. Chaplin believed that Hedda Hopper had advised her to get publicity by having herself arrested, which her second court appearance achieved for her. She was sentenced to thirty days for vagrancy, spending most of the time in hospital on account of her condition.

By the purely Chaplinesque twist of fate, at the very moment that this disturbed young woman was tormenting him and storing up still worse trouble for the future, Chaplin met Oona O'Neill. Oona was the daughter of Eugene O'Neill by his second wife Agnes Boulton, but was only a child when her parents divorced. Oona was gifted with beauty, charm and acute intelligence tempered by remarkable shyness. In the spring of 1942, not quite seventeen, she had been nominated Debutante Number One of the year. Having taken her Vassar entrance examinations, she had decided instead upon an acting career, and arrived in Hollywood where her mother and stepfather were already living. She made a screen test for a role in *The Girl From Leningrad* which was to be produced by Eugene Frenke, the husband of Anna Sten. The test still survives to indicate what a striking screen personality she might have been. The beauty is both radiant and fragile, the personality at once diffident and eager. Even in this forty-year-old fragment of film, the presence remains vivid.

Her agent, Minna Wallace, knew that Chaplin was looking for someone to play Brigid in *Shadow and Substance*. She mentioned Oona O'Neill to Chaplin, who was not optimistic about the prospect of the daughter of America's most celebrated tragic dramatist. Minna Wallace however arranged a dinner party at which she and Oona were joined by Durant (whose father had been a friend of O'Neill's) and Chaplin. Chaplin was instantly enchanted by Oona's looks, appeal, gentleness and smile, but he was still nervous that the role of Brigid was beyond an actress of her years and small experience. Had he at this time seen the Eugene Frenke screen test he might well have felt that, different as she was from the voluptuous Joan Barry, she could have brought a quality of magic to the role.

According to Rollie Totheroh, shortly after the meeting Oona herself arrived at the studio and with that mixture of timidity and determination that is so bewildering and appealing in her refused to be put off by all the efforts of Totheroh and Alf Reeves, who were understandably nervous, after the recent experience with Joan Barry, at the arrival of another youngster who looked even less than her seventeen and a half years. Meanwhile Minna Wallace alarmed Chaplin with reports that Fox were interested in her client. Chaplin offered Oona a contract.

Charles Junior and his brother were at once won by Oona when they met her at the house, but quickly realized that they had an insuperable rival: 'Whenever Oona was with our father a rapt expression would come into her eyes. She would sit quietly, hanging on his every word. Most women are charmed by Dad, but in Oona's case it was different. She worshipped him, drinking in every word he spoke, whether it was about his latest script, the weather or some bit of philosophy. She seldom spoke, but every now and then she would come up with one of those penetrating remarks that impressed even our father with her insight.'[1] The extraordinary, perfect love affair that resulted and which brought Chaplin happiness that compensated for everything else that had happened and would happen to him was not long delayed. Chaplin recalled that – despite his nervousness about the discrepancy in their age – they decided to marry after completing the filming of *Shadow and Substance*. The decision must have been rapid. According to the studio records, *Shadow and Substance* was definitively shelved on 29 December 1942, no more than two months after the meeting at Minna Wallace's house.

Already by November 1942 Chaplin was working on a new idea, which was eventually to become *Monsieur Verdoux*, and no doubt it is the much richer possibilities it offered which made him decide to scrap a year's work on the *Shadow and Substance* script. The idea had taken seed when Orson Welles visited the house and suggested he would like to direct a documentary reconstruction of the career of Landru, the celebrated French wife-murderer, with Chaplin playing the principal role. Welles had as yet done no work on a script, and a few days afterwards Chaplin telephoned him to say that his suggestions had given him the idea for a comedy. Although the film would have only the remotest connexion with the real-life Landru,

Chaplin suggested that Welles might accept a payment of $5000, since his proposition had originally stimulated the idea. The offer was not in any way altruistic: Chaplin had by this time had too much experience of plagiarism claims, and wanted to forestall any such possibility in this case. Welles agreed with the proviso that, after seeing the film, he should have the right to a screen credit: 'Idea suggested by Orson Welles'. Chaplin agreed, though in later years he resented Welles's pride in being the author of the germinal idea for *Verdoux*. Chaplin worked almost continuously on the script from November 1942 until the start of production in April 1946. The production was referred to as *Landru* until March 1943, when it became known as 'Production No 7: Bluebeard'. The title then became simply *Verdoux*; *Monsieur Verdoux* seems to have been finally adopted in June 1946.

The early part of 1943 passed pleasantly, without trouble. Oona and her mother spent a lot of time at the house; so did young Charles and Sydney, who were now approaching draft age. In the weeks after Christmas, Chaplin screened *City Lights*, *The Circus*, *The Idle Class* and *Shoulder Arms* at the studio for the O'Neills and other friends. There was a portent of trouble in May when Joan Barry telephoned the house and informed the butler, for no apparent reason, that she was pregnant. On 4 June she gave the same information to the press, this time adding that Chaplin was the father of her unborn child. Thus began a two-year nightmare which was to be described by one Los Angeles attorney, Eugene L. Trope, as 'a landmark in the miscarriage of justice'.

On the day of Joan Barry's announcement to the press her mother, Gertrude Berry, as guardian of the unborn child, filed a paternity suit against Chaplin, asking for $10,000 for pre-natal care, $2500 a month for support of the unborn child, and $5000 court costs. Chaplin's lawyers countered with a brief statement in his name: 'Miss Barry states her unborn child was conceived in December last. The first claim made upon me by Miss Barry was in May and was accompanied by a demand of $150,000. I am not responsible for Miss Barry's condition.' Chaplin claimed that these May demands specified $75,000 for the child and $75,000 for the mother, with nothing for Barry herself, and were made under threat of exposure to the press. Chaplin indignantly refused to settle, even though Tim Durant, who was acting as middleman, was convinced that it was a *bona fide* once and for all settlement. According to Charles Junior,

Chaplin's refusal was not in consideration of money – he was aware that to fight the case would be much more costly, win or lose – but out of a sense of justice: 'He was indignant because he was innocent. It was all part of the strain of stubborn integrity which runs through him and which is such an admirable and exasperating characteristic.'[2]

Californian law on divorce and paternity always gives the benefit of doubt to the woman, and the mere allegation that a man is father is sufficient grounds for forcing him to support both woman and child until settlement of the suit. So the lawyers on both sides agreed and filed with the Superior Court payments to be made pending the outcome of the case. Chaplin agreed to pay $2500 cash and $100 a week for Barry's support, as well as $500 thirty days before the birth, $1000 at the birth and $500 a month for the succeeding four months. For her part, Barry agreed to permit blood tests on the infant to help determine the child's paternity, when it reached the age of four months. As reported by the *New York Times* the Barry lawyers agreed that 'If at least two of the doctors say "no", the suit would be dropped; if they said "maybe" (a positive "yes" is impossible from blood tests) the girl will be free to press her claims.'

The affair provided a field day for the press. Chaplin, to escape reporters or processs servers, hid out as soon as the story broke in the home of Eugene Frenke and Anna Sten on Layton Drive, Los Angeles; Oona visited him there and also stayed. It remained a long-standing joke with the Frenkes that the lovers were so preoccupied that they forgot to repay the Frenkes' ration coupons which they used up during the stay. They had already decided to marry on 1 June when Oona, having then passed her eighteenth birthday, would no longer need the parental consent which she rightly anticipated would not have been forthcoming from her father, though her mother was wholehearted in her approval of the match. Now Durant and the lawyers felt it would be advisable for Oona to return East until the Barry storm blew over. It was Oona who overruled this, doggedly insisting that at this time more than at any other her place, as the woman Chaplin loved and was loved by, was at his side.

Harry Crocker was entrusted with arrangements for the marriage, and in return was permitted to photograph the ceremony and give the news as an exclusive to his colleague on the Hearst press, Louella Parsons. Always inclined to take a directly contrary view to her arch rival Hedda Hopper, Miss Parsons had remained as friendly towards

Chaplin as Miss Hopper was vituperative – though the peak of Hopper's vilification was yet to come. On Tuesday 15 June Chaplin and Oona, accompanied by Crocker and Catherine Hunter, Chaplin's secretary, drove to Santa Barbara. Soon after eight the following morning they registered at the court house to receive a license, and then made as rapid a getaway as possible to avoid the press who had already been alerted by the court clerk. They were quietly married by a 78-year-old Justice of the Peace, Clinton Pancoast Moore. When they got outside they discovered that Mr Moore had taken down Chaplin's name as 'Chapman'. It was a mistake few people had made in the thirty years since Keystone had telegraphed the Karno Company in quest of a new star. Mr Moore obligingly corrected it.

Chaplin and Oona stayed on in Santa Barbara almost six weeks, and miraculously the press failed to hunt them out. Chaplin veered from depression to bliss. Unrecognized, they went for country walks in the evenings, and Oona read aloud to relieve Chaplin's darker moods.

They returned to Beverly Hills on 26 July, and Chaplin immediately resumed work on the script, now called *Bluebeard*. There was other work to be done at the studio also. Brigadier-General Osborn, Director of the Special Services Division of the army, had requested that Chaplin might make prints of *Shoulder Arms* available to the Armed Forces Institute Film Services. Chaplin was delighted that his 25-year-old picture was still reckoned to have a value for morale, and Totheroh set about revising and restoring a perfect new negative. In January Chaplin saw the new print, as well as *The Gold Rush*, in the company of Oona and a party of friends, and decided that it would be a good idea to do the same for all his old films, in each case assembling the negatives to obtain a good protection print for special use if required at any time. The negatives, when placed in proper order, were to be deposited with Pathé's Hollywood laboratory. Totheroh spent most of the next year or so preparing these definitive negatives and library prints of the First National films. They were to prove invaluable years later when Chaplin decided to reissue a number of his early films with music.

On the night of 2 October 1943 Joan Barry gave birth to a baby girl, whom she named Carol Ann. Meanwhile the Federal courts were concocting a new case against Chaplin in relation to Barry, and during the next weeks were taking depositions from dozens of witnesses, including Chaplin's entire staff, his sons, and even Oona, who had never met Joan Barry. On 10 February 1944 Chaplin was indicted by a Federal grand jury. The charges were that he had violated the Mann Act, a piece of legislaton dating from 1910 and designed to combat commercial prostitution. The Act made it illegal to transport a woman across state lines for immoral purposes, and Chaplin was alleged on 5 October 1942 to have 'feloniously transported and caused to be transported Joan Barry from Los Angeles to the city of New York . . . with the intent and purpose of engaging in illicit sex relations.' A further charge joined Chaplin with six other people, including the police judge who was involved in Barry's first arrest on vagrancy charges, on a rather obscure indictment of conspiring to deprive Miss Barry of her civil rights.

The Mann Act charge was itself pretty far-fetched and depended on proving that Chaplin engaged in sexual relations with Miss Barry on the occasion of his visit to New York for his Second Front speech, and that moreover that had been his intention in paying her fare to New York a couple of weeks earlier. At the trial which began on 25 February, Chaplin's counsel, the celebrated lawyer Jerry Giesler, pinpointed the absurdity of the Government's position. He asked the jury in his summing up if it was likely that Chaplin would transport Barry 3000 miles for the purpose of a single alleged intimacy when she 'would have given her body to him at any time or place'. There was, added Giesler, 'no more evidence of Mann Act violation than there is evidence of murder'. The Government, however, pressed its case doggedly with a procession of witnesses. Barry went on the stand first to assert that intimacy had taken place during the New York visit, and that this meeting had been discussed before her departure from Hollywood for New York. The prosecuting attorney also called the travel agent who had supplied one-way tickets to New York for Barry and her mother; three railroad men who testified that the tickets had been used; the credit manager of the Waldorf-Astoria who confirmed that Chaplin was registered there, as everyone agreed he was, at the time under discussion; the night elevator operator from the hotel; and Chaplin's valet, Edward Chaney. Giesler, for the defence, cross-examined Barry about her visits to Tulsa. J. Paul Getty was called to testify for the defence that he knew Barry and had frequented her company in 1941, and in Tulsa in November 1942.

The last witness, on 30 March, was Chaplin himself, who denied any immoral intent in providing railroad tickets for Joan Barry and her mother, and denied any intimacy with her at any period after

May 1942. Giesler's memoirs recall Chaplin as 'the best witness I've ever seen in a law court. He was effective even when he wasn't being cross-examined but was merely sitting there, lonely and forlorn, at a far end of the counsel table. He is so small that only the toes of his shoes touched the floor.'

The jury of seven women and five men were out almost three hours and took four ballots to arrive at a unanimous vote of 'Not Guilty'. After the trial the judge and the prosecution attorney, Charles Carr, congratulated Chaplin, and he shook hands with each member of the jury and thanked them in turn. He was too moved to speak when one of them, Edythe Lewis, told him, 'It's all right, Charlie. It's still a free country.' At Summit Drive Oona fainted when she heard the news on the radio.

The verdict was an immense relief; but Chaplin had suffered much from the days sitting in court hearing the attorneys sieving through the unsavoury evidence of Barry's love life. During preliminary hearings he had also been furious at the indignity of being fingerprinted while, quite irregularly, the press were permitted to photograph him. This incident was stored up for subsequent use in *A King in New York*.

Between the indictment and the trial, Joan Barry's baby had been submitted to blood tests conducted by three physicians, one representing Barry, one representing Chaplin, and one a neutral observer, Dr Newton Evans. The results were released by the attorneys for both parties on 15 February 1944, and showed conclusively that Chaplin could not be the father of the child. Research had established that parents of blood type O (Chaplin) and A (Joan Barry) cannot produce a child of blood type B, as the baby proved to be. As a result of the tests, Chaplin's lawyer Loyd Wright optimistically filed for a dismissal of the paternity suit. The motion was overruled by Superior Court Judge Stanley Mosk, who enigmatically declared that 'the ends of justice will best be served by a full and fair trial of the issues'. Referring to the previous judge's approval of the blood test, when Mrs Berry's original suit had been filed, Judge Mosk said that it did not appear to him that the court then intended 'more than mere approval of the blood test for the parties and the infant without expressing ultimate determination of the law suit'.

Mrs Berry had of course been party to the agreement to drop the suit if the tests proved negative. This was neatly sidestepped by taking the guardianship of Carol Ann away from her grandmother and assigning it to the court. It was now therefore the Court of Los Angeles that was suing Chaplin on Carol Ann's behalf. The new trial was set for December 1944. Convinced as he was that the results of the blood test must wholly vindicate him, the months of waiting were still an anxious period for Chaplin.

Life with Oona, who was now pregnant with her first child, provided joyful distraction. In May they spent a ten-day holiday in Palm Springs, and passed most of June on the East Coast. On 1 August their first child, Geraldine was born. Shortly afterwards they advertised for a nanny and among the applicants was Edith McKenzie, a Scot who had worked for many years in the United States. When Oona asked her on the phone how old she was Miss McKenzie said evasively, 'Why don't you wait and see me for yourself?' (She was just past forty). Oona saw her and took to this slim, forthright, capable woman at once. Renamed 'Kay-Kay' a few months later by the infant Geraldine, she was to remain for over forty years an indispensable member of the household, and every Chaplin child's closest friend and confidante.

Kay-Kay vividly remembers how Chaplin watched and held his first daughter with as much joyful wonder as a twenty-year-old first-time father. In fact his two sons, now grown up, were both in the army. Less than three weeks after Geraldine was born there was a melancholy reminder of his first unhappy marriage: Mildred Harris died at the age of fory-three in the Cedars of Lebanon Hospital. Chaplin sent a spray of orchids, roses and gladioli to the funeral.

Lion Feuchtwanger, who was among Chaplin's current friends, had commented after the Mann Act trial, 'You are the one artist of the theatre who will go down in American history as having aroused the political antagonism of a whole nation.' On this score Chaplin was reassured when General Eisenhower personally requested the preparation of a dubbed French version of *The Great Dictator* for release in newly-liberated France under the Office of War Information. Chaplin happily gave his consent, and the required prints and tracks were shipped on 21 November.

The Carol Ann Barry paternity trial opened on 13 December 1944 before Judge Henry Willis. Chaplin was so confident that the scientific evidence must win the day that he did not this time hire the skilful Giesler (in the previous trial some friends had advised him that to hire such a heavyweight criminal pleader in itself might imply guilt) but a capable, unsensational attorney, Charles A. (Pat) Millikan. Neither Chaplin nor Millikan had reckoned on being faced by Joseph Scott as attorney for the prosecution. Scott was a craggy-faced old lawyer of the all-stops-out histrionic school. His ardent belief in God, Country and the Republican Party added the strength of personal feeling to his pursuit of the defendant. Scott put Joan Barry on the stand, before a jury of seven women and five men, to describe the events of the night she broke into Chaplin's house brandishing a pistol. She explained that she told Chaplin on that occasion, 'I am almost out of my mind. I have waited and waited. You haven't called me. I don't know what to do.' She insisted that the child was conceived on that occasion, and that she had had relations with no other man since she had met Chaplin. Before she left in the morning of 24 December, she said, Chaplin promised to pay her a regular $25 per week. It was at that point that she had handed over the gun to him. Scott examined Chaplin, who insisted that there had been no intimacy between him and the girl since early in 1942, and that when Barry had told him that she was pregnant and he was responsible, he had replied that it was 'impossible'. Scott's final stroke, was to have the jury gaze for three quarters of a minute at Chaplin and Carol Ann, held in her mother's arms and standing at a distance of eight feet from Chaplin, urging them to recognize facial resemblances. The child was fourteen months old.

Millikan's defence was in principle much stronger, relying simply upon two main witnesses. Dr Newton Evans, the independent physician who had conducted the blood tests, demonstrated the laboratory methods used to arrive at the definite conclusion that Chaplin could not be the father of Carol Ann. A Tulsa lawyer, O. C. Lassiter, described a conversation he had had with Barry on 28 January 1943, when he was Assistant County Counsel and was dismissing an unspecified charge against her. She had told him that she had 'gone overboard' for an oil man – presumably Getty – whom she had accompanied from California to Florida in November 1942; that she had come to Tulsa to be with him, and had spent two nights with him at the Mayo Hotel in Tulsa when he had suggested marrying her if he could get rid of his wife. He had now left, however, and she could not find him. In court Barry denied that such a conversation had taken place.

Logic may not have been on Scott's side but he preferred to appeal to emotion. Throughout the trial he persistently abused Chaplin in terms which shocked even experienced reporters, and which had their effect in wounding and exciting Chaplin. Some instances of his invective were 'grey-headed old buzzard', 'little runt of a Svengali' and 'lecherous hound', Chaplin lied, he said, 'like a cheap cockney cad'. 'The reptile looked upon her [Barry] as so much carrion. Finally he took her up to the house and read her a script about Bluebeard' (a reference which must relate to one of the later meetings of Chaplin and Barry). Scott evidently impressed part of the jury and, more important, he threw Chaplin off balance. At one point Chaplin was stung into crying out to the judge, 'Your Honour, I've committed no crime. I'm only human. But this man is trying to make a monster out of me.' Scott succeeded in manoeuvring Chaplin into a state in which the audience saw him as a man angry and cornered. In his final argument he exhorted the jury:

> There has been no one to stop Chaplin in his lecherous conduct all these years – except you. Wives and mothers all over the country are watching to see you stop him dead in his tracks. You'll sleep well the night you give this baby a name – the night you show him the law means him as well as the bums on Skid Row.

If Scott's abuse was to be taken seriously, it was a name the child would hardly thank them for giving her. Chaplin, along with everyone who knew him, was stunned by this unjust vilification. Even taking into account the publicity surrounding his unfortunate divorces, Chaplin had led a life of exceptional discretion by Hollywood standards, and his time with Paulette demonstrated his essential yearning for domesticity. The sticky label of 'libertine' was rarely more unjustly applied.

The jury may have been impressed by Scott's oratory, but they were less convinced by Joan Barry's evidence. After four hours and forty minutes of deliberation the jury could not reach a verdict: the vote was seven to five in favour of aquittal. Judge Clarence L. Kincaid offered to arbitrate. Scott for the prosecution was prepared to accept the offer, but Chaplin (who had missed the final days of the trial because of a foot injury which hospitalized him) was set on complete exoneration, and refused.

The retrial lasted from 4 April to 17 April 1944, and was heard before Judge Kincaid. It was adjourned on 14 April because of the death of President Roosevelt. This time the jury consisted of eleven women and one man. Joseph Scott stepped up his emotional assault upon the jury even more than at the first trial. The jury, in the words of a writer in *Southern California Law Review*, 'let sentimental consideration turn logic out of doors, and failed dismally in its task of weighing the evidence.' They brought in a verdict of 'Guilty' by an eleven to one vote. The stand-out juror was a housewife called Mary James, who said of her vote: 'I am not upholding Mr Chaplin at all . . . Only I don't think he was the father of the child.'

The evidence of the blood tests was totally disregarded. At that time only ten states, which did not include California, allowed blood tests to be introduced in evidence to disprove paternity. The legal notoriety of the Chaplin case may have encouraged wider subsequent recognition of the test. In 1953 California introduced legislation to prevent pursuance of paternity cases where blood tests had conclusively proved that the defendant could not be father of the child.

Judge Kincaid ruled as a result of the verdict that Chaplin should make payments of $75 a week to Carol Ann – who was now legally entitled to adopt the name of Chaplin – with increases to $100 as her needs grew, until she reached the age of twenty-one. Apart from that the Berry/Barry family finally disappeared from Chaplin's life, though the damage they had done and the embarrassment and smears that he had suffered as a result of the trial were permanent. A year or so later Joan Barry married and had two more children before separating from her husband. In 1953 she was found in a dazed state in Torrance, California, whither she had once trekked from Mexico. She was committed to Patton State Hospital for care.

Through his lawyers, Wright and Millikan, Chaplin filed a motion for a new trial, but after four weeks' consideration the motion was denied on 6 June 1945. Though a further trial might have gratified his sense of justice, Chaplin was repelled and exhausted by the affair, and he knew that nothing could now retrieve the damage to the reputation he had so valued throughout his professional life. His consolation was his new family and, as always, work. He took enormous pleasure in screening for Oona his old films, many of which she had never had the opportunity to see. Apart from all her other qualities, Oona was the best audience he had ever had. However often she saw his films she would giggle with as little inhibition as any child at Charlie's antics; Chaplin, who always saw himself on screen with an objective, critical detachment, would join her.

Despite the irritations and interruptions of the Barry affair, work had continued on the script of *Monsieur Verdoux*, and preparations for production began in 1945. Practically none of Chaplin's earlier drafts and working notes for *Verdoux* have survived, so it is not possible to trace the kind of evolution which we can discover in the case of his other films. Only three manuscript pages in Chaplin's hand, and headed 'Notes for Verdoux', somehow escaped whatever was the fate of the rest of the papers. The use of the name indicates that the notes belong to a late stage of the writing. The name Verdoux seems not to have been adopted until the latter part of 1945 – the main character was originally called 'Varnay', a name which still crops up, through secretarial slips, in the finished script. It is not clear whether the aphoristic notes are suggestions for dialogue, or whether they represent reflections on the philosophic content of the film. In either event it does not seem far-fetched to see in the tone of irony and disillusion Chaplin's personal reaction to his recent months in the pillory:

When all the world turns against a man he becomes holy.

Where there are no facts, sentiments prevail.

Virtues are less acquired than vices.

It is more important to understand crime than to condemn it.

Good is in everything – even in evil.

The most profound eloquence is silence, a deep wordless understanding.

Evil has its attendant good.

In the last analysis there is no reason for anything.

Violence is patience's last resort.

Soul is the possible, and the world is the actual. This concept is the deep inner feeling in man.

The soul is the becoming.
The world is the become.
Life is the state of becoming.

The soul is the still to be accomplished.
The world is the accomplished,
And life is the accomplishing.

The most compleat concept of meaning is beauty.

Living becomes a habit which at times I wish I could break.

A reputation is the concern of cooks and butlers.

The surviving versions of the script are almost exactly in the form of the finished film, except for an opening scene which was never shot, and some emendations to the dialogue required by the censorship of the Breen Office. The only resemblance to the story of Landru is Verdoux's profession, which is that of murdering rich widows and investing their fortunes. The front for his operations is an apparently inoperative furniture business. When he is not otherwise occupied by his demanding business, Verdoux returns to his country cottage, cherished child and invalid wife. He meets a beautiful young woman, down on her luck and working as a prostitute, whom he takes home, intending to use her as a guinea pig for a new poison, but instead persuades her that life is after all worth living. When he meets her again years later, their roles in life have changed: she has become the mistress of an armaments manufacturer, whose business is flourishing on the eve of a new world war; Verdoux's careful investments have been wiped out since the Stock Market crash. At this point Verdoux's past catches up on him and he is arrested and put on trial. At his trial and execution he shows mild surprise rather than remorse, since his mode of life has only carried to logical extremes the philosophies on which contemporary capitalist society is built.

JUDGE: (*to Verdoux*) Have you anything to say before sentence is passed upon you?

VERDOUX: (*rises*) Yes, Monsieur . . . I have . . . However remiss the prosecutor has been in paying me any compliment, he at least admits that I have brains. (*turning to prosecutor*) Thank you, Monsieur . . . I have . . . And for thirty years I used them honestly, but after that nobody wanted them. So I was forced to go into business for myself. But I can assure you it was no life of ease. I worked very hard for what I got, and for the little I received I gave very much . . . As for being a mass murderer, does not the world encourage it? Is it not building weapons of destruction for the sole purpose of mass killing? Has it not blown unsuspecting women and children to pieces, and done it very scientifically? As a mass killer, I am an amateur by comparison . . . To be shocked by the nature of my crime is nothing but a pretence . . . a sham!

> You wallow in murder . . . you legalize it . . . you adorn it
> with gold braid! You celebrate it and parade it! Killing is the
> enterprise by which your System prospers . . . upon which
> your industry thrives. However, I have no desire to lose
> my temper, because very shortly I shall lose my head . . .
> Nevertheless, upon leaving this spark of earthly existence, I
> have this to say . . . I shall see you all very soon.

(This is from the original script: the Breen Office required some
cuts to make the speech more acceptable to the mood of post-War
America.)

Later, awaiting execution, Verdoux tells a reporter who protests
that other people don't conduct their business in Verdoux's way:

> Oh, don't they? That's the history of many a big business. One murder
> makes a villain . . . millions a hero. Numbers sanctify, my good friend.

In an interview shortly before the release of the picture, Chaplin
stated:

> The picture has moral value, I believe. Von Clausewitz said that war is
> the logical extension of diplomacy; M. Verdoux feels that murder is the
> logical extension of business. He should express the feeling of the times
> we live in – out of catastrophe come people like him. He typifies the
> psychological disease and depression. He is frustrated, bitter, and at the
> end, pessimistic. But he is never morbid; and the picture is by no means
> morbid in treatment . . . Under the proper circumstances, murder can be
> comic.[3]

Under the proper circumstances relations with the Breen Office
could be comic too, as well as irritating. Chaplin devotes a dozen
pages of his autobiography to his dealings with the Office over
Verdoux, and the correspondence and a marked copy of the script
remain in the Chaplin archive. In initially disapproving the script in
its entirety, they said they were passing over 'those elements which
seem to be anti-social in their concept and significance . . . the sections
of the story in which Verdoux indicts the 'System' and impugns the
present-day social structure'. (It is interesting that they failed to
acknowledge that the film was supposed to take place in France,
between the wars.) The whole nature of Verdoux's *modus vivendi*,
they found, had 'about it a distasteful flavour of illicit sex, which in
our judgement is not good'. Specific elements to which they raised
objection included a scene which suggested that Verdoux had actually
slept with one of the 'wives' he had murdered; all dialogue which

made it evident that the girl he picked up in the street was a prostitute
and later suggestions that she had become prosperous and was the
mistress of a munitions manufacturer. They wanted to be sure that

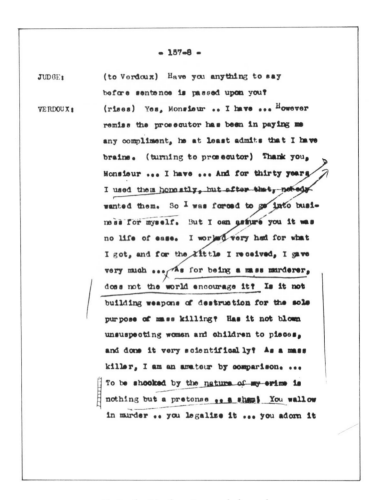

Script for Verdoux's speech from the
dock, marked up by the Breen Office.

there was no 'showing of, or suggestion of, toilets in the bathroom',
objected to a *double entendre* about 'scraping her bottom'; and
required the removal of the word 'voluptuous' and the phrase 'in-

decent moon' which Chaplin had treasured since he savoured it a quarter of a century before in the company of H. G. Wells.

On 11 March 1946 Chaplin accepted Joseph Breen's invitation to go to his office and discuss the script. Breen himself was amiable and even constructive. Chaplin realized however, from the attitude of one of his assistants, a 'tall, dour young man' who greeted him with the words, 'What have you against the Catholic Church?' that a good deal of their anxiety centred upon Verdoux's exchanges with the priest at the end of the film:

VERDOUX: What can I do for you, my good man?

PRIEST: (*benevolently*) Nothing, my son. I want to help you . . . if I can. I've come to ask you to make your peace with God.

VERDOUX: (*affectionately*) Dear father . . . I am at peace with God . . . my conflict, at this moment, is with Man.

PRIEST: Have you no remorse for your sins?

VERDOUX: Who knows what sin is . . . born, as it was, from heaven . . . from God's fallen angel? Who knows what ultimate destiny it serves? (*with politeness*) After all, what would you be doing without sin?

(*footsteps are heard along the corridor*)

PRIEST: They are coming . . . let me pray for you.

VERDOUX: (*politely*) As you wish. But I don't think these gentlemen want to be kept waiting.

(*enter executioner and prison officials*)

PRIEST: May the Lord have mercy on your soul.

VERDOUX: Why not? After all . . . it belongs to him.

The rejected opening sequence of the film began with a montage of scenes showing American business booming: busy brokers on the stock exchange: a business man in his office, all ready for golf; a millionaire on a luxury yacht. A voice over the action explains, 'In the glorious days of '28, everybody made money except those who worked for it'; and Monsieur Verdoux is seen diligently working away as a clerk in a big Parisian bank. A parallel sequence follows, with the stock exchange in panic, the business man shooting himself, the ruined millionaire falling dead over the side of his yacht, a broker swallowing a cyanide capsule and expiring with a grimace of distaste.

In the bank, Verdoux receives with his pay packet a notice of dismissal and the camera moves in to close-up of a hopeless, tragic face. Over dissolves of Depression scenes, the voice continues, 'In the lean years that followed, many changes occurred in the lives of people . . . millionaires became paupers and commodores became stevedores. But Monsieur Verdoux, ex-bank teller of Paris, became something else, a man of many aliases who, in spite of the depression, did well for himself.' Verdoux is next seen busy and prosperous, an elegant *boulevardier* who now goes to work on his next victim.

As work progressed, Chaplin realized that he needed to place the Stock Market crash and Depression later in the film, to explain Verdoux's ruin. A much simpler Stock Market scene was therefore introduced at a later point, and this beginning was abandoned. In its place Chaplin devised a faster, neater opening. Over a shot of a grave marked 'Henri Verdoux, 1880–1937' his voice is heard saying 'Good evening. I was a bank clerk until the Depression of 1930,' and then goes on laconically to explain the nature of his business.

Few of the old collaborators remained. There was still the ever-faithful Totheroh; and half-brother Wheeler Dryden was now promoted to the post of associate director. The other associate director was Robert Florey, a friend and dedicated admirer for thirty years. Since he had written his first book about Chaplin in 1927, Florey had become a director of some distinction in his own right, and had just enjoyed one of his greatest successes with *The Beast With Five Fingers*. He was proud, even so, to accept a subordinate role on a film directed by his lifelong idol, and for Chaplin he was a valuable asset for the technical advice he was able to offer on the French settings. Henry Bergman, a kind of mascot since 1915, was now too ill to work, and died shortly after shooting had begun. Sydney was living in California again, and Chaplin wanted him to play the role of Detective Morrow who arrests Verdoux but unwisely accepts his hospitality in the shape of a glass of poisoned wine. Sydney's wife Gypsy opposed this, since she did not want to see Sydney worried sick by Charlie's extravagance as, she said, he had been during *The Great Dictator*.

Perhaps at some urging of nostalgia, Chaplin decided that the role of the matronly Madame Grosnay might suit Edna Purviance. Edna, who was now over fifty and many years retired, was as much alarmed as flattered by the prospect. On 18 March 1946 she arrived at the

Chaplin studios for the first time in more than twenty years, during which neither Chaplin nor Totheroh had seen her. The reunion was emotional for all three, though Chaplin affected a breezy nonchalance as if they had been together the day before. Edna had grown stout, and there was not much reminder of her old beauty, but she had still the same charm and humour. She read for the part – not badly, Chaplin conceded – and spent the next month at the studio, testing and rehearsing. Gradually it became evident that it would not work: the sophistication of a Continental *grande dame* was not in her line. When Edna returned home, both she and Chaplin were relieved. Her presence was too melancholy a reminder of the old times when everything lay in the future. They were never to meet again, though in the last pages of his autobiography Chaplin quotes with affection two letters she wrote to him in Switzerland in her last years – knowing full well that she would never receive any answer, for Chaplin was no letter writer. Edna died of cancer in 1958 at the age of sixty-two.

The part of Madame Grosnay eventually went to an English actress, Isobel Elsom, who was singing in the chorus of *The Quaker Girl* at the Adelphi at the time that Chaplin was touring for Karno. She had subsequently made a distinguished stage career, and moved to the United States in the late 1930s. The cast mostly called for character actresses, among whom were the formidable Almira Sessions and the Australian-born Marjorie Bennett, who was to appear again for Chaplin in *Limelight*.

It was most probably at the suggestion of Robert Florey, who had directed her nine years before in *Mountain Music*, that Chaplin cast the comedienne Martha Raye in the role of the terrible Annabella, the most indestructible of Verdoux's victims. The decision was taken after a screening of Raye's most recent film, *Four Jills and a Jeep*, in the studio screening room. During her first days on the set the ebullient Martha Raye was awed by Chaplin, who had been a hero for her since her show business childhood. Recognizing that this was inhibiting her work, she took the plunge, and started to address him familiarly as 'Chuck'. He took it in good part and in turn called her 'Maggie'. (Her real name is Margaret Reed). After that she grew even bolder, and alarmed the unit by calling 'Lunch' if she felt the morning's work had gone on too long. Instead of the anticipated fury, Chaplin accepted this in good part also, perhaps because he justly admired the skilful partnering the actress was giving him.

His casting of the young prostitute was less successful. Marilyn

Nash was good-looking and charming, but all too clearly without experience or great natural talent. Chaplin's own doubts about her were indicated by the number of times he re-screened the elaborate test he had shot of her, and the time he spent patiently rehearsing her. Problems with Miss Nash accounted for several lost days on the schedule. On the second day of shooting the scene in which Verdoux takes the girl to his furniture warehouse, Miss Nash left the studio, ill and unable to work. That afternoon Chaplin tested two girls, Barbara Woodell and Randy Stuart, for the role. He settled on Randy Stuart. Marilyn Nash returned to work on the following day, which was Saturday, but for the next four days of shooting Chaplin took the unusual measure of working with both girls in the part, evidently fearing that Miss Nash might be incapable of continuing. Finally however Miss Stuart was paid off and Marilyn Nash completed the film, pleasantly though somewhat without colour.

The filming of *Monsieur Verdoux* was unlike any previous Chaplin film. Apart from this incident, the work proceeded quickly and efficiently, with none of those pauses for reconsideration and reflection which had been so essential to the Chaplin method. The reason was not any change in Chaplin's temperament, or even because he began with a wholly realized script. It reflected rather the change in Hollywood which followed the end of the war. The years 1945 and 1946 saw much union trouble in the industry, and a prolonged strike had forced up studio wages by 25 per cent. Moreover the unions were now imposing tough minimum requirements on staffing, and, even more than during *The Great Dictator*, Chaplin found himself engaging technicians whom he did not require and whose function he did not even understand. For some years the soaring costs of running a studio had necessitated renting out studio space between films. The cost of the idle days that had been part of the studio routine in years gone by would now have been prohibitive.

There were more painful reminders of passing time. Since Christmas Alf Reeves had been ailing and in the first week of April 1946, when production had just officially got under way, he died. Alf had been associated with Chaplin since 1910, at first as his boss with Karno's companies; later as a shrewd, loyal, incorruptible and skilled employee who had discreetly guided the studio's affairs and watched with patient, paternal concern over Chaplin's private life. At the end of March when it was clear that Reeves, now nearing seventy, could not be expected to return to work, Chaplin had interviewed a prospective replacement, John McFadden, who was appointed general manager on 8 April.

McFadden had been recommended to Chaplin by his lawyer Loyd Wright, and arrived at the studio with new-broom efficiency. From the start he aroused the hostility of the unit, but particularly Rollie Totheroh, who was understandably angry when McFadden began to destroy the old footage he had stored (with frequent grumbles) for almost thirty years.

> He told the cutter to get rid of a lot of stuff, to burn it up. 'I'm making a new Chaplin. The old Chaplin is forgotten, see?' He called in *The Gold Rush* after our second release, that was still out making money with the sound track. 'Don't show that stuff to the public any more. That's the old Chaplin; forget that' . . . But Charlie could be taken in by a lot of guys like that, you see.[4]

Relations at the studio became so bad that Chaplin called the unit together and asked for their cooperation. As Totheroh saw Chaplin entrusting property affairs to the new man, and McFadden using studio facilities in ways of which the jealous Totheroh did not approve, he finally plucked up courage to take Chaplin aside:

> I said, 'You know what's going on here? He's just robbing you right and left and what he intends to do later . . . and you're going to give him permission.' It's a wonder Charlie didn't give him his stocks and his bonds to handle. And Charlie said 'Honest?' 'Yes.' 'Well,' he said, 'just keep an eye on him. I'll get rid of him but we're so far into things now I can't very well change in the middle of the stream. He knows about expenses that have already gone out. Just wait.'[5]

One week after the last shot of *Monsieur Verdoux*, with cutting only just begun, McFadden left the studio.

There was no substance in Totheroh's accusations, but they reflected the general dislike of McFadden. Even so, he introduced something which had never been seen before in the Chaplin studios – a shooting schedule. The work was broken down in advance into sixty shooting days and it was to everyone's credit – including McFadden for the practicability of his schedule – that the film fell only seventeen days behind.

Shooting was completed in the first week of September 1946 and during the remainder of the year Chaplin was cutting and working on his musical score with Rudi Schrager. The music – the most notable theme is the perky little '*boulevardier*' motif for Verdoux –

was ready to record by mid-January; but it was six weeks more before Chaplin was satisfied with the RCA Studios' work on recording and dubbing. He had become as perfectionist over sound as he was about his own performances, and perhaps more so than in his judgement of images: contemporary critics pointed out some rather obvious backdrops and some bad cutting matches in *Verdoux*. By the beginning of March the first finished prints of the film were ready and on 11 March 1947 the film was shown to the Breen Office examiners, who passed it without demur. During March Chaplin arranged private showings of the film for friends and visitors, including Gabriel Pascal, and was greatly heartened by their enthusiasm. On 21 March he and Oona, accompanied by Watson the English butler, took a train for New York, nervous but optimistic about the world première there.

The première was at the Broadway Theatre, New York on 11 April, the same day as the West Coast press preview at the Academy Theatre, Hollywood. A Chaplin première still attracted crowds and excitement. Mary Pickford accompanied the Chaplins. Miss Pickford was grabbed by a radio interviewer, and her companions always wondered how she would have continued her statement if she had not been separated from the microphone just as she had begun, 'Two thousand years ago Christ was born and tonight . . .'

The show was a gruelling experience. The bad publicity of the Barry trials and the growing rumbles of political propaganda against him had clearly done their work, and from the start it was apparent that an element of the première audience were there intent on demonstrating their resentment: from the start of the film there was scattered hissing, which stirred in Chaplin all his old terrors of the live audience. Even many of the well-disposed, however, were puzzled by the dark irony of the film. Eventually Chaplin could no longer bear to stay, and waited in the lobby until the film ended, leaving Oona inside with Mary. The supper party afterwards for 150 guests was an ordeal; this time Oona left early.

There was to be a far worse ordeal the following day. United Artists had arranged a press conference for Chaplin in the Grand Ballroom of the Gotham Hotel at 55th Street just off 5th Avenue. The room was crowded and Chaplin started off the proceedings with an attempt at grim jocularity: 'Proceed with the butchery . . . fire ahead at this old grey head.' The first questions were already barbed: Had he not failed to give Orson Welles proper credit for his contribution to *Monsieur Verdoux*? Had *The Great Dictator* been shown in the

Soviet Union, and was it true that he was part of a motion picture combine to transfer American films to the Soviet Union? (Chaplin said that it was definitely untrue.) Then, 'There have been several stories in the past accusing you more or less of being a fellow traveller, a Communist sympathizer. Could you define your present political beliefs, sir?'[6] Chaplin replied,

> Well, I think that is very difficult to do these days, to define anything politically. There are so many generalities, and life is becoming so technical that if you step off the curb – if you step off the curb with your left foot, they accuse you of being a Communist. But I have no political persuasion whatsoever. I've never belonged to any political party in my life, and I have never voted in my life! . . . Does that answer your question?

It did not: the questioner persisted: was he a Communist sympathizer? Again Chaplin attempted a serious answer to the question:

> A Communist sympathizer? That has to be qualified again. I don't know what you mean by a 'Communist sympathizer'. I'd say this – that during the war, I sympathized very much with Russia because I believe that she was holding the front, and for that I have a memory and I feel that I owe her thanks. I think that she helped contribute a considerable amount of fighting and dying to bring victory to the Allies. In that sense I am sympathetic.

At this point the assault was taken over by one James W. Fay, the representative of the Catholic War Veterans' paper and the Catholic War Veterans of New York County. (Some years later Fay was to become President of the League of Catholic Lawyers in New York, and National Commander of the Catholic War Veterans.) Fay's line of questioning had the insuperable advantage of a wonderful absence of logic, which enabled him to side-step Chaplin's careful answers. The dialogue is a horror comic of the Cold War mind:

FAY: Last week you reported, not as a taxpayer . . . you were a well-paying guest. Don't you realize, Mr Chaplin, that veterans while assuming all the obligations of a citizen at the same time pay their share of taxes as well?

CHAPLIN: I didn't say they didn't.

FAY: I know that, but you are giving that implication, sir.

CHAPLIN: I don't see how. I think you have misinterpreted my remark. I never meant it that way.

FAY: Mr Chaplin, you also said you are not a nationalist of any country, is that correct?

CHAPLIN: True.

FAY: Therefore, you feel that you can pay your way on your taxes without assuming any of the moral responsibilities or obligations of the particular country you are living in?

CHAPLIN: When you say, when you do what you are told – when you are living in a country you assume all the responsibilities – wherever you're residing.

FAY: I don't believe you do, Mr Chaplin.

CHAPLIN: Well, that's a – that's a question where we both differ.

FAY: All right. Now, Mr Chaplin, the *Daily Worker* on October 25 1942 reported [that] you stated, in an address before the Artists' Front to Win the War, a Communist front group: 'I'm not a citizen, I don't need citizenship papers, and I've never had patriotism in that sense for any country, but I'm a patriot to humanity as a whole. I'm a citizen of the world. If the Four Freedoms mean anything after this war, we don't bother about whether we are citizens of one country or another.' Mr Chaplin, the men who advanced in the face of enemy fire, and the poor fellows who were drafted like myself, and their families and buddies, resent that remark. And we want to know, now, if you were properly quoted.

CHAPLIN: I don't know why you resent that. That is a personal opinion. I am – four-fifths of my family are Americans. I have four children, two of them were on those beachheads. They were with Patton's Third Army. I am the one-fifth that isn't a citizen. Nevertheless, I – I – I've done my share, and whatever I said, it is not by any means to be meant to be derogatory to your Catholic – uh – uh – uh – GIs.

FAY: It's not the Catholic GIs, Mr Chaplin, it's the GIs throughout the United States!

CHAPLIN: Well, whatever they are, if they take exception to the fact that I am not a citizen and that I pay my taxes and that seventy per cent of my revenue comes from uh – uh – uh – abroad, then I apologize for paying that hundred per cent on seventy per cent.

FAY: I think that is a very evasive answer, Mr Chaplin, because so do those veterans pay their taxes, too.

CHAPLIN: Yes?

FAY: Whether their revenue comes from elsewhere or not.

CHAPLIN: The problem is – what is it that you are objecting to?

FAY: I'm objecting to your particular stand that you have no patriotic feelings about this country or any other country.

CHAPLIN: I think you're . . .

FAY: You've worked here, you've made your money here, you went around in the last war when you should have been serving Great Britain, you were here selling bonds, so it stated in the paper that I read, and I think that you as a citizen here – or rather a resident here – taking our money should have done more!

CHAPLIN: (*after a pause*) Well, that's another question of opinion and, as I say, I think it is rather dictatorial on your part to say as how I should apply my patriotism. I have patriotism and I had patriotism in this war and I showed it and I did a good deal for the war effort but it was never advertised. Now, whether you say that you object to me for not having patriotism is a qualified thing. I've been that way ever since I have been a young child. I can't help it. I've travelled all over the world, and my patriotism doesn't rest with one class. It rests with the whole world – the pity of the whole world and the common people, and that includes even those that object to me – that sort of patriotism.

The questioners who followed Fay were equally determined to pursue Chaplin's political opinions, rather than to talk about the film. Chaplin's replies were forthright and uncompromising. He was asked about his wartime activities:

I spoke what was in my heart, what was in my mind and what I felt was right and manly of me to do. I appealed both to Great Britain and the United States – said that we should have a second front. Our boys were over there and so forth, and I wasn't alone in that. It appears it's come out now that General Marshall and President Franklin Roosevelt and other people were of the same opinion. And then I made several speeches along that line for the unification and for the unity of the Allied cause – which at that time was being disrupted. We know the technique of the Nazis. They started by condemning the Communists, and that was their technique in order to bring around the jingoism and the war that followed – and it was very obvious to see that they were trying to disunite us in this country. We were all fresh at that time, and so the Administration wanted unity – and I made several speeches on behalf of the Administration for that purpose, and I felt that I served that purpose better, doing that sort of thing, than trying to do a floor-show, because that is not quite my business. I'm not very good at that sort of thing. And I thought I would use my effort in another direction. I made several speeches to factory workers and also several records for French distribution and for foreign consumption.

Asked if he was a friend of Hanns Eisler he replied that he was very proud of the fact. Pressed to say if he knew that Eisler was a Communist he said he only knew that 'he is a fine artist and a great musician and a very sympathetic friend'. When eventually some questioners got round to the film, he was asked if he himself shared Verdoux's conviction that contemporary civilization was making mass murderers of us:

Yes ... Well, all my life I have always loathed and abhorred violence. Now I think these weapons of destruction – I don't think I'm alone in saying this, it's a cliché by now – that the atomic bomb is the most horrible invention of mankind, and I think it is being proven so every moment. I think it is creating so much horror and fear that we are going to grow up a bunch of neurotics.

Would he permit his own children to see *Monsieur Verdoux*?

Why not? ... Not all of it's beyond them ... I know there are a lot of pictures that I wouldn't allow my children to see that are supposed to be very forthright, high moral purpose, that I wouldn't send my children because it's absolutely a false notion of life. Something that doesn't exist. A lot of pictures are very dishonest. So-called boy meets girl ...

Chaplin parried the attacks with skill and total honesty. He seemed taken aback, though clearly touched, suddenly to find he had at least one defender. James Agee of *Time* stood up in the balcony. He was so angry that his words were barely coherent, but his sentiments were clear:

What are people who care a damn about freedom – who really care for it – think of a country and the people in it, who congratulate themselves upon this country as the finest on earth and as a 'free country', when so many of the people in this country pry into what a man's citizenship is, try to tell him his business from hour to hour and from day to day and exert a public moral blackmail against him for not becoming an American citizen – for his political views and for not entertaining troops in the manner – in the way that they think he should. What is to be thought of a . . . country where those people are thought well of . . .

Agee followed up this indignant outburst by devoting three successive monthly columns in the *Nation* to *Monsieur Verdoux*. When, later, he arrived in Hollywood to be the writer of John Huston's *The African Queen*, Agee became a personal friend of the Chaplins, and a visitor at Summit Drive.

The transcript of the *Verdoux* press conference was preserved by George Wallach, who was present as a producer-director for radio and recorded the whole affair on a portable sound recorder. After the conference he asked Chaplin if he would like to hear the recording, and Chaplin invited him to his suite on the seventeenth floor of the hotel. He remembered that Chaplin sat cross-legged on a high-back upholstered chair:

> . . . as he listened to the questions and his answers, he relived each and every moment. He would turn to Oona, his wife, who was sitting on the bed, and say 'How was that?' or 'Did you think that was all right?' And she reacted to him rather than to the recording.
>
> Chaplin's back was quite straight and he held his clasped hands under his chin and rocked slightly back and forth – as if he were shadow-boxing with the words coming out of the speaker. He thanked me after the recording had run its course, and I headed back to the studio, where I put together a thirty-minute program that was broadcast that same evening.
>
> Somehow, thinking back after almost a quarter-century to Chaplin sitting in that chair – listening to the recording – I see in him the personification of the universal underdog. The underdog who, somehow, *does* win in the end.[7]

17

LIMELIGHT

Chaplin returned to California. Back home with Oona and the children he rapidly recovered from the ordeal of *Monsieur Verdoux*. He had still confidence in the American public's affection and moreover 'I had an idea and under its compulsion I did not give a damn what the outcome would be; the film had to be made.' Nor did he give a damn about Representative J. Parnell Thomas and the House Committee on Un-American Activities: or at least he was not going to allow them (as so many others in Hollywood did) to curb his opinions or his associations. 'A democracy is a place where you can express your ideas freely – or it isn't a democracy,' he said. In the opinion of his son, Charles, 'He always felt he belonged here in America, with its promise of freedom in thought and belief and its emphasis on the importance of the individual.'[1] Some of his best friends in Hollywood felt that he should have shut up and not made unnecessary enemies, but Chaplin to his credit always valued his friends and feelings more than he did his enemies. He made no secret of his support for the Liberal, Henry A. Wallace. His dinner guests included Harry Bridges, Paul Robeson and the 'Red Dean' of Canterbury, the Very Reverend Hewlett Johnson, whom he had met on his 1931 tour. In the late 1930s he had met Hanns Eisler, a refugee from Nazi Germany, and had remained friendly with him and his wife. Through the Eislers he met Bertolt Brecht.

As early as December 1946, Ernie Adamson, chief counsel for the Un-American Activities Committee, announced that among people who would be subpoenaed to testify at public hearings in Washington would be James Roosevelt, Will Rogers Jr and Chaplin; but no more was heard of it at that time. In May 1947 Chaplin was again quizzed by the press about his unwillingness to take American citizenship, and again he gave the same answer: 'I am an internationalist, not a nationalist, and that is why I do not take out citizenship.' On 12 June Chaplin became the subject of a heated debate in Congress. Representative John T. Rankin of Mississippi (who was also a member of the House Un-American Activities Committee) told the House:

> I am here today demanding that Attorney General Tom Clark institute proceedings to deport Charlie Chaplin. He has refused to become an American citizen. His very life in Hollywood is detrimental to the moral fabric of America. In that way he can be kept off the American screen, and his loathsome pictures can be kept from before the eyes of the American youth. He should be deported and gotten rid of at once.

Chaplin was much more angered by an NBC broadcast given by Hy Gardner. Chaplin immediately filed a $3 million suit in the federal court, alleging that Gardner had defamed him by calling him a Communist and liar, and moreover that NBC had tapped his private telephones. The case was to drag on inconclusively for several years. In July the newspapers learned from Representative Thomas that HUAC now intended to issue a subpoena requiring Chaplin to testify before his Committee. Chaplin did not wait for the subpoena: on 21 July the press reprinted the text of a dignified but sarcastic message which he had sent by telegram to Thomas:

> From your publicity I note that I am to be quizzed by the House Un-American Activities Committee in Washington in September. I understand I am to be your single 'guest' at the expense of the taxpayers. Forgive me for this premature acceptance of your headlines newspaper invitation [*sic*].
>
> You have been quoted as saying you wish to ask me if I am a Communist. You sojourned for ten days in Hollywood not long ago,* and could have asked me the question at that time, effecting something of an economy, or you could telephone me now – collect. In order that you may be completely up-to-date on my thinking I suggest you view carefully my latest production, *Monsieur Verdoux*. It is against war and the futile slaughter of our youth. I trust you will not find its humane message distasteful.
>
> While you are preparing your engraved subpoena I will give you a hint on where I stand. I am not a Communist. I am a peacemonger.

* Investigating Hanns Eisler.

FRANK F. BARHAM, PUBLISHER

TUESDAY, APRIL 15, 1947

Chaplin Should Be Taken at His Word And Barred From U.S.

Charlie Chaplin, self-proclaimed "citizen of the world" and "man without a country," is fast nearing the end of the trail as far as the United States is concerned.

The complacent self-worship of the man, in a New York press conference, is amazing.

In boasting that he was neither a patriot nor an American citizen, he said, in part:

"I am not a nationalist of any country...You might say I am a citizen of the world...I never voted in my life...I did a great deal for the war effort...I made a speech in favor of opening a second front in, 1942...I believe that voting for people...leads to Fascism."

What a moral nonenity this Chaplin is!

In joining the ranks of subversives who have the overthrow of the American way of life as their avowed objective, he insults the American people, the very people who poured millions into his lap.

He has been what he terms "a paying guest" in this country too long.

He has shirked every responsibility of the American citizen.

He brags that he has never cast a vote in his life.

Even permitting him to remain in the United States insults the intelligence of the American people.

He boasts that he is a man without a country.

He should be taken at his word and should be denied the privilege even of being "a paying guest" in the United States.

Leading article from the *Los Angeles Herald-Express*, indicating the violence of McCarthyist attacks on Chaplin.

546

The fearlessness and fierce humour of this message give credibility to Chaplin's description of how he imagined behaving if he were eventually called before the Committee:

> I'd have turned up in my tramp outfit – baggy pants, bowler hat and cane – and when I was questioned I'd have used all sorts of comic business to make a laughing stock of the inquisitors.
> I almost wish I could have testified. If I had, the whole Un-American Activities thing would have been laughed out of existence in front of the millions of viewers who watched the interrogations on TV.[2]

This might have been his greatest performance. Unhappily for history it was not to take place. He was subpoenaed, but three times the date was postponed until eventually he received a 'surprisingly courteous' reply to his telegram, saying that his appearance would not be necessary and that he could consider the matter closed. Perhaps they realized that such a comedian might steal the show.

In November Chaplin was again defying America's Cold War repressions. Deportation proceedings were now proceeding against Hanns Eisler. Chaplin cabled Pablo Picasso asking him to head a committee of French artists to protest to the United States Embassy in Paris about 'the outrageous deportation proceedings against Hanns Eisler here, and simultaneously send me copy of protest for use here'. 'I doubt,' reflected his son Charles,

> if the incongruity of asking a confirmed Communist to intercede for a man accused of Communism in a non-Communist country ever even entered my father's head. He was an artist appealing to another artist to come to the aid of a third artist. But to many people his move smacked of insolence, and the newspapers roundly castigated him for his lack of etiquette rather than for any subversion. How can you call such an open move subversion?[3]

The New York chapter of the Catholic War Veterans did so, however, and sent a telegram to the Attorney General and the Secretary of State demanding 'an investigation of the activities of Charles Chaplin'. The activities in question were the cable to Picasso – 'noted French artist and (self-admitted) Communist' – and an 'alleged attempt to interfere with the activities of a duly elected representative of our citizens'. Almost two years later, when the Senate Judiciary Committee was seeking legislation to expel subversive citizens from the United States, Senator Harry P. Cain revived the

Picasso incident as a reason to deport Chaplin: 'It skirts perilously close to treason,' he declared.

In an atmosphere of growing fear, Chaplin bore up bravely and refused to be intimidated or silenced. Even so it was not surprising that for his new film subject he turned nostalgically backwards to the London of his youth. He even planned to make the film in London, and partly with this in mind decided in the spring of 1948 to go there, taking Oona to show her for the first time the scenes of his boyhood. He had not reckoned with the United States Government, however. When reservations were already made on the *Queen Elizabeth* and at the Savoy, the Immigration Department stalled on Chaplin's application for the re-entry permit which he needed as an alien. Instead they telephoned and asked him to report to the Federal Building. He told them he was busy that day and asked to come the following day, which was Saturday. They replied that they would save him the trouble and call on him. When the deputation arrived, it consisted of a stenographer, FBI man and an immigration officer, who told him that he had the right to demand Chaplin's evidence under oath. The unexpected inquisition lasted for four hours. It began with personal questions about Chaplin's racial origins and sex life. Asked if he had ever committed adultery he countered, 'What is a healthy man who has lived in this country for over thirty-five years supposed to reply?' He found the inquiries into his life, thought and opinions 'most personal, insulting and disgusting'. Asked about his political views he refused as usual to shuffle. He told them frankly, 'that I was decidedly liberal; that I was for Wallace, and that I have no hate for the Communists, and that I believe that they, the Communists, saved our way of life. They were combating 280 divisions of the Germans at a time when we, the Allies, were unprepared.'[4]

Chaplin was told that the re-entry permit would be granted but that he would be required to sign a transcript of the interrogation. Pat Millikan, Chaplin's lawyer, was deeply impressed by the diplomacy with which Chaplin had conducted the affair but advised him not to sign until he was sure he actually intended to sail for England. Chaplin in fact decided against the trip. As soon as wind of his intention to leave the country reached the Treasury, they put in a claim for $1 million's worth of tax and demanded a bond of $1.5 million if he left the country.

To add to his private problems, Chaplin now found himself 'a half-owner in a United Artists that was $1 million in debt'. His co-owner was Mary Pickford. It was a depressed period for Hollywood at large, and most of the other stock-holders had sold back their shares. The repayments had depleted the company's reserves, and *Monsieur Verdoux*, which it had been hoped would bring United Artists back into profit, already promised losses. Chaplin and Pickford found themselves in conflict. Pickford insisted on firing Arthur Kelly, who had resumed his role as Chaplin's representative in the company. In turn Chaplin insisted that Pickford should dispense with her representative also. They then failed to agree an arrangement under which one of them might buy out the other's interest. Various outside offers in turn faded away, and when an Eastern theatre circuit offered $12 million for United Artists, Pickford and Chaplin again failed to agree upon their respective roles in the arrangement. (The circuit's offer consisted of $7 million in cash and $5 million in stock. Chaplin proposed that he should take $5 million cash down and leave the remainder for Pickford. On reflection Pickford decided that since she would have to wait two years for the balance of her money, even though she made two million dollars more, the advantage was Chaplin's.) When they eventually sold out some years later it was for considerably less.

In post-war Hollywood, studio space was too valuable for Chaplin to leave the studio idle between pictures. During the years that Chaplin was preparing *Limelight*, the studio was regularly rented out to small independent production units such as Cathedral Films, who made dozens of religious shorts there such as *The Conversion of Saul* or *The Return to Jerusalem*. One of these rentals was in its way historic. On 5 and 25 May 1949 Walter Wanger rented the sound stage to make some screen tests with Greta Garbo, who had not appeared in a film for seven years, since *Two-Faced Woman* (1942). It was the star's last appearance before the cameras. Historic, or at least ominous, in another way were the rentals of studio space to Procter and Gamble for the production of some of the earliest television commercials.

The secret of Chaplin's fortitude in weathering the storms of the late 1940s was the unqualified success and happiness of his marriage. On 7 March 1946, when their first child Geraldine was nineteen months old, Oona gave birth to a son, Michael. During the time that Chaplin was writing *Limelight* the Chaplins had two more daughters,

Josephine Hannah, born on 28 March 1949, and Victoria, born 19 May 1951. Geraldine's Hollywood birthday parties were family events. On her fourth birthday Rollie Totheroh came to the house and shot 1000 feet of film of the occasion; unfortunately it seems not to have been preserved. Among other relaxations there were still the summer weekends on a new yacht. From time to time friends would be taken down to the studio to see *Monsieur Verdoux* and some of Chaplin's older films. The new generation of Chaplin children were introduced to the films, too; on 5 December 1950 Oona took Geraldine, Michael and Josephine to the studio to see *The Gold Rush* for the first time. Between the births of Josephine and Victoria, Chaplin and Oona made four trips to New York. Their only brief period of separation was on the last of these, in January 1951, when Chaplin made the journey as usual by train while Oona flew.

Most of the time, though, Chaplin was busy with the script of *Limelight* – at this period still called *Footlights*. In all he was to spend more than three years on it – the longest time for any scenario. The title *Footlights* is first mentioned in the studio records in the second week of September 1948, but he had been dictating story ideas since the start of that year. Arthur Kelly, in New York, was asked to register the titles *Limelight* and *The Limelight* on 6 September 1950, and the 'dramatic composition' was sent for copyright five days later. As late as January 1951 Chaplin was still regularly dictating new script material to his then secretary Lee Cobin. The script as completed was filmed virtually without alteration, though before the film was released one or two scenes were eliminated.

Chaplin's approach to *Limelight* was altogether exceptional. He first set it down in the form of a novel running to something like a hundred thousand words. This incorporated two lengthy 'flashback' digressions in which he related the biographies of his two main characters, the clown Calvero and the young dancer Terry Ambrose, before the beginning of the story. Much later Chaplin was to say that the idea for *Limelight* was suggested by his memory of the famous American comedian Frank Tinney, whom he had seen on stage when he first came to New York, at the height of Tinney's popularity. Some years later he saw him again and recognized with shock that 'the comic Muse had left him'. This gave him the idea for a film which would examine the phenomenon of a man who had lost his spirit and assurance. 'In *Limelight* the case was age; Calvero grew old and introspective and acquired a feeling of dignity, and this divorced him from all intimacy with the audience.' Chaplin, in his sixties, must inevitably have taken a subjective view of this peril. Moreover he was in process of witnessing, painfully, how fickle a mass public can be.

The full 'novel' form of *Limelight* indicates, however, that this was a much more complex series of autobiographical reflexions. At one level the young Calvero is the young Chaplin: 'In his youth he yearned to be a musician but could not afford any kind of instrument upon which to learn. Another longing was to be a romantic actor, but he was too small and his diction too uncultured. Nevertheless, emotionally, he believed himself to be the greatest actor living.' At another level though, Calvero, the stage artist who loses heart and nerve and becomes a victim of drink, is Chaplin's own father. Brought up by his mother, Chaplin had in his innocence always thought of her as the injured party, abandoned by her ne'er-do-well husband. Much later – and particularly after his own life provided domestic stability – he began to reconsider his feelings about his father. Perhaps after all Hannah had been unfaithful and promiscuous: the affair with Leo Dryden certainly suggests it. The description of Calvero's marriage

Chaplin's revisions to the
first page of Calvero's story -
a section of the 'novel' version
of *Limelight*.

to Eva Morton, her infidelity and the consequent despair which drives him to alcoholism, is undoubtedly Chaplin's own attempt to explore his parents' problematic relationship.

Terry is also given a biography. It is clear that these flashback stories were never intended to figure in any eventual scenario, but were Stanislavskian studies to provide background for the characters. Terry's mother resembles the adult Hannah Chaplin. She is seen as a woman worn by suffering but still beautiful, bent over a sewing machine, slaving to make a meagre living for herself and her two children. These two children parallel the close sibling relationships that figures so large in the Chaplin history: Charles Senior and his protective brother Uncle Spencer, Hannah and Kate, Chaplin and Sydney, young Charles and young Sydney. Especially since Aunt Kate remains such a mysterious and fascinating figure in Chaplin's childhood, it is intriguing to speculate how much of her and Hannah there is in Chaplin's picture of the relationship of Terry and her elder sister Louise. It has seemed important, for the intimations they may give of Chaplin's own reflections on his family history, to record the content of the *Limelight* 'novel' at some length in the pages that follow. The 'novel' is in itself notable for the Dickensian relish of Chaplin's descriptions of Victorian life and the theatre of his boyhood. The story begins much like the film, with Terry's attempted suicide in Mrs Alsop's lodging house – 'supine, a little over the edge of the iron bed'. Outside a barrel organ plays 'Why did I leave my little back room in Bloomsbury?' In flashback we see the story of Terry's youth.

The daughter of the fourth son of an English lord and a servant girl, Terry lives with her widowed mother and her older sister Louise in a poor room off Shaftesbury Avenue. Louise loses her job in a stationery shop, and the mother is taken off to hospital. Life improves somewhat when Louise starts to bring home a little money. Terry discovers with shock how she earns it, when she wanders with some other children into Piccadilly and sees Louise at work as a street walker.

Before Terry is ten, her mother dies and Louise becomes the mistress of a South American with 'a small, luxurious flat in Bayswater'. She sends Terry to boarding school and pays for her dancing lessons. When Terry is seventeen Louise emigrates to South Africa. Terry becomes a dancer at the Alhambra. On the threshold of success, however, she is struck down with rheumatic fever. When she leaves hospital she goes to work at the stationer's and toy shop where Louise was formerly employed, Sardou

The 1931 world tour. Chaplin at the Majestic Hotel, Nice, between Frank J. Gould and Florence Gould, the noted socialites of the Cote d'Azur and Chaplin's hosts. Sydney is on Mrs Gould's left.

The 1931 world tour. Sydney with May Reeves in front of a snowman Charlie at St Moritz.

Paulette Goddard,
photographed by Hurrell.

Paulette Goddard and Chaplin
at the première of *Modern Times*.

Right: Paulette Goddard,
photographed by Hurrell.

Principal members of the Chaplin unit at about the period of *Modern Times*. Back row: Mark Marlatt, assistant cameraman; Girwood Averill, projectionist; Morgan Hill, assistant cameraman; William Bogdonoff, construction. Front row: Joe Van Meter; Henry Bergman; Roland Totherc Della Steele, secretary and script girl; Allan Garcia, casting.

Chaplin as Napoleon at a fancy-dress
party given by Marion Davies at
San Simeon, 1925. Also in the group
are (left to right) Douglas Fairbanks,
Mary Pickford, William Randolph
Hearst and Princess Bibesco.

Left: set design for the department
store skating sequence in
Modern Times.

Chaplin as Napoleon. When he posed
for a series of photographs in
character in the mid 1930s, Chaplin
appears to have used the old costume
from the Davies fancy-dress party.

The Great Dictator.

The Great Dictator: Chaplin and Roland Totheroh on the camera crane.

The last meeting with Douglas Fairbanks, on the set of *The Great Dictator.*

Above: Chaplin at a music recording session
for *The Great Dictator*.

Below: Chaplin at the New York press conference
for *The Great Dictator*.

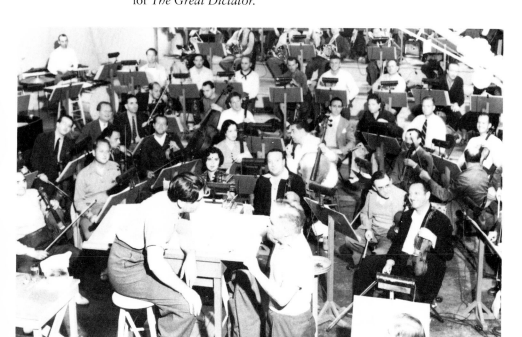

Monsieur Verdoux: Chaplin and
Margaret Hoffmann.

Above left: With Oona in
Hollywood, 1944.

Below left: Chaplin and Martha Raye
in *Monsieur Verdoux*.

Chaplin directing Somerset Maugham's 'Rain' at the
Circle Theatre, Hollywood, 1948. From left to right:
William Schallert, June Havoc, Earle Herdan,
Jerry Kilburn, Chaplin, Jerry Epstein, Sydney Chaplin Jr.

Limelight: Chaplin as Calvero with his half-brother
Wheeler Dryden as the Doctor, and Claire Bloom as Terry.

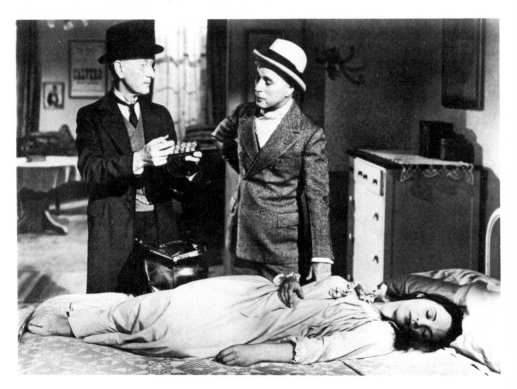

Limelight: the screen debuts
of Geraldine, Josephine
and Michael Chaplin.

Limelight: after thirty-five years
of trying, Chaplin finally
managed to find a place for his
flea circus routine.

Chaplin, Oona:
a conversation in the
summer of 1957

The first script conference for *The Countess from Hong Kong*. From left to right: Chaplin, Marlon Brando, Sophia Loren, Jerry Epstein and Sydney Chaplin Jr

Oona Chaplin.

Chaplin family group. Standing: Josephine, Victoria, Eugene. Sitting: Annie, Christopher and Oona.

Manoir de Ban, Corsier-sur-Vevey, Switzerland.

The Chaplin Studio, Sunset and La Brea, 1983.

Chaplin: Last official portrait, 1977.

and Company: '*a small establishment, overstocked with newspapers, magazines, stationery requisites, indoor games and other miscellany. The shop was close, oppressive, and had a pungent odour of ink, leather goods and the paint of toys . . . Sardou and Company was Mr Sardou, there being no company.*'

It is in Sardou's that she encounters a young composer, Ernest Neville. She loses her job when, out of pity for his evident poverty, she deliberately makes a mistake with his change.

> *Autumn was near, and London was preparing for her coming theatrical season. Dancing troupes, acrobats, trick cyclists, conjurors, jugglers and clowns were renting Soho's clubrooms and vacant warehouses for rehearsals. Theatrical props, costumes and wigmakers were feeling the season's rush. A recumbent giant that would cover the whole stage and that breathed mechanically, was being built in parts for the Drury Lane pantomime, so large that a ballet could enter out of its breast coat pocket.*
>
> *Special devices for Cinderella's transformation scene; pumpkins to be transformed into white horses, contrived by aid of mirrors; paraphernalia for flying ballets, cycloramic tricks, horizontal bars and tight-ropes. Orders for new conjuring tricks, odd musical instruments, padded wigs and slapstick contraptions of all kinds, all to be ready for Christmas.*

Terry, six months after her collapse, desperate for work, takes a job at Northrups' Pickle Factory. Her hands become stained yellow with the pickle and at weekends she wears black gloves to hide them. One Saturday night she walks into a room over a Soho pub where a 'Mr John' is rehearsing some dancers. He is '*a brutish-looking man with a broken nose, a large ugly mouth and a voice low and woolly that sounded like the drawing of a bow over a loose, bass string of a violin.*' Terry asks 'Mr John' for a job. He auditions her, but after dancing she collapses. The dancers are frightened when they see her yellow hands, and take her to hospital where she remains eighteen weeks. Meanwhile 'Mr John' and his wife befriend her, and before leaving with his troupe for an American tour he gives her a sovereign. Leaving hospital she moves into a room at Mrs Alsop's for five shillings a week. (Mrs Alsop wisely requires two weeks in advance; after six weeks Terry is four weeks' rent in arrears.)

While scanning the job advertisements, Terry notices that Sir Thomas Beecham will conduct a new symphony by Mr Ernest Neville. She uses one-and-sixpence of her precious remaining four shillings to buy a gallery ticket. Afterwards she sees Neville leaving the Albert Hall with Sir Thomas Beecham. She speaks to him and reminds him that she was the girl in Sardou's but he does not pursue the conversation. It is at this point that she returns to her room and attempts to commit suicide.

From this point the 'novel' coincides with the scenario of the finished film. Calvero returns to find the girl in a gas-filled room, sends for a doctor, and takes her under his wing. As she begins to recover, he tells her his own life story – the Calvero 'novel'.

Many years ago Calvero had suffered unrequited love for a young woman who had run away with his rival to South Africa, where she married. In course of time her daughter, having run off with a young doctor, arrives in England. Abandoned by her young man the girl, Eva Morton, appeals for help to Calvero, about whom she has heard from her mother. In a short time they become lovers, following a blissful summer's day on the Thames.

> *It was a day of flamboyant color; of white flannels and gay parasols; of baskets of strawberries, bright yellow pears and large blue grapes; it was a day of lemon and pink ices, and cool drinks in long-necked bottles; a day of occasional guitars and the rippling of punts and rowboats, gliding through the water.*
>
> *And so it was that Calvero and Eva spent the week-end at Hanby. On their way back, they stopped for dinner at a small inn at Staines, and spent the night there. Soon after, Calvero gave up his rooms in Belgravia and moved to a flat off Oxford Street, where he and Eva lived as man and wife, and within three months they were married.*

Very soon, however, Calvero realizes that Eva is being unfaithful to him:

> *She . . . understood her own love for him which had a special place in her heart, but which did not wholly occupy it: no man ever could. She realized that her desire was insatiable and verged on being pathological, yet she looked upon it as something separate and apart from herself and her life with Calvero*
> *. . .*
> *Of her unfaithfulness she wanted to tell him. She hated deception because she had a deep regard for him. She wanted to make a clean breast of everything and tell him that she could never be faithful to any man, but she felt that Calvero would not tolerate any compromise. And she was right. His nature demanded the full possession of the thing it loved. His reason might conceive a true justification for her promiscuity, yet to acquiesce to it, he knew that such a love would slowly die from its own poison.**

Matters come to a head when Eva has an affair with a rich Manchester factory owner called Eric Addington. Calvero discovers the affair while playing principal clown in the Drury Lane pantomime, with Addington and Eva watching him from a box. Having introduced some wry comedy

---

* Perhaps seeking to explore the break-up of his parents' marriage, Chaplin undoubtedly also views the problem of the man whose 'nature demanded the full possession of the thing it loved' through the memory of his own experiences with Edna, May Reeves and Paulette.

*about the heartbroken cuckold into his stage business, he afterwards
accuses the couple. Eva leaves him for ever.*

*Calvero begins to drink. The more he drinks the less appeal he has to
his audience. He is advised by his dresser, who was once a famous clown
himself,*

> 'The more you think, the less funny you become. The trouble with me,' he
> continued, '. . . I never thought. It was women that killed my comedy. But
> you – you think too much.'
>
> And the dresser was right. Calvero was instinctively analytical and introspec-
> tive. He had to know and understand people, to know their fallibilities and
> weaknesses. It was the means by which he achieved his particular type of
> comedy. The more he knew about people, the more he knew himself; an
> estimation that was not very flattering; with the consequence that he became
> self-conscious and had to be half-drunk before going on stage.

*Calvero's mind fails under the strain. He wanders for six weeks in a
state of amnesia, and is then confined for three years in an institution.
On his release he is aged and changed. He attempts to make a comeback
in the theatre, but succumbs once more to drink. The audience walks out
on him. 'His engagements grew less, as well as the salary he was asking,
until his vaudeville engagements ceased entirely.' Calvero sinks to work
as an extra, though he remains a celebrity in The Queen's Head where
he mingles with people he knew in his better days – vaudevillians, agents,
critics, jockeys, tipsters. A particular friend is Claudius, the armless
wonder. Claudius recognizes Calvero's impecunious state and offers him
a loan. Calvero is obliged to take the money from Claudius's wallet
himself, and in doing so sees a photograph of a youth. Claudius explains
that it is his nephew whom he has educated since the death of his sister,
the boy's mother. Calvero has to button up Claudius's coat for him before
he goes out into the cold. (Calvero is later able to repay Claudius's loan,
since he stakes half of it on a 3–1 winner.) 'It was after one of these
dialectic – not to say alcoholic – afternoons that he came home and found
Terry Ambrose, unconscious in her back room.'*

*It is from this point that the 'novel' version of the story follows the
essential line of the film script, apart from some inconsiderable differences
of detail and plot mechanism. The result of the friendship and mutual
encouragement between Calvero and Terry is that she is cured of the
psychosomatic fear that she will never be able to dance again, while he
is heartened to attempt a comeback. While Terry's career prospers until
she becomes principal dancer at the Empire, however, Calvero's once
more fades. Terry convinces herself that she is in love with this benefactor,
old enough to be her father; but when she once more meets Neville, the
young composer (she is to dance in his ballet), Calvero understands her
heart better than she does herself, and discreetly disappears from her life.*

555

Calvero is rediscovered, and the manager of the Empire, Mr Postant* arranges a benefit performance for him, at which he will be the star. In the 'novel' version, Chaplin has not yet worked out the mechanics of the end. In the film, the performance takes place, and Calvero has one more triumph with the public. When he takes his bow, carried in the drum into which he has fallen as the climax of the act, the audience applauds wildly, unaware that he has suffered a heart attack. He dies as his protégée dances on the stage, in illustration of the archaic, 1920s-style title that prefaces the film: 'The glamor of Limelight, from which age must fade as youth enters.'

A number of passages exclusive to the 'novel' version of *Limelight* are interesting for their autobiographical and factual references. At one moment Calvero tells Terry that he is going to see a new flat in Glenshaw Mansions – where, of course, the Chaplin brothers had their first bachelor apartment. The illness which is to prove fatal to Calvero is a circumstantial recollection of the elder Chaplin's last days, and the last time his son saw him alive, in the saloon of The Three Stags in Kennington Road:

> The doctors had warned him only a few months ago that further dissipation would be extremely dangerous to his health. It was eleven o'clock in the saloon bar of the White Horse, Brixton, that Calvero, in the midst of his febrile hilarity, collapsed into unconsciousness and was taken to St Thomas's Hospital.

(Charles Chaplin Senior died in St Thomas's.)

Calvero's exhortation to Terry could be the credo of Chaplin's whole working life:

> She must always adhere to the living truth within herself. She must be deeply selfish. That was essential to her art, for her art was her true happiness.

An intriguing scene which was eliminated fom the final film script introduced a historical figure, the great juggler Cinquevalli. Attempting a comeback at the Alhambra, Calvero meets Cinquevalli at the morning rehearsal. The juggler tells him that he intends that evening to perform a new trick with billiard balls that he has been rehearsing for seven years. That night they share a dressing room. Cinquevalli returns from the stage and Calvero asks him how the new trick went.

---

* In 1905 the stage manager of the Duke of York's Theatre, whose kindness to him in his boyhood Chaplin always remembered, was called William Postance.

Cinquevalli says that it received no applause: he had made it look too easy. Calvero says that he should have fumbled it a couple of times. Cinquevalli replies that he is not yet good enough to do that.

'I shall need a little more practice.'
'I see,' said Calvero ironically. 'And now I suppose it'll take another ten years to learn how to miss it.'
Cinquevalli smiled. 'That's right,' he replied.
'That's depressing,' said Calvero.
'Why?' he asked.
'I can't laugh at that. It's frightening. Perfection must be imperfect before we can appreciate it. The world can only recognize things by the hard way.'
'That should be encouraging. The world can only recognize virtue by our mistakes.'
'If that were the truth,' said Calvero, 'I'd be a saint by now.'

To judge from his notes, Chaplin seems to have considered retaining this scene in the film, placing it immediately before Calvero's final appearance on the stage, and setting it in the wings. Finally, though, it was discarded altogether.

Chaplin was fascinated by the problems of creating a ballet, 'The Death of Columbine', for the film. In the past he had always composed his music after the film was finished. In this case the music had to come first. He began to work on the twenty-five minute ballet sequence* with the arranger Ray Rasch in December 1950. Rasch continued to work with him on the ballet several days a week until the following October. A special problem was to compose a forty-five second solo to which André Eglevsky, the dancer Chaplin wanted for the role, could match his choreography for the Blue Bird Pas de Deux. In September the music was recorded with a fifty-piece orchestra under Keith R. Williams. André Eglevsky and his partner Melissa Hayden flew in for two days from New York to hear the music and rehearse some of the dancing. Chaplin was extremely nervous as to their verdict, but they were apparently quite satisfied that his music was suitable for ballet.

Chaplin told his sons that he expected *Limelight* to be his greatest picture and his last. As contented in his family life as he was dis-illusioned with post-war America, he spoke from time to time of

---

* Much shorter in the completed film.

retiring. Had he done so, *Limelight*, going right back to his beginnings, would have been a perfect ending to his career. It was, in any event, to round off the Hollywood period. The film was something of a family affair. As the juvenile lead, the young composer Neville, he cast his tall, handsome younger son by Lita Grey, Sydney Chaplin. Sydney remembered that his father asked him to play the part in June 1948, three years before he was to begin the film. Much later he discovered that his role was that of a starving musician, 'and as at this time I weighed over eighteen stone, had access to plenty of food, and what is called a crew haircut, father suggested that I should go on a diet and grow my hair.'⁵

Charles Junior had a small role as a clown in the ballet. Geraldine, Michael and Josephine were to appear in the opening of the film, as three urchins who watch with curiosity Calvero's drunken return to his home. Geraldine even had a line to speak – her first in movies. In the part of the doctor who looks after Terry after her suicide attempt, Chaplin cast Wheeler Dryden, a lean, somewhat wizened figure, wearing spectacles and with an emphatically British accent. Although Wheeler had been around the studio since *The Great Dictator*, this was the first time that his relationship with the Chaplin brothers had been made public by the studio:

> Our mother and my father separated and Charlie and I never met again until I came to America in 1918 [*sic*]. Charles was already famous.
>
> We both agreed that it would be better for me to make good on my own. This is the first time our relationship has been disclosed.
>
> We have both remained British subjects. Not that we are un-American, but although we are fond of America, we do not feel it necessary to give up our British heritage.⁶

Chaplin's major problem was to find a leading lady. She had to have, said Chaplin, 'beauty, talent and a great emotional range'. She also had to be very young and preferably English.

> An advertisement was placed in the papers reading 'Wanted: young girl to play leading lady to a comedian generally recognized as the world's greatest', and for another year Father saw and tested just about every applicant who seemed even vaguely suitable for the part. It was the first time that Father had written a film in which the girl's part was equal to his, and so it was terribly important that he made the right decision.⁷

Sydney somewhat exaggerates the length of the search: the first girls were interviewed in February 1951 and the choice was made by

August. Sydney himself was given the job of screening applicants, with the help of Chaplin's secretary of the time, Lee Cobin. The playwright Arthur Laurents, who was currently friendly with the Chaplins, recommended the twenty-year-old Claire Bloom whom he had seen in London in *Ring Round the Moon* (Christopher Fry's adaptation of Anouilh's *L'Invitation au château*) at the Globe Theatre. Laurents himself telephoned Miss Bloom to ask her to send some photographs of herself to the Chaplin studio. The idea seemed so fanciful and remote to the young actress that she put the whole thing out of her mind until a few weeks later when she received a cable, 'WHERE ARE THE PHOTOGRAPHS? CHARLES CHAPLIN.' When the photographs arrived, Harry Crocker, who had now rejoined Chaplin as business manager, telephoned from California to say Chaplin wanted to test her for the part. Since the theatre management would only release her from *Ring Round the Moon* for one week, it was agreed that she should fly to New York, and Chaplin would meet her there to make the test. Miss Bloom was chaperoned by her mother; Chaplin brought with him his assistant Jerry Epstein. From the moment he met the Blooms at the airport, Chaplin talked with great excitement of his plans:

> He said the love story – so he described it – took place in the London of his childhood. The opening scenes were in the Kennington slums where he was born. The agents' offices where he had endlessly waited for work, the dressing rooms in the dreary provincial theatres, the digs, the landladies – all his melancholy theatrical memories were to be the film's backdrop. He reminisced about the Empire Theatre, the smart music hall of its day, frequented by the smartest courtesans; he talked of his early triumph as a boy actor in a stage adaptation of *Sherlock Holmes* . . . When we went to his rooms for lunch, he continued with his memories of London and seemed desperate to hear that nothing he had known had changed. In the last few years he had been deeply homesick, he said, but he didn't dare to leave America for fear that the U.S. Government wouldn't allow him to re-enter the country. His family, home, studios, money – everything was in America . . .
>
> In the evening Chaplin would take us and Jerry Epstein to dinner at the most elegant restaurants. At the Pavillon and the '21' Club he spoke endlessly of his early poverty; the atmosphere he was creating for *Limelight* brought him back night after night to the melancholy of those years at home with his mother and brother. He spoke either of the early poverty or of his troubles with the U.S. Government, troubles I wasn't quite able to grasp until I had spent a while in Hollywood.[8]

Chaplin rehearsed Miss Bloom every day throughout the week. A little reluctantly he permitted her to see the script, though she was not allowed to take it to her room but returned it to Epstein every night. Like other players of younger generations, she was surprised by Chaplin's singular method of direction: 'Chaplin was the most exacting director, not because he expected you to produce wonders of your own but because he expected you to follow unquestioningly his every instruction. I was surprised at how old-fashioned much of what he prescribed seemed – rather theatrical effects that I didn't associate with the modern cinema.'[9]

At the end of the week the screen tests were made at Fox Studios. Epstein was behind the camera while Chaplin worked in front of the camera with Miss Bloom: 'I was trying out for the role, Jerry hoped he would please Chaplin as assistant director, and Chaplin was watching the script he had worked on for three years finally come before the camera, so everyone was tense.'[10] She was later to discover that Chaplin's methods in directing the tests were the same that he would use in front of the cameras:

> I was close to panic ... only until I saw that Chaplin intended to give me every inflection and every gesture exactly as he had during rehearsal. This didn't accord with my high creative aspirations, but in the circumstances it was just fine. I couldn't have been happier – nor did I have any choice. Gradually, imitating Chaplin, I gained my confidence, and by the time we came to the actual filming I was enjoying myself rather like some little monkey in the zoo being put through the paces by a clever, playful drillmaster.[11]

Claire Bloom recalled Chaplin's care in choosing the costumes for the tests, talking of the way his mother had worn such a dress or how Hetty Kelly had worn a shawl: 'I quickly realized, even then, that some composite young woman, lost to him in the past, was what he wanted me to bring to life.' She also remembered with amusement the embarrassment of Chaplin and Epstein when they realized that no one had seen her legs, which, since she played a dancer, were going to be important. Somewhat transparently they included a tutu and tights among the costumes she tried, even though no dance sequence was to be included in the tests.

The young actress returned to London with the promise that she would have some news after ten days, and the encouragement that Chaplin had intoduced her to someone in a restaurant as 'a marvellous young actress'. In fact four months passed with no news except for a wire from Harry Crocker saying that she would hear further in a fortnight (which she did not). Despondency – especially after the *Daily Express* printed an article saying that Chaplin did not like the test that had cost him so much to make – gave way to resignation.

Chaplin was much occupied during this period. He arrived back from New York on the 'Santa Fe Chief' on 1 May, and ran the Bloom tests the same evening. Oona was nearing the end of her pregnancy, and on 19 May gave birth to Victoria. Two days later, while mother and baby were still in St John's Hospital, Chaplin moved out of 1085 Summit Drive to temporary accommodation at 711 North Beverly Drive, while the builders moved in to the old home. The growing family and their nurses demanded more room. The pipe organ was usurped. The majestic hall was divided with a new floor to provide more bedrooms. The alterations cost some $50,000 and looked a clear indication of the Chaplins' intention of staying. 'My father,' remembered Charles Junior, 'was so proud of these rooms he liked to take his guests upstairs to show them off.'

He was in fact still not convinced that Claire Bloom was the right choice. Again and again he would run her tests. Often he would invite guests to see some film at the studio, and then slip in the tests as well in order to get their views. Meanwhile he continued to interview other actresses and look at films in which there were likely young candidates. The strongest contender was an actress called Joan Winslow, who was brought from New York to Hollywood to go through the same process of extensive rehearsal and screen testing as Miss Bloom had undergone in New York. She stayed ten days, and was actually shown the Bloom tests. Finally, however, Chaplin made up his mind and Miss Bloom's agent received the fateful call from Harry Crocker. The contract gave her three months' work at $15,000 plus travel expenses and a weekly allowance for herself and her mother.

The Blooms arrived in Hollywood on 29 September 1951, and at dinner at Summit Drive, with Oona and Epstein, Chaplin explained how Miss Bloom would spend the seven weeks till shooting began. Like Chaplin himelf, she had to diet. She was to begin each day by going with Oona to exercise at the gymnasium, then rehearse from eleven until four and round off the day with an hour's ballet class. Generally the rehearsals took place in the garden at Summit Drive. Miss Bloom was again struck by Chaplin's insistence on his boyhood memories. When they went for a costume fitting he told her, 'My mother used to wear a loose knitted cardigan, a blouse with a high neck and a little bow, and a worn velvet jacket.' 'Melancholy,' she noted, 'was a word he was to use frequently when speaking of his plans for *Limelight*.'

The Blooms came to know the Chaplins at a time when their social life was much quieter than in the past. As Charles Chaplin Junior commented:

> It must not be supposed that my father's fight for his convictions was made without sacrifice. When I came back from the East to play my part in *Limelight* I was saddened to see the effect his stand had had on his own life. It was no longer considered a privilege to be a guest at the home of Charlie Chaplin. Many people were actually afraid to be seen there lest they, too, should become suspect.
>
> Tim Durant, the irreconcilable Yankee, solid as a New England rock in his loyalty, was around, and he did his best to bring back some of the old life, noting the irony the while. Once his phone had rung steadily with people calling him, offering him favors, wining him, dining him in the hope that he would extend them an invitation to the Chaplin home. Now it was Tim's turn to phone them and beg them to come up for a game of tennis. But they all backed out. The little tennis house and green lawn where once my father had held a gracious court were practically deserted on Sunday afternoons. I think my father must have been the loneliest man in Hollywood those days.[12]

There were still Saturday night dinner parties for one or two friends. Claire Bloom met there James Agee, the shy film critic who had become a friend since his passionate defence of *Monsieur Verdoux* and had now arrived in Hollywood as a screenwriter; Clifford Odets; and Oona's girlhood friend Carole Marcus, then married to William Saroyan and later to Walter Matthau.

Not many of the old studio staff remained, and once again Karl Struss was to replace Roland Totheroh as cinematographer. As Claire Bloom remembers it,

> the first three days' filming had to be scrapped, because Chaplin was dissatisfied with the camera work of his old associate Rollie Totheroh. He then engaged Karl Struss, a more up-to-date technician, to replace Totheroh, and this cast a gloom over the set. Totheroh had shot most of Chaplin's earlier films and, as he was no longer young, it was clear that this was probably the last job of his career . . . Chaplin, generous and

loyal as he could be in pensioning his workers, was utterly ruthless when it came to the standards he'd set for his film.[13]

Totheroh was credited as 'photographic consultant'. Jerry Epstein remembers him taking special care over the filming of Chaplin himself. 'He would watch everything and say "Head up . . . head up, now . . . We don't want to see those double chins . . . gotta look pretty."'[14]

The visual recreation of the London of Chaplin's memories was all-important. After another designer had submitted some unsuccessful sketches, Chaplin had his production manager call Eugene Lourié. Lourié had emigrated from Russia in 1919, and had worked as a designer in France since silent days. In the 1930s he began an association with Jean Renoir, which continued after Renoir moved to Hollywood during the war. It is possible that Chaplin had noted Lourié's work in Renoir's *Diary of a Chambermaid*, in which Paulette Goddard had starred. Lourié remembers that the production manager telephoned and asked him if he knew London and had worked there (he had, while designing a ballet for the De Basil company in 1933) and told him that the studio would pay minimum rates. Lourié was not told the identity of the producer until he reported to the studio. 'I was pleased. I had a great admiration for Chaplin – but I was sorry I didn't ask for more money.' Chaplin suggested that before making a definite commitment, Lourié should read the script and work for a fortnight on some sketches. This approach impressed Lourié: 'In Hollywood they mostly hire film architects like stage hands.'[15]

Chaplin was pleased with Lourié's drawings.

He had talked to me exclusively about London. I had a nostalgic feeling for the place, although I had lived there only three months when I was designing the ballet for De Basil. Later, though, I visited Georges Périnal there, and he took me all over. He took me to the other bank of the river, where Chaplin had been brought up. I remember that at that time of night the streets were very dark. The only lighted windows were the undertakers' shops. It was very curious to me, those lit windows with coffins inside. Anyway, he liked my ideas, and said, 'Well, start.' Then he took me into his drawing room and played me the music he had composed for the film.

The first set which Chaplin needed, so that he could start rehearsals with Claire Bloom, was the apartment at Mrs Alsop's.

He was very anxious to have the view from the window – high brick houses and sad-looking urban back yards. Instead of using the usual painted backgrounds, I built it three-dimensional in miniature. I took a lot of time to dress it, with drying washing and lights in the windows for the night scenes. In the finished picture though I saw practically nothing of it. It looked to me just like a painted background![16]

After the first day's work in this apartment set, Chaplin took Lourié aside and told him, 'I need more distance between the door and the stove. I rehearse it like a ballet. I need a particular distance to get in all the steps. Can we change it?' Lourié, anticipating possible changes, had made the walls of the set three feet longer than was, apparently, necessary. He was able to make the change without difficulty, so that Chaplin could carry on with his rehearsals the following morning.

He was very impressed. I think from that day he had more confidence in me. At the beginning he was very cautious with me. The second thing which gave him confidence I think was when I showed him the three-dimensional model I made for the set for the pantomime. I made it in very forced perspective, with the ceiling sloping down to two feet from the stage. He liked it. After that he would say, 'Mr Lourié, give me a composition for the frame.'

For the exteriors we could not go to London, of course. Travel was restricted then, and we were working on a shoestring budget. For the street I had to build it or find it. I actually found it. It was a New York brownstone street at the Paramount studio – a very old set, which very much resembled London. I showed it to Chaplin. He said 'It's wonderful.' We slightly remodelled it. We changed the entrances to the houses, and built exteriors for two pubs and the physician's office.

He had a very strong visual impression, though he could not always express it in words. He would draw things, though. I have two or three sketches that he made – I think of street lamps for the Victoria Embankment scene. We used back projection for the scene and one lamp and one bench – the bench may still be around his old studio somewhere.

Vincent Korda was extremely helpful. He sent me lots of research about the old Empire Theatre – old photographs. And he sent out the studio stills man at night to photograph the Embankment. I wanted a point opposite Scotland Yard, with Big Ben in the background. I asked him to photograph the scene every hour from dark until dawn, so that I could choose the light.

Basically the film was shot in the studio. We needed a theatre – several theatres in fact, since he wanted to do a montage of the dancer's international tours. The choice was between using the Pasadena Playhouse or one of the two theatre sets at Universal (it had been built for *Phantom of the Opera*, and was still called 'the Phantom stage') and RKO – Pathé. We chose Pathé. It was a complete theatre, so that we could do the backstage stuff there too. And it's much easier working in a studio than in a real theatre, because you can change things as you please.

I was very excited to find some old backdrops from *The Kid* in the studio. And then I found some old scene painters from the 1880s to make the backdrops for the stage scenes.[17]

Jerry Epstein and Wheeler Dryden were credited as assistant producers, although Eugene Lourié does not remember Wheeler as being very active on the film apart from his appearance as an actor. 'He was around all the time though, because he was then living in a house at the studio.' Robert Aldrich worked on the film as associate director.

I think he was brought in because Chaplin felt he wanted someone with a lot of professional experience of studio work. But Aldrich always wanted more artistic shots. Chaplin did not think in 'artistic' images when he was shooting. He believed that action is the main thing. The camera is there to photograph the actors. I worked with Sacha Guitry, and he had exactly the same approach.[18]

Without any significant departure from the script, Chaplin worked with the same discipline as on *Monsieur Verdoux*. He fell two weeks behind the tight shooting schedule he had given himself, and Claire Bloom's engagement lasted (to her delight) longer than the envisioned three months. Even so the film was finished in fifty-five shooting days, including four days for retakes. This was a very far cry from the interminable shooting histories of *The Kid* or *City Lights*. Sydney Chaplin Junior recorded some impressions of his father at work:

We started with some bedroom scenes which lasted three weeks. Then came the street scenes, and it was while these were being shot that I noticed one of the extras was wearing a strange, mustard-coloured suit which looked to me quite terrible. I called Father's attention to this, and he laughed and said it was strange but he'd had a suit just like it at one time. Of course, the one worn by the extra was rented from a firm of costumiers, but, without quite knowing why, the extra looked at the label in the inside pocket. It read: 'Made for Mr Charlie Chaplin, 1918'.

Another time it was Father who objected to a jacket I was wearing. 'Just look at the length of its sleeves compared with those of your shirt,' he complained. 'Get the tailor to lengthen them (the jacket sleeves) straightaway.' I went away, rolled up my shirt sleeves a little, and came back. 'Now that's more like it,' said Father.

He is, of course a really wonderful director, using the right approach all the time, knowing instinctively how to treat each different artist. There was one old actor who was so nervous of playing with Father that he kept muffing his lines. To put him at his ease, Father muddled his own lines on purpose, and after that the old actor was at ease and the scene was exactly right the next time through.

And, of course, as well as being the film's director Father was also its principal actor. His difficulty was to imagine how he would look in a scene which he wouldn't actually be able to see until it was filmed, and his method was to work out the moves in advance and have his stand-in go through them while he watched through the camera. One moment he'd be behind the camera, the next up 40 ft of scaffolding explaining something to an electrician, the next strolling around on the stage demonstrating some point to another actor . . .

It was hardly surprising that Father ran himself practically ragged. He was always the first to arrive at the studios in the morning and the last to leave at night. His wife Oona would come down about midday with some sandwiches and fruit pie for him. He'd go home at night exhausted and after dinner start right away planning the next day's work.

I only remember one major crisis, that was over a very emotional scene between Father and Claire. He spent the whole day on this scene which on the screen lasts a bare three minutes, and he still wasn't satisfied – chiefly with his own performance. So he spent the next day re-shooting it, and the day after that. Finally there was a terrific take which had all the stage hands weeping and at the end wildly applauding. For the first time in three days Father allowed himself a smile.

The following day the people who were developing the film rang up to say that owing to some technical difficulty that piece of film had been destroyed. Father hit the ceiling when he heard this; but he didn't have the heart to tell Claire. He just said that he still wasn't satisfied and that he wanted to try it again.[19]

Claire Bloom found herself particularly apprehensive about the scene in which she suddenly finds that she can walk again, since she always had difficulty in weeping to order. Chaplin clearly had none of the inhibitions he experienced in directing Jackie Coogan. Before the scene began he criticized her acting and became so angry that she burst into tears. The camera crew had been forewarned and snatched the scene in a single take. 'Chaplin had judged perfectly what would do the job – rather like Calvero understanding what magic would be required to make Theresa walk again.'

In general, however, Chaplin remained patient and understanding with his actors. Eugene Lourié remembered him as being charming to his two sons. Charles Junior, though he evidently worshipped his father, had a different impression:

And now, at last, it was Syd's and my turn to be targets of that drive for perfection which ever since our childhood we had seen focused upon others. After that experience I was more than ever convinced that my father's towering reputation and his seething intensity make it almost impossible for those working under him to assert their own personality. No one in the world could direct my father as he directs himself, but I feel that lesser actors in his pictures might profit from being directed by someone else.

With Syd and me he was, I believe, even more exacting than with the others. As his sons we could not appear to be favored, and so he went to the opposite extreme and even tended to make examples of us. He was especially tough on Syd as the young romantic lead, and sometimes I heard people commiserating with him. But I never heard Syd himself complain. He kept his equanimity and learned from my father and was rewarded by being praised in the reviews for his fine performance.[20]

Sydney and Claire Bloom became romantically attached during the filming. She remembered that away from the set Sydney would be 'wickedly funny about his strong-minded father's eccentricities, but once Sydney reported to begin his role in the film, he lacked all defensive wit and, confronted with those paternal "eccentricities", became nervous and wooden on the set.'[21]

Just before Christmas 1951 the unit moved to the RKO–Pathé studios for the theatre sequences. The backstage scenes were filmed first, and on the last day of the year, Chaplin began to shoot the performance scenes on stage. For the ballet scenes, Melissa Hayden and Claire Bloom were ingeniously doubled: 'When the camera was close enough to permit me to do so [I was required] to wheel into frame and out as fast as possible – whereupon Melissa would take over again. The effect was so convincing that for years afterwards I was complimented on my dancing.[22]

Today the most touching aspect of *Limelight* is the appearance of Buster Keaton in a double act with Chaplin, in a crazy musical duet.* It was the only time the two greatest comedians of silent pictures

---

* Keaton arrived in Hollywood in 1917, more than three years after Chaplin. While Keaton was still working with Roscoe Arbuckle at the Balboa Studios, Chaplin visited their set, was photographed fooling with them and recalled that when Buster was a child performer in vaudeville he had bounced him on his knee while appearing on the same bill.

appeared together, and the only time since 1916 that Chaplin had worked with a comic partner. Keaton plays a crumbling and myopic pianist, who is assailed, the moment he takes his seat at the piano, by an avalanche of tumbling sheet music. Chaplin–Calvero, as the violinist, has his own problems: his legs for some inexplicable reason keep shrinking up inside his wide trousers. The unhappy consequences of Buster's attempt to give his friend an 'A' escalate until the piano strings burst in all directions while Calvero's violin is trodden under-foot. Eventually, after Calvero has produced a new violin, the per-formance begins. Calvero moves from a poignant melody which reduces him to tears to a demonic *vivace* which eventually precipitates him into the pit. He falls into the bass drum, and is carried therein to the stage to take his bow.

Keaton worked on the film for three weeks, from 22 December to 12 January. It was a sweet gesture of Chaplin's to employ him: Keaton had not worked in comedy for years and was all but forgotten. (The previous year, Billy Wilder had introduced him into *Sunset Boulevard* as one of Norma Desmond's Hollywood 'ghosts'.) On the set he was reserved to the point of isolation. He arrived, Jerry Epstein recalls, with the little flat hat he had worn in his own films, and had to be gently told that Chaplin already had a costume and business worked out for him. The whole unit was enchanted to see, however, that once on stage, Chaplin and Keaton became two old comedy pros, each determined to upstage the other. 'Chaplin would grumble,' Eugene Lourié recalls. 'He would say, "No, this is *my* scene."' Claire Bloom, too, felt that 'some of his gags may even have been a little too incandescent for Chaplin because, laugh as he did at the rushes in the screening room, Chaplin didn't see fit to allow them all into the final version of the film.'

Chaplin evidently took particular delight in creating the wonderful pastiches of Edwardian music hall songs and acts. 'Spring Song' led into a charming patter act and dance with Claire Bloom dressed in bonnet and tutu. In 'Oh for the Life of a Sardine' he perfectly parodied the vocal style of George Bastow, one of the last '*lions comiques*' and creator of 'Captain Gingah'. He must, however, have found most satisfaction with 'I'm an Animal Trainer', for here, after more than thirty years of trying, he at last managed to introduce into a film the flea circus business he had first performed on the set of *The Kid*. Chaplin resisted the efforts of his assistants to persuade him to add audience reaction and laughter on the sound track. He was (rightly) convinced that in a full cinema the audience would provide the necessary reaction, and that it would be authentic. He failed to forsee the possibility of the films being shown in thinly-filled cinemas or, worse, on the television screen. Seen in these circumstances, with no laughter or acknowledgement of an audience's presence, the sequences have a somewhat spectral and eerie quality.*

Eugene Lourié was present when the songs were filmed: 'He was very demanding with himself, shooting the vaudeville songs. He'd say, "We'll do it again. I can do it better than that." Sometimes we would shoot fifteen times.'[23] The last shot of the picture was made on 25 January 1952, and Chaplin immediately began cutting and assembling the film. The Blooms – very sad to forsake the family atmosphere of the film and the studio – left California on the 'Santa Fe Chief' on 13 February.

Chaplin spent most of the next three months cutting, and at the beginning of May ordered the rebuilding of several sets for retakes. At this point, yet another Chaplin joined the cast. Some of the new shots required Terry to be seen through the open door of Calvero's apartment, and Oona doubled for Claire Bloom in these scenes. On 15 May Chaplin showed a roughcut to James Agee and Sidney Bernstein, and was gratified by their reactions. By 2 August the final prints were ready for a preview at the Paramount Studios Theatre, which held two hundred people and on this occasion was packed. Sidney Skolsky, the celebrated *Variety* writer, recorded the event two days later:

> The guest list ranged from such celebrities as Humphrey Bogart to Doris Duke to several old ladies and men who had worked with Chaplin since *The Gold Rush* back in 1924 . . . Chaplin and his assistant, Jerry Epstein, ran the picture at two in the afternoon, because Chaplin wanted to check the print personally. Chaplin, who wrote, produced, directed and starred in the picture, had to do everything personally. He even ushered at this preview showing. Then when the lights in the projection room were off and the picture started, this little gray-haired man sat at the dial-controls in the rear of the room and regulated the sound for the picture. It was the most exciting night I have ever spent in a projection room . . .
>
> There was drama and history in the room. There was comedy and drama on the screen, and there was a backdrop of drama running along with the picture *Limelight* itself . . .

---

* The songs are in fact Calvero's dreams or nightmares of his past fame and failure.

The projection room lights went up. The entire audience from Ronald Colman to David Selznick to Judge Pecora to Sylvia Gable stood up and applauded and shouted 'Bravo'. It was as if all Hollywood was paying tribute to Charlie Chaplin . . . Then the little gray-haired fellow walked up to the platform. He said: 'Thank you. I was very scared. You are the first people in the world to have seen the picture. It runs two hours and thirty minutes. I don't want to keep you any longer. I do want to say "Thank you –"' and that's as far as Chaplin got. A woman in the audience shouted, 'No! No! Thank you,' and then others in the audience took these words and shouted them to Chaplin . . . Somehow I think this is the key to *Limelight*. It doesn't matter whether some people think it is good and some people think it is great. The degree doesn't matter. This is no ordinary picture made by an ordinary man. This is a great hunk of celluloid history and emotion, and I think everybody who is genuinely interested in the movies will say, 'Thank you'.

Chaplin had decided that the world première of *Limelight* should be in London and that he would take Oona and the children there for the occasion and a prolonged holiday afterwards. It would be Oona's first visit to England. They planned to miss the Hollywood press show and the New York opening; and left California on the first lap of their journey on 6 September. The night before, Tim Durant gave a send-off clambake party for them at his home. The guests included Arthur Rubinstein and Marlon Brando, who was the only one who arrived in dinner jacket. Chaplin thrilled them with an outstanding party piece, a dance with Katharine Dunham in which he perfectly reproduced and reflected her mannerisms, personality and grace. But Charles Junior sensed that his father was preoccupied, and the following day when Tim Durant drove Chaplin and Oona to Union Station, Chaplin told him that he had a premonition that he would not return.

The Chaplins arrived in New York with Harry Crocker, who was to accompany them to Europe to take charge of publicity, on the 'Santa Fe Chief' on 9 September. A week later they were joined by the four children, accompanied by their nurses, Edith McKenzie ('Kay-Kay') and Doris Foster Whitney. The week in New York was somewhat restricted. Chaplin's lawyer had warned him that a suit was in process against United Artists and that an attempt might be made to serve a summons on him, which could prejudice the entire trip. Chaplin, not for the first time, had to stay in hiding, though he seems to have left the Sherry-Netherlands on one or two occasions, at least. Edith Piaf was playing in New York, and says in her memoirs that Chaplin came to see her performance and visited her backstage.

At Crocker's urging he attended a lunch with the editorial staff of *Time* and *Life*, an event he found frigid and unfriendly and which failed to achieve favourable notices from the magazines. He also attended the New York press show of *Limelight*. There was no repetition of the open hostility of the *Verdoux* press conference, but Chaplin found the atmosphere at the show uneasy and unfriendly. He was gratified, however, by many of the subsequent reviews.

Daily Mail

NO. 17,575   THREE HALFPENCE   FOR QUEEN AND COMMONWEALTH   SATURDAY, SEPTEMBER 20, 1952

U.S. MAY BAN CHAPLIN
Attorney-General Orders an Inquiry Into His Readmission

Comment

TURDAY, SEPT. 20, 1952.

TOO MUCH PLAYTIME?

HE ARCHBISHOP OF CAN-TERBURY has set the cat nong the pigeons with s remarks about tele-sion, although on his turn from America yes-rday he emphasised at he was not "agin"

said : "There is a danger increasing our amenities dlessly when we, as a poor tion, should be concen-ating on getting on with

REASONS ARE KEPT SECRET

Surprise Move as Film Star Brings Family to London

From Daily Mail Reporter

NEW YORK, Friday.

CHARLES CHAPLIN, who left New York for London 48 hours ago, has been barred from re-entering the United States until a Government inquiry decides whether he can return.

The U.S. Attorney-General, Mr. James Mc-Granery, announced in Washington tonight that he had ordered the Immigration Service to bar him until the inquiry. No further statement was made.

SENATOR ACCEPTS CASH AID

Eisenhower May Ask His Team Mate to Quit

From WILLIAM HARDCASTLE
ON THE STEVENSON CAMPAIGN TOUR, Friday.

SENATOR Richard Nixon, Mr. Eisenhower's Vice-Presidential running mate, has accepted a £5,700 elec-tion fund from "millionaire backers" in California.

This disclosure has given Governor Stevenson's chances of being elected President in November an important boost,

On Wednesday 17 September 1952 the Chaplin family embarked for England on the *Queen Elizabeth*. Still evading the process-server, Chaplin boarded the ship at five in the morning, and did not dare show himself on deck. Consequently the devoted James Agee, who had come to see him off, failed to see him as he waved his hat feverishly out of a porthole. Chaplin and Agee were never to meet again: the critic died a couple of years later of a heart attack. Once at sea, process-servers left behind, Chaplin experienced a sense of freedom. He felt 'like another person. No longer was I a myth of the film world, or a target of acrimony, but a married man with a wife and family on holiday.'

The *Queen Elizabeth* had been at sea two days when the radio brought extraordinary news. The United States Attorney General, James McGranery, had rescinded Chaplin's re-entry permit, and ordered the Immigration and Naturalization Service to hold him for hearings when – or if – he attempted to re-enter the country. These hearings, he said, 'will determine whether he is admissible under the laws of the United States'. The Justice Department added that the action was being taken under the US Code of Laws on Aliens and Citizenship, Section 137, Paragraph (c), which permits the barring of aliens on grounds of 'morals, health or insanity, or for advocating Communism or associating with Communist or pro-Communist organizations'. In response to questions, the Attorney General said that this course of action had been planned for some time but that he had waited until Chaplin had left the country before acting. Chaplin, in other words, had no longer the right to return to the place which for the past forty years he had made his home, and to which he had attracted so much love and lustre.

18

Exile

When the *Queen Elizabeth* docked at Southampton, six-year-old Michael Chaplin had been mislaid (he was eventually found in the ship's gymnasium) which gave the reporters time to interview Chaplin before he boarded the train for London. He was tactful in avoiding a direct reply to the American Government's action, since all he possessed was still in the United States and he was terrified that they would devise some means of confiscating it. He indicated that he would return and face any charges:

> The US Government does not go back on anything it says. It will not go back on my re-entry permit.
>
> These are days of turmoil and strife and bitterness. This is not the day of great artists. This is the day of politics.
>
> People are now only too willing to take issue about everything. But I am very philosophical about it all. I try my best.
>
> I do not want to create any revolution. All I want to do is create a few more films. It might amuse people. I hope so . . .
>
> I've never been political. I have no political convictions. I'm an individualist, and I believe in liberty.[1]

He told them that he had an idea for a new film about a displaced person arriving in the New World. A head wound has given the man a complaint called cryptosthenia, which causes him to speak in an ancient language. Since no one can understand him at the immigration barriers, he is allowed to pass all the language tests. Chaplin mimed the interrogation scene for the reporters. Knowing Chaplin's extreme secrecy about the ideas of his films, he cannot have been very serious about this idea: it was simply an attraction for the press.

More seriously he told them about his anxiety to show London to his wife and children, to explore it again himself. He recalled how 'music first entered my soul' (he never varied the phrase) when he heard the street musicians playing 'The Honeysuckle and the Bee'. 'I was seven and now I'm sixty-three, but I'll never forget it.' He appears to have carried with him his first cuttings book, since the newsmen said that he displayed his first notice from 1903 for *Jim, a Romance of Cockayne*.

Although not quite so numerous as on his previous visits, the crowds were there at Southampton, and at Waterloo, where scores of people broke through the police cordons to touch him. More people were waiting outside the Savoy. Mr and Mrs Marriott, the Festival of Britain Pearly King and Queen, brought him a basket of flowers adorned with boots, bowler and walking stick and inscribed from the people of London. At this time Chaplin was especially touched by such sentimental gestures. On the day of his arrival he gave a press conference:

> In Mr Chaplin, face to face, one looks of course for signs of his tragi-comic screen creation. One sees instead a small friendly man, white-haired, his complexion pinker than usual from the lighting of the little stage from which he addresses the hungry journalists through a microphone. When he descends from his stage he is lost. The swarm slowly circles the room with him as its centre, and when someone, guided by a friendly secretary, succeeds in reaching that centre there is ludicrously little time to conduct the personal conversation which, indeed, one shrinks from forcing on him.[2]

The British public and press were enchanted and intrigued by their first sight of Oona. Shy and retiring though she was, a short statement was wheedled out of her: 'I'm happy to stay in the background and help where I'm needed. Perhaps that is why I am the only one of his four wives he took to London, and I am very proud.'

She was asked what Chaplin was like as a husband: 'Charlie is a half-and-half personality. One half is difficult – the other easy. But I find we manage very happily. He is an attentive husband and a wonderful father.' Chaplin had told reporters when the *Queen Elizabeth* docked at Cherbourg, 'I will go back.' In London he said, 'I expect to go back,' and Oona commented: 'It would come as no shock to me if he decided to stay in England.'

After ten years of coldness in America, Chaplin was gratified by the fan letters that awaited him at the Savoy, many of them imploring him to remain. In the *News Chronicle* Lionel Hale, writing 'as a Tory and a friend of America', declared that

> there is always some good in folly, and the good might be that England, and the London streets which are so greatly changed from the days of fog and gas-light and bare-foot boys, might, after so long a time, have once again as one of its gallant inhabitants one of the greatest artists of the era, Mr Charles Spencer Chaplin.[3]

In the House of Commons there were some heated questions to the Foreign Secretary, Mr Eden, with MPs demanding that he make representations to the US Government to allow Chaplin to re-enter the country without let or hindrance. Nor was all American opinion in favour of the Attorney General. A US Congressman visiting Britain spoke of the affair as 'persecution'. A leader in the *New York Times* said that those who had followed Chaplin through the years could not easily regard him as a dangerous person:

> No political situation, no international menace, can destroy the fact that he is a great artist who has given infinite pleasure to many millions, not in any one country but in all countries. Unless there is far more evidence against him than is at the moment visible, the Department of State will not dignify itself or increase the national security if it sends him into exile.[4]

Attorney General McGranery was meanwhile employing the style of innuendo characteristic of McCarthyist technique. 'If what has been said about him is true,' he hinted darkly, 'he is, in my opinion, an unsavoury character.' He claimed that when the public knew the facts on which he was basing his move to bar the comedian from re-entering the United States, it would realize that his action had been justified. McGranery alleged that Chaplin had been accused in the press of being a member of the Communist Party and also of 'grave moral charges'. He declined to be specific about the charges, since he said that this would assist Chaplin in his defence. He would only add further that 'He has been charged with making leering, sneering statements about the country whose gracious hospitality has enriched him.'

McGranery was forced to admit that he had taken his action without consulting any other government departments. It was be-lieved, in fact, that the State Department and many Washington officials had been dismayed by the adverse reaction from all parts of the world. McGranery, though, had evidently been for some time under pressure from right wing and McCarthyist elements. Senator Richard Nixon, using the notepaper of the Senate Committee on Labor and Public Welfare, had written to Hedda Hopper on 29 May 1952 – four months before Chaplin's departure:

Dear Hedda:

I agree with you that the way the Chaplin case has been handled has been a disgrace for years. Unfortunately, we aren't able to do much about it when the top decisions are made by the likes of Acheson and McGranery. You can be sure, however, that I will keep my eye on the case and possibly after January we will be able to work with an Administration which will apply the same rules to Chaplin as they do to ordinary citizens.

The Senator signed himself cordially, 'Dick Nixon'.

Chaplin was invigorated by his explorations of London. From his balcony in the Savoy he could see the river and the new Waterloo Bridge, which he did not like at all, 'only that its road led over to my boyhood'.[5] At that time something still remained of the Kennington he had known as a boy, and on this and subsequent visits Oona was to come to know it as well as he did himself. Alone, he preferred to make his trips on foot or by bus and tube; and he was rarely recognized. On his first evening in London he went to The Scotch House, a pub near Leicester Square, where the landlord was an old Karno colleague, Jimmy Russell, one of many interpreters of the awful boy in *Mumming Birds*, but Russell, to his subsequent chagrin, was not there that night. In the afternoons, while the children made their own excursions with their nannies, Chaplin and Oona would have tea at Fortnums.

Compared with their last years in California these weeks in London were a whirl of social activity. On their first night, they dined at Douglas Fairbanks Junior's house; the Oliviers were also guests. The following evening they went to the Old Vic to see Claire Bloom playing Juliet to Alan Badel's Romeo. Some days later Chaplin took Miss Bloom for a walk around Covent Garden market, and she was touched by the way the market traders all saluted him affectionately with 'Hello, Guv'nor'. The Chaplins went to a Toscanini concert and afterwards met the great old man. They saw Emlyn Williams in his Dickens readings, and afterwards dined with him along with Noël Coward, Alec Guinness and Binkie Beaumont. They were entertained as guests of the Variety Club at the Savoy, and at a lunch given by the Critics' Circle. Chaplin was so much more accessible at this time than on any other London visit before or after that it was confidently predicted that he would appear both in the Royal Variety Performance and the Royal Film Performance. He did not. He had told the *Times* reporter that there was no chance of his appearing again on stage. '"You have to be in constant practice," he said. And the fact that one reminded him of the pleasure it would give and how inconceivable it was that a music-hall actor should ever lose his sense of craft could not persuade him to change his mind.'

Chaplin did however agree to an unscripted half-hour interview on the BBC Light Programme. His interviewers were Dilys Powell, Sir Michael Balcon, Paul Holt, John Mills and Robert Mackenzie. He told them how in his early days he 'used to write with a camera' (in this he anticipated the French director Astruc's concept of the *camera-stylo*). By that he meant that he used to go on the set in the morning without an idea. Then he would start, get excited, and in his excitement begin to invent. He told them that this was a contrast to the long, leisurely and thorough preparations he made for his latest films. Of *Limelight* he told them that he had set the film in London partly out of a feeling of nostalgia, partly because he wanted to say something about kindliness and humanity, for which London seemed to him a fitting setting. The film was not autobiographical except in so far that it, like his other work, inevitably expressed something of its creator's personality.

He had much to say about personality. His conception of a film was as a setting for a striking personality, which the story and everything else existed only to display. In the days of the silent films, he believed, the personality of the actor counted for more than in the present day. So much more was left to the spectator's imagination. The film actors then belonged, as it were, to poetry and to fairyland. 'But we cannot go back to silent films, and perhaps I merely romanticize them.'

This was the only recorded occasion on which he said that he had learnt much about the use of music from Fred Karno, who had used music for its incongruity – some stately eighteenth-century air, perhaps, to accompany the adventures of tramps, to underline the satire.

When the word 'genius' came up more than once, Chaplin laughingly said that it no longer embarrassed him. Indeed he had become quite 'shameless' about hearing himself called one. 'We have so many of them in Hollywood.' He liked to think the word meant merely an individual stylist who did things conscientiously and sometimes perhaps remarkably well. For his own part, he said, he had never written down to the public. He had always done the very best he could.

The world première of *Limelight* was given at the Odeon, Leicester Square, on 23 October, in aid of the Royal London Society for Teaching and Training the Blind, and in the presence of Princess Margaret. The Press Show was held in the theatre the same morning. Claire Bloom appeared with Chaplin at the top of the foyer stairs; when she threw her arms around him and kissed him ('He had finally made me natural with him in life as well') they were warmly applauded. Miss Bloom was working in the theatre in the evening and so could not attend the première, but Chaplin appeared on stage, to great enthusiasm. It was the first film première in Britain to be covered by live television.

Leaving their children happily on the farm of their friend Sir Edward Beddington-Behrens, the Chaplin parents and Harry Crocker moved on to Paris for the French première. There they were even more handsomely fêted. They were invited to lunch with the President, and at the British Embassy; Chaplin was made an officer of the Légion d'Honneur and an honorary member of the Société des Auteurs et Compositeurs Dramatiques. The première was attended by members of the cabinet and the diplomatic corps, though the American Ambassador was a notable absentee. At the Comédie Française, they were guests of honour at a special gala performance of Molière's *Don Juan*. Harry Crocker was anxious about the effect on Chaplin's publicity of a dinner with Aragon, Picasso and Sartre. Later Chaplin and Oona visited Picasso's studio, 'the most deplorable, barnlike garret', stacked with priceless masterpieces by Picasso's contemporaries. Chaplin did not speak French and Picasso did not speak English.

> The interpreters were doing their best but the thing was dragging. Then I had the idea of getting Chaplin alone and seeing if maybe all by ourselves we couldn't establish some kind of communication. I took him upstairs to my painting studio and showed him the pictures I had been working on recently. When I finished, I gave him a low bow and a flourish to let him know it was his turn. He understood at once. He went into the bathroom and gave me the most wonderful pantomime of a man washing

and shaving, with every one of those little involuntary reflexes like blowing the soapsuds out of his nose and digging them out of his ears. When he had finished that routine, he picked up two toothbrushes and performed that marvellous Dance of the Rolls, from the New Year's Eve dinner sequence in *The Gold Rush*. It was just like the old days.

Unfortunately Picasso, violently opposed to all sentimentality, did not like *Limelight*. 'When he starts reaching for the heartstrings, maybe he impresses Chagall, but it doesn't go down with me. It's just bad literature.' He could not reconcile himself either to the physical changes that time had effected in Chaplin:

> The real tragedy lies in the fact that Chaplin can no longer assume the physical appearance of the clown beause he's no longer slender, no longer young, and no longer has the face and expression of his 'little man', but that of a man who's grown old. His body isn't really him any more. Time has conquered him and turned him into another person. And now he's a lost soul – just another actor in search of his individuality, and he won't be able to make anybody laugh.

Picasso's young wife felt that the painter's response to *Limelight* may have been affected by the resemblances between the film's story and their personal situation.

In the United States the vilification continued. The American Legion began a campaign of picketing shows of *Limelight*, and several major theatrical chains – Fox, Loews and RKO – were persuaded to withdraw the film within a short period of its first showings. Hedda Hopper, published a notorious attack in her nationally syndicated column: 'No one can deny [that Chaplin] is a good actor. That doesn't give him the right to go against our customs, to abhor everything we stand for, to throw our hospitality back in our faces . . . I abhor what he stands for . . . Good riddance to bad rubbish.' The American press was not unanimous. *The Nation* (4 October 1952) said: 'Whatever his political views may be . . . Charlie Chaplin can hardly be regarded as an overt threat to American institutions . . . Chaplin is an artist whose shining talent has for decades cast its luster upon his adopted country and brought joy to the world.' On 30 October, the Hollywood Foreign Press Association awarded a scroll of merit to *Limelight*. It was accepted on behalf of his father by Charles Chaplin Junior.

Chaplin was still in touch with the studio and still working, if at a distance, on his film. In November he sent instructions to cut out of *Limelight* the sequences involving the armless wonder, Claudius. As he became more and more convinced that he would not now attempt to return to the United States, he had to face the problem of removing his fortune to Europe. Providently, nearly all his personal assets were contained in a safe deposit box, and immediately before departing for Europe he had made the necessary arrangements for Oona to have access to it. Since he was personally unable to return to the United States, the only solution was for Oona to travel to Hollywood. The ten days that she was away – practically the first time that they had been separated since their marriage nine years before – was a period of terrible anxiety for Chaplin, terrified as he was that the American authorities would discover some way to prevent her leaving the country again. Oona left London by plane on 17 November: at that time New York was still an overnight journey. From New York she flew to Hollywood, accompanied by Arthur Kelly. They arrived on 20 November and left again on 23 November. In only two complete days, Oona, inexperienced as she still was in business affairs, had as far as possible to wind up the Chaplin assets in the United States.

She discovered that since they had left the FBI had interrogated the servants in an attempt to find some evidence of moral turpitude in the household. It was evident that the Bureau was desperate to uncover something – anything – that could substantiate the Attorney General's innuendoes. Everyone connected with Chaplin, including Tim Durant and his lawyer, was questioned, along with all the principals in the Barry case. The details of Paulette's Mexican divorce were re-examined. Even Lita was questioned about her marriage of more than a quarter of a century earlier. She proudly refused to give them any information that could be used to smear her one-time husband.

The most pitiable victim of the FBI harassment was Wheeler Dryden. Since he had first been employed at the studio, he had become devoted to Chaplin. More than devoted, indeed; Wheeler venerated his illustrious half-brother. Even today in the Chaplin archives there remain little packages, neatly wrapped and tied, and labelled in Wheeler's writing, for example, 'Script, incomplete, *but with a note in Mr Chaplin's own hand.*' On the set he would follow Chaplin at a respectful distance, warding off the importunate, seeing that

Chaplin's meditations were not disturbed, bringing him dates and fruit, always ready with anything he needed. Sometimes he might attempt a helpful suggestion, and bore it patiently if Chaplin's dismissal of it was brusque. He carefully collected every discarded relic of the studio and Chaplin; the accumulating hoard of bric-à-brac may have contributed to his estrangement from his wife. (They had married during the making of *The Great Dictator* and had one son, later a well-known jazz musician, Spencer Wheeler.) Though he retained the grand manner of an old English Shakespearean, Wheeler was a timid man. He felt himself abandoned when first Charles and then Sydney left California; and he was terrified by the FBI interrogations. He began to suspect that the FBI were poisoning his food, and refused to leave his house. Ted and Betty Tetrick would from time to time persuade him go out for a walk, but wherever they went he carefully noted down the streets, as if he feared that the Tetricks, too, were going to abandon him. Wheeler died on 30 September 1957, aged 65.

Oona arrived back in London on 27 November 1952, and a few days later the family left for Switzerland. Since Chaplin was not to return to the United States, Swiss residence was likely to be the most advantageous from a financial point of view. While looking for a permanent home, they moved into the Beau Rivage in Lausanne – an old-style grand hotel much favoured by exiled monarchs. From Lausanne they travelled to Rome for the Italian première of *Limelight*. Chaplin was invested with the order Al Merito della Republica, though the occasion was somewhat marred by a demonstration by right-wing extremists who pelted Chaplin with vegetables. Later he said that he had been mostly struck by the comedy of the incident and laughed at it. He refused to prosecute the youthful offenders.

The Chaplins quickly found their house. In January they moved into the Manoir de Ban at Corsier sur Vevey, which they first rented from a former American ambassador. Only a month later they bought it for a reported $100,000. The house is an elegant villa with thirty-seven acres of park, orchard and garden. It has fifteen rooms on three floors. On the ground floor is a handsome drawing room with French doors opening onto a colonnaded terrace which was a focal spot of the household during the summer. At either end of the drawing room double doors lead into the dining room and the library, where Chaplin came to spend more and more of his time when he was at home. A fine elliptical stone staircase (which had a special fascination for the children because the wife of a former owner was said to have been killed by falling down it) leads to the first floor, with guest suites and the main bedrooms. Chaplin's bedroom was simply furnished. He designed the furniture himself. It is in pale wood, with something of the 1930s in its rational austerity, something Edwardian in its proportions and Victorian in its evident sturdiness. The style, as he was accustomed to say, is Chaplin. Oona gave much attention to enlarging and decorating her suite, with its fine views over Lake Leman to the mountains beyond. Her paintings include an Eakins of the artist's studio, in which the nude model is probably Oona's grandmother. The third floor, reached by a more modest staircase or the lift installed by the previous owner, was the realm of the children and their nannies. In the wandering catacombs beneath the house, Chaplin, though no drinker himself, established a cellar, and later built an atmospherically conditioned vault to store his films. One room in the cellars is reserved for the great bulk of Chaplin archives; the scripts, studio records, cutting books and glass negatives of still photographs.

Chaplin felt some anxiety about the cost of staffing such a large estate; while the children were growing up the servants generally numbered around a dozen. In later years the Manoir's domestic machine depended largely on Italians: the butler and cook Gino and Mirella Terni, who arrived in 1958, and the chauffeur Renato, a gentle man of distinguished appearance who took over the post from his brother Mario in 1965.

Chaplin's most urgent need was for a secretary. A friend suggested Rachel Ford. Miss Ford had lived in Paris practically all her life, but remained very British in her appearance and her brisk, no-nonsense approach to life. During the war she had risen to the highest rank possible for a woman in the Free French Army. Afterwards she worked for the European Movement, organizing international conferences. She was persuaded to consider a temporary job with Chaplin because she had inherited from her father a passion for his screen creations. When she arrived at the Manoir, the Chaplins were still unpacking, and Miss Ford felt that she was not at her most presentable: she was wearing a man's boot on one foot and a woman's shoe on the other, having suffered a scald. She was accompanied by a dog on a string – he had lost his leash. She explained in her forthright manner that she could not type, had no experience as a secretary and was only free for a few weeks between conferences. She was to stay for more than thirty years. She was to identify herself wholly with the interests of the Chaplins, who found in her an administrator of integrity, astuteness, skill and unwavering determination. Chaplin was to be delighted by her doggedness, for instance in pursuing any infringement of his copyrights. Miss Ford seemed to find the same invigoration in dealing with legal complexities that others might find in bridge or chess. At her first meeting with the Chaplins, she was dazzled by Oona's beauty and youthfulness and, as someone 'who has never even known what shyness meant' she was struck by the shyness of both of them. From the start it was clear that Miss Ford's role was to be more that of manager than secretary; and a secretary with the typing skills that she disclaimed, Mme Eileen Burnier, was engaged.

Having settled in, Chaplin announced, 'I want to have six months of peace and quietness in this house. We will not go in for big parties, and large receptions, but keep to ourselves.' They were to keep to this resolve, though they saw themselves as part of the local community, went shopping, complained if things went wrong, and from time to time appeared at some festive event (which was always good for the receipts). One serious disadvantage of the house had been overlooked, and was to cause some differences between Chaplin and the local authorities. The Chaplins had seen and bought the property in the quiet of winter, and no one apparently troubled to tell them of the proximity of the Stand de Guémont, where since 1874 the ablebodied male citizens of Vevey had done their training in marksmanship. In 1955 Chaplin lodged a formal protest against the noise nuisance. The canton authorities, eager to accommodate such a distinguished resident, made concessions about certain agreed quiet days, but were adamant that the Stand must stay: 'The township of Vevey will do all in the realm of the possible to diminish the noise due to the proximity of a shooting range. But we stress that under the terms of the Federal ordinance on militia shooting, we must furnish freely a range and we intend to do so.' As long as Chaplin lived the dispute went on, with intermittent protests and the occasional arrival of experts to measure the decibels. The noise nuisance was not ameliorated by the growing traffic on a motorway skirting the estate. In moments of irritability Chaplin would threaten to sell up and move to the Riviera.

Noise or no noise, Chaplin now felt confident about pulling up his last roots in America. Early in March, while the family were on holiday on the Riviera, the studio and the house in Beverly Hills were put up for sale. The studio was sold six months later to a firm of New York real estate agents for $700,000 – considerably less than the asking price. In April Chaplin formally handed back his United States re-entry permit, with a public statement:

> I have been the object of lies and vicious propaganda by powerful reactionary groups who, by their influence and by aid of America's yellow press, have created an unhealthy atmosphere in which liberal minded individuals can be singled out and persecuted. Under these conditions I find it virtually impossible to continue my motion picture work, and I have therefore given up my residence in the United States.

The following February, when the Chaplins arrived at Heathrow for a week's holiday in London, Oona had a British passport. The week before she had renounced her own American citizenship. The final link with the United States would be severed in March 1955, when Chaplin sold off his remaining interests in United Artists.

Chaplin made no concessions to the opinions of the 'yellow press' of America, which naturally howled I-told-you-so when he lunched with Chou-en-Lai in July 1954 while the Chinese Premier was attending the Geneva Conference. Curiosity alone would have forced Chaplin to accept the invitation. A couple of years later when Chaplin was in London preparing *A King in New York* he met Bulganin and Khrushchev at Claridges. The meeting was cordial, though Chaplin diplomatically avoided meeting the American Ambassador, Harold Stassen, who was also present. There were more attacks in May 1954 when Chaplin accepted a £5000 Peace Prize from a Communist World Peace organization. Clearly either to accept or to refuse the prize would have been invidious; Chaplin dealt tactfully with the problem by giving most of the money away. In October he arrived in Paris to present £2000 to the Abbé Pierre to build shelters for the homeless of the city. The following week he came to London and in a ceremony at Lambeth Town Hall gave a further £2000 to the Mayor, Major Herbert White, to be used for the old and poor of the borough. A lot of the Lambeth old and poor turned up for the occasion to give him a riotous local boy's welcome.

There was no question of retirement. Less than six months before his death, terribly frail, Chaplin was still reported to be saying, 'To work is to live – and I want to live.' A year or two before that he had said, 'I can't stop . . . ideas just keep popping into my head.' In his mid-sixties he was exploding with the will and need to work. By the end of 1953 he was talking confidently about his new film, though he would not reveal its subject: 'This industry is a monster which grabs at everything. Every grain of an idea I get I have to hang on to jealously.' He was looking for a boy of twelve to play in it, so clearly the project was already *A King in New York*, which he officially announced (as *The Ex-King*) in May 1954. At that time he thought it would be 'more or less a musical'.

Throughout most of 1954 and 1955 he was working on the script, though in the early part of the time he was still reconsidering *Shadow and Substance* also, so that Isobel Deluz, who was brought in as stenographer for the work, was at times not quite clear which of the two scripts she was supposed to be taking down, or whether it was a memorandum of some general purpose gag or line. She recalled how delighted he was one day when a particularly moving scene he had half-dictated, half-performed, so affected her that she began to cry. 'That's the tear-jerker attack that really wows them at the box-office,' he observed cheerfully.

> Chaplin was never fluent in his dictation, and he seldom finished a sentence. He constantly flipped backwards and forwards in the text or jumped to another sequence. It would go this way:–
>
> 'I love you – I love you,' (He lowers his eyes bashfully). 'That's it, got it. Just like that. I – I love you. Just make a note of that somewhere; may need it later on. Now, got those other pages? All right (reading) good. That's all. I won't do any more today. The tennis pro's arrived. Must get in some exercise or my figure will get fat . . .'

Chaplin would correct the transcripts of the dictation sessions in longhand: the creation of a script was a constantly revolving process of dictation, typing, correction and retyping.

By the autumn of 1955 the script was far enough advanced to begin preparing production, and Chaplin invited Jerry Epstein, his assistant producer on *Limelight*, to be his associate producer in *A King in New York*. Epstein arrived in Europe and joined the household at the Manoir de Ban, where he was to become a favourite and confidant of all the Chaplin children. A new production company, Attica, was established. (When a new company was later set up to handle distribution of all the Chaplin films, it was called Roy Export

Company Establishment, in humorous acknowledgement of Chaplin's determinedly Anglo-Saxon pronunciation of the French title of *A King in New York, Un Roi à New York*.) Studio facilities were to be rented at Shepperton Studios, and in November 1955 Oona arrived in London to arrange accommodation during the production period. She decided on the Great Fosters Hotel at Egham, which had the advantages of being quiet, rich in historical associations, and within easy reach of the studios.

Chaplin, naturally, was to play the main role of the exiled king who arrives in New York full of optimism for his plans for world peace, but is quickly caught up in the materialist frenzy and political paranoia of contemporary America. He needed a leading lady for the role of the go-getting but attractive young advertising agent who persuades him to submit to the lucrative humiliations of acting in television commercials. Jerry Epstein already knew Kay Kendall, who had recently had considerable screen success with her appearances in *Genevieve, Doctor in the House* and *The Constant Husband*. Oona shared his admiration for the comedienne, and Chaplin was infected by their enthusiasm. No doubt his own interest in her was further stimulated by knowing that she was the granddaughter of one of the great idols of the music halls of his youth, Marie Kendall, who had created the song 'Just Like The Ivy'. Epstein incautiously reported to Miss Kendall Chaplin's favourable reaction to his suggestion. Unfortunately he and Oona made the mistake of arranging for Chaplin to see *Genevieve*, which had been a considerable critical and commercial success. Chaplin did not like the film at all, and decided that on no account would he wish to work with Miss Kendall, whereupon Epstein had the uneasy task of deflecting Miss Kendall's hopes. Time has corroborated Chaplin's view of *Genevieve*, though not perhaps of Kay Kendall's elegant talent. He decided upon Dawn Addams, whom he had met when she was filming in Hollywood, shortly before his own departure. She was attractive, and her performance in the film was to prove professional and sporty. The second female role, of the King's estranged Queen, was given to Maxine Audley, an actress with the same aristocratic bearing and fine features as Claire Bloom, and who had recently been playing principal roles at the Shakespeare Memorial Theatre in Stratford.

For the part of the King's long-suffering Ambassador, Chaplin auditioned a number of veteran stage actors and finally chose Oliver Johnston, an actor who had played for most of his career in honourable obscurity, but provided a charming and effective comic foil. Other local character actors in the cast were Jerry Desmonde, who had worked as partner with Sid Field and Norman Wisdom; and Sidney James, who was shortly to establish a new career for himself as a star of the *Carry On* comedies. In the role of the King's lawyer he cast the American–Jewish stage comedian Harry Green – who had, as it happened, begun his career as a real-life lawyer. Green's performance was expert and funny, but Chaplin always had the uneasy sense that Green was upstaging him.

After the King, the most important dramatic role was to be that of the small boy whose parents are victims of the McCarthyist witch-hunt, and whom the King befriends – becoming suspect himself as a result of the association. In late 1953, as we have seen, he was searching for a boy to play this part, and it seems to have been only shortly before embarking on production that he had the idea of casting his own son, Michael: originally he had planned to give Michael the tiny part of the boy in the progressive school who uses his forefinger impartially to form *gateaux* and pick his nose. The boy enjoyed the work: 'I tried hard to do what my father wanted and we got along fine.'[6]

It is important to recognize the courage of Chaplin in undertaking a film, at a time when most men have already retired, in quite new conditions that were far less favourable to creation than the working situation he had known for the past forty years. He was no longer master of his own studio, with familiar craftsmen, who knew his whims, on call. The only official member of the unit who had known the Hollywood studio was Epstein. There were no longer the endless script conferences with the opportunities they provided to test ideas on trusted familiars. Certainly there was no longer the luxury there once had been of time to stop and reflect and try scenes over again some different way. The long pauses between production periods had for long meant that each time Chaplin returned to work there was a marked increase in crewing requirements and production costs. Now the pressures to maintain a tight schedule were aggravated by the added burden of studio rental.

The strains unquestionably show in the finished film. The presence of someone as fearlessly brash as Sutherland or James might have trimmed the script of its wordiness; and someone might have had courage to save Chaplin from mis-pronouncing 'nuclear' as 'nucular'. Circumscribed facilities did not restrain his ambition. His script required the staging of a revolution, while New York had to be recreated from London locations. Georges Périnal was a great photographer who had worked with Clair and Korda and Cavalcanti, but perhaps he lacked Totheroh's resourcefulness and understanding of Chaplin's needs. The London-made New York has a shabby, makeshift look quite absent from the suggestive, mythical cities of *City Lights* and *Modern Times*.

As Chaplin had once taken on the tyranny of European dictators, so now he turned his attack upon the destructive paranoia that had overtaken America. Whether the attack succeeded or failed, the importance of *A King in New York* was that Chaplin was the only film maker with the courage to make it at a time when McCarthyism still prevailed. He was aware before he began the film that he must totally discount the huge American market; in fact *A King in New York* was not screened in the United States until 1976.

The film begins, for old times' sake, with a sub-title: 'One of the minor annoyances of modern life is a revolution.' The exiled King Shahdov of Estrovia seeks refuge in the United States where he hopes to pursue his plans for the peaceful uses of atomic energy. Unfortunately his crooked Prime Minister (Jerry Desmonde) has absconded with the funds that were to have financed these plans. The King and his loyal ambassador Jaume (Oliver Johnston) are initiated into various aspects of contemporary American life – music, movie-going, television and a soirée attended by representatives of the media and intelligentsia. The King visits a progressive school where he meets a precocious child, Rupert Macabee, who reads Marx and assaults the King with a torrent of radical and libertarian oratory. He also encounters an attractive young advertising agent, and ekes out the rapidly diminishing royal funds by appearing in commercials.

The King meets the boy Rupert again, wandering homeless in the wintry streets: he has run away from school to avoid the efforts of the Un-American Activities Committee to question him about his parents' political loyalties and friends. The FBI take the boy away, and the King himself is called before the Committee. His appearance is a fiasco: he manages to get entangled with a fire hose and to soak the Committee with water. He is cleared of any Communist taint but decides to leave America just the same. Before his departure he visits Rupert, but he finds the once spirited child cowed and ashamed. To help his parents he has named names.

Some incidents in the film can be connected with Chaplin's own recent experiences. On arrival at the airport, Shahdov tells reporters how moved he is to be in the United States: all the time he is being fingerprinted by immigration officials. Chaplin had not forgotten his personal humiliation during the Barry affair, when the press was invited to photograph him being fingerprinted. Another incident that can be traced to actual experience is the scene in which the King, fearing a subpoena from the Committee, takes flight at the sight of a sinister pursuer in dark glasses – only to discover, when finally cornered, that the man simply wants his autograph. In his last days in America, fearful of writ-servers, Chaplin slipped out of his hotel each day to lunch at the '21' Club. Al Reuter, the well-known autograph collector and dealer, happened to be working at the club at that time. Al came off duty at 3 p.m. – about the time that Chaplin left the club – and so, on several successive days, he put on his dark glasses and trailed Chaplin, autograph book in hand. Each day Chaplin eluded him until the last, when Al finally caught him and got an autograph from his visibly relieved quarry.

It could be objected – and was widely objected – that fire hoses are as ineffectual against McCarthyism as slapstick against dictators. In a review of the film in the *Evening Standard*, for the most part highly appreciative, the playwright John Osborne wrote:

> In some ways *A King in New York* must be his most bitter film. It is certainly the most openly personal. It is a calculated, passionate rage clenched uncomfortably into the kindness of an astonishing comic personality. Like the king in his film, he has shaken the dust of the United States from his feet, and now he has turned round to kick it carefully and deliberately in their faces. Some of it is well aimed – some is not.
>
> In fact, for such a big, easy target, a great deal of it goes fairly wide. What makes the spectacle of misused energy continually interesting is once again the technique of a unique comic artist.

It is true that some of Chaplin's targets – rock and roll, CinemaScope, sex films – seem marginal to his main theme, and hardly worthy. One part of the film has triumphantly retained its force: the drama of Rupert Macabee, the child robbed of his innate honour. Just as in *The Kid*, Chaplin traces the injustice of a society to its ultimate and most vulnerable victim. The difference is that while The Kid was physically deprived, it is Rupert's conscience and soul that are abused.

Michael Chaplin's performance was admirable: Rupert is a volatile and fiery little pup, as touching in the anger of his protest, 'I'm sick and tired of people asking if I'm this, if I'm that,' as in his final break-down. Chaplin and his wife would afterwards indulge in friendly sparring as to whether Coogan or Michael was the better actor, with his mother always favouring Michael. His parents had wanted Michael to change his name to John Bolton for the role, so as not to trade upon the name of Chaplin, but the child insisted upon his own name. Much later he recalled, 'The only advice my father gave me on acting was: "What you have to try to achieve is to be as natural as possible."'

Shooting lasted from 7 May to 28 July 1956: the twelve-week schedule was the shortest for any Chaplin feature. From August to October Chaplin was in Paris, editing the film. Shortly after his arrival in Paris, on 25 August, he gave a press conference about the forthcoming film, from which American press men were banned. He told the press confidently that it would be his best and funniest film, though he was not giving much away: 'In it I have tried to throw into relief the contrast that exists in a big city, as much in the streets as among the inhabitants.'

One day during the time he was editing in Paris, Chaplin and Oona chanced to eat in the same restaurant as Paulette Goddard and her current husband, the German novelist Erich Maria Remarque. They joined each other, and the meeting was very affable. Remarque and Paulette lived for a time in Switzerland, though the Chaplins and the Remarques never met by design. 'We live on different mountains,' said Paulette.

Work on the film continued thoughout the first half of 1957. On 23 May Oona gave birth to their sixth child who was to be named Jane.*

The film was released on 12 September 1957. Before that Chaplin had previewed it for friends. One of them was J. B. Priestley, who wrote:

> It is always a particular pleasure to hear an artist you admire and like describe what he hopes to do, and then afterwards to see for yourself what he has done. Especially if you are not disappointed in the result.
>
> This new film left me with no feelings of disappointment. Chaplin seems to me to have brought off something very difficult, just as he did in *Modern Times* and *The Great Dictator*.

---

* Chaplin was to have eight children by Oona: Geraldine (1944), Michael (1946), Josephine Hannah (1949), Victoria (1951), Eugene (1953), Jane (1957), Annette (1959) and Christopher (1962).

He has turned film clowning into social satire and criticism, without losing his astonishing ability to make us laugh.

This seems to me – and my standards are high – a wonderful thing to do. Many persons, including a large number who write for a living, will not agree with me. The truth is, this post-war period of ours is rapidly turning into a sour age, in which a great many peevish little men like nothing better than to sneer at anybody of real stature.

And Charles Chaplin has stature. He is, in fact, one of the most remarkable men of our time.

To begin with, he is one of the very few men who have compelled the film industry to serve them, who have been its masters and not its slaves. Sooner or later most film men, no matter how brilliant they may be, are beaten by the front offices, the distributors, the exhibitors, the trade . . .

There is not to my mind a hint of Communist savagery and inhumanity in the satire, for Chaplin, like most genuine artists, is at heart a genial and gentle anarchist and the laughter he provokes only clears and sweetens the air.

Despite Priestley's fears, the British press was largely favourable and at worst respectful. A fine critic who was himself a screenwriter, Paul Dehn, concluded,

Its narrative may be incoherent, its cutting slack, its camera-work primitive and its decor (by glossy Hollywood standards) abominably shoddy, but it says more in its brief, tragi-comic compass than all this year's glossy Hollywood pictures laid end to end; and the more you see it, the more it will have to say – which I take to be a symptom of greatness.

The press was as friendly when the film opened in Paris on 24 September. Chaplin had the American press barred from the première at the Gaumont Palace. This had the effect of excluding one of Chaplin's most loyal and dedicated supporters and devotees, Gene Moskowitz of *Variety*, one of the most generous and best-loved critics in the world. Moskowitz commented sadly, 'For a man demanding liberty and individual freedom of expression for himself, it is a negative action.' Chaplin evidently deigned to communicate with one or two American correspondents. Ed Murrow for one had the opportunity to ask him why he had not shown any positive side of the United States. Chaplin replied frankly:

If you give both sides it becomes bloody dull. I'm not a highbrow – I'm an instinctive artist. Whatever I do is for effect.

The motion picture is not for preachment, and if I've preached here I'm wrong. I'm loading the dice for something more important than politics – the affirmation of the man.

Another American who spoke to Chaplin at this time was Ella Winter who, with her husband Donald Ogden Stuart, had also been forced into exile in these times. The Ogden Stuarts remained friends of the Chaplins until their deaths; shortly before the film was released Ella Winter visited Chaplin in Vevey. Her interview was published in *The Observer* on the same day as Kenneth Tynan's review, which was neither hostile nor admiring. Chaplin had talked incessantly to her about the film.

Chaplin was agog to know how people had liked his new film at a recent private showing. 'Did they laugh? What did they say? Didn't you like the part where . . .?' I reported in detail and he listened avidly. 'It's good, my best picture, it's entertainment, don't you think?' His agile, speckled hands gestured with every word. 'They say a lot about it that's nonsense, it's not political, not "anti" anything.'

'But tell me, didn't you like . . .?' He couldn't get enough. He is always possessed by his work and this picture has given him greater anxiety than his others. It's the first one he has made outside the United States.

'I had to get used to a new crew, different methods of work, but there were advantages – not least that it cost 25 per cent less.' He appreciated many things about the British technicians. 'They're slower, but more thorough . . .

'Of course I do everything. I create the whole thing. A film isn't just a product of mass production to me. I'm an individualist.'

'You haven't chosen colour or a wide screen . . .?'

'No . . . I paint on a small canvas.' He was pacing up and down the porch to keep up with his thought.

'I'd rather see a man stir his teacup with a spoon than see a volcano erupting. I want my camera to be like the proscenium of a theatre, come close to the actor, not lose his contour, bring the audience to him. Economy of action has gone through all my work. People have an idea that motion pictures must be elaborate, vast, spectacular, in some ways perhaps rightly, but I prefer to intensify personality rather than feature grand canyons on a wide screen. I prefer the shadow of a train passing over a face, rather than a whole railway station . . .'

'About America –' I started.

He talked about it in snatches. 'What are they so sore about? There was a time when they put out the red carpet, literally, on every platform when I went from Los Angeles to New York. The crowd adored me. Now all that nonsense . . . people who spend time disparaging me . . . Actually I'm a Puritan. I haven't had the time to live the lives some of them attribute to me . . . or the energy. I've made eighty-five pictures.'*

* *A King in New York* was in fact his eightieth film.

We talked a while about the astonishing face of calumny. Then I asked why, when so many early films appear old-fashioned, his wear well.

'My clowning's realistic, that's why it doesn't go out of date. When I dip my fingers in a fingerbowl and wipe them on an old man's beard, I do it as if it were normal behaviour. So they still laugh at me.' And he laughed at himself as he thought of himself doing it.

'They call me old-fashioned,' he said, a bit wistfully. 'I don't know why. I suppose I ignore the "modern techniques", whatever that is. I don't like camera trickery – that's for technicians or track layers. All it leaves for the actor is to make Magnavox eyes or a CinemaScope mouth. It's too simple to shoot through a nostril or the fireplace. It can hurt an actor's talent, too. I don't like actors to be so swamped. Anyway, that's my preference,' he finished aggressively. 'Others may do it differently; that's my personal taste and my style.

'. . . As for politics, I'm an anarchist. I hate governments and rules and fetters . . . Can't stand caged animals . . . People must be free.'

Suddenly he put a thumb in each armhole. 'Greatest little comedian in the world,' he smiled, and he sat down. Then he was on his feet again. 'My picture isn't political. I'm anxious only that people laugh. The film is a satire; a clown must satirize; I've never made a picture that didn't.' After a moment he added, 'This is my most rebellious picture. I refuse to be part of that dying civilization they talk about.'

In the United States the campaign against Chaplin still persisted. In March 1958 the Hicksville Public Library was obliged to cancel a programme of four Chaplin pictures because of objections by local citizens. When Hollywood Boulevard's 'Walk of Fame' – one thousand bronze stars set into the pavement, each in honour of a different film actor or actress – was laid down, Chaplin's name was omitted because of protests from property owners in the area. In 1956 the American Inland Revenue Service announced that they would seek to claim $1.1 million in back taxes due for the last three years of operation in the United States. By 1958 the estimate had been revised to $542,000 with interest bringing the total to $700,000. In December 1958, however, the claim was definitively settled for $330,000, (with interest, $425,000). So Chaplin paid off the United States.

During these years Chaplin seems to have become more accessible to interviewers – though he had always braced himself to the necessity of grinning and bearing newsmen when there was a new film to be publicized. In one of these interviews, with Frederick Sands, he voiced his satisfaction at being back at work, with no prospect of retirement:

The credit for that goes to Oona. She urged me on, because she found me restive doing nothing.

After taking the decision to go back to work I became a much happier man.

Now I put in a regular six to eight hours of work every day. Usually I finish about five and take a steam bath to keep me fit. In the summer I play lots of tennis . . .

I have no intention of ever retiring again.

I am putting every ounce of energy into writing my memoirs. They will be very long. I have much to tell and at my age I must hurry to complete them.

Every time I think, so much comes back to my mind which I had long forgotten. Seventy years IS a long time.

And then there is my new film, with the little man in the bowler hat back again – in colour.

Asked why he had abandoned the Tramp character in the first place, Chaplin replied:

It's personal. Old friends are like old shoes, you know. All very fine, but we discard them.

Little fellow just didn't fit in . . . there were periods in the atomic age during which I couldn't see room for him.

I was no longer stimulated by him due to the changing of time. You cannot go on composing in one key . . .

But now I shall bring him back – same as he was, yes, the same as he was . . . Of course, a little older.

He talked a good deal at this time about bringing back the Tramp. To another 1959 interviewer he said, 'I was wrong to kill him. There was room for the Little Man in the atomic age.' His interest in the character had been reawakened by working over *A Dog's Life*, *Shoulder Arms* and *The Pilgrim* which, with the assistance of Jerry Epstein, he edited and re-assembled as *The Chaplin Revue*. As severe as ever in the cutting room, he edited out moments which he thought no longer worked well. As a prologue to the omnibus he cut together some of the *How to Make Movies* material of the old Chaplin Studios. This was the first time the public had seen these scenes of the young Chaplin out of costume. As an introduction to *Shoulder Arms* he included some actuality footage of the First World War; and his own reconstruction of the landscapes of battle were not diminished by this juxtaposition. Throughout the work Oona sat beside him, sewing, and he complained humorously that whenever he wanted to throw out some scene, she pleaded for its retention. Chaplin wrote and recorded a new score for the assembly, and for *The Pilgrim* composed a country pastiche, 'Bound for Texas', which was recorded by the popular singer Matt Munro. *The Chaplin Revue* was released in September 1959.

In April 1959 Chaplin celebrated his seventieth birthday. 'I don't feel a day over sixty-nine,' he said. 'If only I could live long enough to do all the things I want to do!' He received over a thousand letters of congratulation from every part of the world. The guests at his birthday dinner included the dancer Noelle Adam who was soon to become the wife of his son Sydney, and Sydney Bernstein, the British cinema and television magnate, who presented Chaplin with a telescope. Another gift gave him some pleasure: thanks to the determined efforts of Miss Ford, the day before his birthday Roy Export and Lopert Films were granted a writ to seize copies of *Modern Times* that were being illegally distributed in the United States.

Chaplin's birthday was reported in newspapers across the world; and he was asked for his views on the future of mankind. 'I hope,' he said, 'we shall abolish war and settle all differences at the conference table . . . I hope we shall abolish all hydrogen and atom bombs before they abolish us first.' In more intimate interviews he never tired of sharing his wonder at the idyllic personal life he had achieved. Two years earlier, at the time of Jane's birth, he had declared, touchingly, 'With Oona to look after me and the children to inspire me, I cannot grow old, and nothing can hurt me.' In a 1959 interview he enlarged upon the secret of his happiness:

I love my wife and she loves me. That is why we are so happy.

If you don't demand too much from each other – that, I think, comes nearest to being a formula for happiness in marriage. The rest takes care of itself through tolerance. In the sixteen years of our marriage, we have been separated only once – for five days [*sic*] when Oona went on a business trip to America.

She is my inspiration, and she is a good critic. She has a natural talent, and her criticism is constructive. To get her reactions to anything I do, I let her see my day's output of work. She never discusses anything or proffers an opinion unless I ask her. Sometimes I disagree with her opinion, only to find a week later that she was right.

We have a profound respect for each other's taste and views, and this makes for a most agreeable atmosphere in the home . . . We can be thoroughly relaxed with each other and enjoy our own company without having to indulge in conversation . . . Oona feels that she has no talents except as a wife and mother.

She is a very busy woman and leaves me at ten o'clock every morning. I just dally over breakfast, which I enjoy. I like my coffee and orange juice and bacon and eggs. Frightfully English, I know. When I've finished, I try to detain Oona with conversation, but she always runs out on me. At ten on the dot she gets up from the table and tells me: 'No, you get to work . . .'

We like to invite friends on Sundays when most of the staff are off, and Oona and I potter about the kitchen preparing our own meal. Oona is a wonderful cook and there is never a mess of dishes in sight . . .

The children? They have a place in our life and we enjoy them. They are very amusing, and they can be very irritating too. We see to it that their lives are fully occupied.

Oona told the interviewer: 'We encourage the children to become independent. We keep them busy with ballet lessons, music, even writing. It's working wonders developing their personalities.' Chaplin added, 'I never get impatient having children around. Far from disturbing me in my work they are an asset. You know, I thrive on youth and merriness. But get this [here he prodded a finger at the interviewer], our happiness is not governed by the children. We would be just as happy – just Oona and I.'

Oona, notoriously reticent in face of the press, made her own contribution to the interview,

I am married to a young man.

People think of Charlie as my father, but age counts for nothing in this house. To me he seems younger every day. There is certainly no father fixation about my feeling for Charlie. He has made me mature and I keep him young.

I never consciously think about Charlie's age for 364 days of the year. Only his birthday is the annual shock for me. But I can feel the way some people stare at me with puzzlement and then look back at him, wondering how we have kept it up; whether it's just a façade.

My security and stability with Charlie stem, not from his wealth, but from the very difference in years between us. Only young women who have married mature men will know what I mean.[7]

About this time the writer Ian Fleming was taken to dinner at the Manoir by Noël Coward. He found it 'wonderful to see two people bask unaffectedly in each other's love'. Shy and reticent as they could be in other ways, the Chaplins would kiss and embrace quite unselfconsciously, whoever was present. On the occasion of this visit, Fleming found Chaplin wearing a plum-coloured smoking jacket: it made him feel 'like a millionaire', he explained. At dinner he entertained his guests with a vivid description, illustrated by mime, of an imaginary film he would make, to be called *Around Romance in Eighty Days*. (This was the era of Mike Todd's much-publicized Jules Verne adaptation.) The film, he said, would be a mixture of half a dozen spectaculars – *Ben Hur*, *South Pacific* and *Anna Karenina* among them. It would include a chariot race. The villain, with huge knives on his chariot wheels would overtake the hero ('a chap called Gulliver or Don Quixote or one of those'). The hero would respond by leaning out of his own chariot to slice a side of ham on the knives. He would then eat the meat to renew his strength to win the race. Chaplin was still talking of reviving the Little Fellow: Mrs Fleming suggested that the theme might be 'the Little Man who never had it so good' (it was also the Macmillan period), and Chaplin seemed to like the idea.[8]

Chaplin and Oona would make occasional trips to London or Paris; there were also family holidays. In July and August 1961 Chaplin took his family to the Far East, and in spring 1962 they made their first trip to Ireland, where Chaplin acquired a taste for salmon fishing. Michael Chaplin recalled a charming comedy scene from the trip:

> When you're seventy-two and you believe that you've had all the experiences and are prepared to sit back and think out the rest of your life, it's maybe a little tough to try to start playing the 'my boy and I are just great pals' type of father . . . but on that Irish holiday my father tried. He took me fishing, ready to show me just how it's done . . .
>
> The object of the lesson was to show me how to cast a fly and play the trout. For fifteen minutes I stood by him on the bank of a stream while he talked about the theory of dropping a hooked piece of feather just where some fish would be coming up for his last breath.
>
> 'The touch,' he said. 'You must have the touch . . . here, I'll show you . . .'
>
> He threw the rod back, the line went swishing through the air, then he whipped the rod forward . . .
>
> A big nothing.
>
> Father tugged, obviously thinking that he'd got the line caught on a branch.
>
> I took a quick glance over his shoulder, right to where he'd just about ripped the back out of his raincoat.

'I think it's caught on your raincoat,' I said, very tactfully . . .

Gratefully, but embarrassed, he unhooked himself and wound the line in.

We plodded home at dusk, with my father coyly trying to hold together the torn halves of his raincoat.[9]

The 1962 holiday – the last on which all the children would be together with their parents – also included visits to Venice, London and Paris. It was widely reported that Chaplin would visit the Soviet Union in the near future. The only foundation for this story was that when he had met a delegation of Soviet writers they had courteously suggested that he might visit Russia and he had as courteously replied, 'With pleasure.'

In June of that year, Chaplin was invested by the University of Oxford with the honorary degree of Doctor of Letters. The only disagreeable note to the occasion was the publicity given to the objections of the historian Hugh Trevor-Roper, who declared that the value of honorary degrees would be degraded by this award to a mere film comedian. This had no effect, however, and on 27 June Chaplin arrived at the Senate House, dressed in a dark suit and academic robes of scarlet and grey, to receive his degree. Others honoured at the same time were Dean Rusk, the American Secretary of State, Yehudi Menuhin and Graham Sutherland. The crowds, though, were for Chaplin. Geraldine, who had come from London where she was studying at the Royal Ballet School, had to battle her way to the door and even then had great difficulty in proving her identity. The Vice-Chancellor greeted Chaplin with the words, 'Illustrious man, without doubt star of the first magnitude, you who have been a source of the greatest pleasure to so many people for so many years . . .'

The Public Orator, A. N. Bryan-Brown, introduced Chaplin with a quotation from Juvenal:

Nil habet infelix paupertas durius in se quam quod ridiculos homines facit.

[The hardest blow poverty yields is that the poor are laughed at.]

Chaplin, he continued, invited laughter,

per bracas illas fluitantes, calceos divaricatos, petasum orbiculatum constantem simul at instabilem, bacillum flexibile, exiguum denique labri superioris ornamentum.

[with his baggy trousers, his turned out boots, his bowler, cane and toothbrush moustache.]

In all his films, said the Public Orator, 'are to be found the humour and generosity of one who sympathizes with the underdog.' Beauty, said Chaplin, in his speech of acceptance, is in the eye of the beholder: 'There are those who can see either art or beauty in a rose lying in the gutter, or the sudden slant of sunlight across an ash-can, or even in the tumbling of a clown.' When it was over, Chaplin said that he would have 'needed a heart of stone' not to be moved by the reception. Sir Maurice Bowra introduced Chaplin to Dean Rusk. 'There was no bitterness between us, no bitterness at all,' he said later.

A note of bitterness was, however, introduced by some elements of the American press. The reactionary *Philadelphia Inquirer*[10] had a report headed 'Buffoonery at Oxford', and found the event 'a snide attempt to place Chaplin on the same plane with Dean Rusk in its distribution of honours that most Americans will find unpalatable.' The *New York Times* however took advantage of the occasion to say, 'We do not believe the Republic would be in danger if the present Administration lifted the ban that was imposed in 1952, and if yesterday's unforgotten little tramp were allowed to amble down the gangplank of an American port.'

Nine days later, the University of Durham followed Oxford's lead and awarded Chaplin an honorary degree of D.Litt. The Durham Public Orator, Karl Britton, was something of a film critic, it seemed. Chaplin, he said, had produced some of the great comic art of the age – comedy 'often enriched and sometimes endangered by sentiment,' and with a political message 'that arose out of a deep view of man's small situation in the world.'

Durham invested Chaplin with his degree on 6 July, after which Chaplin had to hurry back to Switzerland in time for the birth of his eighth child. He arrived home on Sunday 7 July, went to bed that night, but had to get up again around 3 a.m. to rush Oona to the Clinique Montchoisi in Lausanne. At 5.30 a.m. on the morning of 8 July she gave birth to a boy who was named Christopher James. The family was now complete.

Chaplin was fifty-five when Geraldine, his first child by Oona, was born; and seventy-three when their last child, Christopher, arrived.

It was a remarkable and challenging undertaking to bring up a young family at an age when most men are relaxing into the sinecure role of grandfather. Ordinary considerations of age and declining energy seemed irrelevant to Chaplin, but problems still remained in rearing this large brood. Chaplin's dreams had been formed in his youth. It would be natural for him to want to provide for his children the paternal discipline and protection that he had been denied in his own youth, yet for children of the 1960s this ideal could appear somewhat archaic and restrictive. Even though to Oona, Chaplin remained a young man, the generation gap was undoubtedly exaggerated in their household. Despite his life-long dream of domesticity, Chaplin was still dedicated to work, and that work continued, as it had always done, to take precedence over everything and everyone else. The children learned that above all they must never intrude upon Daddy's work; to make sure that they did not was a heavy part of the nurses' charge. Francis Wyndham, a wise and sympathetic observer who knew the Chaplins, remarked another obstacle to ideal domesticity:

> The only flaw in their domestic harmony – occasional misunderstandings with their children as each in turn ceases to be a child – springs from the very intensity and completeness of their mutual happiness. The delight which Charlie and Oona take in each other's company tends to isolate them in a self-sufficient world of love. This atmosphere is utterly charming for their friends, but its effect on a nearer relationship might be unintentionally exclusive. If Chaplin has failed to achieve a wholly unselfish sympathy with his children, he has triumphantly succeeded in eliminating any dichotomy between 'love' and 'admiration' in his attitude towards the woman in his life.[11]

Chaplin may have had problems in being a father; at the same time it is never easy to be the child of a great man. All the Chaplin children to some degree found themselves isolated from their school contemporaries. They lived in a grand house in a park, with servants and money; and the great men of the world paid homage to their parents. With success and fortune, and through bitter experience, Chaplin had learned to mistrust, in the first instance, any proffered friendship or intimacy; and in their turn the children had to learn this unchildlike lesson. Friends were rigorously vetted and rarely encouraged.

Throughout his life Chaplin had been subject to sudden outbursts of temper which were generally soon forgotten. At other times, though, the difficulty he had in delivering a reprimand was a byword at the studio, where someone else was always deputed to perform such unpleasant tasks on Chaplin's behalf. As the children grew up, he found the same difficulty in telling them off when it was necessary. Gentle and shy even in the face of her own children, Oona was no better equipped for the task, and much of the time the task of delivering reproaches and reprimands was deputed to Kay-Kay or Miss Ford, neither of whom felt any inhibitions in the matter. A certain reticence and evasion became characteristic of the relationship between the Chaplin parents and children.

Chaplin tended to be less severe with the younger children than with the older ones born in the United States. If there was any slight resentment among the children about this discrimination, it was from the younger ones who felt deprived of the discipline they saw doled out to their elders. When Chaplin did get angry with them, the older girls were more adept than Michael at deflecting their father's displeasure. Kay-Kay recalled how effectively Geraldine, then aged five, dealt with a prolonged telling-off from her father. Fixing him with a baleful stare, she yanked her baby sister Josephine to her feet, exhorting her, 'C'mon. Let's get out of here.' Chaplin's wrath could not withstand such an exit line.

Geraldine was to be the first rebel, when she left home to study at the Royal Ballet School. Michael soon followed. He became particularly irked by parental intervention in his friendships, and eventually left home. His adventures provided a field-day for the press and acute embarrassment and annoyance to his parents. He became (briefly) a junkie, enrolled in RADA, acted in pictures, recorded pop songs, married and provided Chaplin and Oona with their first grandchild. At one point in 1965 he claimed National Assistance. Chaplin and the rest of the family happened to be passing through London at the time on their way to the annual Easter holiday in Ireland, and Oona was obliged to give the press an uncharacteristically severe statement in which she said, 'the young man is a problem, and I am sorry he was given National Assistance. He has stubbornly refused an education for three years and therefore he should get a job and go to work. If I do not wish to indulge him as a beatnik, that is my privilege – sincerely, Oona Chaplin.'[12]

Despite his aberrations, Michael Chaplin was clearly a young man of individuality, charm and warmth; and before his father's death, he was to be fully reconciled with the family. During the periods of estrangement from Geraldine and Michael, Oona, when she and Chaplin were in London, would make the excuse of shopping expeditions to slip away and visit them. Chaplin was supposed to know nothing of these trips, but there were no real secrets between them and it is pretty certain that he was tacitly aware that she was keeping a maternal eye on their children. They were both grateful, too, for the fatherly concern of Jerry Epstein, who was by this time permanently resident in London.

Chaplin had begun to write his memoirs after finishing *A King in New York*. In 1960 he told Ian Fleming that he had finished five hundred pages and had only some twenty more to go. Fleming may have misunderstood, because three more years of work remained to be done. Chaplin also complained to Fleming that his secretary was forever trying to improve his English. 'He said he was not surprised, as he had taught himself the language and suspected that his secretary knew it far better than he did but, even so, he liked his own version and hoped that some of what he had actually written would survive the process of editing by his publishers.'[13] Chaplin's daily routine while writing the book was to rise at seven, to take a dip in his swimming pool, whatever the weather, to take his breakfast, and afterwards kiss Oona goodbye as if he was going off to his office. He would then work until midday and lunch. The older children took turns to lunch with their parents. After a siesta, Chaplin would return to work until five, when he had tea and, in fine weather, played a little tennis. Dinner at the Manoir was always at seven. When it was over Chaplin would continue to work in the library until ten. *My Autobiography* went through the same cycles of dictation, typing, correction and retyping as the scripts. Chaplin took great delight in reading aloud to visitors the sections he had most recently written. Lillian Ross was so privileged and remembered how on an autumn afternoon in 1962 'I sat with him on his terrace as he read parts of his book manuscript to me, the tortoiseshell-rimmed glasses a bit down on his nose, his reading dramatic to the point of melodrama, his devotion to his subject unselfconscious and complete.'[14]

Since Chaplin had never co-operated with any biographer (at least since his early misfortunes with Rose Wilder Lane in 1916) the autobiography was a major publishing prize. The lucky winner was The Bodley Head. The managing director Max Reinhardt had been introduced to the Chaplins in 1958, and undoubtedly his urging and encouragement were important to its production. Reinhardt was admirably patient. As early as 1958 he had sounded out *The Sunday Times* about serial rights. Leonard Russell, the Literary Editor, recalled delicately asking if Chaplin would be using a 'ghost':

> Mr Reinhardt looked shocked, offended even. Surely we couldn't think that Chaplin, a man who wrote his own scripts, directed his own films, composed his own music, would seek outside help with his own memoirs: every word would be written by Chaplin – he would swear an affidavit on that. 'Never mind,' said Mr Reinhardt, looking for the waiter, 'I hope to have something to show you before very long.'
>
> But years passed, and nothing happened – we thought that Chaplin must have given up. Then early in 1962 Mr Reinhardt produced an uncorrected draft of the first third of the book. We read it. It was magnificent – a splendid serial in itself.
>
> Chaplin, however, wasn't ready to negotiate the newspaper rights: first he must finish the book. There was nothing to do but wait. And while we were waiting, the word got round that Chaplin was writing his autobiography, with the result that frenzied and fantastic offers for the serial rights came from the United Kingdom, from the United States, from most of the countries of Europe. Chaplin ignored them and Mr Reinhardt, presumably, exercised his customary diplomacy.
>
> Mr Chaplin went on writing and rewriting [in point of fact his actual and uninterrupted time on the book was a mere two years] and our frustration deepened.[15]

It was later revealed that when Ian Fleming visited Vevey it was as an undercover agent for *The Sunday Times* with the assignment of wringing an agreement from Chaplin. The mission was bungled since Fleming became far too interested in the author's view of things, and in urging Chaplin to permit no editorial interventions in his work. In the end, however, *The Sunday Times* managed to secure premier publication of the book.

As a trailer, *The Sunday Times* published in their magazine section a profile of Chaplin, by the distinguished theatre critic Howard Clurman, which had already appeared in *Esquire* (November 1962). Clurman had been a guest at the Manoir, and was permitted to read the manuscript of *My Autobiography*. Before he began reading, he was told by Chaplin, 'I'm really surprised how well America comes off!' 'I had supposed when I read a press report to this effect,' Clurman wrote afterwards,

> that his benign attitude might be a matter of tactics (though Chaplin has never been notably tactful), but face-to-face with him I felt sure his moderation was genuine, a mellowness which is not the sign of any weakening, but rather a growth in breadth and wisdom. For the first time in my long acquaintance with Chaplin, I had the feeling that he was not only an artist of genius, but a man who might be considered – or had become – wise.
>
> When I speak of 'wisdom', I do not mean correct in opinion or even reliable in judgement. I mean that Chaplin's whole personality has become integrated and has attained the finest balance that his talents and nature could achieve – and these are sufficiently rich and human enough to make a man to be cherished.
>
> So when Charlie began to let fly with statements which might be added up to a sort of credo, I had no inclination to contradict him, or to test their objective validity. Everything he said – even when paradoxical or perhaps wildly 'wrong' – seemed right for him and could be so interpreted that some basic truth, some corrective to his exaggerations might be distilled from his sallies.
>
> I could not quarrel with his concern about the armaments race. I smiled in comprehension of his anarchistically aesthetic declaration, 'I can't stand Communists with their *system* and systems . . . I hate systems.' Again and again he exclaimed, 'Life is full of poetry', and though this is not exactly a 'scientific' statement, his person made his meaning entirely clear.
>
> He went on to discuss matters of acting craft. He had learned much, he said, from his first director. 'I believe in theatricalism. (His word, not mine.) Theatricalism is poetry . . . I don't believe in The Method.' (I did not tell him that I had heard Stanislavsky say to an actress: 'If my system' – which is also known as The Method – 'troubles you, forget it.') 'I believe in theatricalism,' Charlie continued, 'even in "tricks" – actors' tricks . . . I don't like Shakespeare on the stage; he interferes with the actor's freedom, with his virtuosity.' And as his spirit almost lifted him from his seat, so that I feared that he might become airborne at any moment. I could see that in his way he was more Shakespearean than many professional Shakespeareans . . .
>
> What struck me . . . was that, though I was not at all tempted to interrupt his outbursts, I might easily have done so without offence. In former years I had the impression that, though he was sharply observant, he hardly listened to anyone. He was always 'on' – telling stories, doing imitations, recitations, pantomimes, delivering himself of fire-cracker pronouncements – providing himself and others with a constant spectacle

of irrepressible energy and imagination. No one got a chance to speak in his presence. (Hardly anyone desired to.) But now Charlie was also ready to listen.

As Clurman left the Manoir, he asked Chaplin how his book would end: 'What's the conclusion?'

> 'That I am content to look out at the lake and at the mountains and feel that, with my family around me there is nothing more and nothing better,' he answered. He pointed toward the sky and the open space around – in a gesture which pleaded to say more than his words might convey, while his expression was one of naïve bafflement at his inability to define the ineffable.

While the book was in the last stages of production, Chaplin celebrated his seventy-fifth birthday. This time his message to the world combined melancholy and optimism: 'Where is all the fun, the gaiety, the laughter? Everyone is much too serious these days.' He was still gravely troubled by the existence of nuclear weapons, but now 'I am a humanitarian and therefore I believe in humanity and its ability to survive . . . I think, like the British, we will all muddle through somehow.' During the summer he attended a Callas gala performance at the Paris Opera, and was observed by the press greeting Princess Grace of Monaco on the steps of the theatre. He considered writing an opera himself, and thought *Tess of the D'Urbervilles* a likely subject. He also spoke of writing a slapstick comedy for his son Sydney.

My Autobiography was published in September 1964. The first printing was eighty thousand copies, and the book was selected by the Book of the Month Club in America, and by the largest Italian and German book clubs. Chaplin was reputed to have received an advance of half a million dollars for British and American rights, not to mention the nine pounds of caviare given him by the USSR in consideration of the right to reprint a thousand words in *Izvestia*.

The reviews were almost unanimous about the book, which finally ran to more than five hundred printed pages. The first eleven of its thirty-one chapters, ending at the moment that he signed with the Mutual Company, can stand comparison with any autobiography for their colour and vitality. Chaplin's writing is energetic, and his pleasure in words is infectious. Words he particularly likes, like 'ineffable' and 'concupiscence' he may use too often; but even the occasional slight misapplication of some word can endow it with something new and arresting. His phrasing is vivid. The chronicle of the childhood is such a Dickensian mixture of colour and tragedy that some reviewers were sceptical of its truth. Documentary research constantly vindicates Chaplin's record.

From the twelfth chapter onwards, however, some disappointment is almost inevitable. Chaplin is much more concerned to describe his social life and the celebrities he had known than to reveal anything about his films, the way he made them, life in his studio and his collaborators. Chaplin artlessly exposed himself to charges of snobbery: 'If we were not so preoccupied with our family, we could have quite a social life in Switzerland, for we live relatively near the Queen of Spain and the Count and the Countess Chevreau d'Antraigues, who have been most cordial to us, and there are a number of film stars and writers who live near.'[16]

The preface of the present work has already speculated on the reasons for Chaplin's reticence about his work: his declared belief that 'if people know how it's done, all the magic goes'; the possibility that the ultimate secret of his creation was mysterious even to him; the possibility that he felt that the daily routines of his working life would be simply boring to readers. Even then it was hard to understand how he could devote pages to Randolph Hearst or H. G. Wells, yet not make even a passing reference to loyal collaborators who had given so much to the films; people like Totheroh, Bergman, Mack Swain, Eric Campbell or Georgia Hale. Is it far-fetched to look for a deep-rooted psychological explanation of the increasing reluctance to acknowledge collaborators in his work? The perceptive Francis Wyndham wrote that 'the rich and famous and fulfilled man whom the world sees still considers himself a victim maimed for life by that early catastrophic shock'. Perhaps it was a necessary part of the therapy, essential to his confidence, always to tell himself that he had conquered the world and raised himself from poverty and nonentity to universal fame and affection unaided. No other film maker ever so completely dominated every aspect of the work, did every job. If he could have done so Chaplin would have played every role and (as his son Sydney humorously but perceptively observed) sewn every costume. Chaplin had both the compulsion to do everything and the need to know that he had done everything.

Whatever psychological explanations may be adduced, many were hurt by these omissions in *My Autobiography*. Most vocally offended was Robert Florey, who had begun to write about Chaplin more than forty years before, had published an affectionate biography in 1927 and had maintained his loyalty until this time. His review in *Paris-Match* was very largely an appreciation of those dozens of people left out of the autobiography, including Georgia Hale, Wheeler Dryden, Henry Bergman, Albert Austin, Stan Laurel and Mabel Smith, 'who regularly (if not infallibly) predicted the future for him'.

For all its lacunae the autobiography was a very considerable achievement – wonderfully readable, amiably opinionated, disarmingly frank, sometimes pompous and the next moment self-deprecatory in poking fun at the writer's own human vanities and affections. It was widely translated and the warmth of the reception across the world seemed to give new energy to Chaplin. As soon as the book was finished he set about preparing a new film. Jerry Epstein was to be producer and Universal provided distribution backing. The film was *A Countess From Hong Kong*.

19

A COUNTESS FROM HONG KONG
and the final years

The subject of *A Countess From Hong Kong* was a refurbishment of *Stowaway*, the script Chaplin had written for Paulette almost thirty years before. Only random pages and notes have survived from the original *Stowaway* script: the rest seems to have been cannibalized in compiling the new screenplay. There were few changes to the story. In the early version the Countess came from Shanghai; now she was from Hong Kong. The hero, Ogden Mears, was changed from a big game hunter to a millionaire and diplomat. *Stowaway* would probably have compared very well with the average situation comedy of the late 1930s. The dialogue was crisp and light and Chaplin felt able to adopt it in large part for *A Countess From Hong Kong*.

The new script opens in traditional Chaplin style with a subtitle: 'As a result of two world wars, Hong Kong was crowded with refugees.' Some of the most glamorous of these are employed as taxi-girls at 'The Palace of Beautiful Women' where, for a few dollars, American sailors may dance with former White Russian baronesses and countesses. (Neither Chaplin nor the critics were greatly bothered about the chronology: after two world wars, exiles from the Revolution of 1917 might well be supposed to be past the dancing age.) One of these aristocratic taxi-girls, the beautiful Natascha Alexandroff, finds herself dancing with Ogden Mears, an American millionaire doing the night spots of Hong Kong.

Ogden returns to his suite on the luxury liner after his heavy night out and the next morning discovers that Natascha has stowed away there. The likely embarrassment of the situation is compounded by the news that he has just been appointed United States Ambassador

608

to Arabia. Ogden is softened by Natascha's recital of her sad life story, of how she fled to Shanghai from Russia and became a gangster's mistress at the tender age of fourteen. Now she seeks only the escape that an American passport could provide. Ogden reluctantly hides her in his suite, which results in a succession of alarms and embarrassments. To obtain the nececessary American passport for Natascha, Ogden arranges a marriage of convenience with Hudson, his valet – who is all too clearly not the marrying kind. At Honolulu Ogden's wife comes aboard. Natascha dives over the side of the ship into the harbour. Ogden and his wife come to an amicable divorce agreement. Millionaire and pauper countess are happily reunited in a tango.

While Chaplin was preparing *A Countess From Hong Kong*, the last personal link with his childhood was broken. At 11 p.m. on 16 April 1965 – Chaplin's seventy-sixth birthday – his brother Sydney died in Nice. He was eighty. His death occurred at the Hotel Ruhl, where he and his Niçoise wife Gypsy spent each winter. The following day Chaplin arrived in Nice for the cremation in Marseilles. Sydney's ashes were buried in Montreux.

The two brothers had seen each other frequently during the last years of Sydney's life and no doubt their sessions of reminiscence, as well as delighting Gypsy, Oona and the family, contributed much to *My Autobiography*. Sydney and Gypsy generally visited Switzerland during the summers, and both were adored by the children at Vevey. Gypsy was amusing, charming and elegant, and maintained an intriguing air of mystery: she would never discuss her life before her marriage to Sydney. Sydney, who had never had a family of his own, loved chldren. The young Chaplins for their part were enchanted by his still prodigious facility for inventing gags and jokes. From Nice he would write long letters to the older children, with page upon page of jokes. (He kept carbon copies to be sure that he did not repeat himself next time.) On visits to the Manoir he found a mischievous way of teasing his younger brother. He would tell the girls some mildly off-colour or racist joke and send them off in fits of giggles to retail it to their father. Sydney would then sit innocently by, hearing his brother raging in the distance, 'Never let me hear jokes like that in this house!' Geraldine and Josephine remember too, though, how in old age their cheerful and ebullient uncle would sit at the window of the Manoir watching the beauty of the sun setting over the mountains, and cry.

During the summer of 1965 Chaplin was co-recipient with Ingmar Bergman of the Erasmus Prize. On 11 November he gave a press conference for two hundred journalists at the Savoy Hotel to announce his plans for *A Countess From Hong Kong*. Sophia Loren was present. The writer was there on that occasion:

> Is it thrilling, asked a friend, to see him in the flesh for the first time? And the answer is that somehow it isn't: more of a puzzle rather, to try to find in this spry, well-fed, lively, neatly turned-out figure in dark glasses (and not nearly as small as I had always imagined) either the old Charlie, or a man well on his way toward eighty. Bright-eyed, clear-voiced, quick-talking, he is, if not exactly youthful, fairly ageless. It is, of course, from use that he is able to remain quite untroubled by being the focus of a heavy stampede of pressmen and photographers such as was produced by his press conference at the Savoy . . .
>
> There is never much to be learned from this kind of affair; anyone who is good at it, like Chaplin, knows exactly what he wants to say, and however irrelevant the questions may be, the answers will all quickly come back to the point. And the point in this instance was that Mr Chaplin was going to make a new film. For the first time in nearly half a century he would not be his own producer: 'And it's wonderful. I don't have to worry. I can extend myself as I please, and it is only my fault if the picture doesn't come off.' No expense would be spared. The film would be in colour and have a fourteen-week shooting schedule. What was the budget? 'I don't think that's anybody's business,' he said, but very amiably.
>
> Mr Chaplin had, he said, two great stars, Marlon Brando and Sophia Loren. He had seen Sophia in a film and known at once that she was perfect for the part. What was the film? He really couldn't remember; it was so long ago. Was it *Marriage, Italian Style*? No, no, it wasn't that. Was it *Yesterday, Today and Tomorrow*? Yes. Yes – that was the film. Anyway, she was perfect for the part . . .
>
> The picture would be called *A Countess From Hong Kong*. He had wanted to call it *The Countess*, but someone already had rights on that title. He had had the screenplay since the time of *The Great Dictator*, but he'd up-dated it. He would not say much about the story, except that it is set in the period just after the Second World War, and a lot of the action takes place aboard ship.
>
> Asked to be more precise, Mr Chaplin said he was sorry but he was

tired; which he clearly was not. He would only add modestly that, 'the situation is riotously funny but justified and believable . . . It is not slapstick, but comedy of character, taken from life.

'I have no role myself, thank God! No, it's not the first time I've directed and not played. Around 1924 [*sic*] I made a film called *A Woman of Paris* . . . Of course, I may walk on, like Hitchcock does . . .'

Chaplin said that his son Sydney would play in it. 'He's a very good comedian and I think he will contribute to the lift and hilarity of the screenplay.' (Chaplin always chooses his words carefully, if sometimes curiously.) Inevitably the columnists asked if his son Michael would play. Chaplin was grave. 'I'm not answering any personal questions . . .' and when the newsman tried to insist, 'Don't try to get smart-alecky with me . . .' He was not so solemn when asked about America. He had no plans to go there unless it happened to be in connexion with the picture, but in any case he had no quarrel with Hollywood. 'I wrote a book, and I think America came out of it pretty well. I happen to like Hollywood. Anyway I don't think that's pertaining much to the picture.'

Mr Chaplin answered a few more questions. How did it feel to be at work again? 'Marvellous. Thank God I'm still active. I can still think up two or three laughs. I'm getting on, but right now I have everything before me. The whole world is my oyster.' ('His what?' the reporter who had quizzed him about his son asked a friend.) What did he think about A. J. P Taylor's new book, in which Taylor linked him with Shakespeare as a cultural influence? 'I think he has damn' good judgement,' said Mr Chaplin merrily. ('Linked him with who?' asked the same reporter.)[1]

Shooting began on 25 January 1966. Intrepid as ever, Chaplin – who was to celebrate his seventy-seventh birthday in the course of the filming – now undertook his first film in colour and on the anamorphic screen which he had derided in *A King in New York*. This was also the first time that he had cast and directed major international stars – Sophia Loren and Marlon Brando. As in *A Woman of Paris* he allotted himself only a brief walk-on. He was fortunate to have a director of photography, Arthur Ibbetson, and a designer, Don Ashton, who revered him and were responsive and sympathetic to his demands. Moreover in terms of production the film was comparatively simple. Though the action required skilful playing, it was mostly set in interiors, particularly the adjoining rooms of Ogden's ship-board suite. Despite an interruption when Chaplin suffered a bad bout of 'flu, shooting was completed in fourteen working weeks. Charles Chaplin directed what was to prove his last scene on Wednesday 11 May 1966, fifty-two years and three months after his Keystone debut.

Much later Marlon Brando spoke disparagingly of the experience of working on the film: schooled in 'Method' acting he was bewildered by Chaplin's intuitive and pragmatic approach to performance, and not resourceful enough easily to submit himself to Chaplin's requirement that his actors should reproduce his own interpretation of a part. The film critic Penelope Gilliatt visited the set, and described how Brando one day told Chaplin that he did not understand the character's motivation at a particular point in the action. Chaplin cheerfully replied that he did not understand the motivation either, but that it probably did not amount to much. He went on to explain to Brando exactly how to play the action: that way, he said, it would come off. This sort of thing must certainly have been disconcerting for the actor; but Mrs Gilliatt remarked upon Brando's conscientiousness in following Chaplin's minute instructons on every line or gag. Sophia Loren adored Chaplin and proved wonderfully responsive to his direction. Chaplin thought Patrick Cargill's performance as Hudson the valet entirely admirable: 'I've never done anything as *funny*,' he told Francis Wyndham. In supporting roles he had Tippi Hedren, his son Sydney and Oliver Johnston. Chaplin liked his unit, and it was one of his happiest shooting periods.

Among the visitors to the set during the shooting of *A Countess From Hong Kong* was Kevin Brownlow, the historian of the silent cinema, who had accompanied Gloria Swanson to Pinewood. It was the first time that Swanson had been on a Chaplin set since she appeared in *His New Job* in 1915.*

> Finally, Chaplin had to leave to go on the set. Miss Swanson perched on a ladder to get a better view over the obstructing lights. Sophia Loren, devastating in her low-cut white dress, was joined by Marlon Brando in a blue dressing gown, looking furious. A wave of tension followed him as he shuffled from behind the camera onto the set.
>
> Chaplin seemed oblivious. As he directed Loren, and then Brando, I scribbled down the directions verbatim. He tried to work out a way in which Loren could walk over to Brando, holding a glass. He paid no attention to dialogue. I heard him give only one dialogue direction. He may have written the words, but he could not remember them. 'So-and-so-and-so-and-so etcetera,' would be his delivery of an average line.

* On this occasion, Swanson insisted she had not played in the film.

The associate producer, Jerry Epstein, paced behind him, reading the correct lines from a script. The set was a cabin of a luxury liner; at one point, Chaplin stood by the cabin door and looked across at Epstein.

'This walk lays an egg,' he said, and laughed. Then he stalked back to his director's chair beneath the camera and shouted, 'Go over there, make up your mind, take it.'

The action did not proceed smoothly. Brando, sullen, kept saying, 'All right, all right.' He did not seem to be listening as Chaplin instructed him again. Finally, Chaplin got up and walked back onto the set.

'You go, open the door, "Excuse me-so-and-so-and-so."' He paused, and gave a classical, balletic Chaplin gesture. 'All right, you're here . . . come to the door . . . and say, "I'm etcetera, etcetera."'

Brando came in and did a tolerably good, if lifeless scene, ignoring the Chaplinesque gesture; at the end he uttered, 'Oh, no!'

Chaplin interjected a long-drawn-out, 'O-o-oh, n-o-o-o!' Then he hurried in to make adjustments. 'We'll have to do the same choreography.' He went through the moves, ignoring the dialogue, and then turned to the director of photography, Arthur Ibbetson.

'I think that will be the first close-up till we get it natural and sincere,' he said, crossing his chest with his arm to indicate the limit of the close-up.

He stood by and watched a run-through of the scene. Then he said, 'I think that's all right,' and took his hat off, revealing a shock of pure white hair.

Gloria Swanson leaned forward: 'You can see why actors find him difficult,' she whispered. 'This is a simple scene, and he's making much ado about nothing . . .'

Having worked out a bit of business for Brando, Chaplin did it himself, combining Chaplinesque grace with the suggestive vulgarity of the music hall. He picked up an imaginary glass of Alka-Seltzer and drained the contents, leaning his head right back. Then he gave a funny belch, and laughed at his audience – the rows of technicians, who laughed back. Brando gave no visible reaction. Chaplin did it again; he took the non-existent glass, drank deeply, and burped. It didn't quite work. 'We'll put that on sound,' he said, gesturing vaguely off set.

Then, still thinking out the scene, he walked up and down, clenched fist held at forehead in classical style.*

When Brando tried the scene, he used a real glass with no contents, and took a short draft. Chaplin sprang forward.

'No – you're going to take longer to do that, you know.' The old

---

* In 1982, when searching with his co-director David Gill for material for *Unknown Chaplin*, Brownlow was thrilled to find some shots of Chaplin in the same attitude, taken during the making of *The Count* just fifty years before *A Countess From Hong Kong*.

professional advising the young apprentice. And he demonstrated the whole gesture, going all the way back, swallowing the Alka-Seltzer, and belching at the end of it. Brando followed most of Chaplin's instructions, but he then achieved two startlingly realistic belches which effectively killed the comedy.

Rumours about Brando's temperamental behaviour were circulating widely at this stage of the production. Later, press reports indicated that all was harmonious. But at this point, it was clear that Brando was expected to imitate Chaplin rather than to develop his own performance. For such a great dramatic actor, such direction must have been bewildering.

For the onlooker, however, such direction was miraculous. It was as exciting as watching a Chaplin film no one knew existed; first he played the Brando role, then he skipped over and did the Loren part. One was aggressively masculine, the other provocative and feminine, yet both remained pure Charlie. It is a real loss to the cinema that Chaplin refused to allow a film to be made about the production.

On the way back to London Gloria Swanson reflected:

Well, wasn't *that* a nostalgic time for me. To walk on that set and be greeted with open arms! He looked as fit as a fiddle. He was bouncing in and out of his chair. Frankly, he didn't look a day older than when I'd last seen him, seven years ago. Did you notice that he isn't as articulate with words as he is in pantomime, when showing people what he wants? What an artist. I suppose he is the most creative man it is possible to meet.[2]

A week before the end of shooting, Chaplin got into costume for his final film role. He plays an elderly steward who is a victim of severe *mal de mer*. It was a favourite joke for him, and he played his exit scene in the same silent mime as in his earliest screen appearances.

Chaplin composed seventeen musical themes, which were orchestrated by Eric James and conducted by Lambert Williamson. The theme song, 'This is my Song', was to become a popular hit. The film was ready for release in the New Year. Chaplin had found it 'such fun to do, I thought the whole world was going to go mad for it.' However he had misgivings at the London press show, when the projector kept breaking down and the image was badly focused.* The notices confirmed his worst fears. The kindest adopted a patronizing 'more in sorrow than in anger' tone. A major problem with the film

---

* On the foyer steps he encountered a total stranger. 'They're ruining my film,' he wailed, and passed on.

was that, in the year of *Bonnie and Clyde*, *The Dirty Dozen*, *The Graduate*, *Weekend* and *Belle de Jour*, a gentle romantic comedy was an almost incomprehensible anachronism.

Chaplin, publicly at least, took a bravely truculent stance in the face of the rebuffs and declared to the press that the British critics were 'bloody idiots'. He felt this opinion vindicated when the film opened in Europe. *Paris-Match* said that the film was 'a charming comedy [which] did not deserve the severity of the British Press.' *Le Figaro*'s headline was 'In London Thorns – In Paris Roses', and *Paris Jour*'s was 'Paris makes Chaplin even with London'. In Italy *Unità* also had a headline: 'Demolishing Critical Reviews of British and American Press are Unjustified'; and in Sweden the critic of *Dagens Nyhatet* said 'It is difficult to understand the objections raised by the English critics ... His picture of the world, naïvely warm and generous, unveiling and disarming, uncoils again.' Not all the English-speaking critics were without sympathy. In New York William Wolf wrote in *Cue* Magazine, 'I have returned from a second look at *A Countess From Hong Kong*. Again, I found it charming, funny and a welcome change of pace from our frenetic, super-sophisticated milieu. Chaplin could never be counted on to come up with the expected, and that is a mark of his genius.'

Chaplin spoke at length of his reactions to the reviews in a long interview with Francis Wyndham, which provides fascinating insights into Chaplin's view of the world as he witnessed it in his seventies:

> With my next film, I won't open in London. I'll open in Kalamazoo or somewhere and leave London till later. I don't understand what's happening there now. I think they're swinging drunk. It's a peculiar sort of desperation and somnambulism, a negation of art, of any sort of simplicity. When the swinging thing is over, what will they have left? I don't believe there is such a thing as fashion. Who the hell creates the fashion anyway? Anybody can – something very facile that catches on and everybody imitates. Cynics – so what? Life is cynical if we think only in terms of birth and death. It's too easy. How ironic that my theme song for the *Countess* is a big hit all over the world. They throw away the flesh of the peach ...
>
> Soon they'll come to their senses and start having a good time. Every once in a while you see a ray of light, someone behind the camera with a sensitive hand. But more often on TV than in the cinema. I saw a TV play called *The Caretaker* which was very mysterious and interesting. And I was amused by *Goldfinger*: one scene I thought so funny, when the whole army falls down gassed during the robbery of Fort Knox! But

Dr Zhivago seemed very banal to me – that ridiculous scene when he writes a poem by candlelight! And *Blow-up* was so slow and boring. I wouldn't go on for hours to work up to an eventual striptease. Or pretend that this man doesn't notice a murder.

So much has been done already. I saw a bit of a Beatle film, and it had that old, old gag, a bubble bath! We did all this stop action business in 1914: it was very dull then and nobody paid much attention. Knock 'em down, drag 'em up, all those impossible Keystone gimmicks – it's all right, but they put it on in such a pretentious way now. There's a quick phase for thinking it smart and swinging. It's just what a little boy would do, the most inarticulate thing really, like dribbling. It says nothing – but the intellectuals find it very profound.

The reviews of my pictures have always been mixed. The only one *everybody* praised was *The Kid* – and then they went too far, talked about Shakespeare. Well, it wasn't *that*! But what shocked me about the English reviews of the *Countess* was the fact that they were unanimous. And they seemed so personal, an attack on *me*. All they were interested in was 'Chaplin has a flop'. In the old days, critics could slaughter quite a good play with just one quip. But there was nothing like that – these were so dull! Why couldn't they poke fun at it? Where's *their* humour, for God's sake? They picked on such puerile things to say – 'Brando is wooden' – but that's just the whole point!

I think it's the best thing I've done. I can be more objective about it than the pictures I've acted in, which can be very irksome and give me terrible inferiority complexes. It's full of invention, which I always like, and though it seems to be very simply constructed, it took a long time to motivate it, to work out the cause and effect. And it has great charm – what more do they want? Things like *The Gold Rush* – one, two, three, pantry cakey – it's so easy. A situation comedy like the *Countess* is much more difficult to keep going . . . The humour of the *Countess* may not be mechanical, but the situations are excruciating. The critics now are terrified of being old-fashioned, but this picture is ten years ahead of its time.

I think it is the first time it's ever happened – a realistic treatment of an incredible situation. That was the thing that excited me. My other films were something else entirely, caricatures of Cruikshank's drawings are caricatures. But this is Cruikshank. The characters react realistically in impossible situations . . . At first Brando was frightened of a funny part, terrified of business, but I told him not to worry as the character was meant to be humourless. And he brought off the realism. Except in the belch scene, which we couldn't get right. He thought the point was the belch – but the point was the man's dignified behaviour. And Sophia does a little quiet clowning. She wanted to be much more facetious but I said, give the audience a treat, let them do some of it for you.

Between you and me and the gatepost, it's a very sad story. This man who leaves his icicle of a wife for a girl who's a whore. I think the end, where they're dancing, is tragic. Perhaps his love for her is just a passing thing, as happens to us all.

At first, when I read the reviews, I wondered. Then I went again the next day, and regained all my confidence. Because the audience were loving it . . .

The visual thing in *Countess* is very obvious. That's its great charm, that it *is* obvious. I was always having trouble with people saying, 'Put the camera there', or 'You must have a close-up now'. I want to make films as I *feel* – there aren't any rules. The fuss they make about continuity! You see a handkerchief in somebody's pocket in one shot, and in the next it's gone. Who cares? If the shot is funny, I keep it in. It's a question of values – if the audiences are looking at the *handkerchief* something's wrong with the scene anyhow! In *Shoulder Arms* there's a bit where I have a gun on my back, then I get my finger caught in a mouse-trap and the gun has disappeared then it's back again in the next shot. Glaring – but *nobody* has ever commented on it.

Now I'm working on another film. The trouble is that as I get older, I get more and more interested in beauty. I want things to be beautiful. I'm wondering whether this isn't a moribund period of art. Aesthetics have gone into things like space and science – those beautiful airships: utility at its height. No artist could compete with that.[3]

Chaplin put a brave face on things, but those closest to him understood that he had suffered a severe blow from the criticism of his film. The year brought other irritations. As a result of the publicity attendant on his claim for National Assistance benefits for himself, his wife and child, Michael Chaplin was approached by the publishers Leslie Frewin in March 1965. On 17 April he and his wife Patrice signed contracts agreeing to write his life story in conjunction with two journalists, Charles Hamblett and Tom Merritt, who were to receive a proportion of the royalties. A book was rather swiftly written, in which the two 'ghosts' attributed to young Chaplin an awful, breezy hip style and vocabulary. Michael at first approved the text, but then changed his mind and appealed to the family lawyers, the formidable Richards, Butler and Co. On 26 August Richards, Butler wrote to Leslie Frewin, claiming to avoid and repudiate the agreement of 17 April on the grounds that the plaintiff was a minor. They further alleged that the text contained material seriously defamatory both of the plaintiff and of other persons. Through Richards, Butler (and, as a minor, suing by Patrice as 'his wife and next friend') Michael sought an interlocutory injunction to prevent publication of the book until the trial. The injunction was granted by Mr Justice Waller on 20 September but the Court of Appeal supported the defendant's appeal on 25 October. Michael was given leave to appeal. to the House of Lords and duly lodged his petition. The appeal was withdrawn, however, after the parties got together and agreed on a revised text. Michael agreed to make a substantial contribution from the royalties which would accrue to him when the book was published, to reimburse the publishers for the costs and expenses in which his change of heart had involved him.

Despite the objectionable period style and the title (*I Couldn't Smoke the Grass on My Father's Lawn . . .*) the book, which emerged at the end of the year, is often touching as an intelligent, generous and sensitive youth's reflections on the difficulties of being son to a genius. Despite his resentments at what he perceived as heavy-handed and unsympathetic parental regulation of his life (he instances the employment of private detectives to frighten him off 'unsuitable' friendships), the book still affirms real affecton and admiration for both parents:

> My father is not like any other father. Complex, gifted, strangely creative, his irrationalities have never been those of the average commuter. He was, and is, to put it mildly, a bit of a handful as a father. I first became aware of the general impression that he is an exceptional man through the reactions of other people towards him. Visitors whose names at the time didn't mean a thing but who, in retrospect, turned out to be Noël Coward, Graham Greene, Jean Cocteau, Truman Capote, Ian Fleming, and sundry other types, and who greeted him like a god on furlough from Olympus. There was also a fairly constant traffic of suitably awed interviewers, photographers, intellectuals, painters, actors, socialites and name-droppers; and whenever these showed up at the Manoir de Ban, my father's spread in Switzerland, they cast and, in turn, reflected the aura of greatness around the old guy.
>
> There must have been a time when my unformed infant instincts and undeveloped mind simply sensed and felt this man as a kindly, volatile, moody, gay, self-absorbed, inventive, funny, affectionate, stern, sad, brilliant, autocratic, irrational, snobbish, splendid, silly, unjust, loving, perceptive, indifferent, sensitive, cruel, jolly, extension-in-reverse of my own flesh and thought and feelings; a time when I was, quite naturally, just another limb of the father-octopus. There must have been a time, perhaps in the big house in Beverly Hills, California, which was our home before my father settled in Europe, when I may have been able to take

for granted my surroundings and family and my father as head of the household.

But I cannot remember such a time . . .

To be the son of a great man can be a disadvantage; it is like living next to a huge monument; one spends one's life circling around it, either to remain in the shade, or to avoid its shadow. But then people brought up in an orphanage, when trying to find out where they stand in relation to the world, often spend the rest of their lives searching for such a monument.[4]

While he was still editing *A Countess From Hong Kong*, on 11 October 1966, Chaplin was walking with Jerry Epstein outside Pinewood Studios when he tripped on a piece of uneven pavement and broke his ankle. Epstein helped him into the studio first aid centre, and he was taken to Slough hospital where his foot was encased in a 12-inch plaster. 'This is most humiliating,' was Chaplin's comment. 'It is just a nuisance. I'll be back in a day or so.' He was right. He was outstandingly fit for his age, and was soon about again. But it was the first time in his life that he had broken a limb; and it was the end of that phenomenal mobility that had permitted him to play tennis right up to this time. It is possible that around this time also he had the first of a series of almost imperceptible strokes. From this moment Charles Chaplin was obliged to acknowledge the onset of old age.

Not that old age could stem the phenomenal urge to create. He launched immediately into a new idea, *The Freak*, a dramatic comedy about a young girl who awakes one morning to find that she has sprouted wings. The role was designed for his third daughter, Victoria. Geraldine and Josephine had already embarked on acting careers (both appear briefly in *A Countess From Hong Kong*). Chaplin considered however that Victoria had supremely inherited the gift of comedy. The talent was all the more piquant for her extraordinary, luminous beauty, concentrated in the same searching, melancholy eyes as Chaplin's own Tramp. Over the next two years Chaplin worked doggedly on writing and revising the script, and the wings which Victoria was to wear in the film were made and tried.

In 1969 Victoria met and fell in love with Jean-Baptiste Thierrée, a young French actor who had had a considerable success in Alain Resnais's film *Muriel*, but whose heart was set on making a career as a clown and creating his own circus. Without telling her parents,

Victoria left home to join him: shortly afterwards they were married, and Victoria also dedicated herself to becoming a circus performer. It was for a time a bitter blow to Chaplin, who saw it as a serious set-back to his plans for *The Freak*. Meanwhile Oona and Jerry Epstein, who was to have produced the film, had been forced to recognize that Chaplin's physical strength was not any more likely to be equal to his creative will.

Since *A Countess From Hong Kong*, he had too, suffered a personal bereavement which struck him hard. Charles Chaplin, his elder son by Lita Gray, died at his mother's home in California on 20 March 1968. He was forty-three. Charles Chaplin Junior, as his book about his own relations with his father, *My Father, Charlie Chaplin* (1960) attests, was a charming, warm-hearted young man, whose life had not been fortunate. His career as an actor had not been as rewarding as his brother's; he had acquired a drinking problem during his army service; and he had suffered from two failed marriages. His death resulted from a badly-tended injury received in a fall, which produced a fatal thrombosis.

By the start of the 1970s, Chaplin's energies were engaged on the renewed exploitation of his old films. He had for some time considered leasing out the distribution rights in them. In this way he could secure a very considerable advance and pass on to someone else the task of turning the films to the maximum profit. Both Jerry Epstein and Sydney Chaplin were interested in being involved in such an arrangement. On one occasion Sydney was so sure that he could persuade his father to let him take on distribution that he took to Vevey a potential partner, the producer Sandy Lieberson – who was subsequently to become head of production for, successively, Twentieth Century Fox and Goldcrest Films. Sydney and Lieberson arrived for lunch, which proceeded with great cordiality until Sydney ventured to speak of his proposition, at which Chaplin became enraged. Lieberson still recalls the dreadful embarrassment at being witness to the family row which followed, and their eventual ignominious retreat from the Manoir.

Rachel Ford recommended as a suitable candidate for the distribution deal a former United Artists executive, Moses Rothman, whose effectiveness as a salesman was held in awe throughout Hollywood. Rothman formed a company punningly named Black Inc. to distribute the Chaplin films, and advanced $6,000,000 against the 50 per cent of net proceeds which would go to Chaplin's Roy Export Company

Establishment. Black Inc. were reputed to have recouped the initial advance from sales to Japan alone.

Rothman proved both an astute businessman and a master publicist. Part of the agreement was that Chaplin would assist in publicizing the re-release of the films by discreet and undemanding personal appearances; the acclamation which resulted from these seems to have given Chaplin much interest and satisfaction in his last years. It also provided work to compensate for the set-back to *The Freak*, though it is unlikely that Chaplin ever gave up hope of making the film. In 1970 he composed a new score for *The Circus* and recorded the theme song 'Swing, Little Girl' himself: at eighty he still possessed a pleasant and hardly shaky baritone. In November 1971 Chaplin attested his satisfaction with the Black Inc. deal by throwing in, as a present, *The Kid* and *The Idle Class* (with new musical scores) which had been excluded from the original arrangement.

The world now competed to heap honours upon him. In 1971 the Twenty-fifth Cannes Film Festival made a special award for his total *oeuvre*; at the same time he was invested as Commander of the Légion d'Honneur. Now, at last, America wanted to make amends. The Academy of Motion Picture Arts and Sciences decided to award him an Honorary 'Oscar', and proffered a joint invitation with the Lincoln Center Film Society in New York. The old McGranery prohibitions on his return had long been forgotten. Chaplin was at first hesitant about accepting the invitation: according to Ted Tetrick he was finally swayed by the prospect of inspecting a new camera that was likely to facilitate process work on *The Freak*. The Chaplins decided to have a few days' holiday and rest in Bermuda (where Oona was born and still owned a property she had inherited from her father) before travelling to the United States. They arrived in New York on 2 April 1972, to be greeted at Kennedy Airport by a hundred or so newsmen. Chaplin blew them kisses as he rather slowly descended the steps from the plane and made his way to a waiting limousine, which drove them to the Plaza. That evening Gloria Vanderbilt Cooper, a girlhood friend of Oona's, gave a party for them in her town house. The guests included Lillian Gish, Adolph Green, Geraldine Fitzgerald, Truman Capote and George Plimpton. The following evening the Chaplins attended a cocktail party in their hotel (they arrived late) before going on to the Philharmonic Hall for the gala performance in tribute to him and in aid of Lincoln Center Film Society. The audience consisted of 1500 people who had paid

$10 and $25 admission, and a further 1200 who had paid $100 and $250 for the dressy champagne reception afterwards. They cheered his entrance into the hall; they cheered the films – *The Kid* and *The Idle Class* – and at the end gave him an astonishing and moving ovation. Many of the audience, like Chaplin himself, were in tears. When the applause permitted, he spoke into a microphone: 'This is my renaissance,' he said. 'I'm being born again. It's easy for you, but it's very difficult for me to speak tonight, because I feel very emotional. However, I'm glad to be among so many friends. Thank you.'

The champagne reception proved a greater ordeal. Chaplin had requested that his table not be cordoned off. In consequence, said *Time*, the crowd 'made a surging subway jam of black ties and décolletage, pressing around the table.' Somebody produced a derby and Chaplin mugged a little for the photographers. When Congresswoman Bella Abzug leaned across his table he exclaimed to her in excitement, 'The audience. The audience. *Everybody* was in the audience.' Among those who managed to fight their way to his table were Claire Bloom and Paulette, who talked to him for a couple of minutes. Most of his life Chaplin had been used to crowds and, for all the confusion, *Time* noted that when he left with Oona, protected by policemen, 'his face was alight with pleasure.'

He had initially been nervous about his reception in the United States, but this first experience gave him confidence. The following day he walked in a quiet part of Central Park and lunched at the '21' Club as the guest of a Manhattan Councillor, Carter Borden. When he entered the dining room there was a burst of applause, and a waiter proudly told him that he had served him the last time he lunched at the '21', in 1952. 'Well, thank you,' said Chaplin. 'I didn't think I'd ever be back, you know.' Among those who came to his table to pay their respects was George Jessel, a pillar of the right, and Jack Gilford. He did not remember Jessel and did not know Gilford: 'I didn't know many actors in California,' he recalled; 'I was mostly alone there. It was always hard for me to make friends. I was shy and inarticulate. Doug Fairbanks was my only real friend, and I was a showpiece for him at parties.'

After lunch Richard Avedon, who had photographed Chaplin when he passed through the city in 1952, came to the suite in the Plaza for a new sitting. After that the Chaplins went to Gracie Hall where Mayor Lindsay presented him with the Handel Medallion, New York's highest cultural award. The photographers asked him to smile and Chaplin, now full of the old confidence, cracked back, 'I'm afraid my teeth might fall out,' and cupped his hand beneath his chin.

At the end of the week Chaplin flew to Hollywood with Oona to receive his special Oscar for his 'incalculable effect in making motion pictures the art form of the century'. Candice Bergen accompanied them, on a reporting assignment for *Life*:

> During the flight, he crossed to the other side of the plane to see the Grand Canyon. His face lit up. 'Oh, yes, this is the place where Doug Fairbanks did a handstand on the precipice. He told me about it.'
>
> As they got nearer Los Angeles, he grew more and more nervous, sure he shouldn't have come. He looked fearful and trapped but made a brave attempt to fight it. 'Oh well,' he sighed, 'it wasn't so bad. After all, I met Oona there.'[5]

As he drove through the city he was disappointed to find it changed and unfamiliar. The new owners of his old studio, A. & M. Records, were very proud of the Chaplin connexion, had voluntarily sought to have the buildings declared a national monument and thus protected against alteration, and had established a Chaplin museum in the reception area. They planned to welcome Chaplin back there, and had decorated the place with scores of specially printed flags bearing his portrait. Chaplin could not face it. He arranged to pass the studio on Sunday, when it was closed, and contented himself with looking through the gates.

Some familiar faces from long ago appeared among the worshipping crowds. One was Tim Durant:

> When Charlie arrived, I got a call from a Mrs Walter Matthau. She was a great friend of Oona's and she said, 'I'm giving a lunch for Charlie and would you come next Sunday?' I said, 'Yes, I'll come up right after church. It'll be great to see him' . . . Greer Garson was here in the church, and I asked her to go up with me . . . As I came in, I saw this small table. They were waiting for us: we were a little bit late. I think Lewis Milestone and his wife were there, and one or two others . . . Charlie was across and as I sat down I looked over at him and he seemed to be preoccupied with the people coming up there. He hardly recognized me, you know. We were there about half an hour, and still he didn't respond at all. I tried to catch his eye a few times, and he'd go to move away. He was talking rather aimlessly to people as they came up, not remembering their names, I'm sure. I know how he used to fake that – call them dear friend and so forth. I'd done it myself. I felt, well, Charlie's forgotten about me. I felt rather badly about it, but strangely enough, when the lunch was over he

got up on his feet and he came over to me and looked me right in the eye and said, 'Tim, you and I were buddies once.' Well, tears came to my eyes – I couldn't help it. I sort of grasped him and hugged him and I said, 'Listen, we still are, Charlie.' So I said goodbye to him, and I thought, this is it . . . But then his English secretary called and asked me to come over – they had a cottage at the Beverly Hills Hotel. So I went over there, and as I came in, Charlie opened the front door.

He was talking to a very good-looking young girl, which was typical. She looked about seventeen or eighteen – remember he married all those girls you know, and they all wanted careers and they didn't want Charlie after a while. They weren't as good an audience as I was. Anyway he was talking to her, and the first thing he said to her as he saw me, he said, 'Look at that man there,' he said; 'Now you keep away from him. He's a dangerous man. Don't have anything to do with him, remember that now.'

He was kidding, you know; and I walked in and he introduced me to his granddaughter; and I had a lovely visit with him there.[6]

On another occasion he met Georgia Hale. Georgia had kept her figure and wore blonde shoulder-length hair and long eyelashes. Chaplin affected indignation that she should seem so young while he was suffering the infirmities of age. 'Perhaps, after all, it is your faith,' he told her. 'You should have shared it with me.' It was an ironic joke: in the days of their friendship he had always forbidden her even to speak about religion in his presence.[7]

There was a still more touching reunion. At one of the Hollywood functions which Chaplin attended, Jackie Coogan and his wife were present. They attempted to approach Chaplin's table but Walter Matthau, aiming to protect Chaplin from harassment, fiercely barred their way. 'Either he didn't recognize Jackie,' Coogan's son, Anthony speculates, 'or he *did* recognize him and remembered that there was a time when Jackie could be quite a trouble-maker.' Somehow the Coogans were got past the bodyguard. Jackie was now the bald, stout, 57-year-old man who played Uncle Fester. Chaplin had hardly seen him since he was the Kid, yet he took one look at him and burst into tears. They threw their arms around each other and Chaplin said, 'What a pleasure to see you . . . little boy.' Then, while Jackie and Oona were talking, he gripped Mrs Coogan's arm and pulled her till her face was close to his, and murmured emphatically: 'You must never forget. Your husband is a genius.'[8]

The Oscar show was another great emotional occasion. Chaplin and Oona watched it on a television monitor in a dressing room backstage, delightedly recognizing friends in the audience. Chaplin had had an irrational fear that nobody would turn up. When he accepted his presentation, he was too overcome to stammer out more than a tearful thankyou but he managed a bit of business with a derby, making it spring up from his head as he had in the old silents.

Afterward, as he talked about the ceremony, his eyes were bright and childlike, wide with wonder, round with glee. 'It almost made me cry – and *this* one,' he cocked his head at a beaming Oona, 'this one kept saying, "Oh, don't snivel."

'It was so *emotional* and the *audience – their* emotion. I thought some of them might hiss, but they were so *sweet* – all those famous people, all those artists. You know, they haven't done this to me before. It surpasses everything.'

He looked around for his Oscar and couldn't see it. '*Oh, no,*' he wailed, 'all those sweet people and I've *lost* it.' It was retrieved and put back serenely.

More and more he began to look like an English schoolboy, grinning impishly, rolling his eyes up innocently, pointing a freckled hand to himself, announcing playfully, 'The genius . . .'

Suddenly summoning that old agility, he flew from his chair. Eyes twinkling, he said, with mock impatience, 'Let's go and celebrate, for God's sake!'

And happily humming his song 'Smile!' he took Oona's arm and stepped out grandly through the door.[9]

Two years later, away from the euphoria, Chaplin commented in his book *My Life in Pictures*, 'I was touched by the gesture, but there was a certain irony about it somehow.'

In September 1972 he was given a special award of the Golden Lion of the Venice Film Festival. On the final day of the Festival, St Mark's Square was converted into a huge open-air cinema for a showing of *City Lights*. It was arranged that Chaplin would appear on a balcony overlooking the square for the beginning of the screening, and would then be taken to receive his presentation from the wife of the President of Italy. The schedule was tight, and to avoid delay the police had cleared the route on the Grand Canal between the Square and the Palace. Chaplin's appearance in the Square was the signal for overwhelming enthusiasm. At last the projection began, and Chaplin sat down with the rest to enjoy the film. Oona, Rachel Ford and the rest of his entourage began to be rather agitated about the timing, and urged that they should leave. 'I'll wait until I've seen the fight scene,' he said amiably but firmly. And so he did.

Back in Switzerland he set to work on a new book, *My Life in Pictures*. Max Reinhardt of The Bodley Head had had the idea of a book which might supplement *My Autobiography*, with a greater emphasis on Chaplin's work. This sumptuous collection of private and studio photographs, many never reproduced before, seemed a happy solution. Chaplin evidently enjoyed revisiting the past again, though Rachel Ford was often justifiably nervous for the safety of the precious archives as she watched Chaplin and Reinhardt on their knees in a sea of fragile photographs that washed about the floor. Chaplin's brief caption comments provided some new insights, though occasionally now the phenomenal memory seemed to fail him. Clare Sheridan's son is inexplicably mixed up with his own children, for example; while (never too good on names) he adopted the long-standing error of filmographers, who credited Phyllis Allen with an appearance in *The Kid*. Not the least merit of this fine production was Francis Wyndham's introduction, with its sensitive appreciation and moving portrait of Chaplin in old age. In October 1974 Chaplin was in London for the launch of the book. He told journalists that he would never be able to retire 'because ideas just keep popping into my head'.

He was in London again in March 1975, with most of the family, to receive a knighthood from the Queen. The investiture was unquestionably his occasion. During the long wait for the Queen, the string orchestra of the Welsh Guards introduced the theme from *A Countess From Hong Kong* into their selections from light opera, and just before Her Majesty arrived, a solo pianist played 'Smile'. When it was time for his investiture and the name 'Sir Charles Chaplin' was called out, the orchestra went into the theme from *Limelight*.

Chaplin had hoped to be able to walk the ten-yard distance to the Queen, but his legs were too uncertain and a palace steward wheeled him in a chair. Chaplin said that he was 'dumbfounded' by the Queen's smile. 'She thanked me for all that I had done. She said my films had helped her a great deal.' As he waited with the other guests through the rest of the ceremony, his untiring eye for a gag was caught by the sudden collapse of the bandmaster's music stand. As he left the Palace he had the director's presence of mind in asking the television cameramen not to shoot the now laborious process of climbing into his car.

After the investiture there was a family party at the Savoy. Chaplin now found it tiring to do much talking and spent most of the time sitting quietly, simply watching the others. In the course of the party however there was a telephone call fom the Prime Minister, who said he wished to pay his respects. In due course Harold Wilson arrived with Marcia Williams. At once Chaplin was on his feet, straight-backed and sprightly, the old 'prop smile' as brilliant and charming as sixty years before. An actor's resources are mysterious.

The ideas were still popping into his head: the next one was to compose a musical score for the only one of his great silent features that remained without synchronized sound. After half a century he at last felt able to return to *A Woman of Paris*, which had remained a rather sensitive memory for him since its rejection by the audiences of 1923. Seeing it again, his original enthusiasm for the film was revived. Over-sensitive to the possible response of modern audiences, however, he made some cuts where he thought the film would appear too sentimental. He could have been bolder: the great scene between Marie and Jean's mother over Jean's body was certainly stronger in the original form, with Chaplin's sentiment unrestrained.

The sympathetic Eric James collaborated on transcription and orchestration. Chaplin composed several effective new themes; but the effort of creating eighty minutes of music was too demanding and themes were borrowed from his earlier scores to supplement the new material. The critics of the refurbished *Woman of Paris* were to be ecstatic about the rediscovery of the film, but inclined to dismiss the score as inadequate. This is unappreciative. Like all Chaplin's film scores, this one recreates the method and style of Victorian theatre music – an idiom which seems wholly appropriate to this fine melo-drama, outside time, but at least as closely linked to the nineteenth century as to the twentieth.

Chaplin attended the recording sessions at Anvil Studios at Den-ham. The writer sat with him through one of these sessions; it was here that the idea for the present book was first discussed with him. I had taken him some of the photographs of the Karno fun factory which now appear in this book, and he was particularly intrigued by one of Karno himself, the autocrat at his desk in a cluttered Edwardian office. I asked him if preparing the score for *A Woman of Paris* had been a lengthy job to which he answered, 'Not long – inspiration mostly.' Although he was still quite chubby, he seemed by this time terribly fragile. He could no longer walk unaided. It was clear that his mind was still as lively at it had been, but he was constantly frustrated by the breakdown between the thought and the realization or expression of it. He was terribly sensitive. In a break in the recording some of the musicians pretended to quarrel; this pretence of aggression distressed him acutely.

The score was the last completed work of that phenomenal creation, a working life that had spanned three quarters of a century. After this he did not often leave his home. His son Eugene, who had remained in Vevey, described his father's life in the last years in an interview given to *The National Enquirer*. He said that gout prevented him from walking, and that he no longer cared to have visitors to the house. He read and re-read his favourite Dickens novel, *Oliver Twist*. Sometimes he would tinker a little with the script of *The Freak*. (The final words of *My Life in Pictures* were 'I mean to make it some day.') Sometimes in the evening the family would watch his old films on their 16mm projector. When the others laughed, said Eugene, he would sit up straight and grin happily, 'with a whimsical smile'. While the children were growing up he had stood out against allowing television into the Manoir, but now he grew to appreciate it. He enjoyed watching the news programmes, and even though he did not speak French seemed to have no problem at all in understanding them. He liked to see American films; and with French shows would entertain himself with wicked mimicry of the performers. He did not like to talk about old friends. He had no religion, and never went to church, but he had no fear of death: 'When I go, I go,' he would say. He would sit for hours with Oona, holding hands and hardly exchanging a word. 'She is able to share that strange solitude of his,' said his son.

When the weather was fine, Renato the chauffeur or Gino the butler would drive Chaplin and Oona to a quiet spot by the lake, where they would sit together for an hour or two until the car collected them again. They bought an electric runabout so that he could still inspect his park.

On 15 October 1977 Chaplin made his last trip outside the Manoir. With Oona, Victoria, her husband Jean-Baptiste and their children, he attended a performance of the Circus Knie in Vevey. The visits of the circus had been occasions for the Chaplin family since their arrival in Switzerland. Generally they gave a party at the house for the artists.

Now his strength began to ebb very fast. He needed constant nursing. For weeks Oona insisted on attending him herself, until the family and staff began seriously to fear for her own health and she was persuaded to share the duties with a nurse. At Christmas the family, with the exception of Geraldine, who was working in Spain, assembled at the Manoir for the traditional celebration. There was now a tribe of grandchildren. On Christmas Eve Monsieur Inmoos, came up from the village dressed as Santa Claus, as he had for the past twenty years, to distribute the presents from the tree. (Monsieur Inmoos said that Chaplin saw him many times, but never in any other garb but this.) The children's presents to him were delivered to Chaplin's bedroom, and the door was left open so that he might hear the younger ones' reactions to Santa Claus.

During that night, in the small hours of Christmas Day 1977, Charles Chaplin died peacefully in his sleep.

In Hollywood the young painter Mark Stock, who idolized Chaplin and had made a fine series of lithograph portraits, heard the news on the radio early in the morning of Christmas Day. Somewhere in the deserted city he found fresh flowers. He drove to the gates of Chaplin's old house and left a rose there. He placed another on the gate of the studio. He found that by climbing up the gate he could draw down the studio flag to half mast: it stayed like that for many days. Finally he went to the Hollywood Cemetery intending to place a rose on Hannah's grave; but a spray of fresh blooms already lay there.

The funeral was held on 27 December 1977 at 11 a.m. at the Anglican Church in Vevey. As Chaplin had wished, it was an unpretentious family affair. The service was conducted by Rev. Robert Thomson and Rev. David Miller, in the presence of the British Ambassador, Allen Keir Rothnie. The coffin was covered with a black and silver pall. Immediately after the ceremony Oona left for Crans-sur-Sierre.

Chaplin, with his taste for the macabre, might have found an ideal scenario in the bizarre events that followed barely two months later. On 2 March 1978 the superintendent of the Vevey Cemetery, Etienne

Buenzod, reported for work to find Chaplin's grave opened up and the coffin gone. The world's press competed in fantastic explanations of this crime. Was it the belated revenge of a neo-Nazi group for *The Great Dictator*? An anti-Semitic protest against the burial of a Jew (*sic*) in a Christian cemetery? Or simply fanatical enthusiasts determined to possess the mortal remains of their idol? Within a few days it became clear that it was a case of posthumous kidnapping, as the first telephone call from a mysterious 'M. Cohat' (or 'Rochat') demanded 600,000 Swiss francs for the return of the body.

The culprits eventually proved to be a pathetic pair of Keystone incompetents. Roman Wardas was a 24-year-old unemployed Polish automobile mechanic. Gantcho Ganev, aged 38, was a Bulgarian defector employed as a mechanic in Lausanne. They had been inspired by a news item about the theft of the body of an Italian industrialist, Salvatore Mataressa, and hoped to raise enough money in this way to set themselves up in a garage. Their first mishap was to choose an exceedingly wet night for the exhumation. In the rain it took two hours to dig up the grave and then the ground was much too muddy for them to carry out their original intention of hiding the coffin deeper in the same hole. As it was, they were obliged to struggle through the cemetery with the lead-lined casket, load it on their car and find some other hiding place.

Oona from the start refused to have any dealings with body-snatchers. The family lawyer, Jean-Felix Paschoud, quoted her as saying, 'My husband is in heaven and in my heart.' Perhaps too she remembered the firm line that Chaplin himself had always advocated with kidnappers. The matter had to be treated with delicacy, however, since when the ransom money proved not to be immediately forthcoming, the body-snatchers began to threaten violence against the younger children. After Christopher was threatened with having his legs shot up, he was given an unseen police escort to and from school each day.

From the start Monsieur Paschoud had decided that they were dealing with amateurs: 'If we had parleyed we would eventually have got the coffin back for fifty francs,' he said. The Chaplins and the police had simply to sit it out. In all the kidnappers were to make twenty-seven telephone calls. Geraldine undertook to deal with them, and maintained a fine performance as the weeks went by, keeping the body-snatchers dangling with her vocal representations of grief and concern. A practice 'drop' went farcically wrong. Bit by bit

Wardas and Ganev grew lazy. At first they had moved around and far afield to make their calls but eventually they simply used Lausanne call-boxes. When the police realized this, they waited for a call that was fixed for an appointed time, and then kept watch on every call-box in Lausanne. A number of innocent callers received nasty shocks, but Wardas and Ganev were apprehended.

The coffin was found buried in a cornfield just outside the village of Noville on the eastern end of Lake Geneva, some twenty kilometres from Vevey. It was a place where Wardas was accustomed to go fishing. Oona was touched that they had chosen so peaceful a spot for Chaplin to rest in; and after the coffin was removed, the farmer who owned the land erected a simple wooden cross, ornamented with a cane, in memory.

Wardas and Ganev were put on trial at Vevey in December. The principal witness was Geraldine. Wardas was sentenced to four and a half years' imprisonment and Ganev received a suspended sentence of eighteen months, for 'disturbing the peace of the dead and attempted extortion'.

In the days following Chaplin's death, all the great men of his profession delivered their eulogies. René Clair, doyen of the French cinema, wrote:

> He was a monument of the cinema of all countries and all times. He inspired practically every film maker. I was myself especially sensitive to that extraordinary mixture of comedy and sentiment. It was said that *Modern Times* found its themes in *A Nous la Liberté*. I am happy and proud if I, whom he had so much influenced, was able for once in turn to influence him.
>
> Charles Chaplin, who has given us so many gifts with each of his films, took from us, this Christmas Day, the most beautiful gift the cinema made to us.

Laurence Olivier said, 'He was, perhaps, the greatest actor of all time'; and Jean-Louis Barrault called him

> the supreme example of the perfection of the actor and the creative genius: whether it comes from the theatre or is expressed by the cinema. He is above all an extraordinary mime, and what he teaches, in mime, is that he attains the maximum by immobility, an immobility full and entire. In sum, he has shown us the peak of the art of mime.

The great French film comedian Jacques Tati said,

> Without him I would never have made a film. With Keaton he was the master of us all. His work is always contemporary, yet eternal, and what he brought to the cinema and to his time is irreplaceable.

For Federico Fellini he was

> a sort of Adam, from whom we are all descended . . . There were two aspects of his personality; the vagabond, but also the solitary aristocrat, the prophet, the priest and the poet.

The simplest tribute – yet perhaps also the most touching, because it intimated atonement by the very section of America which, so long ago, had abused and rejected Charles Chaplin – was spoken by Bob Hope:

> 'We were fortunate to have lived in his time.'

NOTES

CHAPTER 1: A London boyhood

1   Suffolk Parish Registers, *passim*.
2   1851 Census return.
3   Will of Shadrach Chaplin at Principal Probate Office, Somerset House.
4   Marriage certificate in General Registry Office.
5   Death Certificate in General Registry Office.
6   Birth Certificate in General Registry Office.
7   Birth Certificate in General Registry Office.
8   Now in possession of Lady Chaplin.
9   Marriage Certificate in General Registry Office.
10 Marriage Certificate in General Registry Office.
11 Marriage Certificate in General Registry Office.
12 Death Certificate in General Registry Office.
13 Birth Certificate in General Registry Office.
14 Birth Certificate in General Registry Office.
15 1871 Census: Parish of St Mary Newington, Schedule 321.
16 Birth Certificate in General Registry Office.
17 Death Certificate in General Registry Office.
18 Marriage Certificate in General Registry Office.
19 *The Era*, 18 June 1887.
20 Programme in collection of Professor E. J. Dawes.
21 *The Era,* August 1890.
22 Letter in Sydney Chaplin Archive, Vevey.
23 *The Era*.
24 Letter from Wheeler Dryden to Edna Purviance. See p. 217.
25 Lambeth Board of Guardians, Lunacy Examinations Book, 1893, p.196, GLC Archives.
26 St Saviour Union (Southwark). Order for Reception of a Pauper Lunatic, GLC Archives.
27 *American Magazine*, November 1918.

28 Renfrew Road (Lambeth) Workhouse Register, GLC Archives.
29 School Register, GLC Archives.
30 Southwark Workhouse Register, GLC Archives.
31 Chaplin. *My Autobiography*, 1964, though correspondence of St Saviour Board of Guardians and Norwood Schools (GLC Archives) establishes the name as 'Hindom' not 'Hindrum' as Chaplin remembered it.
32 *Pearson's Weekly*, 21 September 1921.
33 Letter now in Vevey Archives.
34 Walter Monnington and Frederick J. Lampard. *Our London Poor Law Schools*, London, 1898.
35 *Ibid.*
36 *Strand Magazine*, volume 17, no. 12, pp.88–95.
37 St Saviour (Southwark) Board of Guardians Minutes, GLC Archives.
38 Letter from Dr Shepherd to CC, 1916, in Vevey Archives.
39 Will of Spencer Chaplin, dated 18 May 1897, at Principal Probate Office, Somerset House.
40 St Saviour (Southwark) Board of Guardians Minutes, GLC Archives.
41 Correspondence of St Saviour (Southwark) Board of Guardians, GLC Archives.
42 Renfrew Road (Lambeth) Workhouse Register, GLC Archives.
43 Lambeth Board of Guardians, Lunacy Examinations Book, 12 September 1898, GLC Archives.
44 *Motion Picture Classic.*
45 Renfrew Road (Lambeth) Workhouse Register, GLC Archives.
46 Kennington Road Schools Register, GLC Archives.
47 *Glasgow Weekly Herald*, 9 October 1921.
48 *The Magnet*, 14 July 1900.
49 Armitage Street School Register. The school registers have now disappeared, but the entry was illustrated in a Manchester newspaper in 1921.
50 Alfred Jackson interviewed in *The Star*, 3 September 1921.
51 Charles Douglas Stuart and A. J. Park. *The Variety Stage*, London, 1895.
52 Alfred Jackson, *loc. cit.*
53 *Winnipeg Tribune*, 29 November 1912
54 Renfrew Road (Lambeth) Workhouse Register, GLC Archives.
55 Sydney Hill – Continuous Certificate of Discharge.
56 Sydney Hill – Seaman's Allotment Note.
57 Sydney Hill – Continuous Certificate of Discharge.
58 *Manchester Daily Chronicle*, 14 September 1921.
59 Post Office directories, *passim.*
60 Newspaper cutting, source unidentified.
61 May Reeves. *Charlie Chaplin intime. Souvenirs receuillis par Claire Goll*, 1935.
62 Lambeth Board of Guardians, Lunacy Reception Order, 9 May 1903, GLC Archives.
63 Charles Chaplin Jr. *My Father, Charlie Chaplin*, 1960.

CHAPTER 2: The young professional

1   Charles Chaplin. *My Autobiography*.
2   Letter to Sydney Chaplin, August 1913. See p.97.

3 Bert Herbert interviewed in *the Star*, 3 September 1921.
4 Licensing records, GLC Archives.
5 Edith Scales quoted in *Empire News*, 8 March 1931.
6 Edith Scales, *loc. cit.*
7 *Ashton-under-Lyne Reporter*, 21 November 1903.
8 *Ibid.*
9 Edith Scales, *loc. cit.*
10 *Ibid.*
11 *Ibid.*
12 Sydney Hill – Continuous Certificate of Discharge.
13 Lambeth Board of Guardians, Lunacy Reception Order, 18 March 1905.
14 *The Era.*
15 *The Era Annual*, 1906.
16 Will Murray, interviewed in *Glasgow Weekly Herald*, 10 September 1921.
17 *Ibid.*
18 Dan Lipton quoted in *Daily Graphic*, 1 September 1921.
19 Will Murray, *loc. cit.*
20 Fred Goodwins, article in *Pearson's Weekly.*
21 Interview with Richard Meryman, 1968.
22 In conversation with writer, c.1954.

CHAPTER 3: With the Guv'nor

1 Syndicated newspaper interview.
2 *The Theatre*, London, April 1880.
3 Stan Laurel, quoted in John McCabe's *Charlie Chaplin*, 1978.
4 Fred Goodwins, *op. cit.*
5 Letter in Vevey Archive.
6 Stan Laurel, *loc. cit.*
7 Birth certificate in General Registry.
8 Charles Chaplin. *My Trip Abroad*, 1922.
9 Charles Chaplin. *A Comedian Sees the World*, 1932.
10 Manuscript scenario in Vevey Archive.
11 Newspaper cutting, source unidentified. Most of these early reviews from Karno days are preserved in Chaplin's first cuttings book, but have been pasted in without reference to date or source.
12 Stan Laurel, *loc. cit.*
13 Newspaper cutting, source unidentified.
14 Stan Laurel, *loc. cit.*
15 Alf Reeves interview, *Photoplay*, August 1934. Preserved in Reeves' own cuttings book.
16 Alf Reeves, *loc. cit.*
17 Newspaper cutting, source unidentified.
18 Newspaper cutting, source unidentified.
19 Newspaper cutting, source unidentified.
20 Newspaper cutting, source unidentified.
21 Newspaper cutting, source unidentified.
22 Stan Laurel, *loc. cit.*

23 Newspaper cutting, source unidentified.
24 Letter in Vevey Archive.
25 Newspaper cutting, source unidentified.
26 'Whimsical' Walker. *From Sawdust to Windsor Castle*, 1922.
27 Newspaper interview, source unidentified.
28 Letter from CC to Sydney Chaplin in Vevey Archive.
29 Stan Laurel, *loc. cit.*
30 Newspaper cutting, 1921, source unidentified.

CHAPTER 4: In Pictures

1 Mack Sennett. *King of Comedy* (as told to Cameron Shipp), 1954.
2 Letter in Kevin Brownlow collection.
3 This version is quoted, without source, in John McCabe's *Charlie Chaplin*.
4 Original contract and draft in Vevey Archive.
5 Walter Kerr. *The Silent Clowns*, 1975.
6 *Ibid.*
7 Charles Chaplin. *My Autobiography*.
8 Hans Koenekamp in interview with author, December 1983.
9 *Ibid.*
10 Walter Kerr, *op. cit.*

CHAPTER 5: Essanay

1 Roland Totheroh interviewed by Timothy J. Lyons in *Film Culture*, Spring 1972.
2 *Ibid.*
3 *Ibid.*
4 Fred Goodwins, article in *Pearsons Weekly*.
5 *Ibid.*
6 Lambeth Board of Guardians, Settlement Examination Book, GLC Archives.

CHAPTER 6: Mutual

1 Syndicated newspaper article.
2 *Ibid.*
3 *Ibid.*
4 *Ibid.*
5 Syndicated newspaper interview with Kitty Kelly.
6 Roland Totheroh, *loc. cit.*
7 *Ibid.*
8 *Ibid.*
9 *Ibid.*
10 Terry Ramsaye. 'Chaplin – and how he does it' in *Photoplay*, September 1917.
11 Newspaper interview, source unidentified.
12 Roland Totheroh, *loc. cit.*
13 Edward Sutherland in interview with Robert Franklin.
14 *New York Tribune.*

15 This and subsequent correspondence relating to *Charlie Chaplin's Own Story* is preserved in the Vevey Archive.
16 Langford Reed. *The Chronicles of Charlie Chaplin*, 1917.
17 *Ibid.*
18 *Ibid.*
19 Kevin Brownlow. *The Parade's Gone By*, 1968.
20 Constance Collier. *Harlequinade. The Story of My Life*, 1929.
21 Gerith von Ulm. *Charles Chaplin, King of Tragedy*, 1940.
22 Walter Kerr. *The Silent Clowns.*
23 Mutual press release, 1 February 1917.
24 *Reel Life*, February 1917.
25 Mutual press release, February 1917.
26 Syndicated newspaper interview by Karl Kitchen.
27 Newspaper cutting, source unidentified.
28 Carlyle T. Robinson. *La verité sur Charles Chaplin. Sa vie, ses amours, ses déboires*, 1935 (translated from French original).
29 *Ibid.*
30 *Ibid.*
31 *Ibid.*
32 *Ibid.*
33 *Ibid.*
34 *Cincinnati Star*, 8 February 1917.
35 *NYC Mail*, 23 December 1918.
36 Newspaper cutting, source unidentified.
37 Correspondence in possession of Mrs Wyn Ray Evans, Ritchie's daughter.
38 Newspaper cutting, source unidentified.

CHAPTER 7: Penalties and rewards of independence

1 Interview in *Exhibitors' Trade Review*, 28 April 1917.
2 Letter from Sydney Chaplin to CC, in Vevey Archive.
3 Interview in *Cleveland Leader*, date not known.
4 Lita Grey Chaplin. *My Life with Chaplin*, 1966.
5 Roland Totheroh interviewed by Timothy J. Lyons in *Film Culture*, Spring 1972.
6 Frank Harris in *Contemporary Portraits*, 1924.
7 Detectives' report in Vevey Archive.
8 Edward Sutherland in interview with Robert Franklin.
9 Wyn Ray Evans in interview with author, December 1983.

CHAPTER 8: Escape to independence

1 Charles Chaplin. *My Trip Abroad*, 1922. All subsequent quotations from Chaplin in this chapter are from the same source.
2 Newspaper cutting in Vevey scrapbooks, source unidentified.
3 Newspaper cutting in Vevey scrapbooks, source unidentified.
4 Thomas Burke. 'A Comedian' in *City of Encounters*, 1932.
5 Clare Sheridan. *My American Diary*, 1922.
6 *Ibid.*
7 *Ibid.*

CHAPTER 9: *A Woman of Paris*

1   Edward Sutherland, *loc. cit.*
2   Adolphe Menjou: *It Took Nine Tailors*, 1952.
3   Edward Sutherland, *loc. cit.*
4   *Ibid.*
5   Adolphe Menjou, *op. cit.*
6   Edward Sutherland, *loc. cit.*
7   Cutting preserved in Edna Purviance collection, now owned by Inman Hunter, Esq.
8   Adolphe Menjou, *op. cit.*
9   *Ibid.*
10 Edward Sutherland, *loc. cit.*
11 Adolphe Menjou, *op. cit.*
12 Work notes, Vevey Archive.
13 Adolphe Menjou, *op. cit.*
14 Edward Sutherland, *loc. cit.*
15 Roland Totheroh, *loc. cit.*
16 Adolphe Menjou, *op. cit.*
17 *Ibid.*
18 *Ibid.*
19 *Detroit Free Press*, 16 October 1923.
20 *Boston Globe*, 23 March 1923.
21 *Ibid.*
22 *Ibid.*
23 *Ibid.*
24 *Ibid.*
25 *Los Angeles Times*, 29 January 1923.
26 *Ibid.*
27 *Boston Globe*, 23 March 1923.
28 Charles Chaplin, Jr. *My Father, Charlie Chaplin.*
29 *Ibid.*

CHAPTER 10: *The Gold Rush*

1   Charles Chaplin. *My Autobiography*, 1964.
2   Syndicated press article, June 1924.
3   *Ibid.*
4   Souvenir programme, *The Gold Rush*, 1925.
5   *Ibid.*
6   *Los Angeles Daily News*, 28 October 1924.
7   Georgia Hale in interview with author, December 1983.
8   *Ibid.*
9   *Ibid.*
10 *Ibid.*
11 *Ibid.*
12 *The Star*, 25 September 1925.
13 *The Star*, 28 September 1925.
14 Information from Dr Hans Feld, then critic of *Filmkurier*, Berlin.

CHAPTER 11: *The Circus*

1 Interview with Henry Bergman, in cutting from unidentified source.
2 James Agee. 'Comedy's Greatest Era' in *Life*, 5 September 1949.
3 Harry Crocker in unpublished interview, c. 1955.
4 Press brochure issued by Studio.
5 Robert Florey. *Charlie Chaplin. Ses debuts, ses films, ses aventures*, 1927.
6 *Ibid.*

CHAPTER 12: *City Lights*

1 Harry Crocker, *loc. cit.*
2 Jean Cocteau, *My Journey Round the World*,
3 Interview with Richard Meryman, 1968.
4 Virginia Cherrill, in telephone conversation with author, December 1983.
5 Interview with Richard Meryman, 1968.
6 Carlyle T. Robinson. *La verité sur Charles Chaplin. Sa vie, ses amours, ses déboires.*
7 Georgia Hale in interview with author, December 1983.
8 *Ibid.*
9 Robert Parrish, *Growing Up in Hollywood*.
10 Interview with Richard Meryman, 1968.
11 James Agee, *loc. cit.*
12 Charles Chaplin. *My Trip Abroad.*
13 Interview with Richard Meryman, 1968.
14 Ivor Montagu. *With Eisenstein in Hollywood*, 1967.
15 *Ibid.*
16 *Ibid.*
17 Luis Buñuel. *My Last Breath*, 1983.
18 *Ibid.*
19 Georgia Hale, *loc. cit.*
20 Luis Buñuel, *op. cit.*

CHAPTER 13: Away from it all

1 Charles Chaplin. *A Comedian Sees the World.*
2 The *Daily Express*.
3 Thomas Burke, *loc. cit.*
4 *Ibid.*

CHAPTER 14: *Modern Times*

1 Georgia Hale in interview with author, December 1983.
2 Charles Chaplin. *My Autobiography.*
3 *Screenland*, October 1932.
4 *Chicago American*, 29 September 1932.
5 Charles Chaplin Jr. *My Father, Charlie Chaplin*, 1960.
6 *Budgepost Post*, 16 September 1932.

7   *Boston Globe*, 4 September 1932.
8   Lita Grey Chaplin. *My Life with Chaplin.*
9   Letter to Sydney Chaplin in Vevey Archive.
10 Charles Chaplin, Jr. *My Father, Charlie Chaplin.*
11 *Ibid.*
12 Thomas Burke, *op. cit.*
13 *Ibid.*
14 Charles Chaplin, Jr, *op. cit.*
15 Jean Cocteau: *My Voyage Round the World.*
16 *Ibid.*
17 *Ibid.*
18 *Ibid.*
19 *Ibid.*

CHAPTER 15: *The Great Dictator*

1   Charles Chaplin. *My Autobiography.*
2   The story was published, in English translation, in Peter Cotes and Thelma Niklaus' *The Little Fellow.*
3   Tim Durant in interview with Kevin Brownlow and David Gill, 1980.
4   All quotations from Dan James in this chapter are from an interview with the author, December 1983.
5   Charles Chaplin, Jr, *op. cit.*
6   Dan James, *loc. cit.*
7   Charles Chaplin, Jr, *op. cit.*
8   Dan James, *loc. cit.*
9   Tim Durant, *loc. cit.*
10 Charles Chaplin, Jr, *op. cit.*
11 *Ibid.*
12 *Films*, 1946.

CHAPTER 16: *Monsieur Verdoux*

1   Charles Chaplin, Jr, *op. cit.*
2   *Ibid.*
3   Quoted in Theodore Huff. *Charlie Chaplin* 1951.
4   Roland Totheroh interviewed by Timothy J. Lyons in *Film Culture*, Spring 1972.
5   *Ibid.*
6   All quotations from the press conference are from the transcript by George Wallach, published in *Film Comment*, Winter 1969.
7   *Film Comment*, Winter, 1969.

CHAPTER 17: *Limelight*

1   Charles Chaplin Jr, *op. cit.*
2   Interview with Margaret Hinxman.
3   Charles Chaplin Jr, *op. cit.*
4   Letter to Sydney Chaplin in Vevey Archive.

5   Article in *Everybody's*.
6   Press interview, source unidentified. Wheeler had in fact advertised the relationship in advertisements in *The Stage Yearbook* in the 1920s.
7   Sydney Chaplin Jr, *op. cit.*
8   Claire Bloom. *Limelight and After*, 1982.
9   *Ibid.*
10 *Ibid.*
11 *Ibid.*
12 Charles Chaplin Jr, *op. cit.*
13 Claire Bloom, *op. cit.*
14 Private communication to author.
15 Eugene Lourié in interview with author, December 1983.
16 *Ibid.*
17 *Ibid.*
18 *Ibid.*
19 Sydney Chaplin Jr, *op. cit.*
20 *Ibid.*
21 Claire Bloom, *op. cit.*
22 *Ibid.*
23 Eugene Lourié, *loc. cit.*

CHAPTER 18: *Exile*

1   *News Chronicle*, 24 September 1952.
2   *The Times*, 24 September 1952.
3   *News Chronicle*, 22 September 1952.
4   *New York Times*, 21 September 1952.
5   Charles Chaplin. *My Autobiography*.
6   Michael Chaplin in *I Couldn't Smoke the Grass on My Father's Lawn*, 1966.
7   *Daily Herald*, 16 April 1959.
8   *Sunday Times*, 21 August 1964.
9   Michael Chaplin, *op. cit.*
10 24 June 1962.
11 Introduction to *My Life in Pictures*, 1974.
12 Michael Chaplin, *op. cit.*
13 *Sunday Times*, 21 August 1964.
14 Lillian Ross in *Moments With Chaplin*, 1980.
15 *Sunday Times*, 1964.
16 Charles Chaplin. *My Autobiography*.

CHAPTER 19: *A Countess From Hong Kong*

1   David Robinson: 'Chaplin Meets the Press' in *Sight and Sound*, Winter 1965–66.
2   Kevin Brownlow: *The Parade's Gone By.* (1968).
3   *Sunday Times*.
4   Michael Chaplin, *op. cit.*
5   *Life*, 21 April 1972.
6   Interview with Kevin Brownlow and David Gill, 1980.

7 Georgia Hale, *loc. cit.*
8 Interview with Anthony Coogan, December 1983.
9 *Life*, 21 April 1972.

APPENDIX I
Chaplin chronology

1786		Shadrach Chaplin I (CC's great-great-grandfather) born.
1807–8		Sophia Chaplin (CC's great-grandmother) born.
1814		Shadrach Chaplin II (CC's great-grandfather) born.
1834–5		Spencer Chaplin (CC's grandfather) born.
1839	16 April	Charles Frederick Hill (CC's maternal grandfather) born.
		Mary Ann Terry (CC's maternal grandmother) born.
1854	15 May	Mary Ann Terry (CC's maternal grandmother) marries Henry Lamphee Hodges.
	30 October	Spencer Chaplin marries Ellen Elizabeth Smith (both minors) at St Margaret's Church, Ipswich.
1855	June	Spencer William Tunstill Chaplin (CC's uncle) born.
1858	18 December	Mary Ann Hodges, née Terry (CC's maternal grandmother) widowed by death of Henry Lamphee Hodges, aged thirty-four.
1861	16 August	Charles Frederick Hill (widower) marries Mary Ann Hodges (widow) (CC's maternal grandfather and grandmother) at St Mary's Church, Lambeth.

1863	18 March	Charles Chaplin (CC's father) born at 22 Orcus Street, Marylebone.
1865	6 August	Hannah Harriett Pedlingham Hill (CC's mother) born at 11 Camden Street, Walworth.
1870	18 January	Kate Hill (CC's aunt) born at 39 Bronti Place, Walworth.
1871		Census returns show Charles Hill lodging at 77 Beckway Street, Walworth, with wife, Mary Ann, stepson Henry and daughters Hannah and Kate.
1873	2 October	Death of Ellen Chaplin (CC's grandmother) at 15 Rillington Place, aged thirty-five.
1885	16 March	Sidney John Hill (Sydney Chaplin; CC's brother) born.
	29 April	Sidney Hill's birth registered.
	22 June	Charles Chaplin Senior marries Hannah Hill at St John's Church, Larcom Street.
1886	2 January	Hannah Chaplin ('Lily Harley') appears in Belfast.
	27 May	Hannah Chaplin ('Lily Harley') appears in benefit at South London Palace.
1887	20 June	Hannah Chaplin ('Lily Harley') appears at Folly Theatre Manchester.
	20 June	First recorded professional appearance of Charles Chaplin Senior, at Poly Variety Theatre.
1889	16 April	BIRTH OF CHARLES CHAPLIN.
	Autumn/Winter	Charles Chaplin Senior appearing at several London music halls.
1890		Publication of Charles Chaplin Senior's song successes, 'Eh, boys?' and 'Everyday Life'.
	3 March	Sydney Chaplin enrolled at King and Queen Street School, Southwark (remains until May).
	5 May	Sydney Chaplin enrolled at Addington Street School, Lambeth.
	16 August	Charles Chaplin Senior appearing at Union Square Theatre, New York (remains until 6 September).

	11 November	Sydney Chaplin enrolled at Flint Street School, Southwark.
1891		Publication of Charles Chaplin Senior's song success, 'As the Church Bells Chime'.
	November	Leo Dryden sings 'The Miner's Dream of Home' and is paid £20 for publication rights by Francis, Day and Hunter – 'the most they have ever paid for a song'.
1892	31 August	Birth of Wheeler Dryden (CC's half-brother).
1893		Publication of Charles Chaplin Senior's song success, 'Oui, Tray Bong'.
	19 February	Mary Ann Hill (CC's grandmother) admitted to infirmary. Charles Hill is living at 97 East Street.
	23 February	Mary Ann Hill committed to asylum. Charles Hill is living at 87 St George's Road.
	1 March	Mary Ann Hill removed to Banstead Asylum.
	8 October	Birth of Henrietta Florence Kelly at 12 Guinea St, Bristol.
1895	29 June	Hannah Chaplin admitted (as 'Lilian Chaplin') to Lambeth Infirmary (remains until 30 July).
	1 July	Sydney Chaplin admitted to Lambeth Workhouse (remains until 4 July).
	4 July	Sydney Chaplin transferred to Norwood Schools (remains until 17 September).
	17 September	Sydney transferred to Lambeth Workhouse and discharged to care of father.
	10 October(?)	CC enrolled at Addington Street School, Lambeth.
1896		Publication of Charles Chaplin Senior's song success, 'She Must Be Witty'.
	8 February	Hannah Chaplin (as 'Lily Chaplin') performs at Hatcham Liberal Club.
	30 May	CC and Sydney admitted to Newington Workhouse.
	9 June	St Saviour Parish Board of Guardians requires

		Charles Chaplin Senior to pay 15s. weekly towards support of CC and Sydney.
	18 June	CC and Sydney transferred to Hanwell Schools.
	June/July	Hannah Chaplin admitted to Champion Hill Infirmary.
	1 July	Board of Guardians reports to Local Government Board that Charles Chaplin Senior agrees to contribute to sons' support.
	18 November	Sydney Chaplin transferred to Training Ship *Exmouth*.
1897		Throughout entire year CC remains at Hanwell Schools; Sydney Chaplin at Training Ship *Exmouth*.
	29 May	Death of Spencer Chaplin (CC's grandfather).
	10 August	Hannah Chaplin visits CC at Hanwell.
	16 September	Board of Guardians applies for warrant for Charles Chaplin Senior for non-payment of sons' support, and offers £1 for information leading to his arrest.
	11 November	Reported to Board of Guardians that Spencer Chaplin (CC's uncle) has paid £44.8s. due from Charles Chaplin Senior.
	16 November	Board of Guardians, through Spencer Chaplin, requests Charles Chaplin Senior to take responsibility for sons within fourteen days.
	20 December	Hannah Chaplin and her father Charles Hill seek baptism at Christchurch Nonconformist Church, Westminster Bridge Road. Resulting decision to be baptized on 10 January 1898.
	23 December	Warrant issued against Charles Chaplin Senior for neglecting to maintain his children.
1898	18 January	CC discharged from Hanwell Schools.
	18 January	Charles Chaplin Senior arrested for non-payment of support for sons.

20 January	Sydney Chaplin discharged from Training Ship *Exmouth*.
22 July	CC, Sydney and Hannah admitted to Lambeth Workhouse.
30 July	CC and Sydney transferred to Norwood Schools.
12 August	CC and Sydney transferred to Lambeth Workhouse; CC, Sydney and Hannah discharged from Lambeth Workhouse (Hannah's day's outing).
13 August	CC, Sydney and Hannah readmitted to Lambeth Workhouse.
15 August	CC and Sydney transferred to Norwood Schools.
6 September	Hannah admitted to Lambeth Infirmary.
15 September	Hannah transferred to Cane Hill Asylum.
21 September	Board of Guardians seeks to make Charles Chaplin Senior take charge of his sons.
27 September	CC and Sydney transferred to Lambeth Workhouse, and discharged to care of father.
12 October	Board of Guardians informed that Charles Chaplin Senior has failed to enrol his sons in school.
12 November	Hannah discharged from Cane Hill Asylum.
26 December	CC with Eight Lancashire Lads at Theatre Royal, Manchester.
	Charles Chaplin Senior at Tivoli, Manchester (remains until 7 January 1899).
1899 9 January	CC enrolled at Armitage Street School, Ardwick, Manchester.
5 May	Death of Spencer Chaplin (CC's uncle). Charles Chaplin Senior becomes nominal licensee of Queen's Head.
20 July	Charles Hill (Chaplin's grandfather) admitted to Lambeth Infirmary, from 39 Methley Street.

	2 August	Charles Hill transferred from Lambeth Infirmary to Lambeth Workhouse.
1900	23 April	CC enrolled in St Mary the Less School, Newington (remained until 3 May).
	September	Charles Chaplin Senior's last recorded stage appearance, at Granville Theatre of Varieties, Walham Green.
	12 November	CC enrolled in St Francis Xavier School, Liverpool.
1901	6 April	Sydney Chaplin embarks to Cape as assistant steward and bandsman on *Norman* (returns 31 May).
	29 April	Charles Chaplin Senior admitted to St Thomas's Hospital.
	9 May	Charles Chaplin Senior dies in St Thomas's Hospital, aged thirty-seven.
	1 September	Sydney Chaplin embarks for New York as steward on *Haverford* (discharged in New York, 2 October).
	5 October	Sydney Chaplin engaged as steward on *St Louis*, New York to Southampton (discharged in Southampton, 23 October).
1902	September	Sydney Chaplin embarks for Cape as steward and bugler on *Kinfairns Castle* (returns 25 October).
	8 November	Sydney Chaplin's second voyage as steward and bugler on *Kinfairns Castle* (returns 27 December).
1903	17 January	Sydney Chaplin's third voyage as steward and bugler on *Kinfairns Castle* (returns 7 March).
	24 March	Sydney Chaplin's fourth voyage as steward and bugler on *Kinfairns Castle* (returns 9 May).
	5 May	Hannah Chaplin admitted to Lambeth Infirmary.
	9 May	Hannah Chaplin committed as lunatic (next of kin: son, CC).
	11 May	Hannah Chaplin transferred to Cane Hill Asylum (remains until 2 January 1904).

	6 July	CC plays Sam in *Jim, A Romance of Cockayne* at Royal County Theatre, Kingston.
	12 July	CC plays Sam in *Jim, A Romance of Cockayne* at Grand Theatre, Fulham.
	27 July	CC plays Billy in *Sherlock Holmes* for first time, Pavilion Theatre, East London (H. A. Saintsbury as Holmes).
	10 August	Tour of *Sherlock Holmes*, with CC as Billy, begins at Theatre Royal, Newcastle.
	(?) December	Sydney Chaplin joins cast of *Sherlock Holmes* tour.
1904	2 January	Hannah Chaplin discharged from Cane Hill Asylum; joins sons on tour.
	11 June	First *Sherlock Holmes* tour ends.
	20 August	Production of *From Rags to Riches*, starring CC, announced.
	29 August	Charles Hill (CC's grandfather) admitted to Renfrew Road Workhouse from 24 Chester Street.
	21 October	Charles Hill discharged from Renfrew Road Workhouse.
	31 October	CC joins second *Sherlock Holmes* tour, with Kenneth Rivington as Holmes.
	10 November	Sydney Chaplin embarks on last voyage, as assistant steward and bugler on *Dover Castle* to Natal.
1905	6 March	Hannah Chaplin readmitted to Lambeth Infirmary.
	16 March	Hannah Chaplin committed as lunatic (next of kin: Kate Hill).
	18 March	Hannah Chaplin transferred to Cane Hill Asylum (remains until 9 September 1912).
	22 April	Second *Sherlock Holmes* tour ends.
	12 August	CC joins third *Sherlock Holmes* tour, with H. Lawrence Layton as Holmes (Harry Yorke Company).

	13 September	*Clarice*, with William Gillette, opens at Duke of York's Theatre, London.
	30 September	CC leaves third *Sherlock Holmes* tour.
	3 October	*The Painful Predicament of Sherlock Holmes* added as afterpiece to *Clarice* at Duke of York's: CC plays Billy.
	17 October	*Sherlock Holmes* replaces *Clarice* at Duke of York's: CC plays Billy.
	19 October	Funeral of Henry Irving, CC attends.
	20 November	Royal Gala Performance of *Sherlock Holmes*.
1906	1 January	CC joins fourth *Sherlock Holmes* tour (Harry Yorke Company).
	3 March	Fourth *Sherlock Holmes* tour ends.
	March	CC joins company of Wal Pink's *Repairs*.
	19 March	*Repairs* tour opens at Hippodrome, Southampton.
	12 May	CC leaves tour of *Repairs* at Grand Palace, Clapham.
	May	CC joins *Casey's Court Circus* Company.
	9 July	Sydney Chaplin signs first contract with Fred Karno: one year at £3 per week (£6 if required to work in USA).
	Oct/Nov	Sydney Chaplin with Karno Company in USA.
1907	24 June	Sydney Chaplin signs second contract with Fred Karno: two years at £4 per week, one-year option.
	20 July	Tour of *Casey's Court Circus* ends.
	Autumn	CC attempts single act at Foresters' Music Hall.
1908	February	CC given trial by Fred Karno.
	21 February	CC's first contract with Fred Karno: £3.10s. per week first year; £4 per week second year; third year option at same rate.
		During the year CC and Sydney take flat at 15 Glenshaw Mansions, Brixton Road.
	Autumn	Meets Hetty Kelly.

	Autumn	CC appears in Karno's *Mumming Birds* in Paris.
1909		During the year CC plays in *The Football Match*, *Mumming Birds*.
	3 March	Charles Hill (CC's grandfather) admitted to Renfrew Road Workhouse from 15 Glenshaw Mansions.
	4 September	Charles Hill discharged from Renfrew Road Workhouse.
	31 December	CC plays in *The Football Match* at Oxford Music Hall.
1910		During the year CC plays additionally in *Skating* and *Jimmy the Fearless*.
	19 September	CC signs second contract with Fred Karno, to run from 6 March 1911: three years at £6, £8 and £10 per week and a three-year option.
		Embarks with Karno American Company on SS *Cairnrona*.
	3 October	Karno US tour begins at Colonial Theatre, New York, with *The Wow-Wows*.
	26 December	New York Karno Company presents *A Harlequinade in Black and White* (possibly devised by CC) at American Music Hall.
1911		Karno US tour continues throughout year.
	January	Alf Reeves (Karno tour manager) marries Amy Minister.
1912	June	CC returns to England at end of Karno US tour.
	July/August	CC touring in France and Channel Islands with Karno Company.
	9 September	Hannah Chaplin transferred from Cane Hill Asylum to Peckham House, Peckham Road.
	2 October	CC embarks on *Oceanic* with Karno Company for second US tour.
1913	25 September	CC signs contract with Kessel and Bauman to join Keystone Film Company on 16 December, at $150 per week for one year.

	8 October	CC acquires 200 shares in Vancouver Island Oil Company Ltd (nos. 10826–11025).
	29 November(?)	CC's last performance with Karno Company, at Empress, Kansas City.
	16 December	CC's contract with Keystone Film Company commences.
1914	January	Commences work at Keystone Studios.
	2 February	*Making a Living* released.
	7 February	*Kid Auto Races* released.
	9 February	*Mabel's Strange Predicament* released.
	28 February	*Between Showers* released.
	2 March	*A Film Johnnie* released.
	9 March	*Tango Tangles* released.
	16 March	*His Favorite Pastime* released.
	26 March	*Cruel, Cruel Love* released.
	4 April	*The Star Boarder* released.
	18 April	*Mabel at the Wheel* released.
	20 April	*Twenty Minutes of Love* released.
	27 April	*Caught in a Cabaret* released.
	4 May	*Caught in the Rain* released.
	7 May	*A Busy Day* released.
	1 June	*The Fatal Mallet* released.
	4 June	*Her Friend the Bandit* released.
	11 June	*The Knockout* released.
	13 June	*Mabel's Busy Day* released.
	20 June	*Mabel's Married Life* released.
	9 July	*Laughing Gas* released.
	1 August	*The Property Man* released.
	10 August	*The Face on the Bar Room Floor* released.
	18 August	*Recreation* released.

27 August	*The Masquerader* released.
31 August	*His New Profession* released.
7 September	*The Rounders* released.
24 September	*The New Janitor* released.
10 October	*Those Love Pangs* released.
26 October	*Dough and Dynamite* released.
29 October	*Gentlemen of Nerve* released.
7 November	*His Musical Career* released.
9 November	*His Trysting Place* released.
14 November	*Tillie's Punctured Romance* released.
	Sydney Chaplin arrives at Keystone.
	CC signs contract with Essanay for $1250 per week to make fourteen films in 1915.
5 December	*Getting Acquainted* released.
7 December	*His Prehistoric Past* released.
	At end of month arrives in Chicago.
1915 January	CC working in Essanay Chicago Studio.
1 February	*His New Job* released.
	CC moves to Essanay Studio, Niles, California.
15 February	*A Night Out* released.
11 March	*The Champion* released.
18 March	*In The Park* released.
1 April	*A Jitney Elopement* released.
11 April	*The Tramp* released.
May	Mark Hampton Co. for Charles Chaplin Advertising Service Company sues Art Novelty Co. for producing Chaplin statuettes.
28 May	Board of Guardians seeks to return Hannah Chaplin to Cane Hill Asylum, since sons' payments to Peckham House Hospital are in arrears.

21 June	*Work* released.
12 July	*A Woman* released.
9 August	*The Bank* released.
27 August	Hetty Kelly marries Lieutenant Alan Edgar Horne at registry office in Parish of St George, Hanover Square.
	Keystone sues Chaplin Film Co. along with A. G. Levi and Lemun Film Co. for copyright infringement and accounting of profits relating to *Dough and Dynamite*.
	Himalaya Films, the distributors in France, name Chaplin 'Charlot'.
4 October	*Shanghaied* released.
20 November	*A Night in the Show* released.
18 December	*Charlie Chaplin's Burlesque on Carmen* released.
1916	CC forms Charles Chaplin Music Corporation, with Sydney Chaplin and Herbert Clark (offices at 233 South Broadway, Los Angeles).
22 January	Kate Mowbray (Kate Hill, CC's aunt) dies at 99 Gower Street, London.
20 February	CC appears in benefit at Hippodrome, New York; donates half his fee to Actors' Fund.
25 February	Subscription lists opened on Lone Star Film Corporation ($400,000 7% preferred stock; $25,000 common stock).
26 February	CC signs with Mutual Film Corporation for $10,000 per week, with bonus of $150,000.
27 February	In Boston, Rev. Frederick E. Heath preaches sermon on 'Charles Chaplin's Half Million'.
22 March	CC attacked by London *Daily Mail* for clause in contract forbidding return for war service in British forces.
27 March	Lone Star Studio opened.
22 April	Essanay releases expanded version of *Charlie Chaplin's Burlesque on Carmen*.

	12 May	Chaplin seeks injunction to prevent release of *Charlie Chaplin's Burlesque on Carmen*.
	15 May	*The Floorwalker* released.
	25 May	CC appeals against adverse ruling on *Carmen* case.
	27 May	*Police* released.
	12 June	*The Fireman* released.
	24 June	CC's appeal against *Carmen* ruling fails in Supreme Court.
	10 July	*The Vagabond* released.
	7 August	*One A.M.* released.
	4 September	*The Count* released.
	1 October	CC institutes proceedings to prevent publication of *Charlie Chaplin's Own Story*.
	2 October	*The Pawnshop* released.
	8 November	CC cables requesting to negotiate for rights in Hall Caine's *The Prodigal Son*.
	12 November	Nationwide Chaplin psychic impulse reported in USA.
	13 November	*Behind the Screen* released.
	December	Paderewski visits studio.
	4 December	*The Rink* released.
	9 December	Al Woods cables CC the offer of half of profits plus weekly salary stipulated by CC, to appear in a musical comedy during 1917–18. Woods includes film rights to CC, in consideration of split of profits. Chaplin refuses.
		Publication of *Charlie Chaplin's Own Story* prevented.
1917	22 January	*Easy Street* released.
	8 February	In Cincinnati, hold-up man disguises himself as CC.
	31 March	CC plays in Tragics v. Comics ball game in Washington Park, Los Angeles.

	16 April	*The Cure* released.
	15 May	*Variety* report (incorrectly) Chaplin pictures to be distributed by Artcraft.
	June	John Jasper succeeds Henry P. Caulfield as general manager of Lone Star Studio. Carlyle Robinson appointed press representative.
	17 June	*The Immigrant* released.
		CC signs 'million-dollar contract' with First National Exhibitors' Circuit (salary: $1,075,000 per year).
	4 August	CC issues press statement: 'I am ready and willing to answer the call of my country.'
		British High Command forbids wearing of CC toothbrush moustache in army, as likely cause for ridicule.
	22 October	*The Adventurer* released.
	Autumn	CC begins work on building new studio on La Brea Avenue, Los Angeles.
1918	January	CC moves into new studio.
	15 January	Begins shooting *A Dog's Life* (working title: *I Should Worry*).
	23 January	Harry Lauder visits studio; Lauder and CC shoot 745 feet of comedy together.
	25 January	Lauder visits studio with Douglas Fairbanks.
	7 February	Artificial lights first used in studio (for night scene).
	11 February	*A Dog's Life* abandoned; CC begins new film, *Wiggle and Son*.
	12 February	*Wiggle and Son* abandoned; CC resumes *A Dog's Life*.
	26 March	Begins cutting *A Dog's Life*, 'working night and day'; completes it on 31 March.
	1 April	CC leaves Hollywood for Washington on Liberty Bond Tour.

	8 April	In New York for Liberty Loan appeal (rest of month on Liberty Bond tour).
	14 April	*A Dog's Life* released.
	15 April	John Jasper resigns as studio manager.
	9 May	CC announced to appear at benefit for Child Welfare Association of England and Ireland, but is not present.
	27 May	Begins to shoot *Shoulder Arms* (working title: *Camouflage*).
	8 June	Solar eclipse prevents shooting.
	13 June	Mrs Lee (mother of child actor Frankie Lee) paid $2 for use of her sweater in kitchen scene.
	18 July	CC receives and replies to letter from Henrietta Horne (née Hetty Kelly).
	11 August	Essanay release *Triple Trouble*.
	15 August	CC begins work on *The Bond*.
	22 August	Completes *The Bond*.
	31 August	CC begins cutting *Shoulder Arms* (though shooting continues).
	20 October	*Shoulder Arms* released.
	23 October	CC marries Mildred Harris, and moves into 2000 De Mille Drive.
	4 November	Begins work on *Sunnyside*.
		Death of Henrietta Horne (née Hetty Kelly). CC will not learn of death until 1921.
	7 November	Premature national holiday for Armistice.
	11 November	Holiday for real Armistice.
	15 November	Bishop of Birmingham visits studio.
	16 December	*The Bond* released.
1919	1–18 January	CC and Edna Purviance absent from studio.
	15 January	Statement of intent to form United Artists.
	19–28 January	Studio closed down.

29 January	*Sunnyside* abandoned.
	CC begins work on *A Day's Pleasure* (working title: *Putting It Over*).
5 February	Resumes work on *Sunnyside*.
	Contracts of incorporation for United Artists signed.
15 April	CC completes shooting *Sunnyside*.
17 April	Certificates of incorporation for United Artists filed.
21 May	CC begins rehearsals for *A Day's Pleasure* (working title: *Charlie's Picnic*), but does no shooting until 30 June.
26 May	Elsie Codd, CC's English press representative, arrives in Hollywood.
15 June	*Sunnyside* released.
7 July	CC's first son, Norman Spencer Chaplin, born.
8–9 July	Desultory shooting on *A Day's Pleasure*.
10 July	4 pm: Norman Spencer Chaplin dies.
11 July	Burial of Norman Spencer Chaplin, Inglewood Cemetery.
21 July	CC begins auditioning young children for *The Waif*.
30 July	Begins shooting *The Waif* (first version of *The Kid*).
8 August	Publicity film of CC in aeroplane shot at San Diego.
18 August	Commences 'new version' of *The Waif*.
17 September	Jackie Coogan 'lost and licked'.
	Towards end of month CC apparently abandons work on *The Kid*.
1–4 October	Shoots flea and flophouse material now identified as *The Professor*.
7 October	Resumes work on *A Day's Pleasure* (working title now *The Ford Story*).

	19 October	Completes *A Day's Pleasure*.
	14 November	Resumes work on *The Kid* (now known by definitive title).
	15 December	*A Day's Pleasure* released.
	22–27 December	CC gives Jackie Coogan holiday to visit grandmother in San Francisco, as Christmas present.
1920	14 January	CC begins cutting *The Kid* (though shooting continues).
	18 March	News stories on Chaplin marital troubles.
	4 April	Mildred Harris Chaplin begins divorce proceedings, charging mental cruelty.
	7 April	CC and Louis B. Mayer fight in Alexandria Hotel dining room.
	19 April	CC tests possible replacement for Edna Purviance in *The Kid*.
	9 June	Lillita McMurray (Lita Grey) shoots her first scenes in *The Kid*.
	3 August	Mildred Harris Chaplin's suit for divorce.
		During most of the rest of the year, and while cutting *The Kid*, Chaplin is in New York.
	13 November	Mildred Harris Chaplin granted divorce.
1921	22 January	CC begins preparing *The Idle Class* (working title: *Home Again*).
	6 February	*The Kid* released.
	15 February	CC begins shooting *The Idle Class*.
	29 March	Hannah Chaplin is admitted into America.
	25 July	CC completes shooting *The Idle Class*.
		At end of month CC goes to Catalina with Edward Knoblock and Carlyle Robinson to work on scenario.
	6 August	CC begins work on *Pay Day* (working title: *Come Seven*).

	22 August	Begins shooting *Pay Day*: completes eight scenes (348 feet).
	27 August	Leaves Los Angeles for New York and European trip.
	3 September	Sails from New York on *Olympic*.
	9 September	Arrives in London.
	19 September	Arrives in Paris.
	24 September	Arrives in Berlin.
	25 September	*The Idle Class* released.
	30 September	Weekend with H. G. Wells and family.
	6 October	Returns to Paris. Decorated by French Government.
	7 October	Flies back to London.
	7–9 October	Weekend with H. G. Wells and family.
	10 October	Sails from London in *Olympic*.
	17 October	Arrives in New York.
	30 October	Plagiarism suit brought by L. Loeb *re Shoulder Arms*.
	31 October	CC arrives back in Los Angeles.
	6 November	CC looks for locations for *Pay Day*.
	8 November	Trip with Clare and Dickie Sheridan.
	26 November	Begins shooting *Pay Day*.
1922	27 January	CC begins cutting *Pay Day*.
	7 February	Completes shooting and cutting of *Pay Day*.
	1 April	Begins preparing *The Pilgrim*.
	2 April	*Pay Day* released.
	10 April	CC begins shooting *The Pilgrim*.
	1–6 May	New generator installed at studio.
	15 July	CC completes *The Pilgrim*.
	Summer	Meets Peggy Hopkins Joyce.

	October	CC and Pola Negri meet at Actors' Fund Pageant.
	3 October	Mildred Harris Chaplin files for bankruptcy.
	27 November	CC begins shooting *A Woman of Paris*.
1923	25 January	Jesse Lasky announces that Pola Negri's contract with Paramount would not preclude marriage to Chaplin.
	28 January	Chaplin–Negri press conference to announce engagement.
	26 February	*The Pilgrim* released.
	1 March	Pola Negri breaks engagement.
	2 March	Pola Negri and CC announce reconciliation and re-engagement.
	25 June	CC completes shooting of *A Woman of Paris*.
	28 June	Chaplin–Negri engagement definitively broken off.
	29 September	CC completes editing of *A Woman of Paris*.
	1 October	Première of *A Woman of Paris*, Criterion Theatre, Hollywood.
		New York première of *A Woman of Paris*, Lyric Theatre.
	15 October	CC addresses American Child Health Association in Detroit.
	12 December	*Suspicion*, a play by George Appell and Wheeler Dryden (Chaplin's half-brother) produced at Egan Theatre, Los Angeles.
	29 December	'The Lucky Strike', scenario of *The Gold Rush*, registered for copyright.
1924	January	CC preparing *The Gold Rush*.
	8 February	Begins shooting *The Gold Rush*.
	2 March	Lita Grey signed as leading lady for *The Gold Rush*.
	April	Unit shoots on location at Truckee.
	1 May	Unit returns from Truckee.

	22 September	Studio shooting halted. Does not resume until 2 January 1925.
	19 November	Death of Thomas Ince.
	26 November	CC marries Lita Grey in Guaymas, Mexico.
	22 December	Tests made of Georgia Hale: announcement that she would replace Lita Grey in leading role.
1925	2 January	Shooting of *The Gold Rush* resumed.
	February	First rumours of marital disharmony.
	20 February	CC wins suit against Charles Amador for infringement of a comic character.
	20 April	Begins cutting *The Gold Rush*.
	5 May	Birth of son, Charles Spencer Chaplin.
	26 June	Première of *The Gold Rush* at Grauman's Egyptian Theatre, Los Angeles.
	28 June	'Official' birth date of Charles Spencer Chaplin Junior.
	3 July	CC finishes cutting *The Gold Rush*.
	12 July	Decision in Amador case overturned.
	29 July	CC leaves Los Angeles for New York.
	16 August	New York première of *The Gold Rush* at Strand Theatre.
	1 October	Hannah Chaplin's residence permit temporarily renewed.
	15 October	CC returns to Los Angeles.
	2 November	Begins preparation of *The Circus*.
	31 December	Georgia Hale's contract terminates.
1926	2 January	Commencement of Merna Kennedy's contract.
	11 January	CC begins shooting *The Circus*.
	16 January	Josef von Sternberg begins work on *Sea Gulls*, or *A Woman of the Sea*, produced by CC.
	9 March	Von Sternberg begins shooting *A Woman of the Sea*.

	30 March	Birth of Sydney Earle Chaplin.
	1 June	Von Sternberg completes shooting *A Woman of the Sea*.
	16 June	Raquel Meller visits set of *The Circus*.
	7 September	Chaplin is bearer at Rudolph Valentino's funeral.
	28 September	Fire at studio.
	30 November	Lita Grey leaves Chaplin home, with children.
	5 December	Studio operations temporarily suspended.
1927	8 January	CC sues Jim Tully over biographical article in *Pictorial Review*.
	10 January	Lita Grey files divorce complaint.
	18 January	Chaplin safe and vault opened by receivers.
	March	CC invited by Soviet film organization to visit USSR to escape 'hypocrisy'.
	20 April	CC agrees to pay one million dollars settlement on claim for back taxes.
	2 June	CC answers Lita Grey's complaint.
	9 June	Guards taken off duty, as receiver leaves studio.
	22 August	Hearing of divorce suit. Lita Grey granted divorce (final decree 25 August 1928).
	23 August	CC and Alf Reeves return to studio.
	6 September	Work on *The Circus* resumed after eight months' suspension.
	28 October	Preview of *The Circus* at Alexandra Theatre, Glendale.
	17 November	Further preview at Bard & West Adams Theatre, following reshoots and further editing.
	19 November	*The Circus* completed.
	December	CC works on musical score for *The Circus* with Arthur Kay.
	24 December	CC considering material for next film.
1928	6 January	World première of *The Circus* at Strand Theatre, New York.

	27 January	Première of *The Circus* at Grauman's Chinese Theatre, Los Angeles.
	7 March	Trial of CC's suit against First National for unpaid royalties on *The Kid*. Decision in CC's favour, 17 March.
	5 May	CC begins preparation of *City Lights*.
	28 August	Death of Hannah Chaplin at Glendale Hospital, California.
	1 November	Virginia Cherrill put under contract.
	27 December	CC begins shooting *City Lights*.
1929	25 February	CC becomes ill with ptomaine poisoning; contracts 'flu, and does not resume shooting until 1 April.
	10 June	Work begins to move studio buildings fifteen feet, for widening of La Brea. Last until end July.
	28 June	CC replaces Henry Clive with Harry Myers.
	7 September	CC fires Harry Crocker.
	24 September	Winston Churchill and party visit studio.
	11 November	Georgia Hale brought in to replace Virginia Cherill. Remains on payroll until 30 November.
	12 November	Virginia Cherrill removed from payroll (returns 21 November).
	16 November	Gordon Pollock replaces Eddie Gheller as cameraman.
1930	24 February	Death of Mabel Normand.
	5 October	Shooting of *City Lights* completed.
	8 November	CC begins work on musical score.
1931	19 January	Preview of *City Lights* at Tower Theatre.
	30 January	CC attends world première of *City Lights* at Los Angeles Theatre.
	31 January	CC leaves Los Angeles on start of world trip.
	6 February	CC attends New York opening of *City Lights*, George Cohan Theatre.

13 February	Sails for Europe on *Mauretania* with Ralph Barton and Kono.
19 February	Arrives at Southampton, travels by train to London.
20 February	Visits Hanwell Schools.
27 February	Attends London première of *City Lights*, Dominion Theatre.
March	Visits Berlin, Vienna, Venice.
27 March	Travels from Venice to Paris to receive the Légion d'Honneur.
April	Visits Riviera.
23 April	Alf Reeves reports sackings of studio staff.
28 April	CC in Algiers with Sydney Chaplin and May Reeves, then returns to Riviera.
May	Carlyle Robinson sent from Paris to New York.
30 May	CC in Juan-les-Pins with May Reeves.
20 June	Boris Evelinoff put in charge of Chaplin Paris office.
15 July	Carlyle Robinson put in charge of Chaplin New York office.
August	CC in Spain and Paris.
September	CC in London.
22 September	Meeting with Gandhi.
	Weekend at Chartwell.
10 November	Weekend with Astors at Cliveden.
December	Makes trip to North of England.
26 December	CC in St Moritz with the Fairbankses, Sydney Chaplin and May Reeves, where he stays until March 1932.
1932 January	Carlyle Robinson dismissed.
12 March	CC and Sydney Chaplin leave for Far East. Farewell to May Reeves.

3 April	Edna Purviance, ill and without money, appeals for help to CC.
23 April	CC and Sydney in Singapore; CC becomes ill with fever.
7 May	CC and Sydney leave Singapore for Japan.
14 May	Arrive Tokyo.
2 June	CC, Sydney and Kono leave Yokohama in *Hikawa Maru*.
10 June	CC and Kono arrive in Hollywood. Sydney Chaplin returns to Europe.

[NOTE: The exact dates of Chaplin's itinerary during this 1931–2 trip are extremely elusive: at this distance in time, one must be grateful for sightings *en route* which the foregoing dates largely represent.]

27 June	CC releases article on Economic Solution to press.
July	Until February 1933, Chaplin is occupied in writing series of articles, 'A Comedian Sees the World', for *Woman's Home Companion*.
July	First meeting with Paulette Goddard.
25 August	Loyd Wright (lawyer) files CC's petition objecting to sons working in motion pictures.
27 August	CC in court for petition.
2 September	Decision in CC's favour.
15 October	CC served with subpoena to appear in court, 26 October.
26 October	CC in court on Lita Grey Chaplin's appeal. Decision in his favour.
1933 March	Buys yacht, *Panacea*. Spends much of this summer on it.
25 March	First record of work on *Modern Times*.
21 June	Original and only negative of *A Woman of the Sea* or *Sea Gulls* destroyed in presence of witnesses.
	Work on *Modern Times* and preparations for production continue to end of year.

	23 October	CC speaks for National Recovery Act on Columbia Broadcasting System.
	7/9 December	CC at Hearst Ranch, San Simeon.
	29/31 December	CC at Yosemite.
1934		Preparations for *Modern Times* continue.
	16 May	Kono resigns, is given position with United Artists in Tokyo.
	4 September	Paulette Goddard signs contract with studio.
	11 October	CC begins shooting *Modern Times*.
	16 December	Douglas Fairbanks and Lady Mountbatten visit set.
	28 December	Sound tests of CC and Paulette Goddard.
1935	17 July	Title *Modern Times* officially announced.
	30 August	Shooting on *Modern Times* completed.
	27 November	H. G. Wells arrives in Hollywood as guest of CC; stays until 24 December.
	4 December	CC has row with Al Newman over music for film.
	22 December	Sound for *Modern Times* completed.
	28 December	Preview of *Modern Times* in San Francisco, followed by cuts and redubbing.
1936	5 January	Preview of *Modern Times* at Alexander Theatre, Glendale.
	5 February	*Modern Times* opens at Rivoli, New York.
	12 February	*Modern Times* Hollywood première at Grauman's Chinese Theatre.
	17 February	CC embarks on *Coolidge* with Paulette and Mrs Goddard and Frank Yonamori (valet) for San Francisco *en route* for Honolulu.
	26 February	They arrive in Honolulu but decide to go on to Hong Kong.
	7 March–22 May	Travelling to Yokohama, Kobe, Shanghai, Hong Kong, Manila, Saigon, French Indo-China, Japan.

	22 April	CC erroneously reported dead in Indo-China.
	22 May	Leave Japan for California on *Coolidge*; arrive 3 June.
	11 June	Death of Nathan Burkan, for long CC's lawyer.
		During rest of year CC works on *Stowaway*, *Regency* and Napoleon project. This work continues into 1937.
1937	23 April	Sonores Tobis Films bring suit for plagiarism of *A Nous la Liberté*. (Suit dismissed 19 November 1939.)
	26 May	*Regency* laid aside.
	1 October	Paulette Goddard takes screen test for role of Scarlett O'Hara in *Gone With the Wind*.
1938		Chaplin spends much of year at Pebble Beach, working intermittently on projects.
	October	Begins work on *The Great Dictator*.
1939	9 January	Work begins on sound-proofing studio stages (finished 10 February).
	21 January	Sydney Chaplin arrives in Hollywood from Europe.
	25 March	Wheeler Dryden arrives in Hollywood to work at studio.
	23 June	Title *The Great Dictator* registered.
	9 September	CC begins shooting *The Great Dictator*.
		House Un-American Activities Committee begins investigations.
	15 November	Douglas Fairbanks visits studio with wife: last meeting with CC.
	12 December	Death of Douglas Fairbanks (funeral, 15 December).
1940	28 March	CC completes main shooting of *The Great Dictator*.
	29 March	Begins cutting *The Great Dictator*.
	23 June	Resumes shooting, including final speech.

	3 July	Resumes cutting.
	22 July	Begins work on recording and music.
	5 September	Preview at Riverside Theatre, Riverside, followed by cutting, reshooting and redubbing.
	20 September	Preview at Long Beach, followed by further retakes and redubbing.
	11 October	CC goes to New York; remains until 10 February 1941.
	15 October	World première of *The Great Dictator* at Capitol and Astor Theatres, New York. CC present.
	14 November	Hollywood première of *The Great Dictator*, Carthay Circle Theatre.
1941	26 March– 30 April	CC in New York.
	15 April	Konrad Bercovici brings plagiarism suit over *The Great Dictator*.
	9 June	CC begins work on reissue of *The Gold Rush*, with sound track.
	26(?) June	Puts Joan Berry (Barry) under contract.
		CC working on *Shadow and Substance*.
1942		CC continues work on *Shadow and Substance*.
	18 May	Speech for Russian War Relief in San Francisco.
	19 May	New version of *The Gold Rush* opens at Paramount, Hollywood and Paramount, Los Angeles.
	22 May	Joan Barry's contract cancelled by mutual consent.
	4 June	Paulette Goddard granted divorce (marriage revealed to have taken place in Far East, 1936).
	22 July	CC speaks by radio-telephone to Madison Square Second Front rally.
	12 October	Leaves for New York with Tim Durant and Edward Chaney (valet).
	16 October	Speaks at 'Artists' Front to Win the War' rally, Carnegie Hall.

	30 October	Returns to Los Angeles.
		Meets Oona O'Neill.
	November	Begins work on script for *Landru (Monsieur Verdoux)*.
	25 November	Speaks at 'Salute Our Russian Ally' meeting, Orchestra Hall Chicago.
	3 December	Speaks at 'Arts for Russia' dinner, Hotel Pennsylvania, New York.
	10 December	Returns home from New York and Chicago.
	23 December	Joan Barry breaks into Chaplin house, carrying gun.
	29 December	*Shadow and Substance* shelved.
1943		CC works on *Landru (Monsieur Verdoux)* script throughout year.
	7 March	Broadcasts 'Lambeth Walk' talk to Britain from CBS studio.
		Records speech at Soviet consul's office to be sent to USSR.
	4 June	Joan Barry accuses CC of being father of unborn child.
	16 June	CC marries Oona O'Neill at Carpenteria, Santa Barbara.
	26 June	CC and Oona Chaplin return from Carpenteria.
	14 September	CC's deposition in Barry case.
	2 October	Joan Barry gives birth to girl, Carol Ann.
1944	10 February	CC indicted by Federal Grand Jury on Mann Act charges and for conspiring with Los Angeles police and others to deprive Barry of civil rights in having her held on vagrancy charges.
	14 February	CC in court.
	15 February	Blood tests prove CC not father of Barry's child.
	21 February	CC arraigned.
	25 February	CC in court to plead against Mann Act charges.

	26 February	CC in court – pleads not guilty in Mann Act case.
	9 March	CC in court – pleads not guilty in conspiracy case.
	21 March	Mann Act case opens.
	4 April	CC found not guilty on Mann Act charges.
	4–15 May	CC and Oona in Palm Springs.
	15 May	Violation of civil rights charges dropped.
	29 May– 30 June	CC and Oona absent on New York trip.
	20 July	Death of Mildred Harris.
	1 August	Birth of daughter to CC and Oona, Geraldine Leigh Chaplin.
	26 September	CC dictates article to 'youth of Soviet Russia'.
	13 December	Opening of Barry paternity trial.
	30 December	CC injures foot: in Cedars of Lebanon Hospital until 2 January.
1945	2 January	Paternity suit jury fail to agree (7–5 in favour of CC). Retrial ordered.
	26 January	Work begins on *Landru (Monsieur Verdoux)*. Marilyn Nash tested.
	20 February	CC issues statement to press.
	4 April	Opening of new paternity trial.
	17 April	Paternity trial verdict for Barry (11 votes to 1).
	22–27 April	CC and Oona in Palm Springs.
	10 May	CC files motion for new trial.
	6 June	Motion for new trial denied.
	16 June	CC in court *re* Barry support.
1946	11 February	Script of *Monsieur Verdoux* sent for copyright.
	7 March	Birth of Michael John Chaplin.
	11 March	CC has interview with Joseph Breen.
	18 March	Edna Purviance arrives at studio with view to playing in film.

	7 April	Death of Alf Reeves.
	8 April	John McFadden appointed General Manager of studio.
	10 April	Funeral of Alf Reeves.
	21 May	Begins shooting *Monsieur Verdoux*.
	5 September	Shooting completed.
1947	11 April	World première of *Monsieur Verdoux*, Broadway Theatre, New York.
	12 April	Hostile press conference in New York.
	12 June	Congressman John Rankin demands Chaplin's deportation.
	20 July	CC publicly accepts invitation from House Un-American Activities Committee to testify.
	23 September	Accepts subpoena for HUAC investigations.
	November	Sends telegram to Pablo Picasso in support of Hanns Eisler.
	17 December	Catholic War Veterans urge Justice and State Departments to investigate and arrange for CC's deportation.
1948		By start of year, CC working on story of *Footlights (Limelight)*.
	13 September	Begins dictating *Footlights*: work on script continues throughout following year.
1949	28 March	Josephine Hannah Chaplin born at St John's Hospital, Santa Monica.
	5 May	Walter Wanger rents studio for tests of Greta Garbo.
	3–18 August	CC and Oona on trip to New York.
1950	17 January–13 February	CC and Oona on trip to New York.
	8 April	*City Lights* reissued. Opened Globe Theatre, New York.
	6 September	Title *Limelight* registered.

	11 September	Script of *Limelight* sent for copyright.
	17 September–8 October	CC and Oona on trip to New York.
	December	CC begins working on music for *Limelight*.
1951	11–22 January	CC and Oona on trip to New York.
	February	CC begins interviewing actresses for *Limelight*.
	22–28 April	CC in New York to test Claire Bloom.
	19 May	Birth of daughter, Victoria, at St John's Hospital, Santa Monica.
	21 May	Start of enlargement of house at 1085 Summit Drive. Alterations completed 29 June.
	18 September	Claire Bloom sails on *Mauretania* from London.
	19 November	CC begins main shooting of *Limelight*.
1952	25 January	Main shooting completed.
	15 May	Roughcut of *Limelight* shown to James Agee and Sidney Bernstein.
	2 August	Preview at Paramount Studio.
	6 September	Chaplins leave Hollywood.
	17 September	Chaplin family sails from New York on *Queen Elizabeth*.
	19 September	Re-entry permit rescinded.
	23 September	Chaplins arrive in London.
	23 October	Première of *Limelight*, Odeon, Leicester Square, London.
	17–27 November	Oona Chaplin on trip to Los Angeles to wind up business affairs.
1953	January	Many theatres in USA cancel showings of *Limelight*.
	5 January	Chaplins move into Manoir de Ban, Corsier sur Vevey, Switzerland.
	March	Holiday on French Riviera.

	6 March	*Limelight* named Best Film by Foreign Language Press Critics in USA.
	10 April	CC surrenders US re-entry permit.
	23 August	Birth of son, Eugene Anthony.
	September 18	Studio sold to Webb and Knapp.
1954	10 February	Oona Chaplin renounces US citizenship.
	2 May	CC announces he will make film called *The Ex-King (A King in New York)*.
	27 May	Awarded World Peace Council Prize.
	18 July	Meets Chou En Lai in Geneva.
	10 October	Makes personal appearance in ring of Knie Circus in Vevey.
		Distributes Peace Prize money to poor of Paris and Lambeth.
1955		Preparing *A King in New York*.
	1 March	CC sells remainder of stock in United Artists.
1956	24 April	CC meets Bulganin and Khrushchev at Claridges.
	25 May	Is made honorary member of ACTT.
	May–July	Shooting *A King in New York*.
	15 June	US Inland Revenue Service claims for back taxes.
	10 August	Reissue of *The Gold Rush* in Britain.
	25 August	Press conference in Paris.
	August–October	Editing, recording, dubbing *A King in New York* in Paris.
1957		CC continues work on *A King in New York* during early part of year.
	23 May	Birth of daughter, Jane Cecil.
	12 September	London première of *A King in New York*.
	24 September	CC bars US newsmen from Paris première.
	30 September	Death of Wheeler Dryden, in Hollywood.
1958	13 January	Death of Edna Purviance.

	21 February	CC's name excluded from Los Angeles 'Walk of Fame'.
	November	CC works on *The Chaplin Revue*.
	30 December	Settles US tax claims.
1959	16 April	Seventieth birthday. Chaplin says he will bring back The Little Fellow.
	24 September	*The Chaplin Revue* released.
	3 December	Birth of daughter, Annette Emily.
1960	July	Holiday in Ireland.
	20 December	Death of Mack Sennett.
1961	July	Holiday in Far East.
1962	April	Holiday in Switzerland, Ireland, London, Paris, Venice.
	27 June	Receives honorary doctorate from Oxford.
	6 July	Receives honorary doctorate from Durham University.
	8 July	Birth of son, Christopher James.
1963	June	Roy Export Company wins case against Atlas Films for unauthorized distribution of *The Gold Rush*.
	September	CC seeks suppression of brochure for rejuvenation treatment, quoting CC as successful patient.
1964		CC talks of writing opera, and slapstick comedy for Sydney Chaplin Junior.
	June	Attends Callas Gala at Paris Opera.
	September	Publication of *My Autobiography*.
1965	16 April	Death of Sydney Chaplin Senior.
	2 June	CC receives Erasmus Prize with Ingmar Bergman.
	1 November	London Press Conference to announce *A Countess From Hong Kong*.
1966	25 January	CC begins shooting *A Countess From Hong Kong*.

	11 May	Completes shooting *A Countess From Hong Kong*.
	11 October	CC breaks ankle.
1967	2 January	*A Countess From Hong Kong* opens.
	18 June	Death of Roland Totheroh.
1968		CC works on *The Freak*.
	20 March	Death of Charles Chaplin Junior.
1970		CC composes new score for *The Circus*.
		Black Inc. takes distribution of Chaplin films.
1971	31 October	CC is awarded Grande Medaille de Vermeil by City of Paris.
1972	March	CC's name added to Los Angeles 'Walk of Fame'.
	2 April	CC arrives in New York.
	3 April	Appears at show at Philharmonic Hall, Lincoln Center.
	6 April	Is awarded Handel Medallion, New York.
	16 April	Is awarded Special Academy Award, in Hollywood.
	3 September	Is awarded Golden Lion at Venice Film Festival.
1974	October	Publication of *My Life in Pictures*.
1975	4 March	CC is knighted by HM Queen Elizabeth II.
1976	30 June	CC is reported as saying: 'To work is to live – and I love to live'.
1977	15 October	CC makes last trip from home – to see Knie Circus in Vevey.
	25 December	CC dies in his sleep at Manoir de Ban, Corsier sur Vevey.
	27 December	Funeral at Vevey.
1978	1 March	Theft of body.
	17 March	Recovery of body.
	11–14 December	Trial of Ganev and Wardas for theft of body.

1980	14 January	Leicester Square hoax: *papier maché* statue of CC erected.
	27 September	Parc Charles Chaplin inaugurated in Vevey.
	19 December	Plaque placed on 287 Kennington Road. Unveiled by Sir Ralph Richardson.
1981	14 April	Statue by John Doubleday placed in Leicester Square. Unveiled by Sir Ralph Richardson.
1982	22 August	Bronze replica of Doubleday statue erected in Parc Charles Chaplin in Vevey.

APPENDIX II
Tours of 'The Eight Lancashire Lads', 1898-1900

Chaplin is believed to have been with the troupe throughout the period detailed below. It is possible that the troupe did not perform at all during the weeks for which there is no record.

1898	week commencing:	
	26 December	Theatre Royal, Manchester (*Babes in the Wood*).
1899	2 January	Theatre Royal, Manchester (*Babes in the Wood*).
	9 January	Theatre Royal, Manchester (*Babes in the Wood*).
	16 January	Theatre Royal, Manchester (*Babes in the Wood*).
	23 January	Theatre Royal, Manchester (*Babes in the Wood*).
	30 January	Theatre Royal, Manchester (*Babes in the Wood*).
	6 February	Theatre Royal, Manchester (*Babes in the Wood*).
	13 February	Theatre Royal, Manchester (*Babes in the Wood*).
	27 February	Grand Theatre, Manchester.
	6 March	Grand Theatre, Manchester.
	3 April	Oxford Music Hall, Oxford Street, London.
	10 April	Oxford Music Hall, Oxford Street, London.
	17 April	Oxford Music Hall, Oxford Street, London.
	24 April	Oxford Music Hall, Oxford Street, London.
	1 May	Oxford Music Hall, Oxford Street, London.

	8 May	Oxford Music Hall, Oxford Street, London.
	15 May	Oxford Music Hall, Oxford Street, London.
	29 May	Empire, Cardiff.
	5 June	Empire, Swansea.
	17 July	Empire, Nottingham.
	2 October	Paragon, Mile End Road, London.
	9 October	Paragon, Mile End Road, London.
	16 October	Paragon, Mile End Road, London.
	23 October	Paragon, Mile End Road, London.
	6 November	Oxford Music Hall, Oxford Street, London.
	13 November	Oxford Music Hall, Oxford Street, London.
	20 November	Oxford Music Hall, Oxford Street, London.
	27 November	Oxford Music Hall, Oxford Street, London.
	5 December	Oxford Music Hall, Oxford Street, London.
	12 December	Oxford Music Hall, Oxford Street, London.
	19 December	Oxford Music Hall, Oxford Street, London.
	26 December	New Alexandra Theatre, Stoke Newington, London (pantomime: *Sinbad the Sailor*).
1900	1 January	New Alexandra Theatre, Stoke Newington, London.
	8 January	New Alexandra Theatre, Stoke Newington, London.
	15 January	New Alexandra Theatre, Stoke Newington, London.
	22 January	New Alexandra Theatre, Stoke Newington, London.
	29 January	New Alexandra Theatre, Stoke Newington, London.
	5 February	New Alexandra Theatre, Stoke Newington, London.
	26 February	Empire Theatre, Newcastle-upon-Tyne.

5 March	Empire Palace, South Shields.
12 March	Empire Palace, Glasgow.
19 March	Royal, Holborn (Holborn Empire), London.
26 March	Empire Palace, Edinburgh.
2 April	Empire Palace, Birmingham.
9 April	Empire Palace, Birmingham.
16 April	Tivoli Music Hall, Strand, London.
23 April	Tivoli Music Hall, Strand, London.
30 April	Tivoli Music Hall, Strand, London.
7 May	Tivoli Music Hall, Strand, London.
14 May	Tivoli Music Hall, Strand, London.
21 May	Tivoli Music Hall, Strand, London.
28 May	Tivoli Music Hall, Strand, London.
4 June	Canterbury Music Hall, London.
6 August	Camberwell Palace of Varieties, London.
20 August	Oxford Music Hall, Oxford Street, London.
27 August	Oxford Music Hall, Oxford Street, London.
3 September	Oxford Music Hall, Oxford Street, London.
10 September	Oxford Music Hall, Oxford Street, London.
17 September	Palace Theatre, Hull.
24 September	Empire Palace, Sheffield.
1 October	Empire Palace, Leeds.
8 October	Empire Theatre, Bradford.
15 October	Palace Theatre, Manchester.
22 October	Palace Theatre, Manchester.
29 October	Empire Theatre, Liverpool.
5 November	Empire Theatre, Liverpool.
12 November	Empire Theatre, Dublin.
19 November	Empire Theatre, Dublin.

26 November	Empire Theatre, Belfast.
3 December	Empire Theatre, New Cross.
24 December	According to Chaplin the Lancashire Lads appeared in the pantomime *Cinderella* at the London Hippodrome, which ran from 24 December to 13 April 1901.

APPENDIX III
Tours of 'Sherlock Holmes', 1903-1906

Chaplin is thought to have played the role of Billy throughout these tours, in the absence of any record of performances missed through illness or other causes.

1903   week commencing:

Charles Frohman's Northern Company
H. A. SAINTSBURY as Holmes

27 July	Pavilion Theatre, Whitechapel Road, London.
10 August	Theatre Royal, Newcastle.
17 August	Lyceum Theatre, Sheffield.
26 October	Theatre Royal, Bolton.
2 November	Royal Court Theatre, Wigan.
9 November	Theatre Royal, Ashton under Lyne.
16 November	New Theatre Royal, Stockport.
23 November	Gaiety Theatre, Burnley.
30 November	New Theatre Royal, Rochdale.
7 December	Victoria Theatre, Broughton.
14 December	Theatre Royal, Bury.
21 December	Theatre Royal, Dewsbury.
28 December	Royalty Theatre and Opera House, Barrow.

1904	4 January	Royal Opera House, Wakefield.
	11 January	Queen's Theatre, Leeds.
	18 January	Grand Theatre, West Hartlepool.
	25 January	Grand Theatre, West Hartlepool.
	1 February	Grand Opera House, York.
	4 February	Grand Opera House, Harrogate.
	8 February	Theatre Royal, Jarrow.
	15 February	Theatre Royal, Middlesbrough.
	22 February	Avenue Theatre, Sunderland.
	29 February	Theatre Royal, North Shields.
	7 March	Prince of Wales Theatre, Grimsby.
	14 March	His Majesty's Theatre, Aberdeen.
	21 March	His Majesty's Theatre, Dundee.
	28 March	Paisley Theatre, Paisley.
	4 April	His Majesty's Theatre, Carlisle.
	11 April	Royal Princess's Theatre, Glasgow.
	18 April	Grand Theatre, Glasgow.
	25 April	Grand Theatre, West Hartlepool.
	2 May	Grand Theatre, Hyson Green, Nottingham.
	9 May	Theatre Royal, Aldershot.
	16 May	Theatre Royal, Bradford.
	23 May	His Majesty's Opera House, Blackpool.
	30 May	Royal West London Theatre, Church Street, Edgware Road.
	6 June	Royal West London Theatre, Church Street, Edgware Road.

Charles Frohman's Midland Company
KENNETH RIVINGTON as Holmes

	31 October	New Theatre Royal, King's Lynn (two-day engagement only).

	7 November	Theatre Royal, Shrewsbury.
	14 November	Royal Court Theatre, Warrington.
	21 November	*No engagement traced*
	28 November	Prince of Wales Theatre, Mexborough.
	5 December	Lyceum Theatre, Sheffield.
	12 December	Theatre Royal, Barnsley.
	19 December	*No engagement traced*
1905	2 January	Theatre Royal, Darlington.
	9 January	Theatre Royal, Dumfries (three-day engagement only).
	16 January	*No engagement traced*
	23 January	Theatre Royal, Perth.
	30 January	New Century Theatre, Motherwell.
	6 February	Theatre Royal, Greenock.
	13 February	*No engagement traced*
	20 February	Royal Worcester Theatre, Bootle.
	27 February	Princes' Theatre, Accrington.
	6 March	Theatre Royal, Hyde.
	13 March	*No engagement traced*
	20 March	Theatre Royal and Opera House, Merthyr Tydfil.
	27 March	*No engagement traced*
	3 April	Theatre Royal, Tonypandy.
	10 April	*No engagement traced*
	17 April	Poole's Opera House, Perth.

Harry Yorke's Company
H. LAWRENCE LAYTON as Holmes

	12 August	Theatre Royal, Blackburn.
	19 August	Theatre Royal, Hull.
	26 August	Theatre Royal, Dewsbury.

4 September	Theatre Royal, Huddersfield.
11 September	Queen's Theatre, Manchester.
18 September	Rotunda Theatre, Liverpool.
25 September	Court Theatre, Warrington.

From 3–14 October Chaplin played the role of Billy in William C. Gillette's *The Painful Predicament of Sherlock Holmes* at the Duke of York's Theatre, St Martin's Lane, London.

From 17 October to 2 December Chaplin played the role of Billy in William C. Gillette's revival of *Sherlock Holmes* at the Duke of York's Theatre, London. Royal Gala performance, 20 November.

1906   **Harry Yorke's Company**

1 January	Grand Theatre, Doncaster.
8 January	*No engagement traced*
15 January	New Theatre, Cambridge.
22 January	Pavilion Theatre, Whitechapel Road, London.
29 January	Dalston Theatre, London.
5 February	Carlton Theatre, Greenwich.
12 February	Crown Theatre, Peckham.
19 February	Lyceum Theatre, Crewe.
26 February	Theatre Royal, Rochdale.

Frohman at times had three *Sherlock Holmes* companies touring at the same time. Other boys who played the part of Billy the page included Walter Hicks, Cedric Walters and Ernest Hollern. The last named took over from Chaplin when he left the 1905 tour to play the role at the Duke of York's. Chaplin left the company on 30 September: nevertheless he received a favourable notice in *The Era* for his performance at the Theatre Royal, Preston in the week of 2 October. Presumably his sudden departure had not permitted time to alter the programmes. It is a useful lesson that contemporary documentation must always be regarded with caution.

APPENDIX IV

Tours of 'Casey's Court Circus', 1906-1907

Chaplin is believed to have remained with the company throughout the tour.

1906	week commencing:	
	3 March	Advertisement in *The Era* announces *'Casey's Court Circus'* is 'copyrighted and to be produced shortly'.
	17 March	Advertisement in *The Era* announces *'Casey's Court Circus'* is 'in active rehearsal'.
	14 May	Empire Theatre, Bradford.
	21 May	Olympia Theatre, Liverpool.
	28 May	Coliseum Theatre, Glasgow.
	4 June	Empire Theatre, Newcastle.
	11 June	Empire Theatre, Leeds.
	18 June	*No engagement traced*
	25 June	Empire Theatre, Sheffield.
	2 July	Empire Theatre, Ardwick.
	9 July	Empire Theatre, Nottingham.
	16 July	Palace Theatre, Leicester.
	23 July	Bordsley Palace Theatre, Birmingham.
	30 July	Palace Theatre, Halifax.

	6 August	Richmond Theatre, London.
	13 August	*No engagement traced*
	20 August	Holloway Empire, London.
	27 August	New Cross Empire, London.
	3 September	*No engagement traced*
	10 September	Shepherds Bush Empire, London.
	17 September	Stratford East Empire, London.
	24 September	Surrey Theatre of Varieties, London.
	1 October	Empire, Cardiff.
	8 October	*No engagement traced*
	15 October	*No engagement traced*
	22 October	*No engagement traced*
	29 October	Palace Theatre, Southampton.
	5 November	*No engagement traced*
	12 November	*No engagement traced*
	19 November	*No engagement traced*
	26 November	*No engagement traced*
	3 December	Palace Theatre, Blackburn.
	10 December	Palace Theatre, Bath.
	17 December	Sadlers Wells, London.
	24 December	Empire, South Shields.
	31 December	*No engagement traced*
1907	7 January	*No engagement traced*
	14 January	*No engagement traced*
	21 January	Empire Theatre, Belfast.
	28 January	Empire Theatre, Dublin.
	4 February	Olympia Theatre, Liverpool.
	11 February	*No engagement traced*
	18 February	*No engagement traced*

25 February	*No engagement traced*
4 March	Palace Theatre, West Hartlepool.
11 March	*No engagement traced*
18 March	Zoo and Hippodrome, Glasgow.
25 March	*No engagement traced*
1 April	Empire Theatre, Newcastle-upon-Tyne.
8 April	Hippodrome, Manchester.
15 April	*No engagement traced*
22 April	Empire Palace, Leeds.
29 April	Empire Palace, Birmingham.
6 May	Empire Theatre, Nottingham.
13 May	Hackney Empire, London.
20 May	Holloway Empire, London.
27 May	New Cross Empire, London.
3 June	Stratford Empire, London.
10 June	Shepherds Bush Empire, London.
17 June	Palace Theatre, Leicester.
24 June	Foresters' Music Hall, Bethnal Green, London.
1 July	Surrey Theatre of Varieties, London.
8 July	*No engagement traced*
15 July	Sadlers Wells, London.

APPENDIX V

Three Keystone scenarios

The three shot-by-shot scripts which follow have been recreated from the best available copies of the films, and are believed to represent the complete and original form Chaplin intended. They have been selected to illustrate the rapid progress and variety of Chaplin's approach to film craft in the formative year he spent at Keystone.

CAUGHT IN THE RAIN

Caught in the Rain was probably his first effort as a director: he was only allowed to make it with his own guarantee of $1500 against loss. It is evidently made with great care: Chaplin has conscientiously studied the post-Griffith shot-by-shot method of film construction, and in fact the single reel contains rather more shots than the average Keystone production. The *mise-en-scène* of each shot and scene is already admirable, within the studio formula of only a dozen fixed camera set-ups: the bench, the refreshment stand, the drinking fountain, the road crossing, the saloon doorway, the hotel exterior, the hotel lobby, the balcony and the ground beneath it, and the usual Keystone composite setting of a room on either side of a hallway.

TITLE: A BIG THIRST AND A LITTLE WIFE

1   A bench in the park. Mack Swain and Alice Davenport sit side by side. Mack gets up and exits to –
2   Refreshment stand. Mack takes a drink.
3   The Bench (as shot 1). Alice plucks a rose.

TITLE: A WRECKER OF HOMES

4   A drinking fountain. Charlie, trying to take a drink, soaks himself.
5   The Bench. Alice laughs flirtatiusly; then remembers herself.
6   The Drinking Fountain. Charlie exits to –
7   The Bench. Charlie sits down – on Alice's rose.

TITLE: 'SOMETHING ATTACKED ME IN THE REAR'

8   The Bench. Charlie flirts with Alice, but she is unresponsive.

TITLE: 'WE SEEM TO BE GETTING ALONG WELL TOGETHER'

9   The Bench. Alice remains unresponsive.
10   Refreshment Stand. Mack notices what is going on.

TITLE: 'MY WIFE – WITH A LADY-KILLER!'

11   Refreshment Stand. Mack is clearly angry.
12   The Bench. Alice tells Charlie off.
13   Refreshment Stand. Mack fiercely exits towards –
14   The Bench. Charlie rests his feet on Alice's knee. Mack enters scene and yells at both of them. As he abuses Alice, he keeps hitting Charlie with his elbow.

TITLE: 'TAKE A BACK SEAT – YOU RUSTY ROMEO'

15   The Bench. Mack shoves Charlie into the bushes and goes off with Alice.
16   The Bench. Charlie gets up, brushes himself off and exits.
17   A road. Mack and Alice.
18   Saloon – exterior. Charlie at door of saloon.

TITLE: LOVE IS A THIRSTY BUSINESS

19   Saloon – exterior. Charlie licks his lips, then drags himself into the saloon by his own ear.
20   Hotel – exterior. Mack angrily shoves Alice into the door.
21   Hotel lobby – interior.
22   Saloon – exterior. Charlie emerges, evidently drunk. He leans on a convenient cop (who remains impassive in shock) then strikes a match on him.

TITLE: 'A STRIKING FELLOW LIKE YOU SHOULD BE A MATCH FOR ANYONE'

23   Saloon – exterior. Charlie flicks his match at the cop, but beats a hasty retreat when the cop threatens him with his truncheon.
24   Hotel lobby. Mack and Alice.
25   A road. Charlie crosses, narrowly escaping the cars which rush past him.
26   Hotel corridor with rooms to left and right. Mack and Alice enter room at right.
27   First Hotel Room. Mack and Alice enter.
28   Hotel – exterior. Charlie follows an attractive girl who enters the door. She slams the door in his face, but he enters after her.
29   Hotel lobby. Charlie enters and trips over an old man's gouty leg.
30   First hotel room. Mack and Alice. Mack is drinking.
31   Hotel lobby. Charlie whispers to receptionist, while pointing to a group of girls.

TITLE: 'WHO DOES THE HAT WITH THE FEATHERS BELONG TO?'

32   Hotel lobby. Charlie casually throws the hotel register at the gouty gentleman.
33   First hotel room. Mack and Alice quarrelling.

TITLE: 'AFTER TWENTY YEARS OF MARRIED LIFE I FIND YOU
      FLIRTING WITH A SCAVENGER'

34   First hotel room. Mack and Alice quarrelling.

35   Hotel lobby. Charlie attempts to ascend the stairs, but slides down on his face.
He tries again, and this time bowls over the gouty man who is also making the
ascent. At the next try the gouty man falls on top of Charlie who hits the
receptionist in revenge. He tries again, his body leaning backwards at a
45-degree angle.

36   First hotel room. Mack and Alice still quarrelling.

37   Hotel lobby. Charlie is now wearing the girl's feather hat, d'Artagnan style.
The girl grabs back her hat and goes upstairs, which is incentive enough for
Charlie finally to make the ascent successfully.

38   Hotel corridor (as shot 26). Charlie passes the gouty gentleman, and aims a
passing kick at him.

39   First hotel room. Mack and Alice.

40   Hotel corridor. Charlie inspects lock of first hotel room.

41   First hotel room. Mack and Alice, reconciled at last.

42   Hotel corridor. Charlie attempts to unlock first hotel room with a cigarette
instead of a key.

TITLE: 'AH, LOCKED!'

43   First hotel room. Charlie enters. Mack and Alice, sitting on the bed, are at first
unaware of his presence as he sprinkles the contents of Mack's bottle on his
head as if it were brilliantine, combs his hat, takes a drink, and wipes his
mouth on Alice's hat. Mack finally remonstrates.

TITLE: 'OUT YOU GO – YOU HE-VAMP'

44   First hotel room. Mack throws Charlie out.

45   Hotel corridor. As Charlie emerges from the room the gouty man, passing by,
sees him and hurriedly flees.

46   First hotel room. Mack and Alice are quarrelling again.

47   Hotel corridor. Charlie enters Second Hotel Room, on left.

48   Second hotel room. Charlie does a long undressing routine. He wipes his
shoes on his dickey and his brow on his collar. He then becomes entangled in
his trousers. He is already wearing his pyjamas under his outer clothes.

49   First hotel room. Alice is in bed; Mack exits.

50   Second hotel room. Charlie gets into bed, having first removed hair brush
from between the sheets.

51   Hotel – exterior. Mack comes out of door.

52   Second hotel room. As an afterthought, Charlie puts his boots under the
pillow for safety.

TITLE: MIDNIGHT – THE SLEEP WALKING

53   First hotel room. Somnambulant Alice gets out of bed and opens the door.

54   Hotel – exterior. A sudden shower of rain soaks Mack.

55   Hotel corridor. Alice walks from door of first hotel room to door of second
hotel room.

56   Second hotel room. Alice enters door and sits on bed. Charlie wakens,
alarmed.

TITLE: 'WHOEVER SENT YOU MUST HAVE OWED ME A GRUDGE'

57 Second hotel room. Alice picks up Charlie's trousers and begins to go through the pockets. Charlie snatches them away and hides them under his pillow.

58 First hotel room. Mack re-enters, finds Alice gone, and begins to call out.

59 Second hotel room. Charlie is very alarmed.

60 Hotel corridor. Charlie comes out of his room at the same time as Mack. Charlie affects nonchalance in face of Mack's anger.

TITLE: 'I'M ITCHING TO THROTTLE SOMEONE'

61 Corridor. Charlie and Mack. Mack exits.

62 Second hotel room. Charlie re-enters to find Alice is now in his bed. He collapses on the bed. This awakens Alice, who is shocked by her situation.

63 Hotel corridor. Charlie peeks out of the door of his room, and sees it is empty.

64 Second hotel room. Charlie pushes Alice out into corridor.

65 Hotel corridor. Charlie pushing Alice out of door.

66 Hotel lobby. Mack questions receptionist, then returns upstairs.

67 First hotel room. Charlie enters with Alice.

TITLE: 'KEEP CALM – I'LL BE QUITE ALL RIGHT'

68 First hotel room. Charlie snatches a drink. Alice becomes hysterical.

69 Hotel corridor. Mack returns.

70 First hotel room. Charlie and Alice in consternation. Alice pushes Charlie out of the window.

71 Balcony outside window. Charlie in pouring rain.

72 First hotel room. Alice makes up to Mack.

73 Balcony outside window. Charlie suffering in the rain.

74 Exterior, below the balcony. A policeman yells at Charlie, ordering him down.

75 Balcony. Charlie signals helplessness.

76 Exterior, below the balcony. Policeman fires gun at Charlie.

77 Balcony. Charlie terrified.

78 Exterior, below the balcony. The policeman fires again.

79 First hotel room. Charlie suddenly re-enters through the window.

80 Hotel – exterior. The Keystone Kops arrive.

81 Hotel corridor. Charlie flees from first hotel room, managing to kick the gouty man who happens to be passing.

82 Hotel lobby. The Keystone Kops rush in.

83 Hotel corridor. Charlie rushes back into his room.

84 Second hotel room. Charlie firmly shuts the door behind him.

85 First hotel room. Mack exits.

86 Hotel corridor. Coming out of his room, Mack rushes into arms of the Keystone Kops. They fall like ninepins (or like Keystone Kops).

87 Second hotel room. Charlie listens at door.

88 Corridor. The Kops pick themselves up.

89 Second hotel room. Charlie leaps at the door.

90 Hotel corridor. Charlie's door, bursting open, knocks over the Kops once more. They flee in terror. Charlie kicks Mack into –

91 Second hotel room. Mack is kicked through the door.

92 Hotel corridor. Alice, emerging from her room, faints in Charlie's arms.
93 Second hotel room. Mack in state of collapse.
94 Hotel corridor. Charlie and Alice in state of collapse.

THE NEW JANITOR

Caught in the Rain was released on 4 May 1914. *The New Janitor*, released on 24 September, came less than five months, and fourteen films, later. Chaplin is already much more assured. Again he follows the Keystone ground rules, with a mere eight camera set-ups and ninety shots. Using only seven brief titles, he fashions a brilliant and clear narrative, with suspense and a new element of sentiment. Now Chaplin is creating a real comic drama rather than an animated strip cartoon. The editing builds its own dynamic, in the Griffith manner, rather than simply joining a step-by-step progression of shots. Thus in shots 43 to 56 and 66 to 79, Chaplin skilfully uses cutting between parallel actions to create suspense. At the same time, as in shot 79, he is now prepared to abandon the fast Keystone cutting and allow a piece of dramatic or comic action to run on unbroken as long as it seems to require. Gags and charecter touches, like Charlie's troubles in cleaning the window or his melodramatic response to dismissal, are at once integrated into the story and given time to develop.

1 Stairway and elevator, ground floor. Charlie, the janitor, carrying a broom and feather duster, attempts to enter the elevator in the wake of a well-dressed gentleman, but the elevator boy slams the gate in his face. Charlie toils up the stairs.

TITLE: THE TOP FLOOR

2 Stairway and elevator, top floor. Elevator boy emerges, but darts back into elevator as Charlie, mopping his brow, toils to the top of the stairs.
3 Hallway between two offices. Charlie walks away from camera, twirling his pan and duster behind him.
4 Manager's office (room to left of hall). Manager reads letter.

TITLE:'WILL CALL TODAY TO COLLECT THAT GAMBLING DEBT. HAVE THE MONEY READY FOR ME, OR I'LL EXPOSE YOU. LUKE CONNOR'

5 Manager's office. Manager reads letter, gets up from chair anxiously.
6 Hallway. Charlie hangs hat on hall-stand. It falls off again, and he gives it a back-kick. *[This looks like an accident: retakes were not encouraged at Keystone.]* Enters Manager's office.
7 Manager's office. Charlie enters, knocks on door *after* entering. He removes wastepaper basket, gets it upside down, spilling contents. In retrieving contents, and stuffing them back into basket, he includes a file which Manager has just dropped. Manager is angry. Charlie drops lady-like curtsey on leaving.
8 Hallway. Charlie juggles wastepaper basket but drops it. Picks up broom, pan and duster and enters Boss's office. He gets the brush stuck across the doorway, so carefully steps over it.

9   Boss's office. Charlie walks up and down, dusts telephone.
10 Hallway. Secretary hangs up hat, looks lovingly at Manager's hat hanging there, enters Boss's office.
11 Boss's office. Secretary enters. Charlie continues to dust while casting abstracted, admiring glances at her. Yawning, he inadvertently feather-dusts her bottom as she is bending over her desk.

TITLE: LUKE CONNOR

12 Manager's office. Villainous man enters: altercation with Manager.
13 Boss's office. Still admiring the secretary, Charlie wipes his shoes with his handkerchief. Secretary leaves office by back door.
14 Manager's office. Manager and Connor still arguing. Manager shushes Connor.
15 Hallway. Secretary overhearing conversation.
16 Manager's office. Manager and Connor still arguing.

TITLE: 'I'LL GET IT BY FIVE O'CLOCK'

17 Manager's office. Manager and Connor in conversation.
18 Hallway. Secretary listening.
19 Manager's office. Connor exits.
20 Boss's office. Charlie sits on window ledge cleaning windows, almost falls out, signifies heart palpitations.
21 Exterior window, overlooking street far below. Charlie leans out of window backwards.
    Exterior building at street level. Boss with two ladies.
22 Boss's office. Charlie in window, wringing out cloth.
23 Exterior building at street level. Water falls on Boss and ladies. The ladies are outraged; the Boss shakes his fist in direction of window.
24 Boss's office. Charlie, in window, knocks out his bucket.
25 Exterior window, overlooking street. Charlie's bucket falling.
26 Exterior building at street level. Bucket falls on Boss.
27 Boss's office. Charlie in window talking to (unseen) Boss below. Struggling with the sash, it falls and almost knocks him out of window.
28 Exterior building at street level. Irate Boss enters door.
29 Boss's office. Charlie at window, still shouting down to street, and again almost precipitated out by falling sash.
30 Stairway and elevator, ground floor. Distressed Boss enters lift under amused gaze of lift boy.
31 Staircase and elevator, top floor. Boss storms out of elevator.
32 Hallway. Boss, holding head, charges into office door.
33 Boss's office. Charlie still leaning out of window. Boss rushes in and kicks him. Charlie mildly excuses himself.

TITLE: BOUNCED

34 Boss's office. Boss dismisses Charlie, who runs through a repertory of shrugs, bows, half-turns with startled turns back. He backs towards door, falling over when he gets there.
35 Hallway. Charlie exits backwards through the door, which is slammed on him, knocking him on his back.

Three Keystone Scenarios

TITLE: GOING DOWN

36 Stairway and elevator, top floor. Charlie as usual shut out of lift.

37 Boss's office. Manager enters and gives paper to Boss, still grumbling about his troubles with Charlie.

38 Stairway and elevator, ground floor. Charlie descends stairs, falling on his bottom on last step. Retrieving broom and dustpan, he uses dustpan to protect bottom against further injury.

39 The Janitor's Room. Charlie enters, the dustpan now held to his head.

40 Boss's office. As Manager exits, Boss puts papers in safe.

41 Manager's office. Manager enters, thoughtful.

42 Boss's office. Secretary now at typewriter. Boss picks up hat and stick, instructs Secretary, and leaves.

43 Manager's office. Manager sits at desk, still thoughtful.

44 Boss's office. Secretary tidies up and exits.

45 Hallway. Secretary comes out of office.

46 Manager's office. Manager furtively approaches door.

47 Hallway. Secretary puts on hat and exits.

48 Manager's office. Manager furtively opens door and exits to –

49 Hallway. Manager enters from office.

50 Staircase and elevator. Secretary rings for lift.

51 Hallway. Manager crosses to Boss's office.

52 Boss's office. Manager enters, pulls down blinds, goes to safe.

53 Stairway and elevator. Secretary remembers something, and turns back from elevator.

54 Boss's office. Manager opens safe.

55 Hallway. Secretary approaches office door and opens it.

56 Boss's office. Secretary enters and sees Manager open safe. They look at each other. Manager leaves; the Secretary is very suspicious.

57 Manager's office. Manager enters, takes bag, listens at door.

58 Boss's office. Secretary listening at door. She exits into –

59 Hallway. Secretary crosses, points accusingly at door of Manager's office, then kneels and looks through keyhole.

60 Manager's office. Manager listening at keyhole.

61 Hallway. Shocked, the Secretary recoils from door.

62 Manager's office. Manager goes to open door.

63 Hallway. Secretary retreats into Boss's office.

64 Manager's office. Manager swiftly exits.

65 Hallway. Manager puts on hat, starts to leave, but then goes to door of Boss's office.

66 Boss's office. The alarmed secretary enters, goes to the desk and hides behind it. The Manager enters, makes for the safe, opens it, begins to hurl out the contents, until he finds a wad of notes. At this moment he notices the Secretary. He points at her; she points back. Manager begins to struggle with Secretary, threatening to throw her out of window. She attempts to open the desk to reach for the telephone, but the Manager knocks her to the floor.

67 The Janitor's Room. Charlie, preparing to leave, shrugs.

68 Manager's Room. Manager and Secretary struggling.

TITLE: THE PORTER'S BUTTON

69 Boss's office. As Manager pushes Secretary back across the rolltop desk, her hand reaches for a button at the side.

70 The Janitor's office. Charlie on the point of leaving.

71 Bell ringing.

72 The Janitor's office. Charlie irritatedly mouths 'Shut up.'

73 Boss's office. Manager holds girl over desk, then throws her unconscious to the ground.

74 The Janitor's office. Charlie leaves, with a backward glance.

75 Staircase and elevator, ground floor. Charlie enters . . . indicates indecision . . . indecision . . . but finally sets off up the stairs.

76 Boss's office. Manager returns to rifling safe.

77 Staircase and elevator, top floor. Charlie reaches top landing, collapsing in exhaustion. After taking a breather, he pulls himself to his feet, and exits to left of screen.

78 Hallway. Charlie enters, right of screen. He pauses to light a cigarette, throws down the match and gives it a back-kick. Then, swinging his cane, he enters the Boss's office.

79 Boss's office. Charlie enters, sees man rifling safe, and swipes him on the bottom with his cane, demanding what he has been doing to the girl. Manager produces a gun, but Charlie flicks it out of his hand with his cane. The man hits out, misses, and Charlie fells him with a kick. Charlie turns his back and bends down, but as the Manager prepares to attack him from the rear, points the gun at him between his legs. Charlie neatly rights himself by stepping over his gun arm, and backs the man at gun-point against the safe. They circle each other, and Charlie tells the Manager to pick up the girl, which he does, placing her on a chair. They circle again until the Manager is again backed against the safe. He tries to take advantage of a moment's inattention, but fails to catch Charlie out. Charlie picks up the telephone, but talks into the wrong end of it. They continue to circle each other: when Charlie reaches the window, he fires his gun out of it.

80 Exterior of building at street level. A policeman, flirting with a girl, looks up, attracted by the shots.

81 Boss's office. Charlie accidentally shoots his own foot.

82 Exterior building at street level. Policeman hastily exits.

83 Boss's office. Charlie shoots gun in time to fend off the Manager's counter-attack.

84 Staircase and elevator, ground floor. Policeman rushes upstairs.

85 Hallway. Boss in leisure clothes approaches office.

86 Boss's office. Boss enters, and, misjudging the situation, assaults Charlie, despite the efforts of the Secretary, who has now regained consciousness, to explain all.

87 Hallway. Boss's attack precipitates Charlie into the arms of the Policeman. When Policeman grabs him, Charlie kicks him into –

88 Manager's office. Policeman tumbles into door.

89 Hallway. Policeman re-enters, and grabs Charlie.

90 Manager's office. Manager, Secretary and Boss. Policeman enters, holding

Charlie, but Boss points accusing finger at Manager. As Policeman leads Manager away, Charlie briefly menaces him with the telephone, which he has momentarily mistaken for the pistol. Boss hands Charlie a reward, which he quickly counts before shaking Boss's hand in gratitude.

HIS MUSICAL CAREER

His Musical Career was released on 7 November, towards the end of Chaplin's time with Keystone. At first sight it seems a regression in terms of narrative: in fact, he is boldly experimenting with quite a different style, much closer to that of his maturity. Having recognized that cutting is a convenience, not an obligation, he dispenses with the rapid editing which Keystone inherited from Griffith, and conceives the film in a series of much more extended shots which provide a stage for uninterrupted comedy routines.

TITLE: MR RICH BUYS A PIANO

1 Piano Shop. Charley Chase sells a piano to Mr Rich.
2 Back Room of Shop. Mack and Charlie are piano movers. Mack incredulously gazes at Charlie's antics which include oiling his elbows with an oil can.
3 Piano Shop. Charley Chase treats a Shabby Old Man very differently from Mr Rich.

TITLE: 'IF YOU CAN'T KEEP UP YOUR PAYMENTS, I'LL TAKE BACK YOUR PIANO'

4 Piano Shop. Shabby Old Man sadly leaves.
5 Back Room of Shop. Charlie reposes on piano as Charley Chase enters.

TITLE: 'TAKE THIS PIANO TO 666 PROSPECT STREET AND BRING ONE BACK FROM 999 PROSPECT STREET'

6 Charley Chase regards his unenthusiastic workers.

TITLE: 'NO TIME TO LOSE'

7 Piano Shop. In their struggles with the piano, Charlie manages to leave all the heavy work to Mack.
8 Shop – exterior. Charlie manages to drop entire weight of piano onto Mack – gazes in sympathetic surprise at Mack's struggling form beneath piano.
9 Sidewalk. Mack and Charlie load piano onto cart drawn by minute donkey.
10 Home of Shabby Old Man. Shabby Old Man tells Beautiful Daughter sad tale of piano.
11 CU. Mack and Charlie on donkey cart, with street behind. *[camera apparently mounted on front of cart]*. Charlie uses a clay pipe like straw to drink from Mack's huge jar of beer, while Mack's attention is engaged by traffic.
12 House – exterior. Weight of piano weighs down cart, lifting little donkey into the air.

TITLE: TAKING MR RICH'S PIANO TO 999 PROSPECT INSTEAD OF 666

13 House – exterior. Cart draws up. Mack and Charlie unload piano.
14 Long stairway to house. Mack and Charlie struggle with piano.

697

15 House – interior. Daughter reports arrival of piano. Shabby Old Man delighted.

16 Long stairway to house. Piano slides down stairs.

17 CU. Suffering Mack on stairs.

18 Long stairway to house. Mack and Charlie struggle up with piano.

19 House – interior. Charlie toils in with piano on his back. Shabby Old Man and Daughter are indecisive about where to put it, as Charlie staggers around room.

20 Long stairway to house. Mack and Charlie, relieved of their burden, descend. Charlie falls down last steps.

21 Sidewalk. Mack and Charlie get back on cart. Charlie is almost left behind.

TITLE: COMING TO GET THE OLD MAN'S SUPPOSED PIANO AT MR RICH'S

22 Sidewalk outside Mr Rich's house. Mack and Charlie drive up on cart and dismount. Charlie politely raises hat to donkey.

23 Entrance to Mr Rich's house. Mack and Charlie.

TITLE: THEY WALKED RIGHT IN

24 Mr Rich's House – interior. Mack and Charlie curiously inspect all the ornaments and decorations of the house. They begin to remove the piano. Mrs Rich appears and protests. She calls the Footman, but Mack and Charlie knock him down and exit with piano.

25 Mr Rich's House – exterior. Mack and Charlie carry out piano.

26 Sidewalk. Mr Rich arrives. General Keystone mêlée.

APPENDIX VI

Filmography

The record of the early Chaplin films has been a matter of accretion over the years since 1944, when Theodore Huff compiled his pioneer 'Index to the Films of Charles Chaplin'. Five years before that, in *The Rise of the American Film*, Lewis Jacobs considered that it was already an impossible task to compile an accurate listing of the Chaplin Keystone films. Huff nevertheless achieved a complete record of the Chaplin films, apart from the mysterious *The Professor* which is recorded here for the first time in any filmography. Huff also made a brave beginning in listing the credits and casts of the films; and his remains the basis of all subsequent filmographies. His errors – like crediting Roland Totheroh as Chaplin's cameraman at Essanay – have also been perpetuated.

The early 1970s saw efforts to augment the credits: Denis Gifford's 1974 biography, *Chaplin*, contained the most comprehensive filmography to that date, due to conscientious work in identifying players from the screen. This however introduced some new errors: any passing virago was optimistically identified as Phyllis Allen, while the misapprehension that Edna Purviance appeared as an extra in *Monsieur Verdoux* and *Limelight* was unquestioningly followed by subsequent filmographers. Some of the errors (though not the last) persisted as late as the filmography included in the present writer's *Chaplin: The Mirror of Opinion* (1983).

Inevitably the present filmography relies to an extent upon the work of Huff and his successors, and in the case of the early films cannot claim to be comprehensive or definitive. The source for credits that are included here for the first time is generally the studio records preserved in the Chaplin private archive at Vevey.

The system of numbering established in Uno Asplund's 1971 filmography, *Chaplin's Films*, and adopted by Timothy J. Lyons' *Charles Chaplin: A Guide to References and Resources* and the present writer's *Chaplin: The Mirror of*

Opinion, is again followed here to avoid the confusion which might result from the existence of two systems. As far as may be ascertained, the footages given for films are those of the original release prints.

I THE KEYSTONE FILMS   1914

General Credits:

Production:	The Keystone Film Company
Producer:	Mack Sennett
Photography:	According to Hans Koenekamp, who was at Keystone from 1913 and photographed *Mabel's Strange Predicament*, any Keystone cameraman might work any day on any production. Asked (in 1983) who shot *Tillie's Punctured Romance*, he replied 'Who *didn't?*' Previous filmographies have generally credited Frank D. Williams or E. J. Vallejo *(Making a Living)* with the photography of Chaplin's films, but other members of the Keystone camera team must have also worked on the Chaplin pictures.

1 Making A Living

Director:	Henry Lehrman	
Scenario:	?Reed Heustis	
Cast:	Charles Chaplin	(Slicker)
	Virginia Kirtley	(Girl)
	Alice Davenport	(Mother)
	Henry Lehrman	(Reporter)
	Minta Durfee	(Woman)
	Chester Conklin	(Policeman/Bum)
Released:	2 February 1914	
Length:	1030 feet.	

2 Kid Auto Races at Venice

Director:	Henry Lehrman	
Scenario:	Henry Lehrman	
Cast:	Charles Chaplin	(Tramp)
	Henry Lehrman	(Film Director)
	Frank D. Williams	(Cameraman)
	Billy Jacobs	(Boy)
	Charlotte Fitzpatrick	(Girl)
	Thelma Salter	(Girl)
	Gordon Griffith	(Boy)
Released:	7 February 1914	
Length:	572 ft (released on a 'split reel' with an interest film, *Olives and their Oil.*)	

3 Mabel's Strange Predicament

Director:	Henry Lehrman and Mack Sennett	
Scenario:	Henry Lehrman	
Cast:	Charles Chaplin	(Tramp)
	Mabel Normand	(Mabel)
	Chester Conklin	(Husband)
	Alice Davenport	(Wife)
	Harry McCoy	(Lover)
	Hank Mann	
	Al St John	
Released:	9 February 1914	
Length:	1016 ft.	

4 Between Showers

Director:	Henry Lehrman	
Scenario:	?Reed Heustis	
Cast:	Charles Chaplin	(Masher)
	Ford Sterling	(Rival Masher)
	Chester Conklin	(Policeman)
	Emma Clifton	(Girl)
	Sadie Lampe	(Policeman's Lady Friend)
Released:	28 February 1914	
Length:	1020 ft	

5 A Film Johnnie

Director:	George Nichols	
Scenario:	Craig Hutchinson	
Cast:	Charles Chaplin	(The Film Johnnie)
	Roscoe Arbuckle	(Fatty)
	Virginia Kirtley	(The Keystone Girl)
	Minta Durfee	(Actress)
	Mabel Normand	(Mabel)
	Ford Sterling	(Ford)
	Mack Sennett	(Himself)
Released:	2 March 1914	
Length:	1020 ft	

6 Tango Tangles

Director/Scenario: Mack Sennett

Cast:	Charles Chaplin	(Tipsy Dancer)
	Ford Sterling	(Band Leader)
	Roscoe Arbuckle	(Musician)
	Chester Conklin	(Policeman)
	Minta Durfee	(Check Girl)

Released: 9 March 1914
Length: 734 ft

7 His Favorite Pastime

Director:	George Nichols	
Scenario:	Craig Hutchinson	
Cast:	Charles Chaplin	(Drinker)
	Roscoe Arbuckle	(Drinker)
	Peggy Pearce	(Wife)

Released: 16 March 1914
Length: 1009 ft

8 Cruel, Cruel Love

Director:	George Nichols	
Scenario:	Craig Hutchinson	
Cast:	Charles Chaplin	(Lord Helpus)
	Chester Conklin	(Butler)
	Minta Durfee	(Girl)
	Alice Davenport	(Maid)

Released: 26 March 1914
Length: 1025 ft

9 The Star Boarder

Director:	George Nichols	
Scenario:	Craig Hutchinson	
Cast:	Charles Chaplin	(The Star Boarder)
	Minta Durfee	(Landlady)
	Edgar Kennedy	(Landlady's Husband)
	Gordon Griffith	(Their Son)
	Alice Davenport	(Landlady's Friend)

Released: 4 April 1914
Length: 1020 ft

10 Mabel At The Wheel

Directors:	Mabel Normand, Mack Sennett	
Scenario:	?Mabel Normand, Mack Sennett	
Cast:	Charles Chaplin	(Villain)
	Mabel Normand	(Mabel)
	Harry McCoy	(A Car Racer, Mabel's Boyfriend)
	Chester Conklin	(Mabel's Father)
	Mack Sennett	(A Rube)
	Al St John	(Villain's Henchman)
	Fred Mace	(Dubious Character)

	Joe Bordeaux	(Dubious Character)
	Mack Swain	(Spectator)
Released:	18 April 1914	
Length:	1900 ft	

11   Twenty Minutes of Love

Director/Scenario: Charles Chaplin

Cast:	Charles Chaplin	(Pickpocket)
	Minta Durfee	(Woman)
	Edgar Kennedy	(Lover)
	Gordon Griffith	(Boy)
	Chester Conklin	(Pickpocket)
	Joseph Swickard	(Victim)
	Hank Mann	(Sleeper)
Released:	20 April 1914	
Length:	1009 ft	

12   Caught in a Cabaret

Director:	Mabel Normand	
Scenario:	?Mabel Normand and Charles Chaplin	
Cast:	Charles Chaplin	(Waiter)
	Mabel Normand	(Mabel)
	Harry McCoy	(Lover)
	Chester Conklin	(Waiter)
	Edgar Kennedy	(Café Proprietor)
	Minta Durfee	(Dancer)
	Phyllis Allen	(Dancer)
	Joseph Swickard	(Father)
	Alice Davenport	(Mother)
	Gordon Griffith	(Boy)
	Alice Howell	
	Hank Mann	
	Wallace MacDonald	
Released:	27 April 1914	
Length:	1968 ft	

13   Caught in the Rain

Director/Scenario: Charles Chaplin

Cast:	Charles Chaplin	(Tipsy Hotel Guest)
	Mack Swain	(Husband)
	Alice Davenport	(Wife)
	Alice Howell	(A Woman)
Released:	4 May 1914	
Length:	1015 ft	

14   A Busy Day

Director/Scenario: ?Charles Chaplin

Cast:	Charles Chaplin	(Wife)
	Mack Swain	(Husband)
	Phyllis Allen	(The Other Woman)

| Released: | 7 May 1914 |
| Length: | 441 ft |

15   The Fatal Mallet

Director/Scenario: Mack Sennett

Cast:	Charles Chaplin	(Suitor)
	Mabel Normand	(Mabel)
	Mack Sennett	(Rival Suitor)
	Mack Swain	(Man)

| Released: | 1 June 1914 |
| Length: | 1120 ft |

16   Her Friend the Bandit

| Director: | ? |
| Scenario: | ? |

Cast:	Charles Chaplin	(Bandit)
	Mabel Normand	(Mabel)
	Charles Murray	(Count De Beans)

| Released: | 4 June 1914 |
| Length: | 1000 ft approx. |

17   The Knockout

| Director: | Charles Avery |

Cast:	Roscoe Arbuckle	(Fatty)
	Minta Durfee	(Woman)
	Edgar Kennedy	(Cyclone Flynn)
	Charles Chaplin	(Referee)
	Al St John	(Boxer)
	Hank Mann	(Boxer)
	Mack Swain	(Spectator)
	Mack Sennett	(Spectator)
	Alice Howell	(Spectator)
	Charles Parrott*	(Policeman)
	Eddie Cline	(Policeman)
	Joe Bordeaux	(Policeman)
	*Charley Chase	

| Released: | 11 June 1914 |
| Length: | 1960 ft |

18 Mabel's Busy Day

Director/Scenario: ?Mabel Normand

Cast:	Charles Chaplin	(Tipsy Nuisance)
	Mabel Normand	(Mabel)
	Chester Conklin	(Police Sergeant)
	Slim Summerville	(Policeman)
	Billie Bennett	(Woman)
	Harry McCoy	
	Wallace MacDonald	
	Edgar Kennedy	
	Al St John	
	Charles Parrott*	
	Mack Sennett	
	Henry Lehrman(?)	
	*Charley Chase	

Released:	13 June 1914
Length:	998 ft

19 Mabel's Married Life

Director:	Charles Chaplin
Scenario:	Charles Chaplin and Mabel Normand

Cast:	Charles Chaplin	(Mabel's Husband)
	Mabel Normand	(Mabel)
	Mack Swain	(Sporty Ladykiller)
	Alice Howell	(Mack's Wife)
	Hank Mann	(Friend)
	Charles Murray	(Man in Bar)
	Harry McCoy	(Man in Bar)
	Wallace MacDonald	(Delivery Boy)
	Al St John	(Delivery Boy)

Released:	20 June 1914
Length:	1015 ft

20 Laughing Gas

Director/Scenario: Charles Chaplin

Cast:	Charles Chaplin	(Dentist's Assistant)
	Fritz Schade	(The Dentist)
	Alice Howell	(Dentist's Wife)
	Joseph Sutherland	(Assistant)
	George Slim	
	Summerville	(Patient)
	Joseph Swickard	(Patient)
	Mack Swain	(Patient)

Released:	9 July 1914
Length:	1020 ft

21   **The Property Man**

Director/Scenario: Charles Chaplin

Cast:	Charles Chaplin	(The Property Man)
	Fritz Schade	(Garlico)
	Phyllis Allen	(Hamlene Fat)
	Àlice Davenport	(Actress)
	Charles Bennett	(Actor)
	Mack Sennett	(Man in Audience and Spectator)
	Norma Nichols	(Vaudeville Artist)
	Joe Bordeaux	(Old Actor)
	Harry McCoy	
	Lee Morris	

Released: 1 August 1914
Length: 1858 ft

22   **The Face on the Bar Room Floor**

Director: Charles Chaplin
Scenario: Charles Chaplin, after the poem by Hugh Antoine d'Arcy.

Cast:	Charles Chaplin	(Artist)
	Cecile Arnold	(Madeline)
	Fritz Schade	(The Lover Who Stole Her)
	Vivian Edwards	(A Woman)
	Chester Conklin	(Drinker)
	Harry McCoy	(Drinker)
	Hank Mann	(Drinker)
	Wallace MacDonald	(Drinker)

Released: 10 August 1914
Length: 1020 ft

23   **Recreation**

Director/Scenario: Charles Chaplin

Cast:	Charles Chaplin	(Tramp)
	Charles Murray(?)	(Seaman on Park Bench)
	Norma Nichols	(Girl)

Released: 18 August 1914
Length: 462 ft (released as a 'split reel' with a scenic film, *The Yosemite*.)

24   **The Masquerader**

Director/Scenario: Charles Chaplin

Cast:	Charles Chaplin	(Film Actor)
	Roscoe Arbuckle	(Film Actor)
	Chester Conklin	(Film Actor)
	Charles Murray	(Film Director)
	Fritz Schade	(Villain)

Minta Durfee	(Leading Lady)
Cecile Arnold	(Actress)
Vivian Edwards	(Actress)
Harry McCoy	(Actor)
Charles Parrott*	(Actor)

*Charley Chase

Released: 27 August 1914
Length: 1030 ft

25 His New Profession

Director/Scenario: Charles Chaplin

Cast:		
	Charles Chaplin	(Charlie)
	Minta Durfee	(Woman)
	Fritz Schade	(Uncle)
	Charles Parrott*	(Nephew)
	Cecile Arnold	(Girl)
	Harry McCoy	(Cop)

*Charley Chase

Released: 31 August 1914
Length: 1015 ft

26 The Rounders

Director/Scenario: Charles Chaplin

Cast:		
	Charles Chaplin	(Reveller)
	Roscoe Arbuckle	(His Friend and Neighbour)
	Phyllis Allen	(Charlie's Wife)
	Minta Durfee	(Fatty's Wife)
	Al St John	(Bellhop)
	Fritz Schade	(Diner)
	Wallace MacDonald	(Diner)
	Charles Parrott*	(Diner)

*Charley Chase

Released: 7 September 1914
Length: 1010 ft

27 The New Janitor

Director/Scenario: Charles Chaplin

Cast:		
	Charles Chaplin	(Janitor)
	Fritz Schade	(Boss)
	Jack Dillon	(Villainous Manager)
	Minta Durfee	(Secretary)
	Al St John	(Elevator Boy)

Released: 24 September 1914
Length: 1020 ft

28 Those Love Pangs

Director/Scenario: Charles Chaplin

Cast:

	Charles Chaplin	(Masher)
	Chester Conklin	(Rival)
	Cecile Arnold	(Girl)
	Vivian Edwards	(Girl)
	Edgar Kennedy	(Girls' Friend)
	Norma Nichols	(Landlady)
	Harry McCoy	(Cop)

Released: 10 October 1914
Length: 1010 ft

29 Dough and Dynamite

Director/Scenario: Charles Chaplin (Sennett is generally credited with collaboration on the scenario.)

Cast:

	Charles Chaplin	(Waiter)
	Chester Conklin	(Waiter)
	Fritz Schade	(Bakery Proprietor)
	Norma Nichols	(His Wife)
	Cecile Arnold	(Waitress)
	Vivian Edwards	(Waitress)
	Phyllis Allen	(Customer)
	Jack Dillon	(Customer)
	Edgar Kennedy	(Striking Baker)
	George Slim Summerville	(Striking Baker)
	Charles Parrott*	(Striking Baker)
	Wallace MacDonald	(Striking Baker)

*Charley Chase

Released: 26 October
Length: 2000 ft

30 Gentlemen of Nerve

Director/Scenario: Charles Chaplin

Cast:

	Charles Chaplin	(Impecunious Track Enthusiast)
	Mack Swain	(Ambrose, His Friend)
	Mabel Normand	(Mabel)
	Chester Conklin	(Walrus)
	Phyllis Allen	(His Wife)
	Edgar Kennedy	(Policeman)
	Charles Parrott*	(Spectator)
	Alice Davenport	(Waitress)

*Charley Chase

Released: 29 October 1914
Length: 1030 ft

31 His Musical Career

Director/Scenario: Charles Chaplin

Cast:

Charles Chaplin	(Piano Mover)
Mack Swain	(Ambrose, his Partner)
Charles Parrott*	(Piano Store Manager)
Fritz Schade	(Mr Rich)
Joe Bordeaux	(Mr Poor)
Alice Howell	(Mrs Rich)
Norma Nichols	(Miss Poor)

*Charley Chase

Released: 7 November 1914
Length: 1025 ft

32 His Trysting Place

Director/Scenario: Charles Chaplin

Cast:

Charles Chaplin	(Husband)
Mabel Normand	(Mabel, His Wife)
Mack Swain	(Ambrose)
Phyllis Allen	(Ambrose's Wife)

Released: 9 November 1914
Length: 2000 ft

33 Tillie's Punctured Romance

Director: Mack Sennett
Scenario: Mack Sennett, from the play, *Tillie's Nightmare.*

Cast:

Marie Dressler	(Tillie Banks, a Country Lass)
Charles Chaplin	(Charlie, a City Slicker)
Mabel Normand	(Mabel, his Girl Friend)
Mack Swain	(John Banks, Tillie's Father)
Charles Bennett	(Douglas Banks, Tillie's Uncle)
Charles Murray	(Detective)
Charles Parrott*	(Detective)
Edgar Kennedy	(Restaurant Proprietor)
Harry McCoy	(Pianist)
Minta Durfee	(Maid)
Phyllis Allen	(Wardress)
Alice Davenport	(Guest)
George Slim Summerville	(Policeman)
Al St John	(Policeman)
Wallace MacDonald	(Policeman)
Joe Bordeaux	(Policeman)
G. G. Ligon	(Policeman)
Gordon Griffith	(Newsboy)

Billie Bennett	(Girl)
Rev D. Simpson	(Himself)
*Charley Chase	

Released: 14 November 1914
Length: 6000 ft.

34 Getting Acquainted

Director/Scenario: Charles Chaplin

Cast:		
	Charles Chaplin	(Spouse)
	Phyllis Allen	(His Wife)
	Mack Swain	(Ambrose)
	Mabel Normand	(Ambrose's Wife)
	Harry McCoy	(Policeman)
	Edgar Kennedy	(A Passing Turk)
	Cecile Arnold	(Girl)

Released: 5 December 1914
Length: 1025 ft

35 His Prehistoric Past

Director/Scenario: Charles Chaplin

Cast:		
	Charles Chaplin	(Weakchin)
	Mack Swain	(King Lowbrow)
	Gene Marsh	(Lowbrow's Favourite Wife)
	Fritz Schade	(Cleo)
	Cecile Arnold	(Cave Woman)
	Al St John	(Cave Man)

Released: 7 December 1914
Length: 2000 ft

II THE ESSANAY FILMS   1915–1916

General Credits:

Production:	The Essanay Film Manufacturing Company
Producer:	Jesse T. Robbins
Director:	Charles Chaplin
Scenario:	Charles Chaplin
Photography:	Harry Ensign from *A Night Out* onwards: photographer of *His New Job* unknown.
Assistant Director:	Ernest Van Pelt (believed to have worked on all Essanay films after *His New Job*).
Scenic Artist:	E. T. Mazy (believed to have worked on all Essanay films from *Work* onwards).

36 His New Job

Cast:

Charles Chaplin	(Film Extra)
Ben Turpin	(Film Extra)
Charlotte Mineau	(Film Star)
Charles Insley	(Film Director)
Leo White	(Actor)
Frank J. Coleman	(Assistant Director)
Bud Jamison	(Unpunctual Star)
Gloria Swanson	(Stenographer)
Agnes Ayres	(Secretary)
Billy Armstrong	(Extra)

Filmed at the Essanay Chicago Studios

Released: 1 February 1915
Length: 1896 ft

37 A Night Out

Cast:

Charles Chaplin	(Reveller)
Ben Turpin	(Fellow Reveller)
Bud Jamison	(Head Waiter)
Edna Purviance	(His Wife)
Leo White	('French' Dandy)
Fred Goodwins	

Filmed at the Essanay Niles Studio

Released: 15 February 1915
Length: 1856 ft

38 The Champion

Cast:

Charles Chaplin	(Aspiring Pugilist)
Lloyd Bacon	(Trainer)
Edna Purviance	(His Daughter)
Leo White	(Would-be Briber)
Bud Jamison	(Champion)
Billy Armstrong	(Sparring Partner)
Carl Stockdale	(Sparring Partner)
Paddy McGuire	(Sparring Partner)
Ben Turpin	(Salesman)
G. M. ('Broncho Billy') Anderson	(Enthusiastic Spectator)

Filmed at the Essanay Niles Studio

Released: 11 March 1915
Length: 1938 ft

39   In the Park

Cast:

Charles Chaplin	(Charlie)
Edna Purviance	(Nursemaid)
Leo White	(Elegant Masher)
Margie Reiger	(His Fancy)
Lloyd Bacon	(Hot Dog Seller)
Bud Jamison	(Edna's Beau)
Billy Armstrong	(Thief)
Ernest Van Pelt	(Policeman)

Filmed on location

Released: 18 March 1915
Length: 984 ft

40   A Jitney Elopement

Cast:

Charles Chaplin	(Suitor, the Fake Count)
Edna Purviance	(The Girl)
Fred Goodwins	(Her Father)
Leo White	(The Count)
Lloyd Bacon	(Butler)
Paddy McGuire	(Ancient Servant)
Carl Stockdale	(Policeman)
Ernest Van Pelt	(Policeman)
Bud Jamison	(Policeman)

Filmed at the Essanay Niles Studio

Released: 1 April 1915
Length: 1958 ft

41   The Tramp

Cast:

Charles Chaplin	(The Tramp)
Edna Purviance	(The Farmer's Daughter)
Fred Goodwins	(The Farmer)
Lloyd Bacon	(Edna's Fiancé)
Paddy McGuire	(Farmhand)
Billy Armstrong	(Poet)
Leo White	(Hobo)
Ernest Van Pelt	(Hobo)

Filmed at the Essanay Niles Studio and locations

Released: 11 April 1915
Length: 1896 ft

42 By the Sea

Cast:

Charles Chaplin	(Stroller)
Billy Armstrong	(Holiday-maker)
Margie Reiger	(His Wife)
Bud Jamison	(Jealous Husband)
Edna Purviance	(His Wife)
Paddy McGuire	(Refreshment Stand Proprietor)
Carl Stockdale	(Policeman)

Filmed on location at Crystal Pier

Released: 29 April 1915
Length: 971 ft

43 Work

Cast:

Charles Chaplin	(Decorator's Apprentice)
Charles Insley	(His Boss)
Edna Purviance	(Housemaid)
Billy Armstrong	(Householder)
Marta Golden	(His Wife)
Leo White	(Gentleman Caller)
Paddy McGuire	(Hod Carrier)

Filmed at the Bradbury Mansion studio

Released: 21 June 1915
Length: 2017 ft

44 A Woman

Cast:

Charles Chaplin	(Charlie; and 'The Woman')
Edna Purviance	(Daughter)
Marta Golden	(Mother)
Charles Insley	(Father)
Margie Reiger	(Father's Lady Friend)
Billy Armstrong	(Father's Friend)
Leo White	(Gentleman in Park)

Filmed at the former Majestic Studio

Released: 12 July 1915
Length: 1788 ft

45 The Bank

Cast:

Charles Chaplin	(Janitor)
Edna Purviance	(Secretary)
Carl Stockdale	(Cashier)
Billy Armstrong	(Janitor)
Charles Insley	(Manager)
Lawrence A. Bowes	(Important Customer)
John Rand	(Salesman)

Leo White	(Client)
Fred Goodwins	(Doorkeeper *and* Bank **Robber**)
Bud Jamison	(Chief Bank Robber)
Frank J. Coleman	(Bank Robber)
John Rand	(Bank Robber)
Lloyd Bacon	(Bank Robber)
Paddy McGuire	(Bank Robber)
Wesley Ruggles	
Carrie Clark Ward	

Filmed at the former Majestic Studio

Released: 9 August 1915
Length: 1985 ft

46 Shanghaied

Cast:	Charles Chaplin	(Charlie)
	Edna Purviance	(Owner's Daughter)
	Wesley Ruggles	(Owner)
	John Rand	(Captain)
	Bud Jamison	(Mate)
	Billy Armstrong	(Cook)
	Lawrence A. Bowes	(Seaman)
	Paddy McGuire	(Seaman)
	Leo White	(Seaman)
	Fred Goodwins	(Seaman)

Filmed at the former Majestic Studio

Released: 4 October 1915
Length: 1771 ft

47 A Night in the Show

Cast:	Charles Chaplin	(Mr Pest *and* Mr Rowdy)
	Edna Purviance	(Lady in the Stalls)
	Charlotte Mineau	(Lady in the Stalls)
	Dee Lampton	(The Mischievous Fat Boy)
	Leo White	(Man in Stalls *and* Conjuror)
	Wesley Ruggles	(Man in Gallery)
	John Rand	(Orchestra Conductor)
	James T. Kelley	(Musician *and* Singer)
	Paddy McGuire	(Musician)
	May White	(Fat Lady in Foyer *and* Snake Charmer)
	Bud Jamison	(Edna's Husband in Stalls *and* Singer)
	Phyllis Allen	(Lady in Audience)
	Fred Goodwins	(Gentleman in Audience)
	Charles Insley	(Gentleman in Audience)
	Carrie Clark Ward	(Woman in Audience)

Filmed at the former Majestic Studio

Released: 20 November 1915
Length: 1735 ft

48   Charlie Chaplin's Burlesque on Carmen

Cast: Charles Chaplin   (Darn Hosiery)
              Edna Purviance   (Carmen)
              Ben Turpin   (Don Remendado)
              Leo White   (Officer of the Guard)
              John Rand   (Escamillo)
              Jack Henderson   (Lilias Pasta)
              May White   (Frasquita)
              Bud Jamison   (Soldier)
              Wesley Ruggles   (A Vagabond)
              Frank J. Coleman
              Lawrence A. Bowes

Filmed at the former Majestic Studio

The film was expanded from two reels to four, without Chaplin's authority, after he had left the studio. The new version was assembled by Leo White, who also shot new material for it. Chaplin unsuccessfully took legal action against Essanay.

Released: 22 April 1916
Length: 3986 ft

49   Police

Cast: Charles Chaplin   (Ex-Convict)
              Edna Purviance   (Daughter of the House)
              Wesley Ruggles   (Gaolbird and Thief)
              James T. Kelley   (Drunk)
              Leo White   (Fruit Seller *and* Doss House Proprietor
                                   and Policeman)
              John Rand   (Policeman)
              Fred Goodwins   (Fake Preacher)
              Billy Armstrong   (Dubious Character)
              Bud Jamison   (Dubious Character)

Filmed at the former Majestic Studio

Released: 27 May 1916
Length: 2050 ft

III   THE MUTUAL FILMS   1916–1917

General Credits:

Production: Lone Star Mutual
Producer: Charles Chaplin
Director: Charles Chaplin

Scenario:	Charles Chaplin	

(Story collaboration credit on *The Floorwalker, The Fireman* and *The Vagabond* to Vincent Bryan.)

Photography: *The Floorwalker, The Fireman* and *The Vagabond*: Frank D. Williams. Assistant: Roland Totheroh.

From *One A.M.*: Roland Totheroh

Scenic Artist: E. T. Mazy (said to have worked on *The Floorwalker, The Fireman* and *One A.M.*)

Filmed at the Lone Star Studios, Hollywood.

51 The Floorwalker

Cast:	Charles Chaplin	(Impecunious Customer)
	Eric Campbell	(Store Manager)
	Edna Purviance	(His Secretary)
	Lloyd Bacon	(Assistant Manager)
	Albert Austin	(Shop Assistant)
	Leo White	(Elegant Customer)
	Charlotte Mineau	(Beautiful Store Detective)
	James T. Kelley	(Lift Boy)
Released:	15 May 1916	
Length:	1734 ft	

52 The Fireman

Cast:	Charles Chaplin	(Fireman)
	Edna Purviance	(The Girl)
	Lloyd Bacon	(Her Father)
	Eric Campbell	(Fire Chief)
	Leo White	(Owner of Burning House)
	Albert Austin	(Fireman)
	John Rand	(Fireman)
	James T. Kelley	(Fireman)
	Frank J. Coleman	(Fireman)
Released:	12 June 1916	
Length:	1921 ft	

53 The Vagabond

Cast:	Charles Chaplin	(Street Musician)
	Edna Purviance	(Girl Stolen by Gypsies)
	Eric Campbell	(Gypsy Chieftain)
	Leo White	(Old Jew *and* Old Gypsy Woman)
	Lloyd Bacon	(The Artist)
	Charlotte Mineau	(Girl's Mother)
	Albert Austin	(Trombonist)
	John Rand	(Trumpeter, Band Leader)

| | James T. Kelley | (Musician *and* Gypsy) |
| | Frank J. Coleman | (Musician *and* Gypsy) |

| Released: | 10 July 1916 |
| Length: | 1956 ft |

54 One A.M.

| Cast: | Charles Chaplin | (Drunk) |
| | Albert Austin | (Taxi Driver) |

| Released: | 7 August 1916 |
| Length: | 2000 ft |

55 The Count

Cast:	Charles Chaplin	(Tailor's Apprentice)
	Edna Purviance	(Miss Moneybags, the Heiress)
	Eric Campbell	(The Tailor)
	Leo White	(The Count)
	May White	(Large Lady)
	Charlotte Mineau	(Mrs Moneybags)
	Albert Austin	(Guest)
	Stanley Sanford	(Guest)
	John Rand	(Guest)
	James T. Kelley	(Butler)
	Leota Bryan	(Young Girl)
	Loyal Underwood	(Small Guest)
	Eva Thatcher	(Cook)
	Frank J. Coleman	(Policeman *and* Guest in Pierrot costume)

| Released: | 4 September 1916 |
| Length: | 2000 ft |

56 The Pawnshop

Cast:	Charles Chaplin	(Pawnbroker's Assistant)
	Henry Bergman	(The Pawnbroker)
	Edna Purviance	(His Daughter)
	John Rand	(The Other Assistant)
	Albert Austin	(Customer with Alarm Clock)
	Wesley Ruggles	(Dramatic Customer with Ring)
	Eric Campbell	(Burglar)
	James T. Kelley	(Old Bum *and* Lady with Goldfish)
	Frank J. Coleman	(Policeman)

| Released: | 2 October 1916 |
| Length: | 1940 ft |

57   Behind the Screen

Cast:	Charles Chaplin	(Property Man's Assistant)
	Eric Campbell	(Property Man)
	Edna Purviance	(Aspiring Actress)
	Henry Bergman	(Director of Historical Film)
	Lloyd Bacon	(Director of Comedy Film)
	Albert Austin	(Scene Shifter)
	John Rand	(Scene Shifter)
	Leo White	(Scene Shifter)
	Frank J. Coleman	(Producer)
	Charlotte Mineau	(Actress)
	Leota Bryan	(Actress)
	Wesley Ruggles	(Actor)
	Tom Wood	(Actor)
	James T. Kelley	(Cameraman)
Released:	13 November 1916	
Length:	1796 ft	

58   The Rink

Cast:	Charles Chaplin	(Waiter and Skating Enthusiast)
	Edna Purviance	(Society Girl)
	James T. Kelley	(Her Father)
	Eric Campbell	(Mr Stout)
	Henry Bergman	(Mrs Stout *and* Angry Diner)
	Lloyd Bacon	(Guest)
	Albert Austin	(Chef *and* Skater)
	Frank J. Coleman	(Restaurant Manager)
	John Rand	(Waiter)
	Charlotte Mineau	(Edna's Friend)
	Leota Bryan	(Edna's Friend)
Released:	4 December 1916	
Length:	1881 ft	

59   Easy Street

Cast:	Charles Chaplin	(Vagabond recruited to Police Force)
	Edna Purviance	(Missionary)
	Eric Campbell	(Scourge of Easy Street)
	Albert Austin	(Clergyman *and* Policeman)
	Henry Bergman	(Anarchist)
	Loyal Underwood	(Small but Fecund Father *and* Policeman)
	Janet Miller Sully	(His Wife *and* Mission Visitor)
	Charlotte Mineau	(Ungrateful Woman)
	Tom Wood	(Chief of Police)
	Lloyd Bacon	(Drug Addict)

	Frank J. Coleman	(Policeman)
	John Rand	(Mission Visitor *and* **Policeman**)
Released:	22 January 1917	
Length:	1757 ft	

60   The Cure

Cast:	Charles Chaplin	(Alcoholic Gentleman **at Spa**)
	Edna Purviance	(Fellow Guest at Spa)
	Eric Campbell	(Gentleman with Gout)
	Henry Bergman	(Masseur)
	Albert Austin	(Male Nurse)
	John Rand	(Male Nurse *and* **Masseur**)
	James T. Kelley	(Ancient Bell Boy)
	Frank J. Coleman	(Proprietor)
	Leota Bryan	(Nurse)
	Tom Wood	(Patient)
	Janet Miller Sully	(Spa Visitor)
	Loyal Underwood	(Spa Visitor)
Released:	16 April 1917	
Length:	1834 ft	

61   The Immigrant

Cast:	Charles Chaplin	(Immigrant)
	Edna Purviance	(Immigrant)
	Kitty Bradbury	(Her Mother)
	Albert Austin	(Slavic Immigrant *and* **Diner**)
	Henry Bergman	(Slavic Woman Immigrant *and* **Artist**)
	Loyal Underwood	(Small Immigrant)
	Eric Campbell	(Head Waiter)
	Stanley Sanford	(Gambler on Ship)
	James T. Kelley	(Shabby Man in **Restaurant**)
	John Rand	(Tipsy Diner who **cannot pay**)
	Frank J. Coleman	(Ship's Officer *and* **Restaurant Owner**)
	Tom Harrington	(Marriage Registrar)
Released:	17 June 1917	
Length:	1809 ft	

62   The Adventurer

Cast:	Charles Chaplin	(Escaped Convict)
	Edna Purviance	(A Girl)
	Henry Bergman	(Her Father *and* a **Docker**)
	Marta Golden	(Her Mother)
	Eric Campbell	(Her Suitor)
	Albert Austin	(Butler)
	Toraichi Kono	(Chauffeur)

John Rand   (Guest)
Frank J. Coleman   (Fat Warder)
Loyal Underwood   (Small Guest)
May White   (Stout Lady)
Janet Miller Sully
Monta Bell

Released: 22 October 1917
Length: 1845 ft

IV   THE FIRST NATIONAL FILMS   1918–1923

General Credits:

Production:	Chaplin–First National
Producer:	Charles Chaplin
Director:	Charles Chaplin
Scenario:	Charles Chaplin
Photographer:	Roland Totheroh
Second Camera:	Jack Wilson
Assistant:	Charles ('Chuck') Riesner
Production Designer:	Charles D. Hall

Filmed at the Chaplin Studio on Sunset and La Brea

62a   How to Make Movies

A comedy-documentary showing the premises and personnel of the new Chaplin studios. The film seems never to have been assembled, although a title list was prepared. This was used by Kevin Brownlow and David Gill to reconstruct Chaplin's intended film, and it was seen for the first time in its entirety at the 1981 London Film Festival. Some parts of the film had previously been used by Chaplin in *The Chaplin Revue* however.

63   A Dog's Life

Cast:		
	Charles Chaplin	(Tramp)
	Edna Purviance	(Bar Singer)
	Mut	(Scraps)
	Sydney Chaplin	(Lunch Wagon Owner)
	Henry Bergman	(Man in Employment Agency *and* Lady in Dance Hall)
	Charles Riesner	(Clerk in Employment Agency *and* Drummer)
	Albert Austin	(Crook)
	Tom Wilson	(Policeman)
	M. J. McCarty	(Unemployed Man)

Mel Brown	(Unemployed Man)
Charles Force	(Unemployed Man)
Bert Appling	(Unemployed Man)
Thomas Riley	(Unemployed Man)
Slim Cole	(Unemployed Man)
Ted Edwards	(Unemployed Man)
Louis Fitzroy	(Unemployed Man)
Dave Anderson	(Unemployed Man)
Granville Redmond	(Proprietor of Dance Hall)
Minnie Chaplin	(Dramatic Lady in Dance Hall)
Alf Reeves	(Man at Bar)
N. Tahbel	(Hot Tamaly Man)
Rob Wagner	(Man in Dance Hall)
I. S. McVey	(Musician)
J. F. Parker	(Musician)
Al Blake	
Loyal Underwood	
James T. Kelley	
Fred Starr	
Janet Miller Sully	
Grace Wilson	
(Mrs Tom Wilson)	
Jerry Ferragoma	

Jack Duffy, Richard Dunbar, Edward Miller, Billy Dul, Bruce Randall, Brand O'Ree, Bill White, John Lord, Jim O'Niall, H. C. Simmons, J. L. Fraube, Jim Habif, Florence Parellee, Miss Cullington, Margaret Dracup, Ella Eckhardt, Sarah Rosenberg, Lottie Smithson, Lillian Morgan, Jean Johnson, Fay Holderness, Dorothy Cleveland, J. Miller, Minnie Eckhardt, Mrs Rigoletti.
(People in Dance Hall)

Production started:	15 January 1918
Production finished:	9 April 1918
Released:	14 April 1918
Length	2674 ft

64 The Bond

Cast:		
	Charles Chaplin	
	Edna Purviance	
	Sydney Chaplin	(The Kaiser)
	Henry Bergman	(John Bull)
	Dorothy Rosher	(Cupid)

[Dorothy Rosher worked 17 and 19 August, at a rate of $10 per day.]

Production
started: 15 August 1918
Production
finished: 22 August 1918
Released: 16 December 1918
Length: 685 ft

64a (Chaplin–Lauder Charity Film)

Cast: Charles Chaplin   (Himself)
                Harry Lauder   (Himself)

Filmed: 22 January 1918
Apparently never completed or released
Length: 745 ft (unedited)

65 Shoulder Arms

Cast: Charles Chaplin   (Recruit)
                Edna Purviance   (French Girl)
                Sydney Chaplin   (Sergeant *and* the Kaiser)
                Jack Wilson   (German Crown Prince)
                Henry Bergman   (Fat German Sergeant *and* Field Marshal
                                     von Hindenburg)
                Albert Austin   (American Soldier *and* German Soldier
                                     and Kaiser's Chauffeur)
                Tom Wilson   (Training Camp Sergeant)
                John Rand   (American Soldier)
                Park Jones   (American Soldier)
                Loyal Underwood   (Small German Officer)
                W. G. Wagner, J. T.
                Powell, W. Herron,
                W. Cross, G. E.
                Marygold   (Motorcyclists)
                C. L. Dice, G. A.
                Godfrey, L. A.
                Blaisdell, W. E.
                Allen, J. H. Warne   (Motorcyclists – alternative group*)
                Roscoe Ward, Ed Hunt, M. J. Donovan, E. B. Johnson, Fred
                Graham, Louis Orr, Al Blake, Ray Hanford, Cliff Brouwer,
                Claude McAtee, F. S. Colby, Jack Shalford, Joe Van Meter, Guy
                Eakins, Jack Willis, Charles Cole, T. Madden
                                     (American and German Soldiers)
                Harry Goldman, Jack Willis, Mark Faber, E. H. Devere, Fred
                Everman, A. North, Charles Knuske, O. E. Haskins, Tom
                Hawley, W. E. Graham, James Griffin, W. A. Hackett,
                E. Brucker, J. H. Shewry, Sam Lewis, R. B. McKenzie,
                K. Herlinger, A. J. Hartwell
                                     (Additional players in street set, with
                                     Kaiser's car)

In Cut Sequences

Marion Feducha	(Small Boy)
Alf Reeves	(Draft Board Sergeant)
Albert Austin	(Draft Board Doctor)
Peggy Prevost	(Draft Board Clerk)
Nina Trask	(Draft Board Clerk)

*Since the motorcyclists wore goggles, different groups could be used for different days' shooting. The motorcyclists were paid $5 a day, except for Wagner and Powell, who provided their own bikes and so received $7.50 a day.

Production started:	27 May 1918
Production finished:	16 September 1918
Released:	20 October 1918
Length:	3142 ft

66 Sunnyside

Cast:		
	Charles Chaplin	(Farm Handyman)
	Edna Purviance	(Village Belle)
	Tom Wilson	(Boss)
	Tom Terriss	(Young Man from the City)
	Henry Bergman	(Villager *and* Edna's Father)
	Loyal Underwood	(Fat Boy's Father)
	Tom Wood	(Fat Boy)
	Helen Kohn	(Nymph)
	Olive Burton	(Nymph)
	Willie Mae Carson	(Nymph)
	Olive Alcorn	(Nymph)
	Park Jones	
	Granville Redmond	
	Al Blake	
	Shorty Hendricks	
	Lulu Jenks	
	George Cole	
	David Kohn	
	Tom Harrington	

Zasu Pitts worked in a number of scenes from 4 to 25 November; but her role appears to have been cut from the finished film.

In Cut Sequence

Albert Austin	(Man being Shaved)

Locations: Phelps Ranch, Lasky Ranch, Country Road in Beverly Hills, Bridge in San Fernando Road, exterior of Edna's home.

Production started:	4 November 1918
Production finished:	15 April 1919
Released:	15 June 1919
Length:	2769 ft

67   A Day's Pleasure

Cast:	Charles Chaplin	(Father)
	Edna Purviance	(Mother)
	Marion Feducha	(Small Boy)
	Bob Kelly	(Small Boy)
	Jackie Coogan	(Smallest Boy)
	Tom Wilson	(Large Husband)
	Babe London	(His Seasick Wife)
	Henry Bergman	(Captain *and* Man in Car)
	Loyal Underwood	(Angry Little Man in Street)
	Albert Austin	
	Jessie Van Trump	

At the start of shooting, the role of Charlie's wife was taken by the 495-lb. Tom Wood

Location:	San Pedro pleasure boat, *Ace.*
Production started:	21 May 1919
Production interrupted:	30 July–7 October 1919
Production finished:	19 October 1919
Released:	15 December 1919
Length:	1714 ft

68   The Kid

Cast:	Charles Chaplin	(Tramp)
	Edna Purviance	(Mother)
	Jackie Coogan	(The Kid)
	Baby Hathaway	(The Kid as a Baby)
	Carl Miller	(Artist)
	Granville Redmond	(His Friend)
	May White	(Policeman's Wife)
	Tom Wilson	(Policeman)
	Henry Bergman	(Night Shelter Keeper)
	Charles Riesner	(Bully)
	Raymond Lee	(His Kid Brother)
	Lillita McMurray (Lita Grey)	(Flirtatious Angel)

Filmography

Edith Wilson	(Lady With Pram)
Baby Wilson	(Baby in Pram)
Nellie Bly Baker	(Slum Nurse)
Albert Austin	(Man in Shelter)
Jack Coogan Sr	(Pickpocket *and* Guest *and* Devil)
Edgar Sherrod	(Priest)
Beulah Bains	(Bride)
Robert Dunbar	(Bridegroom)
Kitty Bradbury	(Bride's Mother)
Rupert Franklin	(Bride's Father)
Flora Howard	(Bridesmaid)
Elsie Sindora	(Bridesmaid)
Walter Lynch	(Tough Cop)
Dan Dillon	(Bum)
Jules Hanft	(Physician)
Silas Wilcox	(Cop)
Kathleen Kay	(Maid)
Minnie Stearns	(Fierce Woman)
Frank Campeau	(Welfare Officer)
F. Blinn	(His Assistant)
John McKinnon	(Chief of Police)

Elsie Young, V. Madison, Evans Quirk, Bliss Chevalier, Grace Keller, Irene Jennings, Florette Faulkner, Martha Hall, Estelle Cook, J. B. Russell, Lillian Crane, Sarah Kernan, Philip D'Oench, Charles I. Pierce

(Extras in Wedding Scene)

Elsie Codd (Chaplin's English publicity representative), Mother Vinot (studio sewing lady), Louise Hathaway, Amada Yanez and Baby

(Extras in Alley Scene)

Clyde McAtee, Frank Hale, Ed Hunt, Rupert Franklin, Frances Cochran, George Sheldon

(Extras in Reception Scene)

Sadie Gordon, Laura Pollard, L. Parker, Ethel O'Neil, L. Jenks, Esther Ralston, Henry Roser

(Extras in Heaven Scene)

Production started:	21 July 1919
Production finished:	30 July 1920
Released:	6 February 1921
Length:	5250 ft

68a   Nice and Friendly

Cast: Charles Chaplin (Villain)
      Lord Louis
       Mountbatten (Hero)
      Lady Edwina
       Mountbatten (Heroine)
      Jackie Coogan
      Colonel Robert
       M. Thompson
      Frederick Neilson
      Eulalie Neilson

Improvised sketch, never released.

69   The Idle Class

Cast: Charles Chaplin (Tramp *and* Husband)
      Edna Purviance (Neglected Wife)
      Mack Swain   (Her Father)
      Henry Bergman (Sleeping Hobo)
      Allan Garcia   (His Neighbour on a Park Bench *and*
               Guest)
      John Rand   (Golfer *and* Guest)
      Rex Storey   (Pickpocket *and* Guest)
      Lillian McMurray (Maid)
      Lillita McMurray (Maid)
      Loyal Underwood (Guest)
      Mrs Parker
      Lolita Parker
      Howard Olsen
      Edward Knoblock
      Granville Redmond
      Carlyle Robinson
      Joe Van Meter

Bruce Belamator, William Thompson, William Hackett, Jack Mortimer, B. W. McComber, Charles Aber, Jim Collins, Jack Sydney, Duffy Kirk, Jack Lott, George Bastian, Howard Johnston, Joe Campbell, Richard Brewster, Mrs Ross Lang, Miss Helene Calverley, Margaret Rishell, Miss M. Parsons, Gertrude Pedlar, Ruth Darling, Joe Flores, Miss Grace, Carl Brown, Anita Walton, Miss Egbert, Lura Anson, Catherine Vidor, Gladys Webb, Mary Land, California Truman, Marie Crist, Lottie Cruz, Helen McMullin, Hugh Saxon, Harold Kent, Harold McNulty, Helen McKee, Gladys Baxter, Dolly Rich, Robert Badger, Jack Woods, C. S. Steele, Fred Wilson, E. C. Holkin, Miss Wicks, Mary Ann Bennett, Harriett Bennett, Vera Wilder, Ethel Childers, Anita Simons, Melissa Ledgerwood, Nel Foltz, Ruth Foster, Evelyn Burns, Jean Temle, Bertha Feducha,

Pearl Palmer, Arnold Triller, Jack Underhill, John Sweeny, Clyde McCoy, George Milo, William Moore, George Mistler, J. A. Beaver, Charles Meakins, W. R. Denning, L. Chandler, L. Swisher, R. Pennell, Jules Hanft, Bob Palmer, Walter Bacon, Art Hanson, Harry Tenbrook, Bill Carey, Joe Anderson, Paul Mertz
(Extras)

Production started:	29 January 1921
Production finished:	25 June 1921
Released:	25 September 1921
Length:	1916 ft

70 Pay Day

Cast:		
	Charles Chaplin	(Labourer)
	Phyllis Allen	(His Wife)
	Mack Swain	(Foreman)
	Edna Purviance	(Foreman's Daughter)
	Sydney Chaplin	(Charlie's Mate *and* Lunch Wagon Proprietor)
	Albert Austin	(Workman)
	John Rand	(Workman)
	Loyal Underwood	(Workman)
	Henry Bergman	(Drinking Companion)
	Allan Garcia	(Drinking Companion)

Pete Griffin, Joe Griffin, Harry Tenbrook, Ethel Childers, Edith Blythe, Virginia Bodle, Helen Kapp, La Belle Raymond, Sylvia Menier
(Extras)

Production started:	6 August 1921

Production interrupted by European tour, September–October 1921

Production finished:	23 February 1922
Released:	2 April 1922
Length:	1950 ft

71 The Pilgrim

Cast:		
	Charles Chaplin	(Escaped Convict)
	Edna Purviance	(Girl)
	Kitty Bradbury	(Her Mother, Charlie's Landlady)
	Mack Swain	(Deacon)
	Loyal Underwood	(Elder)
	Charles Riesner	(Thief)
	Dinky Dean (Riesner)	(Horrid Child)

727

Sydney Chaplin	(His Father)
May Wells	(His Mother)
Henry Bergman	(Sheriff on Train)
Tom Murray	(Local Sheriff)
Monta Bell	(Policeman)
Raymond Lee	(Boy in Congregation)
Frank Antunez	(Bandit)
Joe Van Meter	(Bandit)
Phyllis Allen	(Member of Congregation)
Florence Latimer	(Member of Congregation)
Edith Bostwick	(Member of Congregation)
Laddie Earle	(Member of Congregation)
Louis Troester	(Member of Congregation)
Beth Nagel	(Member of Congregation)
Mrs C. Johnson	(Member of Congregation)
Marion Davies	(Member of Congregation)
Miss Evans	
Frank Liscomb	
S. D. Wilcox	
Robert Traughbur	
Carlyle Robinson	
Jack McCredie	
Charles Hafler	
Bill Carey	
Paul Mason	
McNeill	

Sarah Barrows, Donnabelle Ouster, Gallie Frey, Della Glowner, Theresa Gray, Cecile Harcourt, Anna Hicks, Martha Harris, Mary Hamlett, Ethel Kennedy, Emily Lamont, Agnes Lynch, Mildred Pitts, Katherine Parrish, Edna Rowe, Mabel Shoulters, Georgia Sherrart, Rose Wheeler, George Bradford, George Carruthers, J. Espan, F. F. Guenste, Lee Glowner, Harry Hicks, Carl Jensen, Tom Ray, James J. Smith, S. H. Williams, Paul Wilkins, H. Wolfinger

(Extras in Church Scene)

Production started:	1 April 1922
Production finished:	15 July 1922
Première:	26 February 1923, Strand Theatre, New York.
Length:	3647 ft.

71a The Professor

Cast:	Charles Chaplin	(Professor Bosco)
Production started:	30 September 1919	

Production
finished: ?(Film possibly assembled from out-takes from other pictures.)

Never released, but declared by Chaplin to be ready for release in November 1922.

Length: An edited sequence of some 450 feet survives, along with a few out-takes apparently from another sequence. Chaplin's correspondence with Sydney in 1923, however, refers to *The Professor* as a two-reeler – i.e. approximately 2000 feet.

V   THE UNITED ARTISTS' FILMS   1923–1952

72   A Woman of Paris

Production: Regent–United Artists
Producer: Charles Chaplin
Director: Charles Chaplin
Scenario: Charles Chaplin
Photography: Roland Totheroh
Second
   Camera: Jack Wilson
Assistant: Edward Sutherland
Literary
   Editor: Monta Bell
Art Director: Arthur Stibolt
Research: Jean de Limur, Henri d'Abbadie d'Arrast

Cast: Edna Purviance   (Marie St Clair)
                   Adolphe Menjou   (Pierre Revel)
                   Carl Miller   (Jean Millet)
                   Lydia Knott   (Jean's Mother)
                   Charles French   (Jean's Father)
                   Clarence Geldert   (Marie's Father)
                   Betty Morrissey   (Fifi)
                   Malvina Polo   (Paulette)
                   Henry Bergman   (Head Waiter)
                   Harry Northrup   (Man About Town)
                   Nellie Bly Baker   (Masseuse)
                   Miss Delante
                     (?Stella De Lanti) (Revel's Fiancée)
                   Charles Chaplin   (Porter)

Production
started: 27 November 1922
Production
finished: 29 September 1923
Première: 1 October 1923, Criterion Theatre, Hollywood
Length: 7557 ft

73 The Gold Rush

Production:	Chaplin–United Artists
Producer:	Charles Chaplin
Director:	Charles Chaplin
Scenario:	Charles Chaplin
Photography:	Roland Totheroh
Cameramen:	Jack Wilson, Mark Marlatt
Art Director:	Charles D. Hall
Assistant Directors:	Charles Riesner, Henri d'Abbadie d'Arrast, Eddie Sutherland
Production Manager:	Alfred Reeves

Cast:

Charles Chaplin	(Lone Prospector)
Georgia Hale	(Georgia)
Mack Swain	(Big Jim McKay)
Tom Murray	(Black Larson)
Betty Morrissey	(Georgia's Friend)
Kay Desleys	(Georgia's Friend)
Joan Lowell	(Georgia's Friend)
Malcolm Waite	(Jack Cameron)
Henry Bergman	(Hank Curtis)
John Rand	(Prospector)
Heinie Conklin	(Prospector)
Albert Austin	(Prospector)
Allan Garcia	(Prospector)
Tom Wood	(Prospector)
Stanley Sanford	(Barman)
Barbara Pierce	(Manicurist)
A. J. O'Connor	(Officer)
Art Walker	(Officer)
Daddy Taylor	(Ancient Dancing Prospector)
Margaret Martin	(Squaw)
Princess Neela	(Squaw)
Frank Aderias	(Eskimo Child)
Leona Aderias	(Eskimo Child)
E. Espinosa	(Eskimo)
Ray Morris	(Eskimo)
Fred Karno Jr	

Jack Adams, Sam Allen, Claude Anderson, Harry Arras, F. J. Beauregard, William Bell, Francis Bernhardt, E. Blumenthal, William Bradford, George Brock, William Butler, Pete Brogan, R. Campbell, Leland Carr, H. C. Chisholm, Harry Coleman, Harry De Mors, Jimmy Dime, W. S. Dobson, John Eagown, Aaron Edward, Elias Elizaroff, Leon Fary, Richard Foley, Charles Force, J. C. Fowler, Ray Grey, William Hackett, James

Hammer, Ben Hart, R. Hausner, Tom Hawley, Jack Herrick,
Jack Hoefer, George Holt, Tom Hutchinson, Carl Jenson,
Harry Jones, Bob Kelly, John King, Bob Leonard, Francis
Lowell, Clyde McAtee, John McGrath, Chris Martin, John
Millerta, Chris Martin, Mr Myers, George Neely, H. C. Oliver,
William Parmalee, Jack Phillips, Art Price, Frank Rice, E. M.
Robb, C. F. Roarke, J. Ryan, J. J. Smith, Joe Smith, C. B. Steele,
Armand Triller, John Tully, Jack Vedders, John Wallace,
Sharkey Weimar, Ed Wilson, C. Whitecloud, H. Wolfinger,
Dave Wright, Ah Yot, George Young, Ed Zimmer, Lillian
Adrian, Rebecca Conroy, Donnabella Custer, Kay De Lay, Inez
Gomez, Mildred Hall, Gypsy Hart, Helen Hayward, Josie
Howard, Jean Huntley, Gladys Johnson, Helen Kassler,
Geraldine Leslie, Joan Lowell, Ruth Milo, Marie Muggley,
Florence Murth, Lillian Rosino, Edna Rowe, Jane Sherman,
Nina Trask, Mary Williams, Marie Willis, Lillian Reschm,
Nellie Noxon, Dolores Mendes, Cecile Cameron, Joan Lowell,
Betty Pierce, Marta Belfort, Dorothy Crane, Bessie Eade, James
Darby, Frank E. Stockdale, Freddie Lansit, George Lesley,
P. Nagle, M. Farrell, S. Murphy.

(People in Dance Hall)
Shooting began with Lita Grey as leading lady. Georgia Hale
took over the role in December 1924

Production started:	December 1923
Production completed:	21 May 1925
Première:	26 June 1925, Grauman's Egyptian Theatre, Hollywood
Length:	8555 ft

Reissue Version

Director:	Charles Chaplin
Narrator:	Charles Chaplin
Music:	Charles Chaplin
Musical Director:	Max Terr
Editor:	Harold McGhean
Released:	16 April 1942
Length:	8498 ft

74 The Circus

Production:	Chaplin–United Artists
Producer:	Charles Chaplin
Director:	Charles Chaplin
Scenario:	Charles Chaplin
Photography:	Roland Totheroh

Cameramen:	Jack Wilson, Mark Marlatt
Assistant Director:	Harry Crocker
Art Director:	Charles D. Hall
Editor:	Charles Chaplin

Cast:		
	Charles Chaplin	(Tramp)
	Merna Kennedy	(Equestrienne)
	Allan Garcia	(Circus Proprietor)
	Harry Crocker	(Rex, the High Wire Walker)
	Henry Bergman	(Old Clown)
	Stanley Sanford	(Chief Property Man)
	George Davis	(Magician)
	Betty Morrissey	(Vanishing Lady)
	John Rand	(Assistant Property Man *and* Clown)
	Armand Triller	(Clown)
	Steve Murphy	(Pickpocket)
	Bill Knight	(Cop)
	Jack Pierce	(Man operating Ropes)
	H. L. Kyle	
	Eugene Barry	
	L. J. O'Connor	
	Hugh Saxon	
	Jack Bernard	
	Max Tyron	
	A. Bachman	
	William Blystone	
	Numi	(Lion)
	Bobby	(Monkey)
	Josephine	(Monkey)
	Jimmy	(Monkey)

In Cut Sequences

Doc Stone	(Twin Prize Fighters)

Production started:	2 November 1925
Production interrupted:	5 December 1926–3 September 1927
Production finished:	19 November 1927
Première:	6 January 1928, Strand Theatre, New York
Length:	6500 ft

Reissue Version

Director:	Charles Chaplin
Music:	Charles Chaplin
Musical Director:	Eric James

732

Song 'Swing, Little Girl' composed and sung by Charles Chaplin.

Released:	1970
Length:	6431 ft

75 City Lights

Production:	Chaplin–United Artists
Producer:	Charles Chaplin
Director:	Charles Chaplin
Scenario:	Charles Chaplin
Photography:	Roland Totheroh
Cameramen:	Mark Marlatt, Gordon Pollock
Assistant Directors:	Harry Crocker, Henry Bergman, Albert Austin
Art Director:	Charles D. Hall
Music:	Charles Chaplin
Arranger:	Arthur Johnson
Music Director:	Alfred Newman
Editor:	Charles Chaplin

Musical Themes used in addition to original compositions: 'Star-Spangled Banner', 'Hail, Hail, The Gang's All Here', 'Dixie', 'I Hear You Calling Me', 'Home, Sweet Home', 'La Violetera' (Jose Padilla), 'Swanee River', 'How Dry Am I', 'St Louis Blues' (W. S. Handy)

Cast:	Charles Chaplin	(The Tramp)
	Virginia Cherrill	(The Blind Girl)
	Florence Lee	(Her Grandmother)
	Harry Myers	(Millionaire)
	Hank Mann	(Boxer)
	Eddie Baker	(Referee)
	Tom Dempsey	(Boxer)
	Eddie McAuliffe	(Boxer who leaves in a hurry)
	Willie Keeler	(Boxer)
	Victor Alexander	(Knocked-out Boxer)
	Tony Stabeman	(Victorious Boxer, later knocked-out)
	Emmett Wagner	(Second)
	Joe Herrick, A. B. Lane, Cy Slocum, Ad Herman, Jack Alexander	(Extras in Boxing Scene)
	T. S. Alexander	(Doctor)
	Allan Garcia	(Butler)
	Henry Bergman	(Mayor *and* Janitor)
	Albert Austin	(Street Sweeper *and* Burglar)
	Joe Van Meter	(Burglar)
	John Rand	(Tramp)
	Spike Robinson	(Man Who Throws Away Cigar)

Tiny Ward	(Man on Lift in front of Art Shop)
Mrs Hyams	(Flower Shop Assistant)
James Donnelly	(Foreman)
Harry Ayers	(Cop)
Stanhope Wheatcroft	(Man in Café)
Jean Harlow	(Extra in Restaurant Scene)
Mrs Pope (Harlow's Mother)	(Extra in Restaurant Scene)
Florence Wicks	(Woman Who Sits on Cigar)
Mark Strong	(Man in Restaurant)
Mrs Garcia	(Woman at left of table in Restaurant)
Peter Diego	(Man in mix-up with Coat and Hat)
Betty Blair	(Woman at centre of table in Restaurant)
Robert Parrish	(Newsboy)
Margaret Oliver, Charlie Hammond, Milton Gowman	(Extras in Street Scene)

In Cut Sequence

Harry Crocker	(Window Dresser)
Charles Lederer	(Express Boy)
Edith Wilson	(Younger Lady Looking in Window)
Blanche Payson	(Older Lady Looking in Window)

Production started:	31 December 1927
Production finished:	22 January 1931
Première:	30 January 1931, Los Angeles Theatre
London Première:	27 February 1931, Dominion Theatre
Length:	8093 ft

76 Modern Times

Production:	Chaplin–United Artists
Producer:	Charles Chaplin
Director:	Charles Chaplin
Scenario:	Charles Chaplin
Photography:	Roland Totheroh, Ira Morgan
Assistant Directors:	Carter De Haven, Henry Bergman
Art Directors:	Charles D. Hall, Russell Spencer
Music:	Charles Chaplin
Arrangers:	Edward Powell, David Raksin
Musical Director:	Alfred Newman

734

Musical themes used in addition to original compositions: 'Halleluiah, I'm a Bum', 'Prisoners' Song' (C. Massey), 'How Dry Am I', 'In the Evening By the Moonlight' (Bland), 'Je cherche après Titine' (Duncan and Daniderff)

Cast:
	Charles Chaplin	(A Worker)
	Paulette Goddard	(Gamine)
	Henry Bergman	(Café Owner)
	Stanley J. Sanford	(Big Bill *and* Worker)
	Chester Conklin	(Mechanic)
	Hank Mann	(Burglar)
	Louis Natheaux	(Burglar)
	Stanley Blystone	(Sheriff Couler)
	Allan Garcia	(Company Boss)
	Sam Stein	(Foreman)
	Juana Sutton	(Woman with Buttoned Bosom)
	Jack Low	(Worker)
	Walter James	(Worker)
	Dick Alexander	(Convict)
	Dr Cecil Reynolds	(Prison Chaplain)
	Myra McKinney	(Chaplain's Wife)
	Lloyd Ingraham	(Prison Governor)
	Heinie Conklin	(Workman)
	John Rand	(Convict)
	Murdoch McQuarrie	
	Wilfred Lucas	
	Edward le Saint	
	Fred Maltesta	
	Ted Oliver	
	Edward Kimball	

Production started:	September 1933
Production finished:	12 January 1936
Première:	5 February 1936, Rivoli Theatre, New York
London Première:	11 February 1936, Tivoli Theatre
Length:	8126 ft

77 The Great Dictator

Production:	Chaplin–United Artists
Producer:	Charles Chaplin
Director:	Charles Chaplin
Scenario:	Charles Chaplin
Photography:	Karl Struss, Roland Totheroh
Assistant Directors:	Dan James, Robert Meltzer, Wheeler Dryden

Art Director:	J. Russell Spencer
Editor:	Willard Nico
Music:	Charles Chaplin, with paraphrases of Wagner, Brahms
Musical Director:	Meredith Willson
Sound:	Percy Townsend, Glenn Rominger
Coordinator:	Henry Bergman

Cast:		
	Charles Chaplin	(Adenoid Hynkel *and* The Barber)
	Paulette Goddard	(Hannah)
	Jack Oakie	(Benzino Napaloni)
	Henry Daniell	(Garbitsch)
	Reginald Gardiner	(Schultz)
	Billy Gilbert	(Herring)
	Maurice Moskovich	(Mr Jaeckel)
	Emma Dunn	(Mrs Jaeckel)
	Bernard Gorcey	(Mr Mann)
	Paul Weigel	(Mr Agar)
	Grace Hayle	(Madame Napaloni)
	Carter De Haven	(Ambassador)
	Chester Conklin	(Customer in Barber's Shop)
	Hank Mann	(Storm Trooper)
	Eddie Gribbon	(Storm Trooper)
	Richard Alexander	(Storm Trooper)
	Leo White	(Hynkel's Barber)
	Lucien Prival	(Officer)
	Pat Flaherty	
	Harry Semels	
	Esther Michaelson	
	Florence Wright	
	Robert O. David	
	Eddie Dunn	
	Peter Lynn Hayes	
	Nita Pike	
	Jack Perrin	
	Max Davidson	
	Nellie V. Nichols	

Production started:	1 January 1939
First shot:	9 September 1939
Final shot:	2 October 1940
Première:	15 October 1940, Capitol and Astor Theatres, New York
London Première:	16 December 1940, Prince of Wales, Gaumont, Haymarket, Marble Arch, Pavilion Theatres
Length:	11,628 ft

78   Monsieur Verdoux

Production:	Chaplin–United Artists
Producer:	Charles Chaplin
Director:	Charles Chaplin
Scenario:	Charles Chaplin
Photography:	Curt Courant, Roland Totheroh
Cameraman:	Wallace Chewning
Associate Directors:	Robert Florey, Wheeler Dryden
Assistant Director:	Rex Bailey
Art Director:	John Beckman
Editor:	Willard Nico
Music:	Charles Chaplin
Musical Director:	Rudolph Schrager
Sound:	James T. Corrigan
Costumes:	Drew Tetrick
Make-up:	William Knight
Hair Stylist:	Hedvig M. Jornd
Narrator:	Charles Chaplin

Cast:		
	Charles Chaplin	(Monsieur Henri Verdoux)
	Martha Raye	(Annabella Bonheur)
	Isobel Elsom	(Marie Grosnay)
	Marilyn Nash	(The Girl)
	Robert Lewis	(Monsieur Bottello)
	Mady Correl	(Madame Verdoux)
	Allison Roddan	(Peter Verdoux)
	Audrey Betz	(Madame Bottello)
	Ada-May	(Annette)
	Marjorie Bennett	(Maid)
	Helen High	(Yvonne)
	Margaret Hoffman	(Lydia Floray)
	Irving Bacon	(Pierre Couvais)
	Edwin Mills	(Jean Couvais)
	Virginia Brissac	(Carlotta Couvais)
	Almira Sessions	(Lena Couvais)
	Eula Morgan	(Phoebe Couvais)
	Bernard J. Nedell	(Prefect)
	Charles Evans	(Detective Morrow)
	Arthur Hohl	(Estate Agent)
	John Harmon	(Joe Darwin)
	Vera Marshe	(Mrs Darwin)
	William Frawley	(Jean La Salle)
	Fritz Lieber	(Priest)
	Fred Karno Jr	(Mr Karno)
	Barry Norton	(Guest)

Pierre Watkin	(Attorney)
Cyril Delevanti	(Postman)
Charles Wagenheim	(Friend)
Addison Richards	(M. Millet)
James Craven	(Friend)
Franklin Farnum	(Victim)
Herb Vigran	(Reporter)
Boyd Irwin	(Warder)
Paul Newland	(Guest)
Joseph Crehan	(Broker)
Wheaton Chambers	(Druggist)
Frank Reicher	(Doctor)
Wheeler Dryden	(Salesman)
Thérèse Lyon	(Jeannette)
Lester Mathews	(Prosecuting Attorney)
Richard Abbot	(Defence Attorney)
Garnett Monks	(Foreman of Jury)
Joseph Granby	(Court Clerk)
Julius Cramer	(Executioner)
Art Miller	(Guard)
Albert Petit	(Spectator)
Barbara Slater	(Flower Girl)
Ella Ethridge	(Woman in Street)
Christine Ell	(Maid)
Lois Conklin	(Flower Girl)
Alicia Adams	(Flower Girl)
Elisabeth Dudgeon	(Old Hag)
John Harmon	(Joe, friend of Annabella)
Vera Marshe	(Vicki, friend of Annabella)
Daniel de Jonghe	(Waiter)
George Dees	(Waiter)
Carlo Schipa	(Waiter)
Albert D'Arno	(Waiter)
Bert le Baron	(Doorman at Café Royal)
Jean Bittner	(Diner in Café Royal)
Munnel Petroff	(Diner in Café Royal)
Tom Wilson	
Phillips Smalley	

Production started:	April 1946
Opening shot:	3 June 1946
Final shot:	5 September 1946
Production finished:	4 March 1947
Première:	11 April 1947, Broadway Theatre, New York
Length:	11,132 ft

79 Limelight

Production:	Celebrated–United Artists
Producer:	Charles Chaplin
Director:	Charles Chaplin
Scenario:	Charles Chaplin
Photography:	Karl Struss
Photographic Consultant:	Roland Totheroh
Assistant Producers:	Wheeler Dryden, Jerome Epstein
Associate Director:	Robert Aldrich
Art Director:	Eugene Lourié
Editor:	Joseph Engel
Choreography:	Charles Chaplin, André Eglevsky, Melissa Hayden
Music:	Charles Chaplin
Musical Director:	Ray Rasch
Songs:	Charles Chaplin, Ray Rasch

Cast:		
	Charles Chaplin	(Calvero)
	Claire Bloom	(Terry)
	Buster Keaton	(Partner)
	Sydney Chaplin	(Neville)
	Norman Lloyd	(Bodalink)
	Marjorie Bennett	(Mrs Alsop)
	Wheeler Dryden	(Doctor *and* Clown)
	Nigel Bruce	(Mr Postant)
	Barry Bernard	(John Redfern)
	Leonard Mudie	(Doctor)
	Snub Pollard	(Musician)
	Loyal Underwood	(Musician)
	Julian Ludwig	(Musician)
	André Eglevsky	(Harlequin)
	Melissa Hayden	(Columbine)
	Charles Chaplin Jr	(Pantomime Policeman)
	Geraldine Chaplin	(Child)
	Michael Chaplin	(Child)
	Josephine Chaplin	(Child)
	Jack Deery	(Emissary – Dress Circle)
	Major Sam Harris	(Old Fogey in Dress Circle)
	Dorothy Ford	(Patrician Lady in Dress Circle)
	Elizabeth Root, Millicent Patrick, Judy Landon, Sherry Moreland, Valerie Vernon, Eric Wilson, Cyril Delevanti,	

Leonard Mudi,	
Frank Hagrey	(Extras in Dress Circle)
Oona O'Neill	
Chaplin	(Double for Terry, in brief long-shot)
Stapleton Kent	
Mollie Blessing	

Production started:	12 November 1951
Opening shot:	19 November 1951
Final shot:	25 January 1952
Première:	23 October 1952, Odeon Theatre, Leicester Square, London
US Première:	23 October 1952, Astor and Trans Lux Theatres, New York
Length:	12,636 ft

VI   THE BRITISH PRODUCTIONS   1957–1967

80   A King in New York

Production:	Attica-Archway
Producer:	Charles Chaplin
Director:	Charles Chaplin
Scenario:	Charles Chaplin
Photography:	Georges Périnal
Camera Operator:	Jeff Seaholme
Assistant Director:	René Dupont
Associate Producer:	Jerome Epstein
Art Director:	Allan Harris
Editor:	John Seabourne
Assistant:	Tony Bohy
Music:	Charles Chaplin
Arranged by:	Boris Sarbek
Conducted by:	Leighton Lucas
Sound Supervisor:	John Cox
Sound Recording:	Bert Ross, Bob Jones
Sound Editor:	Spencer Reeve
Sound System:	Westrex
Special Effects:	Wally Veevers
Continuity:	Barbara Cole
Make-up:	Stuart Freeborn
Hair Stylist:	Helen Penfold
Wardrobe Supervisor:	J. Wilson-Apperson

Production Controller:	Mickey Delamar	
Production Manager:	Eddie Pike	
Furs:	Deanfield	
Studio:	Shepperton	
Cast:	Charles Chaplin	(King Shahdov)
	Maxine Audley	(Queen Irene)
	Jerry Desmonde	(Prime Minister Voudel)
	Oliver Johnston	(Ambassador Jaume)
	Dawn Addams	(Ann Kay – TV Specialist)
	Sidney James	(Johnson – TV Advertiser)
	Joan Ingrams	(Mona Cromwell – Hostess)
	Michael Chaplin	(Rupert Macabee)
	John McLaren	(Mr Macabee)
	Phil Brown	(Headmaster)
	Harry Green	(Lawyer Green)
	Robert Arden	(Liftboy)
	Alan Gifford	(School Superintendent)
	Robert Cawdron	(US Marshal)
	George Woodbridge	(Member of Atomic Commission)
	Clifford Buckton	(Member of Atomic Commission)
	Vincent Lawson	(Member of Atomic Commission)
	Shani Wallis	(Singer)
	Joy Nichols	(Singer)
	Nicholas Tannar	(Butler)
	George Truzzi	(Comedian)
	Laurie Lupino Lane	(Comedian)
	Macdonald Parke	
Released:	12 September 1957	
Length:	9891 ft	

81 A Countess From Hong Kong

Production:	Universal
Producer:	Jerome Epstein
Director:	Charles Chaplin
Scenario:	Charles Chaplin
Photography:	Arthur Ibbetson
Assistant Director:	Jack Causey
Production Designer:	Don Ashton
Art Director:	Robert Cartwright
Set Decorator:	Vernon Dixon
Editor:	Gordon Hales
Music:	Charles Chaplin

Musical Director:	Lambert Williamson
Musical Associate:	Eric James
Sound:	Michael Hopkins
Sound Recording:	Bill Daniels, Ken Barker
Production Supervisor:	Denis Johnson
Titles:	Gordon Shadrick
Colour:	Technicolor. CinemaScope.

Cast:	Marlon Brando	(Ogden Mears)
	Sophia Loren	(Countess Natascha Alexandroff)
	Sydney Chaplin	(Harvey Crothers)
	Tippi Hedren	(Martha Mears)
	Patrick Cargill	(Hudson)
	Margaret Rutherford	(Miss Gaulswallow)
	Michael Medwin	(John Felix)
	Oliver Johnston	(Clark)
	John Paul	(Captain)
	Angela Scoular	(Society Girl)
	Peter Bartlett	(Steward)
	Bill Nagy	(Crawford)
	Dilys Laye	(Saleswoman)
	Angela Pringle	(Baroness)
	Jenny Bridge	(Countess)
	Maureen Russell	(Countess)
	Jackie Dee	(Girl in Dance Hall)
	Ray Marlowe	(American in Dance Hall)
	Arthur Gross	(Immigration Officer)
	Balbina	(Maid)
	Geraldine Chaplin	(Girl in Ballroom)
	Janine Hill	(Girl in Ballroom)
	Christine Rogers	(Girl in Ballroom)
	Pat Hagan	(Girl in Ballroom)
	Gerry Howes	(Man in Ballroom)
	Anthony Chin	(Hawaiian)
	Burnell Tucker	(Receptionist)
	Leonard Trolley	(Purser)
	Lee Lowe	(Electrician)
	Francis Dux	(Head Waiter)
	Cecil Cheng	(Taxi Driver)
	Ronald Rubin	(Sailor)
	Michael Spice	(Sailor)
	Ray Marlowe	(Sailor)
	Josephine Chaplin	(Young Girl)

Victoria Chaplin	(Young Girl)
Harold Korn	(Officer)
Holly Grey	(Steward)
Kevin Manser	(Photographer)
Marianne Stone	(Reporter)
Lew Luton	(Reporter)
Bill Edwards	(Reporter)
Drew Russell	(Reporter)
John Sterland	(Reporter)
Paul Carson	(Reporter)
Paul Tamarin	(Reporter)
Carol Cleveland	(Nurse)
Charles Chaplin	(An Old Steward)

Released: 2 January 1967
Length: 11,033 ft

VII FILM PRODUCED BY CHAPLIN

A Woman of The Sea (*Working title*: **Sea Gulls**)

Production: Charles Chaplin Film Corporation
Producer: Josef von Sternberg
Director: Josef von Sternberg
Scenario: Josef von Sternberg
Photography: Eddie Gheller, Paul Ivano
Cameraman: Mark Marlatt
Art Director: Charles D. Hall
Assistants: George Ruric, Charles Hammond, Riza Royce

Cast:		
	Edna Purviance	(Joan)
	Eve Southern	(Magdalen)
	Charles French	(Their Father)
	Raymond Bloomer	(Peter, the Fisherman)
	Gayne Whitman	(The Novelist from the City)

The film was never released; on 24 June 1933 the negative was formally burnt.

VIII COMPILATION FILM

80a The Chaplin Revue

Production: Roy Film Establishment–United Artists
Producer: Charles Chaplin
Director: Charles Chaplin
Scenario: Charles Chaplin
Music: Charles Chaplin
Musical
Director: Eric James

Song, 'Bound
For Texas':   Charles Chaplin
Sung by: Matt Munro
Narrator: Charles Chaplin

Compiled from *A Dog's Life, Shoulder Arms, The Pilgrim* and *How to Make Movies*

Released: 25 September 1959
Length: 11,150 ft

IX   UNAUTHORIZED FILMS: ESSANAY PERIOD

49a   The Essanay–Chaplin Revue

5-reel anthology of *The Tramp, His New Job* and *A Night Out*.

Released: 23 September 1916

50   Triple Trouble

Producer: Jesse J. Robbins for Essanay
Directors: Charles Chaplin and Leo White
Scenario: Leo White

Cast: Charles Chaplin   (Janitor)
                Edna Purviance   (Maid)
                Leo White   (Count)
                Billy Armstrong   (Cook *and* Thief)
                James T. Kelley   (Singing Derelict)
                Bud Jamison   (Tramp)
                Wesley Ruggles   (Crook)
                Albert Austin   (Man)

An amalgam, assembled by White, of scenes from *Police* and an uncompleted Essanay Chaplin short, *Life*, with new material directed by White.

Released: 11 August 1918
Length: 2000 ft approximately

50a   Chase Me Charlie

7-reel montage of Essanay films, edited by Langford Reed.

Released: May 1918
Length: 6500 ft approximately

X   OTHER FILM APPEARANCES

His Regeneration (1915)

An Essanay Broncho Billy film, in which Chaplin plays himself.

Filmography

The Nut (1921)

Production:	Douglas Fairbanks–United Artists
Director:	Theodore Reed
Starring:	Douglas Fairbanks

Chaplin appears as himself

Souls For Sale (1923)

Production:	Rupert Hughes–Metro Goldwyn Mayer
Director:	Rupert Hughes

Chaplin appears as himself, along with many other Hollywood stars.

Show People (1928)

Production:	Cosmopolitan–MGM
Director:	King Vidor
Starring:	Marion Davies

Chaplin appears as himself.

The Gentleman Tramp (1975)

Production:	Filmverhuurkantoor 'De Dam' D.V.-Audjeff
Director:	Richard Patterson

Compilation documentary, with newly filmed scenes of Chaplin at home in Corsier sur Vevey.

APPENDIX VII

Shooting schedules and ratios

		SCHEDULES			RATIOS	
DATE	TITLE	SHOOT-ING DAYS	IDLE* DAYS	TOTAL FOOTAGE SHOT	LENGTH OF FINISHED FILM	SHOOT-ING RATIO
1918	A Dog's Life	59	17	35,887 ft	2674 ft	13.4
1918	Shoulder Arms			43,937	3142	14
1919	Sunnyside	76	103	59,559	2769	21.5
1919	A Day's Pleasure			38,921	1714	22.7
1920	The Kid	154	117	278,573	5250	53
1921	The Idle Class	53	78	27,078	1916	14.1
1922	Pay Day	31	164	33,914	1950	17.4
1922	The Pilgrim	51	153	46,166	3647	12.7
1923	A Woman of Paris			130,115	7557	17.1
1925	The Gold Rush	170	235	231,505	8555	27
1927	The Circus	170	467	211,104	6500	32.5
1931	City Lights	179	504	314,256	8093	38.8
1936	Modern Times	147	263	213,961	8126	26.3
1940	The Great Dictator	168	391	477,440	11,628	41
1946	Monsieur Verdoux	80		313,726	11,132	28.2
1952	Limelight	55		239,481	12,636	19

*This is a comparative term. Although the number of 'idle days' recorded in the studio records of each film included some periods of total inactivity, the figure also included time spent on preparation of sets and costumes, rehearsing, cutting and (later) music and recording.

APPENDIX VIII
Chaplin, Epstein and the Circle Theatre

Towards the end of his three-decade residence in the United States, the chance to resume an active contact with the live theatre seems to have revived something of the old passion implanted in Chaplin when he was a boy performer. His contacts with the Circle Theatre also began the association with Jerome (Jerry) Epstein as collaborator, friend and confidant which was to last for thirty years, until Chaplin's death.

Epstein was a friend of Chaplin's younger son Sydney, with whom he was associated in establishing the theatre in 1946. The Circle began in a modest way, giving its performances in the homes of any friends with large enough drawing rooms, but its very first production, *The Adding Machine*, directed by Epstein with Sydney Chaplin in the leading role, attracted favourable notice. Sydney had already introduced Epstein to his father and Oona when they all met at a show of *Les Enfants du Paradis*; and the Chaplins came to see Sydney's performance. 'Charlie was a wonderful audience,' Epstein recalled, 'and he just got to like the theatre. He would come all the time. When he'd nothing else to do, he would drive down in his little Ford, and sit with me in the box office. And then of course all his friends began to come to the theatre and they brought friends. Fanny Brice came; and Constance Collier took us up in a big way, and brought Katharine Hepburn and George Cukor, and Gladys Cooper and Robert Morley and any English people who happened to be in Hollywood. When we did *Ethan Frome* we borrowed props from the studio. Charlie was so impressed by our production of *Time of your Life* that he contacted Saroyan and asked him to give us a play, which he did: it was *Sam Ego's House*.

'Then one day he was watching a rehearsal of *The Skin Game*, and asked "Do you mind if I suggest something . . .?" and of course in no time he had taken over the whole show. He was marvellous. His instinct was amazing – his feeling for the play, stage pictures, timing, exits, entrances, everything.

Of course he acted out every part himself, and some of the actors as a result became little Charlie Chaplins. It was an unforgettable experience for them, though at this stage of the production it was very confusing for them too, altering everything they had already done.

'After that he did five other productions. Of course he had not the patience to do them from the beginning, but he would come in at the end and give his touches. The next one was *Hindle Wakes*. Then he wanted to do *Rain*, which he said had never been done correctly. He considered that Jeanne Eagels' performance had been overrated and that the Reverend Davidson was always done wrong. Sadie was June Havoc – that was the first time we had a real star, but she had come to the theatre and wanted to do the part.

'I had called Albert Camus in North Africa to ask if we could produce *Caligula*, and Charlie did it. It was a disaster: no one understood the play, least of all the actors. Although Charlie's participation was never made public, or printed in the programme, he took it very personally when the play had bad notices, and I had to dissuade him from firing off letters to the press. Sydney was delighted when Frank Eng wrote in his review that he, Sydney, was the only one who understood the play – because he understood no more of it than anyone else!

'Charlie devised some wonderful gags for *School for Scandal* and even added a line. Marie Wilson played Lady Teazle, and the eighteenth-century dresses dramatically showed off her magnificent breasts. I had devised a card game, in which Wheeler Dryden stood behind Marie. Charlie suggested that when Wheeler peered over her shoulder, and Marie held the cards to her, Wheeler should simply say, "Madam, I was not looking at your cards." It really brought the house down.

'Constance Collier would sit in on the rehearsals and there would be some very funny sparring between them. Constance would criticize, and he would become very mad. "But Charlie – you haven't read the play," she would say; and he would snap back, "I don't need to. *I know what it's about*."

'In all, the Circle presented more than a hundred plays. Eventually we had three theatres, the Circle, the Coronet and the Cast. The Cast was attached to the Circle, and shared the same backstage and dressing rooms: one night an actor actually walked onto the wrong stage. Our regular people included Kathleen Freeman and Strother Martin; Alan Pakula directed a very good *Antigone*, and Shelley Winters directed *Thunder Rock*. In 1950 some of our actors broke away to form their own theatre (Charlie was indignant), and that company included Jack Nicholson and Richard Dreyfus.'

The final production of the Circle was *What Every Woman Wants*, which Constance Collier recommended. In her book *Moments With Chaplin*, Lillian Ross gives a vivid picture both of the atmosphere of the theatre, and of Chaplin tirelessly putting his actors – who included his two sons and Ruth Conte – through an energetic five-hour rehearsal. (He thought nothing of working through until 6 a.m. – with Oona calling from time to time to inquire when he was coming home.) Lillian Ross recalls verbatim some of his direction: 'You must not act. You ... *must* give the audience the impression that you've just read the script. It's phoney now. We don't talk that way. Just state it. Don't make it weary. You're too young for that. Let's get away from acting. We don't want acting. We want reality. Give the audience the feeling that they're looking through the keyhole. This will be maudlin and sticky as hell if you act ...' Later he told them, 'Keep it simple. Too many gestures are creeping in. I don't like that. If the audience notices a gesture you're gone. Gestures are not to be seen. And I'm a gesture man. It's hard for me to keep them down ... Thank God, I can see myself on the screen the next day ... I'm essentially an entrance and exit man ... Good exits and entrances. That's all theatre is. And punctuation. That's all it is.'

Epstein felt that a lot of inspiration for *Limelight* came from this contact with the Circle Theatre. 'He had always said, "When I make my film you're going to work with me." I never took it seriously of course; but then when he came to make *Limelight* he took me as his assistant. And after that I just kept on working with him.

'The writer Dudley Nichols – he did *Stagecoach* – was one of our first fans; and as a result of their meetings in the theatre he and his wife became quite friendly with Charlie and Oona. I remember him telling me one day, "You're young. And you'll remember these as the happiest days of your life."'

APPENDIX IX
The FBI v. Chaplin

The extensive files on Chaplin maintained by the Federal Bureau of Investigation over a period of more than fifty years – they total more than nineteen hundred pages – only became available to the author when the present book was practically completed. The information they provide adds little to the material in the body of the book, apart from corroboration and a mass of circumstantial detail in such matters as the Barry trials. In general they reveal much more about the methods of the FBI than about the life of Chaplin. It seems appropriate however to make some comment here upon their contents.

What is alarming in the files is not any investigative skill or deviousness in the methods of the Bureau, but rather the degree of sloppiness and stupidity that many of the reports reveal. An inordinate amount of time seems to have been devoted to processing hearsay, rumours, poison-pen letters and cranky unsolicited correspondence, along with the public revelations of Hedda Hopper, Ed Sullivan and other syndicated gossip columnists. The Bureau's biographical data on Chaplin, which served, periodically rehashed, for more than thirty years, was derived from Gerith von Ulm's 1940 book *Charlie Chaplin, King of Tragedy*, a record only intermittently trustworthy. Throughout the files the Bureau perpetuated such inaccuracies as that Chaplin had married Mildred Harris in London (von Ulm had this right, at least) and that he was Jewish. In this connection, they happily gleaned a piece of colourful misinformation from *Who's Who in American Jewry*, wherein it was claimed that Chaplin was the son of a family called Thonstein, who had emigrated from Eastern Europe and settled in London in 1850. After this they generally headed reports on Chaplin 'alias Charlie Chaplin; alias Israel Thonstein', which gave a nicely sinister touch to things.

The first record of the Bureau's interest in Chaplin dates from 15 August 1922, when an agent called A. A. Hopkins passed on the information that Chaplin had given a reception for a prominent labour leader, William Z.

Foster, who was visiting Los Angeles. The event had been attended by many of the 'Parlor Bolsheviki' and such Hollywood radicals as William De Mille and Rob Wagner. Will Hays had arrived in Hollywood a few months before this to set up the office of Motion Picture Producers and Distributors of America, Inc., a self-regulatory industry body; and Chaplin was alleged to have told Foster in the course of the evening that he had no use for Hays: 'We are against any kind of censorship, and particularly against presbyterian censorship.'

He also pointed out to his guests a pennant bearing the words 'Welcome Will Hays', pinned over the men's lavatory at the studio. J. Edgar Hoover and his associates were so impressed by Agent Hopkins' report on this and other evidence of the infiltration of Communist ideas into the film industry, that they instituted further investigation. Meanwhile Hopkins' information was passed on to Will Hays himself, who recalled broodingly that Chaplin had not participated in the welcoming activities when he arrived in Hollywood, which led him to think that 'the party mentioned is really a little odd in his mental processes to say the least, in the direction which you mention. I did not know he had gone so far, however, as the report indicates.' Hays added a pledge to discuss 'ways and means of making certain that there is no seditious propaganda allowed to get into anything'.

Subsequent reports dealt with the alleged visit to Chaplin of a Communist organizer of the Garment Workers' Union, bearing the sinister name of Plotkin, to appeal for funds for striking railroad workers; and a rumour that Chaplin was the anonymous Hollywood donor of $1000 to the Communist Party of America, at Christmas 1922. Periodically over the next thirty years the Bureau would re-examine their growing file of reports (invariably unsubstantiated) of donations by Chaplin to Communist causes.

These early reports coincided with America's most rabid Red Scare until the 1940s, and in the interim the FBI seem to have lost interest in Chaplin. They were back in action, however, from the moment he spoke at the meeting arranged by Russian War Relief, Inc. on 3 December 1942. The following day an unidentified agent, who had posed as a sympathizer, sent back a detailed transcript of Chaplin's speech which included such enthusiastic phrases as 'I am not a Communist, but I am pretty pro-Communist.'

After this, evidence of 'Red sympathies' was laboriously piled up against him. The Second Front speeches were duly noted. In August 1943 he was Master of Ceremonies at a reception for the distinguished Soviet director Mikhail Kalatozov. In May 1946 he attended a film show and party on a Soviet ship in Long Beach harbour, and jokingly called American customs men 'Gestapo'. On leaving, he was photographed 'with John Garfield, alias Jules Garfinkle and Lewis Milestone, Russian born film director'. The endless rumours of contributions to the Party culminated in Hedda Hopper's inventive sneers about 'Charlie Chaplin, who contributed $25,000 to the

Communist cause and $100 to the Red Cross'. The Bureau 'monitored' his bank account and found a lot of money but no sign of contributions to Communist causes.

Everything was grist to the Bureau's slow-grinding mill. In August 1947 we find Hoover himself requesting by urgent teletype a copy of an article in praise of Chaplin that had appeared in *Pravda*. It hardly seemed to matter to the Director that the item – an appreciative notice of the first Chaplin films to appear in the Soviet Union – had appeared in 1923. A week later, a memorandum proposes that the *Pravda* piece might make an excellent item for the gossip columnist Louella Parsons. In the end it was sent to Hedda Hopper. It is interesting to discover that the FBI was not only using the gossip of these viperish ladies as evidence, but was also feeding information to them. There is at least an acknowledgment that the procedure might be irregular in the instruction (ignored) on the Louella Parsons memorandum: 'To be destroyed after action is taken and not sent to files.'

Nothing, however negative, was disregarded. It was enough for some leftish organization to express its admiration for Chaplin, or to say that it might invite him to attend a function, for an addition to the files. A soldier charged with a security offence snapped 'Sure I'm a Communist . . . so is Charlie Chaplin.' It was reported by the Army to the FBI, and stayed on Chaplin's record to the end; for no detail, however meaningless or insubstantial, was ever erased, once it was on the files. In April 1943 Chaplin was seen at a showing of the Soviet classic, *Baltic Deputy*. He attended a Shostakovich concert. It was recorded as a sign of undesirable radical views that he was signatory to a letter from eight hundred labour, religious and social leaders who urged Roosevelt to prevent racial outbreaks and lauded his stand against discrimination.

At the time of Chaplin's departure from the United States in 1952, all this was summarized in a 125-page report with the classification 'Information pertaining to Questions of Communist Party Membership of Charles Chaplin', 'Individual Associates of Chaplin who are Reported to be Communist Party Members' (they included Hanns and Gerhardt Eisler, Lion Feuchtwanger and Theodore Dreiser), and 'Affiliation of Charles Chaplin with Groups Declared to be Communist Subversive Groups or Reputedly Controlled or Influenced by the Communist Party'.

The investigation into Chaplin's supposed subversive activities was temporarily eclipsed however by the Joan Barry case. Barry made her first public charges that Chaplin was the father of her unborn child on 4 June 1943. The FBI initiated investigations on 17 August, when Hoover put Special Agent Hood on the case to collect evidence to support the Mann Act charges and the case for violation of civil liberties brought against Chaplin and six other defendants. Three days later Hoover issued a teletype requesting that the investigation be expedited, and during the next four months the Bureau were tireless. They interviewed scores of witnesses, and the secret evidence they collected fills more than four hundred pages. One of their most helpful informants was Hedda Hopper. They seemed to have bugged telephones and hotel rooms (with devices they called 'microphone technicals'). They put stops on border posts to prevent Chaplin leaving the country if he had been so inclined.

The Bureau's investigations reveal much more about Joan Barry than emerged in the trials, showing her as perhaps the most pitiable figure in the affair, trapped between the lines of the war which Hoover and the FBI were waging against Chaplin. The files reveal that her true name was Mary Louise Gribble: she had adopted the name of her step-father, Mr Berry, and was variously known as Joan Berry, Joan Barry, Mary Louise Barry, Joan Barratt, Mary L. Barratt, Joanne Berry, Jo Anne Berry, Bettie Booker, Joan Spencer, Mrs Mark Warner, Catherine McLaren and Mary L. Spencer.

This indecision over her names perhaps reflects her real mental confusion, which became increasingly acute towards the end of her association with Chaplin. Chaplin appears to have been considerate and generous during most of their time together; Barry complained that it was his friends, notably Tim Durant (who had first introduced them), who mistreated her in trying to break up the liaison. Perhaps the most singular revelation of the FBI files is the admission that 'never did either BERRY or her attorney request this investigation or express a desire for the Government to take action against CHAPLIN'. It is also revealed that the prosecution did not always have an easy time in presenting Mrs Berry in the required role of a concerned and loving mother: Gertrude Berry was reported to have a drink problem and to quarrel frequently with her daughter; and on one occasion she disappeared from their home.

When the trials ended in failure for the prosecution (the Mann Act jury decided in Chaplin's favour and the civil rights violation charges were dropped on instructions from the Attorney General), the Bureau exchanged letters of commiseration and compliments with the attorneys, and contemplated bringing charges of perjury against some of the witnesses. (After the civil case on Carol Ann Barry's paternity they contemplated, in the same spirit, investigating whether blood tests could be faked by chemical additions to the blood stream. Wiser counsels prevailed.)

With the peak of the McCarthy witch hunts, investigation of Chaplin's suspected subversive sympathies was once more stepped up. Chaplin's friendship with Hanns Eisler, whose brother was a declared Communist, attracted grave suspicion; after his telegram to Picasso seeking support for Eisler the Bureau constituted an investigation 'to determine whether or not Chaplin was or is engaged in Soviet espionage'. Shortly after this, in February 1948, Chaplin applied for a re-entry permit since he planned to visit Britain and then return to California via the Far East. On 17 April officials of the Immigration and Naturalization Service went to his house and conducted an interview which lasted for four hours and was recorded verbatim by a stenographer (cf. p. 548). Chaplin handled the interview with tremendous skill and frankness; a couple of years later the FBI's Los Angeles office said that further interviews with Chaplin were 'not recommended . . . the interview for the most part was inconclusive because CHAPLIN would either deny allegations, explain them in his own manner or state that he did not remember'.

Nevertheless in November 1948 Chaplin was placed on the Security Index. The newspaper morgues were combed anew. Incriminating new evidence was discovered, such as that in 1929 Chaplin had been a member of something called 'The Russian Eagle Supper Club'. News items about his failure to appear in the 1931 Royal Variety Show, and his thoughts on patriotism delivered on that occasion, were brought up against him. There was even an attempt to introduce Hetty Kelly into the case. A disgruntled former employee sent the Bureau off on a wild goose chase involving a fictitious courier who had brought a secret message to Chaplin from an agent in Moscow. A tip-off that there would be a clandestine meeting at Summit Drive launched a surveillance operation on the house, but of course no one arrived.

Despite these setbacks, in November 1949 the FBI had a request from the Assistant Attorney General, Alexander Campbell, for the Chaplin files, since a 'Security-R investigation was pending'. The files were disappointing: on 29 December there came the admission: 'It has been determined that there are no witnesses available who could offer testimony that Chaplin has been a member of the Communist Party in the past, is now a member, or has contributed funds to the Communist Party.' There was some consolation in 1950 when Louis F. Budenz, a former managing editor of the *Daily Worker* and a marathon namer of names, included Chaplin in his list of four hundred 'concealed Communists' and alleged substantial contributions to Party funds. He turned out to be a singularly unreliable witness.

The final phase of the war on Chaplin came in 1952. On 25 August a Mr Noto of the Immigration and Naturalization Service telephoned the FBI to say that Chaplin was intending to sail for England in September, and to ask for information. On 16 September Hoover told the Los Angeles office that Chaplin had been issued with a re-entry permit, and that they should advise head office of any information on his tour abroad. A note at the foot of the message comments, 'INS has advised that even though he was given a re-entry permit, this permit gives no guarantee he will be allowed to return to the United States.' Already, on 9 September, McGranery had met with J. Edgar Hoover and told him that he 'was considering taking steps to prevent the re-entry into this country of Charlie Chaplin . . . because of moral turpitude'. The files on the Barry case were turned up again: 'See that all is included in memo to A.G.,' scribbled Hoover.

On 19 September Attorney General McGranery announced that Chaplin's re-entry permit would not be honoured. The FBI files show however that the Immigration and Naturalization service remained very nervous about their position:

> Mr Farrell stated bluntly that at the present INS does not have sufficient information to exclude Chaplin from the United States if he attempts to re-enter. Mr Mackey interposed that INS could, of course, make it difficult for Chaplin to re-enter, but in the end, there is no doubt Chaplin would be admitted. Mr Mackey pointed out that if INS attempted to delay Chaplin's re-entry into the United States, it would involve a question of detention which might well rock INS and the Department of Justice to its foundations.
>
> Mr Farrell advised further that while INS does not have sufficient information on which to exclude Chaplin if he attempts to re-enter before December 24 1952, INS hopes that under the new Immigration and Nationality Act (Public Law 414, 82nd Congress), effective on and after that date, it will be able to make a case against Chaplin sufficient to exclude him. Mr Farrell expressed the view that if Chaplin's lawyer was astute, he would have Chaplin return to the United States before the effective date of the new law.

Chaplin however did not return. He chose to make his home in Europe. After this the FBI mainly contented itself with monitoring the press reports on his movements and activities. When he handed back his re-entry permit the Bureau were alerted to the possibility that it might be 'an effort on his part to give the impression he is not returning to the United States while actually he may attempt to return unnoticed by United States officials', and cautioned their agents to vigilance. In 1954 the Army Censorship intercepted and passed on to the FBI a letter from Mrs Eisler in Vienna to Oona in Switzerland, in which she expressed a hope that *Limelight* could be shown not only in Austria but also in the Soviet Union and China. In 1955 Charles Chaplin Junior acted in a German film with the export title of *Yankee Business*, which persuaded the Bureau that subversive views might be inherited.

In 1957 the Bureau analyzed the European press reaction to *A King in New York* and concluded that 'the State Department could be put on the spot. Either a move by State to prevent importation of the film or a hands-off policy could subject it to criticism. Any criticism of State would inure to Communist benefit as a discrediting of the United States Government.'

When Chaplin was given his Oxford degree in 1962 the *New York Times* published its editorial speculating that 'We do not believe the Republic would be in danger . . . if yesterday's unforgotten little tramp were allowed to amble down the gangplank of an American port.' This apparently stirred Judge McGranery to ask for the old files once again. The Judge grumbled to the FBI liaison officer that *The Times* had alleged that as Attorney General he had blocked Chaplin's return to the United States. He said that this was simply not true: 'he had insisted that Chaplin be subject to the same hearing procedures as anyone else, and should not be given preferential treatment because of his wealth and notoriety.'

Nine years later Ambassador Davis sent a telegram from Bern to the Attorney General and the Under-Secretary of State, noting that Brandeis University was to honour Chaplin with an award the following year. He 'recommended swift waiving of Chaplin's ineligibility to avoid unfavorable publicity for U.S.'.

Even after this, and Chaplin's return to the United States, the FBI file was not quite closed. The final documents relate to the theft of Chaplin's body in 1978. Somehow it seems appropriate that the FBI's contribution to the investigation was a series of interviews with psychics.

APPENDIX X
A Chaplin Who's Who

AGEE, James. (1909–1955) Screenwriter, novelist, poet, critic. Chaplin's most vigorous and distinguished US defender in the McCarthy years, notably in his *Verdoux* criticisms and *Life* essay, 'The Golden Age of Comedy'. Own screenplays: *The Quiet One* (1950), *The African Queen* (1951), *The Night of the Hunter* (1955).

ALDRICH, Robert. (1918–1983) Director. Associate director of *Limelight*. Was also assistant to Renoir, Milestone, Wellman, Rosson, Polansky, Losey. Own first film: *Big Leaguer* (1953); later work included *Kiss me Deadly* (1955), *Whatever Happened to Baby Jane?* (1962).

ALLEN, Phyllis. Actress, *Caught in a Cabaret, A Busy Day, The Property Man, The Rounders, Dough and Dynamite, Gentlemen of Nerve, His Trysting Place, Tillie's Punctured Romance, Getting Acquainted, Pay Day.* Began career in vaudeville and musical comedy; screen debut 1910 with Selig Company. Keystone 1913–1916; later Fox, Vitagraph.

ANDERSON, G. M. ('Broncho Billy') (1883–1971) The first great Western star, Anderson made some 400 one-reelers between 1907 and 1914. Co-founder of Essanay Company (1907), which engaged Chaplin in 1914–15. Explained principle of own films: 'We don't change the stories – only the horses.' Reappeared on screen 1967 in *The Bounty Killer*. Special Academy Award, 1957. Appears as actor in *The Champion*.

ARBUCKLE, Roscoe. (1887–1933) Actor, *A Film Johnnie, Tango Tangles, His Favorite Pastime, The Knockout, The Masquerader, The Rounders.* Began career in vaudeville and musical comedy, touring with Leon Errol. Film debut, Selig Company 1909. Keystone 1913. Two-reeler partners included Mabel Normand and Buster Keaton. At peak of career earned $1000 a day, but was ruined by scandal in 1921 when an actress, Virginia Rappe, died in the course of a party given by Arbuckle at the St Francis Hotel, San Francisco.

Attempted come-back as director in late 1920s under pseudonym, Will B. Goodrich.

ARMSTRONG, Billy (1891–?). Actor, *The Champion, In the Park, The Tramp, By the Sea, Work, A Woman, The Bank, Shanghaied, Police, Triple Trouble*. Began career in music hall, with Karno companies and Harry Tate Company. Film debut, Essanay 1915; later Horsley, Cub Comedies, L-Ko and Keystone, including *Skirts* (1921).

ARRAST, Henri d'Abbadie. (Argentina, 1897–France, 1968) Research assistant, *A Woman of Paris*, and for a time a regular companion of Chaplin in Hollywood. Had brief and stormy career as director of sparkling social comedies at Paramount: *Service for Ladies, A Gentleman of Paris* (both 1927), *Laughter* (1928), *Topaze* (1933). Retired to Europe.

AUDLEY, Maxine. (b. 1923, London) Actress, *A King in New York*. Stage from 1940; films from 1947 *(Anna Karenina)*.

AUSTIN, Albert. (Birmingham, England, 1885–Hollywood, 1953) Actor, *The Floorwalker, The Fireman, The Vagabond, One A.M., The Count, The Pawnshop, Behind the Screen, The Rink, Easy Street, The Cure, The Immigrant, The Adventurer, A Dog's Life, Shoulder Arms, Sunnyside, A Day's Pleasure, The Kid, Pay Day, The Gold Rush, City Lights*. Also assistant director. Early career in musical comedy and music hall; arrived in America with Karno companies; stock in Denver for two years before film debut with Chaplin at Mutual. Other films as actor included *Suds*. Directed *Trouble* (1922), *A Prince of a King* (1923), both with Jackie Coogan.

AYRES, Agnes. (Agnes Hinkle) (Carbondale, Illinois 1896–Hollywood, 1940) Actress, *His New Job*. Debut at Essanay. Later known as 'The O.Henry Girl'. Starring roles in *The Sheik* (1921), *The Ten Commandments* (1924), *Son of the Sheik* (1926).

BACON, Lloyd. (1889–1955) Director. Actor in *The Champion, In the Park, A Jitney Elopement, The Tramp, The Bank, The Floorwalker, The Fireman, The Vagabond, Behind the Screen, The Rink, Easy Street*. Debut as director with Mack Sennett, 1921. Later films included *The Singing Fool* (1928), *Forty-Second Street* (1933), *A Slight Case of Murder* (1937), *The French Line* (1954).

BAKER, Nellie Bly. (b. 1894) Actress, *The Kid, A Woman of Paris*. Originally employed at the Chaplin Studio as a secretary (she is seen bringing Chaplin his morning mail in *How To Make Movies*) her appearances in Chaplin films led to a career as a character player throughout the 1920s, including von Sternberg's *The Salvation Hunters*.

BARTON, Ralph. (1891–1931) Artist and illustrator. Reported First World War in pictures for British magazine *Puck*, though subsequently developed pathological dislike of British. Illustrated *Gentlemen Prefer Blondes* and *Contes Drolatiques*; many caricatures in *New Yorker, Vanity Fair, Liberty, Harpers*. Accompanied Chaplin – whom he considered 'the greatest man alive' – on the first stage of his 1931 world trip, but returned to New York where he killed himself. In his suicide note he deplored 'beautiful lost Carlotta' (Monterey); but Eugene O'Neill, then married to Carlotta, told reporters, 'I never saw Barton in my life. Mrs O'Neill hasn't seen him in five years. He made no attempt to see her at any time.' Barton was married four times.

BAUMAN, Charles O. Co-founder with Adam Kessel of Keystone. Was bookmaker, exhibitor, producer from 1909 when founded New York Motion Picture Company (with Kessel).

BELL, Monta. (1891–1958) Director. Assisted Chaplin in writing *My Trip Abroad* and was literary editor on *A Woman of Paris*. Early career: reporter on *Washington Post*; actor in stock. Director debut, *The Snob* (1924); later films include *The King on Main Street* (1925), *The Torrent* (1926), *China's Little Devils* (1945).

BENNETT, Marjorie. (d. 1982, Hollywood) Actress, *Monsieur Verdoux, Limelight*. Sister of Enid Bennett and long active in Hollywood as character player.

BERGMAN, Henry. (1868–1946, Hollywood) Actor, *The Pawnshop, Behind the Screen, The Rink, Easy Street, The Cure, The Immigrant, The Adventurer, A Dog's Life, The Bond, Shoulder Arms, Sunnyside, A Day's Pleasure, The Kid, The Idle Class, Pay Day, The Pilgrim, The Gold Rush, The Circus, City Lights, Modern Times*. Coordinator, *The Great Dictator*. Originally on operatic and musical stage; films from 1914 (Henry Lehrman's L-Ko Company). From 1916 worked exclusively at Chaplin studios as actor and assistant. Also owned Hollywood restaurant, 'Henry's'.

BLOOM, Claire. (b. 1931) Actress, *Limelight*. Trained at Guildhall Schools of Speech and Drama, Central School of Speech Training. Stage from 1946: *Ring Round the Moon* (1950); several seasons at Old Vic. Films from 1948 (*The Blind Goddess*), including *Look Back in Anger* (1959), many in USA, and in Europe with director Krzysztof Zanussi. Autobiography, *Limelight and After*, 1982.

BODIE, 'Dr' Walford. (1870–1939). Music hall performer, at first as ventriloquist, later performing 'miraculous' electrical cures for all ills. Chaplin impersonated him during the *Casey's Court Circus* tour.

BRANDO, Marlon. (b. 1934) Actor, *A Countess From Hong Kong*. Studied painting; worked as lift boy; Stella Adler's 'Dramatic Workshop' 1943; summer stock 1944; Broadway 1944 (*I Remember Mama*); films from 1950.

BRUCE, Nigel. (1895–1953) Actor, *Limelight*. Stage (in England) from 1920; films from 1930. Born in US to English parents, Bruce specialized in quintessentially British characters. His most famous screen role was Doctor Watson in numerous *Sherlock Holmes* pictures – a fact which undoubtedly recommended him to Chaplin.

BRYAN, Vincent (1877–?) Writer, assisted Chaplin at Essanay and Mutual. Early career in theatre, writing plays, vaudeville sketches, songs. Began screen career at Keystone; later with Goldwyn.

BURKAN, Nathan. Noted film industry lawyer who represented Chaplin's legal interests from his arrival in Hollywood.

BURKE, Thomas. (1886–1945, London) Novelist and essayist. Their common south London background and mutual admiration brought Burke and Chaplin together; and the friendship resulted in Burke's remarkable study of Chaplin, 'A Comedian', in *City of Encounters*. The most notable film adaptation of a Burke story was D. W. Griffith's *Broken Blossoms*, from *The Chink and the Child*.

CAMPBELL, Eric (1880–1917) Actor, *The Floorwalker*, *The Fireman*, *The Vagabond*, *The Count*, *The Pawnshop*, *Behind the Screen*, *The Rink*, *Easy Street*, *The Cure*, *The Immigrant*, *The Adventurer*. Early career, D'Oyly Carte company, Karno Company. Had appeared in films in London and New York before Hollywood.

CARGILL, Patrick (b. 1918) Actor, *A Countess From Hong Kong*. Sandhurst and Indian Army. Stage, in repertory, from 1939. West End debut in revue, *High Spirits* (1953). Films from 1952.

CARROLL, Paul Vincent. (1900–1968) Dramatist. Author of *Shadow and Substance* (1934), of which Chaplin proposed a screen adaptation.

CHAPLIN, Albert. Younger brother of Charles Chaplin Senior. Emigrated before 1900 to South Africa where he achieved considerable prosperity and raised a large family. Paid funeral expenses for Charles Chaplin Senior.

CHAPLIN, Annette Emily. (b. 1959) Chaplin's youngest daughter. In 1984 made debut as screen actress in *A Sense of Wonder*.

CHAPLIN, Aubrey. (1889–1932) Chaplin's cousin, son of Charles Chaplin Senior's older brother, Spencer. After death of father became youngest licensee in London. Father of Betty and Pauline Chaplin.

CHAPLIN, Betty (May). Daughter of Aubrey Chaplin. Emigrated to USA in 1939, where she married Drew Tetrick, costumier on later Chaplin films.

CHAPLIN, Charles, Senior. (1863–1901) Father of Charles Chaplin. See Chapter I, *passim*.

CHAPLIN, Charles Spencer, Junior. (1925–1968) Chaplin's elder son by his second marriage. Brought up by mother, Lita Grey, though increasingly in contact with father during boyhood and adolescence. Army; indifferent stage and screen career. Appeared in *Limelight*. Wrote *My Father, Charlie Chaplin* (1960) in collaboration with N. and M. Rau.

CHAPLIN, Christopher James. (b. 1962) Chaplin's youngest son. Able musician; in 1984 made debut as screen actor in *Where is Parsifal?*

CHAPLIN, Eugene Anthony. (b. 1953) Chaplin's second son and fifth child by his second marriage to Oona O'Neill. Has worked as recording engineer in Montreux, later as proprietor of curio shop in Vevey.

CHAPLIN, Geraldine Leigh. (b. 1944) First child of Chaplin's marriage to Oona O'Neill. First film appearance in *Limelight*. Appeared in ballroom scene in *A Countess From Hong Kong*. Royal Ballet School and stage experience as dancer. In 1965 made adult film debut in *Par un beau matin d'été*, dir. Jacques Deray. Subsequently many films, notably *Doctor Zhivago* and works by Carlos Saura and Robert Altman.

CHAPLIN, Hannah Harriett Pedlingham. (née Hill) (1865–1928) Chaplin's mother. See Chapters 1, 2, 3 *passim*.

CHAPLIN, Jane Cecil. (b. 1957) Chaplin's sixth child and fourth daughter by marriage to Oona O'Neill. Experimental film maker.

CHAPLIN, Josephine Hannah. (b. 1949) Chaplin's second daughter. As child appeared in *Limelight*. As adult, work on stage and in films and television.

CHAPLIN, Lita Grey. (Lillita McMurray) (b.1908) Chaplin's second wife (marriage dissolved) and mother of Charles Spencer and Sydney Earle Chaplin. See Chapters 10, 11 *passim*.

CHAPLIN, Michael John. (b. 1946) First son of Chaplin and Oona O'Neill. Appeared in *Limelight* and *A King in New York*. Subsequently RADA, work as pop musician and actor. Now works own smallholding in France.

CHAPLIN, Mildred Harris. (1901–1944) Child actress from 1910; reputed to have appeared in the Babylonian sequence of *Intolerance*. Her career prospered after the publicity derived from marriage to Chaplin in October 1918, and she was put under contract by Louis B. Mayer, with whom she had worked in *The Warrens of Virginia* (1918). After the Chaplin divorce her popularity declined rapidly, though she appeared in more than fifty films, the last, Alan Crosland's *Lady Tubby*, in 1933. De Mille used her as an extra, along with other of his former stars, in *Reap The Wild Wind* (1941). Later vaudeville, night clubs. Died of pneumonia, following surgery.

CHAPLIN, Norman Spencer. (Born and died July 1919). Chaplin's first child, by Mildred Harris, born severely handicapped and survived only three days.

CHAPLIN, Oona O'Neill. (b. 1926) Chaplin's fourth wife. Daughter of Eugene O'Neill. See Chapters 16 *et seq.*

CHAPLIN, Paulette Goddard. (Pauline Levy) (b. 1911) Actress, *Modern Times, The Great Dictator.* Chaplin's third wife (1936). On stage from 1927 (chorus of *Rio Rita*); films from 1931. After marriage to Chaplin dissolved, continued to work in films until 1966 *(Time of Indifference).* Married Erich Maria Remarque. See Chapters 14, and 15, *passim.*

CHAPLIN, Pauline (Pauline Mason). (b. 1928) Youngest child of Aubrey Chaplin (q.v.), by second wife, Louise Ella Orton. As licensee of the Princess of Wales, 11 Circus Road, NW8, she represented the fourth generation of Chaplins to manage public houses in London.

CHAPLIN, Spencer. (1834–1897) Chaplin's grandfather; apprenticed as butcher, but became publican. See Chapter 1.

CHAPLIN, Spencer William Tunstill. (1855–1900) Brother of Charles Chaplin Senior and uncle of Charles Chaplin. Publican, notably of The Queen's Head. See Chapter 1.

CHAPLIN, Sydney. (1885–1965) Chaplin's half-brother. See text, *passim.* Films with Chaplin: *A Dog's Life, The Bond, Shoulder Arms, Pay Day, The Pilgrim.* Other films: *Gussle the Golfer* (1914), *Gussle's Day of Rest* (1914), *Gussle Rivals Jonah* (1915), *Gussle's Backward Way* (1915), *Gussle's Wayward Path* (1915), *Gussle Tied to Trouble* (1915), *Submarine Pilot* (1915), *That Springtime Feeling* (1915), *Giddy, Gay and Ticklish* (1915), *Hushing the Scandal* (1915), *No Mother to Guide Him* (1919), *King, Queen, Joker* (1921), *Her Temporary Husband* (1923), *The Rendezvous* (1923), *The Perfect Flapper* (1924), *Galloping Fish* (1924), *The Man on the Box* (1925), *Oh! What a Nurse* (1926), *The Fortune Hunter* (1927), *The Missing Link* (1927), *A Little Bit of Fluff* (1928).

CHAPLIN, Sydney Earle. (b. 1926) Second son of Chaplin by Lita Grey. Actor, *Limelight, A Countess From Hong Kong.* Stage, films; now virtually retired.

CHAPLIN, Victoria. (b. 1951) Chaplin's third daughter. Intended for leading role in *The Freak*, Chaplin's last and unrealized film project. With her husband, Jean-Baptiste Thierrée, formed and runs 'Le Cirque Imaginaire'. Appeared in *A Countess From Hong Kong*, as dancer in ballroom.

CHASE, Charley. (Charles Parrott) (1895–1940) Actor, *The Knockout, Mabel's Busy Day, The Masquerader, His New Profession, The Rounders,*

Dough and Dynamite, Gentlemen of Nerve, His Musical Career, Tillie's Punctured Romance. Early career in vaudeville and burlesque, as Irish monologuist. Film debut, Keystone, 1914. Acted, wrote and directed hundreds of two-reelers for Keystone, Roach (Laurel and Hardy series) and Columbia.

CHERRILL, Virginia. (Virginia Cherrill Martini) (b. 1908) Actress, *City Lights.* Previous career: Chicago society girl. Later films include *Charlie Chan's Latest Case* (1933), *White Heat* (1934), *Troubled Waters* (1935). Husbands include Irving Adler, William Rhinelander Stewart, Cary Grant, Earl of Jersey.

CLINE, Edward. (1892–1961) Actor, *The Knockout.* Stage, then actor and gagman with Sennett. Later notable director of comedy, including *Sherlock Junior* (Buster Keaton) and several films with W. C. Fields.

CODD, Elsie. Chaplin's British press representative from 1918 through early 1920s. Appears as extra in *The Kid.* Seems to have operated from 264 Eastern Road, Kemp Town, Brighton. 'I should like the British press,' she wrote, 'to feel that they can rely upon me as Chaplin's sole press representative for this country for the only true and reliable information about him and his work – that which reaches me direct from the studio.'

CONKLIN, Chester. (Jules Cowles) (1888–1971) Actor, *Making a Living, Mabel's Strange Predicament, Between Showers, Tango Tangles, Cruel, Cruel Love, Mabel at the Wheel, Twenty Minutes of Love, Caught in a Cabaret, Mabel's Busy Day, The Face on the Bar Room Floor, The Masquerader, Those Love Pangs, Dough and Dynamite, Gentlemen of Nerve, Modern Times, The Great Dictator.* Early career, circus clown, vaudeville, stock and road companies. Film debut, Majestic Company, c. 1913; Keystone from 1913; innumerable shorts. Remained in films until 1967 *(Big Hand for a Little Lady).*

CONKLIN, Heinie (or Charles). (1880–1959) Actor, *Modern Times.* Film debut, Keystone; one of original Keystone Kops. Later many silent features.

COOGAN, Jackie. (1914–1984) Child actor, *The Kid.* Discovered by Chaplin when appearing in father's vaudeville act. (See Chapter 7, *passim.*)

COOKE, Alfred Alistair. (b. 1908) Journalist, broadcaster, film critic. Worked with Chaplin on Napoleon script. See pp. 475–6.

COURANT, Curt (or Kurt). (b. c. 1895) Cameraman, *Monsieur Verdoux.* Born and worked in Germany from 1920 (with Fritz Lang, etc), Great Britain from 1933, France from 1937 (with Jean Renoir, Max Ophuls).

CROCKER, Harry. (1895–1958) Actor, assistant, *The Circus, City Lights.* Later Chaplin's publicist. Son of prominent San Francisco banking family, took up screen career. A familiar of the San Simeon circle, was also columnist for Hearst newspapers.

DANIELL, Henry. (1894–1963) Actor, *The Great Dictator*. Stage; then films from 1929, including Cukor's *Camille*, with Garbo. Last film appearance, *My Fair Lady* (1964).

DAVENPORT, Alice. Actress, *Making a Living, Mabel's Strange Predicament, Cruel, Cruel Love, The Star Boarder, Caught in a Cabaret, Caught in the Rain, The Property Man, Gentlemen of Nerve, Tillie's Punctured Romance*. Stage from infancy; films from 1911 (Nestor), with daughter Dorothy D. One of original Keystone Company, 1912. Later with Fox, Sunshine Comedies.

DAVIES, Marion. (1897–1961) Actress, comedienne and long-time mistress of William Randolph Hearst. For years a friend of Chaplin, who made guest appearance in her film *Show People*, directed by another of his friends, King Vidor.

DE HAVEN, Carter. (1886–   ) Assistant director, *Modern Times*; actor, *The Great Dictator*. Long vaudeville career in partnership with wife, Flora. Films from 1915 until early 1920s. Father of actress Gloria De Haven.

DELLUC, Louis. (1890–1924) Pioneer French film critic and author of first serious book-length appreciation of Chaplin, *Charlot* (1921).

DESMONDE, Jerry. (James Robert Sadler) (1908–1967) Actor, *A King in New York*. Variety experience, especially as straight man to comedians like Sid Field and Norman Wisdom. Films from 1946 *(London Town)*.

DORO, Marie. (1882–1956) Actress, played leading role of Alice Faulkner in Gillette's 1905 production of *Sherlock Holmes* at Duke of York's Theatre, London. The adolescent Chaplin worshipped her from afar; much later, as a Hollywood star, met her again. In 1916, when she was working with the Jesse L. Lasky Feature Play Company, Chaplin was guest at a house-warming given by Miss Doro and her husband Elliott Dexter, and presented her with a miniature cine camera he had had specially made.

DRESSLER, Marie. (Leila Koerber) (1869–1934) Actress, *Tillie's Punctured Romance*. Stage career in vaudeville and musicals, notably *Tillie's Nightmare*. When stage career faltered, returned to the screen with singular success (*Let Us be Gay, Anna Christie*, 1929), and at the time of her death was one of Hollywood's top box-office stars.

DRYDEN, Leo. (George Dryden Wheeler) (1863–1939) Music hall star and father of Chaplin's half-brother Wheeler Dryden. Specializing in enthusiastically patriotic and imperialist ballads, he enjoyed huge success in the early 1890s with 'The Miner's Dream of Home'.

DRYDEN, Wheeler. (1892–1957) Chaplin's half-brother, the son of Leo Dryden and Hannah Chaplin. Taken from his mother by Dryden as a baby, Wheeler seems to have been brought up in India. He reappeared in the lives of the Chaplin brothers around 1918, and received a money allowance from the studio, though he made his own career as actor and (occasionally) playwright. Assistant to Sydney Chaplin in his British film ventures in late 1920s. Joined Chaplin Studios as assistant director on *The Great Dictator* and remained until Chaplin's departure from USA in 1952. Last days troubled by paranoid fears of persecution by FBI.

DURFEE, Minta. (1897, Los Angeles–1975, Los Angeles) Actress, *Making a Living, A Film Johnnie, Tango Tangles, Cruel, Cruel Love, The Star Boarder, Twenty Minutes of Love, Caught in a Cabaret, The Knockout, The Masquerader, His New Profession, The Rounders, The New Janitor, Tillie's Punctured Romance*. Musical comedy, vaudeville, stock. Keystone from 1913–16. Married Roscoe Arbuckle. After retirement ran dress shop in Hollywood.

EPSTEIN, Jerry. Chaplin's close associate from *Limelight* onwards. First met Chaplin when running Hollywood theatre, The Circle, in association with Sydney Earle Chaplin; Chaplin directed productions there. Assistant on *Limelight*; associate producer on *A King in New York* and producer on *A Countess From Hong Kong*. Directed *The Adding Machine*.

FAIRBANKS, Douglas. (Elton Thomas Ullman) (1883–1939) Swashbuckling, all-American star of the 1910s and 1920s. Married Mary Pickford; co-founder with Pickford, Chaplin and D. W. Griffith of United Artists. Late in life Chaplin said Fairbanks was the only close friend he had ever had.

FISKE, Minnie Maddern. (1865–1932) One of the most respected American stage actresses of the early twentieth century, Mrs Fiske made her debut at the age of three. Her 1916 essay, 'The Art of Charlie Chaplin' in *Harpers* did much to stimulate the evaluation of Chaplin as a serious artist.

FLOREY, Robert. (1900–1979) French cinephile with passionate admiration both for Hollywood and Chaplin. In 1927 wrote monograph on Chaplin in series *Les Grands Artistes de l'Ecran*. Later, working in Hollywood as assistant to such directors as von Sternberg, Vidor and King, he came to know Chaplin personally. Associate director on *Monsieur Verdoux*. As director, Florey made two horror classics, *The Beast With Five Fingers* and *Murders in the Rue Morgue*.

GARDINER, Reginald. (1903–1980). Actor, *The Great Dictator*. Trained as an architect, but decided to study at RADA instead. Stage debut, London; film debut in *Born to Dance* (1936). Subsequently made career as character actor in American films, playing silly-ass British roles. In 1950s and 1960s returned to the stage, and played Doolittle in Broadway production of *My Fair Lady*.

GILLETTE, William C. (1855–1937) Actor and dramatist, noted for restraint and comedy style. Most famous role was *Sherlock Holmes* which he revived in London in 1905 (Duke of York's Theatre) with Chaplin in the role of Billy.

GODDARD, Paulette, see CHAPLIN, Paulette.

GOODWINS, Fred (1891–?) Actor, *A Night Out, A Jitney Elopement, The Tramp, The Bank, Shanghaied, A Night in The Show, Police*. Journalist, then on stage with George Alexander, Charles Frohman. Screen with Edison, Imp, Horsley companies. Also acted as unofficial press representative for Chaplin at Essanay.

GOULD, Frank J. (d. 1956) American millionaire, son of railway king, George J. Gould, creator of 'Gould System' of railways in American south west. Amateur archaeologist, and Riviera hotelier and host. Wives included Edith, sister of Hetty and Arthur Kelly (q.v.), and Florence Gould (q.v.).

GOULD, Florence. (1895–1983) American philanthropist, art patron, Riviera hostess and collector. Wife of Frank J. Gould. Entertained Chaplin in Nice, where the Goulds were then proprietors of The Majestic Hotel, during his 1931 world tour.

GREY, Lita, see CHAPLIN, Lita Grey.

GRIFFITH, Gordon. (b. 1907) Child actor at Keystone, *Kid Auto Races, The Star Boarder, Twenty Minutes of Love, Caught in a Cabaret, Tillie's Punctured Romance*. Stage at one year with mother, Katherine G. Remained in pictures until 1926: appearances included *Tarzan of the Apes, Huckleberry Finn, Little Annie Rooney*. Later assistant director at Monogram Pictures, and production manager, *The Jolson Story*.

HALE, Georgia. (b. 1906) Actress, *The Gold Rush*. Arrived in Hollywood after winning beauty contest. Worked as extra until von Sternberg made her star of his first film *The Salvation Hunters* (1924). Remained in pictures until 1928 (Paul Fejös's *The Last Moment*). Afterwards worked as dance teacher. Close but intermittent friendship with Chaplin continued until 1943.

HALL, Charles D. (1899–1959) Art director with Chaplin Studios on First National Films, *The Gold Rush, The Circus, City Lights, Modern Times*. Previously worked with Karno companies. Later films included James Whale pictures, among them *The Bride of Frankenstein* and *Showboat*. Continued in films until 1951 (Robert Florey's *The Vicious Years*).

HARRINGTON, Tom. Chaplin's Valet and amanuensis during his early bachelor days in Hollywood.

HARRIS, Mildred, see CHAPLIN, Mildred Harris.

HEDREN, Tippi. (Nathalie Hedren) (b. 1935) Actress, *A Countess From Hong Kong.* Best known for roles in Hitchcock's *The Birds* and *Marnie.* In 1981 made *Roar,* based on her husband and family's experiments in coexistence with wild animals.

HILL, Charles Frederick. (b. c. 1839) Chaplin's maternal grandfather, a boot-maker. See Chapter 1, *passim.*

HILL, Kate. (1870–1916) Chaplin's maternal aunt. See Chapters 1 and 5, *passim.*

HILL, Mary Ann. (c. 1839–1892) Chaplin's maternal grandmother. See Chapter 1, *passim.*

HORNE, Sir Alan Edgar. (1889–1984) 2nd Bt, created 1939; succeeded father, Sir Edgar Horne, 1941. Husband of Henrietta Florence (Hetty) Kelly (q.v.), whom he married in 1915, when he was Captain in Surrey Yeomanry.

INCE, Thomas H. (1882–1924) Outstanding early Hollywood producer, who systematized film-making methods and is credited with the general adoption of the film script. Died mysteriously on W. R. Hearst's yacht: Chaplin has frequently figured as one of several characters in the rumours surrounding the event.

JACKSON, John William. Founder and proprietor of The Eight Lancashire Lads. Previously a school teacher. See Chapter 2, *passim.*

JAMES, Dan. (b. 1911) Assistant on *The Great Dictator.* Educated Yale; worked for family firm of china importers, then became interested in left wing politics. Wrote *Winter Soldiers* (1942), *Bloomer Girl* (1944). While blacklisted worked on scripts of *The Giant Behemoth* and *Gorgo* as 'Daniel Hyatt'. In 1983 published prize-winning novel, *Famous All Over Town* – inspired by experiences as volunteer social work among *chicanos* of East Los Angeles – under pseudonym 'Danny Santiago'.

JAMES, Sidney. (1913–1976) Actor, *A King in New York.* Arriving in Britain from South Africa in 1946, he soon established himself as a popular comedy player, specializing in cockney and American characters. His major success came with the *Carry On* film series.

JAMISON (or JAMIESON), Bud (William). (1894–1944) Actor, *His New Job, A Night Out, The Champion, In the Park, A Jitney Elopement, By the Sea, The Bank, Shanghaied, A Night in the Show, Charlie Chaplin's Burlesque on Carmen, Police.* Before joining Chaplin at Essanay, was café entertainer. Continued in films until 1940 (*Captain Caution*).

JOHNSTON, Oliver. (1889–1966) Actor, *A King in New York, A Countess From Hong Kong.* Son of producer and actor Herbert Jenner, was educated at

RADA. On stage from 1910 till retirement in 1947. Returned to stage in 1951, and played in television, including early series, *The Grove Family.*

KARNO, Fred. (1886–1941) Music hall performer, producer and manager. See Chapter 3, *passim.*

KARNO, Fred, Junior. Son of Fred Karno. Accompanied Chaplin on Karno tours of United States; later worked on *The Gold Rush* and *Monsieur Verdoux.*

KEATON, Joseph Francis (Buster). (1896–1966) One of the great comic stars of the silent screen. Entered films in 1917, after many years since early childhood in vaudeville. Early shorts with Roscoe Arbuckle, then star in his own right. After a series of brilliant feature comedies in the 1920s his career declined with the new economies of sound films. His appearance in *Limelight* teamed the two comic geniuses of the twentieth century.

KELLEY, James T. Actor, *A Night in the Show, Police, The Floorwalker, The Fireman, The Vagabond, The Count, The Pawnshop, Behind the Screen, The Rink, The Cure, The Immigrant, A Dog's Life.* Irish-born stage veteran of stock and vaudeville, who always played elderly and decrepit roles in Chaplin films. Also worked at Universal, Rolin and Roach studios.

KELLY, Arthur. (1890–1955) Brother of Hetty Kelly and Chaplin's representative in United Artists. Began career at twenty-one when he joined Frank J. Gould Enterprises in USA (Gould had married another Kelly sister, Edith). Major in British tank corps in First World War, after which joined United Artists as treasurer. 1924, head of UA foreign sales, and subsequently in charge of domestic sales. 1944, Vice President and US representative for Eagle Lion Pictures. Rejoined UA as Executive Vice President, 1947. Resigned 1950 to establish own television company.

KELLY, Henrietta Florence (Hetty). (1893–1918) Chaplin's first love; subsequently married Alan Edgar Horne (q.v.). See Chapters 3 and 8, *passim.*

KENNEDY, Edgar. (1890–1948) Actor, *The Star Boarder, Twenty Minutes of Love, Caught in a Cabaret, The Knockout, Mabel's Busy Day, Those Love Pangs, Dough and Dynamite, Gentlemen of Nerve, Tillie's Punctured Romance, Getting Acquainted.* Vaudeville and musical comedy, films (at Keystone) from 1914. Credited as inventor of 'the slow burn', he became a comedy star in his own right, notably in sound shorts. Later films included *Duck Soup, A Star is Born.*

KENNEDY, Merna. (1908–1944) Actress, *The Circus.* Musical comedy, as dancer, from childhood. Later films include *King of Jazz* and *Broadway.* Last picture, *I Like It that Way* (1934).

KESSEL, Adam, Junior. Co-founder, with Charles O. Bauman (q.v.), of New York Motion Picture Company and its affiliate, Keystone Film Company.

KNOBLOCK, Edward. (Edward Knoblauch) (1874–1945) Actor and later dramatist and screenwriter. A naturalized British subject, he became friendly with Chaplin through Fairbanks, and was in London at the time of Chaplin's 1921 visit. Appeared as extra in *The Idle Class*.

KONO, Toraichi. (b. 1888) Chaplin's valet and general assistant from 1916–1934. Emigrated to US c. 1906. Appears in *The Adventurer, The Circus*. After leaving Chaplin's service worked briefly in United Artists' Tokyo office.

LAUDER, Sir Harry. (1870–1950) Great Scottish star of the British music halls. Visited Chaplin Studios in 1918 and shot film with Chaplin, intended to raise money for Lauder's war charity fund.

LAUREL, Stan. (1895–1965) Created role of *Jimmy the Fearless*, later taken over by Chaplin, with Karno Company. Accompanied Chaplin on 1910 and 1912 Karno tours of USA. From 1917 in films as star in own right; from 1926 as partner to Oliver Hardy. During vaudeville days did Chaplin impersonation in 'The Keystone Trio'.

LEHRMAN, Henry, nicknamed 'Pathé' by D. W. Griffith. (1886–1946) Director, *Making a Living, Kid Auto Races at Venice, Mabel's Strange Predicament, Between Showers*. Originally tram conductor, then director at Biograph, Imp, Kinemacolor, Keystone, Sterling, L-Ko (Lehrman–Knockout). Continued to direct until 1929 *(New Year's Eve)*; then writer. Was fiancé of Virginia Rappe, whose death in the course of a party precipitated the Fatty Arbuckle trial (1921) in which Lehrmann was main prosecution witness.

LIMUR, Jean de. Research assistant, *A Woman of Paris*. Of aristocratic birth, came to USA after war service as aviator and was actor in Fairbanks's *The Three Musketeers*. Later assistant to De Mille and Rex Ingram, then directed early sound films, *The Letter* and *Jealousy*. Returned to Europe and continued to direct in France and Italy until 1944 *(La Grande Meute)*.

LOREN, Sophia. (Sofia Scicolone) (b. 1934) Actress, *A Countess From Hong Kong*. In films from 1950, became a major international star in the 1960s. Married to producer Carlo Ponti.

LOURIÉ, Eugene. (b. 1895) Art director on *Limelight*. Emigrating to Paris after the Russian Revolution, Lourié trained as a painter, but became involved with emigré film-makers. As a designer he worked with outstanding success with Jean Renoir in the 1930s, and joined him in Hollywood during the 1940s. Later directed monster films, *The Beast From 20,000 Fathoms* (1953) and *The Colossus of New York* (1958).

McGUIRE, Paddy. Actor, *The Champion, A Jitney Elopement, The Tramp, By the Sea, Work, The Bank, Shanghaied, A Night in the Show*. Musical comedy; films from 1915 (Essanay). Later with Vogue and Triangle Keystone companies. Specialized in 'rubes' and Irish characters.

McMURRAY, Lillian. Mother of Lita Grey. Was still living in 1984.

MANN, Hank. (David W. Liebman) (1888–1971) Actor, *Mabel's Strange Predicament, Twenty Minutes of Love, Caught in a Cabaret, The Knockout, Mabel's Married Life, The Face on the Bar Room Floor, City Lights, Modern Times, The Great Dictator.* Stage, then films (Keystone) from 1914. In films until 1957 *(Man of a Thousand Faces)*.

MARCELINE. (1873–1927) French clown. Chaplin saw and admired him when he was appearing in the pantomime *Cinderella* at the newly opened London Hippodrome, where Marceline remained a popular star for several seasons. Chaplin records that he later saw him in the USA when Marceline's talent and confidence had deserted him.

MENJOU, Adolphe (1890–1963) Actor, *A Woman of Paris.* Cornell University, First World War service, then vaudeville and stage. Screen from 1912 at Vitagraph; but only achieved principal roles from 1921 *(The Three Musketeers).* Continued in films until 1959 *(Pollyanna).* Notable later performance in Kubrick's *Paths of Glory.* Reckoned one of Hollywood's best-dressed men. One of the most voluble 'friendly' witnesses in Hollywood Un-American Activities investigations.

MINEAU, Charlotte (b. 1891) Actress, *His New Job, A Night in the Show, The Floorwalker, The Vagabond, The Count, Behind the Screen, The Rink, Easy Street.* Previously with Selig, George Ade Fables, Swedie series; later films include *Sparrows,* with Mary Pickford.

MORRISSEY, Betty. (d. 1950) Actress, *A Woman of Paris, The Gold Rush, The Circus.* Discovered by Erich Von Stroheim, who used her in *Merry-Go-Round* (1922). Screen career continued throughout 1920s, until *The Circus.*

MURRAY, Charles K. (1872–1941) Actor, *Her Friend the Bandit, Mabel's Married Life, The Masquerader, Tillie's Punctured Romance.* Twenty years in vaudeville in Murray and Mack act, then films with Biograph, Keystone. Prolific later career, including *Cohens and Kellys* series.

MURRAY, Tom. (b. 1893–) Actor, *The Pilgrim, The Gold Rush* (Black Larson). Vaudeville, in black-face double act, Gillihan and Murray. Films from 1914, with Eagle Film Company. First Hollywood film, *My Boy,* with Jackie Coogan.

MURRAY, Will. (1877–1955) Managed *Casey's Circus Company* during Chaplin's tour. First stage appearance 1890; first London appearance, 1892. Gymnastic speciality act, Lord, Murray and Lord; then teamed with Arthur Woodville as The Freans. Joined Casey's Court in 1906, and continued to tour the act until 1950. Casey's Court *alumni* included besides Chaplin, Stan Laurel, Stanley Lupino, Jack Edge, Hal Jones, Leslie Strange, George Doonan, the Terry Twins, Jerry Verno, Tom Gamble, Jimmy Russell.

MYERS, Harry. (1882–1938) Actor, *City Lights*. Stage; films from 1908 at Biograph; then Lubin and Vim Comedies series with wife, Rosemary Thelby. Starring roles in 1920s (including *A Connecticut Yankee at King Arthur's Court, Exit Smiling*); continued in films until 1936 *(San Francisco, Hollywood Boulevard)*.

NEWMAN, Alfred. (1901–1970) Composer and musical director. Worked on *City Lights* but walked off *Modern Times* after disagreement with Chaplin. Began his career as a child prodigy at the piano, composed more than 250 film scores, and won nine Oscars (rarely for his best work).

NORMAND, Mabel. (1892–1930) Actress, *Mabel's Strange Predicament, Mabel at the Wheel, Caught in a Cabaret, The Fatal Mallet, Her Friend the Bandit, Mabel's Busy Day, Mabel's Married Life, Gentlemen of Nerve, His Trysting Place, Tillie's Punctured Romance, Getting Acquainted*. Photographic model. Entered films at Vitagraph, then Biograph and Keystone (1912). Features included *Mickey* and *Molly-O*. Later career troubled by scandals; died of tuberculosis.

NORTHRUP, Harry. Actor, *A Woman of Paris*. Character actor much in demand during 1920s (*Four Horsemen of the Apocalypse* etc).

OAKIE, Jack. (Lewis Delaney Offield) (1893–1978) Actor, *The Great Dictator*. After early work as chorus boy in musical comedy and as song-and-dance man in vaudeville, Oakie arrived in Hollywood in 1927 and established himself as a comedian. Debut in *Finders Keepers*. Later films include *It Happened Tomorrow, Lover Come Back* (1962).

O'NEILL, Oona, see CHAPLIN, Oona O'Neill.

PARRISH, Robert. (b. 1916) Actor, *City Lights* (newsboy). Subsequently became film editor and (from 1951) director. Autobiography: *Growing Up in Hollywood*, 1976.

PARSONS, Louella. (1880–1972) Columnist on Hearst newspapers known for her malice but generally (unlike Hedda Hopper) cordial to Chaplin. Was a member of party on Hearst boat trip which proved fatal for Thomas Ince.

PEARCE, Peggy. (b. 1896) Actress, *His Favorite Pastime*; also Chaplin's first Hollywood girlfriend. Films from 1913 (Biograph, Keystone).

PERINAL, Georges. (1897–1965) Director of photography, *A King in New York*. Outstanding cinephotographer whose career began in 1913; notable collaborations with René Clair, Alexander Korda, Michael Powell and Emeric Pressburger.

PICKFORD, Mary. (1893–1979) Dominant star of 1910s and 1920s; wife of Douglas Fairbanks; friend of Chaplin and co-founder of United Artists. Stage debut 1898; film debut 1909 under D. W. Griffith at Biograph. An outstanding businesswoman, she was in constant competition with Chaplin to be the highest earner in Hollywood in the period of the First World War. Retired from acting in 1933.

POLLARD, Snub. (1886–1962) Actor, *Limelight*. Arrived in US from Australia with Juvenile Opera Company; joined Broncho Billy at Essanay in 1913. Subsequently many slapstick shorts. In sound period became character player: career continued until 1961 *(Pocketful of Miracles)*.

POLO, Malvina (or Malvine). Actress, *A Woman of Paris*. Daughter of serial star Eddie Polo (1875–1961) who claimed Italian descent from Marco Polo. Also played half-wit girl in Von Stroheim's *Foolish Wives*.

POSTANCE, William. Stage Manager at Duke of York's Theatre, London, in 1905 when Chaplin played there. Chaplin remembered his kindness, and paid tribute to him in the character 'Mr Postant' in *Limelight*.

PURVIANCE, Edna Olga. (1896–1958) Actress, *A Night Out, The Champion, In the Park, A Jitney Elopement, The Tramp, By the Sea, Work, A Woman, The Bank, Shanghaied, A Night in the Show, Charlie Chaplin's Burlesque on Carmen, Police, The Floorwalker, The Fireman, The Vagabond, The Count, The Pawnshop, Behind the Screen, The Rink, Easy Street, The Cure, The Immigrant, The Adventurer, A Dog's Life, The Bond, Shoulder Arms, Sunnyside, A Day's Pleasure, The Kid, The Idle Class, Pay Day, The Pilgrim, A Woman of Paris*. Afterwards (1926) starred in von Sternberg's *Sea Gulls* (produced by Chaplin; never released) and Henri Diamant-Berger's *Education du Prince* (in France); then retired. The correct pronunciation of 'Purviance' is with the accent on the 'i', pronounced as the letter of the alphabet. Chaplin used to joke that the name was in fact unpronounceable, and that she should change it to Edna Pollolobus.

RAKSIN, David. (b. 1912) Arranger of music for *Modern Times*. Composer, conductor, author, lecturer and teacher. Son of conductor of orchestras for silent films; studied piano in Philadelphia, then composition with Isadore Freed and Arnold Schoenberg. Was working as Broadway arranger when Chaplin asked him to go to Hollywood to assist on score for *Modern Times*. Subsequently remained active in Hollywood, where he composed music for more than a hundred films, including *Laura*. President, Composers and Lyricists Guild of America.

RAYE, Martha. (b. 1916) Actress, *Monsieur Verdoux*. Gifted, wide-mouthed American comedienne. Daughter of vaudeville artists (Reed and Hooper); had experience in musical comedy, radio, vaudeville and band work before making her first film in 1936 *(Rhythm on the Range)*. Many films until 1970; then television work.

REEVES, Alfred. (1876–1946) General Manager, Chaplin Film Corporation, 1918–1946. Son of a lion tamer who lost an arm to the animals; worked in circus, then management for Fred Karno. Managed Karno's US tours from 1905. Chose Chaplin for 1910 tour. Brother of Billie Reeves, Karno player who later did Chaplin imitation.

REEVES, Amy. Wife of Alf Reeves. Karno artist (as Amy Minister) who played the Saucy Soubrette in *Mumming Birds*, and accompanied Chaplin on 1910 and 1912 Karno US tours. Settled in Hollywood from 1918 and befriended Hannah Chaplin during her last days there.

REEVES, Billie. (1866–1945) Brother of Alfred Reeves; Karno player, who preceded Chaplin in *Mumming Birds*. Began his career as a performer at seven, and was acrobat, clown, bareback rider, animal trainer and tamer like his father. Also knockabout skater and member of Fletcher's Skaters. Remained in America after Karno tour, in vaudeville and later in films (Lubin). In one year made fifty-three films, at $1000 each. In 1918 did vaudeville tour with drunk sketch, 'The Right Key But The Wrong Flat'.

REEVES, May. Young woman, apparently of Czech origin, who was Chaplin's companion during much of his 1931 holiday and wrote her memoirs of the period, *Charlie Chaplin intime*, edited by Claire Goll (1935).

REYNOLDS, Dr Cecil. Hollywood neighbour of Chaplin, who played prison chaplain in *Modern Times*. Died by suicide.

RIESNER, Charles Francis. (1887–1962) Actor, *A Dog's Life, The Kid, The Pilgrim*; assistant director, First National Films and *The Gold Rush*. Left Chaplin to direct Sydney Chaplin pictures *(The Man on the Box, The Better 'Ole)*. Later films include Buster Keaton's *Steamboat Bill Jr*. Last film made in Italy, *L'Ultima Cena* (1950). Before joining Chaplin in January 1918 Riesner had ten years experience on the stage; featured on Keith and Orpheum vaudeville circuits, and as star of musical comedy, *Stop, Look, Listen*. His son DEAN RIESNER was a child actor in *The Pilgrim* who later became successful screenwriter.

RITCHIE, Billy. (1877–1921) Vaudeville and musical comedy; then Karno Company. Created role of Drunk in *Mumming Birds*. Following Karno tour, remained in US starring in vaudeville, on Broadway, and Orpheum Circuit. On screen in L-Ko comedies, was persuaded by Henry Lehrman to undertake Chaplin impersonation, Died from injuries received from ostrich during making of a film. His wife WINIFRED RITCHIE, also a former Karno player, was expert in making trick costumes, and worked frequently at Chaplin studios. Daughter WYN married Ray Evins, Hollywood song-writer ('Buttons and Bows' 'Che Sara, Sara' etc). Winifred and Wyn were among Hannah Chaplin's selected Hollywood friends.

ROBINSON, Carlyle T. Chaplin's press representative from 1917 to 1932. Accompanied him on 1921 and 1931 European trips. Appears in *The Idle Class, The Pilgrim*. Was educated in New York, and worked in a bank before turning to journalism. Was obituary reporter for Brooklyn Standard Union before moving to California to work as press agent for motion picture companies.

RUGGLES, Wesley. (1889–1972) Actor, *The Bank, Shanghaied, A Night in the Show, Charlie Chaplin's Burlesque on Carmen, Police, The Pawnshop, Behind the Screen*. Stage, then films at Keystone (1914) as Keystone Kop, and in Sydney Chaplin 'Gussle' shorts. Director from 1917 *(For France)*. Later films include *I'm No Angel*, with Mae West. Last picture, *London Town* (1940), in England.

RUTHERFORD, Margaret Taylor. (1892–1972) Actress in *A Countess From Hong Kong*. Well-loved English character actress. Originally teacher of music and speech; stage from 1925; films from 1936 *(Dusty Ermine)*.

ST JOHN, Al. (1893–1963) Actor, *Mabel's Strange Predicament, Mabel at the Wheel, The Knockout, Mabel's Busy Day, Mabel's Married Life, The Rounders, The New Janitor, Tillie's Punctured Romance, His Prehistoric Past*. Nephew of Roscoe Arbuckle. Musical comedy, then Keystone from 1914. Later, bearded, made career as Western character actor, Al 'Fuzzy' St John, in a career extending to the 1950s.

SAINTSBURY, H. A. (1869–1939) Actor and dramatist. Educated St John's College, Hurstpierpoint, then engaged as clerk at Bank of England. Stage debut 1887. Played wide repertory of Shakespearean roles but his favourite part remained Sherlock Holmes, which he acted more than 1400 times. Chaplin made his first appearances on the legitimate stage under Saintsbury, in Saintsbury's own *Jim, A Romance of Cockayne* and in a touring production of *Sherlock Holmes*.

SENNETT, Mack. (1880–1960) Producer. See Chapter 4, *passim*.

STERLING, Ford. (1880–1939) Actor, *Between Showers, A Film Johnnie, Tango Tangles*. Began career in circus as Keno the Boy Clown; later stock, vaudeville, musical comedy. Films from 1911 at Biograph; then in original Keystone Company (1912). Formed own company in 1914, but later returned to Sennett. Career continued until 1935 *(Black Sheep)*.

STERNBERG, Josef von. (1894–1969) Impressed by Sternberg's first film, *The Salvation Hunters*, Chaplin financed and produced Sternberg's *Sea Gulls* (or *A Woman From the Sea*), starring Edna Purviance. The film was never shown however, and the negative was destroyed in 1933. Later most famous for his films with Marlene Dietrich.

STOCKDALE, Carl. (b. 1874) Actor, *The Champion, A Jitney Elopement*,

By the Sea, The Bank. University of North Dakota; amateur, then professional stage. Films from 1912, at Essanay. Early roles included Belshazzar's Father in Griffith's *Intolerance.* Career continued in sound films until 1941 *(Dangerous Lady).*

STRUSS, Karl. (b. 1891) Photographer, *The Great Dictator, Limelight.* Work as Hollywood cameraman began with Cecil B. De Mille in 1920 and included *Ben Hur* (1926).

SULLY, Janet Miller. Actress, *Easy Street, The Cure, The Adventurer, A Dog's Life.* In 1918 *Motion Picture Magazine* reported that she had just played '68 comedies with George Ovey without a break'.

SUMMERVILLE, George ('Slim'). (1892–1946) Actor, *Mabel's Busy Day, Laughing Gas, Dough and Dynamite, Tillie's Punctured Romance.* Vaudeville and musical comedy; films (at Keystone) from 1913; was also gagman for Sennett. Remained in films as character player until death: most famous later performances in *All Quiet on the Western Front* and *Tobacco Road.*

SUTHERLAND, Edward A. (1895–1974) Assistant director, *A Woman of Paris, The Gold Rush.* Nephew by marriage of Thomas Meighan. Educated Paris and US. Stage and musical comedy. Screen from 1914 in Helen Holmes serial. Director from 1925 *(Coming Through).* Later films included *The Old Army Game* and *Poppy,* both with W. C. Fields. Continued to direct until 1956 *(Bermuda Affair,* in England). Wives included Louise Brooks.

SWAIN, Mack. (1876–1935) Heavyweight actor, *Caught in the Rain, A Busy Day, The Fatal Mallet, The Knockout, Mabel's Married Life, Laughing Gas, Gentlemen of Nerve, His Musical Career, His Trysting Place, Tillie's Punctured Romance, Getting Acquainted, His Prehistoric Past, The Idle Class, Pay Day, The Pilgrim, The Gold Rush.* The son of Mormon pioneers (his middle name was Moroni, from the trumpeter angel on the Mormon temple), he established his own infant minstrel troupe at the age of seven. At fifteen toured with Martin Josey Minstrel Show. 1900, Kempton and Graves Stock Company, Chicago. Films from 1913, at Keystone. Career interrupted by blacklisting, but revived after *The Gold Rush.* Last appearance in 1932, *The Midnight Patrol.*

SWANSON, Gloria. (1897 or 1898–1983) Actress, *His New Job.* One of the greatest Hollywood stars of the 1920s, Swanson for long denied that she appeared in this film. Later she acknowledged it, but claimed that she deliberately tried not to give a comedy performance so as to avoid getting typed as a slapstick artist.

SWICKARD, Joseph. (d. 1938) Actor, *Twenty Minutes of Love, Caught in a Cabaret, Laughing Gas.* In films from 1912; established career as character actor in the 1920s, notably in *The Four Horsemen of the Apocalypse.*

Continued in films until death: last appearance in Frank Capra's *You Can't Take It With You* (1938).

TERRELL, Maverick. (b. 1875) University of Indiana Law School, writer of plays and magazine fiction. Said by Theodore Huff (*Charlie Chaplin*, 1951) to have assisted Chaplin in writing Essanay and Mutual comedies.

TETRICK, Drew (Ted). Hollywood producer and costumier, worked on costumes for *The Great Dictator, Monsieur Verdoux* and planned costumes for *The Freak*. Married to Betty Chaplin (q.v.).

TOTHEROH, Roland H. (1890–1964) Photographer on Chaplin films from 1916 to 1952. Early career as cartoonist; amateur ball player. Photographer at Essanay, shooting Broncho Billy Westerns, from 1913. Retired after Chaplin's departure from Hollywood.

TURPIN, Ben. (1874–1940) Actor, *His New Job, A Night Out, The Champion*. With his puny physique and crossed eyes, one of the most singular figures in silent slapstick comedy. Eleven years in vaudeville with Sam T. Jack's Burlesque Company, then films at Essanay (1915). In later years played support to comedy stars: last appearance with Laurel and Hardy in *Saps at Sea* (1940).

WALLIS, Shani. (b. 1933) Singer in *A King in New York*. Child performer; debut on television, 1948; RADA; stage musicals. Films from 1956 *(The Extra Day)*. Chaplin selected her after seeing her in pantomime at Golders Green Hippodrome.

WELLES, Orson. (b. 1915) Director and actor. Suggested original idea for *Monsieur Verdoux*, and is so credited in the film.

WHITE, Leo. (1887–1948) Actor, *His New Job, A Night Out, The Champion, In the Park, A Jitney Elopement, The Tramp, Work, A Woman, The Bank, Shanghaied, A Night in the Show, Charlie Chaplin's Burlesque on Carmen, Police, The Floorwalker, The Fireman, The Vagabond, The Count, Behind The Screen, The Great Dictator*. With Karno; later in operetta. In films from 1915 (at Essanay); then George Ade Comedies, Billy West comedies, Hal Roach. For Essanay compiled four-reel version of *Charlie Chaplin's Burlesque on Carmen* and *Triple Trouble*. Career continued until 1942 *(Yankee Doodle Dandy)*.

WILLIAMS, Frank D. (b. 1893) Chaplin's cameraman on *The Floorwalker, The Fireman, The Vagabond*. Previously with Essanay and Keystone, where he may also have filmed Chaplin. Highly innovative, Williams is credited with the invention of the travelling matte, and was responsible for trick work on *King Kong* and *The Invisible Man*.

WILLSON, Meredith. (1902–1984) Music arranger, *The Great Dictator*. Accomplished pianist and flautist, studied at New York Institute of Musical

Art (now Juilliard School). Flute and piccolo with J. P. Sousa Band, then first flautist with New York Philharmonic, under Toscanini. Musical director for ABS and NBC. Major Broadway successes with two musicals, *The Music Man* (1957) and *The Unsinkable Molly Brown* (1960).

WILSON, Jack. (John) Second cameraman at Chaplin Studios from First National Pictures to *City Lights*. Wife EDITH WILSON was bit actress in *The Kid*, *City Lights* (cut sequence).

WOOD, Tom. Young, 495-lb. actor in *Sunnyside*. Was originally cast as Charlie's wife in *A Day's Pleasure* but the role was eventually taken by Edna Purviance.

BIBLIOGRAPHY

This bibliography aims only to list some of the major works among the several hundred books that have been devoted to Chaplin's life and career, along with a few early rarities and curiosities. For a comprehensive bibliography the reader is directed to Lennart Eriksson's admirable compilation (see below) and its various updatings.

ADELER, Edwin and WEST, Con. *Remember Fred Karno*, John Long, London, 1939.

AMENGUAL, Barthélemy (and others). *Charles Chaplin*. Premier Plan, 28 Société d'Etudes de Recherches et Documentation Cinématographiques, Lyon, 1952.

ASPLUND, Uno. *Chaplin's Films*. Translated from Swedish, *Chaplin i Sverige*, by Paul Britten Austin. David & Charles, Newton Abbot, 1973.

ATASHEVA, Pera M. (ed.) *Charles Spencer Chaplin* Volume II in a series on film history, edited by Sergei M. Eisenstein and Sergei I. Yutkevitch. Essays by M. BLEIMAN, Grigori KOZINTSEV, S. I. YUTKEVITCH and S. M. EISENSTEIN. Goskinoizdat, 1945.

BAZIN, André *Charlie Chaplin*. Preface by François Truffaut. Collection 7e Art. Editions du Cerf, Paris, 1973.

BESSY, Maurice, and FLOREY, Robert. *Monsieur Chaplin, ou le rire dans la nuit*, Jacques Damase, Paris, 1952.

BESSY, Maurice, and LIVIO, Robin. *Charles Chaplin*, Denoel, Paris, 1972.

BOWMAN, William Dodgson. *Charlie Chaplin. His Life and Art*, Routledge, London, 1931. Reprint: Haskell, New York, 1974.

BROWN, Albert T. *The Charlie Chaplin Fun Book*, 1915.

BROWNLOW, Kevin. *The Parade's Gone By*, Alfred A. Knopf, New York, 1968/Secker & Warburg, London, 1968.

Bibliography

CHAPLIN, Charles. *A Comedian Sees the World*, Crowell, New York, 1933.

CHAPLIN, Charles. *My Autobiography*, The Bodley Head, London, 1964/ Simon & Schuster, New York, 1964/Penguin Books, Harmondsworth, 1966/ Fireside Books, New York, 1978. Translations in Arabic, Armenian, Bulgarian, Chinese, Czech, Danish, Dutch, Finnish, French, Georgian, German (publication in Austria, West Germany and East Germany), Greek, Hungarian, Icelandic, Italian, Japanese, Latvian, Norwegian, Polish, Portuguese, Rumanian, Russian, Serbo-Croat, Spanish, Swedish.

CHAPLIN, Charles. *My Early Years*, The Bodley Head, London, 1979. The first eleven chapters of *My Autobiography*.

CHAPLIN, Charles. *My Life in Pictures*. Introduction by Francis Wyndham. The Bodley Head, London 1974/Grosset & Dunlap, New York, 1976.

CHAPLIN, Charles. *My Trip Abroad*, Harper & Brothers, New York, 1922. Translations in Bulgarian, Chinese, Czech, French, German, Polish, Portuguese, Russian, Spanish, Swedish, Yiddish.

CHAPLIN, Charles. *My Wonderful Visit*, Hurst & Blackett, London, 1922. English edition of *My Trip Abroad*.

CHAPLIN, Charles, Jr. (with N. and M. RAU) *My Father, Charlie Chaplin*, Random House, New York, 1960/Longmans, London, 1960.

CHAPLIN, Lita Grey (with Morton COOPER). *My Life With Chaplin, An Intimate Memoir*, Grove Press, 1966.

CHAPLIN, Michael. *I Couldn't Smoke the Grass on My Father's Lawn*, Leslie Frewin, London, 1966/G. P. Putnam's Sons, New York, 1966.

The Charlie Chaplin Book Street & Smith, New York, 1915.

The Charlie Chaplin Book Sabriel Sons & Co., New York, 1916.

CODD, Elsie. 'Charlie Chaplin's Methods' in *Cinema: Practical Course in Cinema Acting in Ten Complete Lessons*, Volume II, Lesson 2. Standard Art Book Company, London, 1920.

COOKE, Alistair. 'Charles Chaplin' in *Six Men*. Alfred A. Knopf, New York, 1977/The Bodley Head, London, 1978/Berkley Publishing Corporation, New York, 1978/Penguin Books, Harmondsworth, 1978.

COTES, Peter and NIKLAUS, Thelma. *The Little Fellow. The Life and Work of Charles Spencer Chaplin*. Foreword by W. SOMERSET MAUGHAM. Paul Elek, London, 1951/Philosophical Library Inc., New York, 1951. Reprint: Citadel Press, New York, 1965.

DELL, Draycott M. *The Charlie Chaplin Scream Book*, Fleetway, London, 1915.

DELLUC, Louis. *Charlot*, Maurice de Brunoff, Paris, 1921. English translation by Hamish MILES: *Charlie Chaplin*, John Lane/The Bodley Head, London, 1922.

ERIKSSON, Lennart. *Books on/by Chaplin*, Lennart Eriksson, Vasteras, Sweden, 1980. The best and most comprehensive bibliography.

FLOREY, Robert. *Charlie Chaplin. Ses débuts, ses films, ses aventures*. Preface by Lucien Wahl. Collection 'Les Grands Artistes de l'Ecran'. Jean-Pascal, Paris, 1927.

FOWLER, Gene. *Father Goose. The Story of Mack Sennett*, Covici Friede, New York, 1934.

GALLAGHER, J. P. *Fred Karno, Master of Mirth and Tears*, Robert Hale, London, 1971.

GIFFORD, Denis. *The Movie Makers*, Macmillan, London, 1974/Doubleday, New York, 1974.

GOLD, Michael. *Charlie Chaplin's Parade*, Harcourt, Brace & Co., New York, 1930.

HAINING, *The Legend of Charlie Chaplin*, W. H. Allen, London, 1983. Anthology of writings by or about Chaplin.

HEMBUS, Joe. *Charlie Chaplin und seine Filme. Eine Dokumentation*, Wilhelm Heyne, Munich, 1972/1973.

HOYT, Edwin P. *Sir Charlie*, Robert Hale, London, 1977.

HUFF, Theodore. *An Index to the Films of Charles Chaplin*. 'Sight and Sound' Index No. 3, British Film Institute, London, 1944. Revised as *The Early Work of Charles Chaplin*, British Film Institute, 1961.

HUFF, Theodore. *Charlie Chaplin*, Henry Schuman, New York, 1951/Cassell, London, 1952. Reprints: Pyramid Books, New York, 1964/Arno Press, New York, 1972.

JACOBS, David. *Chaplin, The Movies and Charlie*, Harper & Row, New York, 1975.

JACOBS, Lewis. *The Rise of the American Film*, Harcourt, Brace & Co., New York, 1939.

KERR, Walter. *The Silent Clowns*, Alfred A. Knopf, New York, 1975.

LAHUE, Kalton C. *World of Laughter*, Norman, Oklahoma, 1966.

LAHUE, Kalton C. *Kops and Custards*, Norman, Oklahoma, 1967.

LEPROHON, Pierre. *Charlot, ou la Naissance d'un Mythe*, Editions Corymbe, Paris, 1935.

LEPROHON, Pierre. *Charles Chaplin*, Jacques Melot, Paris, 1946.

LUFT, Friedrich. *Vom grossen schönen Schweigen. Arbeit und Leben des Charles Spencer Chaplin*, Rembrandt Verlag, Berlin, 1957, 1963.

LYONS, Timothy J. (and others). 'Chaplin and Sound' in *Journal of the University Film Association*, Vol XXXI, No. 1, Winter 1979. University Film Association, Houston, 1979.

LYONS, Timothy J. *Charles Chaplin: a Guide to References and Resources*, G. K. Hall, Boston, 1979.

McCABE, John. *Charlie Chaplin*, Doubleday, New York, 1978/Robson Books Limited, London, 1978.

McCAFFREY, Donald W. *Focus on Chaplin*, Prentice-Hall, New Jersey, 1971. An Anthology of writings by and about Chaplin.

McCAFFREY, Donald W. *4 Great Comedians: Chaplin, Lloyd, Keaton, Langdon*, Tantivy Press, London/A. S. Barnes & Co., New York, 1968.

McDONALD, Gerald D., CONWAY, Michael and RICCI, Mark. *The Films of Charlie Chaplin*, Citadel Press, New York, 1965.

McDONALD, Gerald D. *The Picture History of Charlie Chaplin*, Nostalgia Press, New York, 1965.

MANNING, Harold. 'Charlie Chaplin's Early Life: Fact and Fiction' in *Historical Journal of Film, Radio and Television*, Vol. III – Number 1, March 1983. Carfax, Oxford, 1983. Valuable contribution to the record of Chaplin's early years.

MANVELL, Roger. *Chaplin*. Introduction by J. H. Plumb. Little, Brown, Boston, 1974/Hutchinson, London, 1975.

MARTIN, Marcel. *Charles Chaplin*. Collection 'Cinema d'Aujourd'hui' no. 43. Editions Seghers, Paris, 1966. New edition, 1972.

MINNEY, R. J. *Chaplin: The Immortal Tramp. The Life and Work of Charles Chaplin*, George Newnes, London, 1954.

MITRY, Jean. *Charlot et la 'fabulation' chaplinesque*, Editions Universitaires, Paris, 1957.

MITRY, Jean. *Tout Chaplin*, Editions Seghers, Paris, 1972.

MONTGOMERY, John. *Comedy Films 1894–1954*. Preface by Norman Wisdom. George Allen & Unwin, London, 1954, 1968.

MOSS, Robert. 'Charlie Chaplin' in *Pyramid History of the Movies*, Pyramid Publications, New York, 1975.

OLEKSY, Walter. *Laugh, Clown, Cry – The Story of Charlie Chaplin*, Raintree Editions, Milwaukee, 1976.

PAYNE, Robert. *The Great Charlie*. Foreword by G. W. Stonier. André Deutsch, London, 1952/Hermitage House, New York, 1952.

QUIGLEY, Isabel. *Charlie Chaplin, Early Comedies*, Studio Vista/Dutton Paperback, London, 1968.

RAMSAYE, Terry. *A Million and One Nights. A History of the Motion Picture*, Simon & Schuster, New York, 1926/Frank Cass, London, 1964.

REED, Langford. *The Chronicles of Charlie Chaplin*, Cassell, London, 1917.

REEVES, May. *Charlie Chaplin intime. Souvenirs receuillis par Claire Goll*, NRF, Gallimard, Paris, 1935.

ROBINSON, Carlyle T. *La vérité sur Charles Chaplin. Sa vie, ses amours, ses déboires.* Translated by René Lelu. Editions de Mon Ciné, Paris, 1935.

ROBINSON, David. *Chaplin: The Mirror of Opinion*, Secker Warburg, London, 1983.

ROBINSON, David. *The Great Funnies. A History of Film Comedy*, Studio Vista/Dutton Paperback, London, 1969.

SOBEL, Raoul and FRANCIS, David. *Chaplin, Genesis of a Clown*, Quartet Books, London, 1977/Horizon Press, New York, 1978.

SADOUL, Georges. *Vie de Charlot. Charles Spencer Chaplin, ses films et son temps*, Les Editeurs Francais Réunis, Paris, 1952, 1953, 1957. Definitive edition: Spes, Lausanne/L'Herminier, Paris, 1978.

SANDS, Frederick. *Charlie and Oona – The Story of a Marriage.* Translated from German, *Herr und Frau Chaplin. Die Geschichte einer Ehe* by Marianne Pasetti. Kindler Verlag, Munich, 1977.

SAVIO, Francesco. (ed.) *Il Tutto Chaplin*, Mostra Internazionale d'Arte Cinematografica di Venezia, Venice, 1972.

SEN, Mrinal. *Charlie Chaplin*, Grantha Prakash, Calcutta, 1974, 1980.

SENNETT, Mack (as told to Cameron SHIPP). *King of Comedy*, Doubleday, New York, 1954.

SULLIVAN, Ed. *Chaplin vs. Chaplin.* Foreword by Walter E. Hurst and Frank Bacon. Marvin Miller Enterprises, Los Angeles, 1965.

TURCONI, Davide. *Mack Sennett, il 're de comiche'*, Mostra Internazionale d'Arte Cinematografica di Venezia, Edizioni dell'Ateneo, Rome, 1961.

TRAUBERG, Leonid. *Mir Naisnanku (The World Inside Out)*, Isskustvo, Moscow, 1984.

TYLER, Parker. *Chaplin, Last of the Clowns*, Vanguard Press, New York, 1947. Reprint: Horizon Press, New York, 1972.

von ULM, Gerith. *Charlie Chaplin, King of Tragedy. An unauthorized Biography*, Caxton Printers, Idaho, 1940. Interesting since largely based on information supplied by Toraichi Kono.

INDEX

Abrams, Hiram 269, 301
Addams, Dawn 586
Adventurer, The 202, 205, 221, 225
Agee, James 361, 410, 542–3, 562, 569, 719
Aldrich, Robert 565
Alexandria Hotel, Los Angeles 129, 252, 260, 267–8, 328
Alexandrov, Grigori 416
Allen, Phyllis 171, 626
Anderson, Andy 454
Anderson, G. M. (Broncho Billy) 134–5, 137–40, 156
A Nous la Liberté 631
Aragon, Louis 375, 578
Arbuckle, Roscoe (Fatty) 107, 109, 114, 120, 124, 139, 253, 354, 374, 379, 568n.
d'Arcy, Hugh Antoine 126
Armstrong, Billy 138, 144, 165
Arnheim, Rudolph 507
d'Arrast, Henri d'Abbadie 307–8, 321, 335, 342, 344–5, 358, 362, 436
Arthur, George K. 286, 351
Ashton-under-Lyne 49–51
Asquith, Margot 438
Astor, Nancy, Lady 288, 422–3, 426
Athletic Club, Los Angeles 131, 188–9, 207, 247, 259
Audley, Maxine 586
Austin, Albert 88, 165–6, 169–70, 172, 174, 177, 189, 193, 195–6, 198, 226, 242, 244, 408, 410, 607
Avery, Charles 114, 124
Ayres, Agnes 136

Bacon, Lloyd 165
Bailiffs, The 75, 85–6
Baker, Eddie 409
Baker, Nellie Bly xxi, 314
Baldwin, Charles 71
balloon ballet in *The Great Dictator* 499–501

Bancroft, Sir Squire 62, 285
Bank, The 126, 146–8, 164, 178, 242, 397, 713
Bara, Theda 149
Barrault, Jean-Louis 631
Barrie, J. M. 63, 261, 285, 426
Barry, Carol Anne 522, 524–6, 528
Barry, Joan 512–3, 517–28, 538, 580, 589
Barrymore, John 389, 414
Barton, Ralph 399, 421–2, 424, 429–30, 443
Bastow, George 52, 568
Bauman, Charles O. 101–3, 106, 131
Beast With Five Fingers, The 534
Beddington-Behrens, Sir Edward 578
Behind the Screen 64, 119, 176–9, 718
Belasco, David 105
Bell, Monta 291, 295, 307, 309, 316, 321
Benchley, Robert 212
Bennett, Marjorie 535
Bergman, Henry 175–8, 196–8, 209, 226, 236, 244, 248, 261, 273, 335, 344–5, 353, 360–1, 365, 367, 371, 381, 401, 404, 413–6, 441, 463–4, 476, 492–3, 534, 606–7
Bercovici, Konrad 271, 416, 485
Bergen, Candice 623
Bernhardt, Sarah 209
Bernstein, Sidney 569, 595
Berry, Gertrude 513, 520, 524
Better 'Ole, The 389
Between Showers 112–13, 119, 701
Bevan, Billy 107
Biograph Studios 106, 116
Birkenhead, Lord 416
Birmingham, Bishop of 248
Birth of a Nation 128, 143, 209
Black, George 437
Black Inc. 620–1
Bloom, Claire 466, 559–63, 565–9, 576, 578, 622
Boardman, Eleanor 348

Bobbs Merrill Publishers 180–5
Bodie, Dr Walford 62, 66–8, 181–2
Bodley Head, The 603, 626
Bodley, Major Ronald 482–3
Bolton, Guy 278
Bond, The 244, 721
Bosco, 'Professor' Leotard 10
Boucicault, Dion 62
Boulton, Agnes 518, 520
Bowra, Sir Maurice 599
Bradbury, Kitty 198
Brando, Marlon 570, 610–14, 616
Brecht, Bertolt 544
Breen, Joseph (Breen Office) 490, 508, 530–3, 538
Briand, Aristide 431, 478
Brice, Fanny 490–1
Bridges, Harry 489, 506, 544
Bristol, Tommy 43, 97
British Broadcasting Corporation 358–9, 577
Broken Blossoms 197, 269, 280
Broun, Heywood 178–9, 212, 277
Brownlow, Kevin xix, 101, 168, 176, 188, 193–4, 227, 300–1, 404, 501, 612
Bruce, Nigel 60
Buñuel, Luis 207n., 363, 417–9
Burkan, Nathan 150, 182, 184–5, 223–4, 299–300, 374
Burke, Thomas 235, 284–5, 287, 420, 424–5, 443–5, 455–6
Busy Day, A 123–4, 704
Butler, David 448
By The Sea 143, 173

Cadle, Harry 64
Caine, Hall 302
Cami 288, 431–2
Campbell, Eric Stuart 165–6, 169–70, 173–4, 176–8, 189, 191–4, 197, 202, 204–5, 606
Campbell, Herbert 9, 75
Cane Hill Asylum 26–7, 41–2, 52, 57, 152
Canterbury Music Hall 5, 26, 282
Cargill, Patrick 612
Carpentier, Georges 288–9
Carroll, Paul Vincent 512–3
Caruso, Enrico 163
Casey's Court Circus 64–68, 76, 126, 181, 283
Casey's Court 44, 64
Caught in a Cabaret 122, 173, 703
Caught in the Rain 121, 123, 125–6, 139, 689, 703
Caulfield, Henry 163, 165, 199
Chaliapin, Feodor 290

Champion, The 120, 124, 140–1, 143, 229, 409, 711
Chaplin, Albert 37
Chaplin, Annette Emily 590n.
Chaplin, Aubrey 250–1, 270, 281, 290, 496
Chaplin, Betty xx, 496–7, 581
Chaplin, Charles Senior xx, 2, 4–13, 15, 19, 21, 23, 24, 26–9, 31, 36–7, 85, 181, 551–2
Chaplin, Charles Spencer *passim*
Chaplin, Charles Jr. 42, 332–3, 447–50, 453–5, 464, 469, 471, 475, 495, 501–5, 509–10, 512, 516–7, 519–21, 544, 547, 552, 556, 558, 560, 562, 566, 570, 620
Chaplin, Christopher James 590n., 599, 630
Chaplin, Ellen Elizabeth xiv, 2
Chaplin, Eugene Anthony 590n., 628
Chaplin, Geraldine Leigh 418, 436, 525, 549–50, 558, 590n., 598, 601–2, 609, 619, 629–31
Chaplin, Gypsy (Mrs Sydney Chaplin) 492, 534, 609
Chaplin, Hannah Harriet Pedlingham xiv, xx, 2–10, 13–28, 33–37, 39, 41–2, 44, 51–8, 96, 98, 115, 132, 151–2, 155, 164, 181–3, 217, 224, 250–1, 269–72, 282, 333, 396, 551–2, 560, 562, 629, 644–9
Chaplin, Jane Cecil 590, 595
Chaplin, Josephine Hannah 550, 558, 590n., 601, 609, 619
Chaplin, Lita Grey xxi, 4n., 255, 261–2, 336–9, 342–6, 348–50, 355, 366–8, 371–9, 382, 436, 447–50, 464, 474, 558, 580
Chaplin, Michael John 549–50, 558, 573, 587, 589–90, 597, 601–2, 611, 617–19
Chaplin, Mildred Harris 245–8, 251–2, 259–60, 262–5, 271, 319, 351, 449–50, 464, 525
Chaplin, Norman Spencer 251–2
Chaplin, Oona O'Neill xix, 518–22, 524–5, 528, 538, 543, 548–50, 560, 566, 569–70, 574, 576, 578, 580–6, 590, 594–602, 609, 620–3, 625–6, 628–31
Chaplin, Paulette Goddard 447, 453–5, 463–4, 466, 469, 472, 476–83, 495, 505, 509–11, 517, 527, 554, 580, 590, 622
Chaplin, Shadrach I 1
Chaplin, Sophia 1
Chaplin, Spencer Senior 1, 2, 23
Chaplin, Spencer William Tunstill 2, 23–4, 26, 115, 281–2, 552
Chaplin, Sydney John xiii, 3, 4, 15, 17–19, 21–7, 30, 34–5, 37–42, 45, 51–8, 62–5, 68–9, 75–7, 82–4, 87–8, 95, 101, 121, 123, 125, 131–4, 144, 151–3, 155–6,

158, 161, 163, 168, 181–3, 187, 192,
206n., 217–19, 221–9, 233–4, 243–4,
248, 250–1, 262, 271–3, 298–301, 358,
360, 376–7, 388–9, 396, 401, 410,
432–5, 438–41, 450–1, 453–5, 473–5,
492, 534, 552, 556, 609–10
Chaplin, Sydney Earle 4n., 368, 447–50,
454–5, 469, 475, 495, 502–3, 510, 517,
520, 552, 558–9, 565–7, 595, 605–6,
611–2, 620
Chaplin, Victoria xix, 550, 560, 590n., 619,
628
Chaplin Revue, The 227, 594–5, 743
Charlie Chaplin in a Son of the Gods 216
Charlie Chaplin's Burlesque on Carmen
149–51, 715
Charlie Chaplin's Own Story 180–5
Charlie Chaplin Glide, The 148, 154
Chase, Charley 107
Chase Me Charlie 744
Cherrill, Virginia xxi, 398–400, 405–9,
506
Chirgwin, G. H. 7
Churchill, Winston 291, 423, 427, 346
Cinderella 32–4
Cinquevalli, Paul 556–7
Circus, The 144, 171, 301n., 363–86, 390,
490, 520, 621, 731
Citizen Kane 494
City Lights xxi, 120, 124, 126, 137, 141,
171–4, 362, 387–415, 418, 420, 426–7,
435, 441, 446, 460, 462, 473–5, 481,
489, 520, 565, 588, 625–6, 733
Clair, René 375, 361
Clarice 59
Clive, Henry 395, 399, 402, 406
Cocteau, Jean 395, 479–82, 618
Cohan Theatre, New York 415
Coleman, Frank J. 165
Collier, Constance 189–91, 483, 503
Collins, May 294
Comedian Sees the World, A 451–2
Comingore, Dorothy 494
Conklin, Chester 107, 112, 120, 215, 233,
467
Converse, Thelma Morgan (Lady Furness)
294, 346, 436
Coogan, Anthony xxi, 254, 624
Coogan, Jack, Senior 252–4, 255n., 259,
266
Coogan, Jackie xxi, 252–4, 258–9, 265–7,
314, 319, 566, 590, 624
Coogan, Lillian 252, 254, 266
Cook, The 354
Cooke, Alistair xvi., 408, 475–6
Count, The 173–4

Countess From Hong Kong, A 162, 205,
433, 482, 607–17, 619, 626, 741
Coward, Noël 576, 596, 618
Crocker, Harry 361–3, 365–9, 371, 381–2,
389–90, 396–7, 399, 403–4, 478–9,
521–2, 559–60, 570–1, 578
Cruel, Cruel Love 119, 702
Cure, The 192–5, 719
Curtain Pole, The 106

Dandoe, Arthur 98–100
Daniell, Henry 502
Davenport, Alice 107, 109, 123
Davies, Joseph E. 515
Davies, Marion 346–7, 361–2, 368, 378,
397, 403, 407, 414, 420, 431, 474, 478–9,
494
Day's Pleasure, A 251, 253, 256–7, 724
Dean, Dinky, *see* Riesner, Dean 298
Delluc, Louis 229
De Mille, Cecil B. 149, 414
Desmonde, Jerry 587–8
Dickens, Charles 84, 90, 443, 628
Dick Turpin 67–8, 115
Dietrich, Marlene 429
Dines, Courtland 336
Dog's Life, A 228–32, 594, 720
Donner Party disaster 334
Doro, Marie 59–60, 238
Dorothy Vernon of Haddon Hall 269
Dough and Dynamite 49, 64, 126–7, 176,
708
Douglas, Major H. 456
Doultons, Lambeth 23, 25
Doyle, Arthur Conan 59
Doyle, Jack 189, 209
Doyle, Johnny 84
Dreiser, Theodore 323
Dressler, Marie 105, 128–9, 133, 237, 243
Drury Lane, Theatre Royal 71–2
Dryden, Leo 13–15, 216–9, 272, 551
Dryden, Wheeler 15, 216–9, 272, 396, 493,
505–6, 534, 558, 565, 580–1, 607
Duke of York's Theatre 45, 59, 61, 63
Du Maurier, Gerald 285
Durant, Thomas Wells (Tim) xxi, 487, 493,
503–4, 506, 509, 512–3, 516–8, 521,
562, 570, 580, 623–4
Durfee, Minta 119–20

Early Birds 42, 74, 76
Easy Street 164, 191–3, 231, 718
"'E Dunno Where 'E Are" 17, 56
Edendale Studios, Los Angeles 108 and
passim

Edison, Thomas 387
Edward, Prince of Wales 260, 436, 438
Eglevsky, André 557
Eight Lancashire Lads, The 28–33, 43, 62, 66, 85, 97, 230, 678–681
Einstein, Albert 155, 414, 429
Eisenstein, Sergei M. 416–7
Eisler, Hanns 542, 544, 545n., 547
Elen, Gus 17, 52
Elizabeth II, H.M. Queen 427, 626
Elsom, Isobel 535
Eltinge, Julian 145, 191
Empire Theatre, Leicester Square 5, 32, 555–6, 559
l'Enfant Prodigue 142
Ensign, Harry 137, 147
Epstein, Jerome (Jerry) xix, 559–61, 563, 565, 568–9, 585–7, 602, 613, 619–20, 747–9
Era, The xx, 4, 6, 7, 36, 46–7, 58, 64, 67
Essanay-Chaplin Revue, The 744
Essanay Film Manufacturing Company 68, 134–55, 165, 199, 410, 458
Evans, Will 71
Evelinoff, Boris 433, 439–40
Evening Standard 589
Exmouth, Training Ship 22, 24, 34

Face on the Bar Room Floor, The 121, 126, 706
Fairbanks, Douglas 168, 191, 195, 237, 244, 259, 267–8, 277–8, 280, 302, 309, 319, 330, 334, 351, 375, 417, 438, 446, 465, 497–8, 622
Fairbanks, Douglas, Jr. 497, 576
Farrar, Geraldine 149
Fatal Mallet, The 704
Fay, James W. 539–41
Fejos, Paul 366
Fellini, Frederico 632
Ferguson, Otis 459
Feuchtwanger, Lion 525
Fields, W. C. 307
Film Johnny, A 119, 136, 176, 701
Fireman, The 170–1, 716
First National Exhibitors' Circuit 151, 165, 185, 221–272 *passim*, 298–301, 522
Fiske, Minnie Maddern 209–12
Fitzmaurice, George 284
Flats 87, 229
Fleming, Ian 596, 602–3, 618
Floorwalker, The 168–70, 716
Florey, Robert 371, 375, 534–5, 607
Folies Bergères, Les 81, 288
Football Match, The 74, 76–7, 82–3, 85, 140

Ford, Rachel xix, 582–3, 595, 601, 620, 626
Forest, Arthur 76
Forsythe, Robert 51
Foster, William C. 165
Francis, Day and Hunter xx, 9, 11–13
Frank, Waldo 288
Freak, The 619–21, 628
Frenke, Eugene 518, 521
Freud, Sigmund 235
Freuler, John R. 156–60, 185
Frohman, Charles 55, 58–9, 62, 85

Gance, Abel 474
Gandhi, Mohandas 438
Ganev, Gantcho 630–1
Garbo, Greta 307, 511, 549
Garcia, Allan 367, 371, 399, 408, 465
Garden, Mary 433
Gardiner, Reginald 496–8, 502
Gentleman of Paris, A 307
Gentlemen of Nerve 126, 708
George V, King of England 427–8
Geraghty, Tom 280, 282–3
Getting Acquainted 126, 710
Getty, J. Paul 512, 517, 523, 526
Giddy Ostend 32
Giesler, Jerry 523–5
Gifford, Denis 66
Gill, David xix, 168, 176, 193–4, 227, 300–1, 404, 501, 613n.
Gillette, William C. 45, 59–60
Gish, Lillian 621
Glass, Montague 273
Glyn, Elinor 347–8
Goddard, Paulette, *see* Chaplin, Paulette Goddard
Godfrey, Charles 9
Gold Rush, The xxi, 155, 271, 296, 334–59, 366, 382, 406, 426, 481, 513, 522, 550, 569, 579, 616, 730
Golden, Marta 144
Goldwyn, Samuel 149, 160, 245, 267
Gone With the Wind 483
Goodman, Paul 507
Goodwins, Fred 68, 78, 138, 145, 147, 199
Gould, Edith *see* Kelly, Edith
Gould, Florence 432–4
Gould, Frank J. 281n., 432–4
G.P.O., The 85–6
Grable, Betty 266
Grauman, Sid 252, 341n., 356, 382
Great Dictator, The 155, 301n, 432, 478, 484–6, 488–510, 513, 525, 534, 536, 538, 581, 590, 610, 630, 735
Green, Harry 587

"Green, Mrs Tom" *see* Scales, Edith
Green, Tom 47, 50, 51
Greene, Graham 618
Grey, Lita (Lillita) *see* Chaplin, Lita Grey
Grierson, John 385
Griffith, D. W. 106, 109, 123, 128, 143, 197, 209, 253n., 267, 269, 280n, 303

Hackett, Francis 261
Hale, Georgia xxi, 350–54, 356–7, 366–8, 386, 406, 414–8, 446, 513, 606, 624
Hall, Charles D. ("Danny") 253, 335, 337, 342, 344, 352, 362, 395
Hamilton, C. E. 45, 60
Hanwell Schools 19, 21–2, 24
Hardy, Oliver 361
Hardwicke, Sir Cedric 512
Harlequinade in Black and White, A 91–2, 242
Harley, Lily, *see* Chaplin, Hannah
Harrington, John P. 11–13
Harrington, Tom 188, 199, 225–6, 246, 262, 270–1, 273, 276, 455
Harris, Frank 188, 263, 290
Harris, Mildred *see* Chaplin, Mildred Harris
Hart, W. S. 267–8
Haven, Carter De 463–4, 476, 501
Hawkes, Sidney (father of Sydney Chaplin) 3, 155, 217
Hayden, Kathleen 434–5
Hayden, Melissa 557, 567
Hays, Will 464
Hearst, Millicent 346
Hearst, William Randolph 135, 346–8, 361–2, 378, 403, 478–9, 606
Hedren, Tippi 612
Herbert, Bert 43
Her Friend the Bandit 122, 173, 704
Hilarity 73
Hill, Charles Frederick xx, 2, 3, 16, 34, 55
Hill, Hannah Harriet Pedlingham, *see* Chaplin, Hannah Harriet Pedlingham
Hill, Kate 3, 22, 41, 56, 151–4, 164, 250, 411, 552
Hill, Mary Ann (née Terry) xiv, 3, 4, 15–16, 19, 34, 40
Hindom, "Captain" xiii–xiv, 21
His Favourite Pastime 119, 702
His Majesty's Guests 74
His Musical Career 127, 697, 709
His New Job 119, 136–7, 139, 176, 612, 711
His New Profession 126, 707
His Prehistoric Past 127, 710
His Trysting Place 709
Hitler, Adolf 484–5, 488–9, 493, 507–8

Hodges, Henry Lamphee 3, 19
Hodges, Joseph 4, 19
Hoover, Herbert 322
Hope, Bob 632
Hopper, Hedda 414, 518, 521–2, 576, 579
Horne, (Sir) Alan Edgar 162, 274
House Un-American Activities Committee 544–5
How To Make Movies 227–8, 594, 720
Huff, Theodore 137, 451, 471
Hunter, Catherine 451, 483, 522
Hunter, Inman xx, 20, 386n.
Hydro, The 192

Ibbetson, Arthur 611, 613
I Couldn't Smoke the Grass on My Father's Lawn . . . 618–9
Idle Class, The 269, 274, 520, 621–2, 726
Immigrant, The 147, 195–202, 204, 304, 719
Ince, Thomas H. 106n., 347–8
Inmoos, M. 629
Insley, Charles 144
In The Park 141, 712
Intolerance 209
Irving, Sir Henry 59, 61, 66, 426
Ivano, Paul 384, 386n.

Jackson, Alfred 29–30, 32, 34
Jackson, John William 28–30, 32–4, 43, 181
Jail Birds 74
James, Dan xxi, 488–90, 492–5, 499, 502–3, 505–6, 516
James, D. L. 487–8
James, Eric 614, 627
James, Lilith 516
James, Sidney 587
Jamison (or Jamieson), Bud 136, 138–9, 141, 165
Jasper, John 199, 238
Jazz Singer, The 389
Jefferson, Stanley, *see* Laurel, Stan
Jim, A Romance of Cockayne 45–7, 574
Jimmy the Fearless 84–5, 87, 127, 141, 146, 242, 274, 397
Jitney Elopement, The 88, 141, 173, 712
Johnson, Arthur 412
Johnston, Oliver 586–8, 612
Joyce, Peggy Hopkins 302–4, 309, 330, 332, 378

Karno, Fred xx, 4n., 34, 42, 68, 71–9, 82–91, 93–4, 96–8, 103, 123, 130, 139–40, 144, 147, 165, 181, 215, 218, 227–9, 242, 304, 369, 387, 402, 408, 410, 502, 522, 535–6, 576–7, 627

Karno, Fred, Jr 88, 335
Kawa, Frank 349, 362
"Kay-Kay" *see* McKenzie, Elizabeth
Keaton, Joseph Francis (Buster) 127, 360, 403, 567–8
Kellerman, Annette 213
Kelley, James T. 165, 170, 178, 193, 196
Kelly, Arthur ("Sonny") 81, 97, 281, 283, 290, 358, 415, 420, 432, 549–50, 580
Kelly, Edith 281n., 432
Kelly, Henrietta (Hetty) Florence 80–1, 97, 162, 274–6, 281n., 290, 432, 560, 645
Kendall, Kay 486
Kennedy, Edgar 107, 119, 124
Kennedy, Joseph 497
Kennedy, Merna 336, 366–8, 371, 378, 414, 474
Kenney, Horace 64
Kerr, Walter 109, 111–2, 118, 191
Kessel, Adam 98, 101–3, 106, 131
Kessel, Charles 101, 103
Keystone Film Company xv, 72, 98, 101–33, 136, 140, 143, 146, 152–3, 170, 188, 215, 218, 317, 409, 458, 464, 502, 522, 612, 616
Krushchev, Nikita 584
Khill, Marcel 479–81
Kid, The 151, 225, 252–65, 267, 274, 285, 289, 292, 298, 301–2, 342, 371, 462, 565, 568, 589, 616, 621–2, 626, 724
Kid Auto Races at Venice 113, 118, 124–5, 131, 369, 700
King, Hetty 31, 69
King in New York, A 64, 144, 147, 478, 511, 524, 584–93, 611, 740
Kingsley, Grace 232–3, 346
Kitchen, Fred 75, 85, 114
Kitchen, Karl K. 161, 327
Knoblock, Edward 273, 277–8, 285–6, 422
Knockout, The 120, 124, 140, 704
Knott, Lydia 313–4, 407
Kono, Toraichi 188, 204, 251, 328, 332, 342, 348–9, 351, 358, 362, 373, 416, 418, 420, 422, 426, 436, 438, 440, 464
Koenekamp, Hans xxi, 113, 116–7, 129–30
Korda, Alexander 505, 588
Korda, Vincent 565
Kustoff, Michael 496–7, 510

Lane, Lupino 152
Lane, Rose Wilder 180–5, 602
Lapworth, Charles 234–5
Lasky, Jesse 149, 191, 325
Last Moment, The 366
Lauder, Harry 155, 161, 230–1, 232n.
Laughing Gas 121, 125, 705

Laurel, Stan 78–80, 84–6, 88, 92–3, 96, 98–100, 215, 361, 607
Laurents, Arthur 559
Lauste, Eugene 387–8
Layton, H. Lawrence 58
Le Brunn, George 11, 13
Lederer, Charles 403
Lee, Florence 407
Lee, Lila 294
Lehrman, Henry 'Pathé' 107–10, 112, 117–8, 120, 175, 215, 397
Lenin 280, 289, 291
Leno, Dan 30, 75, 83n., 96, 114, 189, 283
Lester, "Dashing" Eva xii–xiv, 7
Letellier, Henri 289, 304, 306, 309
Lewis, Sinclair 512
Life 147–8, 151
Life Magazine 571
Limelight xxi, 27, 52, 60, 84, 145, 171, 174, 301, 364, 412, 432, 466, 481, 490, 511, 516, 535, 549–71, 577–81, 585, 626, 739
de Limur, Jean 293, 307–8, 321, 384, 474, 476
Linder, Max 170
Little Fellow, The 20
Lloyd George, David 280, 289, 322, 424
Lloyd, Harold 209, 319, 361
Lloyd, Marie 7, 11, 30–1
Lockwood and Jeffery 182–4
Lohse, Ralph 93–4
Lombard, Carole 352
London, Babe 256
London Suburbia 76, 114
Lone Star Film Corporation 159
Lone Star Studios 164, 199
Loren, Sophia 610–2, 614, 616
Lotinga, Ernie 69–70
"Louise" (mistress of Charles Chaplin Senior) 26–7, 36
Lourié, Eugene xxi, 563–6, 568–9
Low, David 281, 485
Lubitsch, Ernst 321, 324
Lucas, E. V. 285
Lumière, Auguste and Louis 123

Mabel at the Wheel 120, 702
Mabel's Busy Day 122, 125, 705
Mabel's Married Life 112, 121–2, 125, 705
Mabel's Strange Predicament 113–15, 117–18, 139, 701
McAdoo, William Gibbs 267, 269
McCabe, John 92, 98
McCarthy, Senator Joseph 575–6, 588
McCoy, Harry 120–1
MacDonald, Malcolm 422, 428

MacDonald, Ramsay 422, 424, 427–9
McGranery, James 572, 575–6, 621
McKenzie, Elizabeth ('Kay-Kay') xix, 522, 570, 601
McMurray, Edwin T. 371, 375, 450
McMurray, Lillian *see* Spicer, Lillian
Mace, Fred 98, 102–3, 107
Maeterlinck, Madame Maurice 277
Maguire, Paddy 138
Majestic Studios (Bradbury Mansion) 143, 145
Making a Living 109–11, 467, 700
Malone, Dudley Field 288
Manchester Guardian 320, 475
Mann, Hank 209, 409, 467
Mann, Thomas 155
Manoir de Ban, Vevey 294, 581–2, 585, 609, 618, 628
Manon, Charles 63, 71
Maritza, Sari 427, 429
Marriage Circle, The 321
Marsh, Marian 407
Martinetti Brothers 72
Martini, Virginia Cherrill, *see* Cherrill, Virginia
Mary, H.M. Queen 427
Mason, Pauline xxi
Masquerader, The 119, 123, 126, 127, 706
Matthau, Carole 562, 623
Matthau, Walter 562, 624
Maxwell, Elsa 289, 433
Mayer, Louis B. 260
Maynard, Ambrose 5
Mayo, Archie 508
Mayston, Guy 180, 184
Medvedkin, Alexander 144
Meighan, Thomas 220
Melba, Dame Nellie 163
Meller, Raquel 369, 474
Meltzer, Robert 489, 494, 503, 505–6
Menjou, Adolphe 304, 307–13, 315–6, 318–23, 329
Meredith, Burgess 510
Merrill, Flora 456–8
Meryman, Richard 69, 399, 403, 405, 410, 415, 452
Miller, Max 69
Mineau, Charlotte 165
Minney, R. J. 64
Modern Times 39, 141, 149, 171, 176, 412, 431, 454–5, 458–74, 476, 479, 481, 486, 488, 588, 590, 595, 734
Monsieur Verdoux 129, 198, 286, 296, 371, 519–20, 522, 529–38, 542–5, 549–50, 565, 737
Montagu, Ivor 52n., 155, 415–7

Moore, Justice Clinton Pancoast 522
Morgan, Gene 136
Morris Agency, William, 95
Morton, Charles 56
Mountbatten, Lady Edwina 465
Mountbatten, Lord Louis 260
Mowbray, Kate *see* Hill, Kate
Mozart, George 55
Mumming Birds 75–6, 82, 85, 87n., 90, 130, 147, 165, 172, 215, 227, 576
Murray, Charles 209, 464
Murray, D. L. 482–3
Murray, Tom 337, 342, 344, 355
Murray, Will 44, 64–8, 115, 181
Music Box, The 127
Mussolini, Benito 265, 439, 501
Mut (or Mutt) 230, 236
Mutual Film Corporation 156–220 *passim*, 304, 410
My Autobiography xiv, 39n., 79, 275, 452, 602–3, 605–7, 626
Myers, Harry 402, 408
My Father Charlie Chaplin 620 and *passim*
My Life in Pictures 17, 625–6, 628
My Trip Abroad 273n., 291, 295, 307, 452
My Wonderful Visit, see My Trip Abroad

Namara, Marguerite 278
Napoleon Bonaparte, projects for film about 474–9, 482
Napoleon's Return From St Helena 478–9
Nash, Marilyn 536
Nation, The 579
Negri, Pola 288–9, 309, 324–31, 378
New Janitor, The 126, 146, 698, 707
Newman, Alfred 413, 469–70, 472
New Republic, The 261
New Statesman and Nation 508
New Woman's Club, The 74
New York Motion Picture Company 97, 101, 106n.
Nice and Friendly 726
Nichols, George 119–20, 124
Night in a London Club, A 88, 90, 109
Night in a London Secret Society, A, see Wow-Wows, The
Night in an English Music Hall, A, see, Mumming Birds
Night in the Show, A 147–8, 714
Night Out, A 126, 139, 143, 295, 711
Nights in Town 443
Nijinsky, Vaslav 250, 294
Niles, California (Essanay Studio) 134, 137, 139, 141, 180–2
Nilsson, Anna Q. 294
Nixon, Richard W. 576

Normand, Mabel 101, 107–8, 115–7, 120–2, 125, 128–9, 139, 215, 319, 335–6

Oakie, Jack 501–2
Oceanic, SS 96
Odets, Clifford 562
O'Higgins, Harvey 211–2
Olivier, Laurence 576, 631
Olympic, SS 96, 278–9, 280
One A.M. 172–3, 295, 717
O'Neill, Eugene 422, 518
Osborne, John 589

Paderewski, Ignace Jan 163
Painful Predicament of Sherlock Holmes, The 59
Paramount Pictures 222–3
Park, A.J. 30
Parker, Frank 32
Parrish, Robert 409
Parsons, Louella 135, 347, 448, 521–2
Paschoud, Jean-Felix 630
Passion (Madame Dubarry) 324
Pathé Company 106, 109, 175
Pathé Studio (Los Angeles) 565
Pavilion Theatre, Whitechapel Road 47–8, 63
Pavlova, Anna 294
Pawnshop, The 174–5, 717
Pay Day 294–5, 727
"Peace Patrol, The" 412
Pearce, Peggy 119, 129
Pebble Beach 487–8
Perinal, Georges 563, 588
Peter Pan 63
Peters, T. K. 101–2
Photoplay 18
Piaf, Edith 571
Picasso, Pablo 547, 578–9
Pickford, Mary 160, 191, 195, 222, 237, 259, 267–9, 277–8, 302–3, 319, 330, 334, 351, 417, 446, 538, 549
Picturegoer 65
Pierre, L'Abbé 584
Pilgrim, The xxi, 294–300, 302, 434, 594–5, 727
Pink, Wal 63, 114, 144
Police 148–9, 151, 164, 301, 715
Poluski, Will 79
Postance, William xiii–xiv, 59–60, 556n.
Potash and Perlmutter 274
Powell, Dilys 577
Powell, Edward 469, 472
Price, Oscar 267, 269
Priestley, J. B. 590

Prodigal Son, The 302
Professor, The 299–301, 364–5, 490, 493, 728
Property Man, The 121, 125, 706
Pryor, Kathleen 488, 490
Purviance, Edna xix, 138–9, 141–2, 144, 146–7, 149–51, 162–3, 165, 169–70, 173–4, 176–8, 188, 191, 194, 196–9, 201–2, 204, 208–9, 216–20, 225, 229–30, 233–4, 236, 244, 247–50, 253, 261, 269, 273, 296, 302, 304, 306, 311, 313, 319, 335–6, 358, 378, 383–6, 441–3, 446, 451, 474, 534–5, 554

Quarry, Dr M.H. 40–1, 55
Queen Elizabeth, SS 548, 571–4

Rags to Riches 53
Raksin, David xxi, 469–72
Ramsaye, Terry 157, 168–9, 205
Rand, John 165, 174, 193, 273
Rankin, Representative J.T. 545
Rappe, Virginia 374, 397
Rasch, Ray 557
Ray, Man 375
Raye, Martha 535
Recreation 706
Redmond, Granville 232
Reed, Langford 187
Reel Life 157
Reeves, Alfred 75–6, 87–8, 96, 98, 100–1, 141, 216, 227–8, 232, 241, 250–1, 262, 272, 298, 336, 362, 373–4, 401, 404, 407, 410, 415, 434–5, 439, 441–2, 449–51, 453–5, 461, 465, 470, 472–3, 479, 488, 496, 509, 519, 536
Reeves, Amy 87, 96, 228, 271–2
Reeves, Billie 75–6, 82, 172
Reeves, May 40, 433–6, 438–40, 482, 554
Regency 482–3, 486
Reinhardt, Max (theatre director) 289, 513
Reinhardt, Max (publisher) 603, 626
Remarque, Erich Maria 510, 590
Renoir, Jean 563
Repairs 63–4, 68, 114, 144
Reuter, Al xix, 589
Reynolds, Dr Cecil 328
Riesner, Charles (Chuck) 262, 298, 335–7, 348
Riesner, Dean xxi, 298
Ring Round the Moon 559
Rink, The 178–9, 194, 718
Ritchie, Billie 82, 215, 495
Ritchie, Winifred 215–6, 272, 495
Ritchie, Wyn xx, 215, 272, 497

Rivington, Kenneth 55, 60
Roach, Hal 353, 447, 497
Robbins, Jesse T. 134–5
Roberts, Willa 451
Robeson, Paul 544
Robin Hood 269
Robinson, Carlyle 199–202, 205, 234, 253, 273, 275–6, 280, 283, 288, 294, 404, 406–7, 421–2, 424–7, 429, 433, 435–6, 441
Robinson, David 610–11, 627
Rogers, Will 319, 379, 457
Rohauer, Raymond 168
Roosevelt, Franklin D. 237, 458, 510, 516, 527
Roosevelt, Theodore 183
Ross, Lillian 602
Rothenstein, Jenny 431
Rothman, Moses xxi, 620–1
Rounders, The 126, 139, 707
Roy Export Company Establishment 586, 595
Rusk, Dean 599
Russell, Jimmy 84, 576
Russell, Leonard 603

Safety Last 361
Saintsbury, H.A. 45–7, 51, 60, 69
Salvation Hunters, The 351, 366, 383–4
Sands, Frederick 593
Sartre, Jean-Paul 578
Sassoon, Sir Philip 288–9, 422, 424, 428
Saturday to Monday 74
Scales, Edith 47–51
Schenck, Joseph 414, 447, 511
Schrager, Rudi 537
Schwalbe, Harry 298–9
Scott, Joseph 526–8
Sea Gulls 286, 383–6, 451, 743
Seldes, Gilbert 483
Sennett, Mack 101–2, 104–11, 113, 115–7, 119–22, 127–33, 319, 354, 402
Service For Ladies 307
Sessions, Almira 535
Shadow and Substance 512–4, 518–9
Shanghaied 147–8, 170, 178, 198, 714
Shaw, George Bernard 285, 423, 426
Sheik, The 309
Shepherd, May 436–7
Shepherd, Dr Charles Horatio 12, 23
Sheridan, Clare 291–4
Sheridan, Dickie 291–4, 626
Sherlock Holmes xx, 45, 47–8, 51, 53, 55, 58–63, 66, 119, 238, 363, 438, 499, 559, 682–5
Sherwood, Robert 320, 360, 395

Shoulder Arms 91, 228, 241–7, 285, 490, 493, 520, 522, 594, 617, 722
Show People 745
Simpson, Mrs Wallis (Duchess of Windsor) 436
Sinbad the Sailor 32
Skating 74, 83, 85, 178
Skolsky, Sidney 569
Smith, W. H. 39
Smoking Concert, The 90
Sorel, Cecile 289
Southern, Eve 384
Spectator 484, 508
Spicer, Mrs Lillian (Lita Grey's mother) 342–3, 447–8
Spoor, George K. 134–5, 137, 151–2, 156
Spreckels, Geraldine 494
Spring Cleaning 144
Stage, The 63
Stalin, Josef 489, 516
Star Boarder, The 119, 702
Steele, Della 343, 382, 464
Steinbeck, John 488, 506
Sten, Anna 518, 521
Sterling, Ford 102–3, 107–8, 112, 114, 120, 130
Sternberg, Josef von 286, 335, 351, 383–6, 451
Stewart, Donald Ogden 592
Stibolt, Arthur 305–6
Stock, Mark xx, 629
Stowaway 433, 482, 608
Strachey, John 476–7, 479
Struss, Karl 494, 562
Stuart, Charles Douglas 30
Sullivan and Considine Circuit 95–6, 98
Sullivan, Pat 152
Summerville, Slim 209
Sunnyside 141, 248, 256, 723
Sutherland, Edward 176, 271, 306–11, 314–7, 321, 335, 340, 342–4, 362
Swain, Mack 107, 114, 123–5, 127, 136, 273, 336, 339–45, 354, 606
Swanson, Gloria 136, 414, 612–4

Tally, Thomas L. 223
Tango Tangles 120, 701
Tarzan of the Apes 461
Tate, Harry 71
Tati, Jacques 632
Taylor, William Desmond 374
Terni, Gino and Mirella xix, 582, 628
Terr, Max 513
Tetrick, Paul (Ted) xx, 495, 497, 581, 621
Thalberg, Irving 303, 319
Thief of Bagdad, The 269

Thierrée, Jean-Baptiste xix, 619–20, 628
Thomas, J. Parnell 544–5
Those Love Pangs 126, 708
Three Carnos, The 73
Three Musketeers, The 277, 309
Tilden, William 329, 511
Tillie's Nightmare 128
Tillie's Punctured Romance 122, 127–9, 709
Time Magazine 571, 622
Tinney, Frank 550
Totheroh, Roland H. 137–40, 165–8, 176–7, 189, 198, 209, 226, 232, 260, 262, 295, 302, 311, 317, 335, 337, 369–70, 381–2, 441, 467, 494, 519, 522, 534–5, 537, 550, 562–3, 588, 606
Totheroh, Steve xxi
Tramp, The 141–3, 146, 178, 712
Tree, Sir Herbert Beerbohm 62, 189–90
Trevor-Roper, Hugh (Lord Dacre) 598
Triangle Film Corporation 128, 156
Triple Trouble 151, 744
Tully, Jim 308, 337, 341, 345, 350
Turpin, Ben 107, 135, 137–9, 149, 209
Tynan, Kenneth 593
Twelve Just Men 69–70
Twenty Minutes of Love 121–2, 703

Ugarte, Eduardo 417–8
Ulrich, Lenore 329
Underhill, Harriette 246
Underwood, Loyal 193, 198, 226–7, 273
United Artists 267–9, 281n., 302, 436, 482, 505, 538, 548–9, 570, 584
Universal Studios 156, 165, 607
Unknown Chaplin xix, 168, 176, 193–4, 243, 300, 404, 501, 613n.

Vagabond, The 171–2, 205, 716
Valentino, Rudolph 309, 369
Vanbrugh, Dame Irene 59, 63
Van Meter, Joe 408
Varga, Marina 328
Variety (film by E. A. Dupont) 361
Vidor, King 362, 414, 487, 505
"Violetera, La" 205n., 412, 418
Vitaphone 389

Wagner, Rob 202, 225, 232, 237, 451, 508
Waite, Malcolm 352
Walker, Thomas "Whimsical" 46
Wallace, Henry A. 544, 548

Wallace, Minna 518–9
Wallach, George 543
Walton, Clifford 79
Wardas, Roman 630–1
Warner Brothers 389
Way Down East 269
Weber, Jean 474, 476–7
Weber, Lois 245
Weldon, Harry 76–7, 79, 82
Welles, Orson 494, 516, 519–20, 538
Wells, H. G. 274, 285–7, 289–90, 423, 426, 472, 509, 533, 606
West, Billy 215
West, Rebecca 286
Westlake Park, Los Angeles 110, 116, 126, 141, 317
West Norwood Schools 18, 19, 21, 24–6, 41
Weston, Ben 43–4, 79
Wheeler, George Dryden, *see* Leo Dryden
White, Bud (and his bear) 337, 343–4
White, Leo 135, 138–9, 141, 144, 149–51, 165, 170
White, Pearl 120
Williams, Bransby 30
Williams, John D. 223
Williamson, Lambert 614
Willson, Meredith 504
Wilson, Harold 627
Wilson, Jack 232, 262, 302, 335, 451
Wilson, Woodrow 237
Windsor, Claire 294, 378, 414
Winter, Ella 592
Woman, A 123, 145, 713
Woman of Paris, A 288–9, 291, 302–33, 335–6, 383, 407, 411–2, 436, 465, 474, 611, 627, 729
Woman of the Sea see Sea Gulls
Wontdetainia, The 74
Wood, "Wee" Georgie 353
Woolcott, Alexander 277, 382
Work 143–5, 150, 302, 713
Wow-wows, The 88–90, 96, 98, 109
Wright, Basil 508
Wright, Loyd 376, 449, 524, 528, 537
Wyndham, Francis 600, 606, 612, 615, 626

Yonamori, Frank 479
Yorke, Harry 58–9, 63

Zander the Great 346–7
Zukor, Adolph 222–3, 267–9